CONTENTS

LIST OF FIGURES

LIST OF TABLES

LIST OF PLATES

INTRODUCTION

Helen C M Keeley*

Environmental archaeology is a relatively new area of interest which has expanded rapidly over the last two decades. On the recommendation of the Science Panel of the Ancient Monuments Board for England, a series of regional reviews of environmental archaeology was commissioned by the Ancient Monuments Laboratory. The first four of these papers, relating to the north of England, East Anglia, south-west England and York, have already been published in the volume entitled *Environmental Archaeology: A Regional Review* (Keeley H C M Ed. , DAMHB Occasional Paper No. 6, 1984). From 1 April 1984, responsibility for the Ancient Monuments Laboratory passed to the Historic Buildings and Monuments Commission for England. This second volume of *Environmental Archaeology: A Regional Review* is therefore being published under the Commission's auspices.

The volume contains additional reviews which help to complete the national statement of past work, available resources and current needs in environmental archaeology. Two papers provide between them a summary of environmental investigations in the Midlands, describing the extent of research in this important area. A major review of palaeobotanical work in southern England is presented and the paper on environmental archaeology in London provides another useful and interesting urban overview, complementing that of York. A general picture of the application of pedological investigations to archaeology is given in the review of soil science.

It is intended that these retrospective/prospective reviews should be used as aids to planning excavation strategies and research programmes, since they provide recommendations as to areas of work which might be given greater emphasis in the future.

ACKNOWLEDGEMENTS

I would like to thank the Publication Section of the Historic Buildings and Monuments Commission for England for the tremendous effort put into publishing these reviews — especially Alison Cook who took on the enormous task of copy-editing both volumes. I would also like to thank the HBMCE Drawing Office for improving and often redrawing illustrations.

The Science Panel of the Ancient Monuments Board for England (Professors Renfrew, West and Jope) made many apt and useful suggestions for which I am very grateful. I am also most grateful to John Musty and other colleagues in the Ancient Monuments Laboratory for their helpful advice.

Helen C M Keeley (Editor)

The Editor and authors would like to point out that many of the 'forthcoming' and 'in press' entries in the Lists of References may now have been published; however, financial constraints at a late stage of production have made it impossible to update these.

*Ancient Monuments Laboratory, Historic Buildings and Monuments Commission for England, 23 Savile Row, London, W1X 2HE

Chapter 1

A SURVEY OF ENVIRONMENTAL ARCHAEOLOGY
IN THE SOUTH MIDLANDS

Mark Robinson and Bob Wilson

Introduction

Environmental investigations are complementary with conventional excavations for obtaining a proper understanding of the archaeological heritage of the British Isles, and the evidence for both is facing similar threats. This paper attempts to bring together the findings of the many reports, notes and other articles on environmental archaeology in the counties of Bedfordshire, Buckinghamshire, Northamptonshire and Oxfordshire. Its purpose is to give a comprehensive account of what is known about the environmental archaeology of the region and to provide guidelines for future organisation and funding by the Department of the Environment in this part of England. Accordingly, the text has been divided into three sections:

The first provides the geological and archaeological background, gives our definition of environmental archaeology, and describes the history of the subject in the region.

The second and major section describes our current understanding of environment, ecology and culture in the region from the Late Glacial to the Post-Medieval period.

The third section deals with regional needs and priorities of environmental archaeology services which have been, and should continue to be, facilitated by the DOE or the inheritors of its responsibilities.

1   The Background to the Region and Environmental Archaeology

The Geology, Physiography and Soils of the Region; Environmental Remains

The counties of Bedfordshire, Buckinghamshire, Northamptonshire and Oxfordshire are in the heart of Lowland England. The region lies across the central part of the belt of Jurassic and Cretaceous rocks which strikes from Dorset north-east to the Wash. The north-west and south-east borders to the region tend to follow the line of strike, although the projecting south-east corner of Buckinghamshire extends into the Palaeogene sediments of the London Basin. The strata dip to the south-east, each sheet disappearing under the next overlying one. The deposits are entirely sedimentary, being mostly marine clays, sand and limestones (including chalk). Three river systems have shaped the region, the Upper to Middle Thames, the Upper Nene and the Upper Ouse. They have had the effect of cutting down through the clays, creating a landscape of clay vales and plains with limestone, or to a lesser extent, sandstone ridges. The hills tend to run south-west/north-east, with their scarps facing north-west. Superimposed on this landscape in many places are drift deposits.

Figures 1–4 are drawn to illustrate geomorphology and geology and to show location of sites of note. Some information, for example, land contours could not be obtained at the scale the maps were drawn. The figures lack detail and completeness and some information varies from map to map. Readers investigating particular sites should refer to the official survey maps. The geological account has been prepared with reference to the Institute of Geological Sciences solid geology and drift geology maps and memoirs to the maps, Arkell (1939) and Jarvis (1973).

The Solid Geology (Figure 4)

Running in a band along the north-west side of the region is high ground, from part of the Cotswolds in the south-west to Rockingham Forest in the north-east. It is a major watershed, being the source of important tributaries of the Warwickshire Avon, the Welland, the Thames, the Great Ouse and the Nene. The scarp to these hills tends to follow the regional boundary, where the Avon and Welland have cut through the earliest rocks in the region, the clays of the Lower Lias. The Oxfordshire Cotswolds are mostly composed of iron-rich limestone of the Middle Lias in the Banbury area, and the limestones of the Great Oolite and Cornbrash further south. They are drained southwards into the Thames system. In the middle of this belt of high ground, the Great Ouse drains the Great Oolite and Cornbrash eastwards. Further to the north-east the high ground comprises the Inferior Oolite (Northamptonshire Ironstone) and the Great Oolite. The River Nene, however has cut through these limestones into the clay of the Upper Lias, bifurcating the higher ground with a valley running north-east.

At the foot of this range of limestone hills is a broad expanse of Oxford Clay vale. The north-east half is drained to the north-east by the River Ouse. The south-west half is drained by the Thames system, again by rivers running along the line of strike and picking up tributaries from the Cotswolds. There is a general confluence in the vicinity of Oxford.

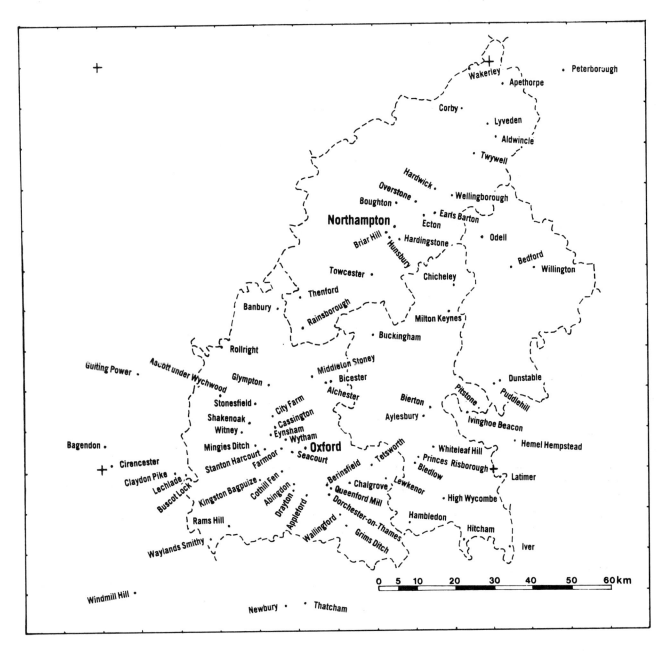

Figure 1   Outline of county boundaries and location map for sites of note in the South Midlands

The next range of hills is not continuous. To the west of Oxford are the Oxford Heights, a ridge of Corallian Sands capped by the Corallian Limestone. The Thames forces its way through this ridge at Oxford. East of Oxford, islands of high ground of Portland Limestone and Lower Greensand rising above Kimmeridge Clay gradually replace the Corallian ridge, while in Bedfordshire there are first Lower Greensand hills around Woburn, then a lower expanse of Lower Greensand further to the north-east.

Beyond the hills is a second clay vale, of Kimmeridge and Gault Clay. It is not nearly as broad as the Oxford Clay vale. The Thames crosses the vale, with tributaries following the line of strike running in from either side. The north-east half of the Gault Clay is drained by the Ouse.

Running along the south-east side of the region is another range of hills, the Downs to the west separated by the Goring Gap, through which the Thames flows, from the Chilterns to the north-east. From the Gault Clay rises a bench of Upper Greensand and then the scarp of the Chalk. On the dip slope of the Chilterns are isolated pockets of sand and gravel of the Reading Beds. Towards the foot of the Chilterns in Buckinghamshire there is a general outcrop of the Reading Beds. In the south-east corner of Buckinghamshire London Clay is present although it is almost entirely covered by drift. The Buckinghamshire dip slope of the Chilterns is drained by the Middle Thames system.

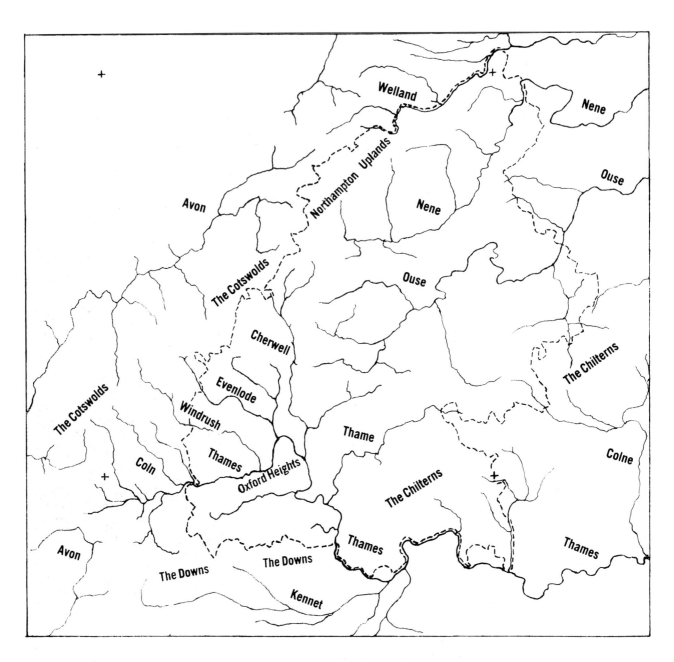

Figure 2   River systems and general topography of the South Midlands

The Drift Geology (Figure 3)

Various sorts of drift deposit cover much of parts of the region. Except in the valley bottoms, there is an extensive covering of chalky boulder clay in east Northamptonshire, east Buckinghamshire and Bedfordshire, extending as far south as the beginning of the Gault Clay. On the dip slope of the Chilterns, Clay with Flints covers much of the Chalk that is not dissected by dry valleys. There are also flint fan gravels and sludged chalk muds spilling down from the Chilterns and Downs.

At the foot of the Chilterns dip slope, in the Boulder Clay region and on top of some of the hills in the region are glacial sands and gravels, which tend to have a high quartzite content. They are very different from the broad flat expanses of Pleistocene terrace gravel which step down to floodplains of the major rivers. Such terraces are most extensive in the Thames Valley, the Upper Thames having four principal gravel terraces but they are also present alongside the Nene and the Ouse. Throughout most of the region, the river terraces have a high limestone content, but where they have been derived from the chalk, flint is more important. The Thames, Nene and Ouse also have broad floodplains which are still regularly inundated. They are covered with alluvial clays to clay loam.

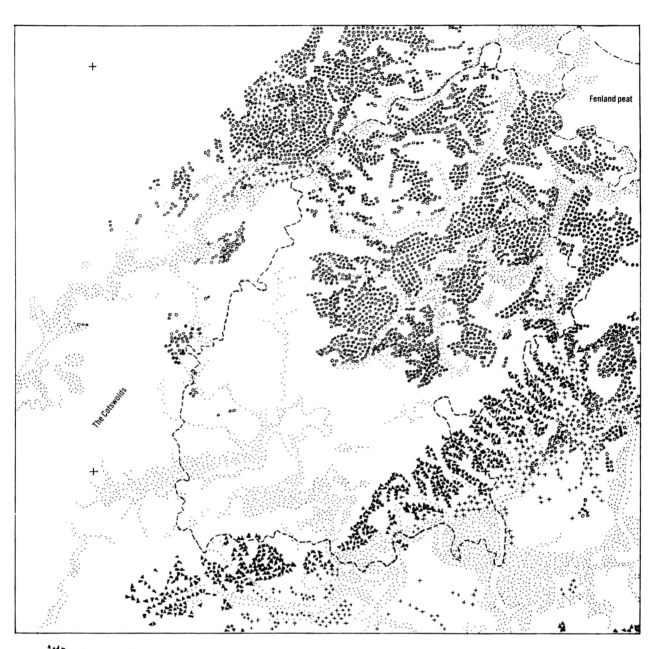

Fenland peat

The Cotswolds

△△▷ Clay with flints

°⊙°° Boulder Clay & morainic drift

River terrace gravels, sands & alluvium

+₊+ Other sand and gravel

Figure 3   Drift geology of the region

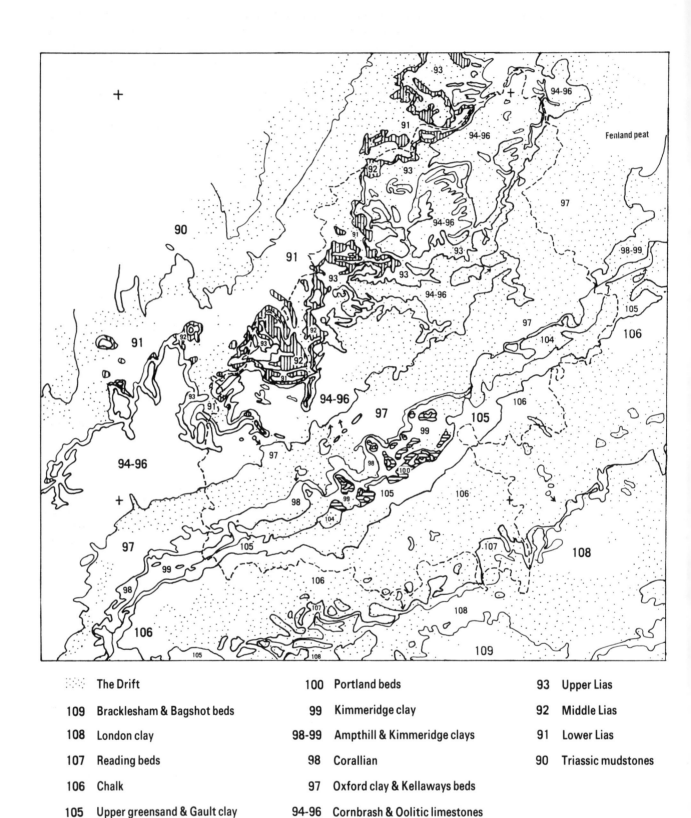

The Drift

109	Bracklesham & Bagshot beds	100	Portland beds	93	Upper Lias
108	London clay	99	Kimmeridge clay	92	Middle Lias
107	Reading beds	98-99	Ampthill & Kimmeridge clays	91	Lower Lias
106	Chalk	98	Corallian	90	Triassic mudstones
105	Upper greensand & Gault clay	97	Oxford clay & Kellaways beds		
104	Lower greensand	94-96	Cornbrash & Oolitic limestones		

Figure 4   Simplified solid and other geology of the region

The Soils

The soils of the region are too complicated for anything more than general trends to be given. As is only to be expected, where limestones, sands or gravels form the parent material, their soils tend to be light and free draining whereas there are heavier soils on the clays, Boulder Clay and Clay with Flints. Most of the region has calcareous to circumneutral soils. Only on the sands, flint or quartz gravels, the Clay with Flints and a few decalcified areas of Boulder Clay do more acidic soils develop. The Upper Greensand gives a fertile acidic soil, whereas the other acid soils tend to be poor. In particular the glacial sands and gravels can give highly acidic podzols. The major areas of very acid soil are on the dip slope of the Chilterns, derived from various parent materials, on the Lower Greensand and Corallian Sands which run in a belt right across the region, and in places in the north-east of the region on glacial sands and gravels and where the boulder clay has become decalcified, for example at Woburn. There is also an important area of acid soil on shallow glacial drift and boulder clay to the west of Oxford at Eynsham Hall and there are some acid soils on sands bedded between the limestones of the Inferior Oolite.

Environmental Remains

Carbonised remains are obviously capable of surviving in all the soils of the region. Bones survive in most soils but unless they were moderately or quickly covered with calcareous sediment they usually become eroded and brittle as a result of rainwater leaching or other weathering. Mollusc shells survive in soils with free calcium carbonate but non-calcareous brown earths were formerly extensive over much of the limestone including parts of the Cotswolds and the river terrace gravels. Shells are not present in these soils. Only in a few parts of the region are soils sufficiently acidic for pollen to be preserved without suffering earthworm disturbance. Pollen and a range of other organic remains including seeds, wood and insect fragments are preserved by waterlogged anaerobic conditions. There is not much peat in the region but a few steep-sided valleys on the high ground of the Corallian which have had their outflow impeded contain small peat fens. Peat also fringes some of the rivers, often beneath a covering of alluvium or river sediments and can be found in cut-off river channels. Organic preservation also occurs in archaeological features which have been dug below the water table. The water table is generally close to the surface on the clays and in the lower river terrace gravels. On the chalk and some of the other limestones, the water table is very deep, but quite often there are thin bands of clay in the sands which result in perched water tables. Occasionally the same effect is seen in the limestones. There is much Post-Glacial alluvium in the valley bottoms while the dry valleys of the chalk often contain Post-Glacial hillwash.

Archaeology in the Region

In recent years most archaeology in the region has been rescue orientated. Originally, it was often dependent on the initiative of local archaeological societies and more specific committees. Gradually, county organisations took over responsibility for co-ordinating work. They undertake surveys and rescue excavations, although separate organisations were created to cover the area of the two new town development corporations. The Department of the Environment provides the main funding for rescue archaeology in the region and through the Inspectorate of Ancient Monuments is a major influence on excavation policy. Significant funding has also been given by local authorities and some of the commercial firms whose activities are destroying archaeological sites.

Rescue archaeology in the region has been directed against five major threats:

1. Urban expansion, especially around Abingdon, and within the area of the new town development corporations of Milton Keynes and Northampton.

2. Re-development of the centre of Medieval towns, especially Bedford, Oxford and Northampton.

3. Gravel extraction from the terraces of the Nene, Ouse and Thames Valleys.

4. Ore extraction in the ironstone region of Northamptonshire.

5. Road building.

A sixth threat, at least as serious as the others, is plough damage, but its effects are insidious, and the DOE has not funded excavations on these sites in the past.

Inevitably, the concentration of archaeological effort into certain areas has resulted in a biased coverage for the environmental archaeology of the region. It seems probable that this bias will be maintained by rescue archaeology in the near future. Destruction of sites continues at an alarmingly high rate and the need for an adequate archaeological response remains imperative.

Environmental Archaeology

A Definition

Environmental archaeology consists of studies directed towards understanding the evolving status of man within and related to diverse ecological systems, including both their biotic and abiotic components. Ecological principles are an important key to the understanding of the environmental archaeology of a region, but often much conventional ecological work has conveniently focussed on entities such as individual plant and animal communities. Our emphasis is upon past human activity which often simultaneously related a number of distinctive ecosystems and thus involved a higher level of biological and social organisation. The overall and special considerations can be termed ecocultural. An ecoculture is here defined as the fundamental organisation of each type of society and the particular ecosystems to which it is passively or dynamically associated. We see the purpose of environmental archaeology as helping to characterise each distinctive ecoculture and, in the case of this survey, tracing the environmental developments which took place in the region.

Associated Disciplines

Environmental archaeology as a self-conscious entity is a comparatively recent subject although it primarily involves well established disciplines, including botany, zoology and pedology. The identification and comment on remains from archaeological sites has taken place for many years. Various other relevant but disparate lines of investigation have taken place. These are listed below with regional examples.

1. *Historical documentation* Much information on the region has been gathered together in the Victoria County Histories.

2. *Archaeological excavations and field survey* The results of very many excavations in the region are given in the county journals of the region: *Bedfordshire Archaeological Journal, Northamptonshire Archaeology, Oxoniensia* and *Records of Buckinghamshire*. There are also various archaeological surveys, for example Benson and Miles (1974).

3. *Geological descriptions* e.g. Arkell (1947), Institute of Geological Sciences maps and memoirs.

4. *Soil surveys* e.g. Jarvis (1973).

5. *Climatic Studies.*

6. *Faunal and floral listing and collection* Species lists and general comments are given in some Victoria County Histories, there are also county floras e.g. Druce (1886) and insect lists e.g. Walker (1906).

7. *Ecological studies* Much ecological investigation has taken place around Oxford eg on the flora of Thames flood-meadows (Baker 1937) and at Wytham Wood, Oxfordshire (Elton 1966, 29–61).

8. *Surveys of agriculture and forestry* e.g. Young (1813), Jones (in Martin and Steele 1954).

9. *Geographical syntheses* Oxfordshire has been well served by regional surveys (Martin and Steele 1954; Emery 1974), the other counties have had limited treatment.

Limitations of the survey

There was insufficient time to make much use of the various lines of investigation listed above. For the same reason environmental research from the bulk of the Paleolithic period has been omitted. Thus the following pages are devoted to the discussion of the information derived from biological remains, soils and sediments of Flandrian Age which have been discovered by the excavation of archaeological or natural deposits.

Historical Development

Until recently, instead of the examination of all potential sources of environmental material, work was largely confined to the identification of larger items found on excavations: mostly bones but occasionally charcoals or a cache of charred grain. Yet even animal bones have had a long history of neglect (Figure 5). Some excavation reports show that bones cannot have been collected or were thrown away without thought of conservation. If bones were examined, the results were little quantified or discussed. Curiously, there seems to have been a decline in standards in the early years of this century, perhaps as a result of a widening of the gap between archaeology and the natural sciences. At the turn of the century A H Cocks, for example, was giving descriptions of species, skeletal elements and bone measurements. He estimated the height of horses and attempted to explain occupational debris in archaeological features (Cocks 1897, on the site at Hedsor, Buckinghamshire; Cocks 1909, on Ellesborough, Buckinghamshire).

After this date bones are not commonly mentioned or collections may be dismissed in a few lines, for example an important group from the Abingdon Causewayed Camp (Dudley-Buxton 1928). Presence of wild species remained of interest to some zoologists (e.g. Newton in Cocks 1921, on Hambledon Villa, Buckinghamshire; Platt 1946, on Poyle Farm,

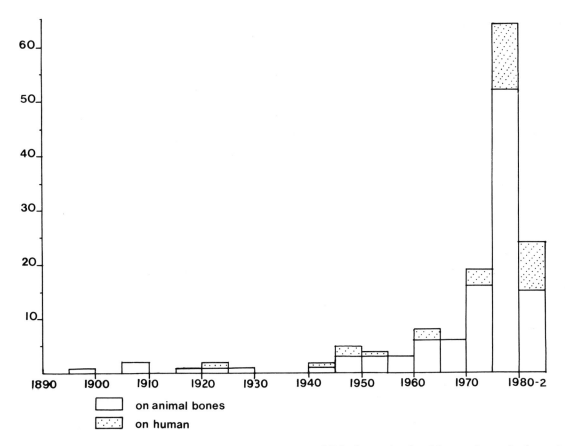

Figure 5   Frequency of reports, notes, or relevant papers published on animal and human bones in the region since 1890

Buckinghamshire) but normally bones of domestic animals were not quantified except in scanty terms. Occasionally there is an exception but the accumulation of some data also led to amusing speculation for instance from measurements of the human skull (Keith 1921).

It is only within the past fifteen years that the sampling of archaeological deposits for biological remains has become at all prevalent within the region. Even when sampling took place, the earlier investigators were usually interested in drawing general climatic conclusions from their results. While these climatic interpretations are sometimes suspect, the results can sometimes be re-interpreted to give local ecological information about the site, for example the Mollusca from the old ground surface beneath a round barrow at the Cop, Bledlow, Buckinghamshire, (Kennard in Head 1934–40, 347–8) comprise a fauna of dry grassland.

Several noteworthy investigations of different aspects of the past environment of the region all aimed at particular problems did, however, take place. An extremely useful pollen sequence was obtained from Cothill Fen, Oxfordshire (Clapham and Clapham 1939). It was one of the sites from which the Post-Glacial vegetational succession for the British Isles was defined in terms of pollen zones (Godwin 1940). Material was examined from many sites in the region by Jessen and Helbaek for their survey of early crops in Britain, which was largely based upon the evidence of seed impressions in pottery (Jessen and Helbaek 1944; Helbaek 1952). Some Oxfordshire sites were included by Cornwall in his project on Bronze Age soil change (Cornwall 1953).

A systematic approach to environmental evidence is apparent in the rescue excavations at Dorchester-on-Thames during 1946–47. Excavators and environmentalists posed specific questions about the past, soil was sieved with a 2mm mesh to recover cremated human bones (Zeuner, Cornwall and Summer 1951). It is unfortunate that biological remains were few or poorly preserved because several decades elapsed before such detailed investigations took place on the Thames gravels again.

A gradual improvement in the quantity and quality of information and discussion is appreciable in bone reports from c1945 onwards. Most of the advances in both reporting and in filling gaps in the cultural record took place on sites around Oxford, but later some detailed work was done in Buckinghamshire and Northamptonshire. Bedfordshire has been neglected.

In the late 1960's and early 1970's, much important work was done on Mollusca and soils in the limestone parts of the region, especially the Chilterns, by Evans (1972). Not only did these investigations result in much information about the past environment on a geological substrate in England from which there was previously little evidence, they also greatly advanced the study of molluscs from archaeological sites. Also in recent years, G W Dimbleby has identified charcoal and undertaken pollen analyses on various sites.

Over the past decade, there has been a considerable increase in the amount of rescue archaeology in the region and a rising awareness of the potential of environmental archaeology. In 1974 the Oxfordshire Archaeological Unit (OAU) created three posts for biologists to work on animal and plant remains from its excavations: M Jones (carbonised plant remains), M Robinson (insects, waterlogged macroscopic plant remains and molluscs) and R Wilson (bones). Their work was concentrated upon major excavations of Iron Age and Roman sites on the Thames gravels, one of the main aims of these excavations being the recovery of biological material. It was intended that the evidence from a wide range of biological investigations should be integrated with the archaeological results. Emphasis was given to the problems of sampling site materials (e.g. Jones M, 1978). The following comprise the main projects during this period: Ashville, Abingdon (Parrington 1978), Farmoor (Lambrick and Robinson 1979), Appleford (Hinchliffe and Thomas 1980) and Barton Court Farm, Abingdon (Miles, forthcoming). In 1979, Jones left the OAU to begin work towards a D Phil on carbonised plant remains but continued to examine material from Oxfordshire. The Ancient Monuments Laboratory of the Department of the Environment assumed responsibility for funding the two remaining specialists. Outside Oxfordshire, the DOE funded many post-excavation projects by other workers (e.g. Harman 1979b) while the AM Laboratory initiated two projects on insects from the Roman town of Towcester, Northamptonshire, and the Roman settlement at Odell, Bedfordshire (Girling, in prep.).

In October 1981 the posts of Robinson and Wilson were transferred from the OAU to the University Museum, Oxford, with beneficial access to museum facilities. For the first time in the area, a committee was instituted to coordinate all relevant interests and the future programme of most of the environmental work occurring locally. DOE funding of the posts stipulated that the area of work should be extended from Oxfordshire to cover threatened sites in Bedfordshire, Buckinghamshire and Northamptonshire.

2   Environmental Archaeology of the Region: The Development of Regional Ecoculture

Introduction

This second section describes two views of diverse aspects of successive ecocultures (p22) of the region. The coverage is broadly, but not always, divided according to the conventionally accepted archaeological periods. At the end of this section, several trends of long duration are discussed. The convention of bc/ad has been used for uncalibrated radiocarbon dates, and BC/AD for dates in calendar years.

Methods

Approaches and General Use of Information

In assessing the work that has been done in the region, it is fortunate that most of the identifications of biological remains seem to be reasonably reliable. Some untrustworthy charcoal identifications have been published: both implausible records, for example horse chestnut from a Bronze Age context, and identifications which have been taken too far. There are, however, sites from which charcoal has been identified by reputable workers.

The archaeological stratigraphy and dating of most of the deposits investigated recently seems reliable. Only the normal precautions need to be taken when considering the evidence from sites. For example, on some there is the possibility of burrowing animals causing contamination of non-waterlogged deposits. The stratigraphy and dating of material from some of the earlier excavations is dubious and it has been treated with caution.

In this section of the survey, Bob Wilson discusses evidence from animal bones, human bones and edible invertebrates, chiefly marine molluscs, and M Robinson covers the remaining types of environmental material. The different nature of our respective lines of evidence has resulted in us developing different approaches.

With bones, the evidence is relatively similar from site to site: the same few species forming the major part of each assemblage. To avoid repetitive summaries of site data, a thematic approach was adopted.

Any discussion of the remaining environmental evidence must be very eclectic, ranging from, for example, the Diptera which fed on a corpse in a stone coffin, to pollen from a peat fen giving widespread information on the tree cover. It is only possible to give an idea of the investigations which have taken place if details are given on a site by site basis before the general discussion for each period.

Robinson has limited his part of the survey to sites within the four counties while Wilson has extended his coverage to include a larger area to give an adequate picture of the regional periphery.

Use of Information from Animal Bones

The use of data from bones requires some further elaboration here. Percentages of the major species in counts of the total number of bones are used because although these are sometimes suspect, they are obtainable from the majority of reports. The figures used here are calculated according to my own assessments of data (e.g. Wilson 1978a, 111) but cannot always be provided consistently for each site. In tables of results (A–I) species percentages are given as minimum and maximum ranges for the sites of each cultural period. A minimum sample size of *circa* 200 fragments for each site assemblage was usually adopted. Exceptions are noted.

The inclusion of other quantitative information depends on the extent to which authors have provided and analysed data – particularly in ways similar or different to my own. Some microfiche publications have not been consulted for a lack of time.

Themes for the Discussion of Animal and Human Bones

Where bones are discussed it would be inept to treat them in the context of 'the physical surroundings of man' as constitutes the self imposed limits of a number of authors and their useful purpose in defining environmental archaeology. Not only do studies of human bones thus rest in a conceptual and practical limbo but the majority of animal bones simply appear to represent merely the physical surroundings of a species whose characteristics do not change. Yet not only is it known that there evolved profound relationships of man with domesticated animals and plants, but these very relationships help to define the ecological status of each ethnic group of man. The relationships should explain the separation of cultural and natural communities and the ability of people to modify their physical surroundings.

The conceptual difficulties and their reorientation stimulated the proposed idea of ecoculture and the definition of it already given at the beginning. Unfortunately any subsidiary conceptual matrix or hierarchy of subcontexts does not exist in any formal or rigorous sense. Consequently it is not possible to give an appropriate weighting to useful explanatory principles and variables or even to say confidently what these all are. However the following simple themes will be found to recur as the evidence for each period is discussed.

(a)   The vegetational succession following the last glaciation is altered in a series of distinctive ecocultures which provide successive but fluctuating changes.

(b)   Toward an open and rural landscape with settlements centred at first on the better drained often calcareous soils or substrates.

(c)   A diversifying prominence of domesticated animals and their associated pastures.

(d)   A general increase in human population and higher ratios of people to animals.

(e)   A decreasing consumption of meat, an expansion of arable agriculture and of subsistence economies based on secondary products or use of live animals.

(f)   Emerging urban aggregations and economies based on urban and rural organisation exchange and external trade.

(g)   Social differentiation and spatial separation of hierarchical elements in societies.

(h)   Division of labour, trade specialisation and intensification, and the creation of industrial environments.

The Late Glacial Period, 13000bc – 8300bc

Tundra

The events of the Late Glacial (late Devensian) will be considered in order to provide a background for more recent developments. By the Late Glacial, c13000bc, the region had already acquired its present day gross morphology, and there was no covering layer of ice. Most of the river gravels and glacial drift had been deposited. An extremely interesting exposure on the Chilterns at Pitstone, Buckinghamshire spanned all three zones of the late Devensian (Evans 1966, 347–53). The Zone I (Older Dryas) deposit consisted of chalk mud and fine rubble lining a channel cut into coombe rock. It contained a sparse fauna of such cold-tolerant open country species as *Pupilla muscorum, Vallonia costata,* and *V. pulchella*. Above this deposit were two horizons of rendzina soil, separated by a little solifluxion debris, Zone II (Alerod) soils. Mollusca were much more abundant in these soils than in the preceding deposit, additional species being represented including *Helicella itala, Trichia hispida* and the now very rare *Catinella arenaria*. The two soil horizons suggest a double oscillation in the Allerod Interstadial, thus confirming pollen evidence from elsewhere in England (Evans 1972, 224–5). Cold conditions returned with Zone III (Younger Dryas) and a thick deposit of flint solifluxion gravels covered everything.

At Mingies Ditch, Oxfordshire, a fauna and flora indicating cold conditions was recovered from organic silt in the bottom of one of the many gravel-filled channels which cross the top of the Devensian gravels of the lower Windrush/Thames floodplain (Robinson, unpublished c). The flow of the Windrush had not yet become restricted to a few well-defined channels and instead consisted of many braided streams working over shifting expanses of gravel. There is also evidence for unstable conditions on the first gravel terrace of the Thames, above river level. At both Thrupp, Abingdon, Oxfordshire (Robinson 1981a; 129, 316–7) and Drayton, Oxfordshire (Robinson, unpublished b), undulating islands of sand covered the limestone river terrace gravels. There was no evidence that this sand had been water-lain. The Mollusca in the sand at Drayton were intrusive but at Thrupp they were all cold-tolerant, terrestrial, open country species. It is possible that the small islands of sandy or loamy drift upon the first terrace of the upper Thames on which the Lashbrook soils developed (Jarvis 1973, 116–17) had a late Devensian wind-blown origin.

By Zone III at Farmoor, Oxfordshire, the flow of River Thames had become confined to major channels. Peat from one, which cut the gravels of the floodplain, gave a radiocarbon date of 8650 ± 250 bc (Coope 1976). The insect fauna from the Farmoor channel was dominated by *Helophorus glacialis*, an arctic-alpine species which no longer occurs in Britain, while the plant remains included fruits of *Betula nana* and calyces of *Armeria maritima*, species which do not occur inland in southern Britain at present, but are characteristic of the late Devensian (Coope 1976; Lambrick and Robinson 1979, 141–2).

At Claydon Pike, over the Oxfordshire border in Gloucestershire, hollows divide the first Thames terrace into islands. In one of these hollows a pool had slowly silted. The bottom half of the pool was a *Chara* marl but as the water became shallower, other plants invaded and a peat rich in *Menyanthes trifoliata* seeds formed. Remains of *Betula nana* were present in the *Chara* marl but interestingly fruits of a tree species of *Betula* occurred in the peat, perhaps suggesting an amelioration of conditions. Unfortunately the sequence did not continue any later (Robinson, unpublished a).

The only pollen analysis on a Late Glacial context in the region was from the bottom sample at Apethorpe, Northamptonshire (Sparks and Lambert 1961–62). Here, the valley of the Willow Brook contains much waterlogged fill, perhaps as a result of stream aggradation. The sequence began late in Zone III and spans a considerable part of the post-Glacial period although there are gaps in the sequence and some of the deposits have been re-worked. *Betula* was the only significant tree pollen in the Zone III sample, which a leaf suggested to be *B. nana*. Otherwise, conditions were open, with high values for Gramineae, Cyperaceae and *Filipendula* pollen.

Discussion Conditions in the region during the Late-Glacial were arctic/sub-arctic. Soil formation occurred during slightly warmer phases but in colder periods, solifluxion took place on slopes and there would have been frost-heaving on level ground. The vegetation was of arctic herbs and a few species of low or creeping shrubs such as dwarf birch. The insect fauna was of a type now found in northern Scandinavia or Siberia. By the end of this period, c8300bc, ground conditions had stabilised, river flow was confined to a relatively few channels and stands of tree birch were probably established in more sheltered localities (tree birch may have been present throughout the late glacial and abundant during the Alerod interstadial c10000 – 8800bc).

The Mesolithic, 8300bc – 3500bc

The Development and Dominance of Woodland

With the warming of the climate after the last glaciation, woodland rapidly became established throughout the British Isles. A calcareous fen filling a valley cut into the Corallian limestone and sands of the Oxford Heights at Cothill, Oxfordshire contains a sequence of deposits beginning in the Pre-Boreal and just reaching into the Atlantic. It was investigated for pollen in the early days of pollen analysis, when the pollen-zone system was just being established for Britain and before detailed identifications could be made on non-tree pollen types (Clapham and Clapham 1939). It remains, however, the most useful pollen diagram from the region across these zones. What is more, the valley floor was sufficiently narrow that the picture given can be regarded as largely reflecting the vegetation on the Corallian Ridge itself. The dating for the sequence is based upon pollen zonation. At the bottom of the sequence, the Zone IV (Pre-Boreal) samples had high values for *Betula* (presumably a tree species) and *Salix* while *Pinus* was well represented. *Betula* was probably the predominant tree on dry ground. The opening of Zone V (the first part of the Boreal) was marked by a dramatic fall in *Betula* and *Salix* pollen frequencies and a rise in *Pinus* to become major component of the woodland. *Corylus* first appeared and it increased in importance, as did *Ulmus*. By Zone VI, (the second part of the Boreal), *Betula* had declined to insignificance, *Pinus* had begun its decline and *Quercus* was soon to appear. In the early part of Zone VI, *Pinus/Ulmus* forest was dominant with *Corylus* abundant, but the proportions of *Quercus* and *Corylus* increased, firstly at the expense of *Pinus*, then perhaps at the expense of *Ulmus* too. Towards the latter part of Zone VI, values for *Corylus* pollen fell and the woodlands was of *Quercus/Ulmus*. *Tilia* and *Alnus*, both thermophilous trees, appeared and soon made their presence felt. The uppermost sample in the sequence from Cothill Fen can be placed just into Zone VIIa (Atlantic). It gives what is probably a good picture of the pre-clearance climax woodland on limestone throughout the region. *Quercus* was the most abundant tree pollen type, at 38% of the arboreal pollen, followed by *Alnus* at 35%, *Tilia*

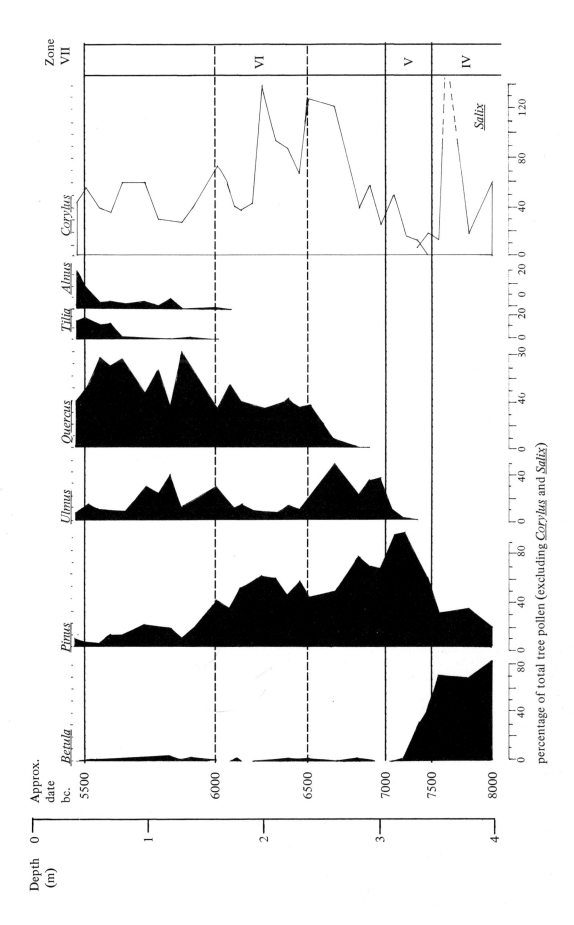

Figure 6   Tree pollen diagram from Cothill Fen (after Clapham and Clapham 1939)

27

at 17% and *Ulmus* at 8%. *Corylus*, not included in the tree pollen sum, was at a proportion of 40% of the total tree pollen. The high value for *Tilia*, when its poor pollen dispersal is taken into account, would suggest that lime was probably the dominant forest tree although much oak and alder was also present. The alder might have tended to grow on the margins of the fen. Some charcoal was present in a sample from towards the bottom of the profile but no evidence for Mesolithic clearance was reflected in the pollen diagram.

A peat deposit with a woodland floral element of an earlier Zone VI character was encountered at Mingies Ditch (Robinson, unpublished c). It had formed in extensive shallows which were once present along the bank of the River Windrush. *Betula, Corylus* and *Quercus* sp. were represented amongst the macroscopic plant remains, seeds of *Betula* sp. were particularly abundant. *Alnus glutinosa* seeds were absent. Stratigraphically later than the previous sample was an accumulation of small branches and peat around a substantial oak log. This deposit likewise seems to have been laid down in shallow water at the river's edge. As with the previous sample, aquatic species were abundant but woodland of a more thermophilous nature was also indicated. *Corylus* and *Quercus* sp. remained but *Betula* sp. was entirely absent, having been replaced by *Alnus glutinosa*, represented by both seeds and catkins. The date of this deposit could be any-thing between later Zone VI to early Zone VIII (the Sub-Atlantic). Similar woodland, but likewise undated, grew on the Thames floodplain at Farmoor, Oxfordshire, where alder catkins and a hazelnut shell were found preserved in what seems to have been a tree root hole. It was from the edge of an old river channel, sealed beneath alluvium of probable late Iron Age date, which was beneath a layer of Roman peat (Layer 1072). The deposit was just to the north-west of F.1182 (Lambrick and Robinson 1979, 8) but was previously unpublished.

The Apethorpe sequence (p26) continued into Zone IV, a tree species of birch apparently being the main component of the woodland (Sparks and Lambert, 1961–62). There was a great reduction in non-tree pollen compared with the Zone III sample. Further up the core, the value for *Betula* pollen fell while there were high values for *Corylus, Pinus* and *Ulmus*, indicating the opening of Zone V. Above this level, the deposits had become mixed. The Mollusca from the Zone IV and early Zone V samples were reedswamp and riverside marsh species, while the macroscopic plant remains indicated a reed swamp of *Schoenoplectus lacustris*. A more interesting molluscan sequence was examined from the edge of the Apethorpe deposit, in which land molluscs were dominant. Unfortunately pollen was absent. The earliest samples containing abundant Mollusca were rich in such woodland species as *Discus rotundatus, Oxychilus cellarius* and *Clausilia bidentata* while open country species were uncommon. *Acicula fusca* and *Vertigo angustior*, now very rare snails in England, were present.

At Higham Ferrers, on the Nene floodplain, Northamptonshire and Harrold, on the Ouse floodplain, Bedfordshire, what were regarded as early Post Glacial deposits were found underneath alluvium and on top of the river gravels (Hall and Nickerson 1966). It is stated that floral and faunal remains were present in both deposits and a skull fragment was found at Higham, but no further details are known.

In the Colne Valley, Buckinghamshire, there are extensive tracts of alluvium over the Pleistocene gravels (Lacaille 1963), Mesolithic artefacts have frequently been found under the alluvium and there is also much peat. Lacaille regarded the valley floor as having become drowned not long after it was occupied. In a section exposed at Iver, there was peat over the gravel covered by shelly marl which was in turn under peaty clay. Early Mesolithic flints were discovered on top of the gravel. Fragments of birch, pine and hazel wood, hazel nuts and red deer bones were recovered from the lower peat. Pollen from the sequence was badly preserved (G F Mitchell in Lacaille 1963, 152–5) but in the lower peat *Corylus* and *Pinus* were the most abundant pollen types (although the abundance of *Pinus* was thought to have been exaggerated by differen-tial decay). Woodland conditions were also indicated by the pollen from the shelly marl, with *Corylus* and *Quercus* the predominant trees. Mitchell regarded these two deposits as being late Boreal rather than final Boreal in date. The molluscs from the shelly marl, identified by A G Davis, were clean flowing water/lake species such as *Bithynia tentaculata* and *Valvata piscinalis*. A nearby excavation by D Allen encountered a band of tufa following the contour and covering the Pleistocene gravels. On the downhill side of the tufa, humified peat covered the gravel. A few Mesolithic flints were found under the tufa and peat. The tufa contained similar clean flowing water/lake molluscs to the shelly marl mentioned above, which is unusual for tufa (Evans 1972, 299) and was an *in situ* deposit which seems to have formed in shallow water along the margin of the lake (Robinson, unpublished d). In the British Isles tufa tends to date from Zone VIIa, the usually forming in swampy pools surrounded by woodland (Evans 1972, 299).

Several other tufa deposits are known from the region, but they have not been examined in detail: Gerard's Cross, Buckinghamshire (Barfield 1977, 319–20); Latimer, Buckinghamshire (Branigan 1971, 102); and several sites in Oxfordshire (Arkell 1947, 247), East Challow, Over Norton, Swerford and Wilcote.

Pre-Neolithic molluscan assemblages were discovered in sub-soil hollows beneath a long barrow at Ascott-under-Wychwood, Oxfordshire on the Inferior Oolitic Limestone of the Cotswolds (Evans 1971, 31–41, 65; Evans 1972, 251–6). In the earliest fill of one of the hollows was a woodland fauna but *Vallonia costata*, an open-country species, was at 10 to 12% of the total. *V. costata* sometimes lives in low numbers in woodland and here is taken to indicate a slight openness. This seems to be confirmed by low values for *Oxychillus cellarius* and *Discus rotundatus* and high values for *Vitea contracta*. In a somewhat later part of the fill to the hollow, the level of *V. costata* was down to 6%, *O. cellarius* and

D. rotundatus were at the normal values for woodland and *Spermodea lamellata*, which is now a relict woodland species, was also present. Fully forested conditions are suggested. During a later part of this closed woodland phase, a decalcified brown-earth formed in which molluscs were not preserved. It is possible that the molluscan sequence represents the natural development of the closed climax woodland of the latter Boreal and Atlantic periods from more open woodland of the earlier Boreal. The second possibility is that there was only a local opening of the forest canopy in the earlier period. Neolithic finds only occurred on the turf line and in pits but Mesolithic flints and charred hazel nut fragments were found in the subsoil hollow, mainly below the brown-earth soil. This occupation of the site by Mesolithic man may have affected the tree cover.

Woodland molluscan faunas have been discovered from the bottom of several soil profiles in the region, but usually they are difficult to date. The molluscs from a sub-soil hollow at Pink Hill, Buckinghamshire on the Chilterns, however, included *Vertigo alpestris* which suggests a Zone VIIa date (Atlantic) (Evans 1972, 312–4). The fauna reflected a closed woodland environment.

Discussion The period under consideration in this chapter is one when the region saw great environmental change, perhaps entirely as a result of natural agencies. Soil formation took place and a general covering of woodland was established throughout the region. The woodland next went through many changes before the climax forests of the Atlantic. In Zone IV, the Pre-Boreal (8300bc – 7500bc) birch woodland was predominant. During Zone V, the early Boreal (7500bc – 7000bc) pine replaced birch to differing degrees, to be joined by elm and hazel early in Zone VI, the mid Boreal (7000bc – 6500bc). In the middle of Zone VI, the later Boreal (6500bc – 6000bc) oak and hazel were probably co-dominant in the woodland with elm, pine and birch varying in importance throughout the region. Towards the end of Zone VI, the final Boreal (6000bc – 5500bc) alder and lime were increasing in importance while pine and birch had become much less important, pine probably to become almost completely absent from the region. Flowering of hazel seems to have been reduced by a complete closing of the high forest canopy. Zone VIIa, the Atlantic (5500bc – 3500bc) was a period of stability compared with the dynamics of ecological succession in the Boreal. Soils would have become fully developed and each part of the region would have been supporting the edaphic climax vegetation. Combining the results from Cothill Fen with the undated Mingies Ditch sample and later samples from Buscot Lock (Neolithic) and Eynsham Hall Camp (Iron Age) it is possible to suggest the following types of climax woodland for the region: lime wood on relatively well drained calcareous soils, alder on the floodplains and oak on acidic gravels and sands. At one time it was assumed that damp oak wood grew on the areas of clay, although there is no evidence yet, and it is possible that lime was dominant on these soils too. Although each woodland type has been named after only one tree species, all the woodland in the region was probably very diverse, with many species contributing to the canopy. In this woodland lived what are now very rare species of mollusc; evidence from elsewhere in the British Isles would suggest that many other invertebrates which are now extremely rare or extinct would also have lived there.

Man was certainly present in the region during the Boreal and Atlantic but there is no evidence that his effect on the woodland was anything other than slight. Evidently hazelnuts were one of the woodland resources expoloited by Mesolithic man in the region.

A Vertebrate Fauna of Transitional Woodland

Nearby Thatcham, Berkshire (King 1962) provides the only good evidence of mesolithic regional fauna. About 464 fragments of bone were identified.

Table 1 Approximate Percentages of Bone Species Fragments at Thatcham

	%
aurochs	2
pig	25
horse	0.6
dog	0.2
'wild' cat	1
red deer	31
roe	15
beaver	20

Other mammals present include badger, fox, wolf, pine marten, elk and hedgehog. Rabbit was identified also but the excavator called this hare which seems an error and the bone may be intrusive. Birds present were crane, teal, gargeny, mallard, goldeneye and possibly smew and blackbird.

Besides the influence of taphonomic factors in deposition of the bones, the hunting pattern may have distorted the evidence of environment, but woodland and marsh habitats and some open water are indicated. King suggested that the presence of elk and aurochs indicates plant communities in transition from birch forest to that of mixed oak. Several other species present, e.g. goldeneye and smew, could also indicate a climate cooler than the present. Fur bearing animals, particularly beaver, appear important in the mesolithic economy.

Climax Mesolithic Woodland Communities

No bone assemblages have been excavated from this period.

The Neolithic and Beaker Periods, 3500bc — 1600bc

Woodland and Agriculturalists

Earlier Neolithic It is reasonable to assume that Neolithic activity of some sort was underway in the region by about 3500bc. No sites have so far been dated this early but it is possible that some of the rather undiagnostic Neolithic flint scatters belong to the earliest (pre-elm decline) Neolithic. There seems to have been an early expansion of settlement on the Cotswolds, up the various tributaries of the Thames, with a proliferation of long-barrows. One such barrow was at Ascott-under-Wychwood, Oxfordshire, where there were two phases of Neolithic activity (Evans 1971, 31—41, 65; Evans 1972, 251—6). A radiocarbon date of 2943 ± 70 bc was obtained from a Neolithic pit which was sealed by a turf line under the barrow. A date of 2785 ± 70 bc was given by charcoal from the soil surface under the barrow. In one place under the barrow, the soil consisted of relatively stone-free mull-humus of the turf line over dark brown calcareous loam (a rendsina) but above a subsoil hollow was decalcified brown earth (in which molluscs were not preserved) sealed by the same turf line. The rendsina showed no evidence of ever having been ploughed and contained a woodland molluscan fauna. In contrast to the Mesolithic samples from this site, the open country species *Vallonia costata* had fallen to 1% of the total. A very shaded environment is indicated, while the presence of *Acicula fusca*, *Vertigo pusilla* and *V. alpestris* along with the high species diversity suggests a complete lack of human disturbance.

Pollen analysis of ancient soils which are neither anaerobic nor highly acidic gives at best equivocal results but more often gives a spectrum of modern pollen or no pollen at all. The brown earth soil above the subsoil hollow at Ascott was subjected to pollen analysis (Dimbleby and Evans 1974, 117–33). Although it lacked free calcium carbonate, the pH of the soil was suitable for earthworms. It is possible that a significant proportion of the pollen at Ascott did in fact come from the Neolithic woodland on the site, protected from subsequent earthworm contamination by the rubble of the barrow mound and preserved from complete decay by the absence of calcium carbonate. In particular, the *Tilia* pollen at 14% and the *Corylus* pollen at 17% of the total pollen sum may reflect components of the pre-clearance vegetation. The Gramineae and *Plantago lanceolata* pollen may have become incorporated into the profile during the Neolithic grassland phase but could also be post-barrow contamination. A high value for Liguliflorae pollen was probably the result of differential decay.

In contrast to the body of the soil profile, the top 5cm, the Neolithic turf line under the Ascott barrow contained an open-country fauna. *Vallonia costata*, *V. excertrica*, *Pupilla muscorum* and *Vertigo pygmaea*, all indicative of open conditions, made up 61% of the fauna while shade-loving species were down to 20% of the total. The large quantity of pot sherds and flint-knapping debris, spreads of charcoal on and in the turf-line, and several pits all suggest that the change in the environment resulted from tree-clearance by Neolithic man. The turf line had a well-developed, stone-free, structure which probably resulted from earthworm sorting under conditions of stable grassland. Limbrey (1975, 185) raised the possibility of lessivation followed by truncation of the soil profile at Ascott prior to the barrow's construction, but the evidence is uncertain. Subsequently, the clearing at Ascott was abandoned and a woodland floor molluscan fauna developed in the quarry ditches of the barrow (Evans and Jones 1973, 107, 112, 116).

The earliest evidence for cultivation in the region comes from the soil beneath the Neolithic chambered tomb of Wayland's Smithy II, on the Downs (Evans 1971, 65; Evans 1972, 262, 265). A radiocarbon date of 2820 ± 130 bc was obtained from charcoal from the surface of the buried soil. The land-snail fauna, examined by M P Kerney, indicated open grassland. The soil, however, was a rendsina with chalk fragments present throughout the profile, strongly suggesting that mechanical disturbance, possibly by cultivation, took place before its burial. Soon after the construction of the barrow, the site became increasingly wooded and remained wooded until almost the end of the Bronze Age (Kerney in Bradley and Ellison 1975, 191).

In contrast, a woodland molluscan fauna was present beneath a Neolithic barrow on the chalk of the Chilterns at Whiteleaf Hill, Buckinghamshire (Kennard in Childe and Smith 1954, 230).

The Abingdon Causewayed Camp, Oxfordshire, on the second Thames gravel terrace produced some occupation debris from the earlier Neolithic (Case 1956) and seems to have been in use between about 3000 and 2500bc (Whittle 1977, 246). Seed impressions on pottery from the site not only give an idea of some of the earliest crops cultivated in the region (Helbaek 1952, 224; Murphy in Case and Whittle 1982): *Triticum dicoccum* and *Hordeum vulgare* but also show some of the woodland species collected for food: *Malus sylvestris* and *Prunus spinosa*. The charcoal examined from some Neolithic contexts in the ditch was mostly *Quercus* but also included *Fraxinus, Corylus, Prunus spinosa* and, interestingly, *Fagus* (Dimbleby in Case 1956, 18). It is the earliest record of beech from the region and with its shallow spreading roots, it might have been a tree well suited to the soils over the relatively compact gravels in some places on the Thames terraces. A further range of taxa, especially shrub species, was subsequently identified from Neolithic charcoal (Western in Case and Whittle 1982).

Charcoal was identified from another causewayed camp at Briar Hill, Northamptonshire (Keepax 1977; Keepax 1980). *Quercus* sp., *Prunus* sp., *Crataegus* type (Rosaceae subfamily Pomoideae), cf *Acer* sp., *Salix/Populus* sp., *Corylus avellana* and *Fraxinus excelsior* were present.

The Later Neolithic: Occupation Sites Rather more later Neolithic sites (that is from towards the end of the 3rd millenium bc onwards) have been investigated. Operations to create a new weir channel for the Thames around Buscot Lock, on the Oxfordshire/Gloucestershire border cut through an old silted up river channel which had possibly resulted from a bend working its way downstream (Robinson 1981a, 80–2, 113–27, 297–315). At the bottom of the profile was peat containing substantial *Alnus glutinosa* logs, animal bones showing signs of butchery, a human femur and a hammer made from the base of a red deer antler. This debris suggests a settlement nearby. A radiocarbon date of 2060 ± 90 bc was obtained from one of the alder logs. The waterlogged deposits were investigated for the full range of preserved plant and invertebrate remains. The majority of the molluscs, seeds and insects were aquatic species but they showed conditions to have been very different from the modern Thames. A clean, well aerated River Thames with rapids in places and much submerged wood had a diverse population of Elmidae including *Macronychus quadrituberculatus* and *Stenelmis canaliculata*, both species which are now very rare in the British Isles and no longer occur in the region.

The pollen (analysed by G W Dimbleby) suggests woodland to have been the predominant non-aquatic environment of the catchment area. Grasses averaged 20% of the total arboreal pollen sum while herbs (excluding Cyperaceae) were only at 6% of tree pollen sum. Likewise, the woodland component of the coleopteran death assemblage was large. Wood and tree-feeding Coleoptera (plus fungus feeders and predators which are strictly associated with wood) made up 17% of the total terrestrial Coleoptera from Buscot, a similar value to that from woodland sites elsewhere. *Alnus* was by far the most abundant pollen type from Buscot and seeds of *A. glutinosa* were the most numerous from a terrestrial species. There was a great range of other indicators for the importance of alder including wood, twigs, catkins, the now rare alder-leaf beetle, *Chrysomela aenea* and galls of the alder-leaf mite, *Eriophyes laevis inangulis*. Alder was probably the predominant forest tree growing on the floodplain, right up to the bank of the river and perhaps extending onto the first gravel terrace as well.

Other forest trees were not well represented by their pollen, perhaps due to the wide expanse of floodplain on either side of the river. The two Buscot samples did, however, contain 36 fruits of *Tilia* sp. between them, sufficient to show that lime was at least of local importance. *Quercus* sp. at 7% followed by *Tilia* sp. at 4% of the arboreal pollen sum were the best represented forest trees after *Alnus* in the pollen results. Lime was perhaps dominant on the limestone hills above Buscot while oak and perhaps alder were more important in mixed woodland on the clay slopes.

The status of secondary woodland at Buscot is uncertain. Some of the *Alnus* could have been re-growth after clearance and *Corylus* was well represented by macroscopic remains, including the nut-feeding weevil *Curculio nucum*, as well as by pollen (at 31% of the total pollen sum, from which *Corylus* has been excluded). However, similar percentages of *Corylus* pollen also occur in Atlantic deposits. Other shrubs represented by macroscopic remains or indicated by insects including *Rhamnus catharticus, Prunus spinosa, Salix* sp. and *Thelycrania sanguinea*. Some of these shrubs do not tolerate deep shade. They probably grew along the bank of the river and around any man-made clearing which provided an illuminated break in the forest canopy.

The seeds included both species which could have formed part of the field layer in a wet alder wood, such as *Eupatorium cannabium* and plants from the ground/field layer of slightly better drained land such as *Mercurialis perennis*. The tree-feeding species of beetles show the full range from seed eating species, leaf feeders, a species which bores into freshly exposed wood containing fermenting sap (*Platypus cylindrus*) through to species of very rotten wood (eg *Melanotus rufipes*), without an excessive preponderance of one type. The remainder of the woodland part of the coleopterous fauna seems balanced, and, from the presence of species which are now rarities, the whole fauna can be regarded as characteristic of the ancient woodland.

Seeds and pollen of grassland or broken ground herbs which are not obviously related to riverbank succession were also present, in particular *Plantago lanceolata* pollen at 1.2% of the total tree pollen sum and some seeds of *P. major*. *Vallonia pulchella* was one of the more abundant species of terrestrial mollusc present in the two samples and it does not live in shady habitats (Evans 1972, 199–200). Dung beetles from the genera *Geotrupes, Aphodius* and *Onthophagus* made up 2.5% of the total terrestrial Coleoptera, although this is a very much lower proportion than from most open country sites. Just how much grazed grassland existed other than small riverside clearings remains uncertain. Small cultivated areas may have been present although the single grain of cereal-type pollen identified is, by itself, insufficient to indicate arable.

An agricultural clearance on the first terrace of the Thames at Thrupp, Oxfordshire, existed around a small penannular enclosure excavated by D Miles which perhaps enclosed an occupation site (Robinson 1981a, 82–4, 128–30, 316–17). A sequence of samples through the enclosure ditch, which contained Abingdon and Peterborough Ware pottery, was examined for molluscs. All contained open country faunas, but whether clearance had been extensive around the site and whether shrub was allowed to colonise after abandonment remains unknown.

M Jones (1980) examined carbonised seeds from two Grooved Ware contexts on the Thames second terrace at Barton Court Farm, Abingdon and at Mount Farm, Berinsfield, Oxfordshire. The finds were from pits which might have been small grain storage pits in settlements. In both cases a few grains of *Triticum dicoccum*, *T. aestivocompactum* and *Hordeum* sp. were identified along with a few weed seeds and many hazelnut shells. In addition, *Malus sylvestris* pips were present at Barton Court. G Taylor identified carbonised hazelnut shells in company with *Corylus*, *Fraxinus* and *Crataegus*-type charcoal from some Neolithic storage pits exposed in a chalk quarry on the Chilterns at Puddlehill, Bedfordshire (Taylor in Field *et al* 1964, 366). No attempt was made to investigate the fill of the pits, which contained Rinyo-Clacton type pottery, for charred cereals.

A later Neolithic occupation site was found at Ecton, Northamptonshire beneath the alluvium of the Nene floodplain. Pollen analysis was undertaken on a section through the alluvium but there was evidence of some earthworm action and the pollen was badly preserved (Dimbleby in Moore and Williams 1975, 27–9). It seems unlikely that much of the pollen from the Neolithic levels was Neolithic in date.

What were regarded as pits associated with a Neolithic encampment were excavated on the Lower Cornbrash limestone at Stacey Bushes, Buckinghamshire (Green 1976). From the fill of one undercut pit, which was interpreted as a clay borrow pit and contained Grooved Ware and Grimston Style pottery, a radiocarbon date of 1830 ± 150 bc was obtained. It is reported that J G Evans found a molluscan assemblage, indicative of shady conditions, in this pit. An unusual range of charcoal was identified (Keepax 1975): probably *Pinus* sp., *Taxus baccata*, *Clematis vitalba*, *Corylus avellana*, *Quercus* sp., and *Crataegus*-type. It seems unlikely that *Pinus* would have been growing on the Cornbrash at a Neolithic date, when most of the other species are characteristic of woodland edge or stages of woodland recolonisation on limestone after clearance. It is possible that the assemblage from Stacey Bushes is mixed, with early Boreal *Pinus* charcoal, later charcoal and Neolithic pottery. The pits might have been tree root holes rather than man-made features.

Later Neolithic Ritual Sites Limited environmental investigations have taken place on several ritual sites of the later Neolithic on the Thames gravels. Soil investigations were carried out at the Dorchester henge complex, Oxfordshire (Cornwall 1953, 141–3) but the conclusions drawn from them can no longer be accepted. *Ilex aquifolium* was present amongst some of the more commonly found types of charcoal from a Peterborough Ware context at the Dorchester complex while charred oak plants were present in another feature of the same date (Stephens and Orr in Atkinson *et al.* 1951, 121–2). The posts from a henge within the cursus at Dorchester, which had been burnt *in situ* were also oak (Robinson, unpublished f). At the other ritual site, the Drayton Cursus, Oxfordshire, a non-calcareous silty clay loam formed a thin covering over the gravel where the cursus crossed the Thames floodplain (Robinson, unpublished g). There was no evidence for flooding on the site during the Neolithic, all the alluvium covering the cursus being later. Preservation by waterlogging in the cursus was very poor, but rotten remains of hazelnuts were present. The illuvial horizon of a truncated sol lessive was discovered beneath the bank of the Devil's Quoits henge on the second Thames terrace at Stanton Harcourt, Oxfordshire (Limbrey 1975, 190). She suggested that wind had been the most important agent of erosion. An alternative interpretation for the truncation of the soil would be that turf had been stripped from the area for use in construction of the bank.

The soil beneath a Neolithic round cairn at Rollright, on the limestone of the Oxfordshire/Warwickshire border, excavated by G H Lambrick, was a red/brown non-calcareous, stone free loam which showed no sign of lessivation (Robinson, unpublished h).

Near another ritual site, a Neolithic mortuary enclosure at Aldwincle, Northamptonshire, Peterborough Ware pottery was found 2.5m down in what had been a marshy area/old stream bed on the Nene floodplain (Metcalf 1973). Associated material included logs, twigs, hazelnuts and mussel shells, but unfortunately they were not investigated.

Possible Neolithic Sites Mollusca from two sites of possible Neolithic date suggest regeneration of woodland after their abandonment. A small prehistoric ditch on the ironstone of the Inferior Oolite at St Peter's Street, Northampton contained a woodland fauna (Evans in Williams 1979, 338–9) while on the chalk of the Chilterns at Pitstone, Buckinghamshire, a rich fauna indicative of a closed woodland environment was discovered in the bottom of a possible Neolithic ditch, which had been truncated by a ploughwash deposit (Evans 1966, 355–6). The ditch (which cut Zone

III deposits already mentioned) contained some species which are extinct or rare in southern Britain at present: *Vertigo alpestris, V. pusilla, Ena montana, Acicula fusca, Balea perversa.* A radiocarbon date of 1960 ± 220 bc was obtained from charcoal buried beneath ploughwash in a nearby exposure at Pitstone (Evans and Valentine 1974).

The Beaker Period Settlements using late Neolithic pottery continued up until about 1800bc in the region, overlapping with users of Beaker pottery from about 2000bc onwards. Few Beaker Period sites have been investigated. On the second Thames terrace site at City Farm, Oxfordshire the banding of *Cepaea* spp. was used very tentatively to suggest grassland conditions (Cain in Case *et al.* 1964–65, 91–4), but molluscs from all the phases of the site were considered together. At Ecton, Northamptonshire on the Nene floodplain near the Neolithic site mentioned above, Beaker pottery was present in an old river channel along with flints, preserved wood and hazelnut shells. At the Hamel, Oxford, a late Beaker burial pit was found beneath alluvium (Palmer 1980, 128–32). A radiocarbon date of 1520 ± 80 bc was obtained from the burial. There was evidence for Beaker occupation on the floodplain, but no evidence of contemporary flooding.

Discussion On the present evidence from the region, some of the earliest agricultural clearances seem to have been on the higher ground of chalk/limestone and only later in the Neolithic were there numerous clearances in the valley bottoms on the river terraces. The woodland may have remained almost untouched on the clay slopes and on the large tracts of boulder clay. Even in the late Neolithic, the woodland in the vicinity of Buscot Lock seems to have retained much of its character from the Atlantic: the presence of lime and species that are now rare. Some of the clearances seem to have been small, as at Buscot, perhaps only a few arable plots and limited pasture. There may have been much larger clearances or extensive open landscapes, for example the arable on the Downs at Wayland's Smithy but such large clearances have not yet been demonstrated in the region by pollen analysis. Regeneration of woodland occurred on some Neolithic sites after their abandonment but the long life of the Dorchester ritual complex suggests a permanent open landscape there. Large ritual sites, however, need not mean general open conditions: the hazelnuts in the bottom of the Drayton Cursus ditch could have been derived from bushes growing alongside the cursus and the cursus need have been no more than a linear woodland clearing.

Most of the buried soils encountered were not ploughsoils, only at Wayland's Smithy did the soil show traces of cultivation. Grassland was probably much more important than arable. The sol lessive under the bank of the Devil's Quoits shows that once clearance interrupted the calcium cycle, the effects of rainwater leaching on soils of low base status began to cause damage. It is unknown whether early podsolization took place on sandy soils of low base type.

Although agriculture was important to Neolithic man, he still seems to have kept a close relationship with the ever-present woodland throughout the period. Where woodland regeneration occurred on abandoned Neolithic sites, Mollusca which are now regarded as woodland relict species and poor colonisers were able to re-establish themselves, suggesting nearby refugia.

Bread wheat, emmer wheat and six-row barley seem to have been the main cereals cultivated in the region during the Neolithic. Although cereals were cultivated, fruit and nuts collected from woodland still made up a significant part of Neolithic man's diet, just as they would have done for Mesolithic man. Far more charred hazelnut shells have been found from Neolithic sites in the region than carbonized grain and chaff. Obviously wood was used for structural purposes, oak seeming to be favoured, while a variety of species was collected for firewood. Charcoal is only of limited use for establishing the composition of the woodland from which it had been obtained but the presence of light demanding and thorny species in part probably reflects man opening up the woodland canopy and grazing pressure at the edge of clearings. It ought to be noted that lime charcoal does not survive well in archaeological contexts and tends to disintegrate to a powder.

Neolithic Woodland Pastoral Communities: the Bones

Animals and Man During Neolithic Despite the long duration of the Neolithic and the variability of species percentage from sites it is best to begin here by treating early and late assemblages as products of an ecoculture whose component ecosystems were very diverse, fluctuated between cleared ground and vegetational climax, and changed slowly as a whole.

Site types of associated human occupation range from groups of a few pits (typically late Neolithic), to house sites (e.g. Fengate, Peterborough), henges (e.g. Dorchester on Thames) and causewayed camps (e.g. Abingdon). All sites so far providing bones are located on chalk, other solid limestones and river gravels or sands.

Bone assemblages are usually small. Intrasite sample variation is shown by reports on material from Abingdon causewayed camp (Dudley-Buxton 1928, Frazer 1956, and Cram 1982). Sheep, pig and smaller animals are probably sometimes under-represented by poor preservation (e.g. Zeuner, Cornwall and Summers 1951) but recovery of small bone fragments elsewhere (Ewbank 1964) and sieved bones (Wilson forthcoming) indicates that most of the available information is moderately reliable to use. Except for an aurochs cranium in a pit at Dorchester (Zeuner *et al.*) there is no good reason to believe that bone samples are unrepresentative because of Neolithic rituals. Percentages from the larger bone collections are therefore considered to be representative of Neolithic meat consumption — with perhaps the exception of red deer bones which may typify small but not large samples.

Table 2 Percentage Ranges of Species Fragments from Four Neolithic Sites[1]

	%
cattle including aurochs (0–23%[2])	9–65
sheep/goat	8–17
pig	23–83
horse	+
dog	0–3
red deer	0–3
roe	+

+   species represented e.g. by antlers

1.   Largest site collections are from:–
     Bedfordshire: Puddlehill (Ewbank 1964 n=174)
     Cambridgeshire: Fengate, Peterborough (Harman 1978c)
     Oxfordshire: Abingdon causewayed camp (Cram 1982)
                Barton Court Farm, Abingdon (Wilson forthcoming)
2.   Estimates based on minimum numbers of individuals or proportions of bone measurements

Other occasional records are of goat (Cram 1982), fox (Ewbank 1964), 'bird' (Dudley-Buxton 1928), pike and vole (*Microtus arvalis*) bones (Wheeler, Wilson forthcoming) but are not necessarily reliable records since some may be of intrusive bones.

The ecological status of species and their abundance is critical for conclusions about Neolithic environments. Domesticated cattle, sheep and pig, comprise the highest proportion of bone debris and obviously their presence is in marked contrast to the Mesolithic fauna at Thatcham. Their percentages and those from most small collections suggest some open country around settlements but, as it will be argued, woods and scrub may have dominated much of the remaining landscape.

Among wild species, intriguingly, there is a paucity of small animal bones. Further in the larger samples, aurochs is more commonly identified than wild pig, or red or roe deer — excluding antler which may often be from shed antlers (Ewbank 1964, Grigson 1976, Harman 1978c, Cram 1982). Wild pig and roe are not always readily identifiable but the bones of red deer and other species should not have been misidentified.

All this suggests that hunting focussed on the largest species and indeed, so far, aurochs appear to have been exterminated in the region by the early Bronze Age. Consequently, red deer and smaller wild species should become more prominent in the archaeological record by the end of the Neolithic. Small groups of bones with higher proportions of red deer support this at some mid to late Neolithic sites e.g. Buscot Lock, Oxfordshire (Wilson in preparation) and Corporation Farm, Abingdon (Carter unpublished).

This possible trend towards hunting smaller species may be related to a recent thesis that bones of pig are particularly abundant in late Neolithic assemblages and therefore indicate considerable scrub and woodland *and* its regeneration (Grigson 1982 a). While the face value of the evidence still allows an acceptance of the hypothesis for the Wiltshire sites, the data must at least be qualified for the Thames Valley by results from a moderate sized *earlier* Neolithic collection of bones from Abingdon causewayed camp (Cram 1982), and which dwarfs the small group identified by Frazer (1956) and cited by Grigson. Also a small early group of pig and cattle bones was noted at Harringworth, Northamptonshire (Harman 1978b).

Thus a substantial management of pigs, and probably presence of scrubland and *possible* woodland regeneration, is apparent during the earlier as well as the late Neolithic. A simple rationalisation of the evidence would be to see pigs and woodland as more common in the valleys than on the chalk downlands, particularly at the early period.

Yet there is a further problem in that if there was a shift to eating more pigs and an increase of woodland is inferred, then this contradicts an overall trend into the Bronze Age of decreased vegetational cover for large mammals. Since however both aurochs and wild pig are conspicuous during the late period at Puddlehill, Buckinghamshire (Ewbank 1964, Grigson 1976) and Fengate (Harman 1978c), the overall decline of large species might have to be conceded to have been delayed by woodland reversion unless some other explanation is found.

Table 3 Percentage Ranges of Neolithic and Beaker Period Bones From the Thames Gravels Between Oxford and Dorchester[1]

(i) major species[2]

	Neolithic		Beaker
	earlier	late	
sample size	692	156—297	20—23
	%	%	%
aurochs	3	0.3—0.6	0
cattle	59	19—35	30—35
sheep/goat	10	10—19	26—30
pig	30	35—66	26—30
dog	0.1	0.7—1	—
red deer	0.1—1	3—9	5—9
roe	0	0.3—0.6	0—9

(ii) Percentages of sheep/goat in sum of sheep/goat and cattle bones

%	%	%
14	34	46

1   These percentages are not from individual sites but from summed site collections with percentage ranges including or excluding antler fragments.
2   In part (i) percentages may be depressed by percentages of pig bones even where partially corrected in column two for piglet bones in a pit at Barton Court Farm.
Earlier Neolithic collections
    Abingdon causewayed camp (Frazer 1956, Cram 1982)
    Dorchester on Thames (Zeuner *et al*. 1951)
Later Neolithic
    Barton Court Farm (Wilson forthcoming) and Corporation Farm, Abingdon (Carter unpublished)
    Mount Farm Berinsfield (Wilson in preparation)
    Dorchester on Thames (Zeuner *et al*. 1951)
Beaker period
    The Hamel, Oxford (Wilson 1980 b)
    Thrupp, Abingdon (Wilson unpublished f)
    Mount Farm, Berinsfield (Wilson in preparation)

An alternative is to examine the faunal evidence on the assumption that, akin perhaps to the environmental indications at Buscot Lock, see pp 31—32, local woodland was never felled extensively or if so regenerated substantially during the earlier period. This alternative would modify the idea of extensive woodland regeneration during the late Neolithic.

An explanation of the latter difference of emphasis may be obtained by agreeing first that the basis of Neolithic subsistence shifted partly from an economy centred around domestic and wild cattle to one favouring *more* pigs and hunting of medium sized game particularly deer. However timing of the shift was early or late according to local activity in clearance and regeneration. Although the scarce representation of sheep in the late Neolithic might support the idea of some woodland regeneration then, the remaining faunal interpretation of Grigson depends on known woodland preferences of, or exploitation by, pigs and the *uncertainty* of whether domestic cattle are to be treated as consumers of grass or woodland foliage. Thus a predominance of cattle bones indicates either much grassland or, much woodland. If the latter, the early Neolithic fauna does not necessarily have to be seen as a sign of widespread clearance in the region and therefore the extent of woodland regeneration was not as great as implied by Grigson.

Only one comparison of the faunal change during the Neolithic in any area of the region is possible. The evidence for the Oxford—Dorchester area is given in Table 2. The lumping of these site assemblages and their sample sizes is undoubtedly questionable but provides some interesting trends where others are not possible or are misleading.

There is no doubt about the increased abundance of pig during the late Neolithic (Table 2i) but the ratio of sheep/goat bones to cattle increases (Table 2ii). As sheep favour grassland and not woodland the results indicate a slow increase of this habitat and not an overall regeneration of woodland: only that which suited pigs. Indeed woodland conversion rather than regeneration may be a better description. Secondary woodland or scrub may have expanded as climax forest was reduced in extent by clearance, woodland management and animal husbandry.

Possibly this type of change encouraged the presence of deer. Although it could have favoured cattle, other environmental factors or selection pressure may have operated against them. For example, the large size of aurochs as a hunting target, and its probable competition with domestic cattle for similar food resources.

This line of argument would therefore associate Neolithic cattle with woodland as well as grassland and scrub. It suggests either, or both, a changing balance of woodland fodder plants, possibly elm and lime, or/and a greater ease of feeding and managing pigs compared to cattle.

To recapitulate and simplify further, the pattern of Neolithic bones indicates the presence of more forest, scrub or perhaps marshland, than in subsequent periods. Woodland fauna and environment is best demonstrated at Buscot Lock, but the majority of bones elsewhere are associated with more 'open' landscapes. 'Open' in the sense of containing stands of primary forest, and secondary woodland, but surrounded by much scrub and some grassland. A plausible vegetational pattern on regional soil and rock illustrated by Barker and Webley (1978, Figure 4) should show greater areas of forest and scrub.

Site information can therefore be reordered as follows to indicate regional differences in the development of Neolithic culture.

(a)   Earlier occupation around Abingdon (Dudley-Buxton 1928, Frazer 1956, Cram 1982 and Wilson unpublished f), and Dorchester (Zeuner, Cornwall and Summers 1951) are associated with a disrupted forest canopy, with much scrubland but limited grass pasture and open ground around settlements. The postulated shift from a relative abundance of domestic cattle and presence of aurochs toward greater numbers of pigs and more sheep and the greater hunting of medium sized animals is therefore evident in this area much earlier than at other sites in the region. Associated vegetational cover for pigs and wild animals remained extensive, albeit altered in character, at least until the late Neolithic as indicated by material from Barton Court Farm (Wilson forthcoming) and Corporation Farm, Abingdon (Carter unpublished), and also at Eynsham (Wilson unpublished c). On average, the extent of grass pasture appears to increase slowly throughout the period. This suggests that Neolithic people and stock were always present but became more widely spread as the woodland retreated.

(b)   Upper Thames occupation at Buscot Lock (Wilson, in preparation) and Rough Ground Farm, Lechlade (G Jones, in preparation) indicates persistent or transformed woodland and little grassland during the late Neolithic.

(c)   Late Neolithic occupation on the Chilterns at Puddlehill (Ewbank 1964, Grigson 1976) where aurochs (and wild pig) and, probably, adjacent woodland remained or possibly had regenerated.

(d)   A similar late Neolithic situation occurred on the fen margins at Fengate (Harman 1978c). Clearance of vegetational cover on the fens or gravels was incomplete.

(e)   The eastern region i.e. Buckinghamshire, Bedfordshire and Northamptonshire therefore appears less occupied and more forested than some areas of the Thames valley. Nevertheless, little is known faunally of large areas of land including the oolitic limestones. Even there the presence of aurochs at Ascott-under-Wychwood, Oxfordshire (Benson pers. comm.) is indicative of persistent woodland in upland areas.

Animal husbandry, and of course hunting, appears directed chiefly toward a supply of meat. Secondary uses of animals, apart from skins or antlers, may have been less important although a predominance of cows at Windmill Hill, Wiltshire (Grigson 1982 b), could indicate dairying was normal Neolithic practice. Sheep rearing and therefore wool production, had no great emphasis, but use of wool would be less obvious if the ratio of domesticated animals to people was high — as the hunting focus on larger animals suggests and because the ecoculture appears capable of sustaining a relatively large number of cattle as well as sheep.

Thus apart from possible difficulties with seasonal requirements, the evidence suggests self sufficiency above subsistence levels which rely heavily on secondary products or arable farming. Both the less studied size of domestic animal bones and the pathological state of human bones would be guides to the level of subsistence.

Little data exists on Neolithic people except from bone debris at Barton Hill Farm, Bedfordshire (Trevor 1962) of a youth aged about 16 years and a woman aged 25–30 years, and at Aldwincle, Northamptonshire (Bayley 1976) of a woman aged 17–25 years at death.

Barker and Webley (1978) have proposed a model of how environmental resources were exploited seasonally. In relation to Abingdon causewayed camp (Cram 1982) however this model seems less applicable. The pigs there appear slaughtered at all ages and therefore at all stages of the year which suggests relatively permanent occupation. The latter is also implied by the suggestion above that the dietary subsistence was at a moderately high level. However the increasing diversity of faunal remains and the changing, possibly more diffuse, settlement pattern suggests that seasonal factors became more important in animal husbandry.

Beaker Episode Few bones appear collected or described for this period and these are from around Oxford and Dorchester-on-Thames. The abundance of major species has been indicated tentatively already in Table 2. Other species records include blackbird (Allison n.d.) and mouse *Apodemus* (Wilson 1980 a) although their dating is not unquestionable.

In this area of the river gravels therefore hunting was still significant during the Beaker period and was focussed on deer and smaller species. A predominance of woodland or scrub is still indicated at this period but probably the extent of grassland increased and was to become most important to the subsequent development of Bronze Age ecoculture.

Human burials at Stanton Harcourt, Oxfordshire, include a 28–30 year old woman 5'5" in height (Powers 1982, 105), a young woman of 5'3", and a further woman of 30–40 years and 5'6" was buried at Ravenstone, Buckinghamshire (Bayley 1981). Skeletal debris from two men aged 20–30 years occurred at Maiden Bower, Buckinghamshire (Brothwell 1976).

Early to Later Bronze Age, 1600bc – 900bc

Man Turns Away From Woodland and Towards Grassland

An Occupation Site The best environmental sequence for the Bronze Age comes from the chalkland of the Downs at Ram's Hill. Oxfordshire, in the extreme south-west of the region (Evans in Bradley and Ellison 1975, 139–49). The evidence is from molluscs, many of them re-deposited in archaeological features. Tree holes on the site contained woodland faunas but it is not known when clearance occurred. A ditched enclosure was constructed on the hilltop, probably in the early Bronze Age but the sherd of Collared Urn upon which the dating rests could have been residual. Mollusca from patches of humus, thought to be fallen turves, in the very bottom of the ditch comprised 65% woodland species and 20% open country species. *Carychium tridentatum* was numerous, perhaps suggesting dank grassland and scrub. The site, therefore, seems to have been built on abandoned agricultural land, reverting after clearance. In the late Bronze Age a box rampart was built around the inner perimeter of the enclosure ditch. The fill of the palisade trench for the revetment contained late Bronze Age pottery and charcoal from which radiocarbon dates of 1060 ± 70 bc and 1030 ± 70 bc were obtained. Both open country and woodland molluscs were present in the soil packing for the posts in the palisade trench. Eventually the rampart fell into disrepair and the molluscs from a layer in the enclosure ditch post-dating the collapse of the rampart but pre-dating the next phase of occupation showed woodland regeneration to have occurred. The profile of the ditch was shallow enough for general rather than local implications to be drawn from these results.

When the site was re-occupied, a double palisade was set in the partly filled enclosure ditch and presumably the trees were cleared. Bronze Age pits from this period contained equal numbers of open country and woodland individuals, but these results are perhaps of only local significance. Three radiocarbon dates of 1050 ± 90 bc, 740 ± 70 bc and 1010 ± 80 bc provide a *terminus post quem* for the double palisade phase. The re-occupation of the enclosure did not last long and Mollusca from the layer which covered the post holes of the palisade in the enclosure ditch, again a layer with a gentle profile, suggest a return to woodland/scrub conditions, with only 10% open country individuals.

Sixty stratified samples from the various Bronze Age phases at Ram's Hill were wet sieved but no cereals or chaff was recovered, only a very few charred weed seeds.

Barrows and Ring Ditches The remaining evidence for this period comes from ritual sites: barrows and ring ditches, but there is no reason to suspect that the environment was different around ritual sites, indeed there is evidence of nearby occupation from several. Molluscan samples were examined from the bottom of an early Bronze Age ring-ditch on calcareous solifluxion deposits in the Great Ouse Valley at Warren Farm, Milton Keynes, Buckinghamshire (Evans in Green 1974, 97–100). Values for *Vallonia costata, V. excentrica* and *Carychium tridentatum* were high, suggesting tall dank grassland in the ditch and a general open country environment. A radiocarbon date of 1500 ± 90 bc was obtained from charcoal in the ring-ditch. A neighbouring ring-ditch on the Ouse gravels at Little Pond Ground also had molluscan evidence for open grassland (Evans in Green 1974, 115–6).

A cache of many hundreds of arable weed seeds associated with a sherd of Collared Urn was identified from an early Bronze Age ring-ditch on the chalk of the Chilterns at Barton Hill Farm, Bedfordshire (Godwin in Dyer 1962, 21). It is not stated whether the seeds were charred. If uncarbonised, they would undoubtedly have been modern, perhaps accumulated by a rodent or ants (*Viola* s. *Melanium* sp. seeds were the most abundant taxon and ants find them particularly attractive).

The following grain impressions from earlier Bronze Age sherds provide better evidence for arable: *Hordeum* sp. (naked), Hitcham, Buckinghamshire; *Triticum dicoccum, Hordeum* sp. (naked), Somerton, Oxfordshire; *T. monococcum*, Long Wittenham, Oxfordshire (Jessen and Helbaek 1944, 18; Helbaek 1952, 226).

Two Bronze Age ring-ditches were excavated on a multiperiod site on the second gravel terrace of the Thames at Ashville, Abingdon, Oxfordshire (Parrington 1978). The cremation burials enclosed by the ring-ditches contained pottery belonging to the Wessex II phase of the Middle Bronze Age. A sample column through one of the ring-ditches was examined for molluscs (Robinson in Parrington 1978, 93; Robinson 1981a, 87–8, 134, 321–2). The ditch evidently silted slowly because the top half of the fill contained Iron Age pottery. The results illustrate well the limited usefulness of molluscan analyses on the higher gravel terraces of the Thames. The poor fauna of the Bronze Age layers was dominated by *Cecilioides acicula*, a subterranean species which could have burrowed in at a later date. Amongst the few remaining molluscs, *Helicella itala* indicates that dry open conditions prevailed in the vicinity of the ring-ditches. Charred grains of *Triticum aestivocompactum, Hordeum* sp. and at least seven species of arable weeds were identified from the ring-ditches (Jones in Parrington 1978, 93–110). The edible tubers of *Arrhenatherum elatius* v. *tuberosum* were present in the cremation pits, while *Quercus* sp. and *Prunus/Crataegus* type charcoal was identified from the Bronze Age features. Crop evidence was also obtained from Oddington, Oxfordshire in the form of an impression of *Hordeum* sp. (naked) on a middle Bronze Age sherd.

A middle Bronze Age barrow was excavated on the Nene floodplain at Earls Barton, Northamptonshire (Jackson 1970; 1972). Radiocarbon dates of 1219 ± 51 bc and 1264 ± 64 bc were obtained for substantial pieces of oak charcoal from the old ground surface under the mound. The barrow had been built from turves of fine loam and the old ground surface was a loam whereas the present soil of the floodplain is an alluvial clay. A similar sequence was discovered at Kings Weir, Wytham, Oxfordshire on the Thames floodplain (Bowler and Robinson 1980). A stone-free red/brown silty loam was found beneath the mound of an early or middle Bronze Age barrow but subsequently, alluvial clay was deposited around the barrow and in its ditches.

An interesting soil was discovered beneath a Bronze Age round barrow next to the Neolithic long barrow at Rollright on the Oxfordshire/Warwickshire border. In contrast to the Neolithic soil, the soil beneath the round barrow was a non-calcareous, shallow, stone-free well-developed sol lessive (Robinson, unpublished h). The sandy eluvial horizon was very distinct from the illuvial clay horizon beneath. On the assumption that extreme lessivation would not have occurred under woodland conditions, grassland must have been present for many years prior to the barrow's construction because ploughing would have caused soil mixing, introducing fragments of limestone.

A sample of Bronze Age soil from beneath the Cop Round Barrow at Bledlow, Buckinghamshire, on the chalk of the Chilterns, contained a small open country molluscan fauna (Kennard in Head 1939–40, 347–8). The charcoal identifications from this site, however, are unreliable. A record of *Aesculus hippocastanum* was claimed from a Bronze Age pit while *Crataegus* was identified to species (*oxycanthoides*) (Mabey in Head 1934–40, 348–9).

Cornwall (1953, 135–8) examined particle size of some ancient soils on the Somerton-Radley gravel terrace. He found loam in a natural hollow and a Neolithic pit at Cassington to have an even distribution of particle size whereas at Stanton Harcourt, the fill of a Bronze Age ring-ditch, the soil beneath a Bronze Age barrow and the soil in the barrow's ditch had a high silt content. He interpreted these results as showing that the Bronze Age soil had been wind sorted and stated that for this to have happened, a drier climate than at present would have been required to give the necessary conditions of sparse vegetation, so that bare soil would be exposed to wind erosion.

These views are no longer accepted, and over-grazing or cultivation would be sufficient to have enabled the erosions to take place (Evans 1971, 15). Another very simple explanation is possible, the natural soil on the second terrace at Cassington may not have the same particle-size distribution as the natural soil on the same terrace 6km or more away at Stanton Harcourt.

Discussion Clearance presumably continued into the Bronze Age from the Neolithic and the landscape would have gradually become more open. Woodland does not, however, seem to have been under great pressure. The sequence from Ram's Hill shows repeated episodes of clearance followed by agricultural abandonment and woodland regeneration. Clearance and prolonged use resulted in the deterioration of some soils, as for example at Rollright, but soil damage alone did not force abandonment of land. Falling productivity may have caused ploughing to cease at Wayland's Smithy in the Neolithic, but the soil would still have been suitable for permanent pasture. The site, however, remained wooded in the Bronze Age. Likewise, the various abandonments at Ram's Hill were not because the grassland would no longer support grazing animals. Instead it seems that man was able to choose good land for arable or pasture, and there was not great pressure to continue using it if productivity fell seriously, or scrub began to invade. There is no evidence that much clearance took place in those parts of the region which had not already seen at least some late Neolithic agricultural activity. Unfortunately, evidence from pollen and waterlogged plants and invertebrates is lacking for this period but it is probably that changes were taking place in the region's woodland. More of the woodland was becoming secondary woodland and even woodland that had never been cleared probably suffered from grazing pressure or experienced management along its margin.

There is not a large amount of evidence for arable from Bronze Age contexts in the region and it seems likely that grassland covered most of the open parts of the landscape. As in the Neolithic, the floodplains of the major river valleys in the region seem to have had large tracts which did not flood and were covered with soils similar to those on the higher gravel terraces.

In general, the cereal crops cultivated in the region remained the same as in the Neolithic but there no longer seems to have been a reliance on woodland plants as a significant part of the diet. Carbonised hazelnut shells are not characteristic of Bronze Age sites. The only new possible crop species identified, *Triticum monococcum*, is as likely to have been a weed or a rogue in a wheatfield or a misidentification.

Bronze Age Pastoralism: the Bones

The chronology of sites is treated generally here but excludes both sites of Beaker period and those clearly of Iron Age. Types of occupation providing bones are diverse and different to Neolithic sites: farmstead systems (Fengate, Peterborough; Corporation Farm, Abingdon); fortified enclosures (Ram's Hill, Berkshire; Ivinghoe Beacon, Buckinghamshire) and ring ditches or barrows (Warren Farm and Bledlow, Buckinghamshire). Most sites occur on river gravels or chalk.

Table 4 Percentage Ranges of Species Fragments From Five Bronze Age Sites[1]

	%
cattle	39–62
sheep/goat	16–40
pig	4–13
horse	0.5–1.6
dog	0.2–4
red deer	0–1.6

1. Site collections used are from:—
    Buckinghamshire: Ivinghoe Beacon (Westley 1968); and Warren Farm, Milton Keynes (Westley 1974).
    Cambridgeshire: Fengate, Peterborough (Biddick 1980).
    Oxfordshire: Appleford (Wilson 1980a: regrouped %s n=159); Corporation Farm, Abingdon (Carter unpublished); and Ram's Hill (Carter 1975 n=144).

Aurochs and goat are not identified. Roe deer appears absent except for occasional antler. Fox is frequently present while hare, badger (Frazer 1940), cat (Westley 1968), wolf, goose (Biddick 1980) and other 'birds', but not any fish, are recorded.

Percentages of bones appear relatively uniform and suggest a less diverse ecocultural system than during the Neolithic. Faunal remains indicating scrub or woodland communities are few, and therefore hunting was less important than previously. A site at Wallingford may be an exception (Wilson unpublished i).

Percentages of probable sheep bones (improbably of goat) and the presence of horse and hare all suggest an open and pastoral landscape around settlements (allowance for arable land there must be made also). The extent of scrub or woodland clearance is uncertain.

As in the Neolithic, cattle are the most important species but since the economic emphasis has shifted away from hunting and pig husbandry and, by implication in part from meat production, dairying (or arable farming) is probably important especially as argued for Grimes Graves, Norfolk (Legge 1981). A predominance of cows and a similar slaughtering pattern to that at Grimes Graves is evident at Corporation Farm (Carter unpublished). Older cattle appear common at Fengate (Biddick 1980) but this conclusion may be influenced by poor preservation of juvenile bones. Future comparisons of Bronze Age and Iron Age information on age and sex of cattle will be useful.

Transhumance from winter pasture on the Fengate gravels to summer grazing on fen meadows is postulated and akin to the medieval pattern (Pryor 1980, 180). Transhumance of cattle to Thames river meadows and sheep to higher ground has also been proposed (Case 1963) but cannot be confirmed and the strict sense of this proposal might be denied by moderate samples of sheep bones from low lying sites in Oxfordshire at Appleford (Wilson 1980a), Corporation Farm (Carter unpublished), Wallingford (Wilson unpublished i) and Lechlade (G Jones in prep.). A more general transhumant dispersal of sheep and cattle is still possible. However, if meadowland sites are relatively well drained and not extensively flooded at this period p 39), one wonders to what degree nomadism need be postulated.

Human burials at Radley, Oxfordshire (Goody 1948), Cassington, Oxfordshire (Trevor 1947) and Aldwincle, Northamptonshire (Denston 1976) indicate that adult males averaged around 5'8" in height and at least two died between 30–45 years of age. The only skeleton which was possibly of a female was of a 20–25 year old individual standing about 5'4" (Wells 1980). This information contrasts with the scanty evidence of early deaths during the Neolithic and suggests a different and possibly an improved mode of life during the Bronze Age although poor oral health is evident too. As a variety of other evidence has long suggested, the bone debris is indicative of a predominantly pastoralist ecoculture as opposed to greater emphasis on hunting and woodland exploitation during the Neolithic, and in contrast to increased arable farming during the Iron Age.

The Final Bronze Age and the Iron Age, *c*900bc Onwards

Agricultural Expansion and the Open Landscape

Final Bronze Age The molluscan sequence at Ram's Hill, on the chalk of the Oxfordshire Downs continued from the late Bronze Age throughout the Iron Age (Evans in Bradley and Ellison 1975, 139–49). At perhaps 900 – 800bc the hilltop was cleared yet again. There was an episode of ploughing which resulted in the formation of a negative lynchet across the top of the Bronze Age enclosure ditch. It is suggested that the ploughing was only transient and related to clearance prior to the establishment of grassland, because a woodland molluscan fauna was present in the ploughsoil. This is not, however, an entirely satisfactory explanation, for the ploughing lasted long enough to create the lynchet. Above, a turf line developed in the ditch, containing an open country fauna indicative of grazed short turf. A turf line was also present underneath the bank of the Iron Age hillfort at Ram's Hill. A system of major land divisions on the Lambourn Downs in Berkshire, dating from the middle/late Bronze Age was related to this grassland phase. At Ram's Hill, the pasture lasted until about 50bc.

The nearby site of Wayland's Smithy was cleared towards the very end of the Bronze Age and ploughed (Kerney in Bradley and Ellison 1975, 191, 200). The duration of the arable phase is uncertain.

Clearance was also taking place on the Thames floodplain, in the Windrush valley, during the late Bronze Age. At Mingies Ditch, Oxfordshire, tree root pits containing very humified peat and charcoal were excavated (Robinson 1981a, 127–8). One pit also contained identifiable wood fragments. The wood and charcoal from this pit were both *Alnus*, a radiocarbon date of 850 ± 90 bc being obtained from the charcoal. The charcoal seems to have resulted from firing tree stumps. There was no evidence as to what sort of activity immediately followed clearance at Mingies Ditch but it is probable that at a later date (but prior to the Iron Age occupation of the site) woodland recolonised the site. A spill of limestone gravel into the upper part of the tree pit resulted in the preservation of mollusc shells and most of them were woodland species, including *Oxychilus cellarius* and *Discus rotundatus*.

There is another site on the Windrush floodplain with evidence for woodland in the late Bronze Age. Tree root fragments, probably alder, which seemed to be in their position of growth, were found in the top of the sandy lime-stone gravel near Witney, Oxfordshire (Hazelden and Jarvis 1979; 1980). A radiocarbon date of 710 ± 85 bc was obtained from these roots. The truncated roots were covered by about one metre of clay alluvium. Hazelden and Jarvis believed the stratigraphy to show that the river truncated the trees by erosion then began to deposit alluvium in the late Bronze Age. This exposure was visited in 1976 and the stratigraphy confirmed, but not their interpretation (Robinson 1981a, 19). The truncation of the roots seemed to have been an artifact of preservation, preservation only occurring below the water table, and there is no reason why the roots should not have grown through some or all of the alluvium. At Mingies Ditch, the tree pits cut through a thin covering of ancient alluvium over the gravel but in turn had a thin alluvial covering of a very much later date.

The River Thames at Wallingford, Oxfordshire, is eroding a late Bronze Age site on the riverbank which is sandwiched between two layers of alluvium (Robinson, unpublished j). The lower layer represents the top fill of an old river channel and the molluscs from it suggest open, terrestrial conditions with occasional flooding. The abundance of *Pupilla muscorum* and *Vallonia excentrica* in the late Bronze Age soil suggests dry, short turfed grassland. The continued presence of a few aquatic molluscs may have been due to infrequent, short episodes of winter flooding. The Bronze Age molluscan fauna is very similar to that from the modern turf line, and at present, flooding probably averages less than one day per year. At some date after the abandonment of the site, conditions first became wetter, the dry ground species being absent, and then substantial alluviation took place. The date of the alluviation is unknown.

A good picture of the late Bronze Age environment on the higher terraces of the Thames is provided by waterlogged deposits in the bottom of a pond of this date at Mount Farm, Berinsfield, Oxfordshire, excavated by G H Lambrick. So far, macroscopic plant and invertebrate remains from this deposit have been identified, (Robinson, unpublished i) but results from pollen analysis are awaited. Wood and tree-dependant Coleoptera, at 4% of the total terrestrial Coleoptera, suggest the landscape to have been relatively unwooded, at least in the vicinity of the site. The presence of seeds from a

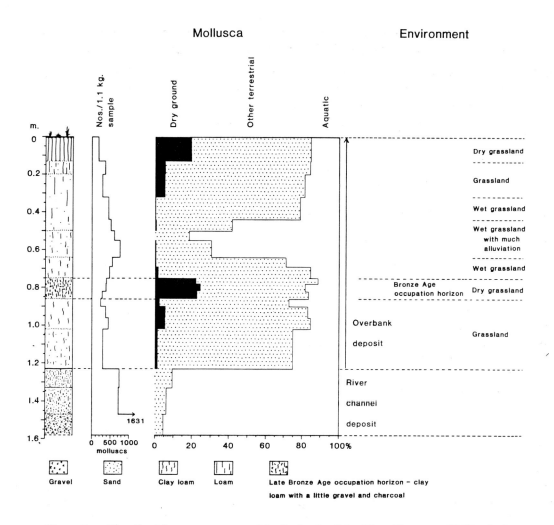

Figure 7 The alluvial sequence exposed in the bank of the River Thames at Wallingford

variety of shrubby species including *Thelycrania sanguinea* and *Crataegus* cf *monogyna* show that some mixed scrub was present but it is unknown whether the scrub took the form of thickets on neglected pasture or was organised into hedges. Various beetles from the families Elateridae and Scarabaeidae which feed on roots in grassland formed 6% of the terrestrial Coleoptera, showing that grassland was important, but the proportion of dung beetles, although indicating the presence of grazing animals, was not very high. It also seems likely that arable farming occurred in the vicinity of the site, and a few glume bases of *Triticum* cf *dicoccum* were rather badly preserved by the waterlogged conditions. Very late Bronze Age or early Iron Age plough marks were present on this site.

Further evidence of arable crops in the region is provided by grain impressions from pottery: *Hordeum* sp (hulled) from Chastelton Camp, Oxfordshire (Jessen and Helbaek 1944, 22); *Hordeum* sp. (naked) from Abingdon, Oxfordshire; and *Triticum monococcum* or *dicoccum* from Radley, Oxfordshire (Helbaek 1952, 227). A pot containing a large quantity of carbonised grain was discovered on the chalk of the north slope of the Chilterns near Dunstable, Bedfordshire from a late Bronze Age site. The grain was identified as 'a primitive form of bread wheat' along with a very few grains of barley (Percival in Hawkes 1940, 489–90), but it is uncertain what Percival meant by his description of the wheat, and it would be better to regard his identification as *Triticum* sp.

Elsewhere on the Chilterns, at Ivinghoe Beacon Hillfort, Buckinghamshire, a late Bronze Age soil was examined beneath the rampart (Dimbleby in Cotton and Frere 1968, 250–1). There was a stone-free, mull horizon over the chalk containing some fragments of *Prunus spinosa* and *Crataegus*-type charcoal. Pollen analysis was undertaken but there was evidence for some modern earthworm activity. Values for tree pollen were low whereas grasses and *Plantago lanceolata* values were high. Interpretation of pollen results from such non-acidic soils is difficult, but even without the pollen, the other results might suggest the rampart to have been built on pasture, perhaps from which a little thorn shrub had to be cleared.

The Pre-Belgic Iron Age Very many pre-Belgic Iron Age sites have been investigated in the region, so it is proposed to sub-divide the area into: the high ground of the Cotswolds and limestone to the north-west of the region; the Downs and Chilterns; the Thames Valley bottom and nearby higher ground; and the Nene Valley bottom with nearby higher ground. Investigations of other parts of the region are lacking.

(a)   *The Cotswolds*   Limited work was done on molluscs and/or charcoal from three hillforts in this part of the region: Lyneham Camp, Oxfordshire (Bayne 1957, 7–9), Madmarston Camp, Oxfordshire (Fowler 1960, 47–8) and Rainsborough, Northamptonshire (Avery *et al.* 1967, 300–6). At Lyneham Camp, the charcoal, identified by G W Dimbleby from beneath the Iron Age rampart was mostly *Prunus spinosa, Crataegus* type and *Frangula alnus*, with a few scraps of *Quercus*. He suggested the wood that was burnt to have been derived from thorn scrub with little indication of true forest species. Possibly it was charcoal from clearance prior to the construction of the hillfort. From Madmarston Camp, Dimbleby identified a large quantity of substantial pieces of *Fagus, Quercus* and *Fraxinus excelsior* charcoal which had been dumped in an Iron Age pit.

(b)   *The Downs and Chilterns*   Short-turfed grassland seems to have persisted throughout the Iron Age on the Downs at Ram's Hill, Oxfordshire (Evans in Bradley and Ellison 1975, 139–49). In contrast, two sections through Grim's Ditch at the western end of the Oxfordshire Chilterns revealed a thin ploughsoil covering the chalk beneath the bank (Case and Sturdy 1959; Robinson in Hinchliffe 1975, 129–132). At the section cut by Hinchliffe, open conditions are suggested by the Mollusca from the Iron Age silting to the ditch. Further along the Chilterns, charcoal was identified from a settlement at Chinnor, Oxfordshire, which was perhaps occupied in the fourth century bc (Richardson and Young 1951, 137). *Corylus* was the predominant species but the list included *Acer pseudoplatanus*, thereby casting doubt on all the identifications. Charcoal of *Acer campestre, Crataegus*-type, *Corylus, Prunus* and *Quercus* was identified from an Iron Age site at Bledlow, Buckinghamshire (Hyde in Head and Piggot 1941–46, 209).

The remaining four Chilterns sites are all ploughwash accumulations from the slopes of the chalk in Buckinghamshire. Truncating the interesting Neolithic ditch, and overlying the Zone III deposits at Pitstone, was ploughwash with early Iron Age pottery at the base (Evans 1966, 355–7). Not surprisingly, open country molluscs predominated. In a nearby section, there was a buried soil beneath the ploughwash. At the bottom of the soil, woodland species were dominant but towards the top the molluscs indicated grassland. *Vallonia costata* and *V. excentrica* being the most abundant. *Pupilla muscorum* and *Helicella itala* were also common. In the ploughwash, *V. excentrica* was dominant and numbers of *P. muscorum* and *V. costata* were greatly reduced (Evans 1966, 357). A section at Pink Hill, near Princes Risborough, showed ploughwash containing probable Iron Age pottery and an open country molluscan fauna (Evans 1972, 312–315). It covered a soil containing woodland molluscs. Hillwash dating from the late prehistoric period onwards was discovered at a second site near Princes Risborough (Evans in Barfield 1977, 319–20). On the other side of the Chilterns, fluvial deposits underlay the Roman villa at Latimer in the Chess Valley (Gilbertson in Branigan 1971, 102–5). Woodland species were present along with aquatic molluscs in the lower sample but the upper sample contained ploughwash and an open country molluscan fauna.

(c)   *The Thames Valley*   A very thorough investigation was made into carbonised plant remains from a substantial Iron Age settlement at Ashville, Abingdon, on the second gravel terrace of the Thames Valley (Jones in Parrington 1978, 93–110). The early Iron Age site consisted of clusters of grain storage pits, and a radiocarbon date of 520 ± 70 bc was made on material from one of these pits. The middle Iron Age settlement had a group of hut circles and more storage pits. The following radiocarbon dates were obtained from middle Iron Age contexts:

220 ± 70 bc	1410 ± 130 bc
100 ± 70 bc	1020 ± 80 bc
ad 80 ± 80	

Only two of these dates fall within an acceptable date range of between *c*350bc to 80bc for the middle Iron Age pottery from the site.

Abundant carbonised plant remains were discovered in the early and middle Iron Age features including weed seeds as well as grain and chaff. *Triticum spelta* and *Hordeum vulgare* (hulled) formed the bulk of the crop species identified while *T. dicoccum* and *T. aestivocompactum* (confirmed by the presence of tough rachis fragments) were present in much smaller quantities. It is possible that the minor species of wheat grew as rogues in the spelt crops. *Bromus* sp. seeds were the most abundant non-cereal taxon and this weed may have been deliberately harvested with the crops. Seeds of *Lithospermum arvense* were especially numerous in one deposit and it is possible that they had been collected for medicinal use.

A mature arable weed flora grew amongst the Iron Age cereal crops, including *Galium aparine. G. aparine* tends to germinate in the autumn and winter, and its presence may be indicative of winter sowing. The weed species suggest that the area under cultivation by the site extended beyond the light well drained soils of the second gravel terrace. As well as such dry ground species as *Scleranthus anuus*, seeds of *Eleocharis palustris* and other plants of marshy places were present. Most interestingly, the proportion of *Vicia* and *Lathyrus* seeds increased throughout the early and middle Iron

Age, which may have resulted from falling nitrogen levels in the soil. The proportion of *E. palustris* also increased, perhaps as a result of increasing arable pressure on wetter soils.

A very different picture from Ashville is presented by the small middle Iron Age settlement on the Windrush flood-plain at Mingies Ditch, Hardwick (Robinson 1981a, 89–95, 138–66, 329–53; Robinson 1981b, 256–9). The site was surrounded by a double-ditched enclosure and a radiocarbon date of 220 ± 90 bc was obtained from waterlogged twigs in the ditch bottom. Beneath the gravel banks of the Iron Age enclosure was about 0.1–0.2m of alluvial clay. It had been worm sorted, concentrating all the riverine Mollusca at the bottom of the profile, while the upper part of the profile had become decalcified. This suggests that there was a long period (possibly lasting more than a millenium) when the site was not regularly flooded. There was no evidence that the Iron Age settlement suffered flooding while it was occupied.

Pollen analysis by G W Dimbleby of peat from the bottom of the enclosure ditches suggested a landscape substantially cleared of trees although willows may have been conspicuously present. Tree pollen formed 4% of the total pollen while shrub pollen, mostly *Salix* comprised another 13% of the total. This picture is confirmed by the Coleoptera. Outdoor wood and tree dependant species made up only 2% of the total terrestrial Coleoptera. The pollen spectra suggest that species-rich grassland was important with Gramineae pollen averaging 34%, *Plantago lanceolata* 6% and *Compositae-Liguliflorae* 7% of the pollen from the four samples. The grassland was likely to have been wet, grading into marsh along the margin of the River Windrush and various minor streams which traversed the area. Seeds of wet grassland or marsh species identified from the waterlogged deposits included *Ranunculus flammula, Lynchnis flos-cuculi, Filipendula ulmaria, Mentha* cf *aquatica, Pulicaria* sp. and various rushes and sedges. Grassland species were well represented amongst the Coleoptera, especially *Phyllopertha horticola*. Elateridae and Scarabaeidae with larvae that feed on roots in permanent grassland made up 7% of the total terrestrial Coleoptera. The Coleoptera provide good evidence for the importance of grassland in the vicinity of the site. Scarabaeoid dung beetles (especially *Aphodius* spp.), which tend to be restricted to dung of large herbivores in the field (rather than in manure heaps), made up 13% of the terrestrial Coleoptera.

There was no evidence for cultivation the form of ploughmarks or the mixing of gravel into the Iron Age soil profile (even though it was shallow and had not been truncated) outside the occupation enclosure. A preliminary examination of an assemblage of carbonised grain, chaff and weeds from the site (mostly *Hordeum vulgare* – hulled, but also *Triticum spelta* and a little *Secale cereale*) suggested that it had been grown on dry ground, probably not on the flood-plain (M Jones, pers. comm.).

Among the macroscopic plant remains from the ditches were abundant seeds, wood and leaves from at least eleven species of shrub and small trees. The pollen, however, did not give even a slight indication for the presence of most of them, but they are entomophilous species, from which pollen has usually only been recorded at very low levels. The strong presence of scrub suggested by the macroscopic plant remains contrasts with the poor evidence for woodland species but substantial indication of grassland from the Coleoptera. This probably reflects the much more local origin of the plant remains compared with the insects, and that the scrub was confined to the vicinity of the settlement. The diversity of woody species, including *Acer campestre* (represented by fruits, wood and leaves), a species of established woodland and old hedgerows that has low colonising powers, suggests that either the scrub had deliberately been planted in the form of mixed hedges around the enclosure or the scrub was of ancient origin. The scrub may have been a relic of the woodland which had been cleared from the site prior to the Iron Age; perhaps selective scrub clearance was used to create hedges around the Iron Age enclosure.

One most important Iron Age find preserved by the waterlogged conditions was the head of a worker honey bee (*Apis mellifera*). This is the only pre-Saxon record of the honey bee from Britain. While it remains unknown whether this bee was domesticated or wild, it provides proof that honey and beeswax would at least have been available for exploitation in the Iron Age (Limbrey 1982).

The charcoal from the site was a mixture of small branches and twigs of assorted hedgerow species, and pieces of oak from more substantial timbers. An oak doorpost to one of the houses was preserved because it had been inserted below the water table.

Some late Bronze Age tree pits on the site were deeper than the deepest Iron Age features yet preservation of organic material in them was very poor, the only identifiable remains being very rotten fragments of wood. By the time of the Iron Age occupation of the site, the water table had risen and there was standing water in the bottom of the enclosure ditches, resulting in good preservation of organic remains. As the ditches began to silt up, so the quality of preservation deteriorated and in some ditch profiles a non-organic deposit built up. Then a gravel trackway belonging to the final phase of occupation was constructed through the entrance to the enclosure. Either just before or just after the abandonment of the site; but stratigraphically later than the gravel road, there was a very distinct recurrence horizon for peat development in the enclosure ditches. It is possible that the construction of the road surface was a response to the rising water table and the abandonment of the site may also have been related to this problem. Perhaps there was a

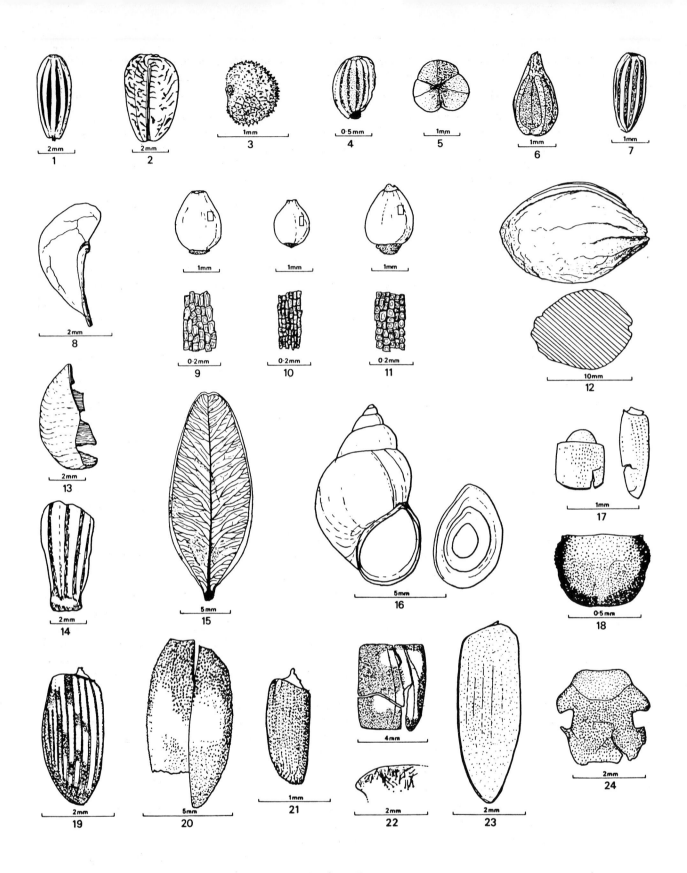

Figure 8   Macroscopic plant and invertebrate remains from Farmoor. *1.* Oenanthe *cf.* aquatica *mericarp (590/4);*
2. Onopordum acanthium *achene (590/4); 3.* Lychnis flos-cuculi *seed (1159); 4.* Lemna *sp. seed (1159); 5.* Valerianella
rimosa *fruit, end on view (1007/1); 6.* V. dentata *fruit (1007/1); 7.* Chrysanthemum leucanthemum *achene (1060/2);*
8. Filipendula ulmaria *achene (43/10); 9–11.* Eleocharis S. palustres *nuts with details of cell patterns (43/10); 12.* Prunus
domestica *stone (1060/2); 13.* Buxus sempervirens *fruit fragment (17/4); 14.* Triticum spelta *glume fragment (17/4);*
15. Buxus sempervirens *leaf (17/4); 16.* Bithynia tentaculata *shell and operculum (Sample Column III 12–22 cm);*
17. Aglenus brunneus *pronotum with head and left elytron (1159); 18.* Carpelimus bilineatus *pronotum (1159);*
19. Aphodius equestris *left elytron (17/4); 20.* Otiorrhynchus ligustici *paired elytra (1072); 21.* Scolytus rugulosus *left
elytron (1060/2); 22.* Hister quadrimaculatus *right elytron and left underside of the front of the pronotum (1159);*
23. Crypticus quisquilius *left elytron (1159); 24.* Tenebrio molitor *head, elytral fragments also found (17/4).*
Iron Age: 1–6, 17–18, 22–23. Roman: 7–16, 19–21, 24.

resumption of flooding. Similar evidence for a rising water table on the Thames floodplain comes from Port Meadow, Oxford, where the fills of Bronze Age ring ditches are ungleyed below the water table whereas Iron Age hut circle ditches of similar depth have gleyed fills and contain preserved organic remains (Lambrick and Robinson, unpublished).

Several hut circles with small compounds attached to them were excavated on the floodplain and first terrace of the Thames at Farmoor. On the basis of the pottery, the date of occupation of the site is likely to have been at some time between about 250bc and 100bc. The following radiocarbon dates were obtained for the site: 180 ± 80 bc, 110 ± 70 bc, 460 ± 100 bc. Peaty deposits had accumulated in the ditches of the floodplain enclosures and in a sump of one of the enclosures on the gravel terrace.

The earliest sample examined was a non-gleyed sandy silt covering the gravel underlying the occupation layer of one of the enclosure complexes on the floodplain (Lambrick and Robinson 1979; Robinson 1978a; Robinson 1981b, 259– 62; Robinson 1981a, 95–104, 166–98, 354–408). It did not contain aquatic molluscs. In contrast, the occupation layer above was a gleyed clay with charcoal flecks, a little pottery and riverine aquatic molluscs. These species, including *Bithynia tentaculata*, were also present in some of the ditches of the floodplain enclosures. *B. tentaculata* lives almost exclusively in lakes and running water, never occurring in small, closed ponds. It would not have been able to breed in water in the bottom of these ditches (which had been traced in their entirety and formed small closed systems). Flooding is regarded as the only likely explanation for the introduction of *B. tentaculata*, implying that the sites were seasonally occupied.

The pollen analyses (by G W Dimbleby) gave an even lower value for tree pollen than the samples from Mingies Ditch, 1.4% of the total pollen. These values suggest that clearance had been very thorough around Farmoor by this date and, unlike Mingies Ditch, there was no evidence to the contrary from macroscopic plant remains for a significant presence of woody species. Only a single beetle out of over 1,000 terrestrial individuals identified fell into the group of outdoor tree and wood dependant species. The pollen indicated the landscape to have been predominantly grassland.

The waterlogged seeds were mostly from plants of disturbed ground but their origin was probably extremely local. There were also seeds of about 35 species which could have grown in grassland, including some which are restricted to wet habitats. Damp pastureland is suggested by *Eleocharis* S. *Palustres* spp., which was well represented. These species (*E. palustris* and *E. uniglumis*) are restricted to places where competition from tall growing species is slight or absent and the water level is at or above soil level in the spring, when rhizome growth takes place (but it can tolerate drier conditions during the rest of the year). *E. palustris* is characteristic of heavily grazed old pasture on the Thames floodplain at present. The importance of pasture at Farmoor in the Iron Age is confirmed by dung beetles of the genera *Geotrupes, Colobopterus, Aphodius* and *Onthophagus.* They made up almost 28% of the terrestrial Coleoptera, a higher proportion than for any other site in the region so far investigated.

There was a wide range of seeds from annual plants of disturbed ground which probably grew around the settlement, but two species which are particularly common in nutrient-rich ground settlements and whose seeds are normally found in large numbers from waterlogged deposits on occupations sites, *Urtica dioica* and *Sambucus nigra*, were almost absent. One or both of these species were well represented from all the other Iron Age and Roman sites in the Thames Valley for which waterlogged seeds have been investigated including Mingies Ditch on the floodplain, and Claydon Pike, which had somewhat similar enclosures to Farmoor. Both species are capable of growing on the floodplain today, sometimes in great abundance, but neither normally grow in grassland. A possible reason for this difference between Iron Age Farmoor and the other sites might be that the Farmoor settlements were temporary. The annual weeds would be able to build up large populations rapidly on the freshly disturbed grassland in the vicinity of the sites but by the time that *U. dioica* and *S. nigra* had become established and flowering in profusion (neither flowers at all in its first year), the settlements had been abandoned and their ditches allowed to silt up.

A few charred grains of *Triticum* sp. and *Hordeum vulgare* (hulled) were the only crop remains identified from the Iron Age features at Farmoor. In view of the evidence for flooding, it would seem most unlikely that the floodplain was cultivated. *Pteridium aquilinum* frond fragments were present in Iron Age samples from both Mingies Ditch and Farmoor. It requires somewhat acidic conditions for sporeling establishment. Limestone heath conditions might have developed on a stone-free soil somewhere over the Thames gravels where there was not an input of calcium carbonate (for instance from the lime-rich floodwaters of the rivers) but it is more likely that the bracken had been brought to the sites from the acidic sands or glacial drift on the hillsides, perhaps as litter for animals.

Some time after the Iron Age sites on the floodplain had ceased to be occupied, the nature of the flooding changed. Rather than being the sort of flooding which occurs on the Thames floodplain today in the vicinity of Oxford, depositing mostly flotsam with very little mineral material, a much greater mineral load was deposited, causing a build up of alluvium over the Iron Age enclosure complexes and a levelling up of undulations in the floodplain. Evidence from the Roman site at Farmoor showed that the main aggradation of alluvium was complete by the fourth century AD.

Excavations by D Miles are continuing on a very large cropmark site towards the top of the Thames Valley at Claydon Pike, Gloucestershire. There are many middle Iron Age hut circles and enclosures on islands of first terrace gravel which are separated from each other by Late Glacial hollows in the gravel surface. An extensive programme of investigations of the carbonised crop and weed remains is taking place. The major cereals are again *Triticum spelta* and *Hordeum vulgare* (hulled) but the assemblages are characteristic of a 'consumer site': weed and chaff-rich with only small quantities of charred material in total (M Jones, pers. comm.). The seeds and insects from a small waterlogged sample suggests wet grassland (Robinson 1981a, 105, 198–9, 409–13; Robinson 1981b, 262; Robinson, unpublished k). There were also many seeds of *Urtica dioica* and *Chenopodium* cf *rubrum*, the former contrasting with Farmoor, the latter probably growing on wet nutrient-rich disturbed ground.

Two more sites give information on possible Iron Age alluviation of the floodplain in the Thames Valley. Plant and invertebrate remains were examined from what seems to have been a river bed/riverside marsh deposit at St. Aldate's, Oxford (Brown and Robinson in Durham 1977, 169–74). A radiocarbon determination of 650 ± 120 bc was obtained on seeds and plant fragments from this context, which, despite the excavator's comments, seems plausible. Sealing these deposits was about 0.6m of clay, which at the time of the excavation was regarded as a man-made causeway (Durham 1977, 90–1, 101–7, 174–9). In view of the extent of this clay layer and in the light of more recent excavations on the Thames floodplain, it seems possible that the clay was a general alluvial deposit. Deposition of clay alluvium may have begun at the Drayton Cursus during the Iron Age. A Roman ditch on the site cut decalcified alluvial clay which covered the Neolithic features (Robinson, unpublished g).

Of the two sites on the sides the Thames Valley, the interest in one of them is alluvial. The 'hillfort' of Cherbury Camp, despite being close to the watershed of the Oxford Heights, is rather low-lying. It is situated on a knoll of limestone surrounded by alluvium. Arkell (1939) noted the abundance of shells of *Oxyloma pfeifferi* when the alluvium had been freshly ploughed and suggested that the marshy conditions they indicate may have contributed to the defences. His inference may well be correct, although the shells on the surface were probably post-Iron Age. The second site is the small hillfort of Eynsham Hall Camp, on the acid soil of the glacial drift of the Wychwood area. Pollen analysis of the soil from the bank showed the site to have been oak woodland after its fortification (G W Dimbleby, pers. comm.).

(d)   *The Nene Valley* The valley of the Willow Brook at Apethorpe contained Zone VIII (sub-Atlantic) deposits which had not suffered re-working (Sparks and Lambert 1961–62). It is possible that some of this sequence belonged to the Iron Age. Herb pollen predominated, with values for tree pollen dropping to less than 10% of the total pollen, although *Corylus* was well represented. *Carpinus* pollen was present. The values for *Artemesia, Chenopodiaceae, Plantago lanceolata* and cereal-type pollen along with various other types of herb pollen suggest grassland and arable to have covered most of the landscape. In the molluscs from this core, *Vallonia pulchella* and other open country snails were well represented amongst the terrestrial and marsh species.

A rather confusing report is given of evidence for flooding in a pre-Belgic context on the Nene floodplain at Grendon (McCormick 1975). At Ecton the alluvium of the Nene floodplain covered Iron Age features (Hollowell 1971, 11).

The remaining Nene Valley sites are all on higher ground of the valley sides. The colour banding pattern of hand-picked shells of *Cepaea nemoralis* from the ditches of pre-Belgic enclosures at Blackthorn, on Northampton Sands (Evans in Williams 1974, 63) and at Wellingborough, on chalky boulder clay (Evans in Everson 1976, 97–8), suggests open conditions. At Blackthorn, a high proportion of *Vallonia excentrica* in a sieved sample confirms the interpretation.

Charred wheat and rye are reported from the Iron Age hillfort of Hunsbury, on the high ground of the ironstone near Northampton (Reid *et al.* in George 1917, 36) but a much more interesting discovery was made at Twywell, on the Great Oolitic Limestone (Jackson 1975, 61). Grain was present in several Iron Age pits on the site but one of the pits contained a considerable quantity of charred grain on the bottom and adhering to the sides. The walls of the pit also showed reddening from heat. On one side of the pit there were alternate layers of carbonised grain and soil between 1 and 5cm thick. The upper and lower layers were 90% *Triticum spelta*, the middle layer 100% *Hordeum vulgare*. The excavator kindly allowed the authors to examine the spelt, which proved to have been stored as spikelets rather than fully threshed. These deposits probably resulted from lighting a fire in this pit to clean it each time it was going to be used for grain storage.

Discussion During the final Bronze Age, c900bc–550bc, there seems to have been increased clearance pressure on woodland. The gravel terraces and floodplain of the River Thames itself were probably largely clear of trees by the beginning of this period although the floodplains of the tributaries such as the Windrush, still seem to have carried alder wood. Clearance was occurring on the Windrush floodplain, although at Mingies Ditch there was a temporary reversal of the trend. On the Downs, tree cover was being removed at Ram's Hill for the last time, as was the woodland at Wayland's Smithy which had survived throughout the rest of the Bronze Age. At both of these sites on the Downs, clearance was followed by ploughing, although at Ram's Hill, pasture subsequently became established. On the Thames gravels, at Mount Farm, there seems to have been both arable and grassland, although the grassland may have been slightly scrubby. The evidence from Wallingford suggests that, for most of the year, conditions on the Thames floodplain were very dry. It is thought likely that, as in the earlier periods, large parts of the floodplains of the major rivers in the region did not flood. On present evidence, the same main cereal crops that were grown in the first part of the Bronze Age, emmer wheat and barley, continued in use, although it is probable that new crops were arriving in the region during the late Bronze Age (Jones 1981, 116—7). Unfortunately, almost all the evidence for conditions in the late Bronze Age comes from the Oxford district, it can only be assumed that similar developments were occurring elsewhere in the region.

Rather more information is available for the pre-Belgic Iron Age. Some woodland seems to have been left on the Cotswolds and limestone hills to the north-west of the region although there was undoubtedly an agricultural expansion in this area. The hillfort of Lyneham Camp was perhaps built on what had been an area of rough grazing with thorn scrub. The Iron Age evidence from the chalk areas of the Chilterns is of ploughsoils under Iron Age earthworks and much hillwash containing Iron Age pottery in valley bottoms. While the only evidence from the Downs so far is for grassland, if the same trends were followed as on the Chilterns, there was also probably much arable.

In the Thames Valley, there were probably still vestiges of tree and scrub cover surviving on the floodplains of its tributaries during the early Iron Age, which also may have had willow swamps in places on their gently sloping river margins. The impression gained from the main Thames terraces and floodplain, however, is of a treeless landscape. The floodplain and at least the lower-lying parts of the terrace seem to have been pastureland. It is difficult to assess the extent of grassland on the higher gravel terraces but arable was certainly important. Open conditions also seem to have been present in the Nene Valley; on the higher ground above the river, arable farming seems to have been important to the site at Twywell.

By the end of the Iron Age, much, if not most of the region was under arable or grass. However, there are still large areas for which no information is available, especially where there are the more highly acidic soils or the more intractable clays. For example, there still could have been extensive tracts of woodland in places on the clay-with-flints and drift/Tertiary deposits of the Chilterns, the Oxford and Gault Clay vales and some of the glacial drift and boulder clay (excluding the chalky boulder clay). Eynsham Hall Camp was constructed in what may have remained oak woodland on the acid glacial drift.

Changes in the river regime of the Thames Valley caused an alteration to conditions in the floodplain during the early and middle Iron Age. The water table at first rose and then there was an onset of extensive flooding. Finally, either at the end of the middle Iron Age or in the Belgic period, alluviation occurred. Similar developments may also have been taking place in the Nene and Ouse Valleys, although at present there is no good evidence for Iron Age flooding, only alluvium, which could be later, covering an Iron Age site.

Spelt wheat and six-row barley seem to have been the main cereal crops of the early and middle Iron Age. Even though spelt has not been recorded from pre-Iron Age contexts in the region, emmer wheat had so declined in importance by the Iron Age that all the finds could even have been rogues/volunteers in other crops. Bread/club wheat seems to have been a minor crop, as was a newcomer, rye. There seems to have been such pressure for arable production at the Ashville site that cultivation extended onto wet, less suitable soils, while the weed flora seems to show declining soil fertility. There is evidence for the winter sowing of cereals in the region during the Iron Age, although there is no reason why this practice should not have been established as early as the Neolithic. Oak seems to have been especially favoured for structural purposes, but a wide range of species, many of them characteristic of thorn shrub, were used for firewood.

In the Thames Valley the environmental evidence has given some indication of site relationships and function. On the wetter parts of the first terrace and on the floodplain were pastoral settlements, dependent upon external sources for their grain. The floodplain sites at Farmoor were probably occupied by transhumant groups from a main settlement elsewhere. In contrast, the sites on the higher terraces, upon which the floodplain sites may have been dependant, were involved in grain production as well as stock rearing.

Iron Age Pastoral and Arable Communities: the Bones

Published collections are common and provide more information than Bronze Age ones. Sites are widespread across free draining calcareous substrata and also occur in areas of heavier ground e.g. Twywell, Northamptonshire (Harcourt 1975) or Bierton, Buckinghamshire (G Jones, unpublished). Reported occupational debris is largely from farmsteads of enclosed type, e.g. Mingies Ditch, Hardwick with Yelford, Oxfordshire, or open type, e.g. Farmoor, Oxfordshire. Few collections are from larger settlements, e.g. Ashville, Abingdon or hillforts, e.g. Rainsborough, Northamptonshire, or *oppida*, e.g. Bagendon, Gloucestershire.

On many sites bones are well preserved, particularly those deposited in storage pits, but those in ditches are more degraded. Less commonly excavated superficial layers usually yield poorly preserved fragments and many teeth (Wilson 1978a, in prep.). Sometimes articulated skeletons are recovered and described: horses and dog (J King 1953), sheep and dog (Wilson 1978a) and 'a small deer' (Tilson 1975).

Table 5 Percentage Ranges of Species Fragments From Twelve Iron Age Sites[1]

	%
cattle	27–50
sheep/goat	25–63
pig	2–22
horse	1–16
dog	0.3–6
red deer	0–2[2]

1. Largest site collections are from:—
Bedfordshire: none
Buckinghamshire: Bierton (G Jones unpublished)
Gloucestershire: Guiting Power (Wilson 1979)
Northamptonshire: Hardingstone (Gilmore 1969a), Moulton Park, Northampton (Orr 1974), Rainsborough (Banks 1967), Wakerley (R Jones 1978) and Hardwick Park, Wellingborough (Orr 1977)
Oxfordshire: Ashville (Wilson 1978a), Barton Court Farm (Wilson unpublished), City Farm (G Jones unpublished), Farmoor (Wilson 1979a) and Mingies Ditch, Hardwick (Wilson in preparation d)
2. Largely antler

Goat is reported (e.g. Banks 1966) but varies from scarcely present to perhaps 5% of sheep/goat remains (Wilson 1978a and in prep.). Roe deer is usually absent from collections (but see Jackson 1961; George 1917). Hare and fox were probably common animals while cat (?wild), pine marten (Wilson in prep. e), beaver (Wilson 1978b) and hedgehog (Wilson 1980 a), occur occasionally.

Rodents are frequently recorded, particularly water vole and mouse (*Apodemus* sp.) but also bank and field voles.

Birds are better known than for previous periods but comprise minute fractions of identified bones (e.g. 0.5%, Wilson 1978 a; and 0.6%, R Jones 1978). Domestic fowl were introduced during the later Iron Age (Bramwell, 1978b). Duck bones include mallard and bones comparable to teal, gargeny, and shoveller (Bramwell in G Jones unpublished) and wigeon (Allison n.d.). Other identifications include goose, crane, blackbird (R Jones 1978), house sparrow (Bramwell 1978b) and raven (Allison n.d.).

Fish bones are rare: chub and pike (Wilson 1978a) although a few soil samples have been sieved for small bones. Marine shells of oyster and mussel are recorded only at Bagendon (Jackson 1961) and these and occasional freshwater mussels (Robinson 1978) appear atypical food items, if indeed they were eaten.

Interpretation of fragment number results is known to be affected by intra site differences among bone scatters (see later in this section) but general comparison to Bronze Age results, shows that the proportions of sheep and horse bones have risen and that of cattle fallen.

Large species indicating woods or scrubland are less abundant and probably these habitats must have retreated further while pasture increased. Wetland species notably ducks are present and may indicate some intensification of hunting but their environmental significance is not clear. Unlike the Bronze Age, the extensive use of meadowlands is well established, particularly at Farmoor (Lambrick and Robinson 1979) where cattle, mostly cows, were relatively abundant (Wilson 1978 a, 136; 1979c).

Yet despite the presence of small game, the Iron Age animal economy is concentrated in the husbandry of domestic animals, especially mammals, more than at any other cultural period except perhaps the Bronze Age. To establish the nature of the ecoculture the evidence is structured as follows.

Many sheep, especially males were slaughtered in abundance at hogget and other immature stages. Similarly bulls and steers were killed relatively young but cows tended to die or were killed after maturation and probably as old animals (Hamilton 1978, Wilson 1978a).

These slaughtering patterns differ from the following Roman period and almost certainly are a consequence of subsistence husbandry and not of well developed marketing patterns (Maltby 1981). Most animals are eaten at small settlements and close to their normal grazing — the latter perhaps varied seasonally.

Consideration of both the length of species life cycles and the estimates of minimum numbers of individuals in site collections suggests a livestock ratio of around 2 sheep:1 cattle. Despite the commonness of sheep bones, therefore, cattle still were the most important Iron Age domestic animal in terms of: meat yield, potential for secondary products, or live use of animals, and because of their fodder requirements.

The small size and conformation of cattle, sheep, and pigs is moderately documented (e.g. Armitage 1978, Gilmore 1969a, Wilson 1978a) and indicate (with pathology R Jones 1978 and Wilson 1978a) considerable environmental pressure on animals, or possibly limited genetic variability or some specific effects of human selection. The evidence of size and the slaughtering patterns give an impression of herds and flocks reproducing to capacity but killed off relatively young because of limited grazing and possibly the latter is linked to a gradual expansion of arable land.

Provision of meat from relatively young animals could be interpreted as a major aim of the economy. Yet the change toward raising more sheep and horses indicates increasing subsistence pressure against rearing cattle for meat, and for greater dependance on secondary products especially dairy and wool, or use of livestock e.g. as draught animals (Wilson 1978a, 118) associated with growing cereals. These trends ought to be correlates of higher human density and lower ratios of livestock to people than previously.

Human population estimates cannot be made easily especially because Iron Age burials had scant ceremony or respect and few survive except as scattered bones. Few burials are described completely. At Ashville, Abingdon, an old man of 5'3" was buried (Edwards 1978) and at Cassington, a Belgic child and a woman of 4'11½" and aged about 25 years (Powers 1982) – interestingly, short statures are indicated like those of animals. Despite the limited skeletal information, however the greater density of settlements, the larger amounts of animal bones and cereal debris all indicate an increased density of people albeit slowly from the Bronze Age.

So a greater demand for secondary products from animals is credible. Legge (1981), from Bronze Age evidence similar to the information from the Iron Age of this region, argues that cows not sheep would be preferred for dairying. Instead, sheep may be reared for wool as well as meat. Certainly spinning and weaving gear is widespread at sites but nevertheless wool does not appear the chief end product of Iron Age husbandry otherwise the slaughtering age would rise as sheep were kept longer to yield larger fleeces.

Butchery of carcasses was probably carried out on the ground and appears primarily concerned with meat removal. An intensive use of bones for food, tallow or glue is not obvious (Wilson 1978a and R Jones 1978). At Mingies Ditch (Wilson in prep. d) many small bone fragments from sheep and pigs occurred close to hearths and houses while large fragments and bones from cattle and horse were spread further away. The pattern indicates not just rubbish dropping, scavenging, or deliberate clearances after cooking and eating but that large carcasses were cut up on the periphery of the occupation area.

Further follow up studies of occupational debris are important because the Iron Age is the first prehistoric period for which there abundant information can be collected and the last before pronounced urban development and cultural imposition have an obvious effect on local economies. Excavations of small settlements therefore appear to present fewer interpretative difficulties. Nevertheless a broad view of the relationships between settlements is already undertaken by single excavation strategies; currently at Lechlade, Oxfordshire (Miles and Palmer 1982).

Unfortunately for the simplistic view of settlement economy, *oppida* and hillforts are still neglected by adequate reporting and faunal signs of social stratification will be more obvious there. At Bagendon the uncommon presence of domestic fowl, roe, and oyster (Jackson 1961) suggests a similar status, economy, or resources which characterise some Romano British sites. Hunsbury, Northamptonshire (George 1917) but perhaps not Rainsborough (Banks 1967) may have been similarly elevated. This hint of status at hillforts may place in better perspective the suggestion that wildlife, notably the hare appears protected by Celtic custom or myth (Wilson 1978 a, 138). Possibly hunting was a pastime associated with status.

As for change during the Iron Age, especially from Belgic influence, the evidence is not very consistent. 'Belgic' site collections occur at Hardingstone, Northamptonshire (Gilmore 1969a), Moulton Park, Northampton (Orr 1974), Puddlehill (Plummer 1976). Bierton, Buckinghamshire (G Jones unpublished), and at Ashville and Barton Court Farm, Oxfordshire. Where cattle appear more abundant this may predate a trend which is conspicuous in Romano British assemblages.

The Belgic and Romano-British Periods, 80bc – AD410

Organised Agriculture, Trade and Towns

The Belgic Period Few sites from this brief transitional period, lasting from 80bc to 43AD, have been investigated in the region. At Ashville, Oxfordshire, on the second Thames terrace, a system of large rectangular ditched enclosures replaced the middle Iron Age village. A radiocarbon date of ad50 ± 90 was obtained on bone from one of these ditches. The two main changes in the carbonised plant assemblages were a decline in wet ground species, possibly as a result of improved drainage or a contraction of the arable area, and the absence of *Triticum aestivocompactum* (Jones in Parrington 1978, 93–110). *T. spelta* and *Hordeum vulgare* (hulled) remained the main crops.

Also on the second Thames terrace quite close to Ashville, at Barton Court, Oxfordshire, a Belgic farmstead was constructed within a square enclosure during the first century BC which lasted into the first century AD. Charred plant remains again showed *T. spelta* and *H. vulgare* (hulled) to be the most important cereals but *T. aestivocompactum* was also reasonably well represented (Jones in Miles, forthcoming). There was a rich somewhat dry ground weed flora and one Belgic pit contained many seeds of *Agrostemma githago*, the first reliable pre-Roman record for this species.

A preliminary investigation has been made of Belgic carbonised plant remains from Bierton, Buckinghamshire, a site on heavy clay (Jones 1981, 107). Unusually, *T. aestivocompactum* was the main cereal crop. It is a species well suited for growing on clay soils, but so is *T. spelta*. The reason for its choice is unknown.

The Roman Period The whole region was within the initial area of Roman conquest after the invasion of AD 43. Sufficient Roman sites have been investigated to consider the region under the same sub-divisions as for the Iron Age, with the addition of: towns; the Ouse Valley; and the North Northamptonshire Ironstone.

(a)   *Towns* Unfortunately, work has so far been limited to the defences of Dorchester and Alchester. Mollusca from the 3rd – 4th century AD outer ditch around Dorchester suggested that it permanently held deep water and was at least linked to the river in times of flood (Kennard in Hogg and Stevens 1937, 70–1). The old ground surface underneath the build-up of the Roman town of Alchester was found to be a flood marsh deposit (Robinson in Young 1975, 161–70). The Mollusca from it included *Vertigo angustior*, which is now extremely rare in Britain and extinct in the region. Two late first century AD ditches contained a slum aquatic mollusc fauna while the seeds and insects suggest wet grazed grassland on the site. There was no evidence for flooding. A seed of *Coriandrum sativum* provided an interesting early Roman culinary find from one of these ditches. The molluscs, seeds and insects showed the later Roman recut of the defensive ditch around the town to have been very different from the first century ditches. It contained moving water and a rich flora of aquatic plants. Amongst the beetles breeding in the ditch was *Hydrophilus piceus*, which now only lives in a few localities in Britian.

(b)   *The Cotswolds* Roman ploughwash was found to fill a ditch on the Oolitic Limestone at Ascott-under-Wychwood, Oxfordshire, (Evans 1972, 342–4) while substantial finds of charred grain have been made from some of the Roman villas on the Oxfordshire Cotswolds. In the early eighteenth century a mosaic pavement at the Stonesfield villa was discovered and found to be covered with between six inches and a foot of black corn (Pointer 1713, 4–5). It was noted to be wheat only, neither mixed with other cereals or earth. Rather than interpreting the find as the burnt contents of a granary, the author, who was chaplain of Merton College, assumed the grain to have been dumped on the mosaic to protect it. 'For the Romans, when they left Britain, did use to burn and demolish their Praetorian Tents and bury their Pavements (or rather cast Tumulus's or Heaps of earth over them) as being too large and cumbersome for carriage, after they were made up; and perhaps not without some thoughts of returning some time or other.' A cache of charred grain thought to be from Stonesfield was identified as mostly *Triticum spelta* grains and chaff, with a little *Hordeum* sp., *Agrostemma githago* and perhaps a few grains each of *T. aestivocompactum* and *T. dicoccum* (Morris 1959). A rather similar accumulation of carbonised grain was identified from the North Leigh villa, but *Secale cereale* grains were possibly present and *T. dicoccum* was absent (Morris 1959). In both cases, the barley grains were reported as naked.

At the foot of the Cotswolds, on the White Limestone of the Wilcote Valley, is the Shakenoak Villa. A great miscellany of biological remains have been identified from this site and they include some important records (various authors in Brodribb *et al.* 1968; 1973; 1978). An assemblage of almost pure threshed *T. spelta* was identified from a third century context by Helbaek and Alvey (in Brodribb *et al.* 1968, 109). The Mollusca from the villa included *Candidula gigaxi* sealed beneath a third century floor (Cain in Brodribb *et al.* 1968, 114–16), an early record for this alien species. Unfortunately the only examples of *Helix pomatia*, the Roman edible snail from this site (or indeed any archaeological site in the region) were from a seventh or early eighth century AD context (Cain in Brodribb *et al.* 1972, 162–3). A vast quantity of charcoal and waterlogged wood was identified from the site (Brodribb *et al.* 1973, 137–41; 1978, 108–10) although it would be prudent to regard most of the identifications apart from those of oak as tentative. The finds included many oak planks, laths and a few off-cuts from massive timbers. There were also oak and beech poles, and many assorted sticks and twigs, mostly of hazel and hawthorn type. Oak, hazel and hawthorn all seem to have been used as firewood from the evidence of the charcoals. Two interesting woods were identified from third century contexts, a lath of *Abies alba*, a non-British species, and a comb of *Buxus sempervirens*. Mollusca from early third century silt on the bottom of one of the fishponds on the site suggest it held still, shallow, water but the deposit may have been from towards the end of the pond's life. The marsh species from the pond provide another record of *Vertigo angustior* from the region (Chatfield in Brodribb *et al.* 1978, 165–8). An assortment of waterlogged plant and insect remains were identified from the fishponds, but for the most part they are only of local interest. Conditions of preservation in one of the ponds, however, were remarkable and included recognisable leaves and stems of several herb species including *Urtica dioica* and *Poterium sanguisorba* (Brodribb *et al.* 1978, 112–16).

(c)   *The Downs and Chilterns* At Ram's Hill, Oxfordshire, on the chalk of the Downs, the Iron Age pasture was ploughed up and c50BC to AD100 a ploughsoil formed (Evans in Bradley and Ellison 1975, 139–49). The ploughsoil covered the tail of the Iron Age rampart while ploughwash filled an Iron Age gulley and the top of the Bronze Age enclosure ditch.

On the Chilterns at Pink Hill, Buckinghamshire, chalky ploughwash continued to accumulate during the Roman period (Evans 1972, 312–16). Charcoals were identified from a Roman villa on the Chilterns at Saunderton, Buckinghamshire (Maby in Ashcroft 1934–40, 426) and a pottery kiln at Hedgerley, Buckinghamshire (Maby in Oakley et al. 1934–40), but in view of the author's identifications from another site (p 38) these identifications must be regarded as suspect. The only reliable charcoal identifications from a Roman site on the Chilterns were from the Latimer villa, Buckinghamshire, in the Chess Valley (Sheldon in Branigan 1971, 168). There was oak, almost all from large timbers, and hazel rods.

(d)   *The Thames Valley* A considerable amount of work has been undertaken on waterlogged and carbonised material from sites on the Thames terraces in Oxfordshire. The site at Farmoor was re-occupied from the later second century AD until the end of the fourth century (dated by pottery and coins) (Lambrick and Robinson 1979; Robinson 1978a; Robinson 1981a, 95–104, 200–29, 354–408; Robinson 1981b, 262–5). The settlement was confined to the first gravel terrace and based around small fields along a ditched droveway leading to the floodplain. Various features, such as wells and ditches, extended below the water table. The pollen analyses (by G W Dimbleby) show that, as in the Iron Age, the landscape was predominantly unwooded. The highest value for tree/shrub pollen in any sample was 12% of the total pollen but the average from the other samples was about 3%. The proportion of outdoor tree and wood-feeding Coleoptera out of the total number of terrestrial individuals, at 1.4%, is very low when compared with woodland sites but more than ten times greater than the comparable value for the Iron Age features at Farmoor.

Rather damp grazed grassland was suggested by a combination of lines of evidence. The dung beetles from the genera *Geotrupes, Aphodius* and *Onthophagus* were almost as important as in the Iron Age at Farmoor, comprising 21% of the terrestrial fauna. Their occurrence in the various Roman samples was, however, by no means uniform, perhaps reflecting differing usages of the small fields.

Many of the weed seeds were probably from plants which grew on disturbed ground around the settlement. Some of the species identified, however, show a particular association with arable agriculture: *Ranunculus arvensis, Agrostemma githago* and perhaps *Anthemis cotula. A. cotula* is often very well represented by its seeds on Roman and Medieval urban sites, where it is thought to have been growing, rather than resulting from threshing debris. Unlike the Iron Age samples from Farmoor, some of the Roman samples contained a significant quantity of cereal remains. In all of these samples, the remains represented the debris from threshing *Triticum spelta*. The fill of a corn-drier was examined for carbonised remains and found to contain five times as many spelt glume bases as wheat grains (Jones in Lambrick and Robinson 1979, 103–4). It is thought that the corn-drier was used to parch the crop, which does not have free-threshing grains, in order to render the glumes brittle enough to thresh. The resultant winnowings had perhaps then been thrown into the corn-drier fire. A late fourth century pit at Farmoor contained a substantial quantity of water-logged spelt chaff and cereal-type pollen. The pollen had remained enclosed within the bracts of the wheat after flowering, and had been brought to the site with the crop (Robinson and Hubbard 1977). A little charred *Hordeum vulgare* was found and a few waterlogged seeds of another arable crop, *Linum usitatissimum.*

Three other species which were present in the waterlogged samples stand out as crops: *Prunus domestica, Anethum graveolens* and *Coriandrum sativum.* Two varieties of plum were found in the Roman samples, one with stones the size and shape of a modern variety of damson, the other from a larger-fruited variety. Another species which might have been cultivated was a non-British umbellifer, seeds (mericarps) of which were present in Roman samples from both Barton Court and Farmoor. They somewhat resembled seeds of *Chaerophyllum aromaticum.*

Macroscopic remains of *Prunus spinosa* and to a lesser extent *Crataegus* type were well represented in the Roman waterlogged deposits. It has already been mentioned for Mingies Ditch how pollen from these entomophilous species tends to be badly represented, so the low frequency of tree/shrub pollen from the Roman samples ought not be surprising. Had natural scrub regeneration been taking place on the site, a much greater diversity of scrub species would have been expected, and the archaeological evidence suggests that the occupation of the site was at its most intensive during this period. Therefore, it is thought that thorn hedges may have been present on the site. Evidence for hedges of another sort came from the discovery of box leaves in two of the Roman features, in one instance along with *Buxus sempervirens* fruit fragments. Box is a plant of chalk and limestone scarps which is regarded as native to Britain, but it is most unlikely to have been growing wild at Farmoor.

In the Roman period at Farmoor, there was a considerable increase in the number of beetles which live in relatively intimate association with man, compared with the pre-Roman sites. Firstly there are those beetles which are capable of invading structural timbers (although they can also inhabit naturally occurring dead wood): in particular *Anobium punctatum.* Secondly, there are various synanthropic species such as *Ptinus fur, Stegobium paniceum* and *Typhaea stercorea.* All of these species can occur in granary refuse and are often associated with hay waste or straw. Another group of species likely to be related to human habitation, the Lathridiidae, were about five times as abundant at Roman

Farmoor compared with any of the earlier sites investigated. They tend to occur in 'sweet' compost such as haystack bottoms and thatch.

Conditions on another Roman site on the first gravel terrace, at Appleford, seem to have been somewhat similar to those at Farmoor (Hinchliffe 1980; Robinson 1978a; Robinson 1981a, 105–7, 229–36, 414–29; Robinson 1981b, 265–6). The site was in use from the late first century AD until the end of the fourth century (on the basis of pottery and coins) and it consisted of three converging droveways with small fields along them. There was not such good evidence from the waterlogged remains for pasture as at Farmoor, but rather better evidence from the Coleoptera for meadow-land. Even though the landscape was predominantly open at Appleford, some scrub was present. It is uncertain whether or not the scrub was in the form of hedges.

Work has only just started on waterlogged samples from the excavation by D Miles of a Roman farmstead or villa on the first terrace at Claydon Pike, Gloucestershire (Robinson, unpublished n). So far, the results correspond reasonably closely to those from other Roman sites on the first gravel terrace, including the presence of *Coriandrum sativum* and a high proportion of dung beetles. The identification of *Foeniculum vulgare* was a not unexpected addition to the culinary herbs/spices recorded from Roman sites in the region. At some time after the end of the Roman period, a silty mollusc-rich alluvium was deposited over the lower-lying features on the site.

At Barton Court, Abingdon, the Belgic farmstead was replaced in the later first century by a Roman timber farm-house within a rectangular enclosure. In about AD270 a small stone corridor-type villa was built on the site, which was on the edge of the second terrace, overlooking the clay slope down to the first terrace. The villa, or at least its farm buildings, continued in use until the end of the fourth century or later (dated by pottery and coins). Carbonised plant remains were examined from all the Roman phases (including two corn-driers) while waterlogged material was investi-gated from two substantial wells which filled up during the fourth century (Robinson 1981a, 107–12, 236–49; 430–67; Robinson 1981b, 266–8; Jones and Robinson in Miles, forthcoming). J R A Greig's pollen analyses showed that the villa was surrounded by an open, relatively unwooded environment. This impression is confirmed by the Coleoptera. Grassland and disturbed ground were the major habitats indicated by the waterlogged plant and insect remains. Dung beetles comprised 16% of the terrestrial Coleoptera and two groups of Carabidae which suggest bare ground or arable were relatively well represented: several species of *Amara*; and *Harpalus rufipes* and *Agonum dorsale*. The carbonised plant remains showed *Triticum spelta* followed by *Hordeum vulgare* (hulled) to have been the major cereal crops. *Vicia faba* v. *minor* was also grown. The weed flora gives some information about the various soils under cultivation. *Rumex acetosella* agg. suggests they included somewhat acidic soils. The abundance of *Anthemis cotula* suggests the cultivation of basic, heavy soils, perhaps on the clay slope, while another mayweed, *Tripleurospermum maritimum*, was perhaps growing in cereal fields on the second terrace. As in the pre-Belgic samples from Ashville, the presence of wet ground species suggests that there was pressure to extend cultivation onto soils less suitable for cereal agriculture.

Remains of three species of arable crops which had been brought to the villa farmyard for processing were found waterlogged: spelt wheat and barley again, but also flax. By far the most numerous of these was flax (*Linum usitatissimum*), represented by seeds and capsule fragments. It seems likely that the capsules were harvested (rippled) and brought to the villa to press for oil or for consumption of the seeds. If the stems were retted for linen, this unpleasant process may have taken place at the site of cultivation. A most interesting discovery amongst the flax remains was silicula fragments of *Camelina alyssum*. This weed is particularly associated with flax cultivation, and its presence in a flax field seriously affects the yield of the crop due to the production of a growth inhibitor on the leaf surface. However, seeds of *C. alyssum* harvested with the linseed would themselves contribute to the oil production on pressing, and it is even possible that *C. alyssum* itself was cultivated as an oil crop.

The apparently contradictory results from the charred and waterlogged samples for the most important crop species illustrate the bias of the different lines of evidence: the parching of cereals tends to result in accidental charring while cereal remains do not preserve very well under waterlogged conditions.

Excluding trees grown for their wood, there were seeds of three more species of cultivated plant: *Anethum graveolens, Coriandrum sativum* and *Prunus domestica*. Another species *Papaver somniferum*, may have been cultivated as an oil or medicinal crop, or could merely have been a weed.

Anobium punctatum was no more abundant than from Roman Farmoor, and likewise the proportion of Lathridiidae and synanthropic species was no greater than at Farmoor (although a new species can be added to the synanthropic group, *Mycetaea hirta*, a fungal feeder which most often occurs in buildings and seems to be partial to the dry rot fungus).

An unusual insight on a piece of woodland exploited by the villa was given by moss which had been packed between the stone lining of one of the wells. The mosses, reported upon by J Dixon, were all woodland species. The most abundant, *Hylocomium brevirostre*, occurs in deep shade on calcareous soil and is at present uncommon. Many other biological remains had been transported with the moss from the woodland floor including pollen, oak galls of Hymenoptera from the sub-family Cynipinae (Robinson 1980a), seeds and the woodland snail *Azeca goodalli*. An 'old

52

woodland' bryophyte flora suggested that the wood had an ancient origin, but a high value of hazel pollen and a low value for forest trees show that by the late third century AD, there had been human interference with the wood. Perhaps it was an oak/hazel coppice and the gall-infested oaks had not reached flowering size. The wood may have been situated on coral limestone to the north of the site, as is the present wood of Bagley, which has a somewhat similar flora and fauna to that from the moss.

Occupation continued throughout the Roman period at Ashville, Abingdon on the second terrace, but the carbonised plant remains showed little difference from the Belgic material (Jones in Parrington 1978, 93–110). The proportion of *Vicia* and *Lathyrus*, however, continued to rise, suggesting that soil fertility fell further.

Macroscopic plant and invertebrate remains have been identified from Roman waterlogged deposits at Mount Farm, Berinsfield on the second Thames terrace (Robinson, unpublished i). The site, excavated by G H Lambrick consisted of a series of trackways and ditched enclosures, within which were ponds and water holes. Preliminary results of pollen analysis by J R A Greig, suggest an almost treeless landscape. This picture is confirmed by the Coleoptera, although the identification of *Salix* capsules in some of the deposits shows that willow trees were locally present. There was a very low value for the selected scarabaeoid dung beetles, only 2.3% of the terrestrial Coleoptera, and there was no indication of the presence of meadowland. In contrast, the values for the two groups of Carabidae which favour bare ground and arable were relatively high. It seems likely that much of the land around the site was cultivated. A more complete picture of the cereals grown on the site will emerge when the carbonised plant remains have been examined, at present only *Triticum spelta* has been identified preserved by waterlogging. One waterlogged sample, however, contained *Linum usitatissimum* threshing debris and a few silicula fragments of that characteristic flax weed *Camelina* sp. This site provided yet another record of *Coriandrum sativum* while a single seed of *Papaver somniferum* was identified. One of the water holes/wells contained many thousands of seeds of *Apium graeolens*. Celery is naturally a local species of wet or marshy ground, especially where conditions are saline. The other plant and insect remains from the deposit suggested the relatively dry conditions that would be expected on the third gravel terrace. Therefore it seems unlikely that celery would have grown wild at Mount Farm. Perhaps the site supplied the nearby town of Dorchester with market garden produce including celery seeds. A few charred seeds of *A. graveolens* were discovered, suggesting some human activity related to them.

Few Roman sites are known on the Thames floodplain. On the site of the Neolithic cursus at Drayton, however, a Roman ditch cut through alluvium and had been filled then covered by the continuing deposition of alluvial clay (Robinson, unpublished g). At a later date, the silt content of the alluvium increased. At Farmoor, further alluvial deposition took place on the floodplain after the end of the Roman period.

Charred and rather badly preserved waterlogged plant remains were examined from a Roman well upon the calcareous sands of the Oxford Heights at the pottery kiln site at the Churchill Hospital, Oxford (Young 1972; Robinson, unpublished m). The charred plant remains represented chaff from the threshing of spelt wheat. The water-logged seeds were all species of neglected ground, several of which tend to be associated with human habitation, for example *Chelidonium majus*. There was also a single seed of *Papaver somniferum*.

(e)   *The Ouse Valley* A series of Roman sites has been excavated in the Ouse Valley which are all related to alluvium. At Bourton Grounds, Buckinghamshire, on the floodplain of the River Twin, a tributary of the Ouse, alluvium sealed a later first century AD occupation site and covered a Roman road, which was still in use during the late third century. The alluvium contained flowing water Mollusca (Evans in Johnson 1975, 49). Alluvium was present under the road, but it seems to have been dumped there to create a causeway. Much further downstream at Bromham, Bedfordshire, on the Ouse floodplain, alluvium completely covered a Belgic and Romano-British site, the latest archaeological features being late third century AD (Tilson 1973).

Of much more local significance, aggradation was taking place in a streamside marsh at the Bancroft villa, Milton Keynes, Buckinghamshire, throughout the Roman period (Keeley 1982; Spencer 1982).

(f)   *The Nene Valley* The only Roman site investigated in the Nene Valley was a 3rd–4th century corn-drier which contained carbonised wheat, at Cogenhoe, Northamptonshire (Alexander 1967).

(g)   *North Northamptonshire Ironstone* Limited investigations were undertaken of carbonised seeds from a Roman site on the Lower Lincolnshire Limestone overlooking the Welland Valley at Wakerley (Arthur in Jackson and Ambrose 1978, 242). *Hordeum vulgare* grains were found in a fourth century corn-drier while a mid third century corn-drier contained *Triticum* sp.

Discussion Woodland need not have been much more abundant in the region than during the nineteenth century although there are large areas for which there is no information. It is probable that the Roman woods were intensively managed: timbers and poles for structural purposes, fuel for pottery kilns. The moss in the Barton Court well seemed to have come from a managed wood and a coppice stool, probably of oak, from which many poles had been cut, was found in a well at Farmoor. Long straight oak poles with widely spaced growth rings had been used for the construction of one of the Farmoor wells and it is likely that they grew under coppice conditions. A wide range of trees and shrubs seem to have been used for firewood but the results from Shakenoak show that oak was favoured for structural purposes. The exotics from Shakenoak, the boxwood and the silver fir, are woods that were possibly imported from outside the region or specially grown.

The agricultural intensification of the Iron Age continued throughout the Belgic period, reaching its peak towards the end of the Roman period. The towns provided a market for surplus agricultural production, the Roman road system (and the rivers) enabled produce to reach the towns or even be exported. On the Cotswolds, previously perhaps somewhat marginal land, were large villa estates on which arable seems to have been important even in the early Roman period. There was also extensive arable on the chalk of the Chilterns and very probably the Downs too. On the gravels of the major river valleys which had been intensively settled throughout the Iron Age, a major agricultural re-organisation seems to have taken place at the start of the Belgic period. Forerunners of the Roman type of droveway settlements appeared on several sites but waterlogged biological evidence is lacking from them at present. The droveways and enclosed fields, possibly with thorn hedges, of the Roman settlements on the Thames gravels are clear indications of more careful land use. The main areas of arable and pasture on the gravels, however, seem to have been open, perhaps only divided by the streams which cross the terraces. The same general trends as in the Iron Age seem to have been shown for the use of the Thames terraces with a concentration on grassland and the exploitation of floodplain grazing by settlements on the edge of the first terrace, while the sites on the higher terraces performed mixed or arable farming.

On the Thames floodplain, even seasonal occupation seems to have ceased by the Belgic period and alluviation continued throughout the Roman period. There is some evidence for stream management in the region during the Roman period on the floodplain, perhaps in order to make the floodwaters drain away more rapidly once river levels had subsided. At Mingies Ditch a stream was dammed and diverted into a ditch while there is possible evidence for a general lowering of the water table at the Roman town of Alchester (Robinson in Young 1975, 169). Conditions on the Ouse floodplain, however, seem to have been suitable for settlement in the Belgic and early Roman periods, right up until the late third century AD in one case. At present there is no definite evidence for Roman inundation of the Ouse and Nene floodplains in the region, although it is thought likely that it was taking place.

Triticum spelta and *Hordeum vulgare* (hulled) remained the main cereal crops throughout the Belgic and Roman periods although *T. spelta* may have been supplanted by *T. aestivocompactum* in a few localities. Cereals were not the only major Roman crops. Seeds of *Linum usitatissimum* were identified from most of the Roman sites from which waterlogged deposits have been examined but they have not been found from any earlier contexts in the region, even though flax was a Neolithic introduction to Britain. *Vicia faba* v. *minor* is also first recorded from a Roman site in the region, but its scale of cultivation is unknown. Horticultural crops also appear for the first time in the Roman period. At least four species of Umbelliferae with seeds that can be used for flavouring seem to have been cultivated:

Coriandrum sativum	*Anethum graveolens*
Foeniculum vulgare	*Apium graveolens*

All but *Apium graveolens*, celery, are likely to have been Roman introductions. *Papaver somniferum* may have been cultivated and several varieties of *Prunus domestica* have been found in Roman deposits. *Prunus avium* and *Malus sylvestris* have also been identified but it is uncertain whether they were from cultivated trees.

It seems that the culinary change which the Romans introduced to Britain spread throughout the region, even down to the most lowly rural sites, not just to the rich villas and the towns. Linseed and opium poppy may have been pressed to provide a northern substitute for olive oil. It is also possible that the Romans introduced the first varieties of 'dessert plum' to Britain. This fruit had apparently been present in the country since Neolithic times but no plum trees have been encountered in pre-Roman deposits in the region.

The introduction of new crops and improved communications with Europe resulted in the appearance of several new weed species in the Roman period such as *Camelina alyssum, Ranunculus arvensis* and *Anthemis cotula. A. cotula* seems to have become a major agricultural weed. The discovery of 248 carbonised seeds of *Agrostemma githago* in the bottom of a late Belgic pit at Barton Court (Jones in Miles, forthcoming), another serious cereal weed which was formerly regarded as a Roman introduction, serves as a warning that many presumed Roman introductions could in fact have occurred just before the Roman conquest.

The entomological evidence shows an increase in synanthropic species and species often associated with structural timbers from all the Roman waterlogged deposits investigated. How much this difference was due to an increase in the number and size of buildings per capita (perhaps there was even indoor housing of some domestic animals) and how much it was due to an increase in the population of the occupation sites is uncertain. It was probably related to some sort of intensification of agricultural exploitation of the area. Grain storage was also changed in this period, from below ground to above ground. Although grain beetles were only present in Roman but not earlier samples, there is no evidence that they reached serious pest proportions on the sites investigated. The major grain pests, such as *Sitophilus granarius* and *Oryzaophilus surinamensis*, which can infest granaries in their millions, have not yet been recorded from Roman sites in the region, even though they have been identified from villas elsewhere.

Two major gaps in the evidence remain. If more Belgic sites had been investigated, it is likely that many more of the developments at present regarded as Roman would be shown to have begun in the century prior to the conquest, even though the conquest probably hastened such developments. The lack of evidence from urban sites means that the synanthropic beetles and imported exotic plants within the towns can only be speculated upon. It would be extremely interesting to know whether some of the Belgic *oppida* in the region developed a characteristically urban insect fauna or whether suitable conditions were only created by the foundation of the Roman towns in the second half of the first century AD.

Romano-British Social and Economic Differentiation: the Bones and Shells

Bone collections from the Romano-British period are numerous. Most are of small to moderate size but exceptionally large ones were made at Shakenoak Villa, Oxfordshire. However collections are not always described adequately. Bone preservation is often exceptionally good where debris occurs in waterholes or wells. Site types yielding bones include villas, farmsteads, villages, military complexes and towns, the last two types including Alchester and Dorchester on Thames, Oxfordshire, and 'Corinium' at Cirencester, Gloucestershire.

Table 6 Percentage Ranges of Species Fragments From Fifteen Romano-British Sites[1]

	%
cattle	31–76
sheep/goat	12–45
pig	3–22
horse	0–12
dog	0.3–5
cat	0–2
red deer	0–18[2]
roe deer	0–4

1. Largest site collections are from:
   Bedfordshire: none
   Buckinghamshire: Latimer (Hamilton 1971)
   Gloucestershire: Cirencester (King 1975)
   Northamptonshire: Overston (Harman 1976c), Thenford (Startin, unpublished)
   Oxfordshire: Alchester (Marples 1975), Appleford (Wilson 1980a), Ashville (Wilson 1978a),
           Barton Court Farm (Wilson, forthcoming), Dorchester on Thames (Grant 1978 and 1981)
           and Shakenoak (Brodribb *et al.* 1968, Cram 1973 and 1978, and Marples 1978).
2. Probably including antler fragments (Latimer Villa)

Other species records of domestic mammals include donkey (Wilson, in prep. e) and goat (e.g. Cram 1978). No fallow deer is identified, but was at nearby Gadebridge Park, Hertfordshire (Harcourt 1974). Hare, fox, badger, pine marten, polecat, otter, cat of uncertain species (e.g. Newton in Cocks 1921), weasel (Marples 1972, see also 1978) and possibly wild pig (Cram 1978) are recorded although the presence of a rabbit skeleton at Hambledon indicates that some identifications there are suspect for the period. Rabbit bones found at Barton Court Farm, Abingdon, were probably deposited following intrusive burrowing (Wilson, forthcoming).

Bird bones are more abundant than previously; chiefly of domestic species; certainly fowl, probably goose, and perhaps ducks and dove/pigeons. Wild geese, wild ducks, golden plover, corncrake, raven, jackdaw, rook/crow, jay, kestrel, buzzard, sparrow hawk and stock dove are listed (Bramwell 1979b, forthcoming, and Eastham 1980). Pheasant is sometimes identified (Field 1977, Hamilton 1971) but is to be doubted unless properly discussed (Coy, pers. comm.).

Freshwater fish bones e.g. pike and eel are found where soil is sieved (e.g. Wilson, Thomas and Wheeler 1979). Among the bony food debris, and commonly for the first time in the development of the regional diet, are large numbers of oyster shells and occasional other marine shells such as Mussel *Mytilus edulis*, whelk and cockle (e.g. Branigan 1971).

Ranges of fragment percentages given in Table 6 appear more diverse than in other periods except the Neolithic. In part this diversity may be due to sampling problems, which affect some percentage results, but it also appears to have a consistent pattern.

As found generally for Roman Britain (A King 1978), percentages of cattle, pig and deer are usually higher and sheep lower than in Iron Age collections. Such differences are most evident at villas: Shakenoak, Oxfordshire (Brodribb et al., Jewell 1968; Cram 1973 and 1978; Marples 1973 and 1978), Latimer, Buckinghamshire (Hamilton 1971), Hambledon (Cocks, and Newton 1921), and Thenford, Northamptonshire (Startin, unpublished), and at large farmsteads like Barton Court Farm (Wilson, unpublished). Possibly Appleford, (Wilson 1980a) could be categorised in this latter group. Overall large farmsteads appear best kept separate from the villa category as deer bones may be less abundant at such sites.

Bones at the majority of small settlements resemble the Iron Age pattern, and this may be followed even in small towns like Towcester (Payne 1980) or the second century military defences at Alchester (Marples 1975). However collections from Dorchester on Thames (Grant 1978 and 1980) and Cirencester (King 1975) contained more cattle debris. Also forty bones from Towcester included a high proportion of horse and cattle (R Jones, unpublished).

Thus the variety of settlement types and their rubbish is a sign of a more differentiated, and probably more stratified society than in the Iron Age. This social differentiation is associated with 'Romanisation' and involves the proportional increases of cattle, pig and deer bones and marine shells on some sites. King (1978) has discussed this material thoroughly but the emphasis given here is slightly different.

Romanisation and its faunal representation is exemplified best by villas and some urban developments and tends to occur away from areas where Celtic sites were common. As is well known, villas were situated on higher ground or on soils over or adjacent to limestones, or sometimes on heavier ground, in the Chilterns and the Cotswolds. Small 'Celtic' settlements are more typical of the gravel terraces of the major rivers of Oxfordshire. This social difference is not yet apparent in the eastern region.

Faunal remains from the villas represent a varied and probably prosperous life style as well as a Roman one. This included the management or hunting of deer and even fish rearing is argued from structural evidence at Shakenoak; sadly no soil was sieved to test this. The hunting of smaller animals such as hare and golden plover is evident both at villas and other sites lower in the social order, for example Barton Court Farm, Lechlade and possibly Abingdon (Wilson et al. 1979, unpublished). A widespread and an intensive use of natural resources is indicated: certainly more than the Iron Age when wild life, notably the hare, appears protected by custom or, doubtfully, a lesser need to hunt.

Romano-British use of resources could reflect a diverse market economy. It indicates a diminished supply of meat from large domestic animals, although the diet is clearly supplemented by smaller ones particularly domestic fowl, and probably geese and ducks. Any shortage of grazing for cattle and sheep can be linked to evidence of expanded arable husbandry and increased cereal consumption (p 72). Fewer cattle and sheep imply great emphasis on secondary products including milk, wool and skins and their derivatives. In general a smaller ratio of domestic animals to people is presupposed.

These suggestions are supported by evidence from Barton Court Farm (Hamilton 1978), Farmoor (Wilson 1979c) and Shakenoak (Cram 1978) that sheep and cattle were killed off at later ages than during the Iron Age. Of course the data may be affected by marketing from rural to urban or military sites, but sample differences of age data due to this factor are not demonstrated yet. In this respect, King (1978, 111) argues that the early military pattern was a reflection of the local economy, for example at Alchester (Marples 1975) and Cirencester (Thawley 1982) so that some assemblages will not be very different to those on rural sites. However urban deposits generally show only a small percentage of horse bones i.e. 0.3% of deposits at Cirencester (King 1975), Dorchester (Grant 1978 and 1980) and Towcester (Payne 1980; but see R Jones, unpublished). The trend is also evident at Alchester. Clearly there was no great preference for horse meat.

General urban butchery at Cirencester has been discussed usefully (Thawley 1982).

Markedly specialised urban refuse comparable to that of the medieval period is not yet known possibly because of only limited urban excavations. However Payne (1980) suggests bones, particularly scapulae, at Towcester were refuse from a butcher.

Perhaps significantly, the most conclusive specialist deposit is one of horn cores of cattle at Kingston Bagpuize Oxfordshire (Armitage 1976; Wilson 1976b): probable refuse of skinning, tanning or use of horn on a probable villa site. Any imagined dominance of urban centres appears better replaced by speculation about a landscape of relatively self contained villa estates and farms, villages possibly with common land, and the occasional small town where some selling or buying of animals was done. Nevertheless if perhaps animals were not abundantly marketed in towns, less perishable products of animal husbandry such as wool, hides, horn and cheese would be distributed more widely, through marketing, and perhaps taxation.

On rural sites percentages of horse bones are high but not very dissimilar to the Iron Age pattern. The 9–12% of horse at Barton Court Farm (Wilson, forthcoming) indicates some marketing of cattle, sheep and pigs, as well as the accumulation of bones of less marketable animals such as draught oxen and horses – thus perhaps explaining the noticeable incidence of pathological bones. While people there ate a good proportion of immature cattle, the oxen and, at least occasionally, the horses were butchered. Possibly butchery of horse carcasses was for products other than meat, but some meat would seem destined for the table or was fed to favoured animals.

Only one cat skeleton is described well (Branigan and King 1965), being found at Latimer while others occurred at Hambledon Villa. Their size indicated both domestic and wild species were present (Newton in Cocks 1921).

Skeletal debris of dogs is much more common. Their wide variation in size at Barton Court Farm, Shakenoak (Cram 1978) and elsewhere (e.g. Payne 1980) indicates their utility and status. At Barton Court Farm dog skulls were buried with two infants. Other remains there suggest dogs were usually buried close to the farmstead where they are likely to have been kept.

Rubbish spreads at farms confirm urban indications of differences between kitchen or table refuse and other types of debris. In the villa phase at Latimer (Hamilton 1971) no horse bones were present, at Shakenoak percentages of horse varied greatly among deposits, while at Barton Court Farm, excepting destruction deposits, the cattle and horse bones predominated in ditch deposits outside the farmstead enclosure ditch. Rubbish disposal cleared large bones away from the farmstead house or confined at least the early stages of butchery of large animals to the farmyard. Articulated vertebrae of cattle occurred in a Romano-British pit just outside the enclosure ditch of the Barton Court farmstead.

The economy of large farms or villa estates varied. Exploitation or management of Shakenoak scrub or woodland communities is strongly marked by deer and goat bones (Brodribb et al. 1968, Cram 1978), and possibly at Latimer and also at Bloxham, Oxfordshire (Knight 1938) but scarcely at Barton Court Farm (no obvious goat, few deer bones). The Shakenoak cattle bones indicated a high proportion of cows, whereas at Barton Court (Armitage, forthcoming, Wilson, forthcoming) and Kingston Bagpuize (Armitage 1976) steers or bulls are abundantly represented and even outnumbered cows. Bones examined by Brodribb et al. (1968), Jewell (1972) and Cram (1978) showed little of the pathology which might be suffered by draught animals yet such abnormalities are apparent at Barton Court Farm.

All these different factors indicate that the environment of Shakenoak included extensive woodland or scrub as well as grass pasture while Barton Court Farm surroundings are largely pastoral and arable. Applebaum (1978) is probably correct in associating woodland coppices with Oxford Clay and heavier ground, but the arguments for the arable economy of Shakenoak are based on more fragmentary evidence than elsewhere. Limited evidence from bones and structures suggests similarities between Shakenoak and Latimer, while Hambledon, Kingston Bagpuize and Barton Court Farm may share a rather different organisation and at least Barton Court Farm had lower status.

The Roman period is an important one for demonstrating ecocultural change from the Iron Age. Besides any themes of marketing, and exploitation of woodland or marginal land, there are indications that the husbandry of normal domestic species benefited as a result of Roman influence.

Because of altered ratios of the sexes in the husbandry of cattle herds, care is needed to demonstrate a size increase of cattle from Iron Age to Roman periods. On average each cattle sex is 5–10cm taller but the species itself ranges greatly in height from 0.96 to 1.39m at the shoulder (Wilson forthcoming). Sheep bones became more robust if not longer at this period (Wilson 1980b) but the bias from flock management and size differences among the sexes is not known. These size changes are associated with increases in horn core length of cattle (Armitage 1976 and 1978) and the prominence of polled individuals among the sheep.

Related explanations of the changes include the human selection of preferred stock, introduction of new breeds, and cross breeding which improves size of animals through natural hybrid vigor. Some knowledge of breeding animals is shown by the extremely wide variation in size of dogs, for example, from 0.24 to 0.60m in shoulder height at Barton Court Farm.

Husbandry and body size of animals would have been improved by winter feeding with hay. These factors combined with possible decreases in pasture from expansion of arable land, suggest that herds and flocks, at least in the areas of arable farming such as at Barton Court Farm, were relatively fewer in numbers, yet were better husbanded than in the Iron Age.

Relatively fewer animals imply more secondary use of animals than previously. However the general reversion to higher proportions of cattle, particularly on Romanised estates or farms, suggests that husbandry or pasture availability was adequate there to maintain a greater meat producing economy. For at least some people at villas a superior range of food was available, but for the overall population the food was probably based on grain supplies and the limited provision of mutton and beef from Celtic agricultural husbandry at a lower level of subsistence than on the estates. Dairying presumably remained important, particularly in urban areas. The rise of pig husbandry is another clue to short supplies of meat and greater dependence on cereals.

Yet it is not known why the proportion of sheep represented remained small while human population density was higher and arable agriculture had expanded. As indicated above, presumably the majority of people were restricted to the land available to them so that Celtic communities are associated with more sheep bones but, not surprisingly, their contribution to total amount of recoverable bones of this period may be relatively small.

Were the few sheep then reared for wool? Certainly the killing of relatively old sheep at Shakenoak and Barton Court Farm suggests that the wool clip was valuable but nevertheless it must have been minor compared to the importance of cattle husbandry.

The presence of draught oxen at Barton Court Farm is shown by two large and deformed metatarsal bones which also indicate that steers or possibly bulls but not cows were used for the purpose. A similar bone from Little Faringdon, Oxfordshire indicates a very tall cattlebeast standing 1.39m at the shoulder although the sex of this individual is questionable (Wilson, unpublished d). Only one comparable bone was recorded at Iron Age Ashville, an obvious focus of arable activity then, but none on other Iron Age sites, where arable activity is less prominent. It is statistically slender but still apposite evidence of the intensification of draught animal use from Iron Age to Roman times and particularly for arable agriculture.

Although large oxen would increase the efficiency of ploughing, and while improvements in animal husbandry include storage of winter feed and breeding changes or selection of livestock, the impression is that these improvements occurred against some environmental pressure on animal populations. Fodder problems are indicated by pathological phenomena such as periosteitis: the incidence in Roman sheep and cattle appears higher than in Iron Age or Saxon samples at Barton Court Farm.

Shells of the liver fluke host snail *Lymneaea truncatula* are associated with Roman waterholes and wells, for example at Appleford (Robinson 1980, 94), as well as damp pasture and suggest that liver fluke was an increased problem because the ecological range of the snail was not only extended but directly linked to a mechanically improved water supply to livestock. It is possible that the greater vulnerability of sheep to liver fluke is a contributory cause of shrinking flocks of sheep at this period — and from meadowland which became increasingly alluviated and flooded. Sheep would be even less favoured by their exclusion from drier tractable land being used for arable — except of course for a season of stubble grazing.

Where data from human skeletons are examined, a number of useful criteria allow further description of environmental pressure and Romano-British culture. Inhumation burials are commonly found, partly from the customs which produced sizeable cemetery groups and probably as a consequence of increased population density of the Romano-British. The largest burial groups reported are from a 4th-5th-century cemetery at Queenford Mill near Dorchester (Harman 1978e) and extensively discussed cemeteries at Cirencester (McWhirr Viner and Wells 1982). Another sizeable group was from Stanton Harcourt (Harman 1980) and smaller groups occur as follows: in Oxfordshire at Appleford (Edwards 1980), Ashville (Edwards 1978), Curbridge (Harman 1976a) and Oxford (Concannon 1972); in Northamptonshire at Wakerley (Bayley 1978); and in Buckinghamshire at Hambledon (Keith 1921) and West Wycombe (Farley and Wright 1979).

A comprehensive review of five late Romano-British sites in the Upper Thames, viz Cassington, Queenford Mill, Radley, Stanton Harcourt, and Curbridge, was provided by Harman, Molleson and Price (1981). The average height of 62 males was 5 ft 6 ins (1.70m) and of 60 females 5 ft 2 ins (1.59m). These are less than Bronze Age and Saxon statures. It is suggested elsewhere in this text (pp 40, 61, 68) that such differences are correlated with the nutritional and subsistence levels of each period. If this rationale is correct, the skeletal data can be taken further.

To begin with, it is suggested that in terms of trophic or ecological feeding levels the Romano-British level of human subsistence is lower than the greater Bronze Age or Saxon emphases on pastoralism. Undoubtedly however, Romano-British arable agriculture is productive enough to sustain a large population and some degree of urban development. The social origin of the skeletons examined in the survey are not certain but it is relevant that shorter stature, child and adolescent mortality, and some pathological symptoms are most evident at Queenford Mill cemetery whose settlement source is probably Dorchester. This suits a previous hint that most village or urban dwellers were less prosperous or more deprived than rural people but signs of population stress are not much less obvious at the other cemeteries. Radley cemetery is an example (Harman *et al.* 1981, 153) and is of interest because some of the inhabitants of Barton Court Farm may have been buried there, and the farmstead is thought to have had a moderate status. Nutrition and general subsistence appear better at Cassington and Stanton Harcourt.

Obviously a variety of criteria are possible in assessing an ecoculture and where detail is supplied in abundance, for example of pathology, the general nature of human existence may be obscured. Nevertheless there is some information from human stature (e.g. Harrison *et al.* 1977, 190) and from animal sizes to show that nutritional or environmental conditions in general were not far below those of most subsequent cultural and modern periods, although the associated technology and other cultural aspects e.g. mortality and medical treatment may be strikingly different.

An illustrative postscript of the potential of studies on a large single group of human inhumations is derived from a cemetery south of the Fosse Way, Cirencester, published recently in splendid detail (Wells 1982). The majority, 207, of the skeletons were of males and only 93 were of females. Males mostly died in their 40s or early 50s with a mean age of 41. Ages of female deaths varied widely but still averaged 38 years. Few juveniles were present and most may have been buried elsewhere. Height estimates of the sexes averaged slightly less than those lower in the Thames Valley.

A low rate of carious tooth decay (5.1%) occurred and suggested that, contrary perhaps to the discussion above, meat was abundant in the diet but not finely milled flours and sugars. Tooth wear was heavy but not excessive compared to other early groups. Calculus or tartar was relatively low and in total the evidence indicated a moderate amount of meat and coarse bread made up the diet.

Osteoarthritic conditions were common and the incidences of localised afflictions was related to different mechanical stresses and a differentiation of sex roles in social behaviour. Fractures of bones and weapon wounds were common among the male skeletons. These were described at length.

Wells suggested that the skeletons were of retired legionaries, officials and prostitutes living in Cirencester and implies that the cemetery was reserved for their burial.

An interesting issue was fostered by the discovery of high concentrations of lead in the bones of the skeletons (Waldron 1982). Intoxication sufficient to cause the death of children was indicated but subsequently it was concluded that most lead accumulated by post-mortem absorption from the soil (Waldron 1983).

The Early to Mid Saxon Period, AD410–AD800

Urban and Agricultural Collapse

Compared with the Roman period, only limited investigations have been made of the early Saxon period. The site of the former Roman villa at Barton Court, Abingdon, Oxfordshire, on the second terrace of the Thames, was occupied by the Saxons from at least the middle of the fifth century AD (on the basis of decorated pottery) and continued into the sixth century. Several sunken huts and a post-built hall-house was constructed on the site. The Saxons also built a wattle-lined well, cut from the bottom of a partly filled Roman ditch, from which waterlogged samples were examined (Jones and Robinson in Miles, forthcoming; Robinson 1981a, 107–111, 250–4, 430–64; Robinson 1981b, 269).

Superficially, there seems to have been very little difference between the general environment around the site in Roman and Saxon times. The pollen (examined by J R A Greig) suggested an open relatively unwooded landscape. It is of particular interest to know whether there was any increase in scrub after the end of the Roman period, showing abandoned land, but the slight rise in tree and shrub pollen from 4.5% to 10% was not sufficient to indicate any change on the basis of only one Saxon deposit. Indeed the Coleoptera showed the reverse trend, with no wood or tree dependent species being present. Pastureland was still probably present, although dung beetles had fallen to 8% of the terrestrial Coleoptera.

The evidence from waterlogged cereal remains takes on a special importance because the presence of residual Roman pottery in the Saxon features would suggest that some of the carbonised seeds could be residual too. Roman material which had not been charred would have decayed in the soil. The only waterlogged cereal was *Hordeum vulgare*, identified from its rachis nodes. It is disappointing that no waterlogged wheat was found because it would be most interesting to know whether spelt continued in use into the Saxon period on this site. However, bread wheat chaff is not as robust as spelt chaff, so it is possible that it is not as easily preserved in a recognisable form. The other arable crop identified was flax, again in the company of *Camelina alyssum* silicula fragments.

Synanthropic Coleoptera and beetles associated with structural timbers were almost absent.

Gravel extraction of the first Thames terrace about 500m to the west of the Roman town of Dorchester, Oxfordshire exposed an early Saxon sunken hut and some Saxon wells. A sample was examined from one of these wells, which was wattle lined and dated to the 5th–6th century AD by pottery. Open conditions were suggested by the Coleoptera, which did not include any tree or wood feeding species. Dung beetles from the super-family Scarabaeoidea made up 10% of the terrestrial Coleoptera, sufficiently high to indicate the presence of at least some pasture nearby. Remains of crops were sparse, but apart from a single grain of *Triticum aestivocompactum*, they were the same two species as for the Saxon well at Barton Court, flax and barley. Beetles which tend to be associated with human habitation were rare (Robinson 1981b, 269–70).

Samples were examined from two early Saxon wells (dated by pottery) excavated by G H Lambrick at Mount Farm, Berinsfield, Oxfordshire on the second terrace of the Thames (Robinson, unpublished i). The Coleoptera indicated an open landscape, with some arable/disturbed ground but rather weaker evidence for pasture. Three crop species were identified: *Linum usitatissimum, Hordeum vulgare* (hulled) and *Vicia faba*. The evidence for *V. faba* was in the form of abundant threshing debris in one of the wells.

Early Saxon grain impressions have been identified from several sites in the region: *Hordeum* sp. (hulled) and *Avena sativa*, Abingdon, Oxfordshire (Jessen and Helbaek 1944, 23); *Avena sativa*, Rothwell, Northamptonshire (Jessen and Helbaek 1944, 23); *Hordeum* sp. Walton, Aylesbury, Buckinghamshire (Monk in Farley 1976, 171–3). Carbonised grain of *Triticum aestivocompactum* and *Hordeum* sp. was also identified from the Walton site.

Charcoal identified from seventh and perhaps eighth century contexts at Shakenoak, Oxfordshire, at the foot of the Cotswolds, was mostly *Quercus* and *Crataegus*-type (Brodribb *et al.* 1972, 131). Stakes and wattles from a Saxon well on the Nene gravels at Aldwincle, Northamptonshire, which gave a radiocarbon date of ad770 ± 70, proved to be of a wide range of trees including *Corylus, Quercus* and *Fraxinus* (Keepax in Jackson 1977, 52–3).

There is little evidence from the river floodplains in the early Saxon period. At Mingies Ditch, Oxfordshire on the Windrush floodplain, the Roman drainage system fell into disuse and silted up, a fine sixth century spear being found in one of the minor streams (Robinson 1981a, 89–95, 329–353). Finally, a thin (but undated) covering of silty alluvium was deposited over the site, filling in the tops of the Iron Age enclosure ditches and the Roman drainage system. This alluvium, which was rich in Mollusca, had not undergone worm sorting.

Aggradation continued to take in the streamside marsh at the Bancroft villa, Milton Keynes, Buckinghamshire, in the early Saxon period (Keeley 1982; Spencer 1982).

Discussion At the end of the fourth century there was a breakdown of communications in the region resulting in the decline of the villa system and the pottery industries. By the mid fifth century there was still limited occupation in some of the towns but they can no longer have been functioning as towns in the Roman sense. After the collapse of Roman administration, some of the Cotswold villas were abandoned to woodland and the Medieval forest of Wychwood grew up on them. There is no direct evidence from the sites investigated for the abandonment of Roman agricultural land and the regeneration of woodland. This is likely to be because most of the very early Saxon sites examined were on the Thames gravels, which always seem to have been valued as agricultural land, and they remained well settled throughout the Saxon period. There was no evidence for an agricultural decline on the gravels but there may have been a general decrease in efficiency: the droveways and ditched field boundaries of the Roman settlements soon fell into disuse.

Hordeum vulgare (hulled) remained one of the main cereal crops, but it is not known to what extent and how rapidly *Triticum aestivocompactum* replaced *T. spelta. Avena sativa* is recorded for the first time in the region from early Saxon contexts. Two species which appeared in the region during the Roman period, *Vicia faba* and *Linum usitatissimum* continued to be cultivated during the early Saxon period, the flax complete with the weed *Camelina alyssum*. The Roman horticultural and orchard crops were not discovered in Saxon contexts, however.

The intensiveness of occupation of sites as reflected by synanthropic beetles fell back to the low level of the Iron Age.

Rural Saxon Period: the Bones and Shells

Reports on moderate numbers of bones are few. Reported sites tend to occupy calcareous substrata. All settlements appear to be small except possibly Dorchester on Thames and St. Peters, Northampton.

Table 7 Fragment percentages from nine Saxon sites[1]

	%
cattle	28–61
sheep/goat	17–54
pig	7–26
horse	0.3–9
dog	0.3–4
cat	0–0.5
red deer	0–2
roe deer	0–0.2

1. Site collections from:
   Buckinghamshire: Chicheley (G Jones 1980); Walton, Aylesbury (Noddle 1976)
   Northamptonshire: St. Peters Street, Northampton (Harman 1979b)
   Oxfordshire: Barton Court Farm (Wilson, forthcoming), and Corporation Farm, Abingdon (Carter, unpublished): Dorchester on Thames (Grant 1978, 1980; Renfrew and Whitehouse 1977); and Mount Farm, Berinsfield (Wilson in preparation e).

Occasional records include goat, otter (Wilson in preparation e) and beaver (Noddle 1976). Fallow deer bones are identified from a Saxon pit (Grant 1981) and antler from middle period material (Grant 1978) while a radius was listed from an eighth to ninth century well at Aldwincle, Northamptonshire (R Jones 1977).

Bird species are poorly known but domestic fowl and geese are present and wild records include crane, plover, raven and redwing (Bramwell 1976a, 1979a, and unpublished).

Remains of fish may be common but only one collection of freshwater fish bones has been recovered by sieving, again from Barton Court Farm, Abingdon (Wheeler, forthcoming). Shells of marine molluscs are mostly absent but where noted at Barton Court Farm, or Marefair, Northampton (Oakley 1979) may be residual Romano-British debris, or if genuine might be regarded as more typical of Roman and medieval periods.

Fragment percentages indicate a relative increase of sheep and a decrease of cattle and horse from the Roman period. Figures from Dorchester however indicate a prevalence of cattle from Roman times (Grant 1978 and 1980; also Renfrew and Whitehouse 1977) as if there was Romano-British continuity, or if environmental conditions there favoured cattle. Similar faunas occur at nearby Mount Farm, Berinsfield and further away at Corporation Farm, Abingdon (Carter unpublished) but not at Barton Court Farm where conditions may have favoured sheep (Wilson forthcoming). Percentages of cattle bones appear less on easterly sites (Noddle 1976, Harman 1979b, 1981a) but the species is still important everywhere.

Saxon cattle and sheep were comparable in size or slightly larger than Romano-British animals. At Dorchester older animals are well represented (Grant 1981) but elsewhere cattle and sheep were also killed off at younger ages (Carter unpublished, Noddle 1976) and particularly at Barton Court Farm. At Corporation Farm bones of cows appear more common than of bulls or steers (Carter unpublished). Therefore the economy and husbandry appear to differ from that in the Roman period and, with the scant evidence of urban development, suggest only a limited marketing of animals and products.

All these factors may be linked to the normally small percentage of horse bones in deposits — about 1%. This relative absence need only be a sign of kitchen or table refuse but most deposits do not have an urban context as do similar groups of Roman and Medieval bones. Thus if as seems, these deposits are to be regarded as rural or farm debris they do not indicate any great use of horses — although Mount Farm, Berinsfield offers an exception with 9% of horse bones (Wilson in preparation e). Otherwise bones of butchered horses might have been prominent in the percentages because there is a continuity or an intensification of hunting, fishing, and domestic dependence on smaller mammals and on birds and fish after the Roman period.

Hunting did not kill a high proportion of deer although 4.6% of red deer occurred in 130 bones from Shakenoak (Cram 1978 v Table 14) an area already identified as partly wooded in the Roman period. In comparison to the earlier and later eras, sites of high status are not represented by published groups of bones. Although diet need not always reflect social differences, the differences found at other periods suggests that Saxon social existence was relatively uniform and unstratified.

Rare or no consumption of marine molluscs is confirmation that, despite exploitation and presumably demand for smaller animals, little trade or transport to coastal areas was available or worthwhile and is in part to be linked with the relative absence of horse. The eating of younger animals and smaller species in some places may indicate meat production and fewer secondary products but, as remarked for the Iron Age, sufficient wool or dairy products could have been obtained from a high ratio of animals to people (and some prominence of cows in the herd structure has been noted already). The higher ratio presupposes a low human density, abundant grazing and requires less arable agriculture to supplement the diet. None of these can be shown directly from the bones but all would imply a higher level of subsistence which would be consistent with increased size of animals.

As well as the presence of large domestic animals, people were as tall or often taller than their Romano-British predecessors. A fifth or sixth century cemetery at Wally Corner, Berinsfield, Oxfordshire indicated an average height of 5 ft 8 ins for 24 males and 5 ft 4 ins for 17 females (Harman unpublished). Similar sized skeletons of less certain date were noted nearer Dorchester on Thames (St. Hoyme 1977) and at Shakenoak (Hughes and Denston 1968, and Denston 1973). Males averaged 5 ft 8 ins and females 5 ft 7 ins at a ninth century site at Beacon Hill, Lewknor, Oxfordshire (Harman 1976b). Further east at Dunstable, Bedfordshire thirteen sixth century males averaged 5 ft 9½ ins (Brothwell 1976b).

This increased stature might have resulted from interbreeding of Saxon and Romano-British peoples or from the ethnic character of the Saxons. Clearly both possibilities are related to genetic constraints on growth but it is probable that either initial cause would be subject to the pattern of rural Saxon nutrition and degree of communal stress. Almost certainly the diet became worse during or just before the medieval period when genetic factors probably remained relatively constant, but environmental conditions were severe and human stature decreased (see medieval section).

Possibly there is some variation of human stature across the region from Wally Corner to Dunstable and might be attributable to either genetic or subsistence patterns, chiefly nutritional, but not to any effect of social stratification and different diet since the status of each of the two groups of burials appears similar.

This kind of rationale suggests that the pattern of rural Saxon subsistence was at a higher level than that of the Roman as well as the medieval period. It is consistent with the general impression that the human population is smaller than in the Roman period and that arable agriculture is less prominent in the Saxon economy (pathology related to the use of draught oxen is however noted – Noddle 1976).

The greater emphasis on exploitation or management of smaller species may therefore be seen as a consequence of limited food supplies from an arable farming sector as well as an indication that the food supply was low in animal protein – or at least as low as that indicated for Roman and possibly the Iron Age periods. Once again, the low incidence of horse bones is a sign that large numbers of this species were not required for draught because arable requirements were low. Reasons for the latter could be sought in the ethnic value system, or in further environmental factors which affected arable farming.

Early and middle period social organisation of the Saxons can be summed up as of: small self contained communities and few urban aggregations; limited social differentiation and stratification; and restricted market systems. These factors are intimately linked with a prominent pastoralist economy in which subsidiary animal products and resources of small species are very important.

In terms of the environment, the extent of woodland may be similar to that in the Roman period. Scrubland reversion is possible if the human population was small but otherwise large areas of grazing would be required to offset the productivity of arable which was not maintained from the Roman period. Although the wetland element is barely apparent (beaver, otter and crane) there is an expectation of a greater prominence of the habitat with the suggested decrease in human population, increased vegetational cover, or altered land drainage as a result of alluviation from previous arable activity (p 60).

The Late Saxon and Medieval Periods, cAD800–AD1500

A Return to Organised Agriculture, Trade and Towns

The Late Saxon Period All the sites investigated from this period, which has been taken as lasting from AD800 to AD1066, were urban. Carbonised seeds were examined from two late Saxon contexts at Marefair, Northampton (Straker, **not** Slater, in Williams F, 1979, 78, microfiche 27, 28). Most of the seeds were *Triticum aestivocompactum*, but *Avena* sp. (either cultivated or wild), *Hordeum* sp. (from the description including at least some hulled *H. vulgare*) and *Vicia faba* v. *minor* were well represented. There were also a few grains of *Secale cereale* and four weed seeds including *Agrostemma githago*. There was only a single fragment of chaff and the low proportion of weed seeds suggests the crops had been thoroughly threshed and cleaned. The diversity of crops suggests that the charred debris was derived from repeated episodes of accidental charring, perhaps in a domestic context.

A few beetles were identified from a waterlogged late Saxon pit at St. Peters Street, Northampton, and the presence of *Bruchus rufimanus* provided confirmation for the use of beans in the town (Girling in Williams J, 1979, 337). This species lays its eggs on the developing bean pods and the adults tend to overwinter inside the dried beans. Interesting use was made of molluscan evidence from this urban site (Evans in Williams 1979, 338–9). A sample from a context between two building phases on the site contained an open country fauna, with high levels of *Vallonia costata* and *V. excentrica* indicating grass cover. The fauna was certainly not one of urban dereliction.

Urban conditions favour a type of preservation which has not been recorded from any earlier sites in the region: phosphatic mineralisation of organic remains in cess pits. Mineralised stones of *Prunus* cf. *domestica* and *P. spinosa* were reported from a tenth century cess pit at Walton, Aylesbury (Monk in Farley 1976, 231).

Several Saxon samples were investigated from excavations by B Durham at All Saints Church, Oxford (Robinson, unpublished o). They include a sample from a large deposit of carbonised grain which had perhaps come from a building that had burnt down. Radiocarbon dates of ad890 ± 70 and ad880 ± 80 were obtained from the grain. The grain proved to be a remarkably pure deposit of threshed *Triticum aestivocompactum*. Out of a total of 4643 seeds, only 0.8% were weeds and a further 1.4% were *Hordeum vulgare* (hulled) grains. The last surviving remains of wood in the timber voids of a mid eleventh century cellar on the site showed it to have been constructed of oak. Finally, charcoal was examined from a fence with a radiocarbon date of ad970 ± 70. The upright posts were oak and the horizontal wattles hazel. The hazel showed much apparent evidence of woodworm damage. This was confirmed on splitting the charcoal open, by the discovery not of the beetles but five individuals of *Theocolax formiciformis*, remarkably well preserved by charring. It is a minute hymenopteran parasite of *Anobium punctatum*.

Waterlogged Saxon deposits were encountered in St. Aldates, Oxford (Durham 1977). Cutting what the excavator regarded as a man-made clay bank was a wattle-lined gully. A radiocarbon date of ad830 ± 110 was obtained from a stake out of the wattles while a date of AD705 ± 74 was provided by a thermoluminescence determination on pottery in the silting behind the wattles. In the gully were abundant flax seeds, capsules and stem fragments and associated arable weed seeds, suggesting that the ditch was used for retting flax (Brown in Durham 1977, 169–172). Sealing this gully were undoubted alluvial silts, containing riverine aquatic molluscs.

The Medieval Period Fortunately, a more balanced range of sites was available for the Medieval period, which has been taken as lasting from AD1066 to AD1500. They will be considered under the headings of urban and rural.

a. *Towns* A sequence of waterlogged twelfth and thirteenth century pits and ditches from the Hamel, a medieval suburb of Oxford, illustrated well the changes that take place when a site becomes urbanised (Robinson in Palmer 1980, 199–206, microfiche 2F12–G6). Samples from mid to late twelfth century ditches contained insect faunas characteristic of damp grassland. Excluding aquatics, about 50% of the individuals of Coleoptera and Hemiptera were outdoor species (species not thought capable of breeding indoors) and the faunas were diverse. Carabidae, Chrysomelidae, Curculionoidea and species of *Aphodius* were well represented. In the late twelfth century, however, there was an abrupt change. The late twelfth to mid thirteenth ditches and pits contained characteristically urban faunas. Species diversity fell and, excluding aquatics, only about 9% of the individuals of Coleoptera and Hemiptera were outdoor species. The following species were numerous in these samples: *Anobium punctatum, Tipnus unicolor, Ptinus fur, Mycetaea hirta* and *Typhaea stercorea.* Only *A. punctatum*, the woodworm beetle was present in the early samples, in which it was rare. The other four species can also be regarded as synanthropic, living in such habitats as rotten thatch or damp corners of buildings. Species of manure heaps and foul plant remains, such as many of the Staphylinidae and *Cercyon* spp., along with species of mouldy plant material were also abundant in the urban samples. The main impression given by the Coleoptera from the urban samples is of filth and decay. Abundant fly puparia confirmed this view. They included *Stomoxys calcitrans*, the stable fly, which commonly breeds in old straw which has been enriched with urine and faeces, and *Musca domestica*, the house fly, which is less fastidious about the type of decaying plant or animal remains in which it breeds.

The insects also gave information on other aspects of the urban site. A late twelfth century pit contained many puparia of *Melophagus ovinus*, the sheep ked. It is a bloodsucking permanent ectoparasite of sheep and will not survive removal from the host for more than a few days. Such a high concentration of these parasites implies some sort of ovine activity on the site. Perhaps sheep were washed there on their way to market, or wool was carded and washed on the site. No grain beetles were found but the bean beetle, *Bruchus rufimanus* occurred in two, perhaps three of the samples.

Limited work was undertaken on waterlogged seeds from the site. They included *Prunus domestica, Corylus avellana, Linum usitatissimum* and *Apium graveolens*. It is uncertain whether *A. graveolens* was cultivated or grew along the ditches on the site. Despite the evidence of *B. rufimanus*, no beans were discovered. Frond fragments of *Pteridium aquilinum* were found. It is unlikely that bracken grew in Oxford, and it had probably been brought to the site, perhaps for use as bedding, from the acid soils on the hills around Oxford.

A sample from a layer of charred plant material from a late twelfth/early thirteenth ditch at the Hamel was examined (Jones in Palmer 1980, microfiche 297–99). It was dominated by cereal rachis fragments and culm nodes but some grain and arable weed seeds were present too. It seems that the charred plant material probably represented burnt straw in the ratio of 85% *Triticum aestivum*, 10% *Secale cereale*, the remainder being *Avena* sp. and *Hordeum* sp.

Waterlogged samples from the Barbican ditch of Oxford Castle, which contained much dumped rubbish, were examined for plant remains including mosses (A Brown, unpublished). The deposits were dated on the basis of pottery to the fourteenth/mid fifteenth century. They produced the usual diverse range of species from many different habitats which tends to be found in urban waterlogged deposits including cornfield weeds, such as *Chrysanthemum segetum*, grassland species, marsh species, weeds that tend to grow around places of human habitation, and cultivated plants. The seeds of edible fruits included *Vitis vinifera* and *Ficus carica*. Interestingly, leaves of *Taxus baccata* and *Buxus sempervirens* were present. Perhaps garden hedge clippings had been thrown into the ditch. There was also much wood in the ditch (Robinson in Hassall 1976, 271). It was mostly *Quercus*, but seven other species were present including, interestingly, a fragment of *Pinus*.

Excavations at Oxford Castle also encountered St. Budoc's Church. Within a twelfth century stone coffin were puparia of flies which had been feeding on the corpse (Varley in Hassall 1976, 306). They included *Muscina stabulans* and perhaps *Hydrotaea dentipes*. Mollusca were examined from a trench excavated to the bottom of Oxford Castle moat, in the grounds of Nuffield College (Grensted 1953). At the very bottom of the ditch was a fauna of clean, flowing, water when the moat was evidently fed from the river. At a later stage, the bottom of the moat became fouled with rotting vegetation, and the fauna was one of stagnant water.

An interesting eleventh century layer of charred plant material was encountered during excavations at Folly Bridge, Oxford (Robinson, unpublished q). It was threshing debris of *Vicia faba* v. *minor* and *Pisum sativum*, consisting of stem, pod and tendril fragments along with a few of carbonised beans and peas. Possibly they had been grown as a mixed crop, the peas using the beans for support.

Not much work has been done on Medieval cess pits in Oxford. A *Ficus carica* seed was identified from a fourteenth century stone-lined pit at Cornmarket Street (Brown in Hassall 1971, 33). Abundant ova of the parasitic nematodes *Trichuris* and *Ascaris* sp. were observed in a sample from a waterlogged late twelfth/early thirteenth cess pit at St. Aldates, Oxford (Marples in Durham 1977, 174).

Carbonised plant remains were examined from thirteenth to sixteenth century contexts at Stert Street, Abingdon, Oxfordshire (Jones in Parrington 1979, 24–25). *Triticum aestivum/aestivocompactum* was the most abundant cereal species followed by *Secale cereale*. *Hordeum* sp. and *Avena sativa* were also present. A few fragments of *Triticum spelta* chaff in the samples could have been residual from Roman activity on the site. The cereal remains were accompanied with what has now been recognised as the expected range of weed seeds.

Mineralised seeds and arthropod remains were discovered in the late fifteenth century fill of what had been a timber lined shaft at Stert Street (Robinson in Parrington 1979, 23–4). The preservation of the items was largely due to the calcium phosphate replacement, which seems to be characteristic of badly drained latrines which contain some calcium carbonate (in this case limestone gravel). The seeds preserved were all fruit: *Vitis vinifera, Prunus* spp. and *Malus sylvestris*. The arthropod remains were mostly fly puparia of Sphaeroceridae and perhaps *Fannia canicularis*, sewage flies and the lesser house fly. Thus both seeds and insects confirm the use of the shaft as a cess pit.

What proved to be a late medieval deposit of *Ulex* sp., preserved by waterlogging, had been dumped on the edge of the Causeway, Bicester. It mostly consisted of shoots with leaves attached, but there were also a few seed pods and seeds (Robinson 1981 c). Bicester itself does not seem a very likely place for gorse to have been growing.

What was perhaps an early fifteenth century drying oven was excavated inside a house at St. Peters Street, Northampton. Carbonised seeds from this structure were mostly wheat, but included smaller amounts of barley and oats (Arthur and Paradine in Williams J, 1979, 337). A directly comparable late fifteenth century kiln was investigated at Marefair, Northampton (Straker 1979; Straker in Williams F, 1979, 78, microfiche 27, 28). In this series of samples, *Hordeum vulgare* (hulled) was the principal cultivated species, with small amounts of *Secale cereale* and *Avena* sp. There was no cereal chaff, but many arable weed seeds and a few possible horse beans were present. It is possible that the Marefair kiln was used for malting barley and the other cereals and weeds were merely contaminants of the main crop. However, it is very likely that the kiln was used to dry/bake more than one commodity resulting in a mixed accumulation of debris which had accidentally become burnt. Also at Marefair, some late fifteenth century grape pips were preserved by bronze corrosion products.

   b. *Rural Sites* Carbonised cereals were extracted from an early thirteenth century pit at the deserted medieval village of Seacourt, Oxfordshire on the Oxford Clay (Arthur in Biddle 1961–2, 195–6). *Triticum aestivum, T.* cf *turgidum, Avena strigosa* and *A. sativa* were well represented, but it would be prudent to regard all these identifications as tentative.

Charred seeds were noted from a late twelfth century context in the village of Tetsworth, Oxfordshire, on the Gault Clay (Robinson 1973, 109–11). The seeds were from a hollow about 6m in diameter, which had repeatedly been lined with clay and showed traces of burning. *Triticum aestivocompactum* was the most abundant species, but *Avena* sp. and *Vicia faba* v. *minor* were also present. It is possible that the feature was a threshing hollow, but unfortunately chaff had not been extracted from the samples.

Moving up the social scale, calcium phosphate replaced seeds were examined from a twelfth century latrine shaft at Middleton Stoney Castle, Oxfordshire (Robinson, unpublished r). They included:

Vitis vinifera	cf. *Malus sylvestris*
Prunus cf. *domestica*	*Ficus carica*
cf. *Pyrus communis*	*Morus nigra*

The occupants of the castle evidently enjoyed a rich and varied diet of fruit.

Prior to the construction of the castle at Middleton Stoney, the soil covering the Lower Cornbrash limestone of the site was a non-calcareous sol lessive, with no evidence of cultivation for at least several centuries beforehand (Evans in Rowley 1972, 129–36). So much limestone was scattered about during the building of the castle that the soil was converted to a calcareous rendzina, and, for the first time, a rich fauna of land snails was able to develop.

Limited investigations were undertaken on waterlogged deposits from the moat of Chalgrove Manor, Oxfordshire (Robinson, unpublished p). The site, which was excavated by P Page, is at the foot of the Chilterns. The waterlogged remains included nutshell fragments of *Juglans regia*, a pip of *Vitis vinifera* and an elytron of *Xestobium rufovillosum*, the death watch beetle. Much charcoal was examined from a variety of contexts on the site. Most of it was rather badly grown branchwood of *Fagus*, which seems to have been used for firewood.

At Oxford, the mid thirteenth century surface of the Thames floodplain was found to be sealed beneath a dumped clay layer upon which the Blackfriar's Priory had been built. The molluscs from the top of alluvium were dominated by *Vallonia pulchella* and aquatic species, suggesting seasonally flooded grassland (Robinson in Lambrick and Woods 1976, 227–31).

Discussion Evidence about the late Saxon environment is restricted because all the sites investigated were in towns. By the ninth century AD, *Triticum aestivocompactum* was firmly established as the main species of wheat. *Hordeum vulgare* (hulled) continued as the other major cereal, although the absence of *Avena sativa* from the late Saxon samples is probably fortuitous. *Secale cereale* was also cultivated. *Vicia faba* v. *minor* and *Linum usitatissimum* continued to be important crops. The discovery of a stone of *Prunus* cf. *domestica* in a late Saxon cess pit at Aylesbury perhaps marks a return to the Roman trend of fruit cultivation.

The evidence from all Saints' Church, Oxford, suggests that large quantities of threshed grain was stored in the towns. The processing of crops was certainly undertaken on the outskirts of towns and quite possibly inside the towns as well. It is understandable why flax retting, a very smelly process, was done on the wet ground at St. Aldates beyond the defences of Oxford rather than in the main town itself.

Oak seems to have remained the major structural timber while the wattle fences at St. Aldates and All Saints provide examples of the use of hazel and oak coppice poles/rods.

It is not appropriate to use the rather limited information from environmental investigations of rural sites dated between 1066 and 1500 to attempt to build up a general picture of the landscape. So many other sources of evidence are available for the Medieval period. The charcoal from Chalgrove does, however suggest the presence of beechwoods on the Chilterns from which the manor house was obtaining its fuel. The ground surface beneath the Blackfriar's Priory, Oxford, showed that the Thames floodplain suffered inundation in the Medieval period. It is thought probable that much of the alluvium which has been noted as covering Roman features in the Thames Valley is of late Saxon or early Medieval date.

The results from the Hamel, Oxford, give an idea of the environmental impact of towns. There was a great input of organic material to the towns: crops, timbers, straw, miscellaneous material such as bracken and gorse. The ultimate fate of much of this material was for it to decay or become ordure. The Hamel was rich in beetles devouring the woodwork of the houses, living in thatch or organic material scattered on floors. There seems to have been much filth on the site infested with beetles and, more unpleasantly, flies, some of which bite. A word of caution is, however, necessary. Insects provide evidence for filth, they do not give evidence of cleanliness. It is likely that some of the upper class or ecclesiastical areas of Medieval towns would have been kept clean, but such areas would be ecological deserts. Evidence for a more pleasant aspect of late Medieval Oxford comes in the form of the box and yew leaves in the Barbican ditch, which were presumably from ornamental shrubs or hedges.

The species of weed seeds identified from Oxford show that the land upon which the town depended was diverse: wet ground, dry ground, acid soil, calcareous soil. Some of the fruit eaten in Oxford had probably been imported from overseas. The weed seeds also suggest that some crop processing took place in the town. The sheep keds from the Hamel point to activity concerning wool, either on or off the sheep.

All the late Saxon crop species remained in cultivation for the most part probably keeping their relative importance. *Avena sativa* is recorded again and there is one record of *Pisum sativum*. It is unfortunate that the identifications of *Triticum turgidum* and *Avena strigosa* must be regarded as suspect. The former seems quite plausible as a Medieval crop in the region whereas the cultivation of the latter would be rather surprising in Lowland England. A rich variety of fruits and nuts was consumed in the region during the Medieval period:

Juglans regia	*Pyrus communis*
Corylus avellana	*Morus nigra*
Prunus domestica	*Vitis vinifera*
Malus sylvestris	*Ficus carica*

It is possible that all these species were cultivated in the region but whether self-fertile varieties of fig (the only sort which fruit in Britain) have seeds robust enough to survive in archaeological contexts is debatable. In the late Medieval period, figs were imported by England from the Mediterranean region and imported raisins greatly supplemented home-grown grapes. Figs and grapes are likely to have been expensive but their consumption seems to have been widespread in late Medieval towns. The results from Middleton Stoney Castle show that even in the early Medieval period, exotic fruits were consumed by the aristocracy in the countryside.

Unlike the earlier periods, much of the evidence for cultivated plants comes from cess pits and therefore provides direct information on diet. Evidence that members of the urban population (or their pigs) were infested with nematode parasites has also come from a cess pit.

Late Saxon and Medieval Urban and Rural Differentiation: the Bones and Shells

At least thirty one sizeable groups from twenty sites and many smaller collections are reported. Typically collections are from urban contexts in Abingdon, Oxford and Northampton. Late Saxon sites are considered in this group.

Table 8 Percentage ranges of species fragments from 20 late Saxon and medieval sites and 31 subgroups of bones[1]

	%
cattle	25–45
sheep	30–60
pig	7–34
horse	0–8
dog	0–9
cat	0–3
red deer	0–2

1. Site collections from:–
    Bedfordshire: St. Johns, Bedford (Grant 1970) and Willington (Grant 1975b)
    Buckinghamshire: Walton (Noddle 1976)
    Northamptonshire: Lyveden (Grant 1975a); Chalk Lane (Harman 1981a); Greyfriars (Harman 1978d), and
    St. Peters, Northampton (Harman 1979b)
    Oxfordshire: Broad Street (Wilson 1975c); Market Place (Wilson, unpublished j), and Stert Street, Abingdon
    (Wilson 1979b); Banbury Castle (Wilson 1976a); All Saints (Wilson, unpublished a); Clarendon Hotel
    (Jope 1958); Greyfriars (Marples, Wilson, unpublished b); The Hamel (Wilson 1980b); Logic Lane
    (Banks 1961); Oxford Castle (Jope 1953 and Marples 1976); and St. Aldates, Oxford
    (Marples 1977); Seacourt (Jope 1962); and Tetsworth (Pernetta 1973)

Compared with deposits of early Saxon bones there are smaller percentages of cattle and greater of sheep and pig. Chronological trends and differences between urban and rural sites are illustrated in Table 9. Results are distinctive enough to describe urban sites and their information separately and as a standard to compare rural ones.

Strongly urban deposits (i.e. of eleventh to sixteenth century period) have more bones of sheep and fewer of cattle, pig, horse and red deer than present on rural sites. Varied percentages of sheep bones occur at Late Saxon sites. Low percentages of sheep bones tend to characterise rural sites e.g. Walton, Buckinghamshire (Noddle 1976), or those commencing their urban development e.g. at Chalk Lane or St. Peters, Northampton (Harman 1979b and 1981a) as already established at Oxford (Banks 1961, Jope 1953 and 1958, Marples 1976 and 1977). However this assessment of urban character is probably complicated by environmental conditions which may favour sheep more in Oxfordshire than in Northamptonshire.

The overall change in animal husbandry and economy towards sheep appears positively related to the re-establishment of urban aggregations and, by implication, population growth and the increased marketing of animals in towns. Yet cattle remain the most important species in the economy and only slowly decline in relative abundance. Urban sheep debris therefore represents some complex of cultural factors: the least necessary farm animals; or more easily produced and marketed surplus; or, the meat by-product of sheep raising for wool, skins, cheese, butter or dung.

The importance of pigs in the urban economy declines over time. A higher percentage of pig (27%) should be noted at eleventh century All Saints' Church, Oxford (Wilson, unpublished a). In general, and as in the Roman period, urban deposits are largely of food debris and horse and dog bones are not prominent.

Cat was a very characteristic urban mammal and the scrawny beasts of the period probably established a niche by preying on vermin but sometimes were hunted in turn for their skins and meat (Wilson, unpublished a). Black rats were present from around the twelfth century (Marples 1977, Wilson 1976a; also in rural areas e.g. Jope and Threlfall 1947 and Pernetta 1973: and possibly earlier; Noddle 1976). House mouse is certainly present in the twelfth to sixteenth century period (Wilson 1979b and Levitan unpublished). Other records possibly as early as the Roman period, for example Wilson, Thomas and Wheeler 1979, are not reliable because the bones were not found in waterlogged deposits which discourage burrowing intrusions.

Rabbit is perhaps the most novel species present and appears introduced during the eleventh to twelfth centuries (Marples 1977 and Grant 1975b). It became a common food and even tends to replace hare in the dietary record (Wilson 1980b).

Wild mammals, particularly deer, are scarcely represented in the eleventh to thirteenth century urban deposits and become even rarer in late ones (Wilson 1980b). Fox occurred at eleventh century All Saints' Church, Oxford (Wilson, unpublished a) and four skeletons from skinned carcasses were found at Church Street (Wilson in preparation c).

Domestic fowl, geese and duck were eaten more abundantly than in earlier cultural periods; domestic fowl becoming relatively more common than geese (Bramwell and Wilson 1980b). Rock/stock dove and swan might be counted among the domesticated species. Wild birds were a smaller part of the diet: wild geese and ducks relatively frequently; also

Table 9 Urban and rural comparison of fragment percentages from the late Saxon to post-medieval period

Period	Late Saxon	Medieval		Post–Medieval Urban[1]				Rural Medieval	
Century	8–11th	11–13th	13–15th	15–16th	17–18th	19th		12–13th	13–14th
Sample No.	9	7	4	3	3	2		4	4
Cattle	25–44	27–41	25–45	30–38	25–35	21–37		25–44	26–37
Sheep	34–60	47–58	43–52	50–59	50–66	50–52		30–43	34–45
Pig	10–27	11–19	8–23	7–13	5–12	9–12		12–34	14–29
Horse	0.6–8	0–3	0–0.3	0–0.2	0.3–1	0–1		0–3	2–7
Dog	2–9	0–2	0–0.6	0	0–3	0–0.4		0–1	0–3
Cat	0–3	0–0.5	0.2–0.5	0–0.6	0–5	0–4		0–0.5	0.3–1
Red Deer	0–0.6	0–0.2	0–+	0–0.6	0	0		0–1	0–2

[1] Post Medieval results have been included here.
Additional sites not listed in Table 8 are:
Oxfordshire: Church Street and Greyfriars (Wilson *et al.* unpublished b).

plover, pigeon, partridge, snipe, woodcock, rook/crow, and smaller birds such as skylark, redwing, and fieldfare (Bramwell 1975, 1978b, and 1979a and, Bramwell and Wilson 1979 and 1980). Other species such as red kite, raven, jackdaw, songthrush, and sparrow (Bramwell in Marples 1977, Bramwell and Harman 1979) may have been eaten, but also their bones and habits indicate that they were a feature of the living urban environment. Several raven skeletons were discovered at late Saxon Chalk Lane, Northampton (Coy 1981).

Marine fish bones among dietary debris begin in the Late Saxon period at Northampton with herring (A Jones 1979a and 1979b) and later cod, ling, conger eel became widespread and abundant; also flat fish, including plaice; also gurnard (Wheeler 1975, Wheeler in Marples 1977 and A Jones op. cit.). A marine mammal vertebra, probably of porpoise, was noted at Oxford Castle (Marples 1976). Fish debris has not been collected commonly and even where recovered is biased in favour of large marine fish although eel and salmon/trout have been identified from late Saxon debris (A Jones 1979a and b).

Sieving soil can add large numbers of eel bones and many freshwater fish species to the record list. Identifications from Stert Street, Abingdon (Wheeler 1979) were of pike, bleak, barbel, dace, chubb, roach, stickleback, perch and ruffe, as well as eel, salmon, and allis shad among the migratory species. Nearly all of these must have been caught locally. In addition spurdog, thornback ray or roker, sprat (also Wilson, Thomas and Wheeler 1979), whiting and mackerel were not then recorded elsewhere in the region. A short supplementary list, is given by Levitan (unpublished).

Marine molluscs, particularly oyster, are conspicuous. Mussel (*Mytilus edulis*), cockle, whelk (e.g. Oakley 1979) and periwinkle (Wilson 1979b) are also found. Quantities of shells appear to vary greatly. Shellfish may not always have been fully reported, but alternatively, large numbers may have been consumed at any one meal thereby producing the uneven record.

The wide range of medieval urban refuse demonstrates human resourcefulness and the corresponding widespread pressure against animal communities. This latter is confirmed by the small size of domestic mammals in Oxford at the Hamel (Wilson 1980b E14, F04) although possibly this is a local effect. The size of animals appears to diminish from the eleventh century into the medieval period proper.

Despite the resourcefulness of humans, a reduction of size is also observed in their skeletons and shows that the problems of medieval existence were shared by people and their animals. For comparison, the mid-late Saxons buried at Beacon Hill, Lewknor, Oxfordshire (Harman 1976b) were tallest: seven males averaging just over 5 ft 8 ins and seven females slightly less than 5 ft 3 ins in height. A small pre conquest group at Eynsham Abbey (Denston 1978) appear similar or smaller in stature. A decrease in stature is more evident with a small *c*12th–13th century group from Faringdon Road, Abingdon (Harman and Wilson 1981): three males averaging 5 ft 6 ins while one female stood only 4 ft 9 ins and the other 5 ft 2 ins. Finally six males buried at the Dominican Priory, Oxford (Edwards 1976) also average 5 ft 6 ins.

Thus on criteria of body sizes, environmental conditions were poorer than in the Saxon period, and about equivalent or poorer than in the Roman period. This level might be reflected in the mortality rates. Child and adolescent deaths were quite common, even to the extent of burials at the Dominican Priory, but a comparison of limited data from Saxon and medieval periods indicates that child and adolescent mortality is relatively high at both periods (e.g. Blackwood 1945; Brothwell 1962; and Harman, unpublished).

Similarly, the kill off patterns of domestic animals might have been distorted by the increased environmental pressure. In optimal conditions relatively young animals might be expected to be marketed to towns. However sheep remains from sites in Oxford show increasing percentages of older sheep are killed as the eleventh to sixteenth century period advances. In addition the results indicate sheep are killed at older age stages than in previous periods (Wilson 1980b, E11–13, also Harman 1981a). Limited studies of other species do not suggest any changes in the slaughtering of cattle or pigs (even at rural Walton: Noddle 1976).

Thus the major part of the animal economy may therefore be largely static from the Saxon period except for the husbandry of sheep. Their killing pattern suggests that any dietary preferences for lamb or hogget were not met. Indeed the combination of the kill off and the evidence of decreased stature indicate that meat and other food demands were not satisfied at all. Marketing of meat is not the paramount concern of husbandry. Marketing and husbandry appear similar to that in the Roman period, rather than to the Iron Age subsistence pattern, yet, if environmental pressure was severe, younger individuals should be better represented as indicated by Iron Age sheep bones. However the medieval reversal of this expected pattern of sheep bones would be explained by a high demand and production of wool, optimally from older animals.

To achieve this, the simple response of keeping fewer sheep to older ages appears contradicted by the evidence of the relative increase of sheep bones. However an increase in the numbers of sheep and kept to older ages could be brought about by decreasing the number of other domestic animals, particularly cattle since the keeping of even one or two fewer would release grazing for a higher number of sheep.

Conversion of arable land to pasture would also assist, but was most unlikely to occur while human population was relatively high. An inability to produce meat and dairy products must be compensated for by cereal cropping. Consequently, for the late Saxon and early medieval period the ratio of domestic animals to people probably decreased while the intensity of arable agriculture increased. After the Black Death these trends probably were reversed but the demand for wool evidently remained high. An export trade would explain the latter trend, while in general at both periods the priorities of wool and cereal production can be considered to have remained high over the area of trade.

Having established some idea of urban debris and its significance, the contrast of rural settlement and environment should become clearer. Site debris of major species (Table 9) shows greater variation than on urban sites because a) animal surplus is marketed elsewhere, b) draught oxen or horses may be consumed locally or buried at farms, c) natural habitats exploited by man or animals are more diverse, and d) status and prosperity are more obvious.

Forested habitats and occupation sites of greater prosperity or status are indicated by the prominence of red and fallow deer bones at the eleventh to twelfth century castle at Ascot Doilly near Wychwood, Oxfordshire (Jope 1959), similarly at Middleton Stoney, Oxfordshire (red deer only: Levitan, unpublished), and later at The Mount, Princes Risborough, Buckinghamshire (King and Lawford 1960) and Lyveden, Northamptonshire (Grant 1975a). Some deer bones will be butchery debris from manorial establishments but at Lyveden also appear to be waste from manufacture of implements.

Venison at Banbury Castle, Oxfordshire was less commonly eaten (Wilson 1976a). Debris from the barbican ditch of Oxford Castle (Marples 1976) was quite ordinary but may have been waste from nearby tenements and not from the Castle.

Another faunal indicator of status is the presence of birds of prey which may have been trained in falconry. The best example is of twelfth to fourteenth century deposits at Deddington Castle, Oxfordshire, which contained skeletons of a peregrine falcon, a kite, a Montague's harrier, several hen harriers, and two buzzards together with the remnants of their trappings (Jope and Threlfall 1947 and Jope unpublished). Sparrow hawk and possibly hobby occurred at Middleton Stoney (Levitan unpublished). Merlin was identified at Copt Hay, Tetsworth, Oxfordshire (Bramwell 1973).

Further associations with status appear to be the presence of peacock and pheasant at Middleton Stoney.

Pig bones tend to be prominent on some rural sites: Ascot Doilly (Jope 1959), Tetsworth (Pernetta 1973), Chalgrove Manor, Oxfordshire (Wilson, in preparation b), and Lyveden (Gilmore 1969b and Grant 1975a). Banbury Castle (Wilson 1976b) should be added to this group of sites and they are all probably associated in some way with some status and woodland pannage. In this respect pig bones at All Saints', Oxford (Wilson, unpublished a) may indicate citizens of moderate status either purchasing pork or keeping tenement pigs. Woodland pannage is clearly more remote from Oxford than from the rurally located sites.

The remaining reports on rural sites are from Hanwell, Oxfordshire (Wilson 1975a), Seacourt, Oxfordshire (Jope 1962), Walton (Noddle 1976) and Willington, Northamptonshire (Grant 1975b). These settlements appear more ordinary in their consumption of pig and presumably in status, prosperity, or access to pig pannage. Nevertheless occasional deer bones are found even at these sites and so indicate some rural character.

Another factor in the separation of site groups is that pigs and deer (and status and woodland) are probably associated with areas of clay or heavy ground. Lyveden is an example and so are sites east of Oxford at Tetsworth (Pernetta 1973) and Chalgrove Manor.

As in the Roman period, the density of rural sites in the early medieval era indicates a greater density of occupation and exploitation of available land. By implication the surrounding natural habitats should decline or be profoundly modified especially in the vicinity of towns. Even when deer and woodland were reserved or protected by custom and legality, red and, later, roe deer virtually disappear from urban deposits of the thirteenth century and later. This decline may also be attributed to the limited prosperity of town dwellers. Deer persist in rural areas at least until the seventeenth century: red deer at Buckingham (Rackham 1975) and roe at Bicester (Wilson in preparation f). Fallow deer were more adaptable or more favoured by men and the occasional bone confirms the persistence of this species by emparkment even in Oxford itself.

In general the disappearance of wild species from the archaeological record appears primarily a sign of human density and hunting intensity but only partly implies the actual destruction of their preferred vegetational habitats. Thus, despite the general demand for meat and any urban rearing of animals, the slow decline of pigs may be the best indication of the reduction of woodland or wetland areas for arable farming by clearance or drainage. Overgrazing by cattle and sheep may also have affected the diversity of wetland vegetation. Inevitably there must have been fewer niches available for wild species.

Wetland areas were useful resources to exploit for food. Of all wild fowl eaten a high proportion of species and numbers of the larger sized birds were sustained by marsh and meadow habitats. Also domestic geese and ducks could graze there.

Rapid declines or regional extermination of birds do not appear quantifiable yet but records of some species and their later absence or rarity suggest they were under threat in the medieval and postmedieval period. For example: whooper swan, gadwall duck, ruff and raven (Bramwell and Wilson 1980). The incidence of crane is of interest. It is just present in early Oxford deposits (Marples, unpublished) and probably declined locally, in numbers although it is noted for twelfth to thirteenth century Walton (Bramwell 1976) and as late as the sixteenth or seventeenth century in Northampton (Bramwell and Harman 1979).

Possibly some species should be treated as chance records of infrequent visits to the country. The unique identification in Britain of the pygmy cormorant *Phalacrocorax pygmeus* at Stert Street, Abingdon, may be an example (Cowles 1981; Bramwell and Wilson 1979). On the other hand the record still demonstrates how far the distribution of the species has contracted to its present Mediterranean and more easterly location and would also be consistent with any other evidence of wetland reclamation although Cowles also attributes the modern absence to climatic deterioration.

Reclamation and use of wetlands ought to fluctuate according to human population density. When and where environmental conditions were severe sheep would have been grazed on meadow beside water where they would be more susceptible to liver fluke. Such grazing is likely not far from The Hamel, Oxford, where early twelfth century structural evidence of field ditches and post holes, two sheep skeletons, and the presence of sheep keds suggest the folding or other husbandry of sheep (but see p 63 also note further evidence of parasites, p 63).

It is hoped that similar skeletal and structural evidence of the organisation of medieval farming will be recognisable from excavations at Chalgrove Manor, Oxfordshire.

Studies of sheep are undoubtedly one key to the medieval economy. Changes in the body form are evident. Polled sheep slowly replace horned varieties including four horned sheep. Short tailed sheep appear replaced by long tailed sheep (Wilson 1980b). Since meat production appears given less emphasis, these physical changes probably resulted from selective breeding for wool quality or quantity.

Finally an overview of medieval ecoculture can be drawn from the suspected economic function of the sheep and the associated trends of urbanisation compared with similar aspects of life in the Roman period. Some idea of the level of subsistence of these ecocultures appears possible.

The predominance of cattle over sheep has already been linked to broad factors of status, prosperity and farming efficiency and is characteristic of the Roman period in the region and to rural sites in medieval times. Conversely greater emphasis on urban development and a lower level of subsistence is more indicative of the medieval period and appears associated with sheep and the wool industry. A fairly direct correlation might be made between increased wool demand and size of the human population, but size of the corresponding sheep and human populations probably is also dependent on the preferences and internal efficiency of each ecoculture. Nevertheless it does appear that medieval people and animals are generally worse off than their Romano-British counterparts.

An 'echo' of this greater medieval emphasis on sheep and urban life is discernible from the bone refuse of Celtic culture, and its Romano-British continuum. Yet, while the Iron Age subsistence pattern shows signs of social stress, the economic constraints of it are certainly different and human existence probably was less severe in total because Celtic society is supposed to be less populous, less stratified, and more self contained communally than Romano-British or medieval societies.

The Post-Medieval Period, AD1500–Present Day

Late and Post-Medieval Urban Industrial Focus

The superficial pattern of bone evidence, namely fragment number percentages (Table 9), indicate little basic ecocultural change from the earlier period but admittedly samples of bones are few and usually urban in origin. In addition, information is limited and incompletely analysed. Nevertheless the urban activity of the late Saxon and early medieval period becomes much more differentiated or at least it is more recognisable in later deposits from Abingdon, Bicester, and Northampton.

Typical post-medieval deposits were excavated from the tenements of the Church Street and Greyfriars sites in St. Ebbes, Oxford (Wilson, R Jones, Marples *et al.*, unpublished). Beef, mutton, and pork were eaten in similar proportions to those in the medieval period although the quantities of meat consumed may have been greater. Certainly more rabbit meat was eaten (also Wilson *et al.* 1979) and so were greater quantities of mussels and cockles, especially as shown by some sixteenth and seventeenth century deposits. Turkey, introduced from North America, makes an appearance during the seventeenth and eighteenth centuries. Peacock is recorded for the second time in the region. Edible crab *Cancer pagurus* is brought to Oxford from the eighteenth century onwards. Some of these items might be delicacies but collectively they may represent continued human pressure on animal sources of food and perhaps a limited protein diet for most people.

Remains from animals which probably lived on the tenements include many of cats and occasional bones (differential recovery problems) of black rat, a skeleton of a hedgehog, and one of a pig which exhibited many deformities suggesting that it was maltreated, or frequently attempted to escape a sty. Other records of animals which may have lived on the tenements include domestic rabbits, and fowl, pigeons and jackdaws. Bones of tawny owl indicate another urban dweller. Two polecat or ferret skeletons also occurred but their ecological status is uncertain. The crania were absent and a probable cut mark indicates that the corpses were skinned — a fate hypothesised for some of the cats: immature individuals are common.

This fragmentary evidence appears consistent with historical documentation of tenements in St. Ebbes containing gardens, orchards, pig sties, waste ground, houses and perhaps the ruins of the Greyfriars.

Brown rat is the last recorded species to arrive in the region and is identified from nineteenth and twentieth century urban contexts in St. Aldates, Oxford (Marples 1977) and Stert Street, Abingdon (Wilson 1979b).

The size of domestic animals increases during the post-medieval period but breed changes are not studied properly except for a late eighteenth century collection of horn cores from medium to long horned cattle buried at Greyfriars (Armitage, unpublished). This type of cattle become common at least from the seventeenth century (Wilson *et al.* 1979). Another clue of attention given to animal breeds or special functions of them was found in two truncated spurs of domestic fowl from Greyfriars and dating to the eighteenth or nineteenth century. These demonstrate the presence of fighting cocks and their fitting with metal spurs (West 1982).

The horn cores too, are signs of an intensification of human activity in specialised and often spatially separate occupations or industries which left behind distinctive debris and sometimes in large quantities. Although butchery and other treatment of carcass products might be the oldest trade of all, the recognition of particular stages in the process is often easiest at post-medieval sites.

While small groups of cattle horn cores are recorded for medieval sites at Northampton (Harman 1979b) and Oxford (Wilson 1980b) the largest deposit known is the late eighteenth century one from Greyfriars, Oxford (Armitage, unpublished). Quantities of whole or halved sheep skulls occur in Oxford and Abingdon (Wilson 1979b and 1980b). Large deposits of sheep metapodial debris are known from other sixteenth to nineteenth century sites in Abingdon and Bicester (Wilson 1975c and unpublished g), but also occurs during the medieval period for example at Buckingham (Rackham 1975).

These deposits are waste from directly dumped slaughter house rubbish, or from processed by-products of early stages of butchery. Such wastes are sometimes associated with tanneries, especially at St. Peters Northampton (Harman 1979b), possibly at the Old Gaol, Abingdon (Wilson 1975c) and probably at Greyfriars, Oxford (Armitage, unpublished). This refuse was part of a wide use of carcass parts for fat, glue, and horn as well as of the skins with which they appear associated indirectly. The extent of butchery differentiation was observed at St. Ebbes where skull debris of calves, but scarcely of older cattle and their horns, was present among domestic refuse. However the degree of epiphysial fusion of bones from the meat joints of the main carcass showed that most of the meat consumed was from older cattle and, therefore, whose heads almost certainly had been put aside for other purposes at the slaughter house.

All of this kind of material is worth further investigation. Differentiation of site rubbish suggests means by which the extent of industrial specialisation can be measured at other historical periods and against other regions. Studies of the more normal information from bones should show the effects of the industrial period on people and animals. Lastly from the use of modern documentation, post medieval bones allow testing of archaeological hypotheses about bones, and for the setting of a standard by which previous levels of subsistence may be assessed. Unfortunately, although understandably, post medieval deposits have been neglected and deserve better attention if only for the reason that it is not possible to round off this survey with a flourishing summary of the significance of this period in the long term development of the region.

A Postscript of Curiosities

A stone chamber within the Provost's lodging at Oriel College, Oxford, which had been used as a cess pit during the late seventeenth century, provided an insight on the diet of an upper class household (Robinson 1982). The Provost's rich meals evidently included:

mustard	plum
black pepper	apple
grape/raisin	fig
raspberry	black mulberry
wild/alpine strawberry	walnut
or hautbois strawberry	hazel/filbert

The pepper (*Piper nigrum*) is the first record of a tropical crop from an archaeological context in Britain. The deposit also contained numerous puparia of *Teichomyza fusca* (sewage flies). The flies suggest a squalid aspect to living conditions in the Provost's lodgings, because the only opening to the chamber was into the house. Each time the lid was lifted, the flies would probably have swarmed to the light.

A corked, but unfortunately broken, seventeenth/eighteenth century wine bottle containing gooseberries was found during excavations at Frewin Hall, Oxford (Robinson in Blair 1978, 76).

A trench in Oxford High Street cut through a nineteenth century cast iron water main which was filled with a mass of shells of the zebra mussel (*Dreissena polymorpha*) (Robinson 1982). The zebra mussel has minute free-swimming larvae capable of passing through filter beds. These larvae would then attach themselves by byssal threads to pipe sides and metamorphose into mussels. The mussels are very efficient filter feeders, and would have been able to feed on impurities in the water. Prior to the chlorination of water supplies in the early years of the twentieth century, these mussels were sometimes a serious pest, either blocking water mains or polluting water supplies when individuals died. It is pleasing to come across an actual example of something often quoted in books, but seemingly rarely seen.

General Developments in the Region

From Woodland to Organised Agricultural Systems

The rise to dominance of woodland shown in the region during the early Post Glacial, then gradual clearance and the creation of an organised agricultural landscape, with a set-back in the early Saxon period, is only what would be expected. Man's relationship with his environment, however, deserves further consideration. It is accepted that throughout the Mesolithic, man was a hunter-gatherer, although the degree to which wild herds were managed and woodland thinned to improve browsing/grazing is debatable. The coming of arable agriculture and domestic animals in the Neolithic has tended to obscure man's continuing dependence upon woodland. Throughout the Neolithic, hunting wild animals and the gathering of plant foodstuffs from woodland was still very much an important part of man's way of life in the region. Even at the end of the Neolithic, much if not most of the landscape remained wooded. Yet probably much of it was actively foraged by domesticated pigs and possibly increasing pressure was placed on natural woodland communities as indicated by the extermination of aurochs in some areas by hunting.

In the Bronze Age, wild animals seem to have provided little of the meat eaten by man and the gathering of hazelnuts declined. Clearance was gradually extended but much woodland was still present, and on occasions, useable grazing land was abandoned to trees. As in the Neolithic, arable agriculture does not seem to have been of nearly such importance as pastoralism in the region during the early and middle Bronze Age. The impression given is that, from the Neolithic until the late Bronze Age, man was not exploiting the region to its full potential given the available technology. Had man's sole concern been maximum food production (and consequently a rapid rise in population), clearance would have been expected to progress more rapidly in the Neolithic, with a much greater concentration upon arable.

In the late Bronze Age, considerable changes began to take place. By the Iron Age, clearance was extensive in the region and arable farming on hillsides was causing serious erosion. Finds of charred grain on some Iron Age sites are enormous compared with the slight presence of carbonised cereals on sites of earlier periods. The proportion of meat in the diet probably decreased and the importance of secondary products and the uses of live animals increased. Population levels probably rose rapidly. It is as if in the late Bronze Age some restraining influence on population growth was removed, resulting in agricultural expansion and a trend towards increased arable.

In the Roman period, arable intensification seems to have continued, which, together with improved technology, communications and organisation, resulted in an agricultural landscape in which each part of the region was used to its best potential. Only in this way could the region support the many small urban centres and the larger walled towns.

In the early Saxon period, there was probably a much lower population level and some abandoned land. Agricultural communities seem to have been more self-sufficient, while the reduced pressure on the land perhaps enabled the amount of animal protein in the diet to rise. By the late Saxon period, however, agricultural expansion was well under-way and the arable/pastoral ratio was perhaps similar to that of the Roman period, or there may have been an even greater concentration upon arable. Domestic animals were probably even more important for secondary products and for traction than they had been in any earlier period.

Later the decrease in size of human and animal bones suggests increased environmental stresses in medieval communities. Conditions generally ameliorated during the following centuries. Urban and rural relationships essentially remained the same in the Post-Medieval period except that a greater differentiation and specialisation of urban society becomes apparent from the remains of industrial and household waste.

Soil Change

The effect of the removal of tree cover and ploughing has caused considerable change to the soils of the region. In general, the pre-clearance soils seem to have been stone-free, perhaps with a relatively high silt content of loessic origin.

Either a consequence of the interruption of the calcium cycle with clearance, or a natural development under woodland conditions, seems to have been the formation of non-calcareous soils over limestone parent material, for instance the soil beneath the Neolithic barrow at Rollright (p 32). The gradual formation of sol lessives was probably widespread after clearance on these soils under grass, for example the soil beneath the Bronze Age barrow at Rollright (p 38) and also under arable on deeper soils where ploughing was shallow. The deep Sutton series soils of the Thames terraces are weak sol lessives (Jarvis 1973, 28, 181). At present there is no evidence for the formation of sol lessives under woodland in the region. On those areas of Glacial Drift and Tertiary Sands in the region which now have very acidic podzols, it is possible that podzolisation was a consequence of ancient agriculture, although at present there is no direct evidence.

Further changes took place as ploughing continued or intensified. The undisturbed natural soil on the gravel terraces of the Thames mostly seems to have been a stone-free silt loam (Robinson in Palmer 1980, 133–4). The modern soils on the terraces are likely to have resulted from ploughing deep enough to mix the soils with the underlying sandy limestone gravel. When this occurred on an extensive scale is uncertain. Late Bronze Age/early Iron Age ploughing at Mount Farm, Berinsfield, Oxfordshire took place in a stony soil and plough marks cut into the gravel (G Lambrick, pers. comm.). Soil depth would have been an important factor. At Rollright, ploughing had destroyed the sol lessive and mixed limestone chippings into the soil by the Roman period. On the Downs and Chilterns, extensive Iron Age ploughing was causing severe erosion and large deposits of hillwash accumulated in the valleys. Again ploughing mixed the chalk bedrock with the soil.

Flooding and Alluviation

Considerable information from many sites has recently been discovered about the Post-Glacial history of the River Thames and its floodplain in the region (Robinson and Lambrick 1984). The channels of the Thames were probably incised to their greatest depth in the early Post-Glacial, when each spring there would have been a complete melt of a whole winter's snow cover. When conditions had become warmer, there would not have been such a large discharge and the river flow would have been more even. The reduced seasonal variation in the flow resulted in the silting up of some channels and little or no overbank flooding. Pedological processes predominated on the floodplains, giving a variety of mainly thin, decalcified soils which have been found sealed or cut by Neolithic and Bronze Age sites. The water table was at least seasonally low. Between the late Bronze Age and the middle Iron Age, the water table rose, culminating in the onset of regular overbank flooding towards the end of the middle Iron Age. In the Belgic period, alluviation began which continued into the Roman period, with the accumulation of c0.5m of alluvial clay. Some of this alluvium subsequently became decalcified. Further and more extensive alluviation began in late Saxon to Medieval times, with the deposition of rather coarser material, which has not been decalcified.

It is thought possible that the reason for the rise in the water table and onset of flooding was due to extensive clearance in the catchment area in the early Iron Age. Removal of tree cover would have caused increased run-off, reducing the amount of water held in the soil and returned to the atmosphere. Flooding and alluviation are issues which ought to be considered separately. The onset of the first phase of alluviation may have been due to a late Iron Age/Roman arable expansion on the Cotswolds, which culminated in the great villas, creating the necessary conditions for soil erosion. The second phase of alluviation was perhaps the result of a later Saxon agricultural recovery followed by the well-documented Medieval arable expansion prior to the Black Death.

Similar developments may have occurred on the floodplains of the other major rivers in the region, the Nene and Ouse. There are several prehistoric sites beneath alluvium on the floodplain of the Upper Nene and at Earls Barton, the old ground surface was a fine loam whereas the present soil of the floodplain is alluvial clay (Jackson 1972). The dates for alluviation of the Nene and Ouse floodplains need not be the same as in the Thames Valley. For example, at Bromham, on the Ouse floodplain, alluvium covered a site which was occupied from the Belgic period to the third century AD (Tilson 1973).

Climatic Change

Apart from the Alerod Interstadial and the climatic amelioration at the end of the last glaciation, there is no convincing evidence from the region for climatic change since the early Post-Glacial period. This is not, however, to say that no slight changes took place. Merely that the evidence for any such changes has so far been obscured by man's effect on the landscape.

Species Change Among Plants and Invertebrates

Obviously the ecological changes in the region since the late Glacial were accompanied by considerable changes in the region. Some of the arctic species were lost very early on, before the arrival of the majority of the thermophilous woodland species. Complete forest cover of the region enabled species with very poor dispersive power outside woodland to colonise, species which today are regarded as characteristic of relict woodland. Some of these are now very rare or extinct in the region. They have been under pressure ever since the Neolithic, although the extent of woodland cover in

PERIOD	NEOLITHIC	BRONZE AGE	IRON AGE		ROMAN		SAXON	MEDIEVAL		POST-MEDIEVAL
ARCHAEOLOGY OF LIMESTONE HILLS	Small scale settlement.		First hillforts.	Further settlement.	Large villas develop.		Economic collapse.	Dense settlement.		Depopulation, slow revival.
	Some agricultural clearances		? extensive clearance	Pastoral emphasis	Much arable		Decline of arable	Arable very extensive		Reversion to grassland
ARCHAEOLOGY OF CLAY SLOPES	Little activity		? settlement begins		Farms present		As for limestone hills			
RIVER CHANNELS	Evidence for silting. No evidence for substantial movement									
WATER TABLE	Probably low	Low	Risen by c. 2200 bp	Further rise		Remaining high				
FLOODING	Little or none		Some sites dry ? starting on others	Much of floodplain		? continuing	Very extensive			
ALLUVIATION	None		? starting →		Well under-way		? reduction or cessation	Extensive – reaches some sites for first time	?	Little
YEARS bp	5000/5400 ← – – 4000	3000	2500	2000	1500		1000	500		100

Figure 9   Summary diagram showing correlation of alluviation and hydrological conditions on the Upper Thames floodplain with human activity in the catchment

Table 10 Crops recorded by period

REGIONAL CROP RECORD		Period								
		Neolithic and Beaker	Early and Middle Bronze Age	Late Bronze Age	Iron Age	Belgic Period	Roman Period	Early Saxon Period	Late Saxon Period	Medieval Period
Arable Crops										
Triticum monococcum L.	Eincorn	−	?	−	−	−	−	−	−	−
T. dicoccum Schubl.	Emmer Wheat	+	+	−	?	?	?	−	−	−
T. cf. *dicoccum* Schubl.	Emmer Wheat	−	−	+	−	−	−	−	−	−
T. spelta L.	Spelt Wheat	−	−	+	+	+	+	?	−	−
T. aestivocompactum Schiem.	Bread/Club Wheat	+	+	−	+	+	+	+	+	+
Secale cereale L.	Rye	−	−	−	+	−	+	−	+	+
cf. *S. cereale* L.	Rye	−	−	−	−	−	+	−	−	+
Hordeum vulgare L. emend.	Six-row Hulled Barley	−	−	−	+	+	+	+	+	+
Hordeum sp.	Hulled Barley	−	−	+	−	−	−	−	−	−
Hordeum sp.	Naked Barley	−	+	+	−	−	−	−	−	−
Hordeum vulgare L. emend.	Six-row Barley	+	−	−	−	−	−	−	−	−
Avena sativa L.	Oats	−	−	−	−	−	−	+	?	+
Avena sp.	Wild or Cultivated Oats	−	−	−	?	?	?	−	−	−
Linum usitatissimum L.	Flax	−	−	−	−	−	+	+	+	+
Vicia faba L.	Celtic/Field Bean	−	−	−	−	−	+	+	+	+
Pisum sativum L.	Pea	−	−	−	−	−	−	−	−	+
Other Crops										
Coriandrum sativum L.	Coriander	−	−	−	−	−	+	−	−	−
Anethum graveolens L.	Dill	−	−	−	−	−	+	−	−	−
Foeniculum vulgare Mill.	Fennel	−	−	−	−	−	+	−	−	−
Apium graveolens L.	Celery	−	−	−	−	−	+	−	−	?
Papaver somniferum L.	Opium Poppy	−	−	−	−	−	+	−	−	−
Prunus domestica L.	Plum/Bullace	−	−	−	−	−	+	−	−	+
P. cf. *domestica* L.	Plum/Bullace	−	−	−	−	−	−	−	+	−
P. avium L.	Cherry	−	−	−	−	−	?	−	−	−
Malus sylvestris Mill.	Apple	?	−	−	−	−	?	−	−	+
cf. *Pyrus communis* L.	Pear	−	−	−	−	−	−	−	−	+
Morus nigra L.	Black Mulberry	−	−	−	−	−	−	−	−	+
Vitis vinifera L.	Grape	−	−	−	−	−	−	−	−	+
Ficus carica L.	Fig	−	−	−	−	−	−	−	−	+
Juglans regia L.	Walnut	−	−	−	−	−	?	−	−	+
Corylus avellana L.	Hazel Nut	?	−	?	−	−	?	?	?	?

+ present.   ? present, but perhaps residual, a weed or collected from the wild;   − not recorded from the region.

the Neolithic provided reservoirs from which they could re-colonise when secondary woodland invaded abandoned clearances. For example, *Ena montana* and several other very rare woodland molluscs were able to establish themselves on what had been a Neolithic site (Evans 1966, 355–6). From the Iron Age onwards, however, woodland cover was probably sufficiently dissected to create problems of colonisation.

Species change would also have taken place in woodland that was never completely cleared, due to the removal of timber, incursions of domestic animals and management. For example oak, a tree with very useful wood which readily seeds itself and has somewhat unpalatable re-growth after felling, expanded at the expense of lime, a much more vulnerable tree. Beech is also a tree which seems to have been favoured by man rather later on. The earliest find of beech in the region is of charcoal from a Neolithic context at the Abingdon Causewayed Camp (Dimbleby in Case 1956, 18). There are sporadic records of beech charcoal from Iron Age and Roman sites on the Cotswolds and Chilterns (although some of them may be unreliable), but there is no reason to suspect it was a very abundant tree. The Medieval site of Chalgrove, at the foot of the Chilterns, however, has produced much beech charcoal. It seems likely that the beechwoods of the Chilterns are of post-Roman origin.

Clearance provided the opportunity for a great expansion of the light-demanding plants of grassland and disturbed ground. Grazing pressure on woodland edges probably favoured thorny shrubs such as *Prunus spinosa*. Most of the early arable weeds are likely to have been native species which were already established on such transient habitats as mud and shingle banks at riversides, e.g. *Chenopodium album* and *Atriplex* spp. (Robinson 1981a, 302). Others, for example *Papaver argemone*, which has been recorded from a Bronze Age context (Robinson, unpublished i), may have been introduced with the crops. In the Belgic period and also the Roman period Mediterranean weeds such as *Agrostemma githago* were introduced. These species seem to have been very dependent on arable for their survival in the region.

The crop species have already been discussed in detail. Periods from which they have been recorded are given in Table 10. Some of the gaps, for example the absence of coriander and fennel from the Medieval period, are simply due to the investigation of insufficient samples from the region.

The rise of synanthropic beetles on Roman sites has also been mentioned. It is very probable that some of the undoubtedly alien grain beetles, such as *Sitophilus granarius*, will be discovered from Roman contexts in the region, just as they have been elsewhere. Remains of exotic species which perhaps never lived in the region, but were imported, first appeared in the Roman period, for example the piece of silver fir wood from Shakenoak (Brodribb *et al.* 1973, 137–8). Likewise in the Medieval period there are the foreign dried fruit.

Some wetland species which are now absent from the region managed to survive into the Roman period such as *Hydrophilus piceus* at Alchester (Robinson in Young 1975, 161–70; Robinson 1979) and *Vertigo angustior* at Shakenoak (Chatfield in Brodribb *et al.* 1978, 165–8). Possibly those species only disappeared due to drainage operations in the Post-Medieval period.

Changes have also taken place in the fauna of grassland in the region, even though the reasons for them remains obscure. *Truncatellina cylindrica* was present during the Neolithic at Thrupp but no longer occurs in the region (Robinson 1981a, 317), while *Onthophagus nutans*, identified from an Iron Age context at Mingies Ditch, is now extinct in Britain (Robinson 1981a, 487). Various plants of disturbed ground which were common in the Thames Valley during the Iron Age to Saxon periods but are now rare or absent are given in Robinson (1981b, 275–8). They include for example, *Hyoscyamus niger* and *Onopordum acanthium* from many occupation sites. The reasons for the decline of some of them are known, for instance the arable weed *Argostemma githago* suffered with improved seed clearing, but the causes for the decline of other species (or even the reasons why they should have been present at all) are uncertain.

Site Gazetteer: Plants, Invertebrates and Soils/Sediments

The sites have been listed according to period, giving their county, reference to the overall authors of publications which include environmental information about the site, and an indication of type of evidence which has been reported upon. Where a question mark precedes the name of a site, it means that the dating evidence is uncertain. The full publication reference is given in the bibliography. Where the author's name is not followed by a date, it means that the information is unpublished but that reference has been made to results from that site in the text under the appropriate period. Some sites listed in the gazetteer have not been mentioned in the text because their results are only of limited interest. The abbreviations used are as follows:

P.	pollen	M.	mollusc
S.	soil/sediment	C.	carbonised
I.	impressions	R.	replaced
W.	waterlogged		

with the following qualifications:

a.	including alluvium	i.	insects
s.	seeds and some other macroscopic plant remains	w.	wood

LATE GLACIAL 13000bc–8300bc

Pitstone	Bucks	Evans 1966	MS
Claydon Pike	Glos	Robinson a	MWis
Apethorpe	Northants	Sparks & Lambert 1961–2	MPWs
Drayton	Oxon	Robinson b	S
Farmoor	Oxon	(Coope 1976	Wi
		(Lambrick & Robinson 1979	SWis
Mingie's Ditch, Hardwick	Oxon	Robinson c	Wis
Thrupp, Abingdon	Oxon	Robinson 1981a	S

MESOLITHIC 8300bc–3500bc

Harrold	Beds	Hall & Nickerson 1966	Sa(W)
?Gerrard's Cross	Bucks	Barfield 1977	S
Iver	Bucks	Lacaille 1963	MPWw(s)
Iver	Bucks	Robinson d	MW
?Latimer	Bucks	Branigan 1971	S
?Pink Hill	Bucks	Evans 1972	MS
Apethorpe	Northants	Sparks & Lambert 1961–2	MPWs
Higham Ferrers	Northants	Hall & Nickerson 1966	Sa(W)
Ascott-under-Wychwood	Oxon	Evans 1971, 1972	MS
Cothill Fcn	Oxon	Clapham & Clapham 1939	P
?East Challow	Oxon	Arkell 1947	S
?Farmoor	Oxon	Robinson e	Ws
Mingie's Ditch, Hardwick	Oxon	Robinson c	Wisw
?Over Norton	Oxon	Arkell 1947	MS(W)
?Swerford	Oxon	Arkell 1947	S
?Wilcote	Oxon	Arkell 1947	S

NEOLITHIC AND BEAKER 3500bc–1600bc

Puddlehill	Beds	Field *et al.* 1964	CswM
?Pitstone	Bucks	Evans 1966	MS
Pitstone	Bucks	Evans & Valentine 1974	MS
Stacey Bushes	Bucks	Keepax 1975, Green 1976	Cw
Whiteleaf Hill	Bucks	Childe & Smith 1954	M
Aldwincle	Northants	Metcalf 1973	(Wsw)
Briar Hill	Northants	Keepax 1977, 1980	Cw
Ecton	Northants	Hollowell 1972	(Wsw)
Ecton	Northants	Moore & Williams 1975	CwPSa
?St. Peter's Street, Northampton	Northants	Williams 1979	M
Abingdon – Barton Court	Oxon	Jones M, 1980, Miles, forthcoming	Cs
Abingdon – Causewayed Camp	Oxon	(Helbaek 1952	Is
		(Case 1956	CwM
		(Case & Whittle 1982	CwIs
Ascott-under-Wychwood	Oxon	(Evans 1971, 1972	MS
		(Evans & Jones 1973	M
		(Dimbleby & Evans 1974	MP
		(Limbrey 1975	S
		(Keepax 1979a	Cw
Cassington	Oxon	Cornwall 1953	S
City Farm, Hanborough	Oxon	Case *et al.* 1964–65	CwM
Devil's Quoits	Oxon	Limbrey 1975	S
Dorchester	Oxon	(Atkinson *et al.* 1951	CwS
		(Cornwall 1953	S
Dorchester Cursus	Oxon	Robinson f	Cw
Drayton Cursus	Oxon	Robinson g	Sa
Mount Farm, Berinsfield	Oxon	Jones M, 1980	Cs
Hamel, Oxford	Oxon	Palmer 1980, Robinson 1981a	Sa

Thrupp, Abingdon	Oxon	Robinson 1981a	M
Wayland's Smithy	Oxon	Evans 1971, 1972	MS
Buscot Lock	Oxon/Glos	Robinson 1981a	(CwMP
			(Wisw
Rollright	Oxon/Warks	Robinson h	S

EARLY AND MIDDLE BRONZE AGE 1600bc—900bc

Barton Hill Farm	Beds	Dyer 1962	?s
Roxton	Beds	Keeley 1974, 1976	S
Bledlow	Bucks	Head 1934—40	CwM
Hitcham	Bucks	Hessen & Helbaek 1944	Is
Milton Keynes	Bucks	Green 1974	M
Earls Barton	Northants	Jackson 1970, 1972	CwSa
Ashville, Abingdon	Oxon	Parrington 1978	CswM
Cassington	Oxon	Atkinson 1946—7	Cw
Long Wittenham	Oxon	Helbaek 1952	Is
Oddington	Oxon	Jessen & Helbaek 1944	Is
Port Meadow, Oxford	Oxon	Lambrick & Robinson	S
Rams Hill	Oxon	Bradley & Ellison 1975	CswM
Somerton	Oxon	Jessen & Helbaek 1944	Is
Stanton Harcourt	Oxon	Cornwall 1953	S
Wytham	Oxon	(Bowler & Robinson 1980)	CwMSa
		(Robinson 1981a)	
Rollright	Oxon/Warks	Robinson h	S

LATE BRONZE AGE 900bc—550bc

Dunstable	Beds	Hawkes 1940	Cs
Ivinghoe Beacon	Bucks	Cotton & Frere 1968	CwPS
Abingdon	Oxon	Helbaek 1952	Is
Chastelton	Oxon	Jessen & Helbaek 1944	Is
Mingie's Ditch, Hardwick	Oxon	Robinson 1981a	MSaWw
Mount Farm, Berinsfield	Oxon	Robinson i	MSWis
Radley	Oxon	Helbaek 1952	Is
Rams Hill	Oxon	Bradley & Ellison 1975	MS
Wallingford	Oxon	Robinson j	MSa
Wayland's Smithy	Oxon	Bradley 1975	MS
Witney	Oxon	Hazleden & Jarvis 1979, 1980	SaWw

IRON AGE 550bc—80bc

Bledlow	Bucks	Head & Piggot 1941—46	Cw
?Gerrard's Cross	Bucks	Barfield 1977	MS
?Latimer	Bucks	Branigan 1971	S
Pink Hill	Bucks	Evans 1972	MS
Pitstone	Bucks	Evans 1966	MS
Claydon Pike	Glos	Robinson 1981a, 1981b,)	MWis
		Robinson k)	
Apethorpe	Northants	Sparks & Lambert 1961—2	MPWs
Blackthorn	Northants	Williams 1974	M
Ecton	Northants	Hollowell 1971	Sa
?Grendon	Northants	McCormick 1975	Sa
Hunsbury	Northants	George 1917	Cs
Rainsborough	Northants	Avery et al. 1967	M
Twywell	Northants	Jackson 1975	Csw
Wellingborough	Northants	Everson 1976	M

Ashville, Abingdon	Oxon	Parrington 1978	CsIsM
Cherbury	Oxon	Arkell 1939	M
Chinnor	Oxon	Richardson & Young 1951	Cw
City Farm, Hanborough	Oxon	Case *et al.* 1964–65	Cw
?Drayton Cursus	Oxon	Robinson g	Sa
Eynsham Hall Camp	Oxon	Dimbleby	P
Farmoor	Oxon	(Lambrick & Robinson 1979)	(CsMP
		(Robinson 1978a, 1981a)	(SaWi
		(1981b)	(mites sw
?Grims Ditch	Oxon	Case & Sturdy 1959	S
Grims Ditch, Mongewell	Oxon	Hinchliffe 1975	MS
Lyneham Camp	Oxon	Bayne 1957	CwM
Madmarston	Oxon	Fowler 1960	Cw
Mingie's Ditch, Hardwick	Oxon	(Robinson 1981a, 1981b)	(CswMP
		(Robinson l)	(Sa
			(Wisw
Port Meadow, Oxford	Oxon	Lambrick & Robinson	S
Radley	Oxon	Helbaek 1952	Is
Rams Hill	Oxon	Bradley & Ellison 1975	MS
St. Aldates, Oxford	Oxon	Durham 1977	(MSa
			(Wis
Stanton Harcourt	Oxon	Hamlin 1966	Cw

BELGIC 80bc–AD43

Bierton	Bucks	Jones 1981	Cs
Ashville, Abingdon	Oxon	Parrington 1978	Cs
Barton Court, Abingdon	Oxon	Miles forthcoming	Cs

ROMAN AD43–AD410

Bromham	Beds	Tilson 1973	Sa
Bancroft, Milton Keynes	Bucks	(Keeley 1982	Sa
		(Spencer 1982	M
Bourton Grounds	Bucks	Johnson 1975	MSa
Bradwell, Milton Keynes	Bucks	Green 1975	M
Hedgerley	Bucks	Oakley *et al.* 1934–40	Cw
Latimer	Bucks	Branigan 1971	Cw
Pink Hill	Bucks	Evans 1972	MS
Saunderton	Bucks	Ashcroft 1934–40	Cw
Cogenhoe	Northants	Alexander 1967	Cs
Wakerley	Northants	Jackson & Ambrose 1978	CsM
Alchester	Oxon	(Young 1975	MWis
		(Robinson 1979	Wi
Appleford	Oxon	(Hinchliffe 1980,)	(IsM
		(Robinson 1978a, 1981a, 1981b)	(Wisw
Ascott-under-Wychwood	Oxon	Evans 1972	MS
Ashville, Abingdon	Oxon	Parrington 1978	Cs
Barton Court, Abingdon	Oxon	Robinson 1980a	W
			galls
			moss
		Robinson 1981a, 1981b,	CsMP
		Miles forthcoming	Wi
			galls
			moss sw
Broad Street, Abingdon	Oxon	Parrington & Balkwill 1975	Cs
Callow Hill	Oxon	Thomas 1957	Cw
Churchill Hospital, Oxford	Oxon	Robinson m	CsWs
Claydon Pike	Oxon	Robinson n	MSa
			Wis

Dorchester	Oxon	Hogg & Stevens 1937	(CwM
			((Wi)
Drayton Cursus	Oxon	Robinson g	MSa
Farmoor	Oxon	(Robinson & Hubbard 1977	PWs
		(Lambrick & Robinson 1979)	(CsMP
		(Robinson 1978a, 1981a, 1981b)	(SaWi
			(mites sw
Madmarston	Oxon	Fowler 1960	Cw
Mount Farm, Berinsfield	Oxon	Robinson i	CsWis
North Leigh	Oxon	Morrison 1959	Cs
Rams Hill	Oxon	Bradley & Ellison 1975	SM
Shakenoak	Oxon	Brodribb *et al.* 1968,	CswM
		1973, 1978	Wi
			moss sw
Stonesfield	Oxon	Pointer 1713	Cs
?Stonesfield	Oxon	Morrison 1959	Cs

EARLY SAXON AD410–AD800

Cainhoe	Beds	Taylor & Woodward 1974	Ww
Bancroft, Milton Keynes	Bucks	(Keeley 1982	Sa
		(Spencer 1982	M
Walton, Aylesbury	Bucks	Farley 1976	CsIs
Aldwincle	Northants	Jackson 1977	Ww
Chalk Lane, Northampton	Northants	Williams & Shaw 1981	Cw
Rothwell	Northants	Jessen & Helbaek 1944	Is
Abingdon	Oxon	Jessen & Helbaek 1944	Is
Barton Court, Abingdon	Oxon	(Robinson 1981a, 1981b)	(CsMP
		(Miles forthcoming)	(Wisw
Bishop's Court, Dorchester	Oxon	Robinson 1981a, 1981b	Wisw
Mingie's Ditch, Hardwick	Oxon	Robinson 1981a	Sa
Mount Farm, Berinsfield	Oxon	Robinson i	Wis
Shakenoak	Oxon	Brodribb *et al.* 1972	CwM

LATE SAXON AD800–AD1066

Walton, Aylesbury	Bucks	Farley 1976	CsRs
Chalk Lane, Northampton	Northants	Williams & Shaw 1981	Cw
Marefair, Northampton	Northants	Straker 1979, Williams F, 1979	Cs
St. James Square, Northampton	Northants	Watson 1981	Ww
St. Peter's Street, Northampton	Northants	Williams J, 1979	WisM
All Saints, Oxford	Oxon	Robinson o	Cisw
Oxford Castle	Oxon	Hassall 1976	Cw
St. Aldates, Oxford	Oxon	Durham 1977	(Sa
			(Wims

MEDIEVAL AD1066–AD1500

Empire Cinema, Bedford	Beds	Keepax 1979b	Cw
Pitstone	Bucks	Evans 1966	M
Lyveden	Northants	Bryant & Steane 1969, 1971	Cw
Marefair, Northampton	Northants	Straker 1979, Williams F, 1979	CsRs
St. Peter's Street, Northampton	Northants	Williams J, 1979	Cs
Bicester	Oxon	Robinson 1981c	Ws
Blackfriars, Oxford	Oxon	Lambrick & Woods 1976	MSa
Chalgrove	Oxon	Robinson p	Csw
			MWs
Church Street, Oxford	Oxon	Hassall 1969	CsWs
Cornmarket Street, Oxford	Oxon	Hassall 1971	Ris

Folly Bridge, Oxford	Oxon	Robinson q	Cs
Hamel, Oxford	Oxon	Palmer 1980	(Cs
			(Wisw
Hell Passage, Oxford	Oxon	Palmer 1976	(Wis)
Middleton Stoney	Oxon	(Rowley 1972	MS
		(Robinson r	(CsRis
			(M
Old Gaol, Abingdon	Oxon	Parrington 1975	Cs
Oxford Castle	Oxon	Grensted 1953	M
Oxford Castle	Oxon	(Hassall 1976	Wiw
		(Brown	(W
			(moss s
St. Aldates, Oxford	Oxon	Durham 1977	(W
			(parasite
			(ova
Seacourt	Oxon	Biddle 1961–2	Csw
Stert Street, Abingdon	Oxon	Parrington 1979	CsRis
Tetsworth	Oxon	Robinson 1973	CsM

POST MEDIEVAL AD1500–Present Day

Church Street, Oxford	Oxon	Robinson 1982	Rs
Frewin Hall, Oxford	Oxon	Blair 1978	Ws
High Street, Oxford	Oxon	Robinson 1982	M
Oriel College, Oxford	Oxon	Robinson 1982	Wis

Needs and priorities for environmental archaeology in the region

Research Priorities and Future Work in the Region

Plants, Invertebrates and Soils

Unless the effort put into environmental archaeology in the region is greatly increased, it will take more than twenty years to achieve most of the aims given below. It must be remembered that some sorts of site are much rarer than others and this has influenced the choice of priority: all Neolithic waterlogged deposits are declared to be of interest but only certain Roman deposits, not because the Neolithic environment is regarded as inherently more interesting than the Roman environment, merely that one cannot afford to be selective about Neolithic deposits. Aims are however, different for some periods. From the late Saxon period onwards, much information about man's environment can more readily be obtained from documentary sources or field survey than 'environmental archaeology'. In the Post-Medieval period, only investigations with very precise and limited aims are likely to be of much value, general investigation of, for example, the full range of plants and invertebrates preserved on a waterlogged Post-Medieval site is unlikely to yield results that would justify the effort expended.

Rescue archaeology will be capable of supplying most of the material necessary for fulfilling the research projects which have been listed. Sometimes threatened deposits will have to be excavated solely for the environmental information they will yield. Occasionally it will be necessary to investigate contexts which are not threatened in order to elucidate problems which have been created by work elsewhere or to provide background information related to threatened sites.

Important Projects – these are not listed in any order of priority.

a. Investigation of any deep peat deposits which can provide a long sequence for pollen and perhaps insects. Just a few deposits of this sort exist in the region, for example at Cothill Fen on the Oxford Heights, where a falling water table is threatening preservation of the post-Mesolithic peat, which has never been investigated. It is possible that suitable peat deposits exist in the Swerford Fault, which would give otherwise unobtainable information about the Cotswolds. Such deposits can provide a background of general vegetational change within a part of the region against which the archaeology of that area can be set.

b. Investigation of any Mesolithic occupation sites to their full potential for plant and invertebrate remains.

c. Investigation of all Neolithic and Bronze Age occupation sites with waterlogged deposits to their full potential for plants and invertebrates. Investigation of other dated waterlogged deposits up until the end of the Bronze Age.

d. Investigation of charred seeds and chaff from Neolithic and Bronze Age sites. Any site of this date producing large quantities of carbonised cereal remains is of considerable importance.

e. Examination of all sealed Neolithic and Bronze Age soils. If they are acidic they should also be investigated for pollen, if they are calcareous they should be investigated for molluscs. In some parts of the region, for example on the gravel terraces of the major river valleys, sealed soils are so rarely encountered that all should be examined up to the Saxon period.

f. Investigation of both carbonised and waterlogged material from hillforts or *oppida* to their full potential.

g. Investigation of waterlogged material to its full potential from Belgic occupation sites. Little work has been done on this transition period and it would be useful to establish whether many of the species thought of as Roman introductions had arrived just before the conquest.

h. Investigation of macroscopic waterlogged material from inside a Roman town. It has yet to be established whether insect faunas from Roman towns in the region have a full urban character and whether various exotic plants were imported by the towns. Such an investigation should provide a useful contrast to the considerable work that has been done on Roman rural sites in the region.

i. Investigation of carbonised seeds and chaff from early Saxon sites which do not have earlier occupation. It is uncertain whether spelt wheat remained in cultivation in the region after the end of the Roman period and residual Roman or Iron Age material has caused confusion on sites so far investigated. Even a relatively small scale investigation would be of value.

j. Investigation of macroscopic waterlogged material and carbonised seeds/chaff from Medieval rural occupation sites. So little work has been done on such sites within the region that even limited investigations would be useful.

k. Investigation of waterlogged material for macroscopic remains from upper class and monastic urban Medieval sites. Insects could be used to assess whether conditions were any cleaner than on lower class urban sites, where filth prevailed. Interesting dietary information could be obtained from plant remains in latrine deposits.

l. Further investigations of archaeological sites interstratified with alluvium, their stratigraphy, the Mollusca in the alluvium and sedimentological studies on the alluvium. Much work still needs to be done in the upper Thames Valley to establish when phases of alluviation occurred, how conditions on the floodplain changed, why the flooding occurred and where the sediments originated. These studies ought to be extended to the Ouse and Nene drainage systems.

m. Investigation of hillwash deposits on the Downs and Cotswolds in order to extend the useful work that has already been done on the Chilterns. In particular, it is important to date such deposits, although molluscan and sedimentological studies are also needed.

n. Pollen analyses of sealed acidic soils from Iron Age to early Medieval date on the Chilterns in an attempt to discover when beech woodland became established there.

o. Extension of the type of major integrated investigations of carbonised and waterlogged remains which have been undertaken on Iron Age to Saxon sites on the Thames gravels to other parts of the region and sites on the other soils. Such investigations are expensive and it will not be possible to undertake them on all suitable sites revealed by rescue archaeology. Priority ought to be given to sites with a long duration of occupation that spans several transitional periods of landscape development, and sites where the environment is likely to have been very different from the Thames gravels.

Other Investigations The projects which have been suggested certainly do not cover all possible environmental archaeology investigations which could be undertaken on threatened sites in the region. It will still be necessary to do some additional work along the following guidelines:

a. Large scale investigations on major archaeological sites where it is thought important that all aspects of their archaeology ought to be examined, for example on extensive 'landscape' excavations. The results of the environmental studies themselves on such sites may not be very original, but they will be associated with much better archaeological information than previously.

b. Limited and carefully planned investigations aimed at answering particular archaeological or environmental problems that a site may raise.

c. Monitoring work on excavations in order to confirm that the sites indeed show the trends that would be expected of them. Full investigations can then be undertaken on unusual sites and 'special' deposits. A particular problem is likely to be presented by the Medieval towns in the region. It is possible that much material suitable for environmental investigations will be excavated in the near future, but with the present resources available, only limited work can be undertaken on urban sites, unless they are to predominate in the work programme. The main aim ought to be to compare results with those obtained for York and London, where very large scale investigations are taking place.

In order to assist with obtaining and interpreting the results from ancient deposits, some research will be required into practical and interpretative methodology. This will include ecological survey of modern habitats for comparative purposes. It will also be necessary to prepare syntheses/reviews of the results from many sites along particular themes. Only by undertaking some methodological and synthetic work will it be possible to maximise the amount of useful information obtained from each site investigated. It should reveal new lines of research and avoid unnecessary work in fields which are either unprofitable or about which sufficient is known already.

Animal and Human Bones

General Excavation Needs Systematic selection and excavation of major sites must obtain a comprehensive view of each and its social and ecological relationships to other sites nearby. The method must allow for problems of site destruction, the variability and complexity of deposition, and the preservation and recovery of bones. Obviously it is necessary for environmentalists and excavators to specify useful and realistic aims of reporting and to anticipate logistical difficulties, such as the use of manpower, at early stages of planning. Consultation and review of aims and their results is important. This already occurs for sites excavated on the Thames gravels by the Oxfordshire Archaeological Unit.

Selective examination and excavation of small or physically restricted sites may yield useful contexts and deposits of particular interest where major excavations are not possible or have low priority.

A ranking of the general usefulness of animal bones from each period, and which therefore is a guide to excavation priorities, is as follows: Mesolithic, Neolithic, Bronze Age, early and middle Saxon, post medieval, and then lastly about equally less useful: iron age, Romano-British and medieval material. Prehistoric human bones are obviously uncommon and to be sought for. Particular interests and problems of the material from each period are outlined below. It must be clear that future studies need well defined objectives before commencement.

Site Type and Excavation Priorities The following types of site deserve greater attention:

a. All types of mesolithic to bronze age site and those of early to middle Saxon period. Also sites of unusual form, should be investigated.

b. Iron Age: hill forts and *oppida*.

c. Romano-British: investigations of the overall organisation of palatial villas, 'Celtic' villages, town, military and religious sites.

d. Saxon and medieval sites: manor farms, deserted medieval villages, castles, specialised (not domestic) urban sites, and monastic sites.

e. Post medieval: farmsteads, and industrial sites processing animal products.

Types of Bone Material

a. Sieved debris This should provide a worthwhile recovery of information on small animals rarely or not yet recorded. Sieving should be planned to give sample control of excavation, and of depositional variables. Unless a specific study of bone degradation is proposed, priority should be given to sieving soil which is well stratified, well sealed, reliably datable and which contains well preserved bones. Only properly rationalised studies which use manpower economically should be undertaken.

b. Normally recovered bones As excavations attain or maintain high standards, this bone material will give diminishing returns of general information, but as the number of available bones increase more specialised studies become feasible.

c. Complete skeletons and other articulated bones Their relative scarcity means that further discoveries will yield valuable information on man and other animals.

d. Backlogs of site material All collections need individual assessments which will maximise the return of information without succumbing to the inherent difficulties associated with sites which may be small, or quickly or poorly excavated. Some of these site collections may be important e.g. from large scale excavation or rubbish pits in towns, because excavations of that type may never be repeated for economic or other reasons. Exceptionally large regional collections of bones which are being studied or require study are those from Church Street, Oxford, and Raunds, Northants.

Methods of analysis While basic report information is collected from every site, particular studies are necessary where they will ease interpretation and increase the informativeness of each collection and subsequent ones. This is a logical extension of beneficial developments already made. For example soil sampling and sieving (see fish bones in medieval section). Current studies of spatial relationships of bone degradation and human activity at Hardwick are providing new areas of evidence and explanation (see Iron Age section).

Advances in analysis satisfy two needs.

a.   The efficiency of general reporting is increased by focusing on problems generated by the variation among data from one or several sites.

b.   There is a greater return to the public of 'real', that is, coherent knowledge rather than of fragmentary details.

Because bone studies are an immature science, many developments of method are required. To some extent these can be achieved by the specialists among themselves. Such developments should, however, and where appropriate, be specifically acknowledged and fostered by the closer co-ordination of excavators, museum, university and Historic Buildings and Monuments Commission administrators and other relevant personnel (Wilson *et al.* 1982 1–5). One area of assistance would be in providing quick, moderately priced means of publication and distribution of more specialised work.

Present Staffing and Fields of Work

Our fields of study at the University Museum, Oxford, are at present: mammal bones (R Wilson); waterlogged macroscopic plant remains including a limited amount of work on wood; insects; and land and freshwater molluscs (M Robinson). The major fields which are not covered are: human bones; bird bones; fish bones; pollen; carbonised plant remains; soils and sediments; and larger projects on wood identification. There are also various other subjects of less general application, such as bryophytes and parasitic nematodes from cess pits, which cannot be covered by us at present.

The region is producing more worthwhile material from rescue archaeology sites in our special fields than we can cope with adequately in every respect, particularly the backlog of bones.

The Extent of the Region

The Department of the Environment originally defined the region which should be covered by Oxford as the counties of Bedfordshire, Buckinghamshire, Northamptonshire and Oxfordshire. The differences between this administrative area and a coherent geographical region of the Upper Thames, Nene and Ouse basins are not great, but some practical modifications to the administrative boundaries could be made.

Since Buckinghamshire to the south of the Chilterns and along the north bank of the Middle Thames is incorporated, the region could be extended to take in the Berkshire bank of the Thames, the Kennet Valley and the dip slope of the Downs. Such an extension has several merits. Alluvial problems will be the same on either side of the River Thames and a long-term study of the Upper Thames alluvium is already being undertaken. Oxford is also a suitable place to work on the waterlogged deposits which are likely to be encountered in the Kennet Valley of Berkshire and the north-east corner of Wiltshire. All of this area is relatively close to Oxford.

Another practical extension is the investigation of material from the Upper Thames gravels beyond Oxfordshire, into Wiltshire and Gloucestershire. Such coverage has been initiated in conjunction with the Oxfordshire Archaeological Unit, which is currently excavating an extensive cropmark site at Claydon Pike, Gloucestershire. A large part of the Gloucestershire Cotswolds falls within the Thames basin, but they are better suited to being covered from the Department of the Environment funded laboratory in Bristol.

That part of the Welland Valley which is in Northamptonshire and the high ground above it would be better served from elsewhere. It is not an integral part of the region and is a long way from Oxford. The north-east extremity of the Nene Valley in Northamptonshire is likewise distant from Oxford.

BIBLIOGRAPHY

Abbreviations: AB = animal bones
                HB = human bones
                MM = marine molluscs

ALEXANDER J, 1967

'Cogenhoe', *Bull Northamptonshire Fed Archaeol Soc* 2, 9.

ALLISON E, n.d.

Identifications (AB) in Wilson R, in preparation e.

APPLEBAUM S, 1978

'The agriculture of Shakenoak Villa' in Brodribb *et al.*, 1978, 5, 186–196.

ARKELL W J, 1939

'The site of Cherbury Camp', *Oxoniensia* 4, 196–197.

ARKELL W J, 1947

The geology of Oxford.

ARMITAGE P, 1976

Report (AB) in Parrington M, 'Roman Finds and animal bones from Kingston Hill Farm, Kingston Bagpuize', *Oxoniensia* 41, 68–69.

ARMITAGE P, 1978

Report (AB) in Parrington M, 1978, 126.

ARMITAGE P, forthcoming

Report (AB) in Miles D, forthcoming.

ARMITAGE P, unpublished

'Report on the cattle horn cores from Greyfriars, Oxford'.

ASHCROFT D, 1934–40

'Report on the excavation of a Romano-British villa at Saunderton, Buckinghamshire', *Rec Buckinghamshire* 13, 398–426.

ATKINSON R J C, 1946–47

'A middle Bronze Age barrow at Cassington, Oxon', *Oxoniensia* 11–12, 5–26.

ATKINSON R J C, PIGGOT C M, SANDERS N K, 1957

Excavations at Dorchester, Oxon. 1.

AVERY M, SUTTON J E G, BANKS J W, 1967

'Rainsborough, Northants. England: excavations 1961–5', *Proc Prehist Soc* 33, 207–306.

BAKER H, 1937

'Alluvial meadows; a comparative study of grazed and mown meadows', *J Ecol* 25, 408–420.

BANKS J W, 1961

Report (AB) in Radcliffe F, 'Excavations at Logic Lane, Oxford', *Oxoniensia* 26–27, 64–67.

BANKS J W, 1966

Report (AB) in Hamlin A, 1966, 22.

BANKS J W, 1967

Report (AB & HB) in Avery M, *et al.*, 1967, 302–305.

BARFIELD L H, 1977

'The excavation of a Mesolithic site at Gerrards Cross, Bucks.', *Rec Buckinghamshire* 20 pt 3, 308–336.

BARKER G, WEBLEY D, 1978

'Causewayed camps and early Neolithic economies', *Proc Prehist Soc* 44, 161–186.

BAYLEY J, 1976

Report (HB) in Jackson D A, 'The excavation of Neolithic and Bronze Age sites at Aldwincle, Northants. 1967–71', *Northamptonshire Archaeol* 11, 70.

BAYLEY J, 1978

Report (HB) in Jackson D A and Ambrose T M, 1978, 234–235.

BAYLEY J, 1981

Report (HB) in Allen D, 'The excavation of a Beaker burial monument at Ravenstone, Bucks. in 1978', *Archaeol J* 138, 72–117.

BAYNE N, 1957

'Excavations at Lyneham Camp, Lyneham, Oxon.', *Oxoniensia* 22, 1–10.

BENSON D, MILES D, 1974

The Upper Thames Valley: an archaeological survey of the river gravels, Oxfordshire Archaeological Unit Survey 2.

BIDDICK K, 1980

Report (AB) in Pryor F, 1980, 217–232.

BIDDLE M, 1961–62

'The deserted Medieval village of Seacourt, Berkshire', *Oxoniensia* 26–27, 70–201.

BLACKWOOD B M, 1945

Report (HB) in Horden D B and Trewecks R C, 'Excavations at Stanton Harcourt, Oxon. 1940 II', *Oxoniensia* 10, 33–34.

BLAIR J, 1978

'Frewin Hall Oxford: a Norman mansion and a monastic college', *Oxoniensia* 43, 48–99.

BOWLER D, ROBINSON M, 1980

'Three round barrows at King's Weir, Wytham, Oxon.', *Oxoniensia* 45, 1–8.

BRADLEY R, ELLISON A, 1975

Rams Hill: a Bronze Age defended enclosure and its landscape, Brit Archaeol Rep 19.

BRAMWELL D, 1973

Report (AB) in Robinson M A, 1973, 115.

BRAMWELL D *et al.* 1975

'The animal bones from the Broad Street and Old Gaol sites (Abingdon)', *Oxoniensia* 40, 120–121.

BRAMWELL D, 1976

Report (AB) in Farley M, 1976, 287–289.

BRAMWELL D, 1978a

Report (AB) in Williams J H, 'Excavations at Greyfriars, Northampton 1972', *Northamptonshire Archaeol* 13, 159.

BRAMWELL D, 1978b

Report (AB) in Parrington M, 1978, 133.

BRAMWELL D, 1979a

Report (AB) in Williams F, 1979, 78.

BRAMWELL D, 1979b

Report (AB) in Lambrick G H and Robinson M A, 1979, 133.

BRAMWELL D, forthcoming

Report (AB) in Miles D, forthcoming.

BRAMWELL D, unpublished

Report (AB) from Thenford Villa, Northamptonshire. Copy held by M Robinson, Oxford University Museum.

BRAMWELL D, HARMAN M, 1979

Report (AB) in Williams J H, 1979, 333.

BRAMWELL D, WILSON R, 1979

Report (AB) in Parrington M, 1979, 20–21.

BRAMWELL D, WILSON R, 1980

Report (AB) in Palmer N, 1980, fiche F08–09.

BRANIGAN K, 1971

Latimer. Also report (MM) 166–167.

BRANIGAN K, KING J E, 1965

'A Roman cat from Latimer Villa', *Annals Mag Natur Hist* 8, 451–463.

BRODRIBB A C C, HANDS A R, WALKER D R, 1968, 1972, 1973 and 1978

Excavations at Shakenoak Farm, near Wilcote, Oxfordshire pts 1, 3, 4 and 5. Also Report (AB) 3, 129–130.

BROTHWELL D, 1962

Report (HB) in Matthews C L, 'The Anglo-Saxon cemetery at Marina Drive, Dunstable', *Bedfordshire Archaeol J* 1, 25–33.

BROTHWELL D, 1976

Report (HB) in Matthew C L, *Occupation sites on a Chiltern ridge: excavations at Puddlehill and sites near Dunstable*, Brit Archaeol Rep 29, 22–24.

BROWN A, unpublished

'Waterlogged plant remains from the Barbican ditch of Oxford Castle'.

BRYANT G F, STEANE J M, 1969

'Excavations at the deserted Medieval settlement at Lyveden, a second interim report', *J Northampton Mus* 5.

BRYANT G F, STEANE J M, 1971

'Excavations at the deserted Medieval settlement at Lyveden, a third interim report', *J Northampton Mus* 9.

CARTER H H, 1975a — Report (AB) in Bradley R and Ellison A, 1975, 118–122.

CARTER H H, 1975b — 'A guide to rates of tooth wear in English lowland sheep', *J Archaeol Sci* 2, 231–233.

CARTER H H, unpublished — Report (AB) for Corporation Farm, Abingdon. Copy held by author c/o Reading Museum, Blagrave Street, Reading.

CASE H, 1956 — 'The Neolithic causewayed camp at Abingdon, Berks.', *Antiq J* 36, 16–18.

CASE H, 1963 — 'Notes on the finds and on ring ditches in the Oxford region', *Oxoniensia* 28, 19–51.

CASE H, BAYNE N, STEELE S, AVERY G, SUTERMEISTER H, 1964–65 — 'Excavations at City Farm, Hanborough, Oxon.', *Oxoniensia* 29–30, 1–98.

CASE H, STURDY D, 1959 — 'Crowmarsh Gifford, Oxon.', *Oxoniensia* 24, 99.

CASE H J, WHITTLE A W R, 1982 — *Settlement patterns in the Oxford region: excavations at the Abingdon causewayed enclosure and other sites*, Counc Brit Archaeol Res Rep 41.

CHILDE V G, SMITH I F, 1954 — 'Excavation of a Neolithic barrow on Whiteleaf Hill, Bucks.', *Proc Prehist Soc* 20, 212–230.

CLAPHAM A R, CLAPHAM B N, 1939 — 'The valley fen at Cothill, Berkshire', *New Phytol* 38, 167–174.

COCKS A H, 1897 — 'The Romano-British dwelling at Hedsor', *Rec Bucks* 7, 545–549.

COCKS A H, 1909a — 'Prehistoric dwellings at Ellesborough', *Rec Bucks* 9, 356–361.

COCKS A H, 1909b — 'Exploration of a 'natural barrow' at Stone', *Rec Bucks* 9, 263–279.

COCKS A H, 1921 — 'A Romano-British homestead in the Hambledon Valley, Buckinghamshire', *Archaeologia* 71, 163–166.

CONCANNON R J G, 1972 — Report (HB) in Hassall T G, 'Roman finds from the Radcliffe Science Library extension, Oxford. 1970–71', *Oxoniensia* 37, 43–45.

COOPE G R, 1976 — 'Assemblages of Fossil Coleoptera from terraces of the Upper Thames near Oxford', in Roe D (ed), *Quaternary Research Association Field Guide to the Oxford Region*, 20–22.

CORNWALL I W, 1953 — 'Soil science and archaeology from some British Bronze Age monuments', *Proc Prehist Soc* 19, 129–147.

COTTON M A, FRERE S S, 1968 — 'Ivinghoe Beacon excavations 1963–5', *Rec Buckinghamshire* 18 pt 3, 187–260.

COWLES G S, 1981 — 'The first evidence of Demoiselle Crane *Anthropoides virgo* and Pigmy Cormorant *Phalacrocorax pygmaeus* in Britain', *Bull Brit Ornith Comm* 101(4), 383–385.

COWLEY L F, 1943–44 — Report (HB) in Grimes W F, 'Excavations at Stanton Harcourt, 1940', *Oxoniensia* 8–9, 61–64.

COY J P, 1981 — Report (AB) in Williams J H and Shaw M, 1981, 134.

CRAM C L, 1973 — Report (AB) in Brodribb *et al.* 1973, 4, 145–164.

CRAM C L, 1978 — Report (AB) in Brodribb *et al.* 1978, 5, 117–160, 171–178.

CRAM C L, 1982 — Report (AB) in Case H J and Whittle A W R, 1982, 43–47.

DENSTON C B, 1973 — Report in Brodribb *et al.*, 1973, 4, 172–183.

DENSTON C B, 1974 — Report (HB) in Green H S, 1974, 93–97.

DENSTON C B, 1976 — Report (HB) in Jackson D A, 'The excavation of Neolithic and Bronze Age sites at Aldwincle Northants., 1967–71', *Northamptonshire Archaeol* 11, 66–69.

DENSTON C B, 1978 — Report (HB) in Gray M and Clayton N, 'Excavations on the site of Eynsham Abbey, 1971', *Oxoniensia* 43, 102.

DIMBLEBY G W, EVANS J G, 1974 — 'Pollen and land-snail analysis of calcareous soils', *J Archaeol Sci* 1, 117–133.

DRUCE G C, 1886 — *The Flora of Oxfordshire.*

DUDLEY-BUXTON L H, 1928 — Note (AB) in Leeds T H, 'A Neolithic site at Abingdon, Berks.', *Antiq J* 8, 476.

DURHAM B, 1977 — 'Archaeological investigations in St. Aldates, Oxford.', *Oxoniensia* 42, 83–203.

DYER J F, 1962 — 'Neolithic and Bronze Age sites at Barton Hill Farm, Bedfordshire', *Bedfordshire Archaeol J* 1, 1–24.

EASTHAM A, 1980 — Report (AB) in Lambrick G, 'Excavations at Park Street, Towcester', *Northamptonshire Archaeol* 15, 112–113.

EDWARDS E, 1976 — Report (HB) in Lambrick G H and Woods H, 1976, 226–229.

EDWARDS E, 1978 — Report (HB) in Parrington M, 1978, 90–92.

EDWARDS E, 1980 — Report (HB) in Hinchliffe J and Thomas R, 1980, 84.

ELTON C S, 1966 — *The pattern of animal communities.*

EMERY F, 1974 — *The Oxfordshire landscape.*

EVANS J G, 1966 — 'Late-Glacial and Post-Glacial sub aerial deposits at Pitstone, Buckinghamshire', *Proc Geol Ass* 77, 347–364.

EVANS J G, 1971 — 'Habitat change on the calcareous soils of Britain, the impact of Neolithic man', in Simpson D D A (ed), *Economy and settlement in Neolithic and early Bronze Age Britain and Europe*, 27–73.

EVANS J G, 1972 — *Land snails in archaeology.*

EVANS J G, JONES H, 1973 — 'Subfossil and modern landsnail faunas from rock-rubble habitats', *J Conchology* 28, 103–129.

EVANS J G, VALENTINE K W G, 1974 — 'Ecological changes induced by prehistoric man at Pitstone, Buckinghamshire', *J Archaeol Sci* 1, 343–351.

EVERSON P, 1976 — 'Iron Age enclosures at Queensway Health Centre Site, Hardwick Park, Wellingborough', *Northamptonshire Archaeol* 11, 89–99.

EWBANK J M, 1964 — Report (AB) in Field N H *et al.*, 1964, 364–366.

FARLEY M, 1976 — 'Saxon and Medieval Walton, Aylesbury: excavations 1973–4', *Rec Buckinghamshire* 20 pt 2, 153–290.

FARLEY M, WRIGHT R, 1979 — 'An early Romano-British inhumation group at West Wycombe', *Rec Buckinghamshire* 21, 85–88.

FIELD N H, MATTHEWS C L, SMITH I F, 1964 — 'New Neolithic sites in Dorset and Bedfordshire, with a note on the distribution of Neolithic storage pits in Britain', *Proc Prehist Soc* 30, 352–381.

FIELD D, 1977 — Report (AB) in Mynard D C and Woodfield C, 'A Roman Site at Walton, Milton Keynes', *Rec Buckinghamshire* 20(3), 377–81.

FOWLER P J, 1960 — 'Excavations at Madmarston Camp, Swalcliffe, 1957–8', *Oxoniensia* 25, 3–48.

FRAZER F C, 1940 — Report (AB) in Head J F, 'Excavation of the Cop Round Barrow, Bledlow', *Rec Buckinghamshire* 8, 344–346.

FRAZER F C, 1946 — Report (AB) in Head J F and Piggott C M, 1946.

FRAZER F C, 1956 — Report (AB) in Case H, 1956, 16–18.

GEORGE T J, 1917 — *Hunsbury*. Also (AB) 33.

GILMORE F A, 1969a — Report (AB) in Woods P J, *Excavations at Hardingstone, Northants. 1967–8*, Northants County Council, 43–55.

GILMORE F A, 1969b — Report (AB) in Bryant G F and Steane J M, 1969, 47–48.

GODWIN H, 1940 — 'Pollen analysis and forest history of England and Wales', *New Phytol* 39, 370–400.

GOODY J R, 1948 — Report (HB) in Williams A, 'Excavations in Barrow Hills Field, Radley, Berkshire 1944', *Oxoniensia* 13, 15–17.

GRANT A, 1970 — Report (AB) in Baker D, 'Excavations in Bedford 1967', *Bedfordshire Archaeol J* 5, 94–96.

GRANT A, 1971 — Report (AB) in Bryant G F and Steane J M, 1971, 90–93.

GRANT A, 1975a — Report (AB) in Bryant G F and Steane J M, 1975, (Lyveden) *J Northampton Mus* 12, 152–57.

GRANT A, 1975b — Report (AB) in Hassall J, 'Excavations at Willington 1973' *Bedfordshire Archaeol J* 10, 38–39.

GRANT A, 1978 — Report (AB) in Bradley R, 'Rescue excavations in Dorchester-on-Thames 1972', *Oxoniensia* 43, 32–36.

GRANT A, 1981 — Report (AB) in Rowley T and Brown L, 'Excavations at Beech House Hotel, Dorchester-on-Thames 1972', *Oxoniensia* 46, 50–55.

GREEN H S, 1974 — 'Early Bronze Age burial, territory and population in Milton Keynes, Buckinghamshire and the Great Ouse Valley', *Archaeol J* 131, 75–139.

GREEN H S, 1976 — 'The excavation of a late Neolithic settlement at Stacey Bushes, Milton Keynes, and its significance', in Burgess C and Miket R (ed), *Settlement and economy in the third and second millennia BC* 11–27, Brit Archaeol Rep 33.

GREEN M J, 1975 — *The Bradwell Roman villa, first interim report*, Occas Papers in Archaeol, Milton Keynes Dev Corp.

GRENSTED L W, 1953 — *Excavations at Nuffield College, August 1953. The Mollusca.* Typescript with specimens in the geological collections of the University Museum, Oxford.

GRIGSON C, 1976 — Report (AB) in Matthews C L, *Occupation sites on a Chiltern ridge: Excavations at Puddlehill and sites near Dunstable*, Brit Archaeol Rep Brit ser 29, 11–18.

GRIGSON C, 1982a — 'Porridge and pannage: pig husbandry in Neolithic England', in Bell M and Limbrey S, *Archaeological aspects of Woodland ecology*, Brit Archaeol Rep Inter Ser 146, 297–314.

GRIGSON C, 1982b — 'Sexing Neolithic domestic cattle skulls and horn cores', in Wilson R, Grigson C and Payne S (ed), 1982, 25–35.

HALL D N, 1973 — 'Rescue excavations at Radwell gravel pits 1972', *Bedfordshire Archaeol J* 8, 67–91.

HALL D N, NICKERSON N, 1966 — 'Sites on the North Bedfordshire and South Northamptonshire Border', *Bedfordshire Archaeol J* 3, 1–6.

HAMILTON J, 1978 — 'A comparison of the age structure at mortality of some Iron Age and Romano-British sheep and cattle populations', in Parrington M, 1978, 126–133.

HAMILTON R, 1971 — Report (AB) in Branigan K, 1971, 163–166.

HAMLIN A, 1966 — 'Early Iron Age sites at Stanton Harcourt', *Oxoniensia* 31, 1–27.

HARCOURT R A, 1974 — Report (AB) in Neal D, *The excavation of the Roman villa in Gadebridge Park, Hemel Hempstead*, Soc Antiq Res Rep 31, 261.

HARCOURT R, 1975 — Report (AB) in Jackson D A, 1975, 88–89.

HARMAN M, 1976a — Report (HB) in Chambers R A, 'A Romano-British settlement at Curbridge', *Oxoniensia* 41, 47–49.

HARMAN M, 1976b — Report (HB) in Chambers R A, 'The cemetery site at Beacon Hill near Lewkenor, Oxon., 1972', *Oxoniensia* 41, 80–83.

HARMAN M, 1976c — Report (AB) in Williams J, 'Excavations at a Roman site at Overston near Northampton', *Northamptonshire Archaeol* 11, 130–131.

HARMAN M, 1977 — Report (AB) in Hunter R and Maynard D, 'Excavations at Thorplands near Northampton, 1970 and 1974', *Northamptonshire Archaeol* 12, 144–145.

HARMAN M, 1978a — Report (HB) in Chambers R A, 'The archaeology of the Charlbury to Arncott gas pipeline, Oxon. 1972', *Oxoniensia* 43, 47.

HARMAN M, 1978b — Report (AB) in Jackson D A, 'Neolithic and Bronze Age activity in the Harringworth area', *Northamptonshire Archaeol* 13, 6.

HARMAN M, 1978c — Report (AB) in Pryor F, *Excavations at Fengate, Peterborough, England; 2nd report*, Royal Ontario Mus monogr 5, 177–188.

HARMAN M, 1978d — Report (AB) in Williams J H, 'Excavations at Greyfriars, Northampton 1972', *Northamptonshire Archaeol* 13, 157.

HARMAN M, 1978e — Report (HB) in Harman M, Lambrick G, Miles D and Rowley T, 'Roman burials around Dorchester-on-Thames', *Oxoniensia* 43, 1–11.

HARMAN M, 1979a — Report (AB) in Williams F, 1979, 77–78.

HARMAN M, 1979b — Report (AB) in Williams J H, 1979, 328–332.

HARMAN M, 1980 — Report (AB) in McGavin N, 'A Roman cemetery and trackway at Stanton Harcourt', *Oxoniensia* 45, 120–122.

HARMAN M, 1981a — Report (AB) in Williams J H and Shaw M, 1981, 132–134.

HARMAN M, 1981b — Report (HB) in Harman M and Wilson R A, 'A medieval graveyard beside Faringdon Road, Abingdon', *Oxoniensia* 46, 59–60.

HARMAN M, unpublished — Report (HB) in Miles D and Brown D, 'Excavations at Wally Corner, Berinsfield, Oxon'.

HARMAN M, MOLLESON T I, PRICE J L, 1981 — 'Burials, bodies and beheadings in Romano-British and Anglo Saxon cemeteries', *Bull Brit Mus Natur Hist (geol)* 35(3), 145–188.

HARRISON G A, WEINER G S, TANNER J M, BARNICOT N A, 1977 — *Human Biology: an introduction into human evolution, variation, growth and ecology* (2nd edition), Oxford University Press, Oxford.

HASSALL T G, 1969 — 'Excavations at Oxford 1968: first interim report', *Oxoniensia* 34, 5–20.

HASSALL T G, 1971 — 'Excavations at 44–46 Cornmarket Street, Oxford, 1970', *Oxoniensia* 36, 15–33.

HASSALL T G, 1976 — 'Excavations at Oxford Castle, 1965–73', *Oxoniensia* 41, 232–308.

HAWKES C F C, 1940 — 'A site of the late Bronze–early Iron Age transition at Totternhoe, Bedfordshire', *Antiq J* 20, 487–491.

HAZELDEN J, JARVIS M G, 1979 — 'Age and significance of alluvium in the Windrush valley, Oxfordshire', *Nature* 282, 291–292.

HAZELDEN J, JARVIS M G, 1980 — 'Reply to R D Wilmot', *Nature* 284, 574.

HEAD J F, 1939–40 — 'The excavation of the Cop Round Barrow, Bledlow', *Rec Buckinghamshire* 13, 313–351.

HEAD J F, PIGGOTT C M, 1941–46 — 'An Iron Age site at Bledlow, Bucks.', *Rec Buckinghamshire* 14, 189–209.

HELBAEK H, 1952 — 'Early crops in Southern England', *Proc Prehist Soc* 18, 194–233.

HINCHLIFFE J, 1975 — 'Excavations at Grim's Ditch, Mongewell, 1974', *Oxoniensia* 40, 122–135.

HINCHLIFFE J, THOMAS R, 1980 — 'Archaeological investigations at Appleford', *Oxoniensia* 45, 9–111.

HOGG A H A, STEVENS C E, 1937 — 'The defences of Roman Dorchester', *Oxoniensia* 2, 41–73.

HOLLOWELL R, 1971 — 'Aerial photography and fieldwork in the Upper Nene Valley', *Bull Northamptonshire Fed Archaeol Soc* 6, 1–21.

HOLLOWELL R, 1972 — 'Ecton Gravel Pit', *Bull Northamptonshire Fed Archaeol Soc* 7, 3.

HUGHES D R, DENSTON C B, 1968 — Report (HB) in Brodribb A C C *et al.*, 1, 116–120.

JACKSON D A, 1970 — 'Earls Barton', *Bull Northamptonshire Fed Archaeol Soc* 4, 47.

JACKSON D A, 1972 — 'The Earls Barton Barrow', *Current Archaeol* 3, 238–241.

JACKSON D A, 1975 — 'An Iron Age site at Twywell, Northamptonshire', *Northamptonshire Archaeol* 10, 31–93.

JACKSON D A, 1977 — 'Further excavations at Aldwincle, Northamptonshire, 1969–71', *Northamptonshire Archaeol* 12, 9–54.

JACKSON D A, AMBROSE T M, 1978 — 'Excavations at Wakerley, Northants. 1972–75', *Britannia* 9, 115–242.

JACKSON W J, 1961 — Report (AB) in Clifford E M, *Bagendon: a Belgic oppidum*, 268–71.

JARVIS M G, 1973 — *Soils of the Wantage and Abingdon District*, Memoirs of the Soil Survey of Great Britain: England and Wales.

JESSEN K, HELBAEK H, 1944 — *Cereals in Great Britain and Ireland in Prehistoric and early Historic times.*

JEWELL P A, 1968 and 1972 — Reports (AB) in Brodribb A C C *et al.* 1968 and 1972, 1, 112–114; 3, 130–131.

JOHNSON A E, 1975

'Excavation at Bourton Grounds, Thornborough 1972–3', *Rec Buckinghamshire* 20 pt 1, 3–56.

JONES A K G, 1979a

Report (AB) in Williams J H, 1979, 335.

JONES A K G, 1979b

Report (AB) in Williams F, 1979, 78.

JONES G G, 1980

Report (AB) in Farley M, 'Middle Saxon occupation at Chicheley, Buckinghamshire', *Rec Buckinghamshire* 22, 99–102.

JONES G G, unpublished a

Report (AB) from Bierton, Aylesbury, Buckinghamshire. Copy held by Buckinghamshire County Museum, Aylesbury, Buckinghamshire.

JONES G G, unpublished b

Report (AB) from East Settlement, City Farm, Hanborough, Oxfordshire. Copy held by County Museum, Woodstock, Oxfordshire.

JONES G G, in preparation

Report (AB) from Rough Ground Farm, Lechlade, Gloucestershire. Copy held by T Allen, Oxfordshire Archaeological Unit, 46 Hythe Bridge Street, Oxford.

JONES M, 1978

'Sampling in a rescue context: a case study in Oxfordshire', in Cherry J F, Gamble C and Shennan S (ed), *Sampling in contemporary British archaeology*, Brit Archaeol Rep 50, 191–205.

JONES M, 1980

'Carbonised cereals from grooved ware contexts', *Proc Prehist Soc* 46, 61–63.

JONES M, 1981

'The development of crop husbandry', in Jones M and Dimbleby G (ed), *The environment of man: the Iron Age to the Anglo-Saxon period*, Brit Archaeol Rep 87, 95–127.

JONES R T, 1977

Report (AB) in Jackson D A, 1977, 53–54.

JONES R T, 1978

Report (AB) in Jackson D A and Ambrose T M, 1978, 235–241.

JONES R T, unpublished

Report (AB) from Towcester *AML Report* 1952.

JONES R T, WILSON R, unpublished

Report (AB) on post medieval bird bones from Church Street and Greyfriars, Oxford.

JOPE E M, THRELFALL R I, 1947

'Excavations at Deddington Castle, Oxon. 1947', *Oxoniensia* 11–12, 167–169.

JOPE E M, unpublished

Draft report on Excavations at Deddington Castle. Copy held by the author and the AM Laboratory.

JOPE M, 1953

Report (AB) in Jope E M, 'Late Saxon pits under Oxford Castle mound: excavations in 1952', *Oxoniensia* 17–18, 110–111.

JOPE M, 1958

Report (AB) in Jope E M, 'The Clarendon Hotel, Oxford', *Oxoniensia* 23, 79–83.

JOPE M, 1959

Report (AB) in Jope E M and Threlfall R I, 'The twelfth century castle at Ascot Doilly, Oxfordshire: its history and excavation', *Antiq J* 34, (3, 4), 269–270.

JOPE M, 1962

Report (AB) in Biddle M, 'The deserted medieval village of Seacourt, Berkshire', *Oxoniensia* 27, 197–201.

KEELEY H C M, 1974

'Soil investigations: Roxton, Beds.', *AML Report* 1669.

KEELEY H C M, 1976

'The soils of Roxton, Bedfordshire', *AML Report* 2104.

KEELEY H C M, 1982 | 'Soil report for the Bancroft site (MK343) Milton Keynes', *AML Report* 3653.

KEEPAX C A, 1975 | 'Stacey Bushes, Milton Keynes', *AML Report* 1894.

KEEPAX C A, 1977 | 'Briar Hill, Northampton, charcoal', *AML Report* 2279.

KEEPAX C A, 1979a | 'Identifications of Charcoal: Ascott-under-Wychwood', *AML Report* 2734.

KEEPAX C A, 1979b | 'Charcoal: Bedford, Empire Cinema', *AML Report* 2859.

KEEPAX C A, 1980 | 'Radiocarbon samples from a Neolithic causewayed enclosure at Briar Hill, Northampton', *AML Report* 3144.

KEITH A, 1921 | Report (HB) in Cocks A H, 'A Romano-British homestead in the Hambledon Valley, Buckinghamshire', *Archaeologia* 71, 159–163.

KING A C, 1975 | *Animal bones in Romano-British archaeology with respect to Cirencester and its region*, BA thesis, Institute of Archaeology Library, London.

KING A C, 1978 | 'A comparative study of bone assemblages from Roman sites in Britain', *Bull Inst Archaeol London* 15, 207–232.

KING J E, 1953 | 'Horse and dog skeletons from Blewburton Hill', in Collins A E P, 'Excavations on Blewburton Hill 1948 and 1949', *Berkshire Archaeol J* 53, 59–64.

KING J E, 1962 | Report (AB) in Wymer J, 'Excavations at the Maglemosan sites in Thatcham, Berks.', *Proc Prehist Soc* 28, 355–361.

KING J E, LAWFORD P, 1960 | Report (AB) in Pavry F H and Knocker G M, 'The Mount, Princes Risborough', *Rec Buckinghamshire* 16, 177–178.

LACAILLE A D, 1963 | 'Mesolithic industries beside Colne waters in Iver and Denham, Buckinghamshire', *Rec Buckinghamshire* 18 pt 3, 143–181.

LAMBRICK G H, ROBINSON M A, 1979 | *Iron Age and Roman riverside settlements at Farmoor, Oxfordshire*, Counc Brit Archaeol Res Rep 32.

LAMBRICK G H, ROBINSON M A, unpublished | 'Bronze Age and Iron Age sites on Port Meadow, Oxford'.

LAMBRICK G H, WOODS H, 1976 | 'Excavations on the second site of the Dominican Priory, Oxford', *Oxoniensia* 41, 168–231.

LEGGE A J, 1981 | Report (AB) in Mercer R, *Excavations at Grimes Graves 1971–72*, HMSO, 79–116.

LEVITAN B, unpublished | Report (AB) in Rowley T, *Excavations at Middleton Stoney, Oxon.* Copy held by author and External Studies Department, Wellington Square, Oxford.

LIMBREY S, 1975 | *Soil science and archaeology.*

LIMBREY S, 1982 | 'The honeybee and woodland resources', in Bell M, and Limbrey S (ed), *Archaeological aspects of woodland ecology*, AEA Symposia 2, 279–286.

MALTBY M, 1981 | 'Iron Age, Romano-British and Anglo-Saxon animal husbandry — a review of the faunal evidence', in Jones M and Dimbleby G (eds) 1981.

MARPLES B J, 1970 | Report (AB) in Hassall T, 1970, 28–31.

MARPLES B J, 1972a | Report (AB) in Rowley T, 1972, 128.

MARPLES B J, 1972b | Report (AB) in Brodribb A C C *et al.*, 1972, 3, 131.

MARPLES B J, 1973a — Report (AB) in Chambers R A, 'A deserted medieval farmstead at Sadlers Wood, Lewkenor', *Oxoniensia* 38, 161.

MARPLES B J, 1973b — Report (AB) in Brodribb A C C *et al.*, 1973, 4, 164–165.

MARPLES B J, 1975 — Report (AB) in Young C J, 'The defences of Roman Alchester', *Oxoniensia* 40, 160.

MARPLES B J, 1976 — Report (AB; MM) in Hassall T, 1976, 302–304.

MARPLES B J, 1977 — Report (AB) in Durham B 1977, 166–167.

MARPLES B J, 1978 — Report (AB) in Brodribb A C C *et al.*, 1978, 5, 169–170.

MARPLES B J, unpublished — Report (AB; MM) from Greyfriars, Oxford. Copy held by Oxfordshire Archaeological Unit, 46 Hythe Bridge Street, Oxford.

MARTIN A F, STEEL R W, (eds) 1954 — *The Oxford Region.*

McCORMICK A G, 1975 — Grendon, Northamptonshire, *Counc Brit Archaeol Group 9 Newsletter* 5, 12–14.

McWHIRR A, VINER L, WELLS C, 1982 — *Romano British cemeteries at Cirencester: Cirencester Excavations II*, Excavations committee, Cirencester.

METCALF W, 1973 — 'Aldwincle', *Northamptonshire Archaeol* 8, 3.

MILES D, forthcoming — *Archaeology at Barton Court Farm, Oxon.*

MILES D, PALMER S, 1982 — *Figures in a landscape: archaeological investigations at Claydon Pike, Fairford/Lechlade – an interim report 1979–82*, Oxfordshire Archaeological Unit, Oxford.

MOORE W R G, WILLIAMS J H, 1975 — 'A later Neolithic site at Ecton, Northampton', *Northamptonshire Archaeol* 10, 3–30.

MORRISON M E S, 1959 — 'Carbonised cereals from the Roman villa of North Leigh, Oxon', *Oxoniensia* 24, 13–21.

NODDLE B, 1976 — Report (AB) in Farley M, 1976, 269–289.

OAKLEY G E, 1979 — Report (MM) in Williams F, 1979, 77–78.

OAKLEY K P, VULLIAMY C E, ROUSE E C, COTTRILL F, 1939–40 — 'The excavation of a Romano-British pottery kiln site near Hedgerley', *Rec Buckinghamshire* 13, 252–280.

ORR C, 1974 — Report (AB) in Williams J H, 1974, 43.

ORR C, 1977 — Report (AB) in Foster P J, Harper R and Watkins S, 'An Iron Age and Romano-British settlement at Hardwick Park, Wellingborough', *Northamptonshire Archaeol* 12, 92–95.

PALMER N, 1976 — 'Excavations on the outer city wall of Oxford in St. Helen's Passage and Hertford College', *Oxoniensia* 41, 148-160.

PALMER N, 1980 — 'A Beaker burial and Medieval tenements in the Hamel, Oxford', *Oxoniensia* 45, 124–225, Microfiche 1 and 2.

PARRINGTON M, 1975 — 'Excavations at the Old Gaol, Abingdon', *Oxoniensia* 40, 59–78.

PARRINGTON M, 1978 — *The excavation of an Iron Age settlement, Bronze Age ring ditches and Roman features at Ashville Trading Estate, Abingdon (Oxfordshire) 1974–76*, Counc Brit Archaeol Res Rep 28.

PARRINGTON M, 1979 — 'Excavations at Stert Street, Abingdon, Oxon', *Oxoniensia* 44, 1–25.

PARRINGTON M, BALKWILL C, 1975   'Excavations at Broad Street, Abingdon', *Oxoniensia* 40, 5–58.

PAYNE S, 1980   Report (AB) in Lambrick G, 'Excavations in Park Street, Towcester', *Northamptonshire Archaeol* 15, 105–112.

PERNETTA J, 1973   Report (AB) in Robinson M A, 1973, 112–114.

PLATT M I, 1946   Identifications (AB) in Corder P and Lacaille A D, 'Belgic pottery from Poyle Farm brickworks near Burnham', *Rec Buckinghamshire* 14, 175.

PLUMMER K, 1976   Report (AB) in Matthews C L, *Occupation sites on a Chiltern ridge: excavations at Puddlehill and sites near Dunstable*, Brit Archaeol Rep 29, 150–151.

POINTER J, 1713   *An account of a Roman pavement lately found at Stunsfield in Oxfordshire, prov'd to be 1400 years old.*

POWERS R, 1982   Reports (HB) in Case H and Whittle A W R, 1982, (Cassington) 148 and (Stanton Harcourt) 105.

PRYOR F, 1980   *Excavations at Fengate, Peterborough, England: the 3rd report*, Royal Ontario Mus monogr 6, Northamptonshire Archaeol Soc monogr 1, 180.

RACKHAM D J, 1975   Report (AB) in Hall R A, 'An excavation at Hunter Street, Buckingham 1974', *Rec Buckinghamshire* 20 (1), 125–133.

RENFREW J M, WHITEHOUSE R, 1977   Report (AB) in May J, 'Romano-British and Saxon sites near Dorchester-on-Thames, Oxfordshire', *Oxoniensia* 42, 79.

RICHARDSON K M, YOUNG A, 1951   'An Iron Age site on the Chilterns', *Antiq J* 31, 132–148.

ROBERTS D F, 1973   Report (HB) in Dickinson T M, 'Excavations at Standlake Down in 1954: the Saxon graves', *Oxoniensia* 38, 256–257.

ROBERTS D F, THOMAS D P, 1950   Report (HB) in Kirk J R and Case H, 'Archaeological notes (Cassington)', *Oxoniensia* 15, 105.

ROBINSON M A, 1973   'Excavations at Copt Hay Tetsworth, Oxon', *Oxoniensia* 38, 41–115.

ROBINSON M A, 1978a   'A comparison between the effect of man on the environment of the first gravel terrace and floodplain of the Thames Valley during the Iron Age and Roman period', in Limbrey S and Evans J G (ed), *The effect of man on the landscape: the Lowland Zone*, CBA Res Rep 21, 35–43.

ROBINSON M A, 1978b   'Molluscan remains', in Parrington M, 1978, 93.

ROBINSON M A, 1979   'An ancient record of *Hydrophilus piceus* (L.) (Col., Hydrophilidae) breeding in Oxfordshire', *Entomologist's Monthly Mag* 115, 28.

ROBINSON M A, 1980a   'Archaeological finds of wasp galls', *J Archaeol Sci* 7, 93–95.

ROBINSON M A, 1980b   Environmental report in Hinchliffe J and Thomas R, 1980, 94.

ROBINSON M A, 1981a   *Investigations of palaeoenvironments in the Upper Thames Valley, Oxfordshire*, University of London Ph D Thesis.

ROBINSON M A, 1981b — 'The Iron Age to early Saxon environment of the Upper Thames terraces', in Jones M and Dimbleby G (ed), *The environment of man: the Iron Age to the Anglo-Saxon period*, Brit Archaeol Rep 87, 251–286.

ROBINSON M A, 1981c — 'Waterlogged plants and invertebrates', *Counc Brit Archaeol Group 9 Newsletter* 11, 62–63.

ROBINSON M A, 1982 — 'Waterlogged plants and invertebrates', *Counc Brit Archaeol Group 9 Newsletter* 12, 178–181.

ROBINSON M A, unpublished   a — 'The Late-Glacial and early Post-Glacial environment at Claydon Pike, Glos'.

ROBINSON M A, unpublished   b — 'A Late-Glacial sand dune at Drayton, Oxon'.

ROBINSON M A, unpublished   c — 'The pre-Iron Age environment of Mingie's Ditch, Hardwick, Oxon'.

ROBINSON M A, unpublished   d — 'The Mesolithic tufa and peat deposits alongside the Alderbourne at Iver, Bucks'.

ROBINSON M A, unpublished   e — 'Further waterlogged deposits at Farmoor, Oxon'.

ROBINSON M A, unpublished   f — 'Soil samples and charcoals from the Neolithic and Bronze Age ritual complex at Dorchester, Oxon'.

ROBINSON M A, unpublished   g — 'The alluvium and buried soil at Drayton Cursus, Oxon'.

ROBINSON M A, unpublished   h — 'The Neolithic and Bronze Age soils of the Rollright Stones'.

ROBINSON M A, unpublished   i — 'The Bronze Age to early Saxon environment of Mount Farm, Berinsfield, Oxon'.

ROBINSON M A, unpublished   j — 'The alluvial sequence and environment of the Thames bank at Wallingford, Oxon. in relation to the late Bronze Age riverside settlement'.

ROBINSON M A, unpublished   k — 'The Iron Age environment at Claydon Pike, Glos'.

ROBINSON M A, unpublished   l — 'The environmental setting of the Iron Age site at Mingie's Ditch, Hardwick, Oxon'.

ROBINSON M A, unpublished   m — 'Plant remains from a Roman well at the Churchill Hospital, Oxon'.

ROBINSON M A, unpublished   n — 'Roman waterlogged deposits at Claydon Pike, Glos'.

ROBINSON M A, unpublished   o — 'Saxon carbonised remains from All Saints Church, Oxford'.

ROBINSON M A, unpublished   p — 'Charcoal and waterlogged remains from a medieval manor house at Chalgrove, Oxon'.

ROBINSON M A, unpublished   q — 'Carbonised pea and bean – threshing debris from Folly Bridge, Oxford'.

ROBINSON M A, unpublished   r — 'A sieved sample from the Middleton Stoney Castle latrine shaft, Oxford'.

ROBINSON M A, HUBBARD R N L B, 1977 — 'The transport of pollen in the bracts of hulled cereals', *J Archaeol Sci* 4, 197–199.

ROBINSON M A, LAMBRICK G H, 1984 — 'Holocene alluviation and hydrology in the Upper Thames Basin', *Nature* 308, 809–814.

ROWLEY T, 1972 — 'First report on the excavations at Middleton Stoney Castle, Oxfordshire 1970–71', *Oxoniensia* 37, 109–136.

ST. HOYME L E, 1977 — Report (HB) in May J, 'Romano-British sites near Dorchester on Thames, Oxfordshire', *Oxoniensia* 42, 75–79.

SPARKS B W, LAMBERT C A, 1961–62 | 'The Post Glacial deposits at Apethorpe, Northamptonshire', *Proc Malac Soc Lond* 34, 302–315.

SPENCER P J, 1982 | Bancroft: MK343, molluscan analysis, *AML Report* 3649.

STARTIN J, unpublished | Report (AB) from Thenford Villa, Northamptonshire. Copy held by M Robinson, Oxford University Museum.

STRAKER V, 1979 | 'Late Saxon and late Medieval plant remains from Marefair, Northampton', *AML Report* 2867.

TAYLOR A, WOODWARD P, 1974 | 'Cainhoe Castle excavation, 1973', *Bedfordshire Archaeol J* 10, 41–52.

THAWLEY C R, 1982 | Report (AB) in Wacher J and McWhirr A, *Early Roman occupation at Cirencester: Cirencester excavs. I* Cirencester Excav Comm, 211–223.

THOMAS N, 1957 | 'Excavations at Callow Hill, Glympton and Stonefield, Oxon.', *Oxoniensia* 22, 11–53.

TILSON P, 1973 | 'A Belgic and Romano-British site at Bromham', *Bedfordshire Archaeol J* 8, 23–66.

TREVOR J C, 1947 | Report (HB) in Atkinson R J C, 1946–47, 26.

TREVOR J C, 1962 | Report (HB) in Dyer, 1962.

WALDRON H A, 1982 | 'Human bone lead concentrations' in McWhirr A, Viner L, and Wells C, 1982, 203–204.

WALDRON H A, 1983 | 'On the post-mortem accumulations of lead by skeletal tissues', *J Archaeol Sci* 10, 35–40.

WALKER J J, 1906 | 'Preliminary list of Coleoptera observed in the neighbourhood of Oxford from 1819 to 1907', *Ashmolean Natural History Society of Oxford Report*, 49–100.

WATSON J, 1981 | 'Identification of waterlogged wood from St. James Square, Northampton', *AML Report* 3551.

WELLS C, 1980 | Report (HB) in Pryor F, 1980, 232–234.

WELLS C, 1982 | Report (HB) in McWhirr A, Viner L, and Wells C, 1982, 135–202.

WEST B, 1982 | 'Spur development: recognising caponised fowl in archaeological material', in Wilson R, Grigson C and Payne S, 1982, 258–259.

WESTLEY B, 1968 | Report (AB) in Cotton M A and Frere S S, 1968, 252–260.

WESTLEY B, 1974 | Report (AB) in Green H S, 131–139.

WHEELER A, 1975 | Report (AB) in Parrington M and Balkwill C, 1975, 112.

WHEELER A, 1979 | Report (AB) in Parrington M, 1979, 21–13.

WHEELER A, forthcoming | Report (AB) in Miles D, forthcoming.

WHITTLE A W R, 1977 | *The earlier Neolithic of Southern Britain and its continental background*, Brit Archaeol Rep Supp 35.

WILLIAMS F, 1979 | 'Excavations at Marefair, Northampton 1977', *Northamptonshire Archaeol* 14, 38–79 and microfiche.

WILLIAMS J H, 1974 (ed) | *Two Iron Age sites in Northampton*, Northants Dev Corp Archaeol Monogr 1.

WILLIAMS J H, 1979 | *St. Peters Street Northampton.*

WILLIAMS J H, SHAW M, 1981   'Excavations in Chalk Lane, Northampton 1975–78', *Northamptonshire Archaeol* 16, 87–135 and microfiche.

WILSON R, 1975a   Report (AB) in Chambers R A, 'Excavations at Hanwell, Banbury, Oxon', *Oxoniensia* 40, 218–237.

WILSON R, 1975b   Report (AB) in Miles D, 'Excavations at West St. Helens Street, Abingdon', *Oxoniensia* 40, 98–101.

WILSON R, 1975c   'The animal bones from the Broad Street and Old Gaol sites (Abingdon)', *Oxoniensia* 40, 105–121.

WILSON R, 1976a   Report (AB) in Rodwell K A, 'Excavations on the site of Banbury Castle 1973–4', *Oxoniensia* 41, 144–147.

WILSON R, 1976b   Report (AB) in Parrington M, 'Roman finds and animal bones from Kingston Bagpuize, Oxon.', *Oxoniensia* 41, 67–68.

WILSON R, 1978a   Report (AB; MM) in Parrington M, 1978, 110–126 and 133–139.

WILSON R, 1978b   'Sampling bone densities at Mingie's Ditch', in Cherry J F, Gamble C and Shennan S, *Sampling in contemporary British archaeology*, Brit Archaeol Rep 50, 355–361.

WILSON R, 1979a   Report (AB) in Saville A, 'Excavations at Guiting Power Iron Age site, Gloucestershire 1974', *Comm for Rescue Archaeol in Avon, Glos. and Somerset, Occ Paper* 7, 141–144.

WILSON R, 1979b   Report (AB; MM) in Parrington M, 1979, 16–20.

WILSON R, 1979c   Report (AB) in Lambrick G H and Robinson M A, 1979, 128–133.

WILSON R, 1980a   Report (AB) in Hinchliffe J and Thomas R, 1980, 84–90.

WILSON R, 1980b   Reports (AB; MM) in Palmer N, 1980, 198 and fiche 1A07 and 2E04–F11.

WILSON R, forthcoming   Report (AB; MM) in Miles D, forthcoming.

WILSON R, unpublished   a   All Saints, Oxford (Wilson unpublished reports AB; MM).

WILSON R, unpublished   b   Church Street and Greyfriars, Oxford (post-medieval).

WILSON R, unpublished   c   Eynsham, Oxon.

WILSON R, unpublished   d   Little Faringdon oil pipeline, Oxon.

WILSON R, unpublished   f   Thrupp, Abingdon, Oxon. (2).

WILSON R, unpublished   g   The Causeway, Bicester, Oxon.

WILSON R, unpublished   h   Wally Corner, Berinsfield.

WILSON R, unpublished   i   Wallingford, Oxon.

WILSON R, unpublished   j   Market Place, Abingdon, Oxon.

WILSON R, in preparation a   Buscot Lock, Oxon (Wilson in preparation reports AB; MM).

WILSON R, in preparation b   Chalgrove Manor, Oxon.

WILSON R, in preparation c   Church Street, Oxford (medieval).

WILSON R, in preparation d   Mingie's Ditch and Smith's field, Hardwick with Yelford, Oxon. (2).

WILSON R, in preparation e   Mount Farm, Oxon.

WILSON R, GRIGSON C, PAYNE S, 1982   'Ageing and sexing animal bones from archaeological sites', Brit Archaeol Rep Brit ser 109, 1–5.

WILSON R, THOMAS R, WHEELER A, 1979   'Sampling a profile of town soil-accumulation 57 East St. Helens Street, Abingdon', *Oxoniensia* 44, 26–29.

YOUNG A, 1813   *General view of the agriculture of Oxfordshire.*

YOUNG C J, 1972   'Excavation at the Churchill Hospital, 1971 interim report', *Oxoniensia* 37, 10–31.

YOUNG C J, 1975   'The defences of Roman Alchester', *Oxoniensia* 40, 136–170.

ZEUNER F E, CORNWALL I W, SUMMERS R F H, 1951   In Atkinson *et al.*, 1951, 119–127.

SUMMARY

A substantial amount of information exists about the past environment of ancient man for the region of the South Midlands, although much of the area and some of the chronological periods are not covered adequately by environmental reports or by current excavations. Some of the extant information is neither reliable nor easy to use. Most of the relevant data has been published since about 1970 in association with rescue archaeology and funded by the Department of the Environment. Recently, special interest and importance has been attached to waterlogged and carbonised organic debris. Studies of all lines of surviving evidence: animal and human bones, molluscs, soils etc, however, are viewed as complementary and necessary parts of environmental archaeology.

Distinctive ecological and cultural variety and change throughout the Post-Glacial period have been described, particularly the development of farming communities and aspects of urban life where detailed historical or other archaeological information is absent.

Environmental archaeology investigations are essential for a proper understanding of the archaeology of the British Isles, and the environmental evidence is facing similar threats to those faced by structural and artefactual archaeological remains. The chief requirements of future work involving the Historic Buildings and Monuments Commission in the region are:

a. Long term planning of environmental archaeology policy for which priorities are suggested.

b. The close co-ordination of administrators, excavators and environmental archaeologists.

c. Funding of the collection and analysis of environmental data.

Chapter 2

A REVIEW OF ENVIRONMENTAL ARCHAEOLOGY IN THE WEST MIDLANDS

J R A Greig, with contributions by S M Colledge and S Limbrey

1 Introduction

This review covers an area which is referred to as 'the Midlands', and which consists of the counties of Hereford and Worcester, Cheshire, Shropshire, Staffordshire and West Midlands. The botanical and general aspects of the environmental archaeology of this area are dealt with at the laboratory in the Department of Plant Biology at the University of Birmingham. Other aspects of environmental archaeology are dealt with by experts at the University and elsewhere, by arrangement. Similarly, work is carried out on material excavated from outside the midlands, in the Birmingham laboratory.

This review has had to be selective rather than comprehensive. It aims to mention most of the main fields of environmental archaeology in which work has been done in the midlands, but some of these, such as the extensive work on Pleistocene deposits, are not fully discussed because they are thought to be peripheral to the main subject. Greater attention has been paid to sites which show the effects of man on the environment, either because they are archaeological sites, or because they show the effects of human occupation e.g. pollen analysis sites.

2 General introduction to the Midlands

2.1 Geology

The generalised geology of the midlands (Hains and Horton 1969, Earp and Hains 1971) is shown in Figure 10. It is of considerable relevance to environmental archaeology because it provides the basic structure of the landscape, modified in places by the overlying drift geology (see next section), which plays a part in determining both the pattern of settlement and the likely preservation of some kinds of evidence like pollen, bones or molluscs.

Using the usual chrono-stratigraphic order, igneous rocks are the first to be discussed. Although there are only a few scattered outcrops of igneous rock, these are important as sources of material for stone implement manufacture such as the picrite which outcrops on Corndon in West Shropshire (although the Group XII axes seem to have been made from rock collected from just across the Welsh border). The camptonite from Griff, near Nuneaton was used for the Group XIV axes (Shotton 1959). Sedimentary rocks of Pre-Cambrian and Cambrian age form small outcrops which are probably not archaeologically significant. The Silurian shales, limestone and sandstone are more significant because they give rise to a gently rolling landscape, as in South Shropshire, with good soil readily formed from the rock, making the area of good potential to early settlers. Old Red Sandstone is important because it underlies a large part of Hereford and Worcester and some of South Shropshire, giving rise to a characteristic red soil, in the area around the Clee Hills. The Carboniferous is represented by very little limestone, but Millstone Grit underlies much of North Staffordshire in the form of intercalated shales and grits which give the high land there, dissected by some river valleys. Coal measures occur in several places, containing sandstone, marl and shales as well as coal itself. Where it outcrops at the ground surface the coal is likely to have been mined for a very long time, and more recently the close juxtaposition of coal, iron ore, and material suitable for founding and refractories was a vital factor in the start of the Industrial Revolution in this area. Likewise, deposits like the Etruria marls have provided the basis for the Staffordshire pottery industry, probably for a very long time.

Permo-Triassic rocks are a very characteristic feature of the midlands; the Bunter sandstones and pebble beds cover large areas, and while they can be cultivated, they are often now left as heathland (Trueman 1971, 169). The Keuper Marl consists of sandstones and clays which often give rise to good soils, and the preservation of waterlogged deposits is enhanced by the impermeability of the ground in places like Droitwich. Salt deposits occur in the area between Nantwich and Northwich, Stafford, Uttoxeter and also at Droitwich, and these have been of very great importance for a long time, which is reflected in archaeological findings e.g. the Very Coarse Pottery (VCP) which appears to have a connection with the salt trade. The muddy and shelly limestones of the Lias occur in the south-east of the midland area, which is a fertile area.

2.2 Drift geology

The effects of glaciation have modified the landscape considerably. Ice sheets and associated periglacial activity have left large deposits, mainly of boulder clay (till) in some places, and of glacial sand and gravel in others (Figure 11). The last glaciation, the Devensian (named after a Celtic tribe thought to have lived in the Chester area), affected the entire north-west of the midlands with ice, and till and gravel are to be found all over the midlands as a result. When the ice retreated, blocks were left behind which melted gradually, giving rise to lakes in Shropshire, Staffordshire and Cheshire.

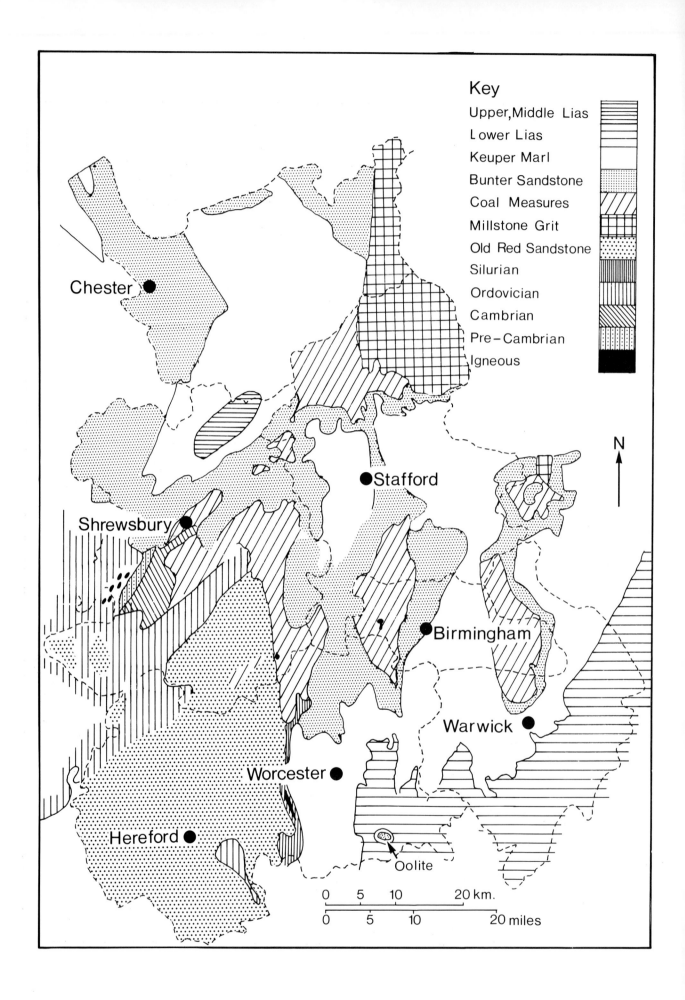

Key

Upper, Middle Lias
Lower Lias
Keuper Marl
Bunter Sandstone
Coal Measures
Millstone Grit
Old Red Sandstone
Silurian
Ordovician
Cambrian
Pre-Cambrian
Igneous

Chester

Stafford

Shrewsbury

Birmingham

Warwick

Worcester

Hereford

Oolite

N

0   5   10   20 km.

0   5   10   20 miles

Figure 10   Simplified geological map of the Midlands

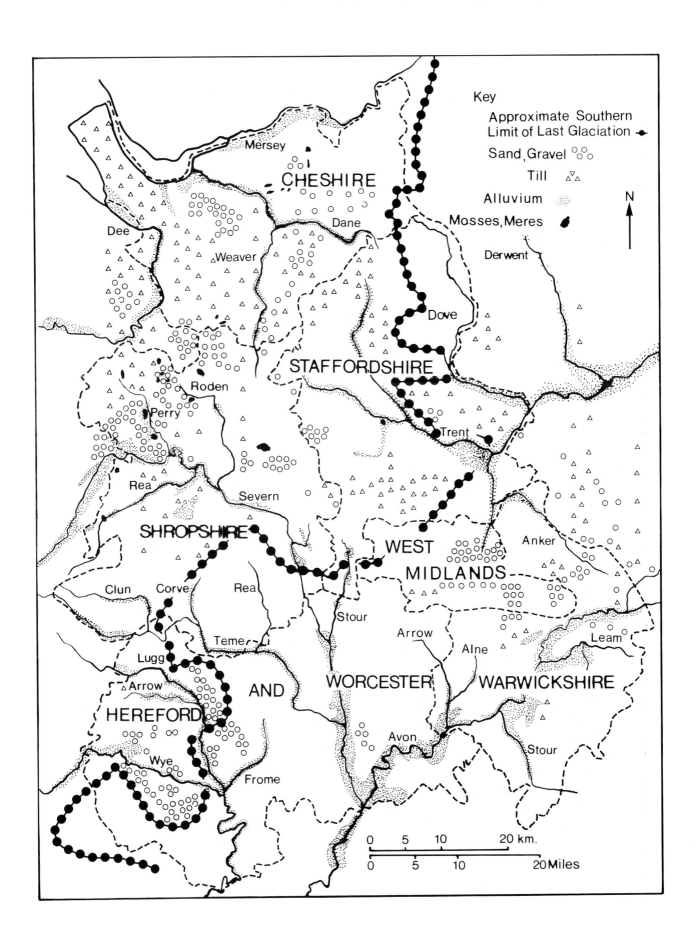

Figure 11   Drift map of the Midlands

The effects of underlying salt beds have also been important in providing or maintaining low-lying areas, with the result that the northern part of the midlands has many suitable sites for pollen analysis, upon which a considerable amount of work has been done, discussed later. The river valleys also contain recent sediment, the alluvium, which is of great archaeological interest because its formation and settlement seem to be interrelated. The drift geology has been used archaeologically as a guide to settlement of areas at various times, and study of place names, for example, has shown that there is evidence of certain areas, evidently more attractive, being settled before less good sites (Gelling 1978, 223). The drift geology is of direct environmental relevance too, since the realisation that useful peat deposits are often incorporated into the alluvium of river valleys, as at Cookley in the Stour valley.

2.3   The landscape

The landscape of the midlands is divisible into the basins of two main river systems, the Severn, Wye and Avon, and the Trent, using the approach of Warwick (1971, 6). It is plausible that this kind of division would have affected the settlement and development of the various parts of the midlands; the river valleys provide natural routes into the areas, and often have good soils, even though they may have been too wet for settlement (Trueman 1971, 163). The landscape map (Figure 12) is based on the river systems, and also shows the ancient forests of Clun, Arden, Delamere and Needwood. These would have been extensive in the past as shown by pollen analyses and some insect studies, and might have proved an important factor in deciding settlement patterns by acting as a barrier, or by covering the best soils at the time. Some of the woods in the midlands have names which appear to be ancient, and refer to much more extensive afforestation at the time of Saxon settlement, sometimes by lime forest (Greig in press b) such as Lindridge.

High ground divides the river basins, and there is some extensive upland like the Long Mynd and Clee Hills in Shropshire, and the Pennine part of East Staffordshire. The altitude as well as the topography would affect the agricultural potential of such upland, perhaps restricting it to pastoral rather than arable farming.

2.4   The archaeological background

The Palaeolithic period is represented by surface finds of implements from gravel quarries and river cuttings. Professor Shotton (Emeritus Professor of Geology, University of Birmingham) has been responsible for much of the research into this period in the midlands. Most of the stone tools have been disturbed by successive glaciations and are not therefore in primary contexts.

Mesolithic surface finds are the main source of evidence about this period (e.g. Saville 1981) and some intensive collecting by local amateurs during fieldwalking has added much to knowledge on the subject. At Middleton on the river Tame there was an extensive spread of microliths in the gravel which filled the river valley. At Rugeley in Staffordshire a Mesolithic cave shelter was excavated by Birmingham University archaeology students, and was thought to have been a temporary hunting site.

Neolithic sites are present, but excavations have been few. Crop marks of possible Neolithic henges and cursus monuments have been photographed, and a barrow from Bromfield, Shropshire has been excavated by Dr Stan Stanford. Neolithic stone axes are well documented from this area and Professor Shotton has been doing petrological identifications (Shotton 1959). Pollen diagrams show the effects of the arrival of Neolithic farmers, although there are few detailed diagrams as yet. It is possible that many Neolithic sites have been lost through soil erosion after early forest clearance, or have been buried beneath alluvial deposits in river valleys.

Bronze Age sites in the midlands seem to be more numerous than was suspected, because survey work is greatly increasing the known number of sites. An important cremation site at Sharpstones Hill near Shrewsbury was excavated in the 1960s (unpublished) and a Bronze Age barrow and cemetery at Bromfield, Shropshire, excavated (Stanford in preparation). Burnt mounds are being investigated where a high concentration of them is being found in Birmingham, and one at Bournville (Cob Lane) has been excavated (Barfield and Hodder 1981). Bronze Age sites, like the Neolithic ones, may have often become eroded away or buried.

Some Iron Age sites are fairly obvious and resistant to destruction, such as the hillforts which are especially abundant in the south-west of the area and which have been extensively researched by Dr Stan Stanford (e.g. Stanford 1974, 1981). Less obvious and more vulnerable are the gravel terrace sites in river valleys which are often only visible from the air in suitable conditions, and which are threatened by gravel extraction and house building. Important rescue excavations have been done at Beckford, near Tewkesbury (Wills in preparation) and Fisherwick, near Tamworth (Smith 1979).

The Roman period is represented by some spectacular sites with standing architecture like Wroxeter, others where it has been reconstructed like The Lunt, the legionary fortress at Chester (DEVA), and a range of smaller 'towns' like Alcester, Droitwich, Mancetter, and Wall. Gravel sites sometimes show signs of Roman or Romano-British occupation, such as Wasperton which is now being excavated.

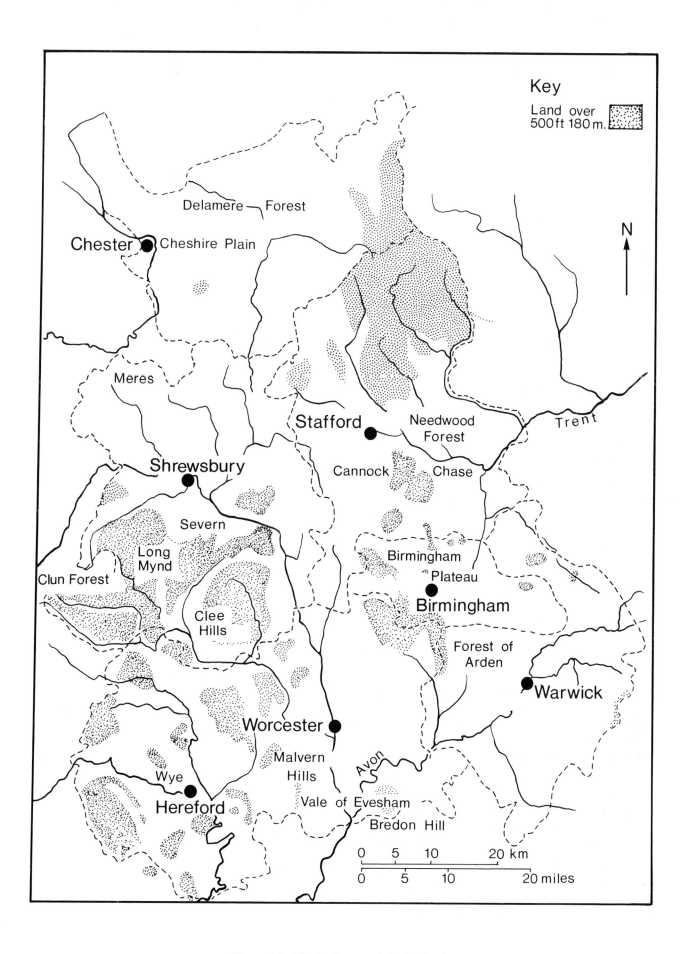

Figure 12   The landscape of the Midlands

Saxon sites are occasionally found in the country e.g. at Wasperton, where there is Saxon as well as Roman occupation. Many of the Midland towns are thought to have Saxon origins, and considerable excavations in the centre of Stafford have shown surprisingly little of the Saxon remains which might have been expected. In the Middle Ages most of the midland towns (apart from Birmingham) were well-developed and interesting archaeological finds occur from time to time, as, for example, a well-preserved barrel latrine at Worcester which was of exceptional environmental interest.

2.5 Archaeological organisations in the Midlands

Birmingham University Field Archaeology Unit (BUFAU) carries out some of the professional archaeological work in the midlands (apart from Cheshire). Members of the Department of Ancient History and Archaeology and the Department for Extramural Studies at Birmingham University also carry out excavations from time to time, and the various local authorities also have archaeologists who excavate. In addition there are many local groups working under the auspices of the Council for British Archaeology (CBA) regional organisation, and whose results appear in 'West Midlands Archaeology' (except for Cheshire).

3 Environmental archaeology in the Midlands

3.1 Introduction

Environmental archaeology seems to have had a late start in the midlands; early works on the subject e.g. Jessen and Helbaek's (1944) classic work on early cereals in Great Britain and Ireland, make little or no mention of the region. Nor has the region provided many deposits of interest to Professor Godwin and his colleagues, there being but one example (Godwin and Dickson 1960–1965). Pollen analysis of mere deposits in Shropshire started early (Hardy 1939) and further work has been done (discussed in 3.7). Most of the early impetus in environmental archaeology in this area has come from Professor F W Shotton and his colleagues and students in the Department of Geological Sciences, many of whom (such as P C Buckland, M A Girling and H K Kenward) have gone on to specialise in environmental archaeology. Much of the work there was mainly concerned with environmental changes connected with the Pleistocene which are outside the scope of this review, but very useful archaeological work has also been done. The study of insect remains, which was started and pioneered by Professor Shotton and Peter Osborne, has resulted in work on insect remains from archaeological sites (e.g. Osborne 1965, 1969, 1971a and b, 1973, 1976, 1977, 1981a and b, and in preparation). G R Coope has done work on the Pleistocene insect assemblages. Other archaeologically relevant work by Professor Shotton and his associates includes mollusc faunal analyses (Shotton 1972), studies of prehistoric alluviation (Shotton 1978) and of stone implement petrology (Shotton 1959). The establishment of a radiocarbon dating laboratory in the 1960s enabled the Department of Geology to make a great contribution to archaeology not only in the form of dates, but also in the understanding of dating methodology and in how best to apply the technique. Botanical work has also been carried out in the Geology Department by Shotton and Strachan (1959), Rowlands (1966), Kelly and Osborne (1964).

Environmental archaeological work in other departments includes that on human skeletal anatomy (e.g. Spence 1967) in the Department of Pathology, and a considerable amount of work being carried out on insect and plant remains from archaeological sites (although not usually in Britain) by Dr P C Buckland and his colleagues in the Department of Geography. Dr K J Edwards has carried out some pollen analysis work on material from Sutton Park, Birmingham.

In 1967 Professor Shotton was instrumental in organising the establishment of a Research Fellowship in the Application of Scientific Techniques to Archaeology. This lasted for three periods of tenure before ending in 1975. The first person appointed, D Peacock, studied the petrology of ceramics. The second, B Noddle, studied animal bones, while the third, J Greig, studied plant remains, and all three are still active in the archaeological field.

With the appointment of S Limbrey to a new lectureship in Environmental Archaeology in 1973, teaching in this field became part of the syllabus in the Department of Ancient History and Archaeology. Dr Limbrey provides advice on soil problems on excavations in the region and has been working on the history of soil development associated with sites such as Beckford, and on the history of alluviation in midland river valleys. This work is now associated with the project on the palaeohydrology of the temperate zone in the last 15,000 years under the auspices of the International Correlation Programme, the Severn Basin having been selected for the British contribution. This project has brought into the region a number of people whose work on fluvial deposits and associated hydrological factors is contributing to our knowledge of the history of the landscape, and will integrate with the information on settlement and land use from archaeological sources.

Some of Dr Limbrey's students have been able to undertake projects on environmental archaeology which would otherwise have been impossible owing to lack of time. The training of students in environmental archaeology has also meant that many of those who are now doing archaeological work in the area, such as the members of BUFAU, have a reasonable understanding of environmental archaeology on site, which once again facilitates the work in the laboratory.

Excavation teams now often include 'environmental assistants' who do sampling, sieving and initial sorting, mainly of charred plant remains, also recovering small bones and artefacts as well. This greatly increases the amount of work which can be contemplated, and efficient sieving and separation techniques have been developed which work even on the rather heavy soils of the midlands, using simple and cheap equipment.

In 1975, a DOE contract post was set up in the Department of Plant Biology, and J Greig was appointed to continue the work he had done as a Research Fellow. In 1977, S Colledge was appointed to a similar post as Research Associate to concentrate on material from midland excavations. She left in 1981 and arrangements are being made to re-fill the post. Most of the various aspects of botanical environmental archaeology are done here, like pollen analysis, the study of waterlogged plant macrofossils, charred grain and seeds. It is hoped to be able to identify mosses, but wood and charcoal, although they often survive, do not often provide enough useful information to be worth the time spent on their study. Very considerable work has been done on building up the best possible reference collections of pollen and seeds, and this seems to have been a worthwhile effort.

The botanical work is only a part of what needs to be done with archaeological material. Other aspects of deposits, such as the sedimentology, insect, mollusc, bone studies, dendrochronology etc need to be done in close collaboration with other specialists working in the relevant fields in order to achieve useful integrated results. Some of these specialists are already working for the DOE as staff, contractors or consultants, and a considerable amount of work is done by people in their spare time, which is very gratefully acknowledged. With this form of collaboration insects, for example, may be extracted from samples here and sent to specialists with their prior agreement, and conversely other specialists send material here for study. The extent of this collaboration can be seen from the frequent co-authorship of papers in the publications lists, and its great value can be seen in the results.

Some work is done on the study of modern materials to compare their pollen and seed content with those found in some archaeological deposits. Such work includes the study of hay from species-rich meadows which may resemble past hay meadows more than most modern grassland, and the study of the pollen content of various straw fractions and some foodstuffs. Similar work on beetle faunas (Osborne in preparation) is similarly proving very useful in demonstrating how they could have arisen.

3.2 Review of environmental work on pre-Iron Age prehistoric sites (Figure 13)

As already mentioned, few prehistoric sites have been excavated in the midlands, and of these, few have been environmentally investigated. Material has been collected from the Sharpstones excavations, such as cremations which were studied by M Nellist and T Spence, although the results have not yet appeared in print.

The burnt mound at Cob Lane, Bournville, is being excavated with consideration for environmental archaeology (Barfield and Hodder 1981) and a radiocarbon date of 1190 ± 90bc (BIRM 1087) has been obtained from charcoal. Peter Osborne has been studying the insect fauna and has found *Ernoporus caucasicus* which is a lime feeder. Initial pollen analysis has been unsuccessful, but pollen may be preserved in other samples.

Excavations at Bromfield revealed Neolithic pits whose contents, studied by S Colledge, included hazel nut shell, wheat, barley and some weed seeds in a charred state, and some other uncharred weed seeds which are probably recent contaminants.

3.3 Hill-forts

At Croft Ambrey (Stanford 1974) bones were recovered by R and D Whitehouse, consisting mainly of remains of cattle, sheep and pigs which often showed signs of butchery. Although most of the meat used would have been beef, swine were commoner than at other Iron Age sites and this was suggested as a sign of surviving woodland around Croft Ambrey. Seeds had been hand-picked rather than being bulk-sieved, but J Greig identified wheat among them. J Sheldon identified all the charcoal as that of oak.

Midsummer Hill, also excavated by Dr Stanford, provided more hand picked grain samples. Grain, spikelet forks and glume bases were identified as either spelt or emmer wheat by S Colledge. She also found barley and brome. Caynham Camp also yielded a very small amount of grain (Gelling 1963) and the Wrekin a small and inconclusive pollen spectrum.

3.4 Gravel sites (Figure 13)

Much more concerted effort has been put into environmental archaeology at these sites, as shown by the results obtained from some of them. This may be because the work on these sites is mostly recent; it had been thought that in hillfort country the surrounding lowland formed an almost impenetrable forest, but air photographs taken in the 1960s by W A Baker showed that there were sites in the Severn and Avon valleys revealed as crop marks.

The site at Beckford was excavated by Oswald and animal remains were reported by Gilmore (1970–2) and Roberts (1970–2) with further excavations by W Britnell in 1974, and by J Wills in 1975–9. The earlier excavation reports

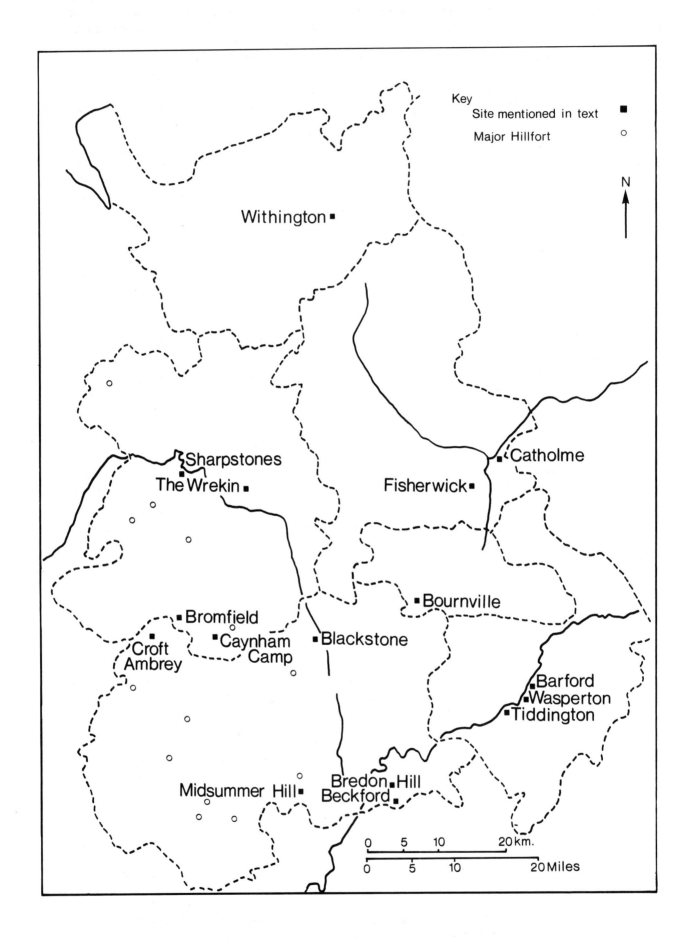

Figure 13   Sites on alluvium, hillforts, and other prehistoric sites

work on animal bones being done (Britnell 1974). In the later excavation a detailed programme for the recovery of charred plant remains was developed by S Colledge and a very large number of contexts sampled. A round-house was investigated square metre by square metre and this botanical work should be one of the most thorough of its kind. Some of the human skeletal material was studied by M Nellist and showed evidence of injury prior to death. Some peat was located in the alluvium a few hundred metres from the excavated area, and was investigated and sampled by means of some machine-cut trenches in 1978. It is now known that the radiocarbon date range of this material is 1800bc–950ad, so it appears to cover the time of the site's occupation (compare the date of 1410 ± 200bc from the site (BIRM 431), Britnell (1974)). Dr S Limbrey is studying the alluvial history of this site. Beckford is a good example of a site of great archaeological importance, a lowland Iron Age (as well as Romano-British) site in the valley below the hillfort of Bredon Hill, which is producing a wealth of environmental information from various studies.

Fisherwick (Smith 1979) was also discovered by aerial photography and was excavated in 1974–5. The site was more promising for environmental archaeology than Beckford would later seem to be, because of the high water table there in the Tame valley. The enclosure ditches of the Iron Age farmstead had waterlogged fills, so waterlogged wood, animal bone, seeds, pollen and insect remains were studied and integrated results were presented in the final report. The wood remains included hedgerow taxa like hawthorn and sloe, nitrophiles like elder, and shrubs of damp habitats like Willow, as reported by P Williams. Some alder and oak showed signs of working. J Startin reported on a fairly small animal bone fauna which was dominated by the remains of cattle, also including swine, sheep/goat, horse and an unspecified deer. J Greig's seed and pollen report shows the presence of a range of plants of damp habitats, and some weeds, while the pollen spectrum adds somewhat to the list, especially in the case of trees and shrubs although the rosaceous taxa whose remains were abundant as wood are hardly represented here. The insect remains which were studied by P J Osborne also showed signs of damp habitats, as might be expected from a ditch fill. The terrestrial fauna, however, was dominated by dung beetles and those of pasture land, giving evidence of pastoral farming around the site. The various lines of evidence are combined in a chapter on the landscape of the Fisherwick area during the Iron Age.

Another gravel site, this time in the Avon valley, is Tiddington, which is being excavated by N Palmer (1982). This is a well-known area of archaeological importance, so there is excavation of areas which are to be developed. An 'environmental assistant' is at present responsible for the day-to-day sampling, sieving and preliminary sorting for charred plant remains, and the finding of possible corn-driers shows the potential for recovering a good assemblage of grain and chaff which should show what grain types were present and how they were being processed. These methods are discussed in 3.8. A well was excavated in 1981 and the material from it studied by M Robinson who reported a large flora which appeared to be representative of the plants which were present in the surroundings at the time, and which might perhaps have been swept into the well when it was back-filled. Interesting plants found there include coriander.

The Wasperton crop-marks were originally thought to represent an Iron Age and Romano-British settlement, but the excavations since 1980 have revealed only Romano-British and Saxon remains (Crawford 1982). Contexts are being sampled and the charred plant remains extracted. Not all the grain is well-preserved, perhaps because some of it was rapidly heated when charred, and also because the soil conditions in such shallowly buried deposits are not ideal for preservation because frost action and disturbance by the soil fauna may have a deleterious effect.

3.5 Small urban settlements, Roman and later (Figure 14)

The Roman settlement at Alcester may have been more extensive than the present-day town, and part of it is known to exist under fields to the south. Excavations have taken place over the years, and P Booth has been excavating on various threatened sites since 1976 with due regard for environmental archaeology. From the earlier excavations of 1964–5, P J Osborne (1971a) obtained a large insect fauna from a sample of about 75kg of organic material and leather scraps. These results are perhaps the first to be obtained with the now-familiar dung/compost heap inhabiting fauna. There were also wood borers including the exotic *Hesperophanes fasciculatus* which might have arrived in this country in articles of furniture brought from South Europe. Another 'first' was the evidence of a range of pests of stored products which had, like *Oryzaephyllus surinamensis*, been thought to have been spread around the world quite recently but which must on such evidence have caused the Romans some problems with the storage of grain. The results of this pioneering work provided the basis for the investigation of insect remains from organic deposits on archaeological sites.

Excavations in the garden behind Lloyd's Bank in 1975 uncovered a well, and samples from this were being studied by B Clayton at Warwick Museum, but it is not known whether the work is complete.

The 'Explosion site' in Bleachfield Street was excavated after the fire in the next-door bottled gas store wrecked the buildings there. A complex succession of 2nd–4th century stone and timber building remains was found, and a well from which S Colledge obtained an interesting list of plants mostly weeds of open ground; the insect remains were not well preserved (AML Report 2577). M Maltby is reporting on bones. When car parks were laid out at the rear of the buildings along the High Street in Alcester, salvage work in drainage trenches permitted the investigation of peaty deposits there, which were similar to those which had already been noted on a building site in Ragley Mill Lane, to the north of the town. The Bull's Head Yard peat had a radiocarbon date of around 190 ad (HAR 2257, 1760 bp ± 90)

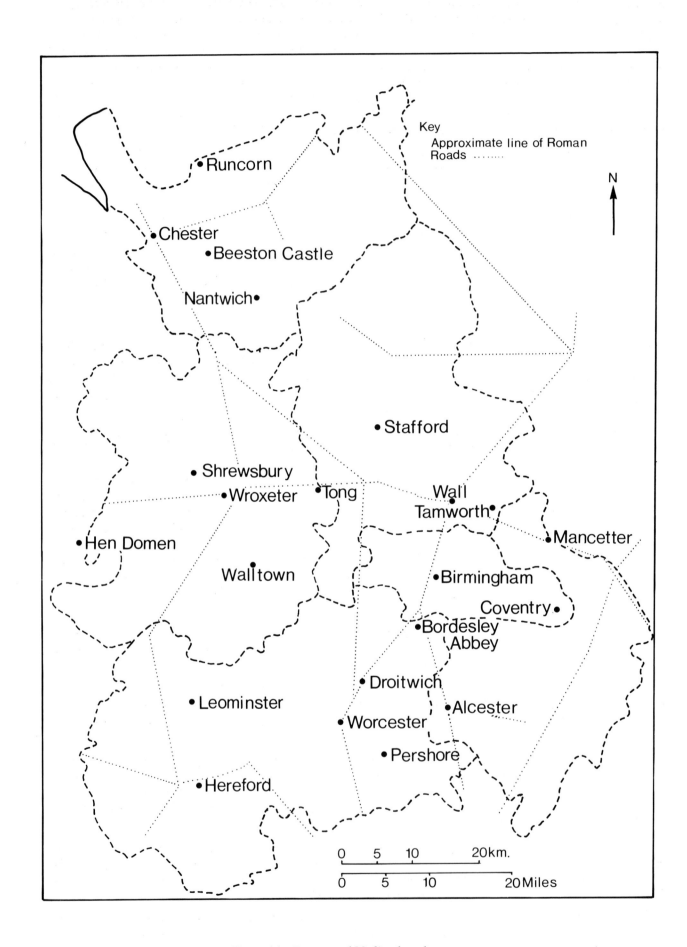

Figure 14   Roman and Medieval settlements

suggesting that these features were an important part of the topography of Roman Alcester, and the pollen spectra obtained from them were comparable and suggestive of a rather open and grassy landscape in the area. Expansion building work at Coulter's Garage provided a third sighting and sampling of these peaty sediments, dated at 2410 ± 110 bp (460 bc) HAR 4905. The seeds and pollen from this section were investigated by L Woodwards and J Greig, and the insect remains by M Girling (AML Report 3110), and these results are about to be published together with the archaeological findings. Burnt layers from Coulter's Garage deposits associated with timber buildings which may have been a granary have been studied by S Colledge who found a very rich assemblage of charred grain, chaff and weed seeds (AML Report 3284) also to be published with the rest of the information about the site. It is possible that dendrochronological work can usefully be done on some of the large timber piles from this building.

Droitwich, thought to be the Roman SALINAE, is another small settlement with many Roman remains. The Bay's Meadow site provided the University of Birmingham with one of its training excavations for several years up to 1976, the remains of a villa. Although environmental archaeology was not undertaken on a systematic basis, various pieces of work have been done. A well, excavated in 1974, provided an extensive fauna and flora; there were many bones of small mammals, and J Rackham has identified numerous remains of water voles, land voles and shrews, with mice only represented by harvest mouse, the earliest record in Britain. The house mouse was not present, nor was the rat. The latter had been considered to have been a post-Roman introduction, their ecological niche having been occupied by the water vole. Since then, J Rackham has found rat remains from Roman well deposits in York, but even so, this fauna is very interesting. The large samples collected also yielded an extensive insect fauna, perhaps the largest of its kind, considering the sample size, which filled several dustbins when it was being transported back to Birmingham. This work is not yet completed, nor is the accompanying seed flora by J Greig. Charred grain deposits from the site have been studied by V Straker (AML Report 2812), who found mainly spelt, some barley, emmer rye and horse bean among the crop plants, and a range of weed seeds. The spelt had mostly sprouted. P J Osborne studied charred insect remains from a grain sample from the granary annexe, which included three species of grain pest. He suggested that infestation may have rendered the grain spoiled and inedible so that it was burnt to destroy it with the pests (Osborne 1977), although a granary fire could have been the cause of charring. The larger animal bones from this site are being studied by B Noddle (1979).

The building of a new fire station necessitated an excavation by A Hunt in Friary Street and the well found there was sampled but it seemed to be 'clean', with little of environmental interest. In the same area of town, the building of an inner ring-road across the site of the bowling green in Rickett's Lane opened that area for excavation by D Freezer, and by J Sawle of the County Museum, in the expectation of finding out about the Roman salt working industry which was thought to have been in that area. Pre-Roman VCP was found, and numerous Roman features, with some medieval ones cut into them, as well as post-medieval ones. A ditch fill, thought to be of late third century date, was investigated and proved to have a rich seed and pollen flora indicating a range of habitats like wetland, grassland, cultivated land and scrub. The ditch formed a boundary around an area thought, on the basis of the bone finds, to have been a place for butchering meat for salting. A very large pit with a fill of fine clay layers is thought to have been an unsuccessful brine pit of 15th—16th century date. This also provided a large and varied seed flora, and a series of pollen spectra exceptionally rich in elm pollen, although these results do not appear to help much with the interpretation. Aquatic molluscs were also present.

Excavations by D Freezer at the site in Hanbury Street uncovered cobble floors and a burnt layer of Roman date which proved very rich in grain and chaff remains. This is such good material that it is being studied as a student project under the direction of S Colledge and G Hillman.

Mancetter is the site of Roman pottery manufacture, and in the 1977 excavations directed by K Hartley a well was discovered and excavated. A large number of samples was collected by the excavator and sent to the laboratory, and one of these has been investigated by S Colledge, showing a flora of grassland plants and weeds of cultivated land. It is not known whether work is still proceeding on this site.

At Wall (LETOCETUM) there have been many excavations, and peat discovered from one of these was studied by C A and J Dickson and H Godwin who obtained two pollen spectra and some rush seeds from the samples. Not much could be concluded from these results (Godwin and Dickson 1964—5) but on a recent visit to the site J Greig observed that it appears to be in a shallow valley with a stream running through, so the peat may well have formed naturally and been covered by later soil movement.

Excavations at Sidbury, Worcester conducted by the Worcester Museum (HWCM 117) in 1977 went down to Roman levels which included a 1st century BC—1st century AD ditch with waterlogged sediment which seems to be potentially interesting (Greig in press a) for the study of urban deposits by means of pollen analysis. S Colledge found two charred wheat grains in a Roman context at this site (reported in Carver 1980).

Wroxeter, another much-excavated site has had some environmental archaeological work done over the years; there is a short charcoal report from early excavations (C Weston in Kenyon 1980). M Monk has been organising a sieving and sorting programme for the recovery of charred plant remains.

3.6 Saxon, Medieval and Post-Medieval Urban results, castles

D G Wilson has studied material from a 13th–14th century cesspit found during excavations in Chester (Wilson 1975) in which a very small sample of 40g produced a flora of 29 taxa including fruit stones and the seeds of poisonous weeds like *Agrostemma githago* which were a problem if they contaminated flour supplies; the various possibilities were discussed.

Apparently similar material has been found at Coventry and studied by I Strachan in the Geology Department but it is not known whether these results are published. Excavations in 1978 by J Bateman in Cox Street by the 15/16th century town wall produced organic material which was studied by S Colledge (AML Report 3348). She found a large weed flora, with lesser signs of plants of grassland and wetland. There were no fruit remains, but *Cannabis sativa* was present. The pollen spectrum was rich in Cerealia pollen so straw remains may have been present, and finds of *Botago* pollen are of interest. The insect remains are being studied by S Colledge and P J Osborne. The overall impression is of 'clean' rather than 'foul' rubbish in this sample.

Hen Domen is just outside the West Midlands area, but a short mention is included. A deep pit was found inside the bailey of this castle, full of organic matter. J Greig helped in the excavations and studied the pollen and seeds, while the associated insect fauna was studied by M Girling, and the flies by P Skidmore (AML Report 2530). The range of grassland and wetland plant remains, but not food, together with a 'compost heap and dung' insect fauna and the finds of horse shoe nails during excavation tend to suggest that stable sweepings may be the source of much of this material. These results have prompted studies into the composition of hay and its likely archaeological remains, which are discussed in 3.8. The excavation and environmental report are in press (Barker in press).

Hereford is another place with extensive medieval remains, mainly excavated by R Shoesmith. Environmental archaeological work has been done there; Hood (1970) reported the identification of various woody taxa from charcoal, while Mitchell (1970) provided a seed flora which included fig, grape, flax and a range of weeds. McCutcheon and Hood (1970) produced a weed seed flora and some mollusc identifications from another sample. Further environmental work on Hereford material has been reported in the reports of the Environmental Archaeology Unit at York.

The Leominster Old Priory excavations of 1979 provided a bone fauna studied by A Locker of both bird bones and fish (AML Report 3277).

The ditch of the twelfth century castle at Nantwich was excavated in 1977, and the organic deposits sampled and studied by S Colledge (AML Report 3347). The most interesting features are, perhaps, the records of *Juglans* pollen at this early time, the Cannabiaceae and *Linum usitatissimum* records, and the presence of so many weed seeds, compared with other ditches which more often produce a flora of wetland plants which would probably have grown in the ditch itself, as at Birmingham (Greig AML Report 2919).

At Shrewsbury, re-development seems to have removed much of the medieval town. At Rigg's Hall, however, excavated by N Baker, tenth and eleventh century pits contained charred plant remains as reported by S Colledge in AML Report 2982. Most of the remains were flower bases and seeds of *Avena sativa*. Other grains include *Triticum aestivo-compactum*, *T. spelta*, *Secale cereale* and *Hordeum vulgare*, and edible plants by *Prunus spinosa*, and a range of other weeds were also present. This represents a useful assemblage because it is vital to know what crops and also weeds were present at various times in order to trace the changes in crop husbandry and in cereal weed floras over the years. This site is early medieval, and it lacks the later medieval typical weeds *Anthemis cotula*, *Centaurea cyanus* and *Chrysanthemum segetum*.

There is a large excavation programme at present being carried out in Stafford, with an 'environmental assistant' doing the sampling and sorting. A large assemblage of charred remains is being collected from deposits of various ages. Waterlogged sites have not been found recently, but in the 1975 excavations in Clark Street by the city walls, M Carver dug some peaty material which had a generally wetland flora (unpublished) which is probably the result of the site's proximity to the King's Pool. The latter is a glacial hollow which has a reported depth of 30m, and has been bored to provide a core for A Morgan to study the beetle remains, and D Bartley the pollen. A core for archaeological investigations was made in 1977 by J Greig and S Colledge, discussed in 3.7.

Excavations in Bolebridge Street, Tamworth, by R Meeson in 1978 revealed organic material, some of which has been examined by S Colledge and J Greig who identified the seeds, and charred material which was examined by S Colledge.

Worcester is another city with archaeological potential, especially for the medieval period. Earlier work includes a bone report (Chaplin 1968–9) and a report on plant remains (Williams 1971). More recently, excavation by M Carver on the post-Roman part of the Sidbury site mentioned earlier (Carver 1980) includes seed reports by S Colledge (1980a) and seed and insect reports by S Colledge and P J Osborne (1980) mainly from cesspits. Excavations near this site in advance of road building in 1975 revealed a few archaeological features which were recorded, and the remains of a barrel latrine which were excavated and whose contents are reported in Greig (1981) with report by P J Osborne on the beetle remains, by P Skidmore on the diptera, by A Jones on the fish bones and by E Crowfoot on the cloth remains. The barrel contents were interpreted as a mixture of domestic rubbish including food remains and perhaps household flooring herbs, and human turds containing the ova of various intestinal parasites. Such finds give the environmental archaeologist the best opportunity to show aspects of past everyday life and to compare this scientifically derived information with what is known from documentary sources.

3.7   Environmental information from non-archaeological sites

Most of this comes from pollen analysis (Figure 15). The midlands is not an area well-known for its pollen diagrams, unlike the fens or the Somerset levels for example, and this is because there are few obvious pollen sites apart from the meres in the north of the area. Recently good pollen analysis sites have been found in small peat deposits which were previously overlooked, as in the Golden Valley, and also in the peats in alluvium which sometimes have excellent sequences. These two types of site are more than usually relevant to the archaeology of their particular areas because they are small wetland areas in which the representation of the pollen of dry land plants may be good, and also because many of these small sites are close to archaeological sites or areas suitable for occupation. This contrasts with some places with good peat, but in uplands which were probably not the main areas of human occupation. The pollen sites are shown in Figure 15. Since this is an archaeological review it is intended to discuss only the archaeological relevance of the results, such as forest, clearance and signs of agriculture, over the last 5000 years only.

Starting with the full forest of the area just before the onset of Neolithic settlement, there is evidence (Greig in press b) that much of the area would have been covered with a forest mainly dominated by *Tilia* although this lime forest seems to have increasing amounts of oak in the north of the midland area. The lime forest also gives way to oak in the west, but the signs are of lime forest still dominating at the western limit of the midlands area, thinning out in Wales. The evidence from pollen diagrams is sparse in various parts of the midlands, but careful searching for sites may fill in some of the gaps. To the east of the midlands area there is an almost complete dearth of pollen diagrams which could be called 'the midland gap', although, once again, careful searching may produce some sites.

After forest maximum come signs of clearance in stages, reflecting successive stages of colonisation of parts of the land. Many pollen diagrams show these effects, such as the Elm Decline marking Neolithic settlement about 5000 years ago. Later clearance episodes need to be carefully dated for them to be archaeologically useful, and few of the pollen diagrams from this area have a good radiocarbon chronology. This is often because the more recent peat is more likely to have been disturbed, by modern root penetration for example, or by peat cutting. The best dating materials, like wood twigs in peat, may not be present at the levels where dates are wanted, and it may require several sampling sessions to obtain the necessary material from the right levels. Turner (1965) has dated clearance levels at Whixall Moss to the Bronze Age. The King's Pool at Stafford is a prime site for pollen analysis since it is right on the edge of the city, and Colledge (AML Report 2535) has a radiocarbon dated sequence. An increase in Cerealia pollen between the dated levels of about 300 ad and 1000 ad may represent the Saxon settlement of the area which culminated in the founding of Stafford itself. The Cannabiaceae curve which starts together with that of *Centaurea cyanus* some time after 1000 ad shows signs of either hop or hemp cultivation in the Middle Ages which is as interesting as the introduction or spread of the cornflower which seems to happen at about this time, according to the results from several sites. The sedimentology of the King's Pool means that the dated (peat) horizons are not always those where pollen changes occur, but there is enough dating evidence to be able to approximate. It is to be hoped that the work on plant macrofossils from the excavations in Stafford can amplify these palynological results.

Cookley, on the Stour valley, was a site discovered by S Limbrey when a water main was being constructed across it in a 3m deep trench, pumped dry. The valley was found to contain peaty sediments which do not appear to have been re-worked or disturbed to any great extent. The sequence goes from the Late-glacial period until recently, and seems to have a good sequence of clearance phases with agriculture including *Vicia faba*, the field bean. The work on this site includes the sedimentology, by S Limbrey, and insects, plant macrofossils and pollen. It will be a major undertaking, but invaluable for archaeological research.

The Severn basin is being studied by sedimentologists, hydrologists, geomorphologists, geologists, palaeobotanists and others as the British contribution to the International Geological Correlation Programme (IGCP). This has stimulated research which impinges upon archaeological interests in the fields of vegetation history, the impact of man on vegetation and soils, land use history, the history of valley floor sedimentation and water supply. Contributions to this research come largely from the Geography Departments of the Universities of Southampton, Reading and Aberystwyth, and the Archaeology, Geology and Geography Departments of Birmingham University. Some work on river valley alluviation in the Avon has been published (Shotton 1978) and other work by F Shotton and P J Osborne on the insect faunas is in preparation, as are results from Bidford on insects, pollen, molluscs and plant macrofossils by J Greig and P J Osborne.

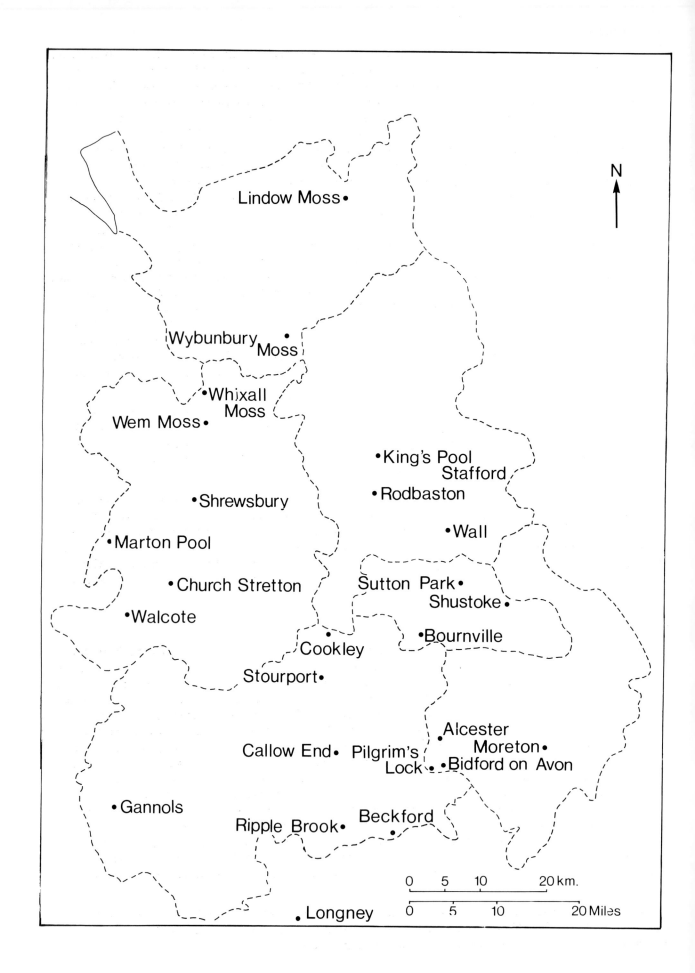

Figure 15 Pollen and beetle sites: 5000 BP–present

3.8 Methods

One particular area of work where methodology is important is in the extraction of charred plant remains, mainly grain, from soil. In the last ten years a range of methods has been proposed, including various kinds of 'seed machine' which were mainly developed in the Near East for the needs of sites there. Midland sites tend to have an appreciable silt and clay content in the soils, especially in the Keuper marl areas shown in Figure 10, and although no 'seed machine' has ever been tried here, it has been felt that it would not be very effective in this soil, and alternative methods have been applied. The method which seems to work here is that the soil is sieved in water on a 0.3–0.5mm mesh sieve, usually made from a gardening sieve lined with commercially-available plastic mesh. This removes much of the clay and silt fractions. The remaining material is dried and then put in water to float off the charcoal and other organic matter. After three 'floats' the stony residue is discarded, and the float is soaked in a 'Calgon' solution to disperse clay, before final drying and sorting. Drying can be difficult, but adaptations of old cupboards, electric light bulbs and aluminium foil are effective. The sampling, sieving and initial sorting are carried out by 'environmental assistants' so that the contractors can spend their time doing the identifications. Non-charred material is only extracted in the laboratory, because it needs more experience and equipment for its handling. It would be hard to give 'recipes' for extracting plant and insect remains, because samples vary so much. Samples are normally measured either by weight or volume, and initially only about 1kg or 1 litre are processed, because some samples are especially rich in remains. Samples are broken down in warm water, put through a coarse sieve to remove large stones etc, and then sieved on meshes such as 0.3m, 2.0mm and 4mm to provide easily sorted fractions. 'Calgon' is used to disperse clay remaining after sieving, and the samples are stored and sorted in alcohol. Insect remains are extracted without paraffin flotation because seeds do not all float, and it is easier to sort through different size fractions rather than a float and a residue with their oily globules, which are hard to get rid of. Samples for plant remain studies are often smaller than those for beetles, so the beetle remains from the small botanical samples may have to be added to the results of the paraffin floating of a much larger sample.

There are not many special methods applied to pollen analysis. Archaeological samples may have a much richer pollen flora than is usually found, for example, in upland peats. The pollen reference collection therefore needs to be very comprehensive. Samples which may contain faeces are usually split during preparation so that one slide can be prepared which has been acetolysed, and one which has not. The latter is examined for intestinal parasite ova which may give a good guide to the likely faecal content of the material.

General work of environmental relevance is the examination of the microscopic and macroscopic content of various materials in order to provide a degree of proof for interpretation. Work on the pollen content of hay, straw, chaff, bread, flour, beans, hops and fruit was considered necessary for the interpretation of some pollen results from towns (Greig in press a). Further work is being done on the pollen and seed content of hay from species-rich meadows in order to establish a link between the amounts of pollen and seeds and the abundance of the plants in the meadows. This should improve the interpretation of material from archaeological deposits, and provide information on what ancient hay meadows were like.

4 Directions of future work

The prehistoric period is one of great changes, to the vegetation, the soils and to the landscape as a whole. There have been few intensive archaeological investigations and still fewer environmental ones, apart from the Beckford work. The direction that future projects should take will be determined by what finally results from Beckford, now sadly hindered by local government cuts. It would be very useful if a similar piece of environmental and archaeological work could be done on a Neolithic or Bronze Age site, if a chance arose. Likewise, the hillfort excavations took place before suitable methods were developed for the large-scale recovery of charred remains, but if one was excavated it would provide a chance to compare results with those from Beckford. The work of Gordon Hillman has shown the potential for interpreting the crop husbandry practises carried out on various parts of a site (e.g. Hillman 1981). All we know at present are the generalities about the commoner crops like emmer and spelt, and their occurrence at sites of different ages. Much of the early work has been based on very small samples, or hand-picked material, often studied by people who never had a chance to see the site, so it is not surprising that the results are often rather uninformative. It would be desirable to have a far more detailed knowledge of what was grown where and when, and about the rarer crops which only come to light in detailed investigation, such as the less usual wheats, rye, field beans, peas, flax, hemp and hops. Intensive charred remains recovery on site, and pollen analysis nearby, should provide some answers. A waterlogged prehistoric Runnymede-type site would be ideal from many points of view, and worth looking for if there are any Midland riverside building works.

The gravel sites on alluvium are interesting, but perhaps the good work already published on some of these (e.g. Lambrick and Robinson 1979) makes the need for information a little less pressing, for Beckford, Blackstone, Tiddington and Wasperton should all add to local knowledge on the subject.

Roman sites with good environmental potential have not often been found. It is tantalising to think what plant remains may have been associated with the organic matter from Alcester (Osborne 1971a), and possibly other such rich sites may appear. Well fills may help provide the general background especially if they have preserved some of the rubbish — the Romans had the infuriating habit, from the environmental point of view, of cleanly disposing of much of their rubbish thus leaving us with less evidence than we would like on some aspects of their life and surroundings (Greig in press a). This contrasts with the insanitary medieval people. Some rich deposits of charred chaff and grain found at Alcester and Droitwich show that there is plenty of potential for work on Roman grain as well as prehistoric. After the Romano-British period there is something of an archaeological gap, and therefore a gap in environmental knowledge. Work on Saxon sites like Stafford, Worcester and Wasperton may help redress this balance, and almost anything environmental dated between 500—1000 AD is of great interest because of rarity value.

Medieval sites are botanically interesting because of the increasing documentation that permits comparison with environmental results. Worcester's barrel latrine provides a very rich plant and animal assemblage, and other such deposits would be interesting for comparative purposes, particularly from different dates. Work on sewage from Taunton shows that a history of the use of many plants from environmental evidence can be pieced together by studying latrines of various ages, so it is hoped that more well-preserved ones will appear. Too often the only remains are a few Calcium phosphate replaced mineralised seeds with a small and uninformative flora. Medieval grain deposits are also of interest because they have not been much studied.

Post-medieval environmental archaeology, such as that on the Birmingham moat (Greig 1980, 1981a) shows some potential. Latrine deposits would be very interesting because of the chance of tracing the introduction of many plants, such as the peppercorns now found from Oxford and Taunton and perhaps even New World introductions like tomato pips.

Waterlogged ditches and pits present problems to the environmentalist. In the past they have been sampled at a close stratigraphic interval and these samples studied, only to find in many cases that the results are uniform. Clearly a more careful approach is needed to economise on time, so now the 'top, middle and bottom approach' is used. The first samples examined are from these three positions on the succession, and only if they greatly differ will the intervening samples be examined. Ditches and pits may also have a rather aquatic flora and fauna which tells little of human activities.

Pollen analysis is very time consuming, but it does provide interesting results. Pollen spectra from waterlogged deposits are always worth doing if macrofossils are also being studied, because of the additional information which becomes available. The construction of pollen diagrams from more or less natural deposits can justify the time spent if there is a nearby archaeological site occupied at the time when the deposit was forming (as at Beckford) or if particular phases of landscape can be dated, as at Cookley. Pollen diagrams are very unpopular with other environmental archaeologists and probably the archaeologists themselves because of their very incomprehensibility and there are various things which can be done to improve the position: careful drawing for clarity is one point, and a grouping of taxa as far as possible in ecological groups is considered important. Separate diagrams summarising the interpretation of the results can also help.

Soil pollen analysis has not often been tried on Midland material because few buried soils have been found, and results have not been very encouraging, perhaps because the soils have not always been acid enough for pollen preservation.

The philosophy behind the study of plant macrofossils is based on obtaining a flora large enough to be representative of the deposit concerned, in the same way that pollen counts need to be around 400 grains. Seed counts sometimes reach thousands before they are considered sufficient, from rich deposits like latrines, otherwise around 5000 may be an average optimum seed count if nothing is superabundant, as some weed seeds are apt to be. The time taken may depend upon the amount of detailed identification of difficult groups that needs to be undertaken, as well as the ease of extraction of the seeds from the matrix.

Combined results from pollen, seeds, beetles flies etc are considered especially important, together with work on modern deposits, for true and detailed interpretation of results. It would be ridiculous to spend large amounts of time extracting and identifying one particular type of remain, while discarding the others in the deposit. It is a matter of policy to try to get the largest possible range of remains identified although this may depend upon the kindness of other specialists.

Problems of soil history in the region concern the changes in profile types in the sandstones and other coarse textured rocks, involving initiation of podzolisation, its progress under changing land use and the history of reclamation and maintenance of podzols under potentially podzolising soils under intensive agriculture. There are a number of reports of podzol profiles buried beneath Roman roads, for example in Sutton Park, perhaps heathland then as now, and by contrast near Hagley in Worcestershire where surrounding cultivated soils are not now podzols. The impression is of the widespread development of heathland in the Midlands, perhaps from the Bronze Age or earlier, and a subsequent history of differentially distributed and perhaps fluctuating reclamation for more intensive agricultural use. On the Keuper Marl and other areas of heavy soils it is the history of drainage problems and associated profile changes which are of interest archaeologically.

Many aspects of environmental archaeology which cannot be dealt with in the Department of Plant Biology can be studied by other DOE staff, consultants, or contractors, or by the kindness of colleagues, and this system provides a good coverage. Animal bones, including those of fish, are perhaps the greatest difficulty, because there is nobody in the Midlands working on them, yet they appear from all but the most acidic-soiled sites. Most bone specialists are kept busy with the work from their own areas, and are understandably unwilling to take on material from still more sites. Insect remains are the next most pressing need.

Future work is hard to predict, because the archaeological programmes are not finalised until months before they start, and often the potential for environmental archaeology can only be assessed as the excavation proceeds. It is therefore impossible to predict the kind of work likely to be done in the future. Some of the types of site that would be especially interesting have been mentioned. Some areas have a great potential interest too, like the Golden Valley in the Wye basin where there are small peat deposits and archaeological remains of a variety of ages, not greatly disturbed by modern development. Fortunately many of the archaeologists working in this area have been trained in the basic ideas of environmental archaeology and are more than willing to take this subject into account even in the planning of excavations, and in supplying the manpower for 'environmental assistants'.

ACKNOWLEDGEMENTS

I am very grateful to those archaeologists, whose environmental reports have been delayed in completion because of the unscheduled insertion of this review into an already over-full work programme, for their patience. I am also grateful to colleagues, including Drs S Limbrey, P C Buckland and S Esmonde Cleary, who have read and commented on parts of the review.

LIST OF REFERENCES

BARFIELD L H, HODDER M, 1981 — 'Birmingham's Bronze Age', *Curr Archaeol* 78, 198–200.

BARKER P, HIGHAM R, in press — *Hen Domen, Montgomery, a timber castle on the Welsh border*, Vol 1, Roy Archaeol Inst, London.

BIRKS H J B, 1965a — 'Late-glacial deposits at Ragmere, Cheshire and Chat Moss, Lancashire', *New Phytol* 64, 270–314.

BIRKS H J B, 1965b — 'Pollen analytical investigations at Holcroft Moss, Lancashire and Lindow Moss, Cheshire', *J Ecology* 53, 299–314.

BRITNELL W, 1974 — 'Beckford', *Curr Archaeol* 45, 293–297.

BROWN A, in press — 'Human impact on former floodplain woodlands of the Severn', in Bell M, Limbrey S, (eds) *Archaeological Aspects of Woodland Ecology*, Brit Archaeol Rep.

CARVER M O H, 1980 — 'The excavation of three medieval craftsmans' tenements in Sidbury, Worcester', *Trans Worcestershire Archaeol Soc* ser 3, 7, 155–219.

CHAPLIN R E, 1968–9 — 'The animal bones from three late- and post-medieval rubbish tips', *Trans Worcestershire Archaeol Soc* ser 3, 2, 89–91.

COLLEDGE S M, 1980a — in Carver M O H, 1980, 212.

COLLEDGE S M, 1981e — 'Charred grain and other seeds' in Stanford S C, 1981, 160–162.

COLLEDGE S M, OSBORNE P J, 1980 — in Carver M, 1980, 207–210.

CRAWFORD G, 1982 — 'Wasperton', *West Midlands Archaeol* 24 (1981 vol), 121–129.

EARP J R, HAINS B A, 1971 — *British Regional Geology: The Welsh Borderland*, HMSO, London.

GELLING P S, 1963 — 'Excavations at Caynham Camp, near Ludlow, final report', *Trans Shropshire Archaeol Soc* 57.

GILMORE F, 1970–1972 — 'Animal Remains', in Oswald A, 'Excavations at Beckford', *Trans Worcestershire Archaeol Soc* ser 3, 3, 7–54.

GODWIN H, DICKSON J H, 1960–1965 — 'Report on plant remains in organic deposits below Roman road (Watling Street) at Wall, monolith cut and examined, with pollen spectrum by C A Dickson', 17–18 in Gould J, 'Excavations in advance of road construction at Shenstone and Wall (Staffs.)' *Lichfield Archaeol Hist Soc Trans* 2–6, 1–18.

GREIG J R A, 1979a — in Smith C (ed), 1979, 81–85, 185–188.

GREIG J R A, 1981a — 'The plant remains', 66–72 in Watts L, 'Birmingham moat, its history, topography and destruction', *Trans Birmingham Warwickshire Archaeol Soc* (for 1978–9), 89.

GREIG J R A, 1981b — 'The investigation of a medieval barrel latrine from Worcester', *J Archaeol Sci* 8, 265–282.

GREIG J R A, in press a — 'The interpretation of pollen spectra from urban archaeological deposits', in Hall A R, Kenward H K (eds), *Environmental archaeology in the urban context*, Counc Brit Archaeol Res Rep 43, London.

GREIG J R A, in press b

'Past and present lime woods of Europe', in Limbrey S, Bell M (eds), *Archaeological aspects of woodland ecology*, Brit Archaeol Rep.

HAINS B A, HORTON A, 1969

British Regional Geology: Central England, HMSO, London.

HARDY E M, 1939

'Studies on the Post-glacial history of British vegetation: 5, the Shropshire and Flint Maelor mosses', *New Phytol* 38, 364–396.

HILLMAN G, 1981

'Reconstructing crop husbandry practices from charred remains of crops', 123–162, in Mercer R (ed), *Farming practice in British prehistory*, Edinburgh University Press.

JESSEN K, HELBAEK H, 1944

'Cereals in Great Britain and Ireland in prehistoric and early historic times', *Det Kongelige Danske Videnskabernes Selskab*, Biologiske Skrifter, Bind III, Nr. 2: 1–68.

MITCHELL G F, 1971

'Seed and fruit stones from pit 1', Note 2 (235–6) in Shoesmith R, 'Hereford City Excavations 1970', *Trans Woolhope Natur Fld Clb*, 40, 225–240.

OSBORNE P J, 1965

'The effects of forest clearance on the distribution of the British insect fauna', *Proc 12th Int Congress Entomology, London, 1964*, 456–7.

OSBORNE P J, 1969

'An insect fauna of Late Bronze Age date from Wilsford, Wiltshire', *J Animal Ecology* 38, 555–566.

OSBORNE P J, 1971a

'An insect fauna from the Roman site at Alcester, Warwickshire', *Britannia* 2, 156–165.

OSBORNE P J, 1971b

'Insect fauna from the Roman harbour', in Cunliffe B, *Excavations at Fishbourne 1961–9*, Res Rep Soc Antiq London 27, 393–396.

OSBORNE P J, 1973

'*Airaphilus elongatus* (Gyll.) (Coll. Cucujidae) present in Britain in Roman times', *Entomologists' Monthly Mag*, 109.

OSBORNE P J, 1976

'Evidence from the insects of climatic variation during the Flandrian period', *World Archaeol* 8, 150–158.

OSBORNE P J, 1977

'Stored product beetles from a Roman site at Droitwich, England', *J Stored Products Res* 13, 203–204.

OSBORNE P J, 1981a

'Some British later prehistoric faunas and their climatic implications' 68–74 in Harding A (ed), *Climatic Change in Later Prehistory*, Edinburgh University Press.

OSBORNE P J, 1981b

'Coleopterous fauna from Layer 1', in Greig J R A, 1981b, 268–271.

OSBORNE P J (in preparation)

'An insect fauna from a modern cesspit. Comparison with probable cesspit assemblages from archaeological sites'.

PALMER N, 1982

'Tiddington Roman settlement: an interim report on excavations 1980–81', *West Midlands Archaeol* 24 (1981), 16–24.

PANNETT D, MORLEY C, 1976

'The origin of the old river bed at Shrewsbury', *Bull Shropshire Conserv Trust* 35, 7–12.

ROBERTS J, 1970–2

'Note on the examination of carbonised seeds from an Iron Age site at Beckford, Worcestershire', 28–29 in Oswald A, Excavations at Beckford, *Trans Worcestershire Archaeol Soc* ser 3, 3, 7–54.

ROWLANDS P H, 1966

Pleistocene stratigraphy and palynology in West Shropshire, unpublished PhD thesis, University of Birmingham.

ROWLANDS P H, SHOTTON F W, 1971

'Pleistocene deposits of Church Stretton (Shropshire) and its neighbourhood', *J Geol Soc* 127, 599–622.

SAVILLE A, 1981

'Mesolithic industries in central England; an exploratory investigation using microlith typology', *Archaeol J* 138, 49–71.

SHOTTON F W, 1959

'New petrological groups based on axes from the West Midlands', *Proc Prehist Soc* 25, 135–143.

SHOTTON F W, 1967

'Investigation of an old peat moor at Moreton Morrell, Warwickshire', *Proc Coventry and Dist Natur Hist Sci Soc* 4, 13–16.

SHOTTON F W, 1972

'A comparison of modern and Bronze Age mollusc faunas from the Warwickshire and Worcestershire Avon', *Proc Coventry Natur Hist Soc* 4, 173–181.

SHOTTON F W, 1978

'Alluvium in the lower Severn-Avon valleys' 27 in Limbrey S, Evans J G (eds), *The effect of man on the landscape: the lowland zone*, Counc Brit Archaeol Res Rep 21.

SHOTTON F W, OSBORNE P J, GREIG J R A, 1977

'The fossil content of a Flandrian deposit at Alcester', *Proc Coventry and Dist Natur Hist Sci Soc* 5, 19–32.

SHOTTON F W, STRACHAN I, 1959

'The investigation of a peat moor at Rodbaston, Penkridge, Staffordshire', *Quart J Geol Soc London* 115, 1–15.

SLATER F M, 1972

'A history of the vegetation at Wem Moss', *Proc Birmingham Natur Hist Soc* 22, 92–118.

SMITH C, 1979

Fisherwick: the reconstruction of an Iron Age landscape, Brit Archaeol Rep 61.

SPENCE T F, 1967

'An anatomical study of cremated bone fragment from archaeological sites', *Proc Prehist Soc* 33, 70–83.

STANFORD S C, 1974

Croft Ambrey; excavations carried out for the Woolhope Naturalists' Field Club (Herefordshire) 1960–1966, Leominster.

STANFORD S C, 1981

Midsummer Hill: an Iron Age Hillfort on the Malverns; excavations carried out for the Malvern Hills Archaeological Committee 1965–1970, Leominster.

TALLIS J H, BIRKS H J B, 1965

'The past and present distribution of *Scheuzeria palustris* in Europe', *J Ecology* 53, 287.

TRUEMAN A E, 1971

Geology and Scenery of England and Wales, revised by Whittow J B, Hardy J R, Penguin, Harmondsworth.

TURNER J, 1962

'The *Tilia* decline: an anthropogenic interpretation', *New Phytol* 61, 328–341.

TURNER J, 1964

'The anthropogenic factor in vegetational history, 1. Tregaron and Whixall mosses', *New Phytol* 63, 73.

WARWICK G T, 1971

'The physical background' in Cadbury D A, Hawkes J G, Readett R C, *A Computer-mapped Flora of Warwickshire*, Birmingham Natural History Society (Academic Press) London, 4–15.

WESTON C, 1980

'Note on the charcoal' 38 in Kenyon K, 'Excavations at Viroconium 1952–3', *Trans Shropshire Archaeol Soc* (for 1975–6) 60, 5–36.

WILLIAMS T J, 1971   'Plant remains in the 15th century cloisters of the college of the vicars choral, Hereford', *Medieval Archaeol* 15, 117–118.

WILSON D G, 1975   'Plant foods and poisons from medieval Chester', *J Chester Archaeol Soc* 58 (for 1973–75), 57–67.

ANCIENT MONUMENTS LABORATORY REPORTS

ARTHUR J R B, 1975   'Seed identification; Beeston Castle, Cheshire', AML Report 1806.

ARTHUR J R B, 1975b   'Seed identification; Victoria Street, Hereford', AML Report 1861.

BAYLEY J, 1974   'Human bone; Beeston Castle, Cheshire', AML Report 1632.

BAYLEY J, 1974   'Human bone; Bromfield', AML Report 1639.

BAYLEY J, 1975   'Human bone; Castle Green, Hereford', AML Report 1877.

COLLEDGE S M, 1978   'An interim report, Clarke Street, Stafford (1975–8)', AML Report 2534.

COLLEDGE S M, 1978b   'An interim environmental report, The King's Pool, Stafford (1977–1978)', AML Report 2535.

COLLEDGE S M, 1978c   'An interim environmental report, Beckford, an Iron Age site (1976–1977)', AML Report 2536.

COLLEDGE S M, 1978d   'Environmental report, Sidbury site, Worcester (1976–1977)', AML Report 2537.

COLLEDGE S M, 1978e   'Environmental report, the Roman well at Alcester, Bleachfield Street', AML Report 2577.

COLLEDGE S M, 1979a   'A final report on the plant remains from Rigg's Hall, Shrewsbury', AML Report 2982.

COLLEDGE S M, 1979b   'A final report on the plant remains from the Sidbury site, Worcester', AML Report 2983.

COLLEDGE S M, 1980b   'Palaeobotanical studies in the West Midlands', AML Report 3096.

COLLEDGE S M, 1980c   'A report on the plant remains from a Neolithic site at Bromfield, Shropshire', AML Report 3112.

COLLEDGE S M, 1981a   'A report on the charred plant remains from the Coulter's Garage site in Alcester', AML Report 3284.

COLLEDGE S M, 1981b   'A report on the charred plant remains from the Midsummer Hill, Herefordshire, excavations', AML Report 3308.

COLLEDGE S M, 1981c   'A report on the micro- and macroscopic plant remains from 'the Crown' car park site in Nantwich', AML Report 3347.

COLLEDGE S M, 1981d   'A report on the plant remains from a 15th Century pit in the Cox Street site, Coventry', AML Report 3348.

CROWFOOT E, 1976   'Examination of textiles, Worcester', AML Report 2124.

EVANS J G, 1976   'Mollusca identification; Cantilupe Street, Hereford', AML Report 2147.

EVANS J G, 1975   'Mollusca identification; Beeston Castle, Cheshire, AML Report 1820.

EVANS J G, 1975b   'Mollusca identification; Wroxeter', AML Report 1825.

GEBBELS A, 1974   'Animal bone; Beeston Castle, Cheshire', AML Report 1714.

GEBBELS A, 1975   'Animal bone; Hereford', AML Report 1918.

GIRLING M A, 1978   'The insect fauna, Hereford', AML Report 2703.

GIRLING M A, 1981   'Insects from Coulters' Garage, Alcester', AML Report 3394.

GREIG J R A, 1976   'Birmingham Moat; environmental report, with a contribution by Dr S Limbrey', AML Report 2058.

GREIG J R A, 1977   'Interim report on the remains found in layer 1, and on the cloth by E Crowfoot, Worcester medieval barrel latrine', AML Report 2439.

GREIG J R A, 1978a   'A report on the plant, beetle, and fly remains from the pit (F1/27) Hen Domen, with reports by M A Girling and P Skidmore', AML Report 2530.

GREIG J R A, 1978b   'A preliminary report on the material recovered in the excavations at Bolebridge Street, Tamworth', AML Report 2532.

GREIG J R A, 1978c   'A report on the seeds and pollen from the Iron Age site at Fisherwick, Staffordshire', AML Report 2539.

GREIG J R A, 1978d   'A report on two pollen spectra obtained from peaty material collected from a section in the bank of the River Alne, near Alcester, Warwickshire', AML Report 2541.

GREIG J R A, 1979b   'Birmingham Moat plant remains; a reconsideration', AML Report 2919.

GREIG J R A, 1980a   'The interpretation of pollen spectra from urban archaeological deposits', AML Report 3097.

GREIG J R A, 1980b   'The investigation of a medieval barrel-latrine from Worcester', AML Report 3229.

GREIG J R A, WOODWARDS L, 1980   'Landscape changes over the last 2000 years, deduced from remains at Alcester, Coulters Garage site', AML Report 3111.

GREIG J R A, 1981c   'A pollen spectrum from Mucking', AML Report 3555.

GREIG J R A, 1981d   'Past and present lime woods of Europe', AML Report 3558.

GREIG J R A, COLLEDGE S M, 1981   'Current environmental archaeology on the midlands', AML Report 3553.

GREIG J R A, 1982   'A small pollen spectrum from the Wrekin (Shropshire) and its limited interpretation', AML Report 3625.

HILLAM J, 1978   'Dendrochronological analysis of Roman timbers from Friary Street 1, Droitwich', AML Report 2552.

JONES R T, 1976a   'Animal bones; Beeston Castle, Cheshire', AML Report 2010.

JONES R T, 1976b   'Animal bones; Cantilupe Street and Castle Green, Hereford', AML Report 2013.

KEELEY H C M, 1974a   'Soil investigations; Red Hill, Lilleshall, Shropshire', AML Report 1703.

KEELEY H C M, 1974b   'Soil investigations; Norton Priory, Runcorn, Cheshire', AML Report 1707.

KEELEY H C M, 1975   'Seed identification; Beckford', AML Report 1896.

KEELEY H C M, 1976   'Soil investigations, Hereford', AML Report 2032.

KEELEY H C M, 1978 — 'Report on a soil sample from Stone House Much Park Street, Coventry', AML Report 2710.

KEEPAX C, 1975 — 'Charcoal identification; Beckford', AML Report 1905.

KEEPAX C, 1976a — 'Soil investigations; Leintwardine', AML Report 2016.

KEEPAX C, 1976b — 'Charcoal identification, Castle Green, Hereford', AML Report 2031.

KEEPAX C, 1976c — 'General environmental investigations; Hereford', AML Report 2033.

KEEPAX C, 1976d — 'Soil investigations; Haughmond Abbey, Shropshire', AML Report 2076.

KEEPAX C, 1976e — 'Wood identification, Beckford', AML Report 2078.

KEEPAX C, PARADINE P J, 1976 — 'The use of the flotation machine at Blackstone, Worcester and the seeds obtained', AML Report 2174.

KEEPAX C, 1978a — 'Wood remains from metal objects; Wroxeter, interim report', AML Report 2597.

KEEPAX C, 1978b — 'Charcoal identification; Hereford, Berrington Street', AML Report 2602.

KEEPAX C, 1978c — 'Wood identification; Droitwich', AML Report 2605.

KEEPAX C, 1979a — 'Charcoal from Blackstone (Hereford and Worcester)', AML Report 2717.

KEEPAX C, 1979b — 'Replaced wood; Wroxeter', AML Report 2864.

KEEPAX C, 1981 — 'Radiocarbon samples from Beckford', AML Report 3436.

LOCKER (GEBBELS) A, 1981 — 'Leominster Old Priory; the fish bones', AML Report 3277.

McPHAIL R, KEELEY H C M, 1978 — 'The soils and pollen of Norton Priory, Runcorn, Cheshire', AML Report 2701.

NODDLE B, 1976 — 'Animal bones, Bewell House, Hereford', AML Report 2082.

NODDLE B, 1979 — 'Animal bones from Droitwich, Bay's Meadow', AML Report 2749.

O'CONNOR T P, 1975 — 'Human Bone, Wootton Wawen churchyard, Warwickshire', AML Report 1922.

STRAKER V, 1979 — 'Macroscopic plant remains from Droitwich, Bay's Meadow', AML Report 2812.

TAYLOR P, KEELEY H C M, KEEPAX C, 1976 — 'General investigations; Wroxeter', AML Report 2067.

THORNTON J H, 1977 — 'Leather examination, Alcester 1964', AML Report 2399.

THORNTON J H, 1978 — 'Examination of leather, Tong Castle, Shropshire', AML Report 2582.

THORNTON J H, 1979 — 'Tong Castle, Shropshire – leather, part 2', AML Report 2814.

Chapter 3   A REVIEW OF LATER QUATERNARY PLANT MICROFOSSIL AND MACROFOSSIL RESEARCH IN SOUTHERN ENGLAND; WITH SPECIAL REFERENCE TO ENVIRONMENTAL ARCHAEOLOGICAL EVIDENCE

Robert G Scaife

1   Introduction

1.1   The background

Detailed knowledge of vegetational and environmental conditions, and their changes can be obtained for the Pleistocene and Holocene periods through the extraction and analyses of sub-fossil microscopic (pollen) and macroscopic (seeds and vegetative structures) plant remains. These data have provided much of the background material relevant to the discipline of environmental archaeology enabling the correct appraisal of man in his surroundings and his effect on, and utilisation of, these environs.

South and South East England has for long been an area with comparatively few sites having been investigated for elucidation of Flandrian vegetational history. This fact has been noted by a number of previous researchers (Smith and Pilcher 1973, Scaife 1980a, 1980b, 1982a).

'There is particular need for such combined studies in South East England since it is likely that it was there that early post-glacial immigrations began. If such combined studies are carried out by future workers, then by an extension of the kind of survey presented here it should be possible to follow routes of migration and to study the patterns of vegetational change in relation to topographic and climatic factors.' (Smith and Pilcher 1973, 912–913).

Evidence from specific regions within the South East similarly needs further and greater elucidation. Sheldon (1978) has indicated this for the Wealden area. J Turner (1970) has pointed to the absence of botanical evidence relating to the nature, extent and impact of prehistoric man on the vegetation of Southern England. It is in the south and south eastern region dominated by chalk lithology, that extensive archaeological evidence for Mesolithic, Neolithic, Bronze Age and later activity exists. Here, further detailed evidence for the nature of primary forest and the secondary effects of their clearance and subsequent land use histories is required. These lacunae in our knowledge have promoted attempts at their elucidation in recent years (Thorley 1971a, Haskins 1978, Scaife 1980b, Waton 1982b) as research dissertations.

These deficiencies relate largely to the analyses of organic peat accumulations providing long pollen and or macrofossil vegetational sequences. Southern England, by virtue of the numerous archaeological field monuments present, has a high relative proportion of buried palaeosols providing pollen data from terrestrial/non-wetland contexts which are directly relevant to archaeological/anthropogenic situations. These are again of localised distribution, being related to the occurrence of archaeological monuments and to the ability of their soils to preserve pollen. Consequently similar lacunae in our knowledge of vegetation and/or land use are evident for some areas. The chalk lands especially, have relatively few sites which have yielded pollen data of note (Dimbleby and Evans 1974, Scaife 1980a, Scaife 1984 and in Tomalin forthcoming). These problems in the occurrence of sites and preservation of pollen will be discussed in the relevant sections of this palaeobotanical review.

1.2   Format for review of available data

The principal aim of this paper is to provide a review of palaeobotanical literature and research which has been carried out, dealing with late Quaternary vegetation and its relation to man. From this it is hoped that areas of knowledge needing elucidation will become apparent and some suggestions for the nature of future research potential and organisation propounded. Three fundamental lines of evidence will be discussed; palynological data from peat mires; palynological data from analyses of palaeosols; and the occurrence of plant macrofossil remains from archaeological excavations. The former provides data on the vegetation environment at a local and regional scale, the latter two on the nature of 'on-site' vegetation and man's activities.

1.3   Region delimited for study

For the principal part of this review, the region under discussion may be defined on structural, geological and lithological criteria. The region of South East and Southern England falls within a primary structural region bounded by the Cretaceous chalk outcrop (see Figure 16). For this reason the area outlined here has been adopted in other botanical or palaeoecological studies and geomorphological discussion (Wooldridge and Linton 1955, Jones 1980, 1981).

This area falls broadly south and south east of a line following the chalk outcrop from the Dorset coast north and north east to the North Sea. The northern limit used for the purposes of most of this discussion is the River Thames.

Geologically the area spans the Mesozoic sequence and the two Caenozoic (Tertiary) basins of Hampshire and London. The former contains both Eocene and Oligocene deposits, the latter having only Eocene. These Tertiary basins may be seen as a result of the major tectonic structural undulations of Wealden pericline dome created by the so-called Late-Cretaceous to Mid-Tertiary or Alpine orogenesis (Wooldridge and Goldring 1953, Gallois 1965, Wooldridge and Linton 1968, 29–32). The denudation and breaching of the Wealden anticline have produced a geological microcosm of varying lithologies of lower to middle Cretaceous age. These occur as concentric outcrop patterns infacing the chalk downland scarps on three sides but breached by the English channel in the east. Such different lithologies have resulted in much variation in soil and vegetation over relatively small areas. These variations and the likelihood of differential anthropogenic activity have further exacerbated the need to understand the characteristics of the vegetation on these diverse soils and lithologies throughout the differing climatic and anthropogenic phases of the Pleistocene and Holocene.

2 Palynology of peat and sediments

2.1 Introduction

Since the pioneer work in the field of pollen analysis in Britain by Von-Post (1916), Erdtman (1928), Godwin (1934) and Godwin, H and M E (1933, 1936) a general picture of the vegetational development of Britain spanning the Quaternary period has been built up. A particularly detailed knowledge of vegetational and environmental changes has been constructed from the analyses of peat deposits and lake sediments from Britain's upland areas. From the early analyses of Godwin (1934, 1940, 1943, 1945a, b), Godwin H and M E (1933, 1936), Burchell and Piggott (1939), Clapham A R and B N (1939) the discovery of broad vegetational seral development formed the basis for Godwin's (1940, 1956, 1975a) classic pollen zonation scheme for the Flandrian (Holocene) period. This scheme was a modification of the numerous continental zonations but was essentially that of Blytt (1876) and Sernander (1908) and Jessen (1935) (see also Zeuner 1946, 73 for summary tables). This scheme gave rise to the Zones I–VIII subdivision which, prior to the advent of radiometric dating resulted in pollen analysis becoming a means of dating. With radiocarbon dating and increased palynological data from the whole country, it has become increasingly evident that the boundaries between Godwin's pollen zones are asynchronous, that is showing marked diachroneity of vegetational development across Britain. Smith and Pilcher (1973) have reviewed the dating of these zones and illustrated the asynchroneity of arboreal vegetational changes. Such asynchroneity resulted from differential rates of migration for different taxa; differential migration from varying glacial refugia; barriers to migration (soils, water, mountains) and latitudinal or altitudinal effects on the growth tolerances of different taxa. Consequently sediments of identical date from spatially disparate sites may show markedly different floras. This is illustrated by Birks *et al.* (1975) who used isopollen maps and principal components analysis constructed from British pollen data spanning the period 5000 bp. This covers the latter part of the Atlantic climatic optimum, the stage of maximum vegetation development prior to extensive anthropogenic interference.

The need for biostratigraphical zonation of pollen diagrams based on the inherent characteristics of the site has been emphasised by a number of workers (Teichert 1958, American Commission 1961, Cushing 1964 in Birks 1973, West 1970a). Once these have been established and delimited, the pollen assemblage zones from a number of diagrams from sites of local proximity may be related in order to form a 'regional pollen zonation scheme'. These in themselves may ultimately form 'chronozones' (West 1970a) representing major and widespread vegetation types at a given date. In Southern England such an approach has been used in recent palynological investigations of valley peats spanning the Flandrian (Thorley 1971b, Haskins 1978, Scaife 1980b, Waton 1982b).

This approach places emphasis on the true use of pollen as a palaeoecological tool assessing the nature of vegetation changes and environment at, or through time dated radiometrically. It is unfortunate that much archaeological literature still views pollen as a dating medium based on rigid zonation frameworks imposed temporally and spatially.

2.2 The problem of pollen preservation in Southern England

The relative paucity (compared to the uplands) of sites analysed in the region of Southern England and the resulting lacunae in our knowledge of aspects of natural and anthropogenic vegetation changes have arisen for the following reasons:

i. Upland Britain has higher rainfall totals and an oceanic regime ideally suited to the creation of anaerobic conditions and organic accumulations. By contrast, the lowland South East Zone is an area having a summer rainfall deficit which is the primary factor accounting for the lack of ombrotrophic and blanket peat bogs.

ii. Absence of major glacial erosion in the south of England (accepting the possibility of English Channel glaciation – Kellaway *et al.* 1975) precluded the deep peat and sediment accumulations which developed in glacial geomorphological situations (glacially overdeepened valleys, corries/tarns, lakes) in upland Britain.

iii. The predominantly calcareous geological strata of much of South and South East England produce strongly alkaline hydrological, peat and sediment conditions. Such alkalinity is generally detrimental to the preservation of pollen and although some results have been forthcoming from calcareous soils (see section 3.D.3) those areas of mire/fen adjacent to the downlands are usually devoid of pollen. The highly pervious nature of the chalklands precludes the presence of surface drainage networks and high ground water tables. Conditions suitable for anaerobic peat accumulation are therefore rare.

iv. In recent years it has become increasingly apparent that human pressure has been largely responsible for disturbance of many of the existing areas of peat in Southern England. Most of this disturbance appears to have taken place in the historic period and in four ways.

Firstly, extensive peat cutting has ruined nearly all of Southern England's extensive peat areas. This occurred in a peasant economy where fuel was scarce due to deforestation and any peat deposits were utilised for burning. This cutting has had a twofold effect. The natural ecological succession is retarded with the plant community reverting to an earlier stage in the hydroseral succession (Rose 1953). Of greater importance to the palaeobotanical or archaeological record is that a truncation of the stratigraphical profile occurs, resulting in an absence of sediment or peats and therefore data relating to more recent periods. These are the upper levels of peat representing periods of archaeological significance.

Secondly, the ever increasing need for agricultural land has resulted in many successful attempts to drain wetland areas. This has been especially prevalent in the extensive fen areas of the Fenlands (Godwin 1978) and the Somerset Levels (Coles 1975 to 1981). In other areas of Southern England many peat mires have vanished especially where they existed adjacent to agricultural land (Scaife 1980b, 1982a). Where these areas have remained subsequent to drainage, a lowered water table has led to peat shrinkage and humification. The extreme consequence is therefore a complete loss of wetlands to agriculture or a modified ecology and cessation of peat formation.

Thirdly, valley carr/swamp woodland associations composed of ecological dominants of *Alnus glutinosa* (alder) or *Salix* spp (willows) were an important constituent of the economy and landscape until comparatively recent times. These 'alder moors' and 'withy beds' were used for coppice and were maintained throughout the historic period. Cessation of 'rural peasant economy' has allowed these plagioclimax communities to regenerate into drier woodland with consequent degradation of the mires.

Fourthly and more recently, the use of nitrogenous fertilisers on fields adjacent to mires has brought about significant changes in acidity and consequently vegetation status of the bogs (Scaife 1980b). This has in some cases been detrimental to the maintenance of the acidophilous vegetation and therefore brought about a reduction in the number of potential palynologically viable sites.

These factors have resulted in a relative scarcity of peat deposits suitable for pollen analysis and palaeobotanical investigation. Exceptions to this are the extensive topogenous valley peat bogs and remnant ombrogenous bogs such as Thursley in Surrey; Cranes Moor in Hampshire; Hothfield Common in Kent; and Amberley Wild Brooks in Sussex. Localised topogenous, soligenous valley mires occur usually as relics of more extensive areas. Many of these are of relatively small extent existing within an agricultural environment (Scaife 1980b). These are, however of considerable value in the elucidation of local vegetation successions and in the understanding of the nature of anthropogenic activities on the surrounding areas.

The data presented in the ensuing section are aimed at providing a corpus of work reviewing the evidence for the botanical and environmental changes for the last 12000 years; that is, the period from the end of the Devensian glacial stage to the present. The majority of those sites mentioned below (section 1) are not related directly to sites of archaeological excavation. These are, however, of fundamental importance to palaeobotany and archaeologists in that they provide the basis for an understanding of the environment of man in the prehistoric period. It is within the greater spans of vegetative data from 'long peat cores' that more local pollen data from archaeological contexts can be placed.

The style of research in the southern region can be categorised into firstly a small number of important detailed regional investigations which have contributed greatly to our knowledge and understanding of vegetational history and succession in Southern England, (Seagrief 1956, Thorley 1971a, Haskins 1978, Scaife 1980b, Waton 1982a and Brooks+, Tilley* in preparation). Secondly there are a number of isolated palaeoecological studies. As noted above peat deposits in Southern England have often been drained, buried and suffered wastage. Such peats are sometimes uncovered accidentally which has resulted in a distinct pattern of pollen yielding sites being discovered and analysed at times.

2.A   Interglacial palynological sequences

A greater portion of palynological literature relating to Pleistocene vegetation changes and the fundamental role of these in elucidating stratigraphies and chronologies can be attributed to R G West's work in East and South East England. The majority of these data fall outside the regional scope of this review, but are nevertheless included in the bibliography at the end of this section for reference purposes.

+ A Brooks, Department of Plant Sciences, Kings College, London.
* A Tilley, Department of Geography, University of Southampton.

Research work which has been specifically related to archaeologically implementiferous sediments of Hoxnian and Ipswichian interglacial age is small. Of note are the analyses of Hoxne, Suffolk (West 1954, 1956b, West and McBurney 1954) and Clacton (Pike and Godwin 1953). These sites are outside the scope of the area of study but are relevant because of their type site status and relationship with other south eastern interglacial sediment sequences and their strongly archaeological connections. West (1954, 1956b) illustrated the early and middle parts of the Hoxne interglacial from the Hoxne brick pit sequence long noted for its Palaeolithic (Acheulian) artefacts (see for example Lubbock (1865), Evans (1897)). At Hoxne, Marks Tey, Essex (C Turner 1970) and Swanscombe, Kent (Kerney 1971) a period of possible deforestation has been hypothesised within the early temperate zone (IIc in West's 1961, 1970a interglacial chronozone sequence). This openness of landscape was first noted and attributed to the possible effects of man at the Hoxne type site (West 1956, West and McBurney 1954) because of the strong archaeological evidence from these levels. Occurrence of this phenomenon at Marks Tey and Swanscombe has resulted in controversy as to its cause. At the former, a more complete sequence of Hoxnian interglacial deposits including annual varved clays has been analysed by C Turner (1970) and show that this phase of openness lasted some 300 years. Turner postulated that fire was the primary cause because charcoal was noted at these sites. This coincidental occurrence at these spatially separated sites has favoured the view of a natural causal agent.

Within the region of study a small number of non-archaeologically related interglacial deposits have been investigated palynologically. These include sequences exposed by coastal erosion including the Ipswichian of Selsey Bill and Stone Hampshire (Reid 1893 and Sparks and West 1970). The latter has been further exposed on the foreshore and re-examined by Brown et al. (1975). At Bembridge, Isle of Wight, plant macrofossils of *Ranunculus hyperboreas* were identified from gravels (Jackson 1924 and Reid and Chandler 1924). Recently, Holyoak and Preece (1983) have examined the Steynewood clay sequence (designated by the authors) in detail and shown a Hoxnian or possibly late or pre-Cromerian age for the sequence, which may possibly be correlated with the Slindon Goodwood raised beach sequence of West Sussex.

R N L B Hubbard has been responsible for increasing our knowledge of vegetation changes from sites which have contained only very small quantities of extractable pollen using sophisticated concentration techniques (Hubbard 1977b). These sites include Stoke Newington, North London; Caddington, Middlesex (Hubbard 1978); Eartham, West Sussex (Hubbard 1978b) and Swanscombe, North Kent (Hubbard 1972, 1977b, 1982). At Eartham, Hubbard recorded a spectrum of 54% tree pollen comprised of 61% *Pinus* and 29% *Quercus* but with a strong herbaceous (Gramineae 31%) element. Re-analyses of this sequence of deposits by the Sussex Archaeological Unit and Mark Roberts (Institute of Archaeology London) have added to the palaeolithic archaeological material outlined by Woodcock (1978a, 1978b, 1981). Sequential samples for pollen analysis adjacent to an *in situ* artefact have been taken and await analysis (Scaife).

Of substantial importance is Hubbard's palynological analysis of the Lower Thames, Boyne Hill sequence at Swanscombe, Kent (Hubbard 1972, 1982). In this, Hubbard casts further doubts regarding the conformity of this sequence to accepted interglacial stratigraphical chronologies. He suggests that a 'double' Hoxnian interglacial is evidenced and correlated with continental European schemes.

The Thames Estuary has been noted for its high frequency of Ipswichian interglacial sites often associated with archaeological evidence, e.g. Bakers Hole (King and Oakley 1936). Here much commercial exploitation of the under-lying chalk and of sand and gravels has exposed a number of brickearth (e.g. Crayford, Kent) and fluvial sequences during the last 100 years. The majority of these are aggradation terraces of the River Thames and its tributaries, often referred to as the 'Taplow' terrace (Zeuner 1959 and Charlesworth 1957). A number of these have yielded plant pollen and macrofossil remains, of importance are those from Ilford, Essex (West 1964); Aveley, Essex (West 1969) and Trafalgar Square under Admiralty buildings (Franks 1960). The former has a more complete sequence spanning the early and mid-temperate zones of *Betula* and *pinus* to mixed oak forest domination. Both Aveley and Trafalgar Square sequences have been referred to the latter part of the mid-temperate zones (IIb and III).

Interglacial pollen data

Thames Valley

Franks J W, 1960 Trafalgar Square.

Gibbard P L, forthcoming. Current analyses of Stoke Newington.

Hubbard R N L B, 1972, Swanscombe, Kent.

Hubbard R N L B, 1977b, Swanscombe, Kent.

Hubbard R N L B, 1975, Yiewsley, Middlesex.

Hubbard R N L B, 1978a, Caddington, Middlesex.

Hubbard R N L B, 1982, Swanscombe, Kent.

Hubbard R N L B, unpublished, Stoke Newington.

Sparks B W *et al.*, 1969 Hatfield, Hertfordshire.

Sutcliff A J, 1976 Relationship of Ipswichian deposits.

West R G, 1964 Ilford, Essex.

West R G, 1969 Aveley and Grays, Essex.

South Coast

Brown R C *et al.*, 1975 Stone, Hampshire.

Holyoak D T and Preece R C, 1983 Bembridge, Isle of Wight.

Hubbard R N L B, 1977a Slindon.

Hubbard R N L B 1978b Eartham, West Sussex.

Jones D K C, 1980 (ed), 1981 Geomorphological review.

Reid C, 1893 Stone, Hampshire.

Reid C, 1892 Sussex coastal Pleistocene deposits.

Reid C, 1899 *Origin of the British Flora.*

West R G and Sparks B W, 1960 Selsey Bill, Sussex.

West R G and Sparks B W, 1960 Coastal interglacial deposits.

Woodcock A G, 1978a Ameys Pit, Eartham, Sussex.

Woodcock A G, 1981 Sussex palaeolithic gravels — archaeology.

Relevant East Anglian pollen data

Pike K V and Godwin H, 1953 Clacton-on-Sea.

Reid E M and Chandler M E J, 1923b Clacton-on-Sea.

Sparks B W and West R G, 1963 Stutton, Suffolk.

Sparks B W and West R G, 1970 Wretton, Norfolk.

Stevans L A, 1960 Nar Valley, Norfolk.

Turner C, 1970 Marks Tey.

West R G, 1956a Ludham, Norfolk. Lower Pleistocene succession.

West R G, 1956b Hoxne, Suffolk.

West R G, 1980 Pre-glacial Pleistocene of the East Anglian coast.

West R G, 1957 Bobbitshole, Ipswich.

West R G and McBurney C M B, 1954 Hoxne.

West R G and Wilson G, 1966 Cromer Forest Bed Series.

Miscellaneous

Duigan S L, 1955 Interglacial plant remains from Wolvercote Channel, Oxford.

Reid C, 1899 *The Origin of The British Flora.*

Walker D, 1953 Histon Road, Cambridge.

West R G, 1954 Reconsideration of the Hoxnian.

West R G, 1961 Interglacial and interstadial vegetation.

West R G, 1970b Pleistocene history of the British flora.

2.B   The Late-Devensian vegetation

This discussion spans the period 12000–8300 BC, that is, the period post that of the full Pleniglacial 'B' phase of the full stadial (Mitchell *et al.* 1973). This period represents the initial climatic amelioration prior to the onset of the Flandrian interglacial. The Late-Devensian, which earlier texts referred to as the late-glacial, embraces the Zones I, II and III of Blytt (1876) and Sernander (1908) and pollen Zones I to III of Godwin (1940, 1956, 1975). The overall chronology of this period may be summarised as follows.

Years bc

	Zone IV	Pre-Boreal	Devensian/Flandrian transition
8800–8300	Zone III	Younger Dryas/Loch Lomond readvance
10000–8800	Zone II	Allerød/Windermere interstadial (Coope and Pennington 1977)
12800–10000	Zone I	Older Dryas

Sediments of this date containing pollen are rare in Southern England. This has resulted in much weight being placed upon evidence from a small number of sites analysed 20–30 years ago when palynological analyses were at a lesser degree of sophistication.

From analyses at Nursling, Hampshire (Seagrief 1956, 1959) and Elstead, Surrey (Seagrief and Godwin 1960) Seagrief concluded on the basis of pollen and macrofossil evidence that the Younger Dryas Zone III was of a landscape comprising a rich herbaceous vegetation with *Pinus* and *Betula* woodland. Scaife (1980b, 1982a) has drawn attention to the fact that these early pollen data were calculated as a percentage of arboreal pollen and not as a percentage of absolute or as a percentage of total pollen. Consequently only the relative inputs of *Betula* and *Pinus* pollen were being compared in Late-Devensian contexts and not the actual relationship of these to the remaining pollen spectrum largely comprising herbaceous taxa. Importantly, therefore, examination of these pollen diagrams by later workers has resulted in an overestimation of the significance of trees (*Betula* and *Pinus*) in the Late-Devensian. The presence of extensive scatters of *Betula* and especially *Pinus* is contradictory to evidence obtained more recently by both Kerney *et al.* (1980) in Kent and in the Isle of Wight (Scaife 1980b, 1982a). In the latter case, sediments spanning the Younger Dryas (Zone III) period have been pollen analysed and calculated as percentages of total pollen providing a more meaningful understanding of the vegetation communities present.

The two sites of Gatcombe Withy Bed (SZ 502858) and Munsley Peat Bog (SZ 526825) in the Isle of Wight provide comparative and corroborative data relating to the changing vegetation of the Late-Devensian and early Flandrian periods. This work suggests that the Younger Dryas had a much more open, herbaceous vegetation than has been inferred in the past. This evidence has been used to show that *Betula* was locally present and that the majority of *Betula* and *Pinus* pollen was derived from longer distance transport (Scaife 1980b, 1982a). Aario (1940) and Ritchie and Lichti-Federovich (1967) showed that up to 35% *Pinus* occurred in *Betula* woodland in the Boreal forest belt, with higher values occurring in tundra environments. These pollen spectra, as well as those of Seagrief (above) and the Lea Valley (Allison *et al.* 1952) are dominated by high frequencies of herbaceous pollen types. This is one of the most interesting features of the Late-Devensian flora, exhibiting a marked floristic diversity with a wide range of phytogeographical elements present. This reflects the variety of microclimatic, edaphic and geological conditions present. Such diversity of herbaceous taxa in Late-Devensian contexts has been noted by Godwin (1953) and evidenced in Southern England floristic analyses by Bell (1969, 1970) in Huntingdonshire, Seagrief's work (above), Haskins (1978) in the Poole Harbour region and Scaife (1980a, b, 1982a) in the Isle of Wight. This diversity has also been shown from pollen and macrofossil analyses of the Lea Valley arctic plant bed and associated deposits (Allison, Godwin and Warren 1952), Reid (1949) and recently by Gibbard and Hall (1982) and Gibbard *et al.* (1982) at West Drayton, Middlesex and Colnebrook, Buckinghamshire where organic deposits occurring as channel fills of the River Colne at West Drayton have been dated at 11230 ± 120 BP and 13405 ± 170 BP. Here again the vegetation is of open aspect with the only woody vegetation being *Salix* at West Drayton.

Very great problems exist in the delimitation and interpretation of the plant communities that might have been growing. As Moore (1980a) has pointed out, the use of pollen in ascertaining the nature of the herbaceous communities present is limited to the precision with which pollen identifications can be made to low taxonomic levels. Exact analogues of the Late-Devensian floristic communities are unlikely to exist today. Those with closest similarities to them may be refuge arctic-alpine plant communities found in upland areas of Britain. These include Cwm Idwal, North Wales (Godwin 1953); Upper Teesdale (Pigott 1956, Holdgate 1955, Turner *et al.* 1973) and in Scotland (Birks 1973). In spite of these problems certain characteristic plant community descriptions have been attempted by pollen analysis. Scaife (1980b, 1982a) illustrates the presence of shrub, dwarf shrub, tall herb, short turf, fen mire, aquatic and disturbed soil plant communities with characteristic but nevertheless diverse phytosociological characteristics.

The openness of the vegetation related particularly to the climate of Zone III indicates that conditions were considerably harsher than postulated by earlier workers. This view, based upon palaeobotanical data, is commensurate with evidence from coleopteran assemblages in Britain from which it is suggested that regionally changing climate and declining temperatures occurred in Zone III. This change may have annihilated earlier Zone II (Allerød/Windermere interstadial vegetation) in Southern England (Osborne 1971, 1972, 1974). Osborne (1971) from coleopteran evidence showed a rigorous climate at 10130 BP from assemblages contained in the River Wandle gravels, Croydon. The status of Zone II vegetation in Southern England is still problematical because of a marked paucity of sites dating to the period 10000 to 8800 BC. Some data have been forthcoming from stratified colluvium burying rendzina soils and some contained wood and charcoal which allowed C^{14} dating of important molluscan faunas (Kerney 1963, Kerney *et al.* 1964) from the North Downs, Kent. These similarly show marked zoogeographical diversity. At one of these sites — Brook, Kent — poorly preserved pollen has been discussed by Lambert (in Kerney *et al.* 1964, 193) and plant macrofossils (Lambert) obtained from a buried Zone II palaeosol dated at 9950 ± factor BC (Q618). It was shown here that pollen of herbs was abundant, being characterised by common Late-Devensian plant taxa with *Pinus* and *Betula* in the Zone II soils. Lambert did however note the possibility that *Pinus* might have been over-represented in the soil because of differential preservation of its pollen. The presence of *Betula* (charcoal) was taken as evidence for local growth of this taxon (Levy p 197 in Kerney *et al.* 1964). West (1976) has carried out an analysis of a spot sample of Allerød date (12250 ± 280 GX-0793) from Sevenoaks, Kent. Pollen preservation was again poor but indicated an open herbaceous vegetation. Pollen data of Zone II age from peat mire stratification have not been forthcoming but tentatively assigned data have been noted in Dorset (Haskins 1978) and in the Isle of Wight (Scaife 1980b).

2.B.1 *Problems/Proposals*

Archaeologically, the Late-Devensian is that part of the Upper Palaeolithic period becoming transitional with the earliest Mesolithic. Open air sites dating to this period are few, posing the question of whether man was in fact present in Southern England and the surrounding continental shelf area. Campbell (1977) has produced a composite pollen diagram based on spatially disparate samples from Hengistbury Head, Dorset. The soils of this site have been subjected to intense podzolisation and disturbance (Macphail 1982) and a reassessment of these pollen data and analysis of recent excavations by Barton (1981, 1983) is being undertaken (Scaife). Detailed work of any excavated Upper Palaeolithic sites would provide valuable data in an attempt to assess whether man was present and surviving in the harsh conditions which are now thought to have existed at the close of the Late-Devensian (Zone III). In order to assess the nature of vegetational colonisation and the rapid environmental change of the ensuing Flandrian interglacial (especially that of the Mesolithic) it is necessary to know further to what extent arboreal and shrub taxa were present as sources for expansion of growth consequent upon climatic amelioration.

Devensian and Late-Devensian

Berkshire

Bryant I D *et al.*, 1983 Early Devensian deposits at Brimpton.

Dorset

Campbell J, 1977 Hengistbury Head.
Haskins L A, 1978 Poole Harbour.

Essex

Baker C A, 1976 Cam Valley, Hertfordshire.
Baker C A, 1978 Bonhunt Water, Hertfordshire.

Hampshire

Seagrief S C, 1956, 1959 Nursling.
Seagrief S C, 1960 Cranes Moor.
Tilley A, in progress Cranes Moor.

Hertfordshire

Allison J *et al.*, 1952 Nazeing.
Gibbard P, 1974, PhD
Godwin H, 1964 Colney Heath.
Reid E M, 1949 Lea Valley.

Isle of Wight

Scaife R G, 1980a, 1980b, 1982a, forthcoming Gatcombe Withy Bed.
Scaife R G, 1980b, 1982a, forthcoming Munsley Peat Bed.

Kent

Kerney M P, 1963 North Downs.
Lambert C A in Kerney M P *et al.*, 1964 Brook Z.II pollen, Sevenoaks.
West R G, 1976 Sevenoaks.

London

Gibbard P *et al.*, 1982 Kempton Park, Sunbury.

Gibbard P and Hall A R, 1982 Lower Colne.

Hall A R, 1982 Isleworth.

Surrey

Brooks A, in preparation Elstead.

Carpenter C P and Woodcock M P, 1981 Elstead.

Seagrief S C, 1956 Elstead.

Seagrief S C and Godwin H, 1960 Elstead.

2.C   Flandrian Chronozone I – The Pre-Boreal and Boreal Mesolithic Forest

Rapidly rising temperatures at c10000 bp initiated the successional rise to dominance of the Flandrian forest. This is contrary to the earlier view that temperatures increased gradually throughout Flandrian I (Pre-Boreal: Godwin's pollen Zone IV and Boreal Zone V and VI) to the Late-Boreal or Atlantic climatic optimum. Coleopteran evidence has shown that temperatures rose rapidly to high mean annual values (Osborne 1974) over a short period of time at the start of the Flandrian. This rapid change, coupled with the openness of vegetation in Zone III initiated a period of expansion of pioneer arboreal vegetation types into the landscape at c10000 bp. The nature of this seral development and the time of arrival of different tree taxa were dependent upon the competition and dispersal characteristics of the species and on the distance of their journey from Devensian refugia. These changes in vegetation were rapid, reflecting a complex reaction of communities to variations in external factors and are problems of dynamic phytosociology. It is within this background of change that early Mesolithic man existed and his impact on the balance of vegetation has been discussed by Smith (1970) in terms of the development of *Corylus* forest or scrub.

The characteristics of this succession have been known from South and South East England since the pioneer work of Erdtman (1928). At Hallstow, Kent he illustrated the early arrival of *Pinus* in the early Flandrian of Southern England as compared to Northern England. Work at Cothill, Berkshire (Clapham and Clapham 1939) provided a long vegetative sequence of early to Middle Flandrian date. A comparative profile from Southampton Water (Godwin and Godwin 1940) peats and sediments of pre-transgression date (see section 2.I) shows a vegetational sequence from Godwin's pollen Zones IV to VII. Early Flandrian peats obtained at Portsmouth (Godwin 1945b) of Pre-Boreal age (pollen Zone IV) were used by Godwin (1940) in his vegetational pollen zone system which has subsequently been used widely and often unquestioningly.

Research analyses by Seagrief (1956) provided data from Cranes Moor, Hampshire; Elstead, Surrey; Godlington Heath, Wareham, Dorset; Nursling, Hampshire and Amberley Wild Brooks, Sussex. Seagrief utilised a number of topogenous mire deposits and at Wareham (Seagrief 1959) Bog, 1 mile north of Wareham, peat of Zone IV (Pre-Boreal) to IIa (Atlantic) date was investigated. At Nursling on the River Test, the peats extend back into the Devensian Zone III with characteristic pollen and macrofossil assemblages, and show the subsequent vegetation history until the Boreal period. At Elstead, Surrey (Seagrief and Godwin, 1960) a similar sequence was found. Re-investigation of this site has subsequently been carried out (Brooks, Kings College, London) and Carpenter and Woodcock (1981). Cranes Moor, Hampshire (Seagrief 1960) has also been reinvestigated by A Tilley (Department of Geography, University of Southampton). Tilley (pers. comm.) has shown that the sediments present extend back in time to Zone III, that is earlier than that shown by Seagrief (1960).

Since these early analyses, further data have been forthcoming from the recent investigations into other areas of Southern England. Improvements in the pollen analysis technique and C^{14} dating have allowed greater correlation between pollen sequences and therefore the establishment of broad vegetation changes (see Scaife 1982a). For example, the recognition of *Juniperus* pollen has provided a useful indicator horizon of the Late-Devensian/Flandrian transition which along with C^{14} dating has allowed more accurate delimitation of Zones III and IV.

Gatcombe Withy Bed, Isle of Wight (SZ 502858) is a valley peat mire, the pollen and stratigraphical analyses of which have produced a complete unbroken sequence of vegetation changes from the late Zone II Devensian to present day (Scaife 1979, 1980b, 1982a). A C^{14} assay of 9970 ± 50 bp (SRR-1433) dates the initiation of woodland colonisation at the beginning of the Flandrian with expansion of *Juniperus* scrub and *Betula* woodland. This is comparable with a similar sequence (truncated by peat cutting) at Munsley Peat Bed (SZ 526825) also in the Isle of Wight. Other comparable pollen diagrams have been constructed from the Poole Harbour area (Dorset) by Haskins (1928). Until recently pollen data of this period other than Erdtman (1928) have been absent from Kent. Turner in Kerney, Preece and Turner (1980) has investigated pollen preservation in tufa forming environs at Folkestone (TR 220379) and Wateringbury, near Maidstone (TQ 68765344). Analyses of these otherwise unlikely pollen preserving deposits have facilitated the comparative approaches of molluscan analysis and palaeobotanical results. Godwin's pollen Zones V and

VI are represented at Folkestone and are dated at between 8120 ± 420 BP (st V 3409) and 7500 ± 100 BP (st-3410) with two C^{14} dates from Zone V of 8980 ± 100 BP (st V 3411) and 9305 ± 115 BP (st-3395). At Wateringbury, pollen spanning Zones IV–VI is present with one C^{14} date in VI with an assay of 8470 ± 190 BP (Q1425).

Organic and inorganic deposits from the Thames Estuary around Dartford, Kent and Tilbury, Essex give biostratigraphical data and sea level change information (Devoy 1977, 1978–9, 1980, 1982). Being from low lying areas the vegetation was dominated by fen elements in addition to the regional terrestrial vegetation. An example of this is the early arrival of *Alnus* prior to 8100 BP, occurrence since confirmed in the Isle of Wight (Scaife 1980b) and Poole Harbour, Dorset (Haskins 1978).

The above analyses have been largely confined to organogenic accumulations (peats) occurring in topogeniously formed anaerobic situations. A large number of valleys in Southern England however contain inorganic sediment fills which have been little utilised for environmental construction despite their importance. Burrin (1981, 1983) has carried out extensive lithostratigraphical investigations of the flood plains of the Rivers Ouse and Cuckmere in Sussex. Pollen analysis of these sediments (Scaife 1983e, Burrin and Scaife 1984; Scaife and Burrin 1983) has shown that the accumulation of these sediments relates to valley side anthropogenic activity. Of note in this section is the basal zone of sites dominated by *Pinus* and *Corylus*. These pollen are of possible Boreal date and are enigmatic in that for these extensive spreads of inorganic sediments to have accumulated, a more open vegetation character for this period has been postulated. Whether or not such openness could have been created by Mesolithic man is not at present clear. What is certain however, is that the investigation of a wider range of such inorganic sequences could provide an alternative data source to the polliniferous peats so rare in Southern England.

In all of the sequences described no indisputable effects of Mesolithic man in the form of local clearance have been seen in the pollen spectra. This may relate to the fact that many of the analyses were carried out some years ago and using a wide sampling interval. The re-investigation of some of these peat sequences in conjunction with field walking of adjacent areas might be of value in ascertaining if earlier Mesolithic man (Pre-Boreal and Boreal) was present and had any effect upon the natural vegetation.

Flandrian Chronozone I

Berkshire

Churchill D M and Dimbleby G W, 1962 Thatcham.
Clapham A R and Clapham B N, 1939 Cothill Fen.
Dimbleby G W, 1959.

Dorset

Seagrief S C, 1956, 1959 Wareham.
Haskins L A, 1978 South East Dorset, Poole Harbour.

Essex

Baker C A, 1976 Newport Pond.
Baker C A, 1976 Bonhunt Water.

Hampshire

Godwin H, 1945b Portsmouth Harbour.
Godwin H and M E, 1940 Southampton Water.
Hodson I M and West R G, 1972 Fawley.
Seagrief S C, 1956, 1959 Nursling.
Seagrief S C, 1960 Cranes Moor.

Hertfordshire

Allison J *et al.*, 1952 Lea Valley.
Brooks A, in preparation Broxbourne and Ponders End.
Warren *et al.*, 1934 Broxbourne.

Isle of Wight

Scaife R G, 1980b, 1982a Gatcombe Withy Bed.
Scaife R G, 1980b, 1982a Munsley Peat Bed.

Kent

Burchell J P T and Piggott S, 1939 Ebsfleet.
Devoy R J N, 1978–79, 1980, 1982 The Lower Thames.

Erdtman G, 1939 Hallstow.
Kerney M P et al., 1980 Wateringbury.
Kerney M P et al., 1980 Folkestone.

London

Scaife R G, 1983c Peninsular House, City of London.

Surrey

Brooks A, in preparation Elstead.
Carpenter C P and Woodcock M P, 1981 Elstead.
Seagrief S C and Godwin H, 1960 Elstead.
Seagrief S C, 1956 Elstead.

Sussex

Burrin P J and Scaife R G, 1984 Sussex Ouse.
Jennings S and Smythe C, 1982 Newhaven.
Scaife R G in Burrin P J, 1983 Sharpsbridge, River Ouse.
Scaife R G and Burrin P J, 1983 Sussex Ouse and Cuckmere.

Thames Valley

Devoy R J N, 1977, 1978–79, 1982.

2.D   Flandrian II – The Late Mesolithic

The Atlantic mesocratic period of Flandrian chronozone II (Godwin's pollen Zone VIIa) corresponds with the late Mesolithic period between c7000 and 5000 bp. This period of 'optimum' hypsithermal conditions was apparently one of vegetation stability with dominant forest and with maximum extension and development of thermophilous deciduous forest. Archaeologically the Mesolithic cultures have a strong coastal orientation which is seen clearly in Dorset (Rankine 1961 and Palmer 1977) and the Isle of Wight (Poole 1936, Basford 1980) dating from a time when sea level was rising relative to land with attainment of the present day sea levels and separation at c7200 bp from the continent (Churchill 1965).

Traditionally the period has been viewed as one of mixed deciduous forest or Quercetum Mixtum with formidable representations of thermophilous elements of *Tilia, Ilex, Alnus, Fraxinus, Lonicera, Hedera* and *Viscum* in woodland of *Quercus* and *Ulmus*. Recent writers including Godwin (1975b) have viewed the vegetation of this period as a polyclimax; that is, a vegetation of different dominant taxa brought about by locally variable edaphic, drainage, topographical and geological factors. This contrasts with the earlier monoclimax tradition of a consistent Quercetum Mixtum vegetation blanketing the landscape. Such a polyclimax approach has been adopted in the interpretation of some peats of Atlantic date from the region.

Haskins (1978) in her analyses of a number of peat sections in the Poole Harbour area has investigated the vegetation changes especially in relation to the spread of *Alnus* and *Tilia* and to structural changes in the woodland. She has shown that the regional expansion of *Alnus* in the Poole area was from 6979 ± 70 bp. This is commensurate with the general dating for this phenomenon which was accepted by Godwin as the delimiting boundary for the Boreal and Atlantic periods (Zones VI and VIIa). Smith and Pilcher (1973) have shown the asynchroneity of this boundary in their summary of C^{14} dated events and therefore the caution which is required in terms of circular argument. This is further illustrated by the apparently early presence of *Alnus* in Southern England as shown by Devoy (1977, 1978–9); Haskins (1978); Scaife (1980b, 1982a) and Waton (1982a, b) for the Lower Thames, Poole Harbour; Gatcombe, Isle of Wight; and Winnall Moors, Hampshire respectively. Because of the relationship of this period to the attainment of Flandrian sea-levels, other submerged coastal peat localities have yielded data for this marked change in the vegetation landscape (see section 2.I). Haskins (1978) has described the characteristics and history of individual arboreal taxa for the Poole Harbour/Wareham low lying areas and has also related the presence of some arboreal taxa to the archaeological soil pollen records and plant macrofossil data from Dorset. Apart from the significant changes in the arboreal constituents, Haskins notes the increased importance of heathland taxa (*Calluna* and *Erica* and *Pteridium*) to which she draws analogy with the heathy oakwoods of today occurring in Hampshire and the London basin (Tansley 1949).

Investigations in the Isle of Wight (Scaife 1980b) have shown the vegetation of the Atlantic from Gatcombe Withy Bed (SZ 502858), Borthwood Farm (SZ 578849) and Brook Bay (SZ 382837). At Gatcombe Withy, the period of Atlantic domination is bracketed by C^{14} dating between 6385 ± 50 bp (SRR-1339) and 4850 ± 40 bp (SRR-1338). Because of the compacted peats used in dating, the former is likely to be of younger nature. Due to the lithological diversity and therefore edaphic variability an attempt was made to recognise different plant communities present in the Atlantic period. This represents the view that the vegetation was a polyclimax mosaic brought about by varying physical controlling parameters.

From the investigation, the following vegetation communities were recognised. These are briefly:

1. Wetlands: Expansion of *Alnus*, as in other pollen sequences, marks the beginning of its domination in Alnetum communities lasting to the present day. Reasons for this expansion were viewed by Blytt and Sernander (1876, 1908 respectively) and later by Godwin (1940, 1956, 1975a, b) as consequent upon climatic change to oceanicity. Devoy (1977, 1978–9) and McVean (1956) have suggested that rising base levels were responsible. Devoy postulated this for the Lower Thames (Tilbury) area and also that a reduction in base level between 7000 and 6670 bp initiated the re-establishment of *Alnus* in previously brackish water areas thereby giving high pollen levels. A corrected date of c7200 BP has been suggested by Barber (1975) for the *Alnus* expansion in Southern England and is in general agreement with those dates obtained by Haskins and Scaife. Such a base level reduction as postulated by Devoy in the South Coast area might have been responsible for reduced water levels in certain lower valley sections at the end of the Boreal/early Atlantic thus explaining the wider existence of Alnetum. High pollen frequencies and abundant macrofossil remains at these sites attest to its autochthonous growth. In addition to *Alnus* and *Salix* as dominant constituents of these Alneta or Saliceta, herbaceous elements of fen type character have been recorded at Borthwood and Gatcombe, Isle of Wight and earlier by Seagrief at Wareham (1959); Godwin at Southampton (1940) and by Clapham A R and B N at Cothill, Berkshire (1939).

2. Base rich soils: The dominance of *Tilia* in this period has been illustrated by many analyses of sites in lowland Britain, and which shows a dramatic expansion at, or slightly after the *Alnus* increase. This genus has been regarded as one of the characteristic thermophiles (Iversen 1960, Godwin 1975a) and as a general indicator of the period of maximum temperatures. Whilst it may have been present at an earlier date (Godwin's Zone VIc) its expansion from c7000 bp illustrates its increased competitive power over *Quercus* such that it became dominant in some areas of base rich and well drained soils. This is especially so in Southern England where its importance and dominance in possibly pure stands has been postulated (Moore 1977, Scaife 1980b, Greig 1982a) being clearly seen in pollen diagrams from the Isle of Wight (Scaife 1980b, 1982a), Dorset (Haskins 1978, Waton 1982a, b), Sussex (Thorley 1971a, 1971b, 1981) and Kent (Webb, 1972).

The evidence from peat mires is enhanced by that of soil palynology of buried soils having a dominance of *Tilia*. This is exemplified at such sites as at Chicks Hill, Dorset (Ashbee and Dimbleby 1958), West Heath, Sussex (Baigent in Drewett 1976 and Scaife in Drewett 1985, Scaife 1983a, Scaife and Macphail 1983), Moor Green, West End, Hampshire (Ashbee and Dimbleby 1976). Areas of poor growth are reflected at some sites by low pollen values as at Winfrith Heath, Dorset (Simmons and Dimbleby 1974, Palmer and Dimbleby 1979) and by Haskins (1978) in her analyses of peats.

Unusually high *Ilex* pollen values for the Isle of Wight (Scaife 1979, 1980b) have been linked to close association with *Tilia*. Both taxa have extremely poor pollen dispersion characteristics being entomophilous (Anderson 1970, 1973). The dominance of these taxa in small bogs/mires in the Isle of Wight attests to the value of analysis of small localised peat accumulations in situations adjacent to terrestrial soils.

3. Meadows on gleyed soils: It is suggested that non-waterlogged meadows and lower valley sides comprised a mixed deciduous wood of transitional character between Tiletum and Alnetum. This was possibly of the character of Quercetum Mixtum described by earlier workers. The dominants may have been therefore *Quercus, Ulmus*, some *Fraxinus* and *Acer*.

4. Clay vales: Those areas of clay lithology (Cretaceous or Tertiary) give rise to heavy soils on which *Quercus* woodland and *Corylus* understorey might have been prevalent plus less well represented elements in the pollen record.

5. The chalklands: The origin and nature of the flora of areas now typically chalk downland grassland have for long been a source of controversy. Recent pollen investigations in Southern England have sought to elucidate these problems. Thorley (1971a, 1981) has indicated the heavily forested nature of the chalklands until the Bronze Age for the area around Lewes, Sussex. Similarly in Dorset and Hampshire, Waton (1982a, 1982b) has investigated a number of sites adjacent to the downlands which again show heavy forestation until a late date. The studies of the writer attempted to ascertain the character of downland vegetation in the Isle of Wight (Scaife 1980b, d, 1982a) (see section 3.D.3). Thorley (1971a, b) has viewed the pre-Neolithic downland vegetation as probably being *Quercus* forest with *Corylus* undershrub. Godwin (1975a, 1975b) has suggested the dominance of *Tilia* as being more suited to the shallower base rich soils of the chalk. This latter argument has also been suggested by Scaife from the Isle of Wight data.

6. Sandy soils of low base status; on areas of Tertiary soils and some Lower Greensand soils (e.g. West Heath, Sussex, see 3.D.2.a) typically podzolised soils are present today. 'On-site' investigation of buried soils under barrows of later date (i.e. post-Atlantic date) has shown that soil deterioration had occurred with heathland and *Corylus* scrub invading localised Mesolithic and/or natural clearances. This evidence is seen more clearly in soil palynology than in the analyses of peat mires.

The presence of *Pinus* in Southern England during the Boreal period has been illustrated by many workers back to Erdtman (1928). Less clear is the possibility of *Pinus* continuing in the region during the ensuing Atlantic and later period. This is a problem of interest and importance because of macrofossil charcoal identifications from a number of archaeological sites (Oakhanger, Hants; Rankine *et al.* 1960; Thickthorne Down, Dorset; Drew and Piggott 1936 and in Sussex; Bell 1981). These have been attributed to the selection and utilisation of *Pinus* timber and its importation from long distance sources. Less clear is the pollen evidence to confirm or deny its local growth in Southern England. Godwin (1944) has demonstrated that *Pinus* possibly remained on the sandy soils of the Brecklands of East Anglia. Forthcoming evidence suggests that some areas of Hampshire and Dorset similarly maintained a *Pinus* element. Pollen percentage of up to 17% at Wyke Ridge, Chesil Beach have been C^{14} dated at 6100 ± 100 bp (Carr and Blackley 1973). Haskins (1978) and Scaife (1980b) for Dorset and the Isle of Wight respectively, have suggested the possibility of local/sporadic occurrence of *Pinus* on low-base-status Tertiary soils and plateau gravels. If present these must have been highly localised in view of the extreme competition from deciduous woodland growing under highly favourable conditions.

2.D.1 *Proposals*

Birks *et al.* (1975) have produced isopollen maps from selected mire data throughout Britain. This represents the vegetation immediately prior to the *Ulmus* decline at 5000 bp. This valuable summary of the spatial variation in the late Atlantic flora covers Southern England. In this region, however, the data base is of minimal extent relating only to a limited number of sites. There is now scope for the application of isopollen trend surface analysis to be carried out on a smaller scale in Southern England. This might help elucidate some of the trends discussed in the above section. Earlier pollen data showing the primary characteristics of the vegetation could be utilised by data transformation from the original pollen diagrams.

Other data on the Atlantic period not referred to above can be found in the Bibliography for Flandrian II (this section).

Flandrian Chronozone II

Dorset

Haskins L A, 1978 Morden 'B'
Sidaway R, 1964 Litton Cheney.
Waton P, 1980, 1982a, 1982b Rimsmoor.

Essex

Baker C A, 1976 Newport.
Baker C A, 1976 Bonhunt Water.
Scaife R G, 1984 and forthcoming Mar Dyke.

Hampshire

Barber K E, unpublished Warwick Slade Bog, New Forest.
Barber K E, unpublished Noads Bog, New Forest.
Barber K E, 1975 Church Moor, New Forest.
Godwin H and M E, 1940 Southampton Water.
Seagrief S C, 1956, 1960 Cranes Moor.
Waton P V, 1982a, 1982b Snelsmoor.

Hertfordshire

Allison J *et al.*, 1952 The Lea Valley.
Brooks A, in preparation Broxbourne, and Ponders End.

Isle of Wight

Clifford M H, 1936 Brook Bay Mesolithic Hearth.
Scaife R G, 1980a, 1980b Gatcombe Withy Bed; Borthwood Farm; Brook Bay, Redway Farm.

Kent

Devoy R J, 1978–79, 1980 Lower Thames valley.
Kerney M P *et al.*, 1980 Folkestone.
Webb J A, 1972 Hothfield Common.

London

Girling M A and Greig J R A, 1977 Hampstead Heath.

Surrey

Carpenter C P and Woodcock M P, 1981 Elstead.

Sussex

Brooks A, in preparation Wellingham, Sussex Ouse.
Thorley A, 1971a, 1971b, 1981 Lewes I and II.
Thorley A, 1971a Amberley Wild Brooks.
Waton P V, 1982a, b Amberley Wild Brooks.

Miscellaneous

Birks H J B *et al.,* 1975 Isopollen maps of 50000 bp.

2.E   The evidence of Mesolithic anthropogenic disturbance in the pollen record

The Mesolithic can be divided into two broad periods of human activity correlations with Flandrian chronozones I (Pre-Boreal and Boreal) and Flandrian II (Atlantic hypsithermal). The former was one of rapid ecological change, the latter was one of relative stability of environment. Evidence, or the lack of it, has been debated from two aspects, that is autogenically or allogenically. The former has been discussed by Simmons (1969) from work in the Pennines (Spratt and Simmons 1976) and especially Dartmoor (Simmons 1964, 1969 and Simmons *et al.* 1981) where man was intrinsically involved in the creation and expansion of forest clearings for wild animals adjacent to waterholes. Hunting and resultant overkill led to the abandonment of these clearings and subsequent woodland regeneration. Such influences of these essentially hunting/gathering societies have been discussed by Simmons (1975a, 1975b) for the upland 'fragile' ecosystems on poorer soils adjacent to peat mires (e.g. Blacklane, Dartmoor, Simmons 1964, 1969). Lack of pollen data from mires in the South and South East England is notable. Evidence of similar character has not been produced for either Flandrian I or II from mire pollen work in lowland Britain probably because the vegetation of better soils here were less susceptible to soil degradation or due to less than adequate pollen coverage of this region. Soil palynology may have illustrated this local soil depletion at Iping Common (Keef, Wymer and Dimbleby 1965) at West Heath (Baigent in Drewett 1976, Scaife 1983a, Scaife and Macphail 1983) and Minsted (Dimbleby in Drewett 1975). This uncertain evidence is not altogether unexpected as these essentially mobile communities with transient/ephemeral settlements are unlikely to have had sufficient direct impact on the closed coniferous or deciduous forests of Southern England. In consequence, the presence of a few herbaceous pollen taxa such as *Plantago* has been discussed (see Smith 1970 for general discussion) in relation to possible anthropogenic disturbances and from specific sites at Gatcombe Withy Bed in the valley of the River Medina, Isle of Wight (Scaife 1980b, 1982a, Tomalin and Scaife 1979) and at Borthwood Farm, Isle of Wight (Scaife 1980) and in the Poole area, Dorset (Haskins 1978).

Pollen analyses of peats and sediments adjacent to known Mesolithic archaeological sites have not produced any marked evidence for occupation activity. Two sites are of note, Broxbourne (Warren *et al.* 1934) and Thatcham, Berkshire (Dimbleby 1959, Lambert in Churchill 1962) both important Maglemosian sites. Radiocarbon dating has placed the latter site at between Pre-Boreal (9850 ± 160 BC Q651) and the early Boreal (7540 ± 160 BC) date although it was noted that the occupation had little or no effect on the river terrace vegetation. *Corylus* nuts and a colour change of the swamp marls from white to grey may indicate wide implications of the impact of Mesolithic man.

Iversen (1941, 1949) suggested that Mesolithic man was controlled to a large extent by his environment. Smith (1970) has suggested that in environmental terms, Mesolithic man may have had a substantial impact on the landscape in spite of his low population numbers. This impact might include the effect of fire, initiated accidentally or deliberately and the greater use of the tranchet axe in deforestation (Radley and Mellars 1964). The characteristic dominance of *Corylus* in the Boreal with *Pinus* is seen at a large number of sites. Strong circumstantial evidence has been given by many writers (see Smith 1970, Jacobi 1978b) and these *Corylus* maxima might be attributed to allogenic factors relating to man's use of fire as an agent for promoting *Corylus* as a food resource, or in game herding and hunting. Such activities and subsequent vegetation destruction might be capable of affecting not only vegetation but also geomorphic parameters.

Such evidence has been forthcoming from Thatcham, Berkshire where a change in the fen marls from white to grey may indicate valley side clearance of forest and subsequent sediment inwash. Similarly, early Flandrian (Boreal) sediments of largely inorganic nature have been discussed from the River Medina, Isle of Wight (Scaife 1980b, 1982a) and at Sharpsbridge on the Sussex Ouse (Burrin 1981, 1983, Scaife 1983e, Burrin and Scaife 1984, Scaife and Burrin 1983). At this site considerable quantities of derived loessic material are present. This valley alluviation has possibly been in response to anthropogenic deforestation since at the time of deposition the landscape was becoming dominated by *Pinus, Corylus, Ulmus* and *Quercus* forest (during pollen zones V and VI). This pre-supposes that dominant forest cover would have had a minimizing effect on surface water run-off and therefore valley side erosion supplying sediments to the valley bottoms. For such alluviation to have taken place, vegetation cover must have been more open than has been generally accepted and with a greater degree of soil instability than has been inferred from the more usual palynological investigations of wholly organic peat sequences. The use of fire on a larger scale than suggested by Dimbleby at Iping (in Keef *et al.* 1965) and at Oakhanger (Rankine *et al.* 1960) seems a more plausible way of explaining the vegetation and soil instability suggested above.

Little evidence has been forthcoming from the few pollen diagrams in the South East for any effects of Mesolithic man on the Atlantic periods vegetation. Here, as noted above, soil pollen analyses have been the sole source of data. The environment in which Mesolithic man lived in the Flandrian chronozone II was substantially different to that of Flandrian I. In contrast to the rapid seral changes in the vegetation through *Betula, Pinus, Quercus* and *Ulmus* forest the Flandrian II has been viewed as one of stability of climate and vegetation. In consequence of this and the establishment of modern day sea-levels, man's environment had changed markedly from one of large areas of low lying fen in the coastal shelf areas to one with closed deciduous woodland and coastal perimeter. It is this latter coastal interface which has a predominantly skewed distribution of Mesolithic sites for the early Flandrian II with coastal and riverine archaeological sites noted in Dorset (Rankine 1961) and the Isle of Wight (Poole 1936, Basford 1980). Few environmental archaeological investigations of these sites have been undertaken in the past, despite the often organic character of the sediments in which artefactual material has been found.

Brook Bay, Isle of Wight (SZ 382387) which is a Mesolithic hearth (Poole 1936) was the subject of some pioneer work on the distribution and character of the Mesolithic cultures and for early macrofossil plant analyses of the Hazel nut beds (White 1921) and pollen analysis of the peats (Clifford 1936). Pollen recorded included *Pinus, Betula, Quercus, Alnus, Corylus* and *Quercus* from the Mesolithic hearth. Plant macrofossils included *Alnus, Corylus, Quercus, Taxus* and *Fraxinus*. This site and Werrar (SZ 506925) also investigated by Poole (1936) have been re-examined by the writer (Scaife unpublished).

2.E.1 *Proposals for Mesolithic research*

a. Further investigation of coastal Mesolithic peat sites lost to Flandrian eustatic changes could provide valuable environmental archaeological data. These might have stronger relevance to the effects of man than otherwise archaeologically unrelated sites. Such investigations are being carried out in a multi-disciplinary fashion at Westward Ho!, Devon but there is the potential for such investigations along the coasts and estuaries of Dorset, Hampshire, Isle of Wight and Kent. Sites could be suggested which might elucidate a possible 'strandlooping' economy of coastally oriented communities.

b. A number of workers have drawn attention to the low quantities of ruderal pollen often found in some pollen spectra of Atlantic age. These may represent the ephemeral activities of Mesolithic man on inland lowland vegetation. Conversely, they might be due to natural/non-anthropogenic factors such as natural tree throw, or herbivore browsing. Recent ideas as to the possibility of Mesolithic man being able to control a semi pastoral/stock rearing economy could be investigated at higher definition by detailed close sampled pollen investigations of known pollen sites. This might be linked to further or continued soil pollen investigations.

c. Investigation of inorganic river flood plain sediment has now proved to be of value. This approach might be used to elucidate regional gaps in our knowledge where peat pollen data have not been forthcoming.

2.F   The Neolithic

It is from the Late-Mesolithic onwards that knowledge of vegetation history and man's anthropogenic impact on the area of Southern England becomes especially scant. This problem has been emphasised by numerous archaeologists and palaeoecologists. J Turner (1970, 98–99) has said:

'It is rather unfortunate that the South-East chalkland, long regarded on archaeological grounds as an area densely settled by Neolithic man should be so poor in plant preserving material'

There is still, despite recent investigations, an absence of botanical evidence showing the nature, extent and impact of Neolithic man on the vegetation. This is important in terms of evidence of initial clearance of forest for arable and pastoral subsistence economies introduced by the Neolithic economy and its secondary effect on the soils and vegetation of Southern England. Because of the large number of vegetation and edaphic possibilities of the lithological microcosm of Southern England, and the marked paucity of data (especially from Kent, East Sussex and Surrey) little conclusive evidence for the effects of this differing land use has been forthcoming from the region. This lacuna results from those factors detailed in Section 2.ii. and also especially from peat cutting which has truncated those upper sections of peat spanning the later prehistoric periods. Examples of this latter effect may be seen in the work of Seagrief already cited, which relates especially to the Late-Devensian/early Flandrian but not post-Atlantic periods and also from Munsley Peat Bed, Isle of Wight (Scaife 1980b, 1982a) and Godlington 'B', Dorset (Haskins 1978) where peats of post-Atlantic date have been removed.

This deficiency is unfortunate as much pollen data have been forthcoming from Northern areas of Britain, the extensive areas of wetlands of the Anglian Fens and Somerset Levels and North West Europe providing evidence of the character and extent of Neolithic anthropogenic impact. The South East centred on the Wessex chalk area is unquestionably regarded as a central place of Neolithic activity. Since the pioneer work of Iversen (1941, 1949) on Neolithic land clearance, much information has come from North West Europe. General reviews of this work may be found in Godwin (1956, 1975a), Smith (1970), J Turner (1970), Evans (1975) and Simmons and Tooley (1981). From this data follows the discussion of a number of phenomena thought to be due to Neolithic man.

2.F.1   *The Ulmus decline in Southern England*

The phenomenon of declining pollen of *Ulmus* at *c*5000 bp has been extensively dated throughout Britain (Smith and Pilcher 1973). The majority of dates fall between the rational dates given by Smith and Pilcher of 5335 ± 120 BP to 4570 ± 120 BP. This decline in *Ulmus* pollen has been recognised throughout NW Europe and has been used to delimit the boundary between the Atlantic and Sub-Boreal pollen Zones VIIa and VIII (Godwin's pollen Zones or VIII/IX of Europe). This boundary also seems to mark the arrival of Neolithic way of economy in Britain although it is still the subject of much controversy (Bradley 1978, Simmons and Tooley 1981). Since Iversen's early discussions (1941, 1949, 1960) five possible explanations have emerged from European pollen analyses:

i.   Climatic causes:– Jessen 1935, Iversen 1941, 1944, 1960, Faegri 1944, Godwin 1956, 1975a, Frenzel 1966.

ii.   Competition factors:– Morrison 1959, Tauber 1965.

iii.   Human influence:– Iversen 1949, Troels-Smith 1954, 1955, 1956, 1960, Smith 1958, Morrison 1959, Sims 1973, 1978, Scaife 1980b, Mitchell 1956.

iv.   Disease:– Aletsee 1959, Troels-Smith 1960, Watts 1961.

v.   Selective pollen filtration:– Tauber 1967.

These causative factors have been discussed in detail by Iversen (1949), A G Smith (1970, 1981), Troels-Smith (1955, 1960), Godwin (1956, 1975a), Tauber (1965), and Ten Hove (1968). Archaeological reviews have been omitted from the above which are source papers written in English language.

In recent years a small number of closely spaced sampled pollen analyses have been carried out on *Ulmus* decline horizons. These have provided greater temporal resolution and understanding of this phenomenon. Moore (1980b) has studied peats of Neolithic age which just post-date the *Ulmus* decline at Llyn Mire. Sims (1973, 1978) has re-investigated Hockam Mere, Norfolk, the site from which Godwin (1944) and Godwin and Tallantire (1951) first recognised the effects of Neolithic man on the vegetation of Eastern England. These sites are, however, removed from the southern region of Neolithic dominance. Some data have been forthcoming from Central South Coast area with Haskins (1978) attempting C^{14} dating of the *Ulmus* decline at Morden Bog. This assay produced a date of 4184 ± 150 BP although this date is likely to be young due to contamination.

In the Isle of Wight at Gatcombe Withy Bed the *Ulmus* decline and an ensuing 'Landnam' and Neolithic agricultural activity have been investigated in detail by close continuous sampling at 2mm intervals of the peats (Scaife 1980b). This site is important representing a peat mire with a small pollen catchment area closely adjacent to archaeological sites. From this work, a degree of resolution not usually found in pollen diagrams was obtained and related to archaeological material obtained within 100 metres of the mire (Tomalin and Scaife 1979). Here, archaeological material was recovered *as a result of palynological investigation of the mire.* From this investigation Scaife (1980b) and Scaife in Tomalin and Scaife (1979) recognised five distinct and differing phases of activity:

i.   Pre-*Ulmus* decline Atlantic period dated 6385 ± 50 (SRR-1339) bp to 4850 ± 45 bp (SRR-1338) of dominant *Quercus, Tilia, Ulmus, Alnus, Corylus, Ilex* and *Fraxinus* with possible local glades created by Mesolithic man. Some flint artefacts may relate to the pollen evidence.

ii.   Primary *Ulmus* decline dated at 4850 ± 50 bp where *Ulmus* pollen declines from > 20% AP to 2%: Herbaceous pollen including cereal pollen becomes present from the immediate *Ulmus* decline levels (*not* before at 2mm intervals) strongly suggestive of an autogenic or allogenic response to human activity.

iii.   Small scale local cereal cultivation during the middle Neolithic, characterised by arable activity taking place within an essential open-canopy forested environment. The pollen of cereal and ruderals shows a series of alternating peaks and troughs suggested as being evidence of ephemeral cultivation of crop patches adjacent to settlement, or even due to crop rotation similarly postulated by Moore (1980a).

iv.   A distinctive phase of local forest clearance of 'Landnam' type in proximity to the site pollen analysed is evidenced by local eutrophication of the peat mire. A marked increase in the presence of cereals and associated ruderals is also seen. Analyses of flint assemblages (Tomalin and Scaife 1979) correspond to this event and are thought to be of Middle Neolithic age and compare favourably with flint assemblages from Arreton Down, Isle of Wight.

v. Subsequent to these phases of transient agricultural activity is a period of Late-Neolithic to early Bronze Age forest regeneration to secondary forest. The writer (Scaife 1980) has suggested that fewer cultivars and the open canopy aspect of this woodland might be indicative of a return to pastoral land usage in the Late Neolithic at least in the area of the site analysed.

Borthwood Farm bog (SZ 378849) was compared with Gatcombe and used to elucidate the differences of local land use during the Neolithic *Ulmus* decline and to show the changes in woodland structure which occurred as a consequence of Neolithic activities (Scaife 1980). It is notable that both of these sites are in close proximity to the chalklands and to the Greensand escarpment (1.2km, and 1.5km respectively). Scaife concluded that the chalklands and the Lower Greensand ridges of the Isle of Wight were probably indistinguishable in terms of anthropogenic activity and remained largely afforested until the late Neolithic or early Bronze Age.

Further evidence of Neolithic activity has been seen in the environmental record at Bohemia Bog (Isle of Wight SZ 513833), a mire of small extent situated on a spring on Greensand lithology in an area previously heathland. The basal peat levels show evidence of forest clearance and cultivation possibly dating to the Late-Neolithic or early Bronze Age although no C^{14} dating is available. This, however, illustrates the possible role of forest clearance in affecting the ecological/hydrological balance with subsequent waterlogging and peat formations. Moore and Willmot's (1976) analysis of Thursley Bog, Surrey (Willmott 1968) has postulated thus for this large relic ombrogenous bog.

Waton (1980, 1982b) has recently similarly carried out close sampled analysis of the *Ulmus* decline at Rimsmoor, Dorset (SY 814922) where deep peat deposits have allowed a fine degree of detail with 1cm of peat formation representing 3.84 years. In direct contrast with the Isle of Wight data but correlating with Haskins' work in the Poole Harbour, Waton concluded that grassland pasture was the principal use of the open areas. From C^{14} dating Waton illustrated that the *Ulmus* decline lasted some 150 years between 3200 ± 70 bc (HAR-3919) and 2740 ± 70 bc (HAR-3920). Waton also notes the enigmatic occurrence of cerealia pollen prior to the *Ulmus* decline but notes that this could be the result of contamination. Waton (1982a, b) has also examined sites at Winnall Moors, Winchester (SU 486799) and Snelsmore in the Berkshire Downs (SU 463704). At the former, the *Ulmus* decline has been dated at 3680 ± 90 bc (HAR-432) showing a marked decline in its pollen followed by subsequently agricultural activity until *c*2575 bc when tree and scrub become more important.

The above analyses of Scaife and Waton illustrate the value of extensive and detailed peat surveys in areas adjacent to archaeological sites with detailed pollen sampling and C^{14} dating. It is noticeable that the above sites are concentrated in the Hampshire Basin region with little detailed work having been carried out in the counties of Kent and Sussex despite obvious areas of Neolithic archaeological importance in both counties (the Medway Megalith group for example).

Thorley (1971) produced pollen diagrams from Amberley and Lewes I and II, Sussex which are noted elsewhere in this review. Thorley (1981) suggests from her Lower Ouse pollen data (Lewes II) that the (adjacent) chalk downland remained well wooded from the early post-glacial to the Middle Bronze Age (*c*1240 bc). Brooks (unpublished) has produced a pollen diagram from the River Ouse at Wellingham also showing the *Ulmus* decline and local vegetation of *Tilia* dominance on the Lower Greensand.

At Hampstead Heath, London, Girling and Greig (1977) have carried out investigations on coleoptera and pollen and seeds respectively which illustrate the *Ulmus* decline and secondary *Ulmus* regeneration discussed below. In addition to the primary *Ulmus* decline, Greig shows that a decline in other arboreal taxa occurred at the same time at this site. This is in accord with the classic work of Iversen's land clearance in Denmark. Plant macrofossils and pollen reflect increasing wetness resulting in the pond's formation. This may result from the local micro-hydrological balance being disturbed as has been discussed above (see Moore and Willmot 1976, Scaife 1980b and Scaife 1983e and Burrin and Scaife 1984, Scaife and Burrin 1983).

2.F.2 *Changes in forest composition resulting from Neolithic activities*

Since Iversen published his classic work *Landnam i Denmarks Stenalder* in 1941, subsequent models by a variety of authors have attempted to elucidate further the natural environment and the effect of Neolithic man upon it. Groenman-van-Waateringe (for example) (1978) has produced two models for the Neolithic Vlaaderingen cultures of the Netherlands which may be applicable in one case to a situation found at Gatcombe Withy Bed, Isle of Wight (Scaife 1980b, 262) with open woodland and well developed undergrowth utilised for grazing without necessarily the use of burning and felling of woodland.

Barker and Webley (1978) attempted to create an overall landscape model for the southern chalklands for the Neolithic period. This was based on the palaeoecological data of soil palynology and molluscan analysis of other researchers. This model postulates that the chalklands, rather than being closed forest in the earlier Neolithic, were actually a mosaic of vegetation types. It was suggested that Neolithic farmers in the region selected areas with soil and vegetation conditions best suited to their cultivation techniques. Such a conclusion is commensurate with the mire palynology described. Scaife (1980b, 263) quotes:

'Evidence for differential pressure of human activity on the Island (Isle of Wight) is seen. This possibly reflects the preference of Neolithic man for special soil conditions, and suitability of areas of cultivation and settlement.'

Apart from the broader speculative models of Barker and Webley (1978), more detailed pollen investigations carried out in the region of Southern England have all discussed the actual nature of changes occurring in the composition of the forest and its structure, showing a degree of diversity of impact by man on different lithology and soils.

2.F.2a   *The High Weald*   A large proportion of the above data refers to the status of the chalklands and immediately adjacent areas. As enigmatic as the historical ecology, and origins of the downlands is that of the high Wealden ridge of Kent and Sussex during prehistoric times (Sheldon 1978). There has been a relative paucity of archaeological artefactual material from this region and the assumption is that the area had remained largely forested until deforestation resulting from the Wealden iron industry.

Burrin (1981, 1983) has shown that a number of valleys in the Southern Weald area have extensive thicknesses of valley sediments. Sedimentological analyses of River Ouse and River Cuckmere sediments have shown that these are of aeolian characteristics and possibly reworked loessal origins. This phenomenon has emphasised the uncertainty regarding causal factors responsible for valley alluviation and river flood plain development. Geomorphological and palynological investigations of the biostratigraphy and lithostratigraphy were undertaken by Burrin (1981 and Scaife 1983e, Burrin and Scaife 1984, Scaife and Burrin 1983). Results from one of the sites studies at Sharpsbridge near Newick, Sussex show that valley alluviation in this area has been largely in response to anthropogenic valley side forest clearance dating back to the Mesolithic. It has been suggested that prehistoric man was capable, albeit inadvertently, of making a significant impact on flood plain hydrology. This study, in addition to elucidating and suggesting the nature of the vegetation and extent of man's impact upon an area previously not studied, also illustrates the potential value of palynological investigation of primarily inorganic flood plain sediments. This contrasts markedly with most river valley pollen analyses which concentrate on biogenic deposits rather than minerogenic sediments. The implications of pollen transfer and origins in such sediments has been discussed (Scaife in Burrin and Scaife 1984), and from this it seems that pollen in such deposits may be of local origin, pollen incorporated into the rivers sediment load possibly being readily destroyed by abrasion over greater distances.

2.F.3   *Neolithic proposals*

a. Further close contiguous sampling of Neolithic peat dated horizons in areas of archaeological activity is much needed in order to add to our knowledge of Neolithic agricultural practices. Sampling at 4cm or even 8cm intervals is no longer an adequate method of assessing the true nature of Neolithic anthropogenic activity.

b. Correlations could be made between vegetative data from pollen and macrofossil analyses with that of archaeological concentrations and possibly with Neolithic polished axe distributions.

c. Closer study could be made of the history of secondary woodland brought about by anthropogeny. This would provide a more realistic assessment of the tree vegetation and environment of the Neolithic and Post Neolithic. This is important in terms of woodland economy not only from the point of view of coppicing as illustrated by Somerset Levels work but also in woodland pastoralism. Palynological investigations have for too long concentrated upon agriculture in terms of pastoralism or cereal cropping in open clearings, whereas it is likely that certain agricultural practices or periods may be reflected by closer ecological investigation of woodland phases (see earlier discussion on late Neolithic woodland regeneration).

Neolithic data from mires

Berkshire

Clarke A in Bradley R *et al.*, 1980 Pollen from Aldermaston Wharf.

Dorset

Haskins L A, 1978 Poole Harbour.
Waton P V, 1980, 1982a, 1982b Rimsmoor.

Essex

Baker C A, 1976 Newport.
Scaife R G, forthcoming Mar Dyke.

Hampshire

Waton P V, 1982a, 1982b Whinnall Moors, Snelsmore.

Isle of Wight

Scaife R G in Tomalin and Scaife 1979, Scaife 1980a, b Gatcombe Withy Bed.
Scaife R G, 1980b Borthwood Farm.
Scaife R G, 1980b Bohemia Bog and Ninham Bog.
Shackley M, 1976 Shide Bridge, Newport.

Kent

Devoy R J, 1980 Lower Thames.
Webb J A, 1972 Hothfield Common.

London

Girling M and Grieg J R A, 1977 Hampstead Heath.

Lower Thames

Devoy R J N, 1977, 1978–79, 1980, 1982

Sussex

Brooks A, in preparation Wellingham.
Burrin P J and Scaife R G, 1984 Sharpsbridge, Sussex Ouse.
Scaife R G 1983e.
Scaife R G and Burrin P J, 1983 Sussex, Ouse.

2.G   Bronze Age and Post-Bronze Age mire data

As with the Neolithic, our knowledge of the overall effect of Bronze Age man on the environment remains somewhat enigmatic, with our primary source of environmental data coming from soil palynology (see section 3.D) and molluscan analyses. Added to this problem is the fact that the majority of Bronze Age field monuments are situated on the Wessex chalklands which are not conducive to pollen preservation. Also, the majority of field monuments found are burial mounds which may be placed on atypical areas of human activity. Although it has been postulated (Bowen 1961, 1975b, 1978) that the extensive Wessex chalklands were areas subjected to sophisticated land allotment, those sites analysed for environmental data relate almost solely to material preserved by mortuary practices. It has become clear with recent pollen work that these upland areas were of substantial importance to the Bronze Age peoples by virtue of the extensive forest clearance and establishment of the downland areas as they exist today albeit, with some regional variation in the date of the forest clearance. In Kent, Kerney *et al.* 1964 show a period of clearance at 1000 bc; in Sussex, Thorley (1981) suggests middle Bronze Age; in the Isle of Wight, Scaife (1980b, 1984 and forthcoming in Tomalin) suggests early Bronze Age and in the Hampshire/Wessex region, Waton (1982a) has shown late Bronze Age deforestation. Palaeoecological studies have been preoccupied with the status of these upland areas. The preservation of molluscan assemblages has allowed environmental reconstruction (Thomas 1982) but not specific data on the vegetation of the downlands. Botanically, the studies of Thorley (1971a) in Sussex, Scaife (1980) in the Isle of Wight and Waton in Hampshire and Dorset have sought to elucidate the actual nature of the vegetation more clearly. Burgess (1974) has stressed again the differences outlined by Cyril Fox's highland/lowland division of the country, suggesting a predominantly pastoral highland zone contrasting with the more arable lowlands. Although this is suggestive of overall differences across the country, such differences are apparently applicable to a lesser extent (but still importantly) to the highland/lowland division of Southern England.

Godwin (1964) was the first person to produce pollen data from a lowland peat mire in Kent and apply C^{14} dating. Godwin related his pollen diagrams from Frogholt near Folkestone and Wingham near Canterbury to the problem of downland vegetation because of the proximity of his sites to the chalklands. At Wingham, basal peat deposits in a valley showed a largely deforested landscape at the time of peat inception (3105 ± 110 bp Q-110). Thus an early date for deforestation and subsequent arable agriculture and pastoral farming is indicated. Peat at Godwin's other site of Frogholt began to accumulate after 2980 ± 130 bp (Q-354), that is representing the later Bronze Age and Iron Age periods. This similarly showed an open landscape dominated by agriculture which he correlated with the commencement of more efficient Iron Age agriculture. In view of recent palynological literature dealing with pollen dispersion and pollen infiltration to small peat mires, and after recent studies of similar small mires in Southern England, it is possible that this evidence relates not to the downland areas but to areas closely adjacent to the mires. This is of value in as much as it still provides valuable data relating to lowland prehistoric agriculture. Thus, a predominantly arable economy was shown, which contrasts with recent evidence of grassland/pastoral environs of the downlands.

The impact of the Bronze Age activity on the environment of these lowland areas has been dealt with by a number of workers on different aspects from data from pollen diagrams spanning this period. Analysis of Thursley peat bog, Surrey by Willmott (1968) and Moore and Willmot (1976) has been discussed in terms of the possibility of Bronze Age man causing peat initiation by effecting higher water tables by deforestation and disrupted hydrological balance. The effect of agricultural activity on local hydrology and river alluviation has been demonstrated in Sussex (Burrin and Scaife 1984 and Scaife and Burrin 1983). Where increased Bronze Age activity caused large inputs of sediments to the river systems (River Ouse and Cuckmere), and in the Isle of Wight (Scaife 1980b) with silica inorganic constituents within valley peats similarly correlated with adjacent agricultural phases.

Haskins (1978, 269) has related the large numbers of Bronze Age monuments in Dorset to pollen analysis of the Poole Harbour area (Haskins regional pollen Zone G). She states that 'it appears that Bronze Age man effected considerable changes in the vegetation of the Poole Basin'. Here extensive woodland clearance resulted in a marked decline in tree pollen with only patches of *Quercus, Alnus* or *Betula* growing in topographically favourable conditions. The vegetation became one of open grassland and heathland possibly concentrated around areas of greatest barrow distribution/density and areas of *Corylus* scrub.

Palynological investigation of lowland valley peat bogs and fens in the Isle of Wight (between 1974–1980, Scaife 1980b) illustrated the differences between agricultural activity on the downlands and that taking place on the Lower Greensand areas. It was suggested that changes in woodland structure initiated with early Neolithic disturbance were subsequently maintained and enhanced in the Bronze Age. Data including diverse herb assemblages from Gatcombe Withy Bed, Borthwood Bog, and Bohemia Bog, Isle of Wight suggest arable and possible mixed agricultural practices. In contrast to Haskins, however, throughout the lowland areas of the Isle of Wight there is evidence of extensive forest and continuity of woodland dominated by *Tilia* and *Ilex* on the well drained soils of the Lower Greensand. *Quercus, Corylus* and possibly *Fraxinus* remained on heavier soils. Many of the mires remained dominated by Alnetum and Salicetum. Although some suggestions as to dating of changes in land use are given in this work, further radiocarbon assays are required to elucidate further the apparent differences of activity resulting from topographic and edaphic variability, and the settlement of the marginal environs in response to population pressure. Scaife (1980b) has emphasised that Bronze Age man had an impact on a whole variety of ecotypes which might be related to a dual agricultural system of arable agriculture in the lowlands and pastoralism on the upland downlands. The overall effect on the vegetation appears to have been dependent upon the edaphic and lithological characteristics of the area. Such studies might be related to evidence of later Bronze Age land apportionment coming from field and aerial surveys (Bowen 1961, 1975a, b, 1978, Ellison and Harriss 1972, Fleming 1971).

In contrast to the marked vegetation changes described above, Baker *et al.* (1978) and Oxford (1974) illustrate the continuity of *Tilia* climax woodland in the area of Epping Forest and which remained until the *Tilia* decline. Some continuity has also been noted by Waton (1982a) for Snelsmore where the immediate landscape remained wooded with only limited clearing occurring after the late Bronze Age. Waton suggests that this variability reflects the distribution of deposits capping the chalk, or possibly more favourable areas of occupation in other areas.

2.G.1 *The Tilia decline*

Almost as significant as the *Ulmus* decline is a similar reduction in *Tilia* pollen in the pollen record. This phenomenon has been widely recognised in both British and European pollen analyses and as such it has been used as the delimiting factor between the Sub-Boreal (pollen Zone VIb) and sub-Atlantic (Zone VIII) periods. The assumed synchroneity was based on the premise that *Tilia* declined as a result of significant climatic change. Further research has shown that an anthropogenic factor is the most likely cause as the *Tilia* decline is inversely related to the abundance of herbaceous and ruderal pollen. Moore (1977), and Greig (1982a), have discussed the distribution of *Tilia* in England, and as this taxon has a southern distribution pattern its importance has already been noted in pollen spectra from the region under discussion. Baker *et al.* (1978) have summarised the C^{14} dating of the *Tilia* decline phenomenon and shown that this was asynchronous throughout the country with dates from as early as the late-Neolithic at Mordon Carr, Durham (Bartley *et al.* 1976) to Anglo-Saxon in Epping Forest (Baker *et al.* 1978). Three C^{14} dates for the decline of *Tilia* have been obtained from the Isle of Wight (Scaife 1980b). An earlier decline of Neolithic date (4010 ± 110 bp SRR-1435) precedes a second decline of later Bronze Age date (3280 ± 80 bp SR-1434) at Borthwood Farm Bog. A second later Bronze Age date (2910 ± 130 bp SRR-1436) at Bohemia Bog and a marked *Tilia* and *Ilex* decline at Gatcombe Withy Bed attest to its widespread significance. That this is due to anthropogenic causes is evidenced by the increased frequency and occurrence of cultigens consequent upon the clearance of *Tilia* woodland. The majority of dates fall within the later Bronze Age and may indicate land clearance for agriculture. Bowen (1975b) has suggested that deliberate allotment of arable land occurred at an earlier date than generally held and evidence from such sites as Martin Down, Hampshire shows a middle Bronze Age date (1200 BC) for Celtic fields and ranch boundaries. The *Tilia* decline in pollen catchments analysed may lend weight to Bradley's (1978) postulations that later Bronze Age expansion took place at the interface between natural zones. In this context, the areas discussed have fertile soils and lie midway between the heavy clay vales and the already extensively cleared downland tracts. Such clearances might have preceded the major increase of arable farming at *c*1200 BC (Bradley 1978). The *Tilia* decline has also been noted in pollen diagrams from the Poole Harbour–Wareham district (Haskins 1978), Sharpsbridge, Sussex (Scaife 1983e, Burrin and Scaife 1984 and in press) and by Waton at Rimsmoor, Dorset and at Snelsmore, Hampshire, Wellingham, Sussex (Brooks unpublished) and Lewes I and II, Amberley Wild Brooks (Thorley 1971a, 1971b, 1981) in Sussex.

2.G.2 *Miscellaneous studies*

Bronze Age pollen data have produced evidence of a predominantly pastoral environment at Aldermaston Wharf and Knights Farm, Burghfield, Berkshire (Lobb in Bradley *et al.* 1980). Some pollen data relating to the Iron Age have also been forthcoming from the same upper middle Thames region at Farmoor by Dimbleby in Lambrick and Robinson (1979).

Bronze Age data from mires

Dorset

Haskins L E, 1978 Poole Harbour.
Waton P V, 1980, 1982a, 1982b Rimsmoor.

Essex

Baker C *et al.*, 1978 Epping Forest.
Oxford P M, 1974 Epping Forest.

Hampshire

Waton P V, 1982a, 1982b Snelsmore and Whinnal Moor.

Isle of Wight

Scaife R G, 1980a, b Gatcombe Withy Bed, Bohemia Bog, Borthwood Bog, Ninham Bog.

Kent

Devoy R J, 1980
Godwin H, 1960 Wingham.
Godwin H, 1962 Wingham and Frogholt.
Webb J A, 1972 Hothfield Common.

London

Girling M and Greig J R A, 1977 Hampstead Heath.

Surrey

Moore P D and Willmot A, 1976 Thursley Bog.
Willmot A, 1968 Thursley Bog.

Sussex

Burrin P J and Scaife R G, 1984 Sharpsbridge.
Scaife R G, 1983e Sharpsbridge.
Scaife R G and Burrin P J, 1983 Sharpsbridge.

2.H Roman and Post Roman vegetation changes

Pollen analysts have in the past been generally pre-occupied with those changes in the vegetation record brought about by natural and anthropogenic causative factors. This, with a few exceptions has generally concerned the earlier parts of the present interglacial in relation to prehistoric man's activities and for the earlier Pleistocene glacial/inter-stadial or interglacial sequences. It is in the post Iron Age period that vegetational and ecological sequences can be verified, augmented or superseded by the available historical documentation. Thus, the writings of Pliny, Columella, Strabo, Diodorus Siculus and Theophrastus have provided valuable accounts of domesticated plants in the Roman empire. In Southern England, Murphy (1977) has made use of these discussions. The Post Roman to Norman period represents an episode of special paucity of data and is a period during which urban archaeology and associated environmental data collection has been particularly forthcoming (see Hall *et al.* Volume I and Armitage *et al.* this volume). Such a case is not true of the rural environs where little data are available for the nature of land use in the Anglo Saxon to Norman phase. It is through this period and after that analyses of peat sequences have not been fully utilised.

As noted (Section 1) the use of peat mire communities whether of *Sphagnum*, or Cyperaceae bog or the tree/fen carr communities has in a large number of cases brought about the destruction of these peats by either peat cutting or draining and the promotion of withy bed. It is possible to delimit the changing economic usage of these plant communities as for example shown by dated 'cut' *Alnus* stakes and waste twigs at Gatcombe Withy Bed, Isle of Wight (490 ± 90 bp i.e. HAR-2839 1460 AD) (Scaife 1980b, 96). This illustrates the removal of coppice which promoted the further growth of *Alnus* and *Salix* during the late Medieval. This coppicing has been suggested as relating to the charter for the building of Newport subsequent to the destruction of the old capital of the Isle of Wight (Newtown) and Newport by the

French invasion of 1377 AD. This would undoubtedly have required a considerable quantity of coppice for the construction of wattle and daub buildings. This example serves to show the detail which might be possible from those upper levels of peat often rapidly dismissed for the earlier evidence of prehistoric, climatic and vegetational palaeoecology.

The value of archival documents is well known to historical documentary specialists. From the Domesday Survey of 1086 onwards documentation of the economy can provide much detail of land management and agricultural structure. Consequently, the translation of the Domesday text (Darby and Campbell 1962) provides a source for much environmental reconstruction. From 1580 onwards the 'English' County maps of Saxton, Speed, Morden and later tithe maps and estate plans before the first Ordnance Survey of 1795 (Isle of Wight) and publication of 1812, portray graphically the remaining wild wood and those areas which by this date had become enclosed hunting/royal forests. Detailed historical studies have been carried out in Southern England based on documentary evidence. (Jones J, 1978 in the Isle of Wight and Flower 1977 in the New Forest) Macphail (1979) and Haskins (1978) have discussed the diminution/ fragmentation of heathlands in the counties of Surrey and Dorset respectively. Haskins (1978, Chapter XIII) has examined very effectively the changing land use patterns within Dorset Poole Basin area with special reference to the extent of heathland, agricultural land use, woodland management and woodland extension by plantation.

Such detail cannot be obtained from the pollen analyses of peat (and even less so soil) sequences although it can be noted that Barber (1976a) has achieved greater resolution of climatic, vegetation and land use changes during the last 1000 years in North West England. This lack of detail has largely occurred as a result of the often relatively broad sampling intervals used by palynologists. Although peat humification and compaction as might be expected are less in the upper levels of peat mires — if draining has not caused desiccation — a sampling interval of 4cm or more would be too great to add precision.

There is consequently little pollen data which deal with the Roman and post Roman. Barber (1975), Haskins (1978) and Scaife (1980b) have noted the changing character of the vegetation in general terms. Scaife, (1980b, 284) has noted that subsequent to the *Tilia* decline (see section 2.G.1) in the late Bronze Age in the Isle of Wight a degree of replacement by *Fraxinus, Betula* and *Sorbus/Crataegus* occurred; that is expansion of scrub vegetation. It was also illustrated that arable agricultural activity subsequent to the *Tilia* decline remained unchanged throughout the Iron Age and Romano British period. From c1700 AD Barber, (1975) Haskins, (1978) and Scaife, (1980b) have noted the distinct and useful increase in the percentages of *Ulmus* and *Pinus* pollen. The former relates to the increase in *Ulmus glabra* growing in the hedgerows and the latter to the planting of exotic elements in estates and Forestry Commission plantations after 1919.

2.I   Proposals/suggestions for continued mire palynology

Palynological investigations of local, small topogenous mires (bogs and fens) have proved invaluable to the elucidation of Flandrian palaeobotany and ecology. It has been demonstrated (Tomalin and Scaife 1979, Scaife 1980b) that concentrated field survey in areas otherwise thought to be unproductive for such studies can provide information relating to not only natural palaeovegetation community characteristics, but can also provide data on the local effects of archaeological/prehistoric activity on the landscape. In the past, undue emphasis has been placed upon the analysis of peat bogs of the ombrogenous type occurring in the wetter areas of highland Britain, or the rare larger mires such as exist at Thursley or Cranes Moor. These give a palynological spectrum which may relate to the multitudinous plant communities present over a wide spatial area of the pollen catchment. Similarly, they mask or blur the individual nature of localised anthropogenic control on the vegetation landscape. In contrast, analytical investigation of local peat mires of small extent and therefore of limited pollen catchment characteristics can show a higher degree of resolution for these events — such as local 'Landnam' agriculture in the Neolithic period. Where these events are present, higher degrees of resolution can be obtained by close contiguous sampling of the peats spanning those temporal horizons of interest. The availability of small sample size C[14] dating could be advantageous in the discrimination of archaeological events seen in the pollen record. A better understanding of the character of Neolithic and Bronze Age agriculture and land management can be forthcoming if such investigations are carried out. Because of pressures on time and on expertise such detailed work has not often been undertaken. Examples of such are, however Moore's (1980b) analysis of Llyn Mire (Shropshire) sampled at 25mm. Contiguously, Scaife's (1980b) analysis of the 'Primary *Ulmus* decline' and 'Landnam' phase at 2mm contiguous intervals in the Isle of Wight and Turner's (1964) earlier investigations of Bronze Age shifting cultivation in Northumberland and Tregaron Bog, Wales. In the case of Gatcombe, Isle of Wight, such detailed investigations resulted in the discovery of Mesolithic and Neolithic flint scatters in fields adjacent to the site analysed for pollen. These facilitated comparison with anthropogenic activity viewed in the pollen record. Such analyses have potential for providing greater understanding of a wide variety of archaeological/land use phenomena if applied to analyses of peats occurring adjacent to known or suspected archaeological sites. This might include elucidation of the extent to which Mesolithic man affected the vegetation at his places of encampment both in Flandrian chronozones I and II. Neolithic activity is an obvious choice with such work having been undertaken to illustrate the nature of the early arrival of subsistence arable and pastoral economies. Potential is available for elucidation of many post-Neolithic phenomena if problem areas could be formulated by archaeologists and/or historical geographers and industrial archaeologists and linked to sites with plant-macrofossil and palynological potential for investigation.

Extensive peat mires provide regional vegetation characteristics for the main arboreal and herbaceous taxa present through a given time. Such generalities of the nature of the vegetation have resulted from the monoclimax theory upheld for many years suggesting more/less uniform vegetation type and cover over wide areas at a given time under given climatic conditions (e.g. Godwin's Quercetum mixtum of the Atlantic zone VIIa). It has become more realistic to assess the vegetation as a polyclimax phenomenon functionally related to the varying physical controls within the ecosystem. In consequence, vegetation as might be expected was a mosaic of varying types growing in edaphically and local microclimatically suited niches and in chance occurrences (e.g. refugia) of less deterministic logic. The analysis of more than one mire of small pollen spectral extent enables a finer understanding of local vegetation character and extent. This has also greater potential to the environmental archaeologist by giving a more realistic local view of vegetation and environmental conditions relating to the archaeological site under examination. From this, it can be further suggested that such investigations could and should be used to verify many rather hypothetical site catchment analyses which were undertaken with little knowledge of the palaeoenvironment.

2.J   Flandrian base level changes

In spite of the relative paucity of detailed analyses in this region, it is of note that there was much early palaeobotanical interest along the south coast of England. Early discussion centred on the discovery of plant macrofossils obtained from submerged coastal deposits (e.g. Mounts Bay, Cornwall, Borlase 1757). These submerged forests have for long been known and in 1838, Clarke recorded the following arboreal taxa (wood) types in Poole Harbour, Dorset:– *Betula, Pinus, Quercus, Alnus, Fagus, Corylus.* Similar plant remains were found in Portsmouth Dockyard excavations (James 1847). Narthorst (1873) discovered a number of arctic floras in south coast localities. During the 1890s Clement Reid produced a series of comprehensive data recording sub-fossil plant material from Sussex (1892), Stone, Hampshire (1893) and *Pinus* charcoal found within peats at Parkestone, Dorset (1895) and from a midden site at Corfe, Dorset. In 1899 Reid produced the now classic text *The Origin of the British Flora* and *Submerged Forests* in 1913.

Geomorphologically, numerous raised beaches and marine cut platforms/erosional surfaces have been identified along the south coast. These features relate to the changing sea levels brought about by tectonic and glacio-eustatic causes. (See Greensmith and Tooley 1982, Jelgersma 1966). These have created much debate and literature on the history of the North Sea Basin and the history of the English Channel and European mainland separation from Britain and on the dating of the various middle and late-Quaternary raised beaches such as Goodwood-Slindon (Sussex). For a review of these data see D K C Jones (1980, 1981).

There has been evidence forthcoming from Southern England for the details of Pleistocene palaeogeography, (West R G 1972) especially spanning the last (Devensian) cold stage. Glacio-eustatically lowered sea-levels exposed much of the continental shelf in response to a falling sea level of at least 100m. Marked erosive incision possibly resulted from fluvial discharge from the landmass subjected to periglacial phenomenona during the Wolstonian and Devensian cold stages. With the close of the Devensian, the Flandrian transgression of the sea was initiated resulting in the re-establishment of sea-level at OD (of present levels). This has been of considerable importance to the discipline of archaeology, palaeoecology and palaeobotany affecting the nature and time of arrival (or not) of the British flora and in presenting a barrier or restriction to the movement of peoples from the continental mainland. This establishment of sea levels at c6500–7000 bp had a profound effect on the distribution of the Mesolithic population (Akeroyd 1966 and see section 2.D).

In order to assess the dating and events of this transgressive phase, palaeobotanical, palynological, C^{14} dating and sedimentological data have been used. From these analyses, sea level change data have been forthcoming and 'height-time/date' curves have been constructed from the Thames (Devoy 1977, 1978–79, 1980, 1982). Devoy (1982) has reviewed the data on sea level change in the southern region and from his important researches in the lower Thames valley basin has established a sequence of five marine transgressions. These he has dated as follows:

Thames	V	c.1750 bp
Thames	IV	?2600 bp?
Thames	III	3850–2800 bp
Thames	II	6575–5410 bp
Thames	I	8200–6970 bp

This is the most recent work at present and is being widely used in archaeologically related work (see Straker this volume).

Much detailed work has also been carried out along the Essex coast. Here, Greensmith and Tucker (1969, 1971, 1973, 1980) and Greensmith and Tooley (1982) have extensively studied and dated sediments relating to eustatic changes. Comparative North Sea Basin and continental work comes from the eustatic change curves plotted for the

Lower Somme, France (Ters 1973), in Holland (Jelgersma 1961, 1966 and Jelgersma and Pannekoek 1960) and earlier work in Southern England by Akeroyd (1966, 1972) and West R G (1972).

Data from earlier Pleistocene deposits containing plant microfossils and macrofossils have also been researched along the south coast. The earlier investigations of Reid have been mentioned. More recent work includes continued research and reappraisal of deposits at Stone, Hampshire (Brown *et al.* 1975) dating those to the Ipswichian interglacial. These therefore correlate with known Ipswichian sequences at Selsey Bill, Hampshire (West and Sparks 1960). Kellaway *et al.* (1975) and Morzadec-Kerfourn (1975) have examined the Quaternary history of the English Channel, work which has become controversial in view of the possibility of the glaciation of the Channel. South coast Flandrian information of sedimentological, geomorphological and palaeoecological nature has been produced by Everard (1954a, 1954b), Dyer (1972, 1975), Hodson and West I M (1972), Devoy (unpublished BSc dissertation, University of Durham) and Scaife (unpublished).

Much data not referred to in the above brief account are indicated in the site appendix given at the end of this section.

Literature relevant to eustatic changes

General and local continental sources

Akeroyd A V, 1966 Post-Devensian of Southern Britain, related to Mesolithic man.
Churchill D M, 1965 Southern Britain at 6500 years ago.
Greensmith J T and Tooley M J, 1982 Movements over the last 15000 years.
Jelgersma S, 1961 Holocene and sea level changes in the Netherlands.
Jelgersma S, 1966 The last 10000 years.
Jelgersma S and Pannekoek A J, 1960 Netherlands' sea level change.
Reid C, 1899 *Origin of the British Flora.*
Reid C, 1913 *Submerged forests.*
Suggate R and Willis E, 1958 C^{14} dating of eustatic changes.
Ters M, 1973 Lower Somme, France sea level change curve.
West R G, 1972 Land and sea levels in South East England during the Pleistocene.

East coast and Thames estuary region

Devoy R J, 1977, 1978–79, 1980, 1982 Thames Estuary and reviews.
D'Olier B, 1972 Thames Estuary.
Godwin H and M E, 1934 Submerged forests of the Essex coast.
Greensmith J T and Tucker E V, 1969, 1971, 1973, 1980 Essex coast.
Reader F W, 1911 Flint implements of submerged peats.
Warren S H S *et al.,* 1936 Archaeology of Essex coastal submerged forests.

The Solent region

ApSimon A *et al.,* 1976 Pleistocene raised beaches on Portsdown Hill.
Brown R C *et al.,* 1975 Pleistocene deposits at Stone.
Dyer K, 1972, 1975 Buried channels in the Solent.
Everard C E, 1954b Solent River geomorphological study.
Everard C E, 1954a Peat and gravels in Southampton Water.
Godwin H, 1945b Portsmouth Harbour.
Godwin H and M E, 1940 Southampton Water.
Hodson I M and West R G, 1972 Fawley Holocene deposits.
Mottershead D, 1977 South coast.
Palmer L S and Cooke J H, 1923 Pleistocene deposits of Portsmouth area in relation to early man.
Reid C, 1893 Pleistocene deposits at Stone.
Scaife R G, Unpublished data on peats dredged from Solent by fishing vessels.
West I M, 1980 Solent sedimentological study.

Sussex

Hodgson J M, 1964 Low level Pleistocene sands of West Sussex Plain.
Hubbard R N L B in Shephard Thorne 1977 Slindon Goodwood raised beach deposits.
Jennings S and Smythe C, 1982
Reid C, 1892 Pleistocene of the Sussex coast.
West R G and Sparks B W, 1960 Selsey Bill.

Miscellaneous

Behre K E and Mencke B, 1969 North Sea 'moorlog'.
Borlase W, 1757 Submerged forests in Mounts Bay, Cornwall.
Clarke W R, 1838 Submerged forests at Bournemouth.
Godwin H, 1943, 1945 Coastal peat beds of the North Sea basin.
Warren S H, 1919 Dating of implements and submerged peat surfaces.
Kellaway G A *et al.,* 1975 Channel Tunnel boreholes and sedimentology.
Morzadec-Kerfourn M T, 1975 Pollen analyses of Channel Tunnel boreholes.
Narthorst A G, 1873 Arctic floras in South Coast localities.

3   Soil pollen analysis as a technique in environmental archaeology

3.A   Introduction

The use of archaeologically buried soils for providing environmental evidence has been particularly important in Southern England, especially as this area has had in the past a paucity of palaeo-vegetation data (for reasons see section 2.2) and a contrastingly high number of archaeological field monuments. G W Dimbleby has been largely responsible for the development of the technique of pollen analysis of terrestrial mineral soils (Dimbleby 1954, 1956, 1957b, 1961b, 1962a, 1965d and Dimbleby and Evans 1974).

With the advent of C^{14} assay, the use of pollen as a dating technique has been superseded, allowing pollen analysis to fulfill its primary function as a tool for establishing the ecological setting of an area before and immediately prior to 'fossilization' of that prehistoric soil by construction of monuments such as tumuli or linear earthworks. The problems of alkalinity in peats resulting from calcareous lithologies are similarly applicable to the palynology of soils. Acid soils, especially podzols having a pH of less than 5.5 are particularly suited for the application of soil palynology often containing high absolute frequencies of pollen per gram weight. With soils, however, the degree of stratification present in a profile is not resolvable to the degree that peat profiles (which accumulate *upwards*) can be. This is because the progressive movement of soil and organic materials down through the profile result in broad ecological/vegetation changes being represented *downwards* from a ground surface (excepting 'raw' humus accumulation). Where extensive soil degradation/soil acidification has resulted in an organic (Ah) surface accumulation due to break down of soil-faunal mixing, this may be stratified in the character of mire of telmatic peats although these may be greatly humified.

In soils of pH around c.5.5 and above, soils have a high level of bacterial and actinomycete activity in temperate climes. Pollen in such soils is subject to rapid attack and deterioration and mixing by soil faunal activity. The consequent result is that differential preservation occurs in favour of pollen types having a robust exine. Examination of earthworm casts (Dimbleby 1961b and Ray 1959) show that pollen passes through the worm gut without destruction and that such soils containing earthworms show a characteristic pollen spectrum of homogeneous nature throughout the depth of the profile. Dimbleby and Evans (1974) have compared molluscan analyses and soil pollen and concluded that contained pollen is co-eval with the time of burial of such soil profiles. Dimbleby has carried out research on contemporary soil profiles to assess the above problems (Dimbleby 1957b, 1961a, b, 1965d, Dimbleby and Gill 1955). Furthermore the construction of the Overton Down, Wiltshire and Wareham, Dorset experimental earthworks have and should provide further and invaluable information on pollen movement in calcareous and podzolic soils.

Overton Down (Dimbleby 1965e, Dimbleby 1966a)
Morden Bog, Wareham (Dimbleby in Evans and Limbrey 1974)

3.B   Mesolithic soil palynology

The absence of Mesolithic structures precludes the possibility of having preserved palaeosols other than by natural agencies such as from blown sand. In consequence, and in spite of the abundance of Mesolithic flint scatters representing the transient settlements of these peoples, little direct archaeologically related pollen analyses have been carried out. Consequently, those sites which have been investigated have become of substantial importance in the understanding of the immediate/local environmental impact of Mesolithic man.

For the purposes of discussion of the Mesolithic phase, the period can be divided into two broad periods of differing environment. The first spans the close of the Late-Devensian at *c*10000 bp to the Atlantic period at *c*7000 bp. The second spans *c*7000 to 5300 bp after which the first proven effects of Neolithic man are seen on the vegetation. These two periods comprise the Flandrian chronozone I (Pre-Boreal and Boreal) and the Flandrian chronozone II (Atlantic). These major phases of vegetation change as shown by the 'long pollen diagrams' of the Flandrian peats (section 2.C and D) are reflected to a lesser extent in that soil pollen data which exist for the Mesolithic period. With absolute dating these data are valuable in their showing of terrestrial plant communities and the extent and possible nature of man and his economy. This is important in differentiating between natural ecological seral succession in Flandrian I and in assessing man's role as an allogenic factor in both edaphic and biotic development of his environment.

3.B.1 *Flandrian I*

Of those sites listed, Iping Common (Keef *et al.* 1965) analysed by Dimbleby is of greatest note. Here, soils of Mesolithic date have been preserved by blown sand of possible Atlantic date. The analysis of this site shows a typical and often quoted Boreal – *Pinus* – *Corylus* forest in level 'c' and an earlier Boreal (layer d) again dominated by *Corylus* but with the stronger role of *Betula*. The importance of Iping as an archaeological and environmental site lies in the fact that these Maglemosian peoples were able to bring about a change from the dominant *Betula/Pinus* woodland to *Corylus* and heathland at least on a local scale by use of fire and possibly animal herding.

The former possibility has been noted in relation to the possible effects of fire causing valley side soil instability and fluviatile erosion and deposition in Sussex (Scaife and Burrin 1983, Burrin and Scaife 1984). The second case of stock herding or rearing is altogether more problematical, but evidence for such does come from a number of sites in Southern England in the Flandrian II chronozone.

3.B.2 *Flandrian II*

Dimbleby (1975, 1976) and Simmons and Dimbleby (1974) have suggested the usage of *Hedera* as green-winter fodder for herded animals. If this evergreen was collected at the end of autumn it would be in flower so that pollen might be liberated on the archaeological site. Thus, an anthropogenic cause might be responsible for the high APF of *Hedera* found at Iping and in the lower soil levels of Minsted Bronze Age barrow (Dimbleby 1975) and at West Heath, West Sussex (Baigent 1976, Scaife 1983a and Scaife in Drewett 1985) and at Addington, Kent (Dimbleby 1965c).

Utilisation of natural food resources by Mesolithic/Maglemose man himself has been generally discussed by Smith (1970) and Jacobi (1978b). Some evidence has been forthcoming from the region under review. In addition to the high *Corylus* pollen percentages at Iping (Keef *et al.* 1965) and at West Heath (Baigent 1976 and Scaife 1985) and from peat sequences, *Corylus* macrofossil remains have been recovered from archaeological contexts and utilized for C^{14} dating. The following sites have recorded carbonised *Corylus* nuts which have also been used to provide determination of date of habitation.

i.   Oakhanger C^{14} 6300 ± 120 BP (Rankine *et al.* 1960)

ii. Thatcham, Berkshire 8080 ± 170 BC (Q658) (Wymer 1962)

iii. Iping Common 4340 ± 120 BC (Keef *et al.* 1965).

Although *Corylus* was a markedly dominant taxon in Southern England during this period it is very likely that these macrofossil remains occur on archaeological sites because of their utilisation by Mesolithic man as a food resource and their natural resistance to decay (especially when carbonised).

Dimbleby has raised the question of the extent of the influence of Mesolithic man on the soils and vegetation. The sites of Oakhanger (Rankine *et al.* 1960) and Iping (Keef *et al.* 1965) occur on the Lower Greensand giving rise to easy loss of soil structure and increasing acidity and eventual establishment of heathland vegetation on podzolic soils. This, he says, is in contrast to those settlements on more fertile soils where forest regeneration would have been likely as at Addington, Kent (Dimbleby 1965c). Micromorphological work on soils underlying the Bronze Age barrows of West Heath Cemetery (Macphail 1981) in conjunction with pollen investigations (Scaife 1983a, Scaife and Macphail 1983, Scaife in Drewett 1985) has similarly indicated that Mesolithic communities (dated at 6150 ± 70 BC from Barrow I – Drewett 1976b) caused soil acidification and heathland consequent upon the opening up of forest. It is also suggested by Scaife (1983a and Scaife in Scaife and Macphail 1983) that these ecologically sensitive soils may have supported heathland taxa throughout the early post-glacial, thus being able to expand their relative dominance through natural or anthropogenic disturbance. This question remains unresolved and requires further analyses of deep soils and investigation of peat mires in the vicinity of these areas. Furthermore, the relatively small number of sites analysed reflects the paucity of buried and sealed profiles of this age. It has for long been suggested that Mesolithic man was dominated by his environment and had little effect on the environment (Iversen 1941, 1949). The most that could be expected in the pollen record of these essentially nomadic hunting and gathering economies is therefore evidence of transient forest clearance. The above has suggested that Southern England may provide evidence of his greater influence on the vegetation and soils by deliberate and accidental means.

A strong coastal distribution of the Mesolithic cultures has been demonstrated in this region (Poole 1936, Rankine 1961, Palmer 1977, Basford 1980) reflecting possible utilisation of the coastal economic resource base of these ecotonal areas. A striking pattern of Lower Greensand distribution on the Isle of Wight (Poole 1936) and on light sandy soils in the Weald (Clarke 1932) has similarly been shown. Initially, the latter case was viewed as being due to ease of clearance of forest growing on lighter soils. Bradley (1970) and Evans (1975) point out that extensive fieldwork has shown that artefacts are not as closely related to soil typology as previously thought and that distribution reflects ease of recovery in non-flint soils. Jacobi (1978a) has shown that Mesolithic man was active in all differing lithologies of the

Weald. If this is the case our knowledge of the ecological impact of Mesolithic man is scant, being based on a handful of sites located on predominantly sandy soils.

Mesolithic soil pollen

Flandrian chronozone I

    a.   Iping Common, West Sussex; Dimbleby G W, 1976, Dimbleby in Keef P A M *et al., 1965.*

Flandrian chronozone II

    a.   Addington, Kent; Dimbleby G W, 1965c.

    b.   Iping Common, West Sussex; Dimbleby G W, 1975, 1976; Keef P A M *et al.,* 1965.

    c.   Minsted, West Sussex; Dimbleby G W, 1975.

    d.   Oakhanger, Selborne, Hampshire; Dimbleby G W, 1962b; Rankine W F *et al.,* 1960.

    e.   West Heath, West Sussex; Baigent J, 1976; Scaife R G, 1983; Scaife R G in Drewett P L, 1985; Scaife R G and Macphail R, 1983.

3.C   Neolithic — soil palynology

Evidence of vegetation relating to the Neolithic period in Britain has largely come from the analyses of peat mires as discussed in section 2.F. The status of the vegetation immediately prior to the impact of Neolithic peoples has been summarised by Birks *et al.* (1975) using isopollen maps for 5000 bp. It is into this forested environment that Neolithic man moved bringing with him the first subsistence economy of pastoralism and arable agriculture. Dating of these events has been discussed (section 2.F) and the period of *c*5500 to 3000 BP is that under discussion.

The environmental background from terrestrial archaeological sites is scant even in comparison with the Mesolithic data. This gap in knowledge can be attributed to the lack of settlement sites which have been excavated in this region. Drewett (1978) has discussed this for Sussex. Despite numerous flint scatters possibly representing ephemeral or local settlement sites in areas away from the chalk these have provided little archaeological excavation or suitable buried profiles for soil pollen investigations. This is in spite of the use by Neolithic peoples of earthen structures (funerary) for the first time in England. This problem has been further exacerbated by the strongly distributed nature of Neolithic monuments on the chalklands and therefore on calcareous soils unsuitable for pollen preservation; such distributions have been clearly shown in Sussex (Drewett 1978), Kent (A Clark 1982) and the Isle of Wight (Basford 1980). This generally precludes the use of palynological investigation due to the problems of soil alkalinity degrading the pollen and intense faunal (especially earthwork) action homogenising the rendzina profiles. This is unfortunate as the nature of development of the downland vegetation has been of constant interest, being discussed in recent literature by Thorley (1971a, 1981), Waton (1982a, b), Scaife (1980b, 1984) and from the archaeological viewpoint (Barker and Webley 1978).

The Neolithic chalklands It was suggested in early literature that the downland vegetation was in fact the natural climax plant community, having remained so since the last cold stage (e.g. Wooldridge and Linton 1933). However, as recent investigations have shown, these are plagioclimax communities being brought about by clearance of primary forest which had colonised during the early and middle Flandrian (section 2.C and D). Grassland sward ecosystems became established and maintained by grazing and anthropogenic pressures. These data result from modern phytosociological studies showing that soils and woodland recolonisation take place on reduction or removal of anthropogenic pressure. This has been substantiated by palaeoecological data from molluscan evidence (Evans 1972, Kerney *et al.* 1964 and Thomas 1982).

From the various lines of evidence it has suggested that forest clearance of the downland areas was not a synchronous occurrence, having taken place between the early Neolithic in Wiltshire and Sussex (Bell's work at Bishopstone 1977, and J G Evans 1972), to the early Bronze Age in the Isle of Wight (Scaife 1980b, 1984 and forthcoming in Tomalin) and the middle Bronze Age around Lewes (Thorley 1971b, 1981). Barker and Webley (1978) have produced a model of the character of vegetation on a downland catena utilising molluscan data. This is based on the site catchment hypothesis and fails to take into account such anachroneity of changing patterns of vegetation. Based on molluscan data it is not possible to determine exact composition of the vegetation but only broader environmental parameters. Thus, their model must remain largely speculative in its scope.

Dimbleby and Evans (1974) have produced an important paper illustrating that pollen can be preserved albeit in small quantities in calcareous soils. Although some contradiction is present with the molluscan evidence, Dimbleby (in Dimbleby and Evans 1974) has shown the value of investigating rendzina type soils under archaeological structures.

Analyses have been carried out in Wiltshire at eight sites in the Neolithic core area. These include Ascott-under-Wychwood (long barrow); Avebury (henge); Beckhampton (long barrow); South Street (long barrow); Horslip (long barrow); Durrington Walls (henge) and the causewayed enclosures of Knap Hill and Windmill Hill. References to these are given in the appendix at the end of this section. Dimbleby has suggested that pollen present may be subject to differential preservation and faunal intermixing so that no stratigraphical/temporal sequence is present. However, it does have value in that pollen present is likely to be of coeval date (3–4 years) with burial of the profile, thus providing on the spot detail of vegetation ecology. Analyses of this nature have not been carried out in the region of study and such a research programme would verify the spatial variability of the extent of remaining downland primary forest during the Neolithic period. Many earthwork structures of this date are present on the downlands including long barrows, causewayed enclosures and flint mines (spoil heaps). These monuments are especially frequent in Sussex with Grinsell (1934) listing thirteen known long barrows. Five certain causewayed enclosures are known in Sussex and eleven flint mining complexes (Drewett 1978). In the Isle of Wight only two long mounds exist on the chalk. With small excavations or augering these could provide a valuable insight into downland history across those areas peripheral to the Central Wessex Neolithic area/heartland.

Non calcareous lithologies Soil pollen studies on Neolithic non-calcareous lithologies are similarly scant. Of primary note is the investigation of a possible Neolithic butchery site and its associated flint scatter and assemblage at Rackham, Sussex (TQ 04901520) by Dimbleby and Bradley (1975). Because this site is on the Sandgate Beds of the Cretaceous Lower Greensand sequence, pollen preservation had occurred enabling the elucidation of vegetation change and soil development. Charcoal from the hearths gave an assay of 2000 ± 140 bc (HAR-360) being therefore of Late-Neolithic date. Dimbleby showed that the soils had originally been brown earths under closed deciduous forest canopy. An initial localised clearance of this forest is seen in the pollen diagram by an increase in heliophytic herbs in the lowest (oldest) levels of the pollen stratigraphy. This also initiated some soil acidification leading to preservation of the pollen. Subsequently there was a regeneration of forest dominated by *Quercus, Alnus* and *Corylus* with *Tilia, Ulmus* and *Ilex* again growing on soils of possibly brown earth character. With the beginning of permanent clearance after the Late-Neolithic clearance, *Calluna* reached overall dominance and was associated with strong soil acidification and podzolisation. This process would have eliminated earthworm activity but not prior to Neolithic artefacts having been buried by such activity.

At High Rocks, Sussex, excavated by J Money, the Mesolithic/Neolithic remains have been dated by two C^{14} assay at 3710 ± 150 bc (BM-40) and 3780 ± 150 bc (BM-91) and this is an important site for the early dated record of *Fagus*, a species of problematic and enigmatic origins in England (Dimbleby 1960). This paucity of knowledge has been brought about by the poor pollen dispersion characteristics of this taxon. The importance of this site also lies in its dated chronology lying between, or at the Mesolithic/Neolithic transition.

The 'Longstone' Mottistone, Isle of Wight (Hawkes 1957, Smith 1979) is one of the few Neolithic megaliths occurring off the chalk in the region of study. This sub-megalithic barrow is sited on the Lower Greensand ridge adjacent to the chalk downland scarp. A Neolithic buried land surface shows minor evidence of leaching as might be expected from forest clearance on these soils and lithologies. Results of pollen analysis of a single 'spot sample' taken from the upper level of this buried profile has indicated that the area was of open character with some *Betula, Quercus* and *Ulmus* represented in the low arboreal pollen frequencies (Scaife 1980b). The dominant ecotype being herbaceous gives an impression of a pastoral area or an abandoned site with high values of Gramineae and *Plantago lanceolata* pollen. A high proportion of *Calluna* pollen is commensurate with soil acidity on the potentially acidic sub-strates and may indicate that unlike other areas of Greensand which had Neolithic activity within deciduous woodland (Scaife 1980a, 1980b, Scaife in Tomalin and Scaife 1979) the area had possibly been subjected to a greater anthropogenic disturbance. It must, however, be noted that this spot sample requires confirmation by a full analysis and may also be representative of a small spatial area. This site does however provide evidence of markedly contrasting environments within the sphere of Neolithic activity from that of other Isle of Wight areas pollen analysed in detail. This is illustrative of the need for a greater number of analyses from a range of field monuments on as many and/or all differing lithologies within the region.

3.C.1 *Further suggestions for research*

a. Concerted attempts to elucidate at least the coeval vegetation of the downlands of Sussex, Hampshire, Dorset and the Isle of Wight need to be made by analyses of soils buried beneath these field monuments. Work of similar character to that of Dimbleby and Evans (1974) would provide evidence for the peripheral chalk areas of Southern England. This would add weight to the pollen investigations of peat mires spanning this period. Such research should also be undertaken along with plant macrofossil analyses and molluscan work.

b. Dimbleby and Bradley (1975) have shown that valuable data can be forthcoming from Neolithic archaeological sites even though no evident buried palaeosols are present (i.e. at Rackham, Sussex). The paucity of any 'on site' palynological data from Southern England must necessitate the investigation and/or retention of soil monoliths from all available excavations of Neolithic archaeological sites.

c. Where standing monuments of Neolithic date are found/known on non-calcareous strata their value is greatly enhanced by the possibility of pollen preservation. These phenomena are rarely known and few analysed. An obvious area for the study of local vegetation from a small geographical area could be the Medway valley megalith complex (Coldrum, Kits Coty, Lower Kits Coty and Chestnuts). Minor excavation of such field monuments solely for the recovery and analysis of an archaeological soil ought to be amply repaid by botanical and/or faunal investigations.

d. As shown in the subsequent section dealing with the Bronze Age, the analyses of pre-Bronze Age barrow soils and the archaeological evidence fail to show the presence of any substantial Neolithic activity in present day heathland environs (Scaife and Macphail 1983). This absence needs clarifying to assess whether soil material has been removed by downslope movements as a result of agriculture, or whether poor soils in these areas were responsible for a real absence of Neolithic occupation.

3.C.2 *Work in progress*

North Marden, Sussex. Scaife for P L Drewett.
Selmeston, Sussex. Scaife for P L Drewett.
Longstone, Isle of Wight. Scaife with D J Tomalin.

Neolithic soil pollen

A. *Causewayed enclosures*

Knap Hill, Wiltshire; Dimbleby G W, 1965a; Dimbleby G W and Evans J G, 1974.
SU 121636.
Windmill Hill, Wiltshire; Dimbleby G W and Evans J G, 1974; Dimbleby G W, 1965b.
SU 087715.
Etton, Maxey, Cambridgeshire; Dimbleby G W, unpublished; Scaife R G, 1983; Scaife R G in French C, 1983.

B. *Henges*

Durrington Walls, Wiltshire; Dimbleby G W and Evans J G, 1974; Dimbleby G W, 1971.
SU 153435
Avebury, Wiltshire; Dimbleby G W and Evans J G, 1974.
SU 101698.

C. *Long barrows*

Ascott-under-Wychwood, Oxfordshire; Dimbleby G W and Evans J G, 1974.
SP 299175.
Beckhampton Road, Wiltshire; Dimbleby G W and Evans J G, 1974.
SU 066677.
Horslip, Wiltshire; Dimbleby G W and Evans J G, 1974.
SU 086705.
Longstone, Isle of Wight; Scaife R G, 1980b; Scaife R G and Tomalin D J, 1979.
South Street, Wiltshire; Dimbleby G W and Evans J G, 1974.
SU 091693.

D. *Open sites*

High Rocks, Tunbridge, Kent; Dimbleby G W in Money J, 1960.
Rackham, Sussex; Dimbleby G W, 1976; Dimbleby G W and Bradley R, 1975.
TQ 04905120.

E. *Models of Neolithic activity/land use*

Central Wessex; Barker G and Webley D, 1978.
Dorset and Hampshire; Haskins L E, 1978; Waton P V, 1982a, 1982b.
Isle of Wight; Scaife R G, 1980b.
Sussex; Thorley A, 1971a, 1971b, 1981.

3.D   Bronze Age — soil palynology

3.D.1 *Introduction*

Archaeologically the Bronze Age period has for long been hampered by a lack of settlement evidence. In spite of recent settlement finds such as Belle Tout (Bradley 1970) and Bishopstone (Bell 1977) in Sussex and others, most of our knowledge both from purely archaeological grounds as well as environmentally has been derived from ritual/funerary sites and associated artefacts. The physical background for this period has been stressed with the basic division between highland and lowland zones outlined by Sir Cyril Fox (1932). This division employed socio-economic similarities such as the links between Southern England and North Western France. Fox has suggested that altitude would affect crop ripening and be relevant to other factors of congenial living. The lowlands were in contrast rich in tractable soils sought by prehistoric man, a fact reflected therefore in higher population densities.

With these population changes came the widespread acceptance of round burial mounds covering inhumations and cremations. After a period of 'Beaker folk' co-existence and trade with the indigenous Neolithic population, there developed the early/middle Bronze Age with a food vessel producing tradition (Ashbee 1960). Round barrows became the significant funerary means of burial and are one of the commonest and most easily recognisable field monuments. Ashbee (1960) estimated that some 18000 occur in Britain with 6000 in Wessex (Grinsell 1941). In the South and South East, earthen barrows are found in two contrasting environments; the chalk downlands and on areas of elevated heaths. In addition to burial of cremations/urns or inhumations was the burial of many Bronze Age ground surfaces by the construction of the mound. These have allowed both pedological investigation (see Macphail this volume) and micro and macro botanical investigations.

As noted, the distribution of barrows is on both chalklands and heathland soils, a fact well illustrated by examination of distribution maps for Sussex, Isle of Wight and Dorset. Grinsell (1934, 1940) estimated that there were more than 1000 round barrows in Sussex the majority of Bronze Age date and of which 95% were situated on chalk, the remainder being on the Wealden heathland areas. There is therefore a skewed distribution pattern both in archaeological terms and in the environmental data which have been forthcoming. Palynologically this is even more evident due to the problems of lack of pollen preservation in chalk soils. This problem has been recognised archaeologically and has given rise to the proposed Sussex Archaeological Unit's work in the Cuckmere Valley and Sussex coastal plain.

3.D.2 *Heathland acid substrates*

On the lowland Greensand substrates of the Weald, acid podzolic soils and heathlands are widespread, giving the Surrey, Sussex, Hampshire and Dorset Heath areas. In recent years barrows have been excavated for rescue reasons (especially that of white sand extraction used in glass manufacture). This has provided a wealth of data.

a. *West Heath, Sussex* (SV 786226) was initially recorded by Grinsell in 1940 and is one of a series of cemeteries and isolated barrows on the Folkestone series of the Lower Greensand. Two phases of excavation were carried out by P L Drewett (Sussex Archaeological Unit) to keep ahead of sand extraction (1973–1975 and 1980) (Drewett 1975c, 1976a, b, 1981). This scheme also embraced the excavation of an outlying barrow at Minsted (Drewett 1975a). Of the eleven barrows present, I–IV were excavated between 1973–5 and the pollen analysis carried out by Baigent (in Drewett 1976b). For the later excavations (Drewett 1985) detailed pollen analyses of barrows V, VIII and IX have been carried out (Scaife 1983a and in Drewett). Due to unfortunate circumstances the published pollen diagram of barrow I (Baigent in Drewett 1976) is inverted and back to front. From the pollen analysis of these barrows, a view of the changing ecological character of West Heath has been established. Initially, and not represented in the soil profile or pollen spectrum, the natural vegetation cover of the Atlantic period is likely to have been deciduous forest overlying brown earth soils. The soils occurring under possible stands of *Tilia* would have been subject to faunal mixing and have a pH and nature not conducive to pollen preservation. Early anthropogenic activity, possibly corresponding with Mesolithic artefactual material found by Drewett (1976a, b), resulted in the opening of the forest and subsequent soil acidification. This allowed the formation of humus iron podzols and pollen preservation in these soils. *Corylus* woodland became an important coloniser of the clearings within a background of *Quercus, Tilia, Ulmus* and *Fraxinus* woodland. This vegetation community appears to have continued until at least the time of Bronze Age barrow construction. Heathland taxa remained as ground flora and in clearings within this woodland throughout. It is, however, evident from the pollen analysis and from pedological investigation (Scaife and Macphail 1983) that a number of soil truncations have taken place. It is suggested that a major hiatus may be present with early–middle Bronze Age soil formation superimposed on the earliest periods of soil acidification. Both archaeological and pollen evidence point to a lack of Neolithic influence. This problem, noted in the preceding section (VIb) requires elucidation. Work in the River Cuckmere valley (Scaife 1983e, Burrin and Scaife 1984, Scaife and Burrin 1983) would suggest perhaps that Neolithic artefactual material may have been removed from the slopes by colluvial processes consequent upon forest clearance.

Although West Heath is a nucleated barrow group, with a relatively long history (2100–1450 BC and forthcoming dating for outer barrows) it does not appear from the pollen data that chronologies of barrow construction at this site are possible by study of vegetation change through the time span covering their construction. Pollen analysis of turves forming these barrows in some cases shows greater variation with the *in situ* profile than between barrows. It seems likely, therefore, that analyses of such cemeteries in detail are of more value for elucidation of local vegetation variation than in assessing longer temporal variations with the aim of outlining a chronology of barrow construction.

Excavation and pollen analysis of the nearby *Minsted* barrow by Drewett and Dimbleby respectively (Drewett 1975a, 1975b) provide comparative evidence of soil and vegetation from a nearby area. This barrow was situated on the Lower Greensand, Folkestone beds, again on a well developed humic iron podzol. This barrow was one of the two outlying barrows of the Iping Common group of 12 and was similarly excavated for rescue reasons. Pollen analysis by Dimbleby 1975) showed 2 periods of vegetation history, a Mesolithic phase and the pre-Bronze Age barrow environment. The latter illustrated a wooded landscape with some heathland component. At this site, as at West Heath, no evidence of arable farming was apparent in terms of cereal or allied ruderal pollen. Keatinge (1983) has also carried out palynological investigations on a buried sub-barrow BA soil on nearby Trotton Common and adjacent pond sediments. These data similarly showed the importance of woodland and the dominance of *Tilia* in that area.

b. *Moor Green Barrow, West End, Hampshire* (Ashbee and Dimbleby and ApSimon 1976). An early Bronze Age turf barrow covered by ditch dug material covered a primary cremation burial (removed in 1888) and an old land surface. Dimbleby recorded his highest known absolute pollen frequencies (pers. comm.) of 7.5 million grains per gram. This showed the vegetation and ecological setting of the barrow at the time of construction and the sequence of soil development prior to the barrow's construction. Dimbleby concluded that the earliest vegetation was predominantly *Corylus* and *Quercus* forest with a high proportion of *Tilia*. This subsequently gave way to an increase in open more heliophilous taxa, *Calluna* and Gramineae, in response to anthropogenic deforestation and development of *Betula* scrub. It was in this *Betula* scrub woodland that the barrow was constructed with local clearances created by the use of fire.

c. *Ascot, Berkshire* (Grinsell 1936, 55, Bradley and Keith-Lucas 1975). One of a group of four barrows near Bracknell (SU 14687) situated in an area still surrounded by heathland and forest on the Tertiary Bagshot sands. Bradley and Keith-Lucas (1975) have studied the structure of the barrow, its mode of construction and the environment in which it was built. A date of 1480 ± 70 bc (HAR-478) was obtained from an isolated patch of charcoal in the Ah horizon of the old land surface. Pollen analysis showed that *Calluna, Pteridium, Ilex* and other heathland taxa were the autochthonous vegetation of the site growing on podzolic soils. The area possibly cleared by fire was surrounded by extended and little modified mature forest comprising *Tilia* and *Alnus* and associated *Salix, Ilex* and *Corylus*. Some evidence of cereal cultivation was shown by the presence of cereal type pollen and herbaceous taxa. The arrival of these apparently had little effect upon the heathland vegetation and hence it was suggested that cultivation was taking place in newly formed clearings where podzolisation and soil depletion had already occurred. It was suggested that these clearings were maintained by contrivance of burning or grazing or by cultivation in a number of periods.

d. *Isle of Wight* The Isle of Wight has a primary concentration of barrows of early Bronze Age date in three major chalkland areas (see section 3.D.3). Outside these are two areas in which barrows are situated on acid substrates. To the south of the Island is Luccombe Down (NGR SZ 573779) an area of podzolic soils occurring on the gravel angular flint cappings of the chalk (Wooldridge and Linton 1968), Cox (1982) has carried out soil pollen analysis on one of a group of six barrows and shown that *Calluna* heathland was at least as extensive as it is today. Localised patches of cultivation and pastoralism were also postulated. This confirms evidence (Scaife 1980b) from peat mires that increased soil leaching and heathland development occurred on sandy substrates in response to a change in land use.

A second area of heathland on Headon Warren (SZ 315857) has barrows constructed on the Tertiary Headon Beds. An unexcavated barrow dated 1800–1400 BC (Tomalin pers. comm.) was pollen analysed by Scaife (1980b) and is a contrast to the Luccombe Down data (Cox 1982). Here a buried brown earth containing much charcoal was revealed by plough clipping. The pre-barrow vegetation was characterised by low AP (9% of total pollen) and a notable herbaceous content (91% TP). Soil faunal mixing was likely because of the soils' characteristics. The environment was shown to be one of pastoral and waste-ground with *Plantago lanceolata, Rumex* Luguliflorae and Gramineae dominant. Trial excavation and conservation work on a second nearby barrow was undertaken by D J Tomalin (county archaeologist) in 1979. Samples from this await further investigation by the author.

e. *Dorset* Because of the presence of acidic podzolic soils associated with heathlands of Dorset a considerable amount of pollen data has been forthcoming from barrow excavations. Until recently this work has largely been carried out by G W Dimbleby and on the following sites.

f. *Knighton Heath, Poole* Two barrows excavated in autumn 1949 by H J Case were situated on plateau gravels overlying the Bagshot Beds. The environment is one of heathland in which a number of Bronze Age barrows have been recorded (Grinsell 1941). A pre-barrow leached/podzolic soil was sampled for pedalogical examination (Cornwall in Case 1952) and pollen analysis (Dimbleby 1952). This showed a predominantly heathland environment, commensurate with the humus podzols present. Thickets of *Corylus* and occasionally *Quercus* were suggested as remnants in damper places. From the herbaceous pollen from the two barrows, Dimbleby was able to show minor, but real differences between the time of construction of the barrows.

g. *Black Down, Portesham* (Thompson and Ashbee 1957). Excavated in 1955 as a result of gravel extraction. The barrow was situated on the Bagshot series which, being acidic, were dominated by heathland vegetation. The pre-barrow soil showed a considerable degree of leaching and was pollen analysed by Dimbleby (in Thompson and Ashbee 1957). This analysis showed an early period of forest dominated by *Quercus, Tilia, Ulmus* and *Betula*. Subsequently open conditions are indicated in the pollen diagram by *Pteridium*, Gramineae and weeds of cultivation. Subsequent abandonment of this cultivated land is shown by increased percentages of *Corylus* and *Alnus* and heathland taxa pollen. Also noted are high values of *Hedera* pollen, suggested as being a possible phase of re-clearance of scrub during the Bronze Age. In later work, Dimbleby has suggested that *Hedera* was utilised as a fodder crop (Dimbleby 1976, Simmons and Dimbleby 1974, Palmer and Dimbleby 1979) and similar high values of *Hedera* have been found in profiles at other sites.

h. *Chicks Hill, East Stoke Parish, Dorset* (Ashbee and Dimbleby 1959). A barrow excavated on Tertiary sands (Barton, Bagshot and Bracklesham beds) with soils of podzolic character. Pollen and charcoal analysed by Dimbleby showed the barrow to have been built on a grassland/heathland community with a substantial quantity of *Corylus, Quercus* and *Alnus.* Some agriculture cereal cropping in the neighbourhood was indicated but probably not on the site itself.

i. *Canford Heath, Poole* (SZ 01889586) (Horsey and Shackley 1980) one of a group of forty barrows situated on heathland to the North of Poole Harbour. The barrow was situated on a Pleistocene gravel capped spur and C^{14} dated at 1110 ± 110 bc (HAR-2279). An old land surface was present, being a mature humus iron podzol. Pollen analysis was carried out by Haskins (1978 and in Horsey and Shackley 1980) showing that the environment in which the barrow was constructed was heathland with *Corylus* scrub, and with adjacent alder carr in nearby wetter valley bottoms.

j. *Miscellaneous* Row Down, Lambourn, Berkshire – pollen analysis by Dimbleby (1962). Knighton Heath, Dorset (Dimbleby forthcoming).

3.D.3 *The Downlands/chalklands*

As shown by Dimbleby and Evans (1974) and discussed in section 3.C the pollen analysis of calcareous soils can be of value, providing data on vegetation coeval with or, immediately prior to barrow or mound construction continuing work of this type has been slow to develop for periods other than the Neolithic, with priority being given to terrestrial molluscan research on such soils. In contrast to the podzolic soil profiles discussed (section 3.D.2) two attempts at elucidating the status of the downlands vegetation have come from the Isle of Wight.

a. *Apes Down* (SZ 455872). In 1976 Tomalin (forthcoming) excavated a ring ditch/ploughed out bell barrow situated 2km north of Gallibury Down and in the bottom of a dry chalk valley. The site is dated at *c*1600 bc and contained a primary crouched inhumation. Although largely ploughed out by a recent arable cropping, a small area of an undisturbed rendzina soil profile was present. Spot samples for pollen analysis were taken from this profile and from the ditch. The former produced pollen in countable quantities. On the basis of assumptions laid down by Dimbleby and Evans (1974) and Dimbleby (1969a), this investigation (Scaife 1980b, 1984) illustrated that the Apes Down valley had been cleared of forest by *c*1600 bc with only minor amounts of *Betula* and *Corylus* present. The environment was predominantly pastoral as shown by *Plantago lanceolata* and Liguliflorae pollen and *Pteridium aquilinum* spores. This latter may have been introduced by man as a fertiliser or as fodder. This analysis noted that some pollen was present in a fine condition of preservation, but with a predominance of degraded pollen and differential destruction being an important factor in the interpretation of such pollen spectra.

b. *Newbarn/Gallibury Down* (SZ 442855) is a Bronze Age barrow situated on the crest of the chalk downland 7km south west of Newport and 2km south west of the Apes Down ring ditch. Excavated between 1977 and 1979 (Tomalin 1979 and forthcoming) a primary burial has been dated at *c*1700–1600 BC (C^{14} dating forthcoming).

This site is important in that it is situated at 199m above sea level on top of the highest part of the chalk downlands. It was however sited on top of a small area of clay with flints capping to the chalk. Although subject to ploughing disturbance, a section of old ground surface was preserved by a capping of tenacious clays thrown from the primary inhumation burial. Initial pollen analysis (Scaife 1980b, 1984) showed a predominantly open environment with low arboreal pollen frequencies (10% TP) dominated by pollen of taxa with long distance distribution characteristics, and by autochthonous pastoral herbaceous component. The latter was dominated by Gramineae, *Taraxacum*/Liguliflorae, *Plantago lanceolata*. It was concluded that the downland was essentially a pastoral environment. Full analysis of these soils has been completed (Scaife 1984 and Scaife forthcoming b) confirming the earlier data. The pollen diagram from this site is the only one from a chalkland Bronze Age site and shows in addition minor evidence of cereal agriculture.

Future plans at this site involve the excavation or partial investigation of Gallibury Hump, a well preserved barrow adjacent to the first destroyed site. In addition to this barrow cemetery and on the surrounding downland is a complex pattern of field systems (Tomalin 1980). Proposals have been made for the detailed mapping and investigation of this complex of agricultural and funerary monuments and settlement to obtain a model of the functioning Bronze Age and later environment and economy. Pollen and macrofossil investigations of differing dates on site/field monuments might help to further knowledge of the nature of land use relating to land allotment and its continuity.

3.D.4 *Further proposals for Bronze Age work*

a. We can see a markedly skewed pattern of evidence resulting from the archaeological distribution of field monuments on two major and differing lithological areas. Some with the greatest potential number of barrows and therefore preserved Bronze Age palaeosols occur on those positions least suited to preservation of pollen. In exceptional cases, as illustrated by Gallibury/Newbarn Down, pollen diagrams and palaeoecological data can be retrieved where barrows and/or field system banks have been sited on clay cappings. Every attempt should be made to examine these soils to provide on the spot vegetation data of the kind which analysis of peat sections cannot. This may provide information on the degree of clearance and nature of agricultural practice pertaining.

b. The greater number of Bronze Age barrows is situated directly on the chalk substrate. Although pollen is either absent or at least sparse and requires specialist techniques of extraction or concentration, the result of such work can be of value. Dimbleby and Evans (1974) have proven thus, but in spite of this few such profiles have been analysed because of the problems associated with the preservation, extraction and interpretation of such pollen and information.

c. From the analyses of West Heath Cemetery, Minsted, Moor Green, it is evident that these barrows were constructed upon soils that were already badly degraded by the early Bronze Age. Because of the absence of Neolithic archaeological and palaeoecological evidence from these southern heathlands it is not clear whether Beaker/early Bronze Age forest clearance initiated conditions of soil degradation or whether Neolithic colonisation of these areas promoted intense degradation and colluviation. Intensified studies of the valley bottoms adjacent to such areas might elucidate this problem (for example, see the Sussex archaeological unit Cuckmere project).

d. Extensive downland field systems are present in Southern England, (Bowen, 1961, 1972, 1975b) and Bowen and Fowler (1978) and Ellison and Harriss (1972, 911—962). Pollen and plant macrofossil research could help in understanding of their origins and use.

e. Bronze Age barrows on acid sub-strates provide valuable sources of data on the nature of the environment prior to barrow construction but can also provide evidence assessing the post-construction history. Such work in conjunction with pedological investigation is needed to assess the nature of movement of organic materials (including pollen) in the soils.

Bronze Age soil pollen

Barrows

Berkshire

Ascott: Bradley R and Keith-Lucas M, 1975
Row Down: Dimbleby G W, 1962

Dorset

Ashley Heath: Dimbleby G W, 1954
Black Down, Portesham: Dimbleby G W, 1957a; Dimbleby G W, 1961a
Canford Heath, Poole: Haskins L A, 1978; Haskins L A in Horsey I and Shackley M, 1980
Chicks Hill, East Stoke Parish: Ashbee P and Dimbleby G W, 1959; Dimbleby G W, 1961a, 1962b
Hengistbury Head: Scaife R G forthcoming in Barton R N E.
Knighton Heath: Dimbleby G W, forthcoming.
Poole: Dimbleby G W in Case H, 1962.
Turners Puddle Heath: Dimbleby G W, 1954, 1969a, 1971, 1976; Dimbleby G W, 1953

Hampshire

Beaulieu: Dimbleby G W, 1954
Burley Moor: Dimbleby G W, 1962b
Moor Green, West End: Ashbee P, Dimbleby G W, ApSimon A M, 1976

Isle of Wight

Apes Down: Scaife R G, 1980b, 1984 and forthcoming in Tomalin D J
Gallibury Down: Scaife R G, 1980b, 1984 and in Tomalin D J, forthcoming
Headon Warren: Scaife R G, 1980b and Scaife forthcoming b
St. Boniface Down: Cox J, 1982

Sussex

Minsted: Dimbleby G W, 1975
Trotton Common: Keatinge T, 1983
West Heath: Baigent J in Drewett P L, 1976; Scaife R G, 1983a; Scaife R G in Drewett P L, 1985, Scaife R G in
          Scaife R G and Macphail R I, 1983

Other field monuments

Hampshire

Crockford 'A': Tubbs C R and Dimbleby G W, 1965
Matley Wood: Dimbleby G W, 1956, 1976

Surrey and Kent

Blackheath Common; Headley Heath; Ockham Common; Wotton Common: Macphail R I, 1979

General discussions

Dimbleby G W, 1962b Heathlands.
Scaife R G and Macphail R I, 1983

3.E   Iron Age – soil palynology

3.E.1   *Introduction*

In Section 3.G.1 an anthropogenic cause for the 'Tilia decline' has been demonstrated with this relating to a later Bronze Age utilisation for agriculture of more well drained lowland soils. These phases of encroachment fall within the later Bronze Age at *c*1000 BC (Scaife 1980b, 280–285). This phenomenon may be linked to archaeological evidence of field systems. Bowen (1975a, b) suggests that deliberate allotments of arable land had been established by the middle to Late Bronze Age. At Martin Down, Hampshire for example, a middle Bronze Age date of 1200 BC for Celtic field systems and ranch boundaries has been established (Bowen 1975b) showing a shift towards agricultural systems of a larger scale. In the later Bronze Age there also occurred a larger network of linear banks and ditches and cross ridge dykes which have been suggested as representing the divisions of large tracts of land for pastoral agriculture. Similarly, hill forts had become an increasingly important phenomenon by, or during the later Bronze Age sometimes in conjunction with cross ridge dykes. With the exception of a small number of burial mounds in the south east of this date (e.g. Lexdon) the potential for analyses of buried soils lies with old land surfaces below the artificial mounds of these linear earthworks and banks created by hillfort construction.

Despite the relatively recent realisation of the extent of such phenomena it is unfortunate that the potential of these sites has not been fully utilised for environmental data. This no doubt reflects the fact that many of these were constructed on calcareous substrates or on lowland clays of circumneutral pH where conditions are not conducive to preservation of pollen. Those few analyses which have been carried out in the south and south east are as follows:

3.E.2   *Caesar's Camp,* Keston, Kent (Fox 1969)

Pollen analysis (Dimbleby 1962b, 1969b) of this site excavated by Fox related the prehistoric soil to the vegetation of the time, and to the different phases of rampart construction. This revealed dense *Quercus* woodland with *Corylus, Betula* and *Ilex* in Stage I of the inner rampart. Once constructed there is evidence of partial clearance of the forest within the enclosure, with some cultivation taking place.

3.E.3   *The New Forest*

Tubbs and Dimbleby (1965) have drawn attention to the archaeological relevance of the numerous linear earthwork features present. They suggest that these are relics of former agriculture in the area. Former archaeological excavations in the forest have been concerned largely with the excavation of Bronze Age barrows and Romano-British kiln sites. Forty abandoned fields and systems have been located (Jones, Pasmore and Tubbs unpublished) dating back to the Bronze Age as at Crockford. Dimbleby (in Tubbs and Dimbleby 1965) undertook pollen analysis as a potential guide to the dating of some of these linear monuments and to determine vegetation changes and land use prior to the construction of the various banks. Sites analysed and tentatively dated are as follows:

a. Setley:– Medieval, showing a deforested landscape though with some *Quercus* regeneration with no evidence of cultivation.

b. Crockford B:– Medieval, showing a completely open landscape dominated by Gramineae and with evidence of arable cropping.

c. Hinchelsea:– Medieval showing two phases, of cereal cropping giving way to bracken (*Pteridium*) dominance with advanced podzolisation.

d. Holmsley:– Iron Age banks and ditches with vegetation data possibly back to the Bronze Age with forest dominated by *Quercus,* and *Tilia* with some *Ulmus.* These were replaced by *Pteridium* and some heath taxa.

e. Pilley:— Iron Age. A more complex sequence of banks and enclosed fields of possibly different ages. Pollen data illustrated an opening of the forest to grassland and heathland prior to burial of this soil.

f. Crockford A:— Bronze Age pollen spectrum indicating relatively wooded conditions with *Alnus, Tilia* and *Ulmus*.

3.E.4 *Miscellaneous*

Eide (1981) has produced some pollen diagrams from similar bank structures within the forest. Dimbleby (pers. comm.) has examined a stake hole filling from Ranscombe Camp, Sussex, built on Calcareous chalk soils. High frequencies of Liguliflorae were present, a fact noted and discussed in Dimbleby and Evans (1974).

Iron Age soil pollen data

Hampshire

New Forest Linear banks: Eide K, 1981; Tubbs C R and Dimbleby G W, 1965.

Kent

Keston Camp: Dimbleby G W, 1961a, 1969b

Sussex

Ranscombe Camp: Dimbleby G W, unpublished.
Seaford Head: Scaife R G, in preparation.

3.F   Roman and Post-Roman to Medieval

3.F.1 *Introduction*

Pollen analyses of sediments dating to this period (directly from archaeological contexts) have been sparse from the area of Southern England. Interest in medieval archaeology in recent years has, however, resulted in a greater number of deposits of this age available for pollen and macrofossil analyses. Such data have come from rescue archaeology in urban environments. In recent years a better understanding of the problems of pollen found in British urban Roman and post-Roman contexts has been forthcoming from work by Greig (1981, 1982b) and Scaife 1979, 1980c, 1982b, c, Ayers and Murphy 1983d, in Macphail 1981). These highlight the problems of the derivation of, and possible interpretation of those pollen spectra found in a number of different archaeological settings.

3.F.2 *London*

Continued rescue archaeology in the City of London and surrounding areas has provided considerable potential for environmental analysis (see Chapter 5 this volume). Palynological investigations have been undertaken on deposits of the following nature.

a. *'Dark Earth'* (Scaife 1980c and Scaife 1981b). Pedological investigation in conjunction with botanical results have been obtained in order to elucidate the nature and possible origins of this wholly anthropogenic deposit of Roman to Medieval date. There are comparative pollen and phytolith analyses from York (Bedern) and GPO 75 (London) Roskams (1981) and Macphail (1981, 1983). Pollen preservation for the London samples was poor, grains being heavily degraded and resulting in differential preservation in favour of pollen taxa/grains with robustness of exine. The studies did, however, suggest a polygenetic origin resulting from the possibility of these soils being used for market gardening or farming within the city area to inclusion of domestic waste and ordure to these soils in the urban waste areas.

b. *Broad Sanctuary,* Westminster (TQ 299797) (Scaife 1979, 1982c). Trenching activities in 1979 revealed a stream channel containing organic sediments and urban refuse. This deposit was excavated by the Inner London Archaeological Unit and dates between the fourteenth and seventeenth centuries. Pollen preservation was good in these deposits and provided information and pollen spectra from the areas adjacent to London's Thorney Island (Scaife 1979). This study illustrates the problems associated with the interpretation of urban pollen spectra and the possible origins of many unexpected types of ethno-economic usage (e.g. *Linum, Cannabis, Humulus* and *Fagopyrum*). Substantial quantities of cereal pollen and associated arable weeds are likely to have been derived from animal feed-stuffs or more likely resulting from dumped ordure into the stream channel. The latter is substantiated by nematode parasite eggs (*Ascaris* and *Trichuris* spp) recorded in the pollen preparations (Scaife 1979, 1982c). See also Pike and Biddle 1966. It has been suggested also that many pollen types recorded may have resulted from pollen input from floor sweepings, bedding, roofing materials and a wide range of other urban usage.

c. *Work in Progress* St James Yard, Westminster (Greig) associated with the Broad Sanctuary sequence but being of earlier date. A series of cess pits has been sampled for pollen analysis in the City (forthcoming Scaife). It is expected that these will provide data on diet and further elucidate the origins and types of pollen found in urban situations, such as Broad Sanctuary (above) and the 'Dark earth'. Other sites sampled between 1980–1983 (Scaife) include Pudding Lane: late Roman-Saxon alluvial sediments; Trig Lane – Roman and post-Roman and peats obtained at Peninsular House, 1979 (Scaife 1983c).

d. *Wilson's Wharf, Southwark* (TQ 33198028). Peats and sediments of Late Bronze Age to Iron Age date have been pollen analysed and C^{14} dated (Scaife AML Report 3499). These have shown the local vegetation of the Southwark marshes and provide important evidence for later Bronze Age activity which has been substantiated more recently by the first Bronze Age artefactual material from this south bank region. The three sequential dates obtained span the period.

e. *Temple of Mithras* This well known and publicised excavation by W F Grimes in 1954 has recently been pollen analysed (Scaife 1982b). Samples obtained by W F Grimes from the underlying gravels at the time of excavation were rich in pollen of ruderals and marginal aquatic taxa.

   Armitage, Locker and Straker have reviewed the city and outer London regions (this volume) and have provided further detail on these sites.

3.F.3 *Other urban areas*

Little pollen work has been carried out on other urban areas in Southern England. *Newport*, Isle of Wight: Excavations of medieval remains in this town started in 1978 (Pyle Street) and subsequent Gas Board excavations revealed wooden (*Ulmus*) pipes for the purpose of carrying Newport's first water supply. These date to a lease granted in 1618 to Phillip Flemming 'for the Convenient Carrying and conveying of wholesome spring water' (Tomalin and Scaife forthcoming). The pipes were entrenched through earlier deposits of Medieval date containing 'midden material'. This is tentatively ascribed to the late-Norman period. A single pollen sample (Scaife 1980d and in Tomalin and Scaife forthcoming) provides data on urban palynology. From this, the regional vegetation is not clearly evident, but primary inputs of anthropogenic pollen were dominant. The predominant herbaceous element in the spectrum (82% total pollen) was suggested as resulting from urban ruderals and an arable pollen association of cereal, Cruciferae and Polygonaceae pollen. The latter may result in urban contexts from cess pits, animal fodder and animal excreta (Greig 1979, 1982b, 62–3, Scaife 1979, 1981b, 1982c). A further possible source of the arable pollen component has been indicated. J P Jones (1978) has shown from documentary evidence (albeit 200 years later) that corn winnowing was a common phenomenon in Newport's High Street to such an extent that bye-laws were passed restricting this process to the outer areas of the town. It is likely, therefore, that these cereal pollen and allied taxa are the direct product of this activity and it has been shown (Robinson and Hubbard 1977) that cereal pollen may be readily transported in the bracts of cereals. Two caryopses of *Hordeum vulgare* were recovered in the samples.

3.F.4 *Roman villas*

Soil pollen analyses, from two Romano-British villas have been carried out in Sussex (Fishbourne) and the Isle of Wight (Combley).

a. *Combley Roman Villa,* Arreton, Isle of Wight (NGR SZ538738). This villa has been excavated by Fennelly (1976) and a second phase of excavation in 1979/80 by Basford (Isle of Wight County archaeology). Pollen analysis has been carried out on organic material which accumulated as a result of waterlogging of the villa in the second century AD (Scaife 1980b). This illustrated a strong arable component possibly resulting from local crop processing adjacent to the villa. A sequence of samples relating to earlier first century occupation of the site await analysis (Scaife).

b. *Fishbourne Roman Villa* (Greig 1971). Greig has found pollen in what were thought to be garden soils within the villa grounds/perimeter. A range of ruderals and local vegetation was indicated but unfortunately no evidence for the possibility of cultivated exotic plants was forthcoming.

c. *Miscellaneous Studies* Barber (1976b) has investigated two pollen samples from a Roman well in Portchester Castle. This analysis showed quantities of non-arboreal pollen, reflecting the environment in close proximity to the well. It is likely that many of the herb pollen recovered relate to the urban pollen sources described above.

3.F.5 *Proposals for work*

The interpretation of pollen spectra from urban contexts presents various problems relating to their mode of origin and to theoretical palynological questions. Interpretations have to be based on an understanding of both natural pollen productivity, the dispersal of pollen of urban plant taxa and on the archaeological or archaeoenvironmental connotations which can be placed on the large number of pollen types encountered in such studies.

Continued analyses of such palynologically unsatisfactory contexts and environments have increased our knowledge of the problems of producing new data accounting for the presence of certain pollen types which are ubiquitously found. Continued investigation of the range of urban 'every day life' contexts should continue in order to ascertain the nature of, origins and possible use of certain urban areas. This has been illustrated by the studies of dark earths, medieval stream channels and midden deposits. Pollen and macrofossil investigations of cesspits provide data on ordure which contributed to the waste urban areas and to possible diet and disease.

Romano-British and urban palynological data

Hampshire

Fishbourne Roman Palace; garden soil: Greig J R A, 1971
Portchester Castle Roman well: Barber K E, 1976b

Isle of Wight

Combley Roman villa: Scaife R G, 1980b
Newport High Street Medieval: Scaife R G, 1980d, Scaife R G, forthcoming b

London

Broad Sanctuary Westminster: Scaife R G, 1979; Scaife R G, 1982c
Dark Earth deposits: Scaife R G, 1979; Scaife R G in Macphail R I, 1981b
New Palace Yard, Westminster: Greig J R A, forthcoming
Temple of Mithras: Scaife R G, 1982b; Scaife R G in Grimes W F, in preparation

Miscellaneous

Winchester: Parasite eggs; Pike A W and Biddle M, 1966

4   The investigation of plant macrofossils

4.1   Introduction and development of the subject

Prior to, and for long after the development of pollen analysis as a technique (Von-Post 1916), the study of plant macrofossils was the primary means of working out chronostratigraphic sequences. Early work of this nature was carried out on the blanket peats of Scotland by Geikie (1874, 1881) and Lewis (1905, 1906, 1907, 1911) who produced a basic climatic division for the present interglacial on the basis of interstratified blanket peat and tree growth in upland areas. In Southern England buried/submerged forests occur and were known to earlier workers, (see Section 2.1) and which relate to eustatic changes. To Blytt (1876) and Sernander (1908) can be attributed the classic zonation schemes of the Late-glacial and Holocene periods. With the application of pollen analysis to the dating (prior to C^{14}) of organic deposits to already established macrofossil sequences, chronologies for Britain and Europe were established. With realisation of the fact that vegetation changes were by no means synchronous and not necessarily due to climatic but often anthropogenic causes, regional assemblage zonation has released plant macrofossil and pollen analysis to its rightful role as providing palaeoenvironment/vegetation data.

In this discussion, plant macrofossils will be largely related to those data directly related to archaeological contexts. Whereas pollen data described in previous sections, with some minor exceptions, are derived from regional and local vegetation, plant macrofossils are usually of autochthonous origin and therefore good indicators of environment and vegetation. This applies more specifically to natural accumulations containing plant material and is not the case where purely anthropogenic inputs of plant materials, for whatever anthropogenic cause, occur. With this latter group, similar problems of interpretation as with pollen exist. Studies of plant macrofossils in conjunction with pollen analysis and stratigraphy can obtain higher degrees of resolution of environmental interpretation. Consequently, many of those papers discussed in Section 1 may contain data on plant macrofossils of non-anthropogenic relevance. Dimbleby (1978) points out that in archaeological contexts, macrofossils will provide evidence on the sites' vegetation and to agricultural and ethnobotanical utilisation of the plant resource base for which there are an infinite variety of uses by man.

Development of plant macrofossil analyses in Southern England have, like palynology, been subject to absence of plant materials due to poor media for preservation. Consequently substantial gaps exist in our knowledge for certain periods and from some regions. Evidence from past work is of a rather disjunct nature in terms of detail and extent. Various stages in the development of our knowledge can be seen and are itemised below:

a. Early historical development includes work on submerged forests and natural biogenic accumulations (James 1847, Narthorst 1873, Reid 1893, Borlase 1857) and the early innovative work on Roman fruits and seeds from archaeological excavations at Silchester (Reid 1902, 1903, 1905, 1906, 1907); Blashenwell, Corfe Castle (Reid 1896); Dorset peat mosses (Reid 1895).

b. Cecil E Curwen (1938) was innovative in his early discussions as to the mode of agriculture practised by prehistoric farming communities. For the time of its writing, his work was of substantial breadth and formed a basis for discussion over many years since publication. His data from Britain and Europe utilised flint artefactual materials (sickles), querns, ploughs, field systems and available plant macrofossil data. From this he produced an outline of prehistoric agricultural development for Britain. In writing his synthesis, Curwen also drew upon the limited quantities of charred/carbonised cereal grain in southern Britain. These included a number of Wiltshire sites of Iron Age date (Fifield Bavant, Swallow-cliffe, All Cannings Cross and Lidbury) and Dorset (Maiden Castle). Curwen tried to integrate studies of prehistoric agriculture with known and extensive field systems in Sussex at Plumpton Plain and New Barn Down.

c. A considerable hiatus was followed by the work of Helbaek who carried out a survey of prehistoric plant husbandry in Great Britain and Ireland (1939) and published with Jessen in 1944. Due to the impending war, plant material was not examined from Southern England. This included important remains from Windmill Hill. In 1951 Helbaek investigated this material and grain and cereal chaff impressions in pottery. This research was published in 1952 and details the state of knowledge for Southern England at this date. After this work, there were few people researching in this field of prehistoric crops and only sporadic reports accrued where excavators noted obvious carbonised plant remains on site. Much of the identification of these carbonised plant remains can be attributed to J R B Arthur (1954, 1963a, b, 1977).

d. Jane Renfrew at Southampton University (Archaeology) was responsible for the establishment of further investigation into plant macrofossil assemblages from a range of differently dated and situated archaeological sites in the Southampton/Hampshire region. These studies include those of Murphy (1977) on the Iron Age and Roman agriculture of Hampshire; Green (1979a) researched the medieval urban seed assemblages and characteristics of preservation; and Monk (1977) investigated plant assemblages from the M3 rescue archaeological project. These studies are notable in that they adopt a scientific recovery technique with greater detail and objectivity to analysis and interpretation of plant assemblages.

Similarly investigations of the upper Thames basin, Oxfordshire have been undertaken through the Oxford archaeological unit (M Robinson and M Jones). The result of these recent approaches to the environment and crop cultivation of the South East Zone has allowed modern and updated accounts of the status of our knowledge – M Jones (1981), Robinson (1981), and Dennell (1976).

4.2   The macrofossil reviews

In 1938, E C Curwen produced his paper the 'Early Development of Agriculture in Britain', an innovative account for the time it was written, when few detailed data were available in Britain. In his account, Curwen discussed the forthcoming evidence from the Near East and Egypt in addition to carbonised cereals, artefacts (detailed classification of flint sickles), corn drying ovens, ploughs and field systems. As with later reviews, Curwen dealt with the problem of post-Neolithic agriculture in a chronological fashion. He postulated an early Neolithic to middle Bronze Age pastoral agricultural stage with stock raising (ox, sheep, goat, pig), and cereal cropping. His evidence for this was of grain and impressions from Whitehawk Camp, Sussex. Curwen formulated the idea that with the later Bronze Age came settled villages, an idea he based on the presence of field systems in Sussex. He commented that 'this marks a major turning point in the history of agriculture in Britain', with the introduction of two-ox ploughs, crop rotation and manuring. Curwen (1938, 40) provides detail of known Late Bronze Age and early Iron Age carbonised grain and pottery impressions including the following southern English sites:

Lidbury, Wiltshire
Fifield Bavant, Wiltshire
All Canning Cross, Wiltshire
Park Brow, Sussex
Corfe Mullen, Dorset
Winkelbury, Dorset
Maiden Castle, Dorset

These data provide an adequate summary to this date of agricultural crops, and draw to some extent on the earlier seminal work of Percival (1934).

Table 11 Southern English site data referred to by Helbaek (1952/3)

Neolithic	Whitehawk Camp, Sussex
	Maiden Castle, Dorset
	Abingdon, Oxfordshire
Early Bronze Age	Lambourn Downs
Middle Bronze Age	Telscombe, Brighton
	Itford
	? Bloxworth Down
	Bere Regis Down
	Long Wittenham, Oxfordshire
	Loughlanghan, Oxfordshire
Late Bronze Age	Lancing, Sussex
	Plumpton Plain, Sussex
	Hassocks, Sussex
	Luxford Lake, Dorset
	Abingdon, Oxfordshire
Early Iron Age	Maiden Castle, Dorset
	Radley, Oxford
	Chastleton Camp

In 1939, Hans Helbaek visited England to examine carbonised grain and pottery impressions in British and Irish museums. This resulted in Jessen and Helbaek producing a wide ranging account of archaeobotanical data in tabulated form spanning the Neolithic to Saxon periods. Data from Southern England were not included, especially of note being those from the excavations of Windmill Hill and Avebury containing *Triticum vulgare* and from Late Bronze Age/Iron Age at Theale Berkshire. Sites referred to by Helbaek (1952) in the region of this study are listed in *Table 11* along with a list of taxa discussed individually. Jessen and Helbaek (p62) concluded that two main routes of immigration of the cultivated plants to Britain were from the Mediterranean via Iberia and France and from South West Asia via Central Europe. The importance of Southern England for the elucidation of early arable practices was suggested:

'If one would attempt to separate the earliest finds of grain in England, it must be such as are available from the camp sites in the south of the country for instance Windmill Hill, Hembury, Haldon, Belvedere, Abingdon, Whitehawk and Maiden Castle.'

Helbaek (1952) produced his classic review of 'Early Crops in Southern England' because of the absence of information mentioned above. This review included data from eleven counties and again detailed in written and tabulated form, data from the Neolithic. Helbaek concluded that Neolithic Britain grew equal proportions of *Hordeum* and *Triticum* and that emmer was the predominant crop. Bronze Age agriculture saw a predominance of *Hordeum* over *Triticum* and subsequent growth of spelt (*T spelta*). As noted these studies formed the pillar stones of archaeobotanical crop literature until recent palaeobotanical investigations based upon statistical sampling, more refined plant macrofossil extraction techniques and a greater understanding of crop processing techniques.

Green (1981a) has published a review of work undertaken on Wessex plant remains (Hampshire, Dorset, Wiltshire, Devon, Somerset and Berkshire). Green's review outlines the sources of information which have been made available since those works referred to above. Green (*ibid,* 129) notes that Helbaek and the later reassessment by Dennell (1976, 11—23) have over emphasised the divisions between the Iron Age to Saxon periods by overgrouping of data when finer divisions need to be made. Consequently he has grouped Iron Age data into three more relevant periods, noting that in spite of the relatively small quantities of pottery grain impressions looked at by Jessen and Helbaek these are data which are comparable with more recent archaeological excavations. The predominant cereal taxa of *Triticum dicoccum* and *Hordeum vulgare* have similar periods of importance and decline. Green (1981a) has attempted statistical (presence) analyses, which although subject to some inherent (statistical) problems have been used to elucidate the periods of agricultural/crop importance for this region. Major cereals and the crops — *Pisum sativum, Vicia faba, Lens* and other herbs, oil seed, fibre crops and associated weeds — are discussed. This shows successfully that the archaeological evidence for crops from Wessex during the Iron Age, Roman and Saxon periods is more complex than indicated by earlier works 'especially in light of those species that were previously thought to have been late Iron Age introductions but that were clearly present from the earliest Iron Age'. Similarly with supposed Saxon introductions, these have been found in Roman contexts. An important but often overlooked discussion is that of spatial variability of crop type in contrast to the more often discussed temporal chronologies of agricultural change. Both Green (1981a) and Murphy (1977) make this point based on the Wessex evidence.

Grose J D and Sandell R E (1964) produced a catalogue of prehistoric plant remains from Wiltshire. This is, however, based on records extracted from Godwin's (1956) *History of the British Flora,* with the addition of later records from Windmill Hill and Wilsford, Wiltshire. Other review sources are those of Percival (1921, 1934) and Salisbury and Jane (1940) and more recently Jones' (1980) review of the plant macrofossil remains from Neolithic grooved ware contexts from throughout Britain.

4.3 Suggestions for macrofossil strategy

It is unfortunate that since the research of Murphy, Green and Monk at Southampton University, advances in detailed site work in the south of England have been limited, although F Green (who remains in Wessex as director of the Test Valley Archaeological Unit) continues when possible. Contract workers for the Department of the Environment and researchers/botanists attached to archaeological units attempt to keep pace with the work load. In view of our lack of data for all periods in many areas of this region and in view of recent advances in the study of crop processing techniques, a continued programme of sampling strategies and adequate recovery techniques is required. This might furnish a much greater understanding of prehistoric agricultural practices.

4.4 Full and Late Devensian plant macrofossil analyses

Analyses where they occur, have provided invaluable accurate taxonomic data on those arctic and sub-alpine elements of the vegetation present during the Full-Devensian and Late-Devensian periods. These have been shown to represent a marked phytogeographical and floristically diverse flora dominated by cold tolerant heliophytes. Other interesting aspects have been noted in the flora and include the halophytic taxa now restricted to coastal and montane distribution patterns as relics of the Devensian flora. Bell F G (1969, 1970) has discussed these in detail in her work in Huntingdonshire. Much seed data have come from a number of 'classic' localities in the Lea Valley/Ponders End Arctic Plant Bed series dating to circa 28000 ± 1500 bp (Reid 1916, Reid and Chandler 1923). Also at Colney Heath in Hertfordshire, Godwin (1964) has illustrated an open late-glacial flora without trees but with characteristic diversity of floral elements present. This site falls within the Late-Devensian and is radiocarbon dated at 13560 ± 210 bp.

Recent work has been forthcoming from Middle Devensian river deposits beneath the Upper Floodplain terrace of the Middle Thames at Isleworth, West London. A similar picture of treeless vegetation with some dwarf shrubs has been shown from combined palynological, coleopteran and plant macrofossil analyses by Kerney *et al.* (1980). A radiocarbon date of 43140 ± $^{1520}_{1280}$ bp (BIRM-319) was obtained and places this sequence chronologically at the time of the Upton Warren interstadial complex. A further sequence but of slightly younger date has similarly been investigated by Gibbard *et al.* (1982) from beneath the Upper Floodplain terrace at Kempton Park, Sunbury. Here sediments dated at 35230 ± 185 bp again contain a flora indicative of the cold stage of the full-Devensian.

Outside the Thames valley and its tributaries, such data are few, with only a very small number of insubstantial seed and plant records coming from palynologically analysed sequences by Seagrief (1959) and Seagrief and Godwin (1960) at Nursling, Hampshire and Elstead, Surrey respectively. These records come from the basal waterlogged peats and sediments of Late Devensian and early Flandrian age/date. A more detailed investigation (Gibbard and Hall 1982) has been carried out on organic and plant bearing levels within floodplain gravels of the River Colne, at West Drayton, Middlesex. Radiocarbon dates of 11230 ± 120 bp and 13405 ± 170 bp are of the Late-Devensian substage. Although these dates indicate that the flora should be representative of the Late Devensian interstadial, the macrobotanical evidence is not commensurate with the flora which might be expected. Instead, an absence of arboreal taxa and the presence of cold tolerant herbs is shown.

Miscellaneous

Terrestrial, that is non waterlogged plant macrofossils of this date are understandably few due to the problems of lack of a preserving medium and strong oxidation in soils. Where present, these are usually as charcoals occurring in buried palaeosols as at Brook, Kent. Here Levy (Kerney *et al.* 1964) has identified wood and charcoals of *Betula* and *Salix* while Lambert identified a number of seeds relating to fen, aquatic and dry land habitats. These were dated to the Allerød Zone II (10000–8000 bc).

Plant macrofossil remains

Applebaum S, 1972 Crops and plants.
Arthur J R B, 1954 Prehistoric wheats in Sussex.
Curwen C E, 1938 Prehistoric agriculture.
Curwen C E, 1938 Early development of agriculture.
Dennell R, 1974 Evidence for prehistoric crop processing.
Dennell R, 1976 Prehistoric crop cultivation in Southern England.

Dennell R, 1976 Economic use of plants as shown by archaeological materials.

Green F J, 1979a Southampton and Winchester urban Medieval plant assemblages.

Green F J, 1979b Mineralisation of seeds in urban Medieval contexts.

Green F J, 1981a Iron Age and Roman and Saxon plant remains from Wessex.

Grose J D and Sandell R E, 1964 Prehistoric plant remains in Wiltshire. (Taken from Godwin H, 1956)

Helbaek H, 1940 Anglo-Saxon and Prehistoric crops in Southern England.

Helbaek H, 1952 Early crops in Southern England.

Hinton P, 1984 Plant remains from Sussex.

Hubbard R N L B, 1975 Palaeo economies.

Hubbard R N L B, 1976b Crops and climate.

Hubbard R N L B, 1976a Prehistoric crop processing.

Jessen K and Helbaek H, 1944 Prehistoric cereals in Great Britain and Ireland.

Jones M, 1978 Bronze Age, Iron Age and Roman plant remains at Ashville, Oxford.

Jones M, 1981 The development of crop husbandry.

Keepax C, 1975 S.E.M. of wood replacement by corrosion products.

Keepax C, 1977 Contamination problems in seed assemblages.

Monk M, 1978 Anglo-Saxon crops in Southern England.

Monk in Fasham P J and Monk M, 1978 Seed sampling strategies.

Percival J, 1934 Wheat in Great Britain.

Reynolds P J, 1974 Iron Age storage pits.

Reynolds P J, 1979 Butser Hill Iron Age Farm project.

Robinson M, 1978 Land use and crops of the Upper Thames Valley.

Robinson M, 1981 Iron Age to Saxon crops of the Upper Thames Valley terraces.

4.A   The Neolithic

4.A.1   *The cereals*

Hillman (1981) discussing Neolithic crop husbandry, comments upon the sparse evidence of crops available for any detailed investigation of the means of agricultural subsistence in Britain. Such a view pertains especially to Southern England despite the importance of this region to the early Neolithic way of life. Such is this paucity of knowledge that recent works still rely upon those earlier seminal works discussed (Section 4.2).

Curwen (1938) related *Triticum* as being the only Neolithic grain found in Britain. Liddell's excavations of Hembury causewayed enclosure, Devon in 1931—2 yielded *T. vulgare* (Percival 1934, 10) found in 'cooking pits'. Jessen and Helbaek (1944) list occurrences of bread wheat (*T. vulgare*) ascribed to a primitive form now taxonomically ascribed to *T dicoccum* (see Helbaek 1952, 201). Helbaek provided substantially more data with identifications of 150 Neolithic grain impressions, representing five cereals from two cultural phases at four localities. The Neolithic type site of Windmill Hill provided 127 impressions of four cereal types being dominated by *Triticum dicoccum* schubl. and only two certain impressions of *T monoccum*. The latter he considered as being weeds of the *T. dicoccum* fields. *Hordeum vulgare* (var. *nudum*) and hulled barley constituted 8.4% of the total sample of impressions (wheat formed 91.6% of the total) and therefore subordinate in agricultural importance. It should be noted however, that such often stated preferences may only relate to particular edaphic and/or cultural preferences of this local area, further emphasising the necessity of continued objective scientific data collection.

Triticum spelta the hexaploid form of substantial note in cereal subsistence in later Wessex periods, has been recorded at Hembury Causewayed enclosure (Devon) and is an only occurrence and apparent anomaly. Recently revived discussion (Smith I F *et al.* 1964 and Hillman 1981) suggests its contemporaneity with Neolithic stratigraphy. Whilst *no* records of this more advanced taxon have been forthcoming from the region under review, circular argument refuting its presence in *any* Neolithic context should be removed and a greater objectivity and appraisal of larger volumes of plant material obtained from bulk extract in techniques.

Hillman (1981) rightly concludes that C^{14} dating of the material would solve this important problem of dating. This should be more readily feasible with small C^{14} sample counting techniques. Dennell (1976) has reassessed the data of Helbaek from Windmill Hill for the Neolithic and later periods using the same information base. Dennell's work adds little to available information relating to the Wessex area, showing simply a heterogeneity of cropping activity with lighter calcareous soils being more suited to cultivation of *Hordeum*. In contrast, heavier clay regoliths in the Frome—Bath area were possibly more favourable to *Triticum*.

Arthur (in Bell 1977, 273) working at Bishopstone, Sussex has isolated Neolithic cereals from a number of contexts at this multiperiod site. *Triticum dicoccum* schubl. (grain and spikelets), *Triticum* sp (resembling *T. aestivum*) and *Hordeum vulgare* L ssp. *hexasticum* were recorded and were in addition to associated arable weeds — *Chenopodium album, Arctium, Atriplex patula, Polygonum convolvulus, P aviculare, Stellaria media.*

M Jones (1980) reviewed and discussed the nature of carbonised grain found in grooved ware contexts. This discussion arises out of Wainright and Longworth's Durrington Walls assessment of grooved ware cultures subsisting through strandlooping economy — an argument based upon lack of cereals in grooved ware contexts. Jones notes that four sites of this nature have been processed by modern flotation techniques and all were found to contain carbonised/charred grain. Jones examined material from pits containing domestic refuse at Mount Farm, Dorchester on Thames; Barton Court Farm, Abingdon and Down Farm adjacent to the Dorset cursus, Woodcutts. Taxa indicated as being of importance include *Triticum dicoccum* schubl, *T. aestivo-compactum, Hordeum vulgare* var. ssp *nudum* and eight edible starch seeds including *Malus sylvestris* and *Corylus avellana.* The strong representation of woodland plants is noted by Jones as indicative of exploitation of woodland resources.

4.A.2 *Other plant remains*

Because of the purported introduction of cereals by Neolithic man into Britain with an agricultural subsistence life style, attention has been focussed on the character of these early cereals. No less important are the allied crop remains and weeds recovered from these sites.

Again, Helbaek (1952) provides a source for the few known finds of other plant macrofossils of possible economic significance. The work of Arthur (in Bell 1977) and M Jones (1980) has been noted above. Salisbury and Jane (1940) discuss the nature of the downland vegetation from the occurrence of charcoal from Maiden Castle Dorset of Neolithic, early and late Iron Age date. It was suggested from these data that the Dorset downland was swathed in a vegetation of *Quercus, Corylus* type. Neolithic taxa present were *Populus, Rhamnus catharticus, Sorbus aria* and *Taxus baccata.* An immediate reply to this paper by Godwin and Tansley (1940) followed with criticism of this work.

As Hillman (1981) points out, no pulse crops have yet been recovered from Neolithic sites in Britain although it has been shown that they formed a substantial part of Neolithic economy in North Europe and the Middle East. Occurrence of later legumes as for example *Vicia faba* L (see section 4.B) indicates that better plant macrofossil recovery techniques may result in a fuller knowledge of this problem.

Analyses of Bryophyte remains from archaeological contexts have been substantially neglected. Williams (1976b) provides one of the few studies from Silbury Hill, Wiltshire (SU 100685). These were extracted from the heap of stacked turves at the centre of the mound. Williams confirmed the existence of calcareous grassland at least in the neighbourhood of the Silbury mound.

4.A.3 *Proposals*

1. Continued and better extraction techniques for plant macrofossils might provide better data relating to cereal and pulse crops, and to the spatial variability of Neolithic agriculture in relation to edaphic variations.

2. Bryophytes provide sound vegetational environmental data. Such work has notably been shown by Dickson (1973) and there is considerable scope for increasing this data base.

Neolithic plant macrofossil remains

Devon

Fox A, 1963 Hembury charcoals.

Dorset

Morgan G C, 1979 Mount Pleasant charcoals.
Salisbury E J and Jane F W, 1940 Maiden Castle charcoals.

Oxfordshire

Jones M in Parrington M, 1978 Farmoor

Sussex

Arthur J R B in Bell M, 1977 Bishopstone excavations. Seeds and crops.
Cartwright C, 1977a Bishopstone excavation charcoals.
Cartwright C, 1977b Offham charcoals.

Wiltshire

Dimbleby G W, 1966b Fussells Lodge charcoals.
Williams D, 1976b Silbury Hill Bryophytes.

Miscellaneous and general

Godwin H and Tansley A C, 1940 Prehistoric charcoals.
Helbaek H, 1952 Crops.
Jessen K and Helbaek H, 1944 Crops.
Jones M, 1980 Cereals from grooved ware contexts.
Percival J, 1934 Wheat origins.

4.B   The Bronze Age

Jessen and Helbaek (1944) and Helbaek (1952) in their review of cereals in Great Britain suggested that *Hordeum* sp (83%) was the predominant crop in Southern England with *Triticum monococcum* and *T dicoccum* also being cultivated. These scant data relate largely to the south and south east zone. Helbaek (1952) notes the inadequacy of known data as an adequate basis for judgement despite his attempt to assess the relative importance of crops in the Early, Middle and Late Bronze Age. This lack of early information reflects the paucity of excavated settlement sites in this region.

4.B.1   *Cereals*

Itford Hill, Sussex (NGR TQ 44670541) produced a large quantity of carbonised grain which was recovered from a pit. This proved to be exclusively *Hordeum vulgare* L *var. hexastichum* (Arthur 1954) and some *Triticum dicoccum* in association (Helbaek 1957).

Recent advances in macrofossil extraction and detailed excavations of occupation sites have provided a much greater body of evidence. This work has been centred on the Sussex downlands with excavations by the Sussex Archaeological Unit and by Bell. Bell's excavation at Kilne Combe (Bell 1981, 1983) produced carbonised/charred cereals and crop debris (rachis and glume fragments). Hillman (in Bell 1981, 179) has identified *Hordeum hexastichum, Triticum* sp, *Hordeum* sp indeterminable, *Triticum aestivo-compactum* and *T cf. dicoccum* despite poor preservation due to abrupt charring. The possibility of free threshed wheat here is interesting as this provides possible evidence for early bread/club wheat cultivation. Hillman (pers. comm.) has commented that there is no reason why it should not have been growing in Southern England as it has been found in a substantial number of North West European Neolithic contexts.

Hinton (Hinton in Drewett 1982) has produced important work for later Bronze Age chalk downland economy from the recently excavated Black Patch site (Sussex TQ 495008). Here, hut platforms and enclosures within rectangular field systems have been C[14] dated with a range of 1070 ± 70 bc−830 ± 30 bc. Earlier seed investigations by Arthur (Arthur 1982a) identified cereal debris including *Triticum spelta* L, *Hordeum vulgare* L and *Hordeum* sp indet. Bulk flotation and hand flotation of undisturbed soils from huts having pits containing large deposits of charred grain, ponds and fence post-holes were carried out. Well preserved *Hordeum vulgare* L emend LAM was the major constituent in pits (3 and 12). This was hulled barley and no naked barley was present. *Triticum* sp was, however, predominant with *T. dicoccum* schubl. and some *T monoccum* rachis fragments (Hinton 1982, 383).

In addition to cereal remains was an important list of other plant macrofossil identifications. *Vicia faba* L *var minor* is an interesting carbonised occurrence which adds to increasing records of this taxon as a crop of importance in the Neolithic Bronze Age and Iron Age (Hillman 1981, Murphy 1982, Scaife 1982d). Details of weeds and wild taxa recorded are too plentiful to summarise (Hinton 1982, 384) but as Hinton notes, all records are appropriate to light dry calcareous soils with the majority being arable field taxa. Hinton's paper is furthermore important in its attempt at assessing the economic importance of the crop plants identified and relating it to samples from other regional sites. The study showed that *Hordeum* was the most frequently occurring cereal followed by emmer and spelt. The absence of naked barley and probable absence of einkorn.

4.B.2   *Other studies*

Allison and Godwin (1949) reported on the presence of large numbers (50) of onion couch − *Arrenatherum tuberosum* (Gilib) Schultz in association with small quantities of cereal (*Hordeum*) from Rockley Down, Wiltshire. Its presence was noted as being a possible weed associated with cultivation.

Recent records of *Vicia faba* L in pre-Iron Age contexts have been forthcoming. Hillman (1981) has recorded a Neolithic pottery impression from Cardiganshire, Wales. In England, Hinton (above) and Murphy (pers. comm.) have also identified remains dated to the late Bronze Age. Scaife (1982d) has identified an early Bronze Age record from a pottery food vessel urn from Newbarn/Gallibury Down, Isle of Wight (Tomalin 1979 and forthcoming). In spite of these few limited records, it seems likely that horse beans were a crop in Britain from the Neolithic and presence of spelt and beans is interesting for the late Bronze Age.

Plant macrofossils from West Heath barrow cemetery (Drewett 1985) of Middle Bronze Age date have been analysed by Hinton. Charred seeds and flowers of *Erica* and *Calluna* and other heathland vegetation elements corroborate pollen data discussed in Section 2.D.2a. Charcoals (Cartwright in Drewett 1985) have also been studied.

In contrast to the above data is that recent evidence from low lying waterlogged environments in the Middle Thames and its tributary areas. Robinson (in Bradley *et al.* 1980) provides data from Aldermaston Wharf and Knights Farm Burghfield, Berkshire along with pollen data (Lobb in Bradley *et al.* 1980). Evidence for cultivation and economy is enigmatic being represented by plants of open ground. The plant macrofossil evidence from ponds at Knights Farm illustrates an area of grassland and pasturage. At Aldermaston, however, there was some indication of heathland development. Charcoal from an oven provided the earliest date of 1680 ± 50 bc (BM 1593) for this site. Later dates are for occupation at Knights Farm, 740 ± 80 bc (HAR-1011) and 600 ± 80 bc (HAR 1012). Economic evidence is from flotation analysis at Aldermaston where quantities of grain were found in 35% of pits. This contrasts with other regional/site evidence for pasturage. Bradley concludes that the implication is for a whole range of agriculture practices without any degree of uniformity of cereal to pastoral agriculture.

Further data come from Bronze Age and post-Bronze Age settlement at Ashville Trading Estate, Abingdon (excavated by Parrington). Detailed plant macrofossil discussion and dates are given by Jones for the Bronze Age and successive periods. Jones shows the presence of bread/club wheat and barley and associated arable and weed spp, charcoals and edible tuberous roots of onion couch. Charcoals comprised hawthorn and blackthorn used for cremation pyre and suggested by Jones as representing the most easily available wood for this purpose. For complete discussion of the evidence from this region see references to Jones in the review of environmental work in the Middle Thames Valley Section.

Willis (in Bradley and Ellison 1975) recovered a small number of seeds and plant remains from Rams Hill Bronze Age defended enclosure. Bradley discusses land use models (chapter 6) and the landscape in its whole context (*ibid*, 190–204) of field systems and boundary location.

Charcoal remains have been identified from some sites: Chicks Hill, Dorset (Dimbleby in Ashbee and Dimbleby 1958).

4.B.3 *Proposals*

There has for long been a problem of understanding Bronze Age settlement and its related activity. Recent detailed excavation and large scale flotation has provided evidence for cropping. An increased and better understanding of land apportionment in Wessex has also resulted from the work of Bowen and Fowler (1978) and Ellison and Harriss (1972), and this might be further linked to pollen data for the *Tilia* decline and to attempts to elucidate fully the style of agriculture which subsequently resulted.

Bronze Age plant macrofossils

Berkshire

Curwen C E, 1938 Theale crops.
Robinson M in Bradley R *et al.,* 1980 Aldermaston Wharf and Knights Farm.

Dorset

Ashbee P and Dimbleby G W, 1958 Chicks Hill; charcoals.
Green F J in Horsey I and Shackley M, 1980 Seeds from Canford Heath barrows.

Isle of Wight

Scaife R G, 1982d Gallibury Down. *Vicia faba* L. pottery impression.
Scaife R G, in Tomalin D J forthcoming, Gallibury Down plant remains (wood, charcoals, pottery impression, pollen).

Oxfordshire

Jones M, 1978 Ashville Trading Estate.

Sussex

Arthur J R B, 1954 Plumpton Plain cereal grain.
Arthur J R B, 1970 Belle Tout seed impressions.
Cartwright C R in Drewett P L, 1976b West Heath charcoals.
Cartwright C R in Drewett P L, 1985 Charcoals from West Heath Excavations (1979).
Helbaek K, in Burstow and Holleyman, 1957 Cereals from Itford Hill.
Hillman G C in Bell M, 1977 Seeds from Bishopstone excavations.
Hinton P, 1982 Seeds from Black Patch.

Hinton P in Drewett P L, 1985 Seeds from West Heath.
Salisbury E J, 1957 Itford Hill charcoals.

Wiltshire

Allison J and Godwin H, 1949 Plant remains and tubers.
Dimbleby G W in Ashbee P, 1963 Wilsford Shaft; notes on plant remains.

General

Godwin H, 1975a Barley in the Bronze Age.
Helbaek H, 1952 crops of southern Britain.
Jessen K and Helbaek H, 1944 Crops.

Barrow distribution

Grinsell L V, 1932, Surrey.
Grinsell L V, 1938–40 Hampshire.
Grinsell L V, 1934, 1940 Sussex.

4.C   Iron Age and Romano-British

4.C.1   *Introduction*

It is not proposed to outline here in detail the very real increases in data which have occurred in recent years back to 1975. These periods have a history of more detailed research being a function of the relatively large number of sites excavated. Reid's (1901–1907) work on Roman seed remains from Silchester is notable for its depth and awareness at this early period of archaeological study. Jessen and Helbaek (1944) and Helbaek (1952) give adequate reviews of the earlier finds of Iron Age plant macrofossils and seed impressions from Maiden Castle, Dorset; Worth Matravers, Dorset; Prae Wood, Hertfordshire; Radley, Oxfordshire and Winkleby, Fifield Bavant, Little Salsbury, in Wiltshire.

Since these early researches, much work has been undertaken in the Wessex area providing much greater detail of information on agricultural practices in the Iron Age and Roman periods. In addition to Dennell's (1976) reappraisal of Helbaek's information source, recent investigations have been reviewed by Green (1981a) for the Iron Age to Saxon of Wessex. He discusses the nature of preservation of the evidence in the region and produced a statistical analysis of the key crops and exotic foods and weeds as represented by data from the Wessex area. From his conclusions, Green suggests that the archaeological evidence for cropping in Wessex is one of greater complexity than shown by earlier work. In consequence he has separated the Iron Age into three divisions to show the changing balance of cultivation throughout this period.

M Jones (1981) has similarly reviewed the main crops and agricultural practices in terms of crop husbandry again spanning the Iron Age to Saxon period. This work includes much detail taken from Southern England although its geographical scope is outside that of the present study.

4.C.2   *Wessex*

Detailed site investigations have been undertaken in Wessex by Murphy (1977) Monk (1978) and Green (1979a) and in the Middle Thames region by M Jones and M Robinson (this volume chapter 1). Murphy (1977) has in his dissertation *Early Agriculture and environment on the Hants. Chalklands, 800 BC–400AD* analysed ten sites of Iron Age and Roman date. In doing so he has reviewed the techniques of sampling and flotation and associated problems of contamination by recent plant materials. This thesis also includes a valuable listing of all plant macrofossils of this date known to him in 1977. Interestingly he has discussed the possibility of pre-Roman horticulture (*ibid*, 177) and the principal factors probably affecting the crops produced.

In Dorset, the Iron Age Settlement at Gussage All Saints (excavated by Wainwright) contained pits, ditches, post-holes a gulley and burial the macrofossils from which were investigated by Evans and Jones (1979b). *Triticum* spelta and some *T aestivo-compactum, Hordeum hexasticum* L indeterminable *Avena* p and a range of other weeds and other crops including *Vicia faba* were present.

Monk (1978) and Monk in Monk and Fasham (1980) have utilised cereal and other wild grasses found at Micheldever Wood settlement and banjo enclosure (SV 5277370) and Winnall Down (SU498303) (Fasham and Monk 1978) to appraise sample recovery and the presentation of data in terms of prehistoric economy. This was carried out using flotation machines for extraction of remains from pits, post-holes, building gullies and ditches. Monk showed that of 640 samples analysed at Micheldever Station, 541 (85%) produced charred plant remains. The majority of these came from pits and at Winnall Down 143 samples, 110 (77%) yielded charred material. The function of the ubiquitous Iron Age pit is assessed in terms of the evidence for pit grain storage in relation to discussions of contemporary experimental pits (Reynolds 1974, 1976) and to seasonality of crop storage.

4.C.3 *Thames Valley*

Robinson (1981) has revealed data from the upper Thames Valley derived from excavations of the Oxford Archaeological Unit. The recent excavations of two floodplain sites preserving waterlogged plant remains at Mingies Ditch (Allen and Robinson 1979) and at Farmoor (Lambrick and Robinson 1979) are of note for the study of plant remains and coleopteran assemblages. This was especially so at Farmoor comprising middle Iron Age farmsteads and associated ditches, illustrating (from a range of multidisciplinary evidence) a middle Iron Age economy of essentially pastoral character with seasonal occupation of the flood plan and pastoral enclosures. Few carbonised cereals were recovered but those of *Triticum* sp and *Hordeum* showed that these inhabitants used cereal grain. Robinson postulated that the local environment would have been unsuited for arable agriculture. After a break in the Belgic and during the Romano British phase, grazed pasture was predominant but in more controlled form, enabling land to support a greater head of animals than in the Iron Age. A more varied land use has been suggested from evidence of corn driers, fruits and gardens.

In addition to Farmoor, another native droveway settlement has been investigated/excavated at Appleford (SU523936) and a small Roman villa at Barton Court (SU516978) (Robinson 1986). At the latter site, Jones (in Jones and Robinson 1986) found *Triticum spelta* and *Hordeum* (6 row) to be most abundant. Seeds of other cultivated species were also present including *Papaver* which was noted as of interest in its possible agricultural context. Broader environmental evidence suggested the absence of woodland from the immediate vicinity of the site (Robinson 1981, 267).

Ashville Trading Estate, Abingdon, Oxfordshire has similarly produced substantial quantities of waterlogged and charred plant fossils. M Jones (1978) suggested that the peak of activity was reached in the early Iron Age with *Triticum spelta* and *Hordeum vulgare*. Some lesser crops — emmer and club wheat — were present. These data contrast with the predominantly pastoral aspect portrayed above for the Farmoor site. These studies have a precision of identification and knowledge of crop processing which was obtained from analysis of the chaff debris. A detailed appraisal of those data in relation to plant identification, species concerned and their broader environmental interpretations based on multidisciplinary approaches must be sought in the source papers and in this volume (chapter 1). Brief inclusion of this work was felt justified here.

4.C.4 *Sussex*

Arthur (in Bell 1977) has recorded Iron Age and Roman grain (T *Spelta, Hordeum disticum, Avena* sp and *Pisum*) from pits at Bishopstone multiperiod site. At Bullock Down (Arthur 1982b) *Triticum spelta* and Roman *Hordeum vulgare* have also been identified. Wood charcoal remains from Sussex have been consistently identified by Caroline Cartwright (Sussex Archaeological Unit) for different periods. Iron Age/Romano-British data include those from Bishopstone (Cartwright 1977a) Ranscombe Hill (Cartwright 1978b), Harting Beacon (Cartwright 1978a).

4.C.5 *Kent*

A small amount of information has been forthcoming from Kent.

a. *Wilmington Gravel pit* produced 50 oval pits one of which contained a substantial quantity of charred remains and associated chaff deposits. The principal taxa (Hillman unpubl) were *Triticum dicoccum*, and T *spelta* in equal proportions. Minor records included *Hordeum vulgare* and *Avena* and other Gramineae and Leguminosae. Hillman regards this as a typical assemblage where a mixture of emmer and spelt relate to the diminishing utilisation of these grains by early Iron Age people. From study of the caryopses and a small amount of chaff it was concluded that grain possibly represented the primary product of grain processing, perhaps an accidentally charred grain store.

b. *Keston Camp, Kent* (Hillman in press). Remains identified were small in number and comprised *Triticum spelta*, *Avena* (wild or cultivated) and the cereal weed *Lolium temulatum* (Darnel). The germinated state of the spelt grains was noted and discussion given.

Iron Age and Roman plant macrofossils

Dorset

Evans A M and Bowman A, 1968 Tollard Royal Cereals.
Evans A M and Jones M, 1979 Seeds and Cereals from Gussage All Saints.
Salisbury E J and Jane F W, 1940 Maiden Castle Charcoals.

Hampshire

Green F, 1981b Old Down Farm.
Monk M and Fasham P J, 1980 Micheldever.
Murphy P, 1977

Isle of Wight

Scaife R G, unpublished Cereals, Newchurch Corn Drier and Rock Roman Villa.

Kent

Arthur J R B and Metcalf C R in Johnston D E, 1972 Chalk, Gravesend.
Hillman G C, in press Cereals from Keston Camp.
Hillman G C, unpubl Wilmington gravel pit cereals.

Oxfordshire

Jones M in Lambrick G and Robinson M, 1979 Farmoor Cereals.
Jones M, 1978 Ashville Trading Estate.
Robinson M in Lambrick G and Robinson M, 1979 Waterlogged seeds from Farmoor.

Sussex

Arthur J R B in Bell M, 1977 Bishopstone.
Arthur J R B and Rudling D, 1979 Frost Hill, Beachy Head Cereals.
Cartwright C R, 1977a Bishopstone Charcoals.
Cartwright C R, 1978b Ranscombe Hill Charcoals.
Cartwright C R, 1978a Harting Beacon Charcoals.
Greig J R A, 1971 Fishbourne Palace seeds.
Hinton P, forthcoming Cereals from Boxgrove and Goring.
Hinton P, forthcoming Daub impressions from Chichester.
Reid C in St John Hope W H, 1901–1908 Seeds from Roman Silchester.

Wiltshire

Arthur J R B, 1963 Downton Roman Villa cereals.

General

Applebaum S, 1966 Peasant economy and agricultural types.
Applebaum S, 1954
Green F J, 1981b Iron Age, Roman and Saxon crops in Wessex.
Helbaek H, 1952 Crops in Southern England.
Jessen K and Helbaek H, 1944 Prehistoric crops.
Monk M in Fasham P J and Monk M, 1978 Iron Age pits and grain.
Murphy P, 1977 Iron Age and Roman agriculture on the Wessex chalklands.
Murphy P, 1981 East Stratton, Winchester.
Reynolds P J, 1974 Crop storage pits.
Reynolds P J, 1979 Butser Hill Iron Age Farm experiment.
Willcox G H, 1977 Exotic plants in Roman London.

4.D   Saxon and post-Saxon

Data relating to the Saxon and Medieval periods have recently been published in that literature noted in preceding Sections; Wessex, (Green 1981, 129–153) the Upper Thames terraces work of the Oxford archaeological unit (Robinson 1981) and more generally in relation to the development of crop husbandry in England (M Jones 1981). Consequently data are not reviewed in detail.

A substantial proportion of data relating to the Saxon and post-Saxon/medieval periods has come from rescue excavations funded by the Department of the Environment (DOE) over the last 15 years. Increasingly the relevance of environmental archaeology has been shown for urban situations. Plant macrofossil evidence has come from Post-Roman urban settlements at Winchester, Southampton (Hamwih). Plant remains come from different preservation contexts and include an aerobic preservation in waterlogged deposits, carbonisation/charring of cereal crops and from cesspits. Keeley (1978) and Green (1979a, 1979b) have examined these modes of preservation in urban contexts. Green (1979a, 1979b) has specifically examined the preservation of seeds in cesspits and garderobes and in other situations (pits, middens) where ordure accumulated. This illustrated the process of mineralisation of seeds and gives data on dietary habits/food consumption.

In contrast to the work discussed above, Arthur (nd, 1963a) has investigated plant remains from medieval building materials from Larkfield, Sittingbourne and Tenterden in Kent. This plant material consisted of chopped dried plants and cereal straw in building plaster. The former comprised a substantial list of arable weeds and ruderals and the latter was dominated by *Triticum turgidum* (Rivet wheat). This taxon was also recorded at Maidstone, Chillington House and Bicknor, Kent (Arthur 1960, 1961).

In Kent, the Graveney Boat has provided a substantial macrofossil record (Wilson 1975) with 60 plant taxa from this boat dated at 1003 ± 40 BP (BM-715). The sample included autochthonous salt marsh vegetation and inputs from the local and regional area. Of primary interest was the presence of *Humulus lupulus* L (hop) from which it was suggested that the boat was carrying a cargo of hops. A valuable review of early hop growing and brewing is given in the paper.

Saxon to Medieval plant macrofossils

Hampshire

Green F J, 1979a Urban Southampton and Winchester.
Green F J, 1979c Mineralisation of seeds from latrines.
Monk M A, 1980 Melbourne Street, Southampton.

Isle of Wight

Scaife R G, 1980d Newport High Street seeds (Medieval).

Kent

Arthur J R B, 1960 Maidstone; plant remains in plaster.
Arthur J R B, 1961 Bicknor Court plant remains.
Arthur J R B, 1963 Larkfield; plant remains in clay.
Arthur J R B, 1965 Tonge Manor; plant remains.

General

Green F J, 1979b Collection and interpretation of botanical remains.
Green F J, 1981a Review of Wessex crops.
Monk M A, 1978 Plant economy of Anglo-Saxon Southern Britain.

5   The experimental framework

The basis of our interpretation of archaeobotanical data relies on a number of implicit assumptions based upon the concept of a uniformitarianist approach. The necessity of understanding and therefore analysis and research of modern analogues to past vegetation may provide the necessary information required for the interpretation of archaeobotanical assemblages. The use of source reference collections for the identifications of material both botanical and zoological is of utmost importance at the level of primary data collection. In consequence, therefore the availability of and ability to extend these collections is of substantial importance to the correct and increasingly greater competence in the identification of archaeological materials.

At the stage of raw data interpretation, such analyses have to be based upon a knowledge of both present day analogues where they exist and upon that experience gained from previous analyses of similar contextual materials. The interpretation of pollen spectra and their temporal change is extremely complex, being subject to a whole range of factors of differing production, dispersion and depositional aspects; the results emerging have for long been appraised in literature relating to theoretical palynology. Such discussions have dealt essentially with pollen analyses carried out in rural and usually non-archaeologically related contexts. Furthermore, the bulk of this theoretical work has come from European and particularly Scandinavian workers. Research such as that of Tauber (1965, 1967a, 1967b) has provided invaluable data on the nature of pollen dispersion in woodland environs and the incorporation of airborne pollen into fossilizing sediments. Similar research in the opposing environs of the arctic tundra zones has also been carried out. The former studies in essentially forested conditions are pertinent to interglacial stages whereas the latter are related to glacial stadial environs. This work, in addition to that by Andersen attempting the correlation/interrelationship of differential pollen production rates and the creation of mathematical indices for correction of pollen rain data, may provide a means of 'adjusting' pollen diagrams such that those people not versed with the interpretation of palynological data may view pollen data in a more realistic light. Although the technique of correction has been little used (although see Baker C A *et al.* 1978), because palynologists tend to regard this as yet another inaccuracy to the already multiplicity of factors present, its approach if realised could have popular appeal to the archaeologist in aiding the understanding of complex pollen data.

Such an approach can only, however, be utilised if sufficient research into the pollen production/dispersion/filtration of environments relevant to those being studied is carried out. In Southern England some research of this character has been undertaken, the results of which could provide source data, but which have unfortunately not been published. Whether or not these correction ('R' Values) factors are of interest or use is a source of dispute and debate. It can, however, be argued that the fundamental research on pollen dispersal and sedimentation relating to a range of habitats in Southern Britain could provide a useful tool in the interpretation of pollen spectra from palaeo contexts.

Studies recounted above deal solely with natural environments of woodland ecosystems or tundra landscapes and are studies showing the exponential decay of pollen away from woodland fringes. Of greater relevance to the archaeologist/archaeoenvironmentalist is a more detailed understanding of the incorporation of pollen into environments more clearly related to man. Such work has not been forthcoming because of the enormous complexities involved. At the greatest extreme, it has been seen that the pollen encountered in urban waterlogged situations is representative of a multitude of different natural, semi-natural and purely anthropogenic inputs (ethnobotanical may also be included). Whilst there is no means of producing any realistic medieval analogues in London or Southern Britain, it is suggested that modern pollen rain studies of pollen dispersion in wasteland urban areas could prove useful to the understanding of production rates and dispersal characteristics of urban ruderal plants. Such studies could be pursued even into European, more analogous towns and cities. Previous studies of pollen in urban environments have been solely the domain of the aerobiologist providing the daily pollen count statistics clearly known to hayfever sufferers.

In *rural areas* experimental palynological data have been put into operation but only on a relatively small scale in the Morden Bog, Wareham and Overton Down, Wiltshire earthwork projects. These studies seek mainly to provide data on the movement of pollen and other objects in the soils of two contrasting environments. They do not seek to provide data on the range and spatial representation of vegetation around a point in varying vegetation communities or ecosystem types. Such work would amply repay surface pollen studies of a substantial number of 'vegetational' communities on different lithologies in the region under discussion. As with urban areas it would be naturally impossible to provide close analogues with those prehistoric habitation sites for which pollen analytical research is often carried out. It is unfortunate, however, that the site of the popularised BBC television programme 'Living in the Past', on the Marlborough Downs, Wiltshire should not have been pursued to a greater length in this matter, with studies of pollen input to a small woodland during both occupation and the re-invasion of woodland consequent upon human abandonment. Modern pollen rain studies have been carried out by Caroline Evans (formerly Department of Plant Sciences, Kings College, University of London) at the Butser Hill Iron Age experimental farm. These data are not available but refer to broad vegetation patterns and related pollen spectra around the area of the Butser Hill Camp. Reynolds (1979) suggests the value of this experimental site to pollen analysis. To clarify this, the nature of pollen dispersal of the proto and early cereal crops could be studied in detail using spaced pollen traps. Such data could assist with the interpretation of pollen found adjacent to localised Neolithic and Bronze Age settlement.

From the macrofossil viewpoint, contemporary experimental work is less possible but can be viewed in two different ways. Firstly, Hillman has produced detailed accounts (Hillman 1981) of ethnobotanical practices in the Near East, that is those areas where cereal cropping had possibly developed. Secondly, there is no possible way in which analogues can be found in Southern Britain. These data are, however, a valuable source of reference for comparison with those assemblages of archaeologically charred cereal remains which occasionally occur in British sites. Here, the use of total extraction methods of not only full caryopses but additional waste chaff may help to elucidate the prehistory of crop economy.

Conclusion

Throughout this paper, specific archaeological periods have been used to summarise the archaeobotanical knowledge for these broad periods. It is appreciated by the writer that the transition between successive periods may be less distinct than initially thought by archaeologists. Similarly, the temporal delimitation of those periods has been subject to substantial modification caused by greater sophistication in the radiocarbon dating technique, the greater number of dates now available for Southern England and the reassessment of lithic and pottery typologies. Such broad archaeological terminology has been similarly utilised in recently published county archaeological reviews, thus perpetuating a degree of circularity. Whilst these county reviews show varying degrees of concern and policy considerations in relation to the destruction of sites by urban and rural land use development pressures (for example see Groube and Bowden 1982, and Basford 1980). Others have provided little in terms of these problems (Leach 1982). All do, however, give reviews of archaeology and topics of county relevance. By contrast, the rate of environmental archaeology has been dealt with in a variety of ways or not at all, and in all cases insubstantially. Only in three volumes have specific archaeobotanical or pollen analytical reviews been provided. Renfrew J (in the *Archaeology of Hampshire* ed. Shennan and Schadla Hall 1981) has outlined briefly the macrofossil analyses carried out for that county. In the same volume, Barber also details recent palynological work and some associated problems. Scaife (1980a) in *The Vectis Report* (Basford 1980) adopted a similar approach, providing an outline of work and results, thus detailing an environmental background to the archaeology discussed. Only in Basford (1980) have suggestions concerning certain environmental (as well as archaeological) work been given.

Throughout this review, an attempt has been made to bring together the majority — as almost certainly much work still remains in 'hidden' journals — of pollen and, to a lesser extent, plant macrofossil data. This is because plant macrofossils have been reviewed successively by a number of writers but such has not been the case with palynological data. Where possible, at the end of each section, short proposals and ideas where further data might be of value have been provided. There is of course an almost infinitely large number of potentialities which might be suggested according to the interests of the archaeologist and archaeoenvironmentalist. This synthesis of published data allows an insight into the problems evident for the archaeobotanical and botanical construction of Southern British environments. Section 1 has highlighted the fact that Southern England is an area with problems posed by its lithological, geomorphological and climatic placement. Such problems have for long been expounded as the reasons for the lack of data from the south. Scanning/viewing of the 'mini-gazetteers' relating to different periods shows that in total more pollen data are actually present than might have been thought. However, very striking deficiencies in our knowledge of the vegetational environmental and anthropogenic character of the landscape are clearly seen.

Firstly, there are the spatial/county deficiencies where for reasons of physical landscape, data of palynological or plant-macrofossil value are not present or, as is more often the case, there is lack of concern by archaeologists for the information which can be accrued from the analyses of environmental data. In such areas where the latter cause is prevalent, work carried out by non-archaeological research bodies (e.g. University graduate and post-graduate research or private interest) is relied upon to provide a background environmental data base for the archaeologist. Such an approach may be unsatisfactory because this research may have been carried out with no archaeological background, in isolation from archaeologists, and in areas where prehistoric and later activity had not occurred. Consequently those areas rich in archaeological sites/field monuments are frequently those which are least suited to palaeobotanical investigations in the eyes of researchers looking for pure records of ecological change.

Secondly, this review again clearly shows that deficiencies in our knowledge occur for certain archaeological/anthropogenic phases. This has arisen because of a combination of factors discussed above, with a bias toward the unsuitability of certain lithologies and environments in Southern England. For example, it has been seen (Section 3) that Bronze Age barrows are especially frequent in nucleated cemeteries on the chalk downlands with a second grouping occurring on acid heathlands of the Wealden Mesozoic and Hampshire Basin Tertiary provinces.

These two environments contrast the problems of pollen and plant macrofossil preservation. A substantial number of pollen diagrams (although not enough) have been constructed from the sandy environments. In contrast only a single diagram from a chalk downland barrow exists (Scaife 1984) despite the vastly greater number of barrows and excavations of barrows which have been carried out on chalkland tumuli. This is in part a reflection of both problems discussed above. The almost religious belief that chalk rendzina soils are only of value in preserving snails and not pollen is not however, always the case. In consequence archaeologists often fail to consider the need or value of palynological investigation. In reality however it has to be noted that the problems of pollen preservation in calcareous soils do require considerable experience in extraction, identification and interpretation of such pollen spectra obtained.

Broadly changing spheres of interest within the archaeological discipline during the post World War 2 period have influenced the data available for analysis of specific archaeological periods. The phase of barrow rescue excavation provided much of the data relating to the Bronze Age environment. The increasing importance of urban and especially medieval archaeology during the 1970s and the creation of rescue archaeological units in conjunction with post excavation environmental research have established the discipline of environmental archaeology. Urban rescue archaeology has been one of the earlier spearheads for the assessment of environmental archaeology, with the establishment of units in York and the City of London. Palynologically such environments (previously totally dismissed by non-archaeological pollen analysts) are now more fully appreciated and understood (see Section 3.F.).

In the rural situation rescue archaeology has become of concern both for terrestrial situations brought about by mineral extraction or road construction or through deep ploughing of threatened archaeological sites. The uneven distribution of rescue units dealing with these pressures has had a profound effect causing regional gaps in detailed knowledge. Kent, despite its size, has a paucity of data due largely to lack of communication between archaeologists and environmental workers. In contrast Sussex has, through the auspices of the Sussex Archaeological Field Unit and its interaction with University research, maintained a high standard of environmental studies. With the advent of 'project funding' it is likely that those differences in 'interest' between archaeological directors and excavators (and therefore the environmental data source) will become less significant as each potential project needs to be viewed in terms of its overall value to archaeology and associated disciplines. This presents few real problems so long as a constant dialogue is maintained between archaeological site directors and environmental specialists. As such, the system of project funding should maintain a dialogue at the outset on project proposal, design, application and operations. Continuance of such a system can only create a greater awareness of a site's potential (or lack of it from any aspects) and help to establish greater integration of palaeobotanical work into earlier stages of archaeological reports and operations.

In the rural context the detailed excavation and researches on the Somerset levels under the supervision of Professor J Coles has brought about the recent upsurge in interest amongst archaeologists for 'wetlands'. This move towards an understanding of the preservation potential and indeed the degree of prehistoric movement and activity in these ecotypes bring archaeology and environmental archaeology closer to those researches carried out in many University departments of Geography and Botany, where peat and sediment waterlogged sites have for long been used as a source of past vegetational data. The continuation of the Somerset levels excavations and the establishment of the Fenlands Research Committee to obtain information from these unique wetlands can be seen as a valuable move towards an understanding of the total environment and economy of prehistoric man. It is the opinion of the writer that such investigations of Wetland areas on a scaled down nature in other areas of lowland Britain could be fruitful. Scaife (1980b) has shown that intensive fieldwork in a relatively small area (Isle of Wight), apparently containing little in the nature of organic deposits, can yield valuable environmental data from waterlogged sites closely adjacent to areas of archaeological interest. In one case an extensive flint scatter and site were located as a direct result of interesting palynological evidence.

The opinion often expressed in the past that Southern England is sterile or devoid of peat/organic deposits of use to palynologists, has occurred because of the fact that large lake and peat mires typical of northern and upland England are, with a few exceptions, not present. A small amount of palynological work of non-archaeologically related nature sought to establish the broad data base of vegetational changes for Southern England. Such work gave rise to the 'standard' Godwin Zonation Scheme for the Flandrian (Post-Glacial) period. Such sites have frequently suffered the ravages of peat cutting and drainage in a rural peasant economy, and are therefore rarely available, having been either destroyed completely or had their upper and therefore archaeologically relevant layers removed. The writer (1980b, 1982a) has shown that other Wetland habitats were maintained in this economy for different uses. It is from 'Withy Beds', that is *Alnus/Salix* Carr woodland of valley bottoms within predominantly agricultural areas, which can provide more complete sequences of vegetational and environmental change. This is so much the case that the sole complete Flandrian sequence (11000 bp to present) comes from Gatcombe Withy Bed, Isle of Wight (see Section 2). This typically small peat site, surrounded at present by agricultural land, contains clear evidence for not only the late-Devensian and Flandrian vegetational development but also the effects of Neolithic and Bronze Age agriculture on the valley sides within 100m of the peat accumulation. This exemplification is by no means unique to this area and the knowledge that old Withy Beds/Carr woodland could provide invaluable data throughout Southern England must be recognised. It is evident, however, that such possibilities may not be present in a few years; Coles *et al.* have talked of the Somerset levels and the Fenlands as dying landscapes. Such a situation is happening to lowland valley peat bogs of the character described. Cessation of this rural economy — *Salix* coppice and older wood for hurdles, basketry, thatch, gunpowder, etc., — has allowed these areas to regenerate and become wild. Furthermore, improved systems of land drainage and the use of nitrate fertilisers have had a profound effect on the ecology of these areas.

Archaeologically such areas could be of great interest. It is striking to compare the character of many Danish peat bogs containing remarkable archaeological, artefactual (and human) remains with that of southern English peat mires. Cadavers contained within peat are by no means unknown from England (Glob 1969, 101). This evidence as might be expected, comes from the period where peat cutting for fuel was commonly carried out — that is also a period prior to the full realisation of man's ancestry. Is there a Tollund or Grauballe man in Kent, Sussex, Hampshire or the Isle of Wight?*

Although not so spectacular, archaeological material has recently been forthcoming from peat bogs in the Isle of Wight where a Roman Kiln has been discovered which is stratified within waterlogged peat accumulations. This is significant in as much as it was through close co-operation (where possible) with farmers that machine ditching activities on a *small farm* resulted in its discovery. Although watching briefs are often established on motorway schemes and in premier areas such as the Somerset levels this find illustrates that a greater co-operation between County Council departments, farmers, archaeologists and environmental researchers could fill some of those glaring gaps revealed in the various sections of this review of Southern England.

*Written prior to the discovery of Lindow Man in Cheshire (1984)

Appendix 1

ANCIENT MONUMENTS LABORATORY REPORTS

I WOODS AND CHARCOALS

3503	Watson J	Identification of mineral replaced wood found on two iron objects from Canterbury, St. Pancras. AML site 99.
3505	Watson J	Wood identification of a waterlogged statue from Ickenham, Kent. AML site 63.
3522	Watson J	Identification of waterlogged wood from Stanwell, Heathrow airport.
1652	Keepax C A	Wood identification; Eynsford Castle, Kent.
1933	Keepax C A	Charcoal identification; Brooklands, Weybridge, Surrey.
1930	Keepax C A	Charcoal identification; Bridge By-pass, Canterbury.
1934	Keepax C A	Charcoal identifications; Camber Castle, Sussex.
2027		Charcoal identification; Avebury.
2287	Keepax C A	Charcoal identification; St Augustines Abbey, Canterbury.
2401	Keepax C A	Wood identification; Silchester.
2466	Morgan R	Tree-ring analysis of wood from excavations at Silchester 1976.
2595	Keepax C A	Identification of wood; Runnymede Bridge.
2692	Keepax C A	Identification of charcoal; Knights Farm, Berks, 1978.
2693	Keepax C A	Identification of charcoal; Knights Farm, Berks, 1975.
2694	Keepax C A	Identification of charcoal; Danebury, Hants.
2734	Keepax C A	Identification of charcoal; Ascott-under-Wychwood, Avon.
2776	Keepax C A	Identification of wood from Reliquary; Winchester.
2861	Keepax C A	Identification of charcoal and seed; Christchurch X17, Dorset.
3002	Hillam J	Dendrochronological analysis of well timbers from 16 Watling Street, Canterbury.
3004	Hillam J	The dating of well timbers from Allen and Hanburys, Ware, Herts. — Interim Report.
3005	Hillam J	Dendrochronological analysis of well timbers from the St. Radigund's site, Canterbury.
3064	Keepax C A	Late Neolithic/Early Bronze Age charcoal from Greenhill, Otford.
3074	Keepax C A	Charcoal from a cremation at Lambourn, Bronze Age barrow.
3089	Keepax C A	Charcoal from a Saxon burial at Romsey Abbey, Hants.
3143	Keepax C A	Replaced wood and charcoal from an Anglo-Saxon site at Portway, Andover.
3210	Keepax C A	Charcoal from Stonehenge, Wilts.
3209	Keepax C A	Charcoal from an ironworking bloomery at Ashdown Forest.
3242	Keepax C A	Identification of a charcoal sample, Eltham Palace.
3245	Keepax C A	Wood remains from Romano-British coffins at Poundbury, Dorset.
3246	Keepax C A	Bronze Age charcoal samples from Pingewood, Berkshire.
3438	Keepax C A	Identification of radio carbon samples from Hambledon Hill, Dorset.
3357	Morgan R	Winchester — preliminary examination of wood.
3691	Watson J	Wood identification of a 'paddle' from Danebury, Hants.
3410	Watson J	Identification of waterlogged wood for Kent Museum Service.

II   SEEDS

1745	Paradine P J	Seed identification; Stonar, Sandwich, Kent.
2653	Monk M	Carbonised cereal grains and seeds from Avebury Saxon pit.
2884	Paradine P J	Plant remains; Herons House, Berkshire; Bronze Age.
3000	Scaife R G	Preliminary oval of Carbonised cereal from Harlington Wall Garden Farm.
3102	Scaife R G	Medieval pollen and macrofossil plant remains from Newport, Isle of Wight.
3239	Paradine P J	Eltham palace site; seeds.
3301	Paradine P J	Christchurch; later impressions from pots.
3668	Paradine P J with Girling M A	Insect and plant remains at Pingewood, Berks.
3501	Scaife R G	An early Bronze Age record of *Vicia faba* (horsebean) from Newbarn Down, Isle of Wight (NB: now renamed Gallibury Down).
3517	Scaife R G	Identification of C11 and C12 carbonised crop remains from Gatehouse nurseries, West Drayton Manor House, Middlesex.

III   POLLEN

2231	Greig J R A with Girling M	Palaeoecological investigations of a site at Hampstead Heath, London.
2846	Greig J R A	Barton Court, Oxon; pollen report.
3001	Scaife R G	Pollen analysis of some Dark Earth samples (London and York).
2999	Scaife R G	Pollen analysis, Waltham Abbey Building Society (WAB 1979).
3070	Scaife R G	Pollen analytical investigation of Broad Sanctuary, Westminster.
3102	Scaife R G	Medieval pollen and macrofossil plant remains from Newport, Isle of Wight.
3279	Scaife R G	Pollen analysis, Moulsham Street, Chelmsford, Essex.
3499	Scaife R G	Pollen analysis and radiocarbon dating of Wilson's Wharf Iron Age peat deposits.
3502	Scaife R G	Pollen analysis of Roman peats underlying the Temple of Mithras, London.
3942	Scaife R G	Interim report on the pollen analysis of Etton Neolithic Causewayed enclosure.
4001	Scaife R G	Stratigraphy and preliminary palynological results of peats from Peninsular House, City of London.
4002	Scaife R G	Palynological investigation of barrows V, VIII and IX, West Heath Bronze Age barrow cemetery, West Sussex.

IV   EXPERIMENTAL AND MISCELLANEOUS

2130	Keepax C A	A brief experiment on the recovery of seeds from modern soil.
2131	Keepax C A	Investigations into soil samples and some comments on modern contamination at Winklebury, Hants.
2134	Keeley H C M	Cost effectiveness of methods of recovering macroscopic organic remains from archaeological deposits.
3316	Keepax C A	Samples of replaced organic materials from Christchurch X.17, Anglo Saxon Cemetery.
3167	Green, F	Environmental draft report, Ludgershall Castle.

Appendix 2

Sampling – some informal notes

The taking of samples for both archaeobotanical and archaeozoological analytical research has been the subject of considerable recent discussion. This has been especially in relation to the central Southern England region. Several writers have discussed the theoretical and conceptual viewpoints. It has to be said, however, that while expertise in sampling strategy both from the statistical and conceptual viewpoints are the 'norm' in environmental specialists, the broader views of much sampling on archaeological sites leaves a lot to be desired. In such cases the complexities of statistical/philosophical literature on the implications of detailed random sampling are of little practical value. More fundamental concern with the basic techniques of sampling and interpretation, as found in Renfrew *et al.* and Keeley and Macphail (1981) dealing with seeds and soils respectively, may provide a simple but valuable basis to the field archaeologist. The ideas of archaeologists are often not commensurate with the reality of data retrieved by the environmental archaeologist (and *vice versa*).

A negative sampling strategy for the archaeologist: or how to keep on the right side of your environmental analyst

Each and every environmental archaeologist, as in every profession, will adopt those techniques which he has developed or has found satisfactory to the needs of his analyses. Such idiosyncrasies cannot be delimited! However the following are generally scorned.

i.   DO NOT SEND SAMPLES BY POST – OR SECURICOR! Let the environmental analyst take/retrieve his own samples. This is necessary so that points of stratigraphical note to the archaeologist can be seen. 'Visual Contact' with the site is of value for two reasons.

    a.   stratigraphical changes often divided into discrete contexts by the archaeologist, whilst of different textural calibre, may, however, be to the environmentalist part of a continuum of process. An example of such may be the hydroseral changes in a topographical basin from lake sediments to peat and wood peat as the vegetation succession and sediment accumulation occur through time. Pedologically the contrasting layers in a podzol profile are part of a whole which may not be immediately apparent to the archaeologist. Conversely, the archaeologist may portray a context sequence in a different light providing therefore background to environmental interpretation.

    b.   interpretation of archaeobotanical assemblages as seen above depend to a large extent on the doctrine of uniformitarianism. It often aids the palaeoenvironmentalist to see the region and local area and its topography and vegetation. Such a general viewpoint leads often to a more realistic interpretation of archaeobotanical assemblages.

From a more altruistic viewpoint many archaeologists do not realise the expenditure and therefore monetary cost (as shown clearly by H C M Keeley 1978) of analysing both pollen and plant macrofossil assemblages. The often great enthusiasm for an excavation by an archaeologist can provide enough sample material to keep an unsuspecting environmentalist at work for many months or years! On-site sampling by the analyst may thus curb this by optimum sampling strategy, simply, therefore not inundating himself with months of work, while the excavator has subsequently become equally enthusiastic about another archaeological site. A final point is that, whilst most analysts enjoy looking at their relevant materials – in the writer's case, pollen – the analysis of materials received through the post can be a trial of patience against drudgery if he has no insight into where the samples were obtained from.

Environmental analysts are notorious in the eyes of the pure archaeologist for burrowing into nicely/squarely cut baulks. In consequence the micro/macrobotanist is often summoned to the site in its 'last throes'. As a result, where a fine example of man's heritage exposed archaeologically may often appear to the analyst as a heap of rubble or as a completely empty trench SOME ENVIRONMENTAL ARCHAEOLOGISTS MAY ALSO APPRECIATE ARCHAEOLOGY. As Otto Lillianthal said whilst dying having attempted to fly from a hot air balloon – 'Sacrifices have to be made'. Little trenches in the sides of big ones really are not that bad!

ii.   Where the sampling strategy has broken down due to the unavailability of the analyst because (a) he is out at other sites or (b) the telephone lines are mysteriously engaged then PROVIDE THE RIGHT SORT OF SAMPLE. A few general and simple rules apply.

    a.   pollen grains are small (av. 25–28nm), therefore some samples of 1cc may contain many millions of pollen grains. In soil or organic deposits these may have accumulated over a long time span. Therefore DO NOT PROVIDE SACKS OF SAMPLES OF 15 KILOS weight (as happened to the writer with the aid of a sack barrow for transport). Wheelbarrows are definitely not required in pollen analysis.

Generally, samples of 3–5ml are adequate for most pollen analysts. As little as 0.5cc to 1cc is generally adequate for *organic samples/deposits*. It is however beneficial to have auxiliary samples as even the most experienced decanter of

177

supernatant liquid may inadvertently 'drain' the samples. Where pollen is known to be present but is in low absolute pollen frequencies larger (sometimes up to 100 gm) samples may be required. In such circumstances, it is more than necessary for the analyst to extract his own samples from the site.

iii. for the analyses of plant macrofossils — especially those of seeds — larger samples of excavated material are required by virtue of the greater size of these items and the often infrequent occurrence of preserved items. There are two basic situations in seed preservation, that of charring and that of waterlogging. Charring occurs where fire — usually anthropogenically initiated — has occurred on an occupation site where habitation, storage or kiln drying contexts are involved. Such charring results in the carbonisation or semi-carbonisation of plant remains, which being 'C' are inert and stable.

The value of such charred grain and associated chaff is widely recognised and discussed in detail (Hillman 1981a, Hubbard 1975a, 1976a). The extraction of such material often present in diminutive quantities has resulted in the design and operation of seed flotation devices (Williams 1976a). Such devices have been sporadically used with great success on Southern England rescue archaeological sites (Fasham and Monk 1978). The greater realisation and utilisation of such equipment could provide valuable data from those areas seen to have insufficient prehistoric crop data. Such activities are pursued in the regions by both university departments and archaeological field units, but not at the more local level of archaeological societies. Thus it seems probable that many archaeobotanical data are being lost with flotation techniques: care must also be taken so that highly diagnostic chaff material is not lost through sieving at too coarse a grade. As shown by the Southampton workers and widely used by seed analysts, sieve size of 250μ in conjunction with 1mm for separating the larger fraction is adequate for total recovery.

Sampling strategy plays a similarly important role. Argument over random (objective) v. subjective point sampling still exists. It is pertinent to point out that both exhibit certain advantages according to specific site characteristics. It is clear that quantities of charred grain will not be left simply because they are found outside of a random number thrown against a representative grid. Conversely, large areas of old ground surfaces of possible agricultural usage might be sampled randomly in order to assess the background count, and any possible spatial variability. As Hubbard (*unpublished document 'Cretin's guide to environmental sampling') has poignantly pointed out, random sampling must take account of the fact that archaeological sites are the product of man and therefore subject to controls in location and not random occurrences to be sampled randomly.

Waterlogged archaeological or associated palynological contexts are substantially different. Whilst large quantities of material may be used in the flotation of soils, in waterlogged situations far smaller volumes are required. Seeds are preserved in often fine condition and in high frequencies, requiring therefore substantially less sample (0.5 to 2kg).

Archaeologically, such waterlogged and anaerobic conditions are often pits, cesspits and latrines and stream channels. Discrete archaeological contexts are usually point/spot sampled. In non-archaeologically related palaeoecological and in normal palynological practice, serial sampling is usually carried out contiguously or utilizing a sampling interval. Where sediments are deposited over time, the temporal dimension is added to information gained. Such serial sampling has been little applied by archaeobotanists even in situations where waterlogged deposits have accumulated over time spans. Exceptions to this possibility are of course specific cases of spot sampling of remains deposited at one point in time — charred grain or seeds. In such cases points in time are the essence of the study. Sampling of 'normal' archaeological contexts using a single point sample technique is of more limited value than temporal sequences which show more clearly the position of a single point in that sequence as shown by the spot sample.

Box monolith columns may be used to achieve such a sequence in temporal/stratigraphic sequences.

*A notably serious and useful document

LIST OF REFERENCES

AARIO L, 1940

'Waldgrenzen und Subrezenten Pollenspektren in Petsamo, Lappland', *Ann Acad Sci Fenn* A 54(8), 1–120.

AKEROYD A V, 1966

Changes in relative Land and Sea level during the post glacial in Southern Britain with particular reference to the post-Mesolithic period, unpublished MA thesis, University of London.

AKEROYD A V, 1972

'Archaeological and historical evidence for subsidence in Southern Britain', *Phil Trans Roy Soc London* A 272, 151–169.

ALETSEE L, 1959

'Zur Geschichte der Moore und Wälder des nördlichen Holsteins', *Nova Acta Leopoldiana* 21(139), 1–51.

ALLEN T E, ROBINSON M A, 1979

'Hardwick with Yelford, Mingies Ditch', *CBA Group 9 Newsl* 9, 115–117.

ALLISON J, GODWIN H, 1949

'Bronze Age plant remains from Wiltshire. Data for the study of post-glacial history, XII', *New Phytol* 48, (2) 253–254.

ALLISON J, GODWIN H, WARREN S H, 1952

'Late Glacial deposits at Nazeing in the Lea Valley, North London', *Phil Trans Roy Soc London* B 236, 169–240.

AMERICAN COMMISSION ON STRATIGRAPHIC NOMENCLATURE, 1961

'Code of Stratigraphic nomenclature', *Amer Assoc Petroleum Geol Bull* 45, 645–655.

ANDERSEN S TH, 1970

'The relative pollen productivity and pollen representation of North European trees, and Correction factors for tree pollen spectra', *Danm geol Unders Ser II* 96, 1–99.

ANDERSEN S TH, 1973

'The differential pollen productivity of trees and its significance for the interpretation of a pollen diagram from a forested region', in Birks H J B and West R G (eds). *Quaternary plant Ecology*, 109–115, Blackwell, Oxford.

APPLEBAUM S, 1954

'The agriculture of the British Early Iron Age as exemplified at Figheldean, Wiltshire', *Proc Prehist Soc* 20, 103–14.

APPLEBAUM S, 1966

In Thomas C (ed) *Peasant economy and types of agriculture in rural settlement in Roman Britain* CBA Res Rep 7, 99–107.

APPLEBAUM S, 1972

'Crops and plants', in Finberg H P R (ed) *The Agrarian History of England and Wales,* 108–121, Cambridge University Press.

APSIMON A, GAMBLE C, SHACKLEY M, 1976

'Pleistocene raised beaches on Portsdown, Hampshire', *Proc Hampshire Fld Clb Archaeol Soc* 33, 17–32.

ARTHUR J R B, n.d.

Plant remains taken from Medieval building material, Oxford: private publication.

ARTHUR J R B, 1954

'Prehistoric Wheats in Sussex', *Sussex Archaeol Collect* 92, 37–47.

ARTHUR J R B, 1960

'Maidstone, Chillington House – plant remains in wall plaster', *Archaeol Cantiana* 74, 194–196.

ARTHUR J R B, 1961

'Plant remains from Bicknor Court', *Archaeol Cantiana* 76, 192–193.

ARTHUR J R B, 1963a | 'Larkfield, Kent: plant remains in late 14th century clay', *Archaeol Cantiana* 78, 192–193.

ARTHUR J R B, 1963b | 'The cereals' (p. 328) in Rahtz P A 'A Roman Villa at Downton', *Wiltshire Archaeol Natur Hist Mag* 58, 303–341.

ARTHUR J R B, 1965 | 'Special note on the plant remains from Tonge, Kent' (p. 268) in Forde D M, 'Tonge Medieval manor – summary of results, 1965', *Archaeol Cantiana* 80, 265–269.

ARTHUR J R B, 1970 | 'Appendix I' in Bradley R 'The excavation of a Beaker settlement at Belle Tout, East Sussex, England', *Proc Prehist Soc* 36, 373–375.

ARTHUR J R B, 1977 | 'Plant remains', in Bell M, 'Excavations at Bishopstone, Sussex', *Sussex Archaeol Collect* 115, 273–275.

ARTHUR J R B, 1982a | 'The seeds from the 1977 trial excavation', in Drewett, P L, 'Later Bronze Age downland economy at Black Patch, East Sussex', *Proc Prehist Soc* 48, 381–382.

ARTHUR J R B, 1982b | In Drewett, P L, *The archaeology of Bullock Down, Eastbourne: the development of a landscape*, Sussex Archaeol Collect Monog 1, 22–24, Sussex Archaeol Soc, Lewes.

ARTHUR J R B, RUDLING D R, 1979 | 'The Romano-British site on Frost Hill, Beachy Head, East Sussex', *Bull Inst Archaeol London* 16, 43–49 (see p. 45).

ASHBEE P, 1954 | 'The excavation of a round barrow on Canford Heath, Dorset', *Proc Dorset Natur Hist Archaeol Soc* 76, 39–50.

ASHBEE P, 1960 | *The Bronze Age round barrow in Britain,* London.

ASHBEE P, 1963 | 'The Wilsford Shaft', *Antiquity* 37, 116–120.

ASHBEE P, DIMBLEBY G W, 1959 | 'The excavations of a round barrow on Chicks Hill, East Stoke Parish, Dorset', *Proc Dorset Natur Hist Archaeol Soc* 80, 146–159.

ASHBEE P, DIMBLEBY G W, APSIMON A M, 1976 | 'The Moor Green barrow, West End, Hampshire: Excavations 1961', *Proc Hampshire Fld Clb Archaeol Soc* 31, 5–18.

ATKINSON R J C, 1970 | 'Silbury Hill, 1969–1970', *Antiquity* 44, 313–4.

BAIGENT J, 1976 | 'Appendix I: Pollen Analysis' in Drewett P L 1976, 'The excavation of four round barrows of the Second Millennium BC at West Heath, Harting 1973–1975', in *Sussex Archaeol Collect* 114, 144–147.

BAKER C A, 1976 | 'Late Devensian periglacial phenomena in the Upper Cam Valley, north Essex', *Proc Geol Ass* 87, 285–306.

BAKER C A, MOXEY P A, OXFORD P M, 1978 | 'Woodland Continuity and Change in Epping Forest', *Fld Stud* 4, 645–669.

BARBER K E, unpublished data | *New Forest pollen data from Warwick Slade Bog and Noads Bog,* Department of Geography, University of Southampton.

BARBER K E, 1975 | 'Vegetational history of the New Forest: A preliminary note', *Proc Hampshire Fld Clb Archaeol Soc* 30, 5–8.

BARBER K E, 1976a | 'History of Vegetation', in Chapman, S B (ed) *Methods in Plant Ecology* 5–83 Blackwell Scient. publics.

BARBER K E, 1976b

'Two pollen analyses on Sediments from Well (pit) 135', in Cunliffe B W, *Excavations at Portchester Castle Vol II Saxon,* Res Rep Soc Antiq London 33, 297–299.

BARKER G, WEBLEY D, 1978

'Causewayed Camps and Early Neolithic Economies in Central Southern England', *Proc Prehist Soc* 44, 161–186.

BARNES M, 1974

Vegetational history of Pevensey Marshes, Sussex, Unpublished MA thesis, Institute of Archaeology, University of London.

BARTLEY D D, CHAMBERS C, HART–JONES B, 1976

'The Vegetational history of parts of South and East Durham', *New Phytol* 77, 437–468.

BARTON R N E, 1981

'Some conjoinable artefacts from a new Mesolithic site at Hengistbury Head, Dorset', *Proc Dorset Natur Hist Archaeol Soc* 103, 13–20.

BARTON R N E, 1983

'Hengistbury Head: Palaeolithic and Mesolithic Project', *Proc Dorset Natur Hist Archaeol Soc* 105, 137–139.

BASFORD H V, 1980

'The Mesolithic' in *The Vectis report: a survey of Isle of Wight Archaeology,* 12–14, Isle of Wight County Council.

BEHRE K E, MENCKE B, 1969

'Pollen analytische Untersuchungen an einen Bohrkern der Süderlichen Doggerbank', Deutsche Akad. Wissenschafter zum Berlin Inst für Meers Kinde, pp 122.

BELL F G, 1969

'The occurrence of Southern, Steppe and Halophyte elements in Weichselian (last-glacial) floras from Southern Britain', *New Phytol* 68, 913–922.

BELL F G, 1970

'Late pleistocene floras from Earith, Huntingdonshire', *Phil Trans Roy Soc London, B* 258, 347–378.

BELL M, 1977

'Excavations at Bishopstone', *Sussex Archaeol Collect* 115, 1–291.

BELL M, 1981

Valley Sediments as evidence of prehistoric land-use: a study based on dry valleys in South East England, unpublished Ph D thesis Institute of Archaeology, University of London.

BELL M, 1983

'Valley sediments as evidence of prehistoric land-use on the South Downs', *Proc Prehist Soc* 49, 119–150.

BIRKS H J B, 1973

Past and present vegetation of the Isle of Skye; a palaeoecological study, Cambridge University Press.

BIRKS H J B, DEACON J, PEGLAR S, 1975

'Pollen maps for the British Isles 5000 years ago', *Proc Roy Soc B.* 189, 87–105.

BLYTT A, 1876

Essay on the immigration of the Norwegian flora during alternating rainy and dry periods Cammermeyer, Christiania.

BORLASE W, 1857

'An account of some trees discovered underground on the shore at Mounts Bay in Cornwall', *Phil Trans Roy Soc* 50, 51–53.

BOWEN H C, 1961

Ancient Fields. A tentative analysis of vanishing earthworks and landscapes, London: Brit Assoc for the Advancement of Science, 80 pp.

BOWEN H C, 1972

'Air photography: some implications in the South of England', in Fowler E (ed) *Field Survey in British Archaeology,* 38–49, London CBA.

BOWEN H C, 1975a

'Air photography and the development of the landscape in central part of southern England', in Wilson, D M (ed), *Aerial reconnaissance for archaeology*, CBA Res Rep 12, 103–118.

BOWEN H C, 1975b

'Pattern and interpretation: a view of the Wessex landscape' in Fowler P J (ed), *Recent Work in rural archaeology*, 44–55, Moonraker Press, Bradford on Avon.

BOWEN H C, 1978

' 'Celtic' fields and ranch boundaries in Wessex', in Limbrey S and Evans J G (eds) *The effect of man on the landscape: the Lowland Zone.* CBA Res Rep 21, 115–123.

BOWEN H C, FOWLER P J (eds), 1978

Early land allotment in the British Isles: a survey of recent work, Brit Archaeol Rep 48, Oxford.

BRADLEY R, 1978

The prehistoric settlement of Britain, Routledge and Kegan Paul Ltd, London.

BRADLEY R, ELLISON A, 1975

Rams Hill: a Bronze Age defended enclosure and its landscape, Brit Archaeol Rep 19, Oxford.

BRADLEY R, KEITH–LUCAS M, 1975

'Excavation and pollen analyses on a bell barrow at Ascot, Berkshire', *J Archaeol Sci* 2, 95–108.

BRADLEY R, LOBB S, RICHARDS J, ROBINSON M, 1980

'Two late Bronze Age settlements on the Kennet gravels: excavations at Aldermaston Wharf and Knight's Farm, Burghfield, Berkshire', *Proc Prehist Soc* 46, 217–295.

BROOKS A, unpublished

'Pollen data from Elstead, Surrey; Broxbourne and Ponders End, Hertfordshire and Wellingham, Sussex,' Dept of Plant Sciences, King's College, University of London.

BROWN R C *et al.,* 1975

'Stratigraphy and environmental significance of Pleistocene deposits at Stone, Hampshire', *Proc Geol Ass* 86, 349–363.

BURCHELL J P T, PIGGOTT S, 1939

'Decorated prehistoric pottery from the bed of the Ebbsfleet, Northfleet, Kent', *Antiq J* 19, 405–420.

BURGESS C, 1974

'The Bronze Age' in Renfrew C (ed) *British Prehistory, a new outline,* 165–232, Duckworth, London.

BURRIN P J, 1981

'Loess in the Weald', *Proc Geol Ass* 92, 87–92.

BURRIN P J, 1983

The character and evolution of floodplains with specific reference to the Ouse and Cuckmere, Sussex, unpublished PhD thesis, London School of Economics, University of London.

BURRIN P J, SCAIFE R G, 1984

'Aspects of Holocene Valley Sedimentation and flood plain development in Southern England', *Proc Geol Ass* 95(1), 81–96.

BYRNE S, 1975

Environmental Changes in Poole Harbour during the Flandrian, unpublished BA dissertation, University of Durham. (ref Mottershead D N).

CAMPBELL J B, 1977

The Upper Palaeolithic of Britain, Oxford.

CARPENTER C P, WOODCOCK M P, 1981

'A detailed investigation of a pingo remnant in Western Surrey', *Quaternary Stud* 1, 1–26, (City and North London Polytechnic publication).

CARR A P, BLACKLEY M W L, 1973

'Investigations bearing on the age and development of Chesil Beach, Dorset, and associated area' *Trans Inst Brit Geogs* 58, 99–111.

CARTWRIGHT C R, 1977a

'The Charcoals' in Bell M, 'Excavations at Bishopstone' *Sussex Archaeol Collect* 115, 275, 277.

CARTWRIGHT C R, 1977b | 'Charcoals and other environmental evidence from on-site flotation', in Drewett P L, 'The Excavation of a Neolithic Causewayed enclosure on Offham Hill, East Sussex, 1976', *Proc Prehist Soc* 43, 232–234.

CARTWRIGHT C R, 1978a | 'Charcoal identifications' in Bedwin O, 'Excavations inside Harting Beacon Hill-Fort, West Sussex, 1976', *Sussex Archaeol Collect* 116, 240.

CARTWRIGHT C R, 1978b | 'Charcoal', in Bedwin, O, 'The excavation of a Romano-British site at Ranscombe Hill, South Malling, East Sussex, 1976', *Sussex Archaeol Collect* 116, 253.

CHARLESWORTH J K, 1957 | *Quaternary Era,* London: Arnold.

CHURCHILL D M, 1962 | 'The Stratigraphy of Mesolithic Sites III and IV at Thatcham, Berkshire, England', *Proc Prehist Soc* 28, 362–370.

CHURCHILL D M, 1965 | 'The displacement of deposits formed at sea level 6500 years ago in Southern Britain', *Quaternaria* 7, 239–249.

CLAPHAM A R, CLAPHAM B N, 1939 | 'The Valley fen at Cothill Berkshire. Data for the study of post-glacial history II', *New Phytol* 38, 167–174.

CLARK A, 1980 | 'Knight's Farm: Table 1, pollen and spores', in Bradley R *et al.,* 'Two Late Bronze Age settlements on the Kennet gravels: Excavations at Aldermaston Wharf and Knight's Farm, Burghfield, Berkshire', *Proc Prehist Soc* 46, 279–280.

CLARK A, 1982 | 'The Neolithic of Kent: a review', in Leach, P (ed), *Archaeology in Kent to AD 1500,* CBA Res Rep 48, 25–30, London.

CLARKE J G D, 1932 | *The Mesolithic age in Britain,* Cambridge University Press, London.

CLARKE W R, 1838 | 'On the peat bogs and submarine forests of Bournemouth, Hampshire and in the neighbourhood of Poole, Dorsetshire', *Proc Geol Soc* 2, 599–601.

CLIFFORD M H, 1936 | 'A Mesolithic flora in the Isle of Wight', *Proc Isle Wight Natur Hist Archaeol Soc* 2, 582–595.

COLES J *et al.,* 1975 onwards | *Somerset Levels Papers,* Vol 1 (1975), Vol 2 (1976), Vol 3 (1977), Vol 4 (1978), Vol 5 (1979), Vol 6 (1980), Vol 7 (1981).

COLES J, 1983 | 'The Fenland project', *Antiquity 57,* 51–52.

COOPE G R, PENNINGTON W, 1977 | 'The Windermere interstadial of the Late-Devensian', *Phil Trans Roy Soc London* B 280, 227–339.

COX J, 1982 | *Pollen analysis of a Bronze Age barrow on the Isle of Wight,* unpublished undergraduate dissertation, King's College, University of London.

CURRY D, HODSON F, WEST I M, 1968 | 'The Eocene Succession in the Fawley Transmission Tunnel', *Proc Geol Ass* 79, 179–206.

CURWEN C E, 1938 | 'The early development of agriculture in Britain', *Proc Prehist Soc* 4(2) 27–51.

CUSHING E J, 1964 | In Birks H J B, *The past and present vegetation of the Isle of Skye; A palaeoecological study,* Cambridge University Press.

D'OLIER B, 1972 | 'Subsidence and sea level rise in the Thames Estuary', *Phil Trans Roy Soc London* A 272, 121–130.

DARBY H C, CAMPBELL E M J, 1962   *The Domesday Geography of South-East England* Cambridge University Press.

DENNELL R, 1974   'Botanical evidence for prehistoric crop processing activities', *J Archaeol Sci* 1, 275–284.

DENNELL R, 1976   'Prehistoric crop cultivation in Southern England: a reconsideration', *Antiq J* 56(1), 11–23.

DEVOY R J N, 1977   'Flandrian sea level changes in the Thames estuary and the implications for land subsidence in England and Wales', *Nature* (London), 270, 712–715.

DEVOY R J N, 1978–9   'Flandrian sea level changes and vegetational history of the Lower Thames estuary', *Phil Trans Roy Soc London* B 285, 355–407.

DEVOY R J N, 1980   'Post-glacial environmental change and man in the Thames estuary: a synopsis', in Thompson F H (ed), *Archaeology and Coastal Change* Occas Pap Soc Antiq new ser. 1, 134–148.

DEVOY R J N, 1982   'Analysis of the geological evidence for Holocene sea-level movements in south-east England', *Proc Geol Ass* 93, 65–90.

DICKSON J H, 1973   *Bryophytes of the Pleistocene. The British record and its chorological and ecological implications.* Cambridge University Press.

DIMBLEBY G W, 1952   'Appendix III,' in Case H, 'The excavation of two round barrows at Poole, Dorset', *Proc Prehist Soc* 18, 158–159.

DIMBLEBY G W, 1953   In Piggott S, 'A Bronze Age barrow on Turners Puddle Heath', *Proc Dorset Natur Hist Archaeol Soc* 75, 34–35.

DIMBLEBY G W, 1954   'Pollen analysis as an aid to the dating of prehistoric monuments', *Proc Prehist Soc* 20, 231–6.

DIMBLEBY G W, 1956   'The importance of historical checks in interpreting the effect of vegetation upon soil development', *12th Congr/Int/Union for Res organ* 1, 181–186.

DIMBLEBY G W, 1957a   'Pollen analysis', in Thompson M W and Ashbee P 'Excavation of a barrow near the Hardy monument, Black Down, Portesham, Dorset', *Proc Prehist Soc* 23, 124–136.

DIMBLEBY G W, 1957b   'Pollen analysis of terrestrial soils', *New Phytol* 56, 12–28.

DIMBLEBY G W, 1959   In Wymer J J 'Excavations on the Mesolithic site at Thatcham, Berkshire – 1958', *Berkshire Archaeol J* 57, 1–33, (pollen 25–33).

DIMBLEBY G W, 1960   'Appendix D. Pollen', in Money J, 'Excavations at High Rocks, Tunbridge Wells, 1954–1956', *Sussex Archaeol Collect* 98, 212–217.

DIMBLEBY G W, 1961a   'Soil pollen analysis', *J Soil Sci* 12, 1–11.

DIMBLEBY G W, 1961b   'Transported material in the soil profile', *J Soil Sci* 12, 12–22.

DIMBLEBY G W, 1962a   In Biek L, 'Row Down, Lambourn, Berkshire', *Berkshire Archaeol J* 60, 25–29.

DIMBLEBY G W, 1962b   'The development of British Heathlands and their soils', *Oxford Forestry Memoir* 23.

DIMBLEBY G W, 1965a   In Connah G, 'Excavations at Knap Hill, Alton Priors, 1961', *Wiltshire Archaeol Natur Hist Mag* 60, 21.

DIMBLEBY G W, 1965b   In Smith I F, *Windmill Hill and Avebury: Excavations by Alexander Keiller, 1925–1939,* 38–40, Oxford University Press.

DIMBLEBY G W, 1965c   'Pollen analysis at a Mesolithic site at Addington, Kent' *Grana Palynologica* 4, 140–148.

DIMBLEBY G W, 1965d   'Post-Glacial changes in soil profiles', *Proc Roy Soc London* B 161, 355–362.

DIMBLEBY G W, 1965e   'Overton Down Experimental Earthwork', *Antiquity* 39, 134–6.

DIMBLEBY G W, 1966a   In Jewell P A and Dimbleby G W 'The experimental earthwork on Overton Down, Wiltshire, England: The first four years', *Proc Prehist Soc* 32, 313–342.

DIMBLEBY G W, 1966b   In Ashbee P 'The Fussell's Lodge long barrow excavation', *Archaeologia* 100, 65.

DIMBLEBY G W, 1969a   'Pollen analysis' in Brothwell D and Higgs E (eds), *Science and Archaeology,* 2nd edit, 167–177. Thames and Hudson, London.

DIMBLEBY G W, 1969b   'Report on pollen analysis', in Fox, N P, 'Caesar's Camp, Keston', *Archaeol Cantiana* 84, 196–199.

DIMBLEBY G W, 1971   In Wainwright G J and Longworth I, *Durrington Walls: Excavations 1966–1968,* London Soc Antiq.

DIMBLEBY G W, 1974   In Evans J G and Limbrey S, 'The experimental earthwork on Morden Bog, Wareham, Dorset, England: 1963–1972', *Proc Prehist Soc* 40, 171–172.

DIMBLEBY G W, 1975   'Pollen analysis', in Drewett P L 'The excavation of a turf barrow at Minsted, West Sussex, 1973', *Sussex Archaeol Collect* 113, 61–62, 65.

DIMBLEBY G W, 1976   'The history and archaeology of heaths' in Sankey J H P and Mackworth-Praed H W (eds), *The Southern Heathlands,* Surrey Naturalists Trust, 38–52.

DIMBLEBY G W, 1977   *Plants and archaeology,* John Baker, London.

DIMBLEBY G W, 1979   In Lambrick G and Robinson M, *Iron Age and Roman riverside settlements at Farmoor, Oxfordshire,* Oxford Archaeol Unit Report No. 2, CBA Res Rep 32, 77–147.

DIMBLEBY G W, forthcoming   In Petersen, *Excavations at Knighton Heath,* British Archaeol Rep.

DIMBLEBY G W, unpublished   *Pollen data from a post-hole – Ranscombe Camp, Sussex.*

DIMBLEBY G W, BRADLEY R J, 1975   'Evidence of pedogenesis from a Neolithic site at Rackham, Sussex', *J Archaeol Sci* 2, 179–186.

DIMBLEBY G W, EVANS J G, 1974   'Pollen analysis and land snail analysis of Calcareous soils', *J Archaeol Sci* 1, 117–133.

DIMBLEBY G W, GILL J M, 1955   'The occurrence of podzols under deciduous woodland in the New Forest', *Forestry* 28, 95–106.

DODD J P, 1979   'Hampshire agriculture in the mid-nineteenth century', *Proc Hampshire Fld Clb Archaeol Soc* 35, 239–260.

DREW C D, PIGGOTT S, 1936   'Excavation of a long barrow 136a on Thickthorn Down, Dorset', *Proc Prehist Soc* 11, 177–96.

DREWETT P L, 1975a   'The excavation of a turf barrow at Minsted, Stedham, West Sussex', *Inst Archaeol Bull* 12, 24–26.

DREWETT P L, 1975b   'The excavation of a turf barrow at Minsted, West Sussex, 1973', *Sussex Archaeol Collect* 113, 54–65.

DREWETT P L, 1975c   'The excavation of three round barrows of the Second Millennium BC at West Heath, West Sussex', *Inst Archaeol Bull* 12, 19–26.

DREWETT P L, 1976a   'The excavation of barrow IV at West Heath Common, West Sussex, 1975', *Inst Archaeol Bull* 13, 58–62.

DREWETT P L, 1976b   'The excavation of four round barrows of the Second Millennium BC at West Heath, Harting, 1973–1975', *Sussex Archaeol Collect* 114, 126–150.

DREWETT P L, 1978   'Neolithic Sussex' in Drewett P L (ed) *Archaeology in Sussex to AD 1500* CBA Res Rep No. 29, 23–29.

DREWETT P L, 1981   'The excavation of five round barrows at West Heath, Harting, West Sussex', *Bull Inst Archaeol* 18, 26–32.

DREWETT P L, 1982   'Later Bronze Age downland economy and excavation at Black Patch, East Sussex', *Proc Prehist Soc* 48, 321–400.

DREWETT P L, 1985   'Excavations of barrows V–IX at West Heath, Harting, 1980', *Sussex Archaeol Collect* 123, 35–60.

DUIGAN S L, 1955   *Interglacial plant remains from Wolvercote Channel, Oxford.*

DYER K, 1972   'Recent sedimentation in the Solent Area', *Extrait du Mémoire du BREM* 79, 271–280.

DYER K, 1975   'The buried channels of the Solent River, Southern England', *Proc Geol Ass* 86, 239–245.

EIDE K S, 1981   *Some aspects of pedogenesis and vegetation history in relation to archaeological sites in the New Forest,* unpublished PhD thesis, Institute of Archaeology, University of London.

ELLISON A, HARRISS J, 1972   'Settlement and land use in the prehistory and early history of southern England: a study based on locational models', in Clarke D L (ed), *Models in Archaeology* 911–962, London.

ERDTMAN G, 1928   'Studies in the post-arctic history of the forests of North West Europe. I. Investigation in the British Isles', *Geol Fören Stock Förh* 50, 123–92.

EVANS A M, BOWMAN A, 1968   In Wainwright G J 'The excavation of a Durotrigian farmstead near Tollard Royal in Cranborne Chase, Southern England', *Proc Prehist Soc* 34, 146.

EVANS A M, JONES M K, 1979   'The plant remains' in Wainwright G J, *Gussage All Saints: An Iron Age Settlement in Dorset,* London HMSO (DOE Archaeol Rep No 10), 172–175.

EVANS J, 1897   *The ancient stone implements, weapons and ornaments of Great Britain,* 2nd Edition Longmans, Green, Reader and Dyer.

EVANS J G, 1972   *Land snails in archaeology,* Seminar Press, London.

EVANS J G, 1975   *The environment of Early man in the British Isles,* Paul Elek, London.

EVERARD C E, 1954a   'Submerged gravel and peat in Southampton Water', *Proc Hampshire Fld Clb Archaeol Soc* 18, 263–285.

EVERARD C E, 1954b · 'Solent River: a geomorphological study', *Trans Inst Brit Geog* 20, 41–58.

FAEGRI K, 1944 · 'On the introduction of agriculture in Western Norway', *Geol Fören Stock Förh* 66, 449–462.

FASHAM P J, MONK M A, 1978 · 'Sampling for plant remains from Iron Age pits: some results and implications' in Cherry J F, Shennan S and Gamble C, *Sampling in Contemporary British Archaeology,* Brit Archaeol Rep 50, 363–371.

FENNELLY L R, 1976 · 'Combley Roman Villa' in Goodburn R *et al.* (eds) 'Roman Britain 1975', *Britannia* 7, 364–366.

FLEMING A, 1971 · 'Territorial patterns in Bronze Age Wessex', *Proc Prehist Soc* 37, 138–166.

FLOWER N, 1977 · *Forestry land use in the New Forest,* unpublished PhD thesis, University of London.

FOX A, 1963 · 'Neolithic charcoal from Hembury', *Antiquity* 37, 228–229.

FOX C, 1932 · *The personality of Britain,* National Museum of Wales, Cardiff.

FOX N P, 1969 · 'Caesar's Camp, Keston', *Archaeol Cantiana* 84, 185–199.

FRANKS J W, 1960 · 'Interglacial deposits at Trafalgar Square, London', *New Phytol* 59, 145–152.

FRENZEL B, 1966 · 'Climatic change in the Atlantic/Suboreal transition on the Northern Hemisphere: botanical evidence' in Sawyer, J S (ed), *World climate from 8000 to 0 BC Proc Int Sympos Imperial College, London* 1966, 99–123, Roy Met Soc London.

GALLOIS W, EDMUNDS F H, 1965 · *British regional geology; the Wealden District,* Geol Survey.

GEIKIE J, 1874 · *The Great Ice Age,* W Isbister & Co, London.

GEIKIE J, 1881 · *Prehistoric Europe,* Stanford, London.

GIBBARD P L, 1974 · *Pleistocene stratigraphy and vegetational history of Hertfordshire,* PhD thesis, University of Cambridge.

GIBBARD P L, COOPE G R, HALL A R PREECE R C, ROBINSON J E, 1982 · 'Middle Devensian deposits beneath the Upper Floodplain terrace of the River Thames at Kempton Park, Sunbury, England', *Proc Geol Ass* 93(3) 275–289.

GIBBARD P L, HALL A R, 1982 · 'Late Devensian river deposits in the Lower Colne Valley, West London, England', *Proc Geol Ass* 93(3) 291–299.

GIBBARD P *et al.,* · *Current pollen investigations on Stoke Newington.*

GIRLING M, GREIG J R A, 1977 · 'Palaeoecological investigations of a site at Hampstead Heath, London', *Nature* (London) 268, 45–47.

GLOB P V, 1969 · *The bog people,* Faber and Faber, London.

GODWIN H, 1934 · 'Pollen analysis. An outline of the problems and potentialities of the method', *New Phytol* 33, 278–305.

GODWIN H, 1940 · 'Pollen analysis and the forest history of England and Wales', *New Phytol* 39, 370–400.

GODWIN H, 1943 · 'Coastal peat beds of the British Isles and North Sea', *J Ecol* 31, 199–247.

GODWIN H, 1944 · 'Age and origins of the "Breckland" heaths of East Anglia', *Nature* (London) 154, 6–10.

GODWIN H, 1945a — 'Coastal peat-beds of the North Sea region, as indices of land and sea-level changes', *New Phytol* 44, 29–69.

GODWIN H, 1945b — 'A submerged peat in Portsmouth Harbour', *New Phytol* 44, 152–155.

GODWIN H, 1953 — 'British Vegetation in the Full-glacial and late-glacial periods' in Lousley J E (ed), 59–74, *The changing Flora of Britain.*

GODWIN H, 1955 — 'Vegetational history at Cwm Idwal: a Welsh plant refuge', *Svensk Bot Tidskr* 49, 35–43.

GODWIN H, 1956 — *The history of the British flora,* 1st Edition, Cambridge University Press.

GODWIN H, 1960 — In Greenfield E 'A neolithic pit and other finds from Wingham, East Kent', *Archaeol Cantiana* 74, 58–72.

GODWIN H, 1962 — 'Vegetational history of the Kentish Chalk downs as seen at Wingham and Frogholt', *Veroff Geobot Inst Rubel Zürich* 37, 83–99.

GODWIN H, 1964 — 'Late Weichselian Conditions in South-Eastern Britain: organic remains at Colney Heath, Herts', *Proc Roy Soc London* B 160, 258–275.

GODWIN H, 1975a — *The history of the British flora,* 2nd Edition, Cambridge University Press.

GODWIN H, 1975b — 'History of the natural forests of Britain: establishment, dominance and destruction', *Phil Trans Roy Soc London* B 271, 47–67.

GODWIN H, 1978 — *Fenland: its ancient past and uncertain future,* Cambridge University Press.

GODWIN H, GODWIN M E, 1933 — In Clarke G, 'Report on an early Bronze Age site in the South-Eastern Fens', *Antiq J* 13, 281–289.

GODWIN H, GODWIN M E, 1936 — 'Pollen analysis at sites on the Essex coast', in Warren S H, *et al*, 'Archaeology of the submerged land-surface of the Essex Coast', *Proc Prehist Soc* 2, 185–186.

GODWIN H, GODWIN M E, 1940 — 'Submerged peat at Southampton. Data for the study of post-glacial history V', *New Phytol* 39, 303–307.

GODWIN H, GODWIN M E, CLIFFORD M H, 1936 — In Clarke J G D, 'Report on a Late Bronze Age site in Mildenhall Fen, West Suffolk', *Antiq J* 16, 29–50.

GODWIN H, TALLANTIRE P A, 1951 — 'Studies in the post-glacial history of British Vegetation. XII: Hockham Mere, Norfolk', *J Ecol* 39(2) 285–307.

GODWIN H, TANSLEY A G, 1940 — 'Prehistoric charcoals as evidence of former vegetation, soil and climate', *J Ecol* 29, 117–126.

GREEN F J, 1979a — *Medieval plant remains: methods and results of archaeobotanic analyses from excavations in Southern England with especial reference to Winchester and urban settlements of the 10th–15th centuries,* unpublished M Phil thesis, University of Southampton.

GREEN F J, 1979b — 'Collection and interpretation of botanical information from Medieval excavations in Southern England' (Festschrift for Maria Hopf), ed Korber Grohne, *Archaeo-Physika* 8, 39–55.

GREEN F J, 1979c — 'Phosphate mineralisation of seeds from archaeological sites', *J Archaeol Sci* 6, 279–284.

GREEN F J, 1980

In Horsey I and Shackley M, 'The excavation of a Bronze Age round barrow on Canford Heath, Poole, Dorset', *Proc Dorset Natur Hist Archaeol Soc* 102, 33–42.

GREEN F J, 1981a

'Iron Age, Roman and Saxon crops: The archaeological evidence from Wessex', in Jones M and Dimbleby G W (eds) *The Environment of Man: the Iron Age to the Anglo-Saxon period,* Brit Archaeol Rep (Brit Ser) 87, 129–153.

GREEN F J, 1981b

In Davies S M, 'Excavations at Old Down Farm, Andover – part II: Prehistoric and Roman', *Proc Hampshire Fld Clb Archaeol Soc* 37, 140.

GREENSMITH J T, TOOLEY M J (eds), 1982

'IGCP project 61. Sea level movements during the last deglacial hemicycle (about 15000 years)', *Proc Geol Ass* 93(1).

GREENSMITH J T, TUCKER E V, 1969

'The origin of Holocene shell deposits in the Chenier plain of Essex, England', *Marine Geology* 7, 403–425.

GREENSMITH J T, TUCKER E V, 1971

'The effects of late Pleistocene and Holocene sea level changes in the vicinity of the River Crouch, East Essex', *Proc Geol Ass* 82, 301–322.

GREENSMITH J T, TUCKER E V, 1973

'Holocene transgressions and regressions on the Essex Coast, outer Thames estuary, *Geol en Mijnb* 52, 193–202.

GREENSMITH J T, TUCKER E V, 1980

'Evidence for differential subsidence on the Essex Coast', *Proc Geol Ass* 91, 169–175.

GREIG J R A, 1971

'Pollen analysis of the garden soil' in Cunliffe B, *Excavations at Fishbourne 1961–1969,* Res Rep Soc Antiq London, 27, 372–376.

GREIG J R A, 1979

'Pollen from the lower silts', in Kenward, H K, and Williams, D, *Biological evidence from the Roman warehouses in Coney Street, The archaeology of York* 14/2, 52–53.

GREIG J R A, 1981

'The investigation of a Medieval barrel-latrine from Worcester', *J Archaeol Sci* 8, 265–282.

GREIG J R A, 1982a

'Past and present lime woods of Europe', in Bell M and Limbrey S (eds) *Archaeological aspects of Woodland ecology,* 23–55, Assoc Environ Arch Symposia Vol 2, Brit Archaeol Rep (Int Ser) 146.

GREIG J R A, 1982b

'The interpretation of pollen spectra from urban archaeological deposits', in Hall A R and Kenward H (eds) *Environmental archaeology in the urban context,* CBA Res Rep 43, 47–65.

GREIG J R A, forthcoming

New Palace Yard: London, Westminster, pollen investigation.

GRINSELL L V, 1932

'Some Surrey Bell-Barrows', *Surrey Archaeol Collect* 40, 56–64. Analysis and List (1934) 42, 27–60.

GRINSELL L V, 1934

'Sussex barrows', *Sussex Archaeol Collect* 75, 216–275 (supplementary paper 1940, 81, 210–214).

GRINSELL L V, 1936

'An analysis and list of Berkshire barrows', *Berkshire Archaeol J* 40, 20–58.

GRINSELL L V, 1938–40

'Hampshire barrows', *Proc Hampshire Fld Clb Archaeol Soc* 14, 9–40, 195–229, 346–365.

GRINSELL L V, 1940 — 'Sussex barrows, supplementary paper', *Sussex Archaeol Collect* 81, 210–214.

GRINSELL L V, 1941 — 'The Bronze Age round barrows of Wessex', *Proc Prehist Soc* 7, 73–113.

GROENMAN–VAN–WAATERINGE W, 1978 — 'The impact of Neolithic man on the landscape in the Netherlands', in Limbrey S and Evans J E (eds), *The effect of man on the landscape: the lowland Zone,* CBA Res Rep 21, 135–146.

GROSE J D, SANDELL R E, 1964 — 'A catalogue of prehistoric plant remains in Wiltshire', *Wiltshire Archaeol Natur Hist Mag* 59, 58–67.

GROUBE L M, BOWDEN M C B, 1982 — *The archaeology of Rural Dorset,* Dorset Natur Hist Archaeol Soc monogr 4.

HALL A R, 1982 — In Kerney M P, Gibbard P L, Hall A R and Robinson J E 'Middle Devensian river deposits beneath the upper floodplain terrace of the River Thames at Isleworth, West London', *Proc Geol Ass* 93, 385–393.

HASKINS L E, 1978 — *The Vegetational History of South-East Dorset,* unpublished PhD thesis, Department of Geography, University of Southampton.

HAWKES J, 1957 — 'The Longstone, Mottistone', *Antiquity* 31, 147–152.

HELBAEK H, 1940 — 'Studies on prehistoric and Anglo-Saxon cultivated plants in England', *Proc Prehist Soc* 6, 176–178.

HELBAEK H, 1952 — 'Early crops in southern England', *Proc Prehist Soc* 18(2), 194–233.

HELBAEK H, 1957 — 'The carbonized cereals' in Burstow E P and Holleyman G E, 'Late Bronze Age settlement on Itford Hill, Sussex', *Proc Prehist Soc* 23, 206–209.

HILLMAN G C, 1981a — 'Reconstructing crop husbandry practices from charred remains of crops', in Mercer R (ed), *Farming practice in British prehistory,* 123–162, Edinburgh University Press.

HILLMAN G C, 1981b — In Smith A G *et al.* 'The Neolithic', in Simmons I G and Tooley M J (eds) *The environment in British prehistory,* 184–191.

HILLMAN G C, in press — *Carbonised charred cereal remains from Keston Camp, Kent.*

HILLMAN G C, unpublished — 'The charred plant remains from Iron Age pits at Wilmington, Kent' (from excavations by B Philp).

HINTON M P, 1979 — 'The environmental samples' in Freke D in 'Excavations in Tanyard Lane, Steyning, 1977', *Sussex Archaeol Collect* 117, 147–149.

HINTON M P, 1982 — In Drewett P L 'Later Bronze Age downland economy and excavation at Black Patch, East Sussex', *Proc Prehist Soc* 48, 382–390.

HINTON M P, 1984 — 'Seeds from archaeological excavations: results from Sussex' *Sussex Archaeol Collect* 122, 3–11.

HINTON M P, 1985 — 'Macro plant remains', in Drewett P L, 'The excavation of barrows V–IX at Weat Heath, Harting, 1980', *Sussex Archaeol Collect* 123, microfiche 2, 39–41.

HODGSON J M, 1964 — 'Low-level pleistocene marine sands and gravels of the West Sussex coastal plain', *Proc Geol Ass* 75, 547–561.

HODSON I F, WEST I M, 1972 — 'Holocene deposits of Fawley, Hampshire, and the development of Southampton Water', *Proc Geol Ass* 83, 421–441.

HOLDGATE M W, 1955 — 'The Vegetation of some British Upland fens', *J Ecol* 43, 389–403.

HOLYOAK D T, 1980 — *Late pleistocene sediments and biostratigraphy of the Kennet Valley, England,* unpublished PhD thesis, Department of Geography, University of Reading.

HOLYOAK D T, PREECE R C, 1983 — 'Evidence of a high Middle Pleistocene sea-level from estuarine deposits at Bembridge, Isle of Wight England', *Proc Geol Ass* 84(3) 231–244.

HORSEY I, SHACKLEY M, 1980 — 'The excavation of a Bronze Age round barrow on Canford Heath, Poole, Dorset', *Proc Dorset Natur Hist Archaeol Soc* 102, 33–42.

HUBBARD R N L B, 1972 — 'An interim note on the pollen record at Swanscombe', *Proc Roy Anthropol Inst for 1971,* 79.

HUBBARD R N L B, 1975a — 'Assessing the botanical component of human palaeoeconomies', *Inst Archaeol Bull* 12, 197–205.

HUBBARD R N L B, 1975b — 'Pollen analysis of the pleistocene deposits at Yiewsley: some interim results', in Collins D, *'Early Man in West Middlesex: the Yiewsley Palaeolithic Sites'* 15–19. London, HMSO.

HUBBARD R N L B, 1976a — 'On the strength of the evidence for prehistoric crop processing activities', *J Archaeol Sci* 3, 257–265.

HUBBARD R N L B, 1976b — 'Crops and climate in prehistoric Europe', *World Archaeol* 8(2) 159–168.

HUBBARD R N L B, 1977a — In Shephard-Thorn E R and Wymer J J, *INQUA guidebook for excursion AS: South East England and Thames Valley,* 71. Section on Slindon by Shephard-Thorn E R and Kellaway G A, publ Geo-Abstracts.

HUBBARD R N L B, 1977b — 'On the chronology of the Lower Palaeolithic in Southern Britain', *Abstract of the Xth INQUA Congress, Birmingham,* 216.

HUBBARD R N L B, 1978a — In Sampson C E, *Palaeoecology and archaeology of an Acheulian site at Caddington, England,* Southern Methodist University, Dallas, Texas.

HUBBARD R N L B, 1978b — In Shephard-Thorn E R and Kellaway G A, *Quaternary deposits at Eartham, West Sussex,* Brighton Polytechnic Geog Soc, 4.

HUBBARD R N L B, 1982 — 'The environmental evidence from Swanscombe and its implications for palaeolithic archaeology' in Leach P (ed) *Archaeology in Kent to AD 1500,* CBA Res Rep 48, 3–7.

IVERSEN J, 1941 — 'Landnam i Danmarks Stenalder', *Danm geol Unders* R11, 66, 1–67.

IVERSEN J, 1944 — '*Viscum, Hedera* and *Ilex* as climatic indicators', *Geol Fören Stock Förh* 66, H3.

IVERSEN J, 1949 — 'The influence of prehistoric man on vegetation', *Danm geol Unders,* ser IV, 3(6), 1–25.

IVERSEN J, 1960 — 'Problems of the early post-glacial forest development in Denmark', *Danm geol Unders,* ser IV, 4(3), 6–32.

JACKSON J F, 1924

'Description of the Pleistocene deposit near Bembridge', *Proc IoW Natur Hist Archaeol Soc* 1, 290–291.

JACOBI R J, 1978a

'The Mesolithic of Sussex' in Drewett P L (ed) *Archaeology in Sussex to AD 1500*, CBA Res Rep No. 29, 15–22.

JACOBI R J, 1978b

'Population and landscape in Mesolithic lowland Britain' in Limbrey S and Evans J G, *The effect of man on the landscape: the lowland Zone*, CBA Res Rep 21, 75–85.

JAMES H, 1847

'On a section exposed by the excavation at the New Steam Basin in Portsmouth Dockyard', *Quart J Geol Soc* 3, 249–251.

JARMAN H N, LEGGE A J, CHARLES J A, 1972

'Retrieval of plant remains from archaeological sites by froth flotation' in Higgs E S (ed), *Papers in economic prehistory* 39–48.

JELGERSMA S, 1961

'Holocene sea-level changes in the Netherlands', *Meded geol Sticht* ser (6)7, 1–100.

JELGERSMA S, 1966

'Sea level changes during the last 10,000 years' in Sawyer J S (ed), 54–71, *World climate 8000–0 BC,* Roy Met Soc.

JELGERSMA S, PANNEKOEK A J, 1960

'Post-glacial rise of sea-level in the Netherlands (A preliminary report)', *Geologie en Mijnbouw* 39, 201–207.

JENNINGS S, SMYTHE C, 1982

'A preliminary interpretation of coastal deposits from East Sussex', *Quaternary Newsl* 37, 12–19.

JESSEN K, 1935

'Archaeological dating in the history of North Jutland's vegetation', *Acta Archaeol* (Copenhagen) 5, 185–214.

JESSEN K, HELBAEK H, 1944

'Cereals in Great Britain and Ireland in prehistoric and early historic times', *Det Kongelige Danske Videnskabernes Selskab Biologiske Skrifter* 3(2), 1–68, Copenhagen.

JOHNSTONE D E, 1972

'A Roman building at Chalk, near Gravesend', *Britannia* 3, 112–148.

JONES D K C, 1980

The shaping of Southern England, Academic press, London.

JONES D K C, 1981

The southeast and southern England, Methuen, London.

JONES J P, 1978

Isle of Wight 1558–1642, unpublished PhD thesis, University of Southampton.

JONES M, 1978

'Plant remains' in Parrington M *The excavation of an Iron Age Settlement, Bronze Age Ring ditches and Roman features at Ashville Trading Estate, Abingdon (Oxfordshire) 1974–1976,* CBA Res Rep 28, 93–110.

JONES M, 1980

'Carbonised cereals from grooved ware contexts', *Proc Prehist Soc* 46, 61–63.

JONES M, 1981

'The development of crop husbandry' in Jones M and Dimbleby G W (eds), *The environment of man: the Iron Age to the Anglo-Saxon period,* Brit Archaeol Rep (Brit Ser) 87, 95–127.

JONES M AND ROBINSON M, 1986

'The crop plants', in Miles, D (ed), *Archaeology at Barton Court Farm, Oxon,* CBA Res Rep 50, microfiche 9:E10–9:E14.

KEATINGE T H, 1983

'Development of pollen assemblage zones in soil profiles in south-eastern England', *Boreas* 12, 1–12.

KEEF P A M, WYMER J J, DIMBLEBY G W, 1965 — 'A Mesolithic site on Iping Common, Sussex, England', *Proc Prehist Soc* 31, 85–92.

KEELEY H C M, 1978 — 'The cost-effectiveness of certain methods of recovering macroscopic organic remains from archaeological deposits', *J Archaeol Sci* 5, 179–183.

KEELEY H C M, MACPHAIL R I, 1981 — 'A soil handbook for archaeologists', *Inst Archaeol Bull* 18, 225–241.

KEEPAX C, 1975 — 'Scanning electron microscopy of Wood replaced by iron corrosion products', *J Archaeol Sci* 2, 145–150.

KEEPAX C, 1977 — 'Contamination of archaeological deposits by seeds of modern origin with particular reference to the use of flotation machines', *J Archaeol Sci* 4, 221–229.

KELLAWAY G A, REDDING J H, SHEPHARD–THORN E R, DESTOMBES J P, 1975 — 'The Quaternary history of the English Channel', *Phil Trans Roy Soc London A* 279, 189–218.

KERNEY M P, 1963 — 'Late glacial deposits on the chalk of south-east England', *Phil Trans Roy Soc London B* 246, 203–254.

KERNEY M P, 1971 — 'Interglacial deposits in Barnfield pit Swanscombe and their molluscan fauna', *Quart J Geol Soc* 127, 69–93.

KERNEY M P, BROWN E H, CHANDLER T J, 1964 — 'The late-glacial and post-glacial history of the chalk escarpment near Brook, Kent', *Phil Trans Roy Soc London B* 248, 135–204.

KERNEY M P, PREECE R C, TURNER C, 1980 — 'Molluscan and plant biostratigraphy of some late Devensian and Flandrian deposits in Kent', *Phil Trans Roy Soc London B* 291, 1–43.

KING W B R, OAKLEY K, 1936 — 'The Pleistocene succession in the lower parts of the Thames Valley', *Proc Prehist Soc* 2, 52–76.

LAMBERT C A, 1964 — In Kerney M P, Brown E H and Chandler T J 'The Late-glacial and post-glacial history of the chalk escarpment near Brook, Kent', *Phil Trans Roy Soc London B* 248, 193–197.

LAMBRICK G, ROBINSON M, 1979 — *Iron Age and Roman riverside settlements at Farmoor, Oxfordshire,* Oxford Archaeol Unit Rep No. 2, CBA Res Rep 32, 77–147.

LEACH P E, 1982 — *Archaeology in Kent to AD 1500,* CBA Res Rep 48.

LEVY J F, 1964 — In Kerney M P *et al.* 'The late-glacial and post-glacial history of the chalk escarpment near Brook, Kent', *Phil Trans Roy Soc London B* 248, 197–198.

LEWIS F J, 1905 onwards — 'The plant remains in the Scottish peat mosses. Part I. The Scottish Southern Uplands', *Trans Roy Soc Edinburgh* 31, 699–723, Part II (1906) 45, 335–60, Part III (1907) 46, 33–70, Part IV (1911) 47, 793–833.

LUBBOCK J, 1865 — *Prehistoric times: as illustrated by ancient remains and the manners and customs of modern savages,* (1st Edition) Williams and Norgate, London.

MACPHAIL R I, 1979 — *Soil Variation on selected Surrey heaths,* unpublished PhD Thesis, CNAA Kingston Polytechnic.

MACPHAIL R I, 1981 — *Soil report on West Heath cemetery (1980), West Sussex, parts I and II,* AML Report No. 3586.

MACPHAIL R I, 1982 — *Preliminary soil report on Hengistbury Head, Bournemouth, Hants,* AML Report No. 3811.

MACPHAIL R I, 1983 — 'The micromorphology of dark earth from Gloucester, London and Norwich: an analysis of urban anthropogenic deposits from the late Roman or early medieval period in England', in Bullock P and Murphy C P (eds), 'Soil Micromorphology', *A B Acad Publ, Berkhampstead* 1, 245–252.

MCVEAN D N, 1956 — 'Ecology of *Alnus glutinosa* (L) Gaertn. VI Post-glacial history', *J Ecol* 44, 331–333.

MITCHELL G F, 1956 — 'Post-Boreal pollen diagrams from Irish raised bogs', *Proc Roy Ir Acad B* 57, 185–251.

MITCHELL G F, PENNY L F, SHOTTON F W, WEST R G, 1973 — *A correlation of Quaternary deposits in the British Isles,* Geol Soc Special Report No. 4.

MONK M A, 1978 — *The plant economy and agriculture of the Anglo-Saxons in Southern Britain: with particular reference to the Mart settlements at Southampton and Winchester,* unpublished M Phil thesis, University of Southampton.

MONK M A, 1980 — In Holdsworth P, *Excavations at Melbourne Street, 1971–1976,* Southampton Arch Res Committee Rep 1 CBA Res Rep No. 33, 128–133.

MONK M A, FASHAM P J, 1980 — 'Carbonised plant remains from two Iron Age sites in Central Hampshire', *Proc Prehist Soc* 46, 321–344.

MOORE P D, 1977 — 'Ancient distribution of lime trees in Britain', *Nature* (London) 268, 13–14.

MOORE P D, 1980a — 'The reconstruction of the late glacial environment: some problems associated with the interpretation of pollen data', in Lowe J J, Gray J M and Robinson J E (eds), *Studies in the late glacial of North West Europe,* 151–155.

MOORE P D, 1980b — 'Resolutions limits of pollen analysis as applied to archaeology', *MASCA J* 1 (4), 118–120.

MOORE P D, WILLMOT A, 1976 — 'Prehistoric forest clearance and the development of peatlands in the Uplands and lowlands of Britain', *V Int peat Congress, Poznan, Poland 1976.* 1–15.

MORGAN G C, 1979 — 'Charcoals' in Wainwright G J, *Mount Pleasant, Dorset: Excavations 1970–1971,* Rep Res Soc Antiq London 37, 253.

MORRISON M E S, 1959 — 'Evidence and interpretation of landnam in the North East of Ireland', *Bot Notiser* 112, 185–204.

MORZADEC–KERFOURN M T, 1975 — In Destombes J P, Shephard-Thorn E R and Redding J H, 'A buried valley system in the Strait of Dover', *Phil Trans Roy Soc London A* 279, 243–256.

MOTTERSHEAD D N, 1977 — 'The quaternary evolution of the South Coast of England', in Kidson C and Tooley M J (eds) 'The Quaternary History of the Irish Sea' 290–320, *Geol J Special Issue* No. 7, 299–320.

MURPHY P, 1977 — *Early agriculture and environment on the Hampshire Chalklands c. 800 BC to 400 AD,* unpublished M Phil thesis, University of Southampton.

MURPHY P, 1981 — In Fasham P J, 'Fieldwork and excavations at East Stratton along the Roman Road from Winchester to Silchester', *Proc Hampshire Fld Clb Archaeol Soc* 37, 173–174.

MURPHY P, 1982 — In Case H J and Whittle A W R, *Settlement patterns in the Oxford region: excavations at the Abingdon Causewayed enclosure and other sites.* CBA Res Rep No. 44, 47–49.

NARTHORST A G, 1873 — 'On the distribution of arctic plants during the post-glacial epoch', *J Bot London* 2, 225–228.

NICHOLS H, KELLY P M, ANDREWS J T, 1978 — 'Holocene palaeo-wind evidence from palynology in Baffin Island', *Nature* (London) 273, 140–142.

OSBORNE P J, 1971 — 'Appendix on the insect fauna of the organic deposits within the Wandle gravels' in Peake D S, 'The age of the Wandle gravels in the vicinity of Croydon', *Proc Trans Croydon Natur Hist Sci Soc* 14(7), 147–175.

OSBORNE P J, 1972 — 'Insect faunas of Late Devensian and Flandrian age from Church Stretton, Shropshire', *Phil Trans Roy Soc London B* 263, 327–67.

OSBORNE P J, 1974 — 'An insect assemblage of Early Flandrian age from Lea Marston, Warwickshire, and its bearing on the contemporary climate and ecology', *Quaternary Research* 4, 471–486.

OXFORD P M, 1974 — *A pollen analytical investigation into the vegetational history of Epping Forest,* unpublished BA dissertation, Department of Geography, King's College, London.

PALMER L S, COOKE J H, 1923 — 'Pleistocene deposits of the Portsmouth area in relation to early man', *Proc Geol Ass* 34, 253–282.

PALMER S, 1977 — *Mesolithic Cultures of Britain,* Poole, Dolphin Press.

PALMER S, DIMBLEBY G W, 1979 — 'A Mesolithic habitation site on Winfrith Heath, Dorset', *Proc Dorset Natur Hist Archaeol Soc* 101, 27–49.

PERCIVAL J, 1921 — *The wheat plant,* Duckworth, London.

PERCIVAL J, 1934 — *Wheat in Great Britain,* (2nd Edition 1948), Duckworth, London.

PIGOTT C D, 1956 — 'The vegetation of Upper Teesdale in the Northern Pennines', *J Ecol.* 44, 545–586.

PIKE A W, BIDDLE M, 1966 — 'Parasite eggs in Medieval Winchester', *Antiquity* 40, 293–297.

PIKE K V, GODWIN H, 1953 — 'The interglacial at Clacton-on-Sea', *Quart J Geol Soc London* 108, 261–272.

POOLE H F, 1936 — 'Outline of the Mesolithic flint cultures of the Isle of Wight', *Proc Isle of Wight Natur Hist Archaeol Soc* 2, 551, 581.

RADLEY J, MELLARS P, 1964 — 'A Mesolithic structure at Deepcar, Yorkshire, England and the affinities of its associated flint industries', *Proc Prehist Soc* 30, 1–24.

RANKINE W F, 1961 — 'The Mesolithic age in Dorset and adjacent area', *Proc Dorset Natur Hist Archaeol Soc* 83, 91–99.

RANKINE W F, RANKINE W M, DIMBLEBY G W, 1960 — 'Further excavations at a Mesolithic site at Oakhanger, Selborne, Hampshire', *Proc Prehist Soc* 26, 246–262.

RAY A, 1959 — 'The effect of earthworms on pollen distribution', *J Oxford Univ Forestry Soc* 7, 16–21.

READER F W, 1911 — 'A Neolithic floor in the bed of the Crouch River and other discoveries near Rayleigh, Essex', *Essex Naturalist* 16, 249–264.

REID C, 1892   'Pleistocene deposits of the Sussex coast and their equivalents in other districts', *Quart J Geol Soc* 48, 344–361.

REID C, 1893   'A fossiliferous Pleistocene deposit at Stone, on the Hampshire coast', *Quart J Geol Soc* 49, 325–9.

REID C, 1895   'On charred pinewood from Dorset peat mosses', *Proc Dorset Natur Hist Archaeol Soc* 16, 14–16.

REID C, 1896   'An early Neolithic kitchen-midden and tufaceous deposit at Blashenwell near Corfe Castle', *Proc Dorset Natur Hist Archaeol Soc* 17, 67–75.

REID C, 1899   *Origin of the British Flora,* London, Dulace and Co.

REID C, 1902   In St John Hope W H, 'Excavations on the site of the Roman city of Silchester, Hampshire, in 1901: With a note on the plant remains of Roman Silchester', *Archaeologia* 58(1), 17–36.

REID C, 1903   In St John Hope W H, 'Excavations on the site of the Roman city at Silchester, Hants. in 1902', *Archaeologia* 58(2), 425–428.

REID C, 1905   In St John Hope W H and Fox G E, 'Excavations on the site of the Roman city at Silchester, Hants in 1903 and 1904', *Archaeologia* 59(2), 367–370.

REID C, 1906   In St John Hope W H, 'Excavations on the site of the Roman city at Silchester, Hampshire, in 1905', *Archaeologia* 60(1), 164.

REID C, 1907   In St John Hope W H, 'Excavations on the site of the Roman city at Silchester, Hants, in 1906', *Archaeologia* 60(2), 449.

REID C, 1908   In St John Hope W H, 'Excavations on the site of the Roman city of Silchester, Hampshire in 1907', *Archaeologia* 61(1), 210–213.

REID C, 1913   *Submerged forests,* Cambridge University Press.

REID C, 1916   'Plants of the Late Glacial deposits of the Lea Valley', *Quart J Geol Soc* 71(2), 155–161.

REID E M, CHANDLER M E J, 1923a   'The Barrowell Green (Lea Valley) Arctic Flora', *Quart J Geol Soc London* 79, 604–605.

REID E M, CHANDLER M E J, 1923b   'The fossil flora of Clacton-on-Sea', *Quart J Geol Soc London* 79, 619–623.

REID E M, CHANDLER M E J, 1924   'On the occurrence of *Ranunculus hyperboreus* Rottb. in Pleistocene beds at Bembridge, Isle of Wight', *Proc Isle of Wight Natur Hist Archaeol Soc* 1, 292–295.

REID E M, 1949   'The late-glacial flora of the Lea Valley', *New Phytol* 48, 245–252.

RENFREW J M, MONK M, MURPHY P, 1976   *First aid for seeds,* RESCUE publication No. 6.

REYNOLDS P J, 1974   'Experimental Iron Age storage its: an interim report', *Proc Prehist Soc* 40, 118–131.

REYNOLDS P J, 1976   *Farming in the Iron Age*, Cambridge University Press.

REYNOLDS P J, 1979   *Iron-Age farm: the Butser experiment,* Brit Mus publication.

RITCHIE J C, LICHTI–FEDEROVICH S, 1967   'Pollen dispersal phenomena in Arctic-Subarctic Canada', *Rev Palaeobotan Palynol* 3, 255–266.

ROBINSON M A, 1978   'A comparison between the effects of man on the environment of the first gravel terrace and floodplain of the Upper Thames Valley during the Iron Age and Roman periods', in Limbrey S and Evans J G (eds), *The effect of man on the landscape: the lowland zone,* CBA Res Rep 21, 35–43.

ROBINSON M, 1979   In Lambrick G and Robinson M, *Iron Age and Roman riverside settlements at Farmoor, Oxfordshire* CBA Res Rep 32.

ROBINSON M, 1980   In Bradley R, Lobb S, Richards J and Robinson M, 'Two Late Bronze Age settlements on the Kennet Gravels: Excavations at Aldermaston Wharf and Knights Farm, Burghfield, Berkshire', *Proc Prehist Soc* 46, 277–282.

ROBINSON M, 1981   'The Iron Age to early Saxon environment of the Upper Thames terrace', in Jones M and Dimbleby G W (eds), *The environment of man: the Iron Age to the Anglo-Saxon period,* Brit Archaeol Rep (Int Ser) 87, 251–277.

ROBINSON M, 1986   'Waterlogged plant and invertebrate evidence', in Miles, D (ed), *Archaeology at Barton Court Farm, Oxon,* CBA Res Rep 50, microfiche 9:C1–9:C4.

ROBINSON M, HUBBARD R N L B, 1977   'The transport of pollen in bracts of hulled cereals', *J Archaeol Sci* 4, 197–199.

ROSE F, 1953   'A survey of the ecology of the British lowland bogs', *Proc Linn Soc London* 164, 186–211.

ROSKAMS S, 1981   'GPO Newgate Street, 1975–9: The Roman levels', *London Archaeol* 403–407.

SALISBURY E, 1957   'Charcoals' in Burstow G P and Holleyman G A 'Late Bronze Age settlement on Itford Hill, Sussex', *Proc Prehist Soc* 23, 205.

SALISBURY E J, JANE F W, 1940   'Charcoals from Maiden Castle and their significance in relation to the vegetation and climatic conditions in prehistoric times', *J Ecol* 28, 310–325.

SCAIFE R G, 1978   *Unpublished pollen data from peats dredged from the Solent by fishing vessels.*

SCAIFE R G, 1979   *Pollen analytical investigation of Broad Sanctuary, Westminster, London,* AML Report No. 3070.

SCAIFE R G, 1980a   'Pollen analysis' in Basford H V, *The Vectis report: A survey of Isle of Wight Archaeology,* 56–59, Isle of Wight County Council.

SCAIFE R G, 1980b   *Late-Devensian and Flandrian palaeoecological studies in the Isle of Wight,* unpublished PhD thesis, King's College, University of London.

SCAIFE R G, 1980c   *Pollen analysis of some dark earth samples, 1979,* AML Report No. 3001.

SCAIFE R G, 1980d   *Medieval pollen and macroscopic plant remains from Newport, Isle of Wight.* AML Report No. 3102.

SCAIFE R G, 1981a   *Pollen analysis and radiocarbon dating of Willsons Wharf Late Bronze Age and Iron Age peat deposits, Southwark, London,* AML Report No. 3499.

SCAIFE R G, 1981b

In Macphail R I, 'Soil and botanical studies of the 'Dark Earth' ', in Jones M and Dimbleby G W (eds), *The environment of man: the Iron Age to the Anglo-Saxon period*, Brit Archaeol Rep (Brit Ser) 309–331.

SCAIFE R G, 1982a

'Late-Devensian and early Flandrian vegetation changes in southern England', in Limbrey S and Bell M (eds) *Archaeological aspects of Woodland ecology*, Brit Archaeol Rep (Int Ser) 146, 57–74.

SCAIFE R G, 1982b

Pollen analysis of Roman peats underlying the Temple of Mithras, London, AML Report No. 3502.

SCAIFE R G, 1982c

In Mills P S, 'Pollen report' 360–365, in 'Excavations at Broad Sanctuary, Westminster', *Trans London Middlesex Archaeol Soc* 33, 345–365.

SCAIFE R G, 1982d

An early Bronze Age record of Vicia faba, L (horsebean) from Newbarn Down, Isle of Wight, AML Report No. 3501.

SCAIFE R G, 1983a

Palynological analyses of West Heath barrows, V, VII and IX, Sussex, AML Report No. 4002.

SCAIFE R G, 1983b

Interim report on the pollen analysis of Etton Neolithic Causewayed enclosure, AML Report No. 3942.

SCAIFE R G, 1983c

Stratigraphy and preliminary palynological results of peats from Peninsular House, City of London, AML Report No. 4001.

SCAIFE R G, 1983d

'Pollen analysis' in Ayers B and Murphy P, 'A Waterfront excavation at Whitefriars car park, Norwich, 1979', *East Anglian Archaeol* 17, 38–39 (with fiche).

SCAIFE R G, 1983e

Appendix III, in Burrin P, *The character and evolution of flood plains with specific reference to the Ouse and Cuckmere, Sussex*, unpublished PhD thesis, London School of Economics, University of London.

SCAIFE R G, 1983f

'Pollen analysis of ditch peat fill at Etton Neolithic causewayed enclosure' 445–449 in French C A I, *An environmental study of the soil, sediment and molluscan evidence associated with prehistoric monuments on river terrace gravels in North West Cambridgeshire*, unpublished PhD thesis, Institute of Archaeology, University of London.

SCAIFE R G, 1984

Bronze Age soil pollen data from Gallibury Down (formerly Newbarn Down), Isle of Wight, AML Report No. 4240.

SCAIFE R G, 1985

In Drewett P L, 'Excavations of West Heath barrows V–XI, West Sussex', *Sussex Archaeol Collect* 123, 51–59.

SCAIFE R G, forthcoming a

In Preece R C, *Eastham, Worcestershire Pollen data from basal tufas of early Flandrian age*.

SCAIFE R G, forthcoming b

In Tomalin D and Scaife R G, 'The excavation of the first piped-water system at Newport, Isle of Wight and its associated urban palynology'.

SCAIFE R G, forthcoming c

In Wilkinson T J, 'Pollen analytical investigation of a 6m peat section exposed at Mar Dyke, Essex during M25 motorway construction'.

SCAIFE R G, BURRIN P J, 1983

'Floodplain development in and the vegetational history of the Sussex High Weald and some archaeological implications', *Sussex Archaeol Collect* 121, 1–10.

SCAIFE R G, MACPHAIL R I, 1983   'The post-Devensian development of heathland soils and vegetation'. In Burnham P (ed), *'Soils of the heathlands and chalklands'*, South East Soils Discussion Group (SEESOIL) 1, 70–99.

SCAIFE R G, TOMALIN D J, 1979   'A Neolithic flint assemblage and associated palynological sequence at Gatcombe, Isle of Wight', *Proc Hampshire Fld Clb Archaeol Soc* 36, 25–33.

SEAGRIEF S C, 1956   *A pollen-analytic investigation of the Quaternary period in Britain,* unpublished PhD thesis, University of Cambridge.

SEAGRIEF S C, 1959   'Pollen diagrams from Southern England: Wareham, Dorset and Nursling, Hampshire', *New Phytol* 58, 316–325.

SEAGRIEF S C, 1960   'Pollen diagrams from Southern England: Cranes Moor, Hampshire', *New Phytol* 59, 73–83.

SEAGRIEF S C, GODWIN H, 1960   'Pollen diagrams from Southern England: Elstead, Surrey', *New Phytol* 59, 84–91.

SERNANDER R, 1908   'On the evidence of post-glacial changes of climate furnished by the peat mosses of Northern Europe', *Geol Fören Stock Förh* 30, 465–478.

SHACKLEY M L, 1976   'Palaeoenvironmental evidence from a late third millennium BC peat bed at New Shide Bridge, Isle of Wight', *J Archaeol Sci* 3, 385–390.

SHELDON J, 1978   'The environmental background', in Drewett P L (ed), *Archaeology in Sussex to AD 1500,* CBA Res Rep 29, 3–7.

SHENNAN S J, SCHADLA HALL R T, 1981   *The archaeology of Hampshire from the palaeolithic to the Industrial Revolution,* Hampshire Fld Clb Archaeol Soc Monogr 1.

SIDAWAY R, 1964   'A buried peat deposit at Litton Cheney', *Proc Dorset Natur Hist Archaeol Soc* 85, 78–86.

SIMS R E, 1973   'The anthropogenic factor in East Anglian vegetational history: an approach using APF techniques', in Birks H J B and West R G (eds), *Quaternary Plant Ecology,* Blackwells, Oxford, 223–236.

SIMS R E, 1978   'Man and Vegetation in Norfolk', in Limbrey S and Evans J G (eds), *The effect of man in the landscape: the lowland zone,* CBA Res Rep 21, 57–62.

SIMMONS I G, 1964   'Pollen diagrams from Dartmoor', *New Phytol* 63, 165–180.

SIMMONS I G, 1969   'Environment and early man on Dartmoor, Devon, England', *Proc Prehist Soc* 35, 203–219.

SIMMONS I G, 1975a   'Towards an ecology of Mesolithic man in the uplands of Great Britain', *J Archaeol Sci* 2, 1–15.

SIMMONS I G, 1975b   'The ecological setting of Mesolithic man in the highland zone', in Evans J G and Limbrey S (eds), *The effect of man on the landscape: the highland zone* CBA Res Rep 11, 57–63.

SIMMONS I G, DIMBLEBY G W, 1974   'The possible role of ivy (*Hedera Helix* L) in the Mesolithic economy of Western Europe', *J Archaeol Sci* 1, 291–296.

SIMMONS I G, TOOLEY M (eds), 1981

The environment in British Prehistory Duckworth, London.

SMITH A G, 1958

'Pollen analytical investigation of the mire at Fallahogy Td, Co Derry', *Proc Roy Ir Acad B* 59, 329–343.

SMITH A G, 1970

'The influence of Mesolithic and Neolithic man on British vegetation: a discussion', in Walker D and West R E (eds), *Studies in the Vegetational history of the British Isles,* 81–96, Cambridge University Press.

SMITH A G, 1981

'The Neolithic', in Simmons, I G, and Tooley, M J, *The environment in British prehistory*, 125–209, Duckworth, London.

SMITH A G, PILCHER J R, 1973

'Radiocarbon dates and the vegetational history of the British Isles', *New Phytol* 72, 903–914.

SMITH I F, 1979

Long barrows in Hampshire and the Isle of Wight, Royal Commission on Historical Monuments, HMSO London, 70–71.

SMITH I F, *et al*, 1964

'New Neolithic sites in Dorset and Bedfordshire with a note on the distribution of Neolithic storage pits in Britain', *Proc Prehist Soc* 30, 352–382.

SPARKS B W, WEST R G, 1963

'The interglacial deposit at Stutton, Suffolk', *Proc Geol Ass* 74, 419–32.

SPARKS B W, WEST R G, 1970

'Late pleistocene deposits at Wretton, Norfolk, I. Ipswichian interglacial deposits', *Phil Trans Roy Soc London B* 258, 1–30.

SPARKS B W, WEST R G, WILLIAMS R B G, RANSOM M, 1969

'Hoxnian interglacial deposits near Hatfield, Herts', *Proc Geol Ass* 80, 243–267.

SPRATT D A, SIMMONS I G, 1976

'Prehistoric activity and environment on the North York Moors', *J Archaeol Sci* 3, 193–210.

STEVENS L A, 1960

'The interglacial of the Nar Valley, Norfolk', *Quart J Geol Soc London* 115, 291–316.

SUGGATE R, WILLIS E, 1958

'Radiocarbon dating of the eustatic rise in ocean level', *Nature* (London) 181, 1518–1519.

SUTCLIFF A J, 1976

'The British glacial-interglacial sequence', *Quat Newsl* 18, 1–7.

TANSLEY A, 1949

The British Isles and their vegetation, Cambridge University Press.

TAUBER H, 1965

'Differential pollen dispersion and the interpretation of pollen diagrams', *Danm geol Unders* II 89, 1–69.

TAUBER H, 1967a

'Investigation of the mode of pollen transfer in forested areas', *Rev Palaeobot Palynol* 3, 277–287.

TAUBER H, 1967b

'Differential pollen dispersion and filtration', *Proc Congr Int Ass Quat Res* 7, 131–134.

TEICHERT C, 1958

'Some biostratigraphical concepts', *Bull Geol Soc Am* 69, 99–120.

TEN HOVE H A, 1968

'The Ulmus fall at the transition Atlanticum-Suboreal in pollen diagrams', *Palaeogeog palaeoclim palaeoecol* 5, 359–469.

TERS M, 1973

'Les Variations du niveau marin depuis 10,000 ans, le long du littoral Atlantique Francais', in *Le Quaternaire: geodynamique, stratigraphie et environment.* Christchurch NZ. Congress International de L'INQUA, 114–135.

THOMAS K D, 1982 — 'Neolithic enclosures and woodland habitats on the South Downs in Sussex, England', in Bell M and Limbrey S (eds), *Archaeological aspects of woodland ecology,* Brit Archaeol Rep (Int ser) 146, 147–170.

THOMPSON M W, ASHBEE P, 1957 — 'Excavation of a barrow near the Hardy Monument, Black Down, Portesham, Dorset', *Proc Prehist Soc* 23, 124–136.

THORLEY A, 1971a — *An investigation into the post-glacial history of native tree species in South East England using the pollen analysis technique,* unpublished PhD dissertation, King's College, University of London.

THORLEY A, 1971b — 'Vegetational history of the Vale of Brooks', *Inst Br Geog Conf* Part 5, 47–50.

THORLEY A, 1981 — 'Pollen analytical evidence relating to the vegetation history of the chalk', *J Biogeog* 8, 93–106.

TILLEY A, unpublished — *Pollen data from Cranes Moor, Hants,* Department of Geography, University of Southampton.

TOMALIN D J, 1979 — 'Barrow excavation in the Isle of Wight', *Current Archaeol* 68, 273–276.

TOMALIN D J, 1980 — 'The Neolithic' in Basford H V, *The Vectis Report: A survey of Isle of Wight Archaeology,* 15–17, Isle of Wight County Council.

TOMALIN D J, forthcoming — *Excavation of a Bronze Age barrow on Gallibury Down, Isle of Wight.*

TOMALIN D J, SCAIFE R G, 1979 — 'A Neolithic flint assemblage and associated palynological sequence at Gatcombe, Isle of Wight', *Proc Hampshire Fld Clb Archaeol Soc* 36, 25–33.

TROELS–SMITH J, 1954 — 'Ertebollekultur–Bondekulture', *Åarb Nord Oldkynd Hist,* 1953, 5–62.

TROELS–SMITH J, 1955 — 'Pollenanalytischen Untersuchungen Zur einigen Schweizerischen Pfahlbauproblemen', in Guyan W U (ed) (Herausgeber), *Monographien zur ur und Frühgeschichte der Schweiz,* Basel 11, 59–88.

TROELS–SMITH J, 1956 — 'Neolithic period in Switzerland and Denmark', *Science,* New York 124, 876–879.

TROELS–SMITH J, 1960 — 'Ivy, mistletoe and elm. Climatic indicators – fodder plants', *Danm geol Unders* IV 4, 1–32.

TUBBS C R, DIMBLEBY G W, 1965 — 'Early agriculture in the New Forest', *Advancement of Science* 22, 88–97.

TURNER C, 1970 — 'The Middle Pleistocene deposits at Marks Tey, Essex', *Phil Trans Roy Soc B* 257, 373–435.

TURNER J, 1964 — 'The anthropogenic factor in vegetational history. I. Tregaron and Whixall Mosses', *New Phytol* 63, 73–90.

TURNER J, 1970 — 'Post-Neolithic disturbances of British vegetation', in Walker D and West R G (eds), *Studies in the Vegetational history of the British Isles* 97–116, Cambridge University Press.

TURNER J, HEWETSON V P, HIBBERT F A, LOWRY K H, CHAMBERS C, 1973 — 'The history of the vegetation and flora of Widdybank Fell and the Cow Green reservoir basin, Upper Teesdale', *Phil Trans Roy Soc London B* 265, 327–408.

VON–POST L, 1916   'Om skogstradspollen i sydenvenstia torfmosselager-folider (foredrags referat)', *Geol För Stock Förh* 38, 384–394.

WALKER D, 1953   'The interglacial deposit at Histon Road, Cambridge', *Quart J Geol Soc London* 108, 273–282.

WARREN S H, 1919   'The dating of surface flint implements and the evidence of the submerged peat surface', *Proc Prehist Soc* 3, 94–104.

WARREN S H, CLARKE J G D, GODWIN H, GODWIN M E, MACFADYEN W A, 1934   'An early Mesolithic site at Broxbourne sealed under Boreal peat', *J Roy Anthrop Inst* 64, 101–28.

WARREN S H *et al.*, 1936   'Archaeology of the submerged land-surface of the Essex coast', *Proc Prehist Soc* 2, 178–210.

WATON P V, 1980   'Rimsmoor, Dorset: pollen record from late Boreal to present in eighteen metres of peat', *Quat Newsl* No 30, 25.

WATON P V, 1982a   'Man's impact on the chalklands: some new pollen evidence', in Bell M and Limbrey S (eds) *Archaeological aspects of Woodland Ecology,* Brit Archaeol Rep (Int Ser) 146, 75–91.

WATON P V, 1982b   *A palynological study of the impact of man on the landscape of Central Southern England with special reference to the chalklands,* unpublished PhD Thesis, Department of Geography, University of Southampton.

WATTS D, 1961   'Post-Atlantic forests in Ireland', *Proc Linn Soc London* 172, 33–38.

WEBB J A, 1972   *A palynological study of a valley bog in Hothfield Common (Ashfield) Series,* unpublished BSc thesis, Department of plant sciences, King's College, University of London.

WEST I M, 1980   'Geology of the Solent estuarine system', in *The Solent Estuarine System: An assessment of present knowledge* NERC publication series C No. 22, 6–19.

WEST R G, 1954   'The Hoxne Interglacial reconsidered', *Nature* (London), 187.

WEST R G, 1956a   'Vegetational history of the Early Pleistocene of the Royal Society Borehole at Ludham, Norfolk', *Proc Roy Soc London B* 155, 437–453.

WEST R G, 1956b   'The Quaternary deposits at Hoxne, Suffolk', *Phil Trans Roy Soc London B* 239, 265–356.

WEST R G, 1957   'Interglacial deposits at Bobbitshole, Ipswich', *Phil Trans Roy Soc London B* 241, 1–31.

WEST R G, 1961   'Interglacial and interstadial vegetation in England', *Proc Linn Soc* 172, 81–89.

WEST R G, 1964   'Interglacial deposits at Ilford, Essex', *Phil Trans Roy Soc London B* 247, 185–212.

WEST R G, 1969   'Pollen analyses from interglacial deposits at Aveley and Grays, Essex', *Proc Geol Ass* 80, 271–282.

WEST R G, 1970a   'Pollen zones in the pleistocene of Great Britain and their correlations', *New Phytol* 69, 1179–1183.

WEST R G, 1970b   'Pleistocene history of the British flora', in Walker D and West R G (eds) *Studies in the Vegetational history of the British Isles,* 1–11, Cambridge University Press.

WEST R G, 1972   'Relative land sea level changes in South East England during the pleistocene', *Phil Trans Roy Soc London A* 272, 87–98.

WEST R G, 1976   In Skempton A W and Weeks A G, 'The Quaternary history of the Lower Greensand escarpment and Weald Clay Vale near Sevenoaks, Kent' 513, *Phil Trans Roy Soc London A* 283, 493–526.

WEST R G, 1980   *Pre-glacial pleistocene vegetation and stratigraphy of the East Anglian Coast,* Cambridge University Press.

WEST R G, McBURNEY C M B, 1954   'The Quaternary deposits at Hoxne, Suffolk and their archaeology', *Proc Prehist Soc* 20, 131–154.

WEST R G, SPARKS B W, 1960   'Coastal interglacial deposits of the English Channel', *Phil Trans Roy Soc London B* 243, 95–133.

WEST R G, WILSON G, 1966   'Cromer forest bed series', *Nature* (London) 209, 497–8.

WHITE H J O, 1921   *Geology of the Isle of Wight,* HMSO London.

WILLCOX G H, 1977   'Exotic plants from Roman waterlogged sites in London', *J Archaeol Sci* 4, 269–282.

WILLIAMS D, 1976a   'Preliminary observations on the use of flotation apparatus in Sussex', in Drewett P L (ed) 'Rescue archaeology in Sussex' *Inst Archaeol Bull* 13, 51–59.

WILLIAMS D, 1976b   'A Neolithic moss flora from Silbury Hill, Wiltshire', *J Archaeol Sci* 3, 267–270.

WILLMOT A, 1968   *The palynological and stratigraphical record of Ockley Bog, Thursley Common,* unpublished undergraduate dissertation, Department of Plant Studies, University of London.

WILSON D G, 1975   'Plant remains from the Graveney boat and the early history of *Humulus lupulus* L in W Europe', *New Phytol* 75, 627–648.

WOODCOCK A G, 1978a   'The archaeological material from Ameys Pit, Eartham, Boxgrove', *Brighton polytechnic Geog Soc* 4, 9–10.

WOODCOCK A G, 1978b   'The palaeolithic in Sussex' in Drewett P L (ed), *Archaeology in Sussex to AD 1500,* CBA Res Rep 29, 8–14.

WOODCOCK A G, 1981   *The lower and middle palaeolithic periods in Sussex,* Brit Archaeol Rep (Brit Series) 94, 418 pp.

WOOLDRIDGE S W, GOLDRING F, 1953   *The Weald,* London, Collins.

WOOLDRIDGE S W, LINTON D L, 1933   'The loam terraces of South East England and their relation to its early history', *Antiquity* 7, 297–310.

WOOLDRIDGE S W, LINTON D L, 1955   *Structure surface and drainage in South East England,* (1955, 1964, 1968 impressions) G Philip and Son, London.

WYMER J J, 1962   'Excavations at the Maglemosian Sites at Thatcham, Berkshire, England', *Proc Prehist Soc* 28, 329–361.

ZEUNER F E, 1946   *Dating the past: an introduction to geochronology,* Methuen, London.

ZEUNER F E, 1959   *The Pleistocene Period,* Hutchinson, London.

Chapter 4

ARCHAEOZOOLOGY IN WESSEX
Vertebrate remains and marine molluscs
and their relevance to archaeology

Jennie Coy and Mark Maltby

Introduction

Archaeozoology

This review discusses the study of animal bones in Wessex. Marine shells have only been systematically studied for a few settlements but are included here as most of the remarks made for bones apply to some extent to shells as well.

The investigation of bones and shells from archaeological excavations does not fit easily into what is today often called 'environmental archaeology'. This is because, although clues to the surrounding environment may accumulate from their study, bones and shells are normally associated with settlement activities. Collection is usually from excavated contexts within settlements whereas sampling for, e.g., terrestrial molluscs and pollen, may be from the surrounding terrain and from buried soils and can therefore be more directly related to physiographic areas or ecosystems.

On the other hand the breadth of information which can be extracted from bone fragments is greater than for most other environmental material. As well as providing information to complement that from the other environmental archaeology disciplines, bones can answer other questions – relating, for example, to diet; use of skin, horn, bone, and antler; domestication; animal improvements and husbandry; settlement organisation and activities; ritual and dietary taboos; and redistribution of animals and their products. Bone fragments may also become artefacts. In addition, incremental information from bones, teeth, and shells has potential for the study of seasonality, climate, and husbandry.

Archaeozoology (the study of animal remains from archaeological excavations) is now studied as a science in most countries of the developed world. It now links itself more and more closely with the philosophy and techniques of archaeology. These links, especially with rescue archaeology, are better in Britain than in many other countries and much of this review is an account of a joint evolution that has taken place over recent years.

Wessex

The region referred to as 'Wessex' in this review is the Council for British Archaeology's Group 12 Area comprising Wiltshire, Dorset, Hampshire, Isle of Wight, and Berkshire. Geographically Wessex has little meaning except as a region for military purposes, civil defence, censuses, electricity boards, or economic planning (in each case it never quite coincides with the Group 12 area). To the historian it usually means the Saxon kingdom of Alfred. To many the name evokes the world of Thomas Hardy's Wessex novels. Archaeologically too, Wessex has varied in size from the small area associated with the 'Wessex culture' (Piggott 1938) to a region that also included Somerset, Gloucestershire, and Surrey (Grinsell 1958).

Using Europe as a framework Wessex is geographically, in the greater part, an extension of the lowlands of Holland and Northern France with the separation of Britain and the Isle of Wight phases in post-glacial development. The study of animal remains, like that of archaeology, cannot be divorced from continental European studies. Bones can make an important contribution to the study of trade as well as to comparative studies. For example, comparisons between material from Saxon Southampton (Hamwic) and Dorstat, Holland, and between medieval Winchester and Normandy have provided interesting contrasts, stimulating wide-ranging discussions about their implications.

Within Britain, Wessex has many features in common with other parts of lowland Britain although agricultural activities may have been influenced by the mildness in parts of the region which are today climatically unmatched except by parts of the South West, and west Wales.

The geographical variety of Wessex is worth a brief description here. Most of Wessex consists of a fairly definite physical region – the **Hampshire Drainage Basin** – which includes some smaller, more westerly, basins and their drainage areas. This is sometimes known as Central Southern England and as such comprises most of Dorset, the south-eastern half of Wiltshire, most of Hampshire, and small portions of Somerset and west Sussex.

Within this the **chalk uplands** represent a definable area, with its own survival problems in hard winters and dry summers, but with great variety; the differences between valley bottom, downland, and hill-slope added to climatic alleviation near the coast, produce a complex pattern of zones, and, presumably, a variety of human and animal adaptations.

The **tertiary lowlands** are even more complicated, consisting of river valleys, coastal alluvium, gravel plateaux, heathlands, and heavy clay woodlands. The coastline itself is one of the most varied in the British Isles. Although it has been subjected to extensive modern ecological studies — something that will help the formulation of archaeological theories within the region — these primarily demonstrate the great complexity of the ecosystems involved.

Clay vales provide both unity and diversity and might be regarded as a sub-region in themselves. Their agricultural potential is important, each major town in them having a very different hinterland and important links with it.

Town sub-regions provide a major contribution to material remains available for study in Wessex and the position and significance of **Southampton** and **Winchester** demand special attention. If both France and Britain are included in the backcloth, Southampton is very near the centre of the area with a position of centrality of extra-European significance and an expanding range through medieval history. The north west coast of France has also for long been closely linked economically. Documentary evidence from medieval Southampton points to the considerable European, Mediterranean, and (via Italian merchants) even more extensive trading. The significance of trade for bones has been discussed elsewhere (Coy 1982a).

Southampton Water, topographically a drowned river valley and, with respect to salinity, a partially mixed estuary (Dyer 1973), provides a complexity of ecosystems which makes environmental interpretation for Southampton today difficult enough (N.E.R.C. 1980) and simplistic statements about the past dangerous. The complex interface here between sea and rivers combines with particular climatic advantages compared with most of Wessex. The Southampton area sometimes receives the high temperatures of the warmest parts of the South West without the high level of rainfall.

Winchester has served as a major market and administrative centre, being at times of regional, national, or even international significance. The geographical and ecological relationships of Winchester and Southampton are of more than regional significance. Cultural and ecological differences will prove difficult to disentangle through study of the faunal remains from Winchester and Southampton but it is important to make the attempt.

The role of other town sub-regions within Wessex in the Medieval and Post-medieval Periods is still relatively unknown. Excavation in other Wessex towns such as Dorchester, Christchurch, Poole, Alton, Newbury, Romsey, and Andover are providing much information, including that from bones although access to material, as for Southampton and Winchester, is almost solely as a result of development and therefore subject only to limited research design.

Any faunal remains from the **Isle of Wight** might be expected to shed light on its relatively unknown past and by comparison give insight into mainland interpretation. Geographically it provides a complexity all of its own which makes it a geologists' and ecologists' laboratory. Its potential for the testing of archaeological theories, including those relating to archaeozoology, is so far relatively unrealised.

Such geographical discussions are ultimately of crucial relevance to faunal work and this account is included here to set a regional and sub-regional background to the ensuing archaeozoological discussions. Their relevance will be taken up again in the final section.

Past developments in archaeozoology in Wessex

Palaeontological studies

This is not the place for a discussion of all the post-glacial palaeontological evidence for vertebrates and marine molluscs from Wessex, although the archaeozoological picture must always be viewed against the background of developing knowledge of post-glacial fauna as a whole.

The development of archaeozoology in Wessex as in the rest of Britain was partly rooted in palaeontological studies of fossil vertebrate remains from valley gravels and cave deposits. During the nineteenth century the foundations of the work in terms of accuracy of identification and precise recording of context were taking place. The remains of 'Claudius' elephants' were shown by Owen to be bones of the cave bear; Buckland recanted and his 'relics of the flood' were recognised as bones from valley gravels, subjected to searching study and restudy, and carefully documented in local journals such as the *Wiltshire Archaeological and Natural History Magazine*. With the close link between Natural History and Archaeology that existed in the local societies of the time much discussion took place on whether or not remains such as those of the aurochs, *Bos primigenius*, in the Wessex gravels, were associated with evidence of man. However, contextual mistakes were often made.

Since that time palaeontology has moved on and the study of post-glacial mammals has now been firmly integrated to include evidence from palaeontology, archaeology, and modern mammal populations by such workers as Yalden (1982), who includes a discussion of the important Mesolithic material from Thatcham, Berkshire.

The origins of archaeozoology

Excellent tools for osteologists developed during the mid-nineteenth century, such as the accumulation of comparative skeleton collections (now often dispersed) in museums and universities and the publication of works on comparative osteology, fuelled by evolutionary studies of the age. On the continent this was the time of the pioneering archaeozoological work of Rütimeyer on the fauna of the Swiss Lake Villages.

Pitt-Rivers' treatment of animal bones from Cranborne Chase set a standard for much future Wessex work and established the importance of measuring bones and comparing them for size with 'standards' of known modern breeds (e.g. Pitt-Rivers 1887, Vol I, 171; Vol. II, 209; 1898 Vol. IV, 208).

By the early years of the twentieth century Pitt-Rivers' work and that of Ewart in the North had firmly established archaeozoology as a supporting speciality in the developing science of archaeology in what has been called the 'Relic and Monument Phase' of archaeological investigation (Binford 1981, 4).

The work of J W Jackson

Dr J Wilfrid Jackson produced many specialist reports for archaeologists between 1913 and 1961. The major ones have been listed by Bishop (1982). Many of them were for key Wessex excavations – e.g. All Cannings Cross Farm, Wiltshire; Woodhenge, Wiltshire; Maiden Castle, Dorset; and the Glastonbury Lake Village. In his numerous shorter papers Jackson frequently referred to these key reports. He was also very much aware of the work of Pitt-Rivers, that of Rütimeyer and Ewart, and the evolution of archaeological theories; his 1948 Little Woodbury report, for example, discusses Clark's paper on sheep and swine husbandry (Clark 1947).

Jackson's work was important and influential in the development of archaeozoology and its relationship with archaeology in Britain. He was himself an experienced excavator and his writings reflect the care which he took to find parallels (both in Britain and abroad) for the bones he studied. Jackson cannot be criticised for the fact that archaeologists often read too much into these parallels.

His work established the basic format of a 'bone report' which would consist of a listing of identified bone for the different phases of the site, their dimensions and breed parallels, and a note of any pathological and genetic abnormalities – he noted the presence of hornless cattle and those lacking mandibular second premolars and third molar cusps in the Wessex Iron Age.

Jackson noted the relative absence of sheep on Neolithic sites but his discussion of specific ratios was never firmly based. He sometimes acknowledged this by suggesting that larger samples would be needed to investigate this aspect. Animal sizes were also much discussed and Jackson was one of the first to detail a decrease in cattle size during the prehistoric period. Examination for butchery marks was cursory but it was important for the time that he should have suggested that bones were food remains as indicated by their broken state and by splitting of skulls and longbones, moreover he occasionally mentions butchery marks on individual bones as having been made when 'disjointing' or 'stripping off flesh'.

The uses of animals are discussed but Jackson's recognition of butchery on dog bones at Highfield pit dwellings did not lead him to suggest that they were eaten but he puts forward that the main use of horses at Little Woodbury would be traction, with no supporting evidence from the bones, showing an overprojection of twentieth century lifestyles back into the past. Jackson often implies other uses of animals, past functions of particular archaeological features, and the seasonality of certain deposits. His work should be examined critically because such analysis facilitates an appreciation of the conceptual shifts which have taken place as archaeozoology has evolved.

In many of the site reports to which Jackson contributed there is an associated account of the bone and antler objects. The original material is usually identified to species and anatomical element where possible. In this, and in many other ways, the archaeological reports of the first half of this century are the culmination of a co-operative effort between archaeologists and specialists. Although writing basically zoological bone reports, Jackson appreciated the complexities of archaeological stratigraphy and phasing and was aware of contemporary developments in archaeological theory and method. He lived into the 'rescue archaeology' era and most of the work discussed below, which owed something to the foundations he had laid, was written in his lifetime.

Postwar developments

Although considerable excavation of animal bone continued after the main period of Jackson's work into the early 1970s and excavators continued to procure bone reports, there was as yet little involvement of bone analysts in research design before and during excavation. During this time Addyman saved bones from Ludgershall Castle and Southampton, Biddle from Winchester, Collis from Owslebury, Cunliffe from Portchester, and Wainwright from Mount Pleasant, Marden, Durrington Walls and Gussage All Saints. But the specialists to study their material were not then always available and little was done to continue the really close integration with archaeology seen in the prewar years or to encourage developments in archaeozoology.

Archaeozoological reports written for excavations which took place in Wessex from c1957 to 1975 suffered considerable publication delays. Despite these factors Harcourt's work provided a valuable approach to zoological and veterinary matters (e.g. Harcourt 1969; 1971a; 1971b; 1979a; 1979b; AML Report 1626). He was, however, unable to publish such systematic records of bone fragmentation and the frequencies of the different anatomical elements as did Grant (1971; 1975; 1976; 1977). In the last of these reports Grant mentions the many factors which affect the bone assemblage – fragmentation, gnawing, butchery, erosion, and evidence of different kinds of human activity, although these were not systematically recorded. Her analysis of the very large sample of bones from Danebury and the final Portchester volume are shortly to be published.

It is symptomatic of both the rapid progress of archaeozoology and the state of the archaeological publication backlog (Wainwright 1982, 25) that we are now having to plan retrieval of bones for new excavations in Wessex before we have the results from the old.

In 1975 the Faunal Remains Project (FRP) was set up at the Department of Archaeology, University of Southampton, with a contract from the Ancient Monuments Laboratory (AML) of the Department of the Environment. After some years spent analysing both backlog and recently-excavated material the Research Aims of the Project were restated in 1980 as an attempt to work along the following lines:

To obtain an appreciation of *continuity and change* in the wild and domestic species in Wessex and their exploitation through time, paying particular attention to changes which might have occurred during long periods of supposed stability and to interfaces between recognised periods.

Investigation of the significance of *urban/rural differences* in some periods.

Investigation of the changes in exploitation of *wild versus domestic animals*.

Some attempt to discover the relative role of *marine resources* – especially marine fish and Mollusca.

Some investigation of more *specialised techniques* from other sciences which might be useful in archaeozoology in Wessex.

A full discussion of these aims in 1980 stressed the importance of obtaining a final assessment of phasing from the archaeologist before bone work began. This phasing would rely on full stratigraphic information, typology of other finds, especially pottery, and radiocarbon dates where available. Although it was clear that bones would ultimately play a role in defining such phases, in the current state of archaeology there was a need to study clearly stratified and securely dated groups of bones in order to build up knowledge of the basic characteristics that went with particular periods. This was necessary before changes in husbandry which did not mirror changes in other attributes of a settlement (e.g. buildings, pots, documents) could be identified.

The Project's work is still focussed on these aims, particularly the investigation of continuity and change, with considerable attention being given to detailed analyses within the Iron Age and Saxon periods.

During the whole of its existence, however, the approach of the FRP has continually been adapted to take account of the rapid changes taking place in the discipline of archaeozoology. In particular, our own experience and the work of others have repeatedly demonstrated that the aims outlined above cannot be achieved without a full appreciation of the factors that create variability in our samples. The following section on 'recent developments and current themes' is therefore structured to show how recent Wessex work has attempted to analyse such variability in order to remove the biases in the data. This in turn ensures more reliable answers to the broader questions relating to animal exploitation (many of which are the same ones asked by Jackson). An attempt has been made below to show that more reliable answers are becoming available, at least for the Iron Age, Romano-British, and Saxon periods.

Recent developments and current themes

Archaeozoology in the 1980s – A change in concepts

The conceptual shifts which have taken place between monument-based research at Cranborne Chase and the type of archaeological study taking place today have been discussed by many proponents of the 'New Archaeology'. Intrinsically linked with modern archaeological developments is the concern to develop a better understanding of the formation of archaeological assemblages by developing methodologies based on rigorous and scientific analysis of the data from fieldwork and excavation. Such 'middle range research' is

'designed to control for the relationship between dynamic properties of the past about which one seeks knowledge and the static material properties common to the past and the present'

(Binford 1981, 29)

It involves experimental, rather than inferential, studies. These must be intellectually independent of our general theories of the past, something very difficult to achieve and archaeozoology is no exception. The very decisions on *which* data to collect are inextricably bound up with general theories or assumptions. Jackson's results and some postwar work in Wessex had been used by archaeologists to infer wide-ranging theories (e.g. Murray 1970) which made it difficult to develop methods for investigating faunal remains in intellectually independent ways. This independence must be the hallmark of any progressive archaeozoology.

Binford's discussions on changing conceptual frameworks relating to faunal remains suggest that we should now stop treating hunter-gatherer sites as if they were monuments and referring everything in them as relating to man (Binford 1981, 18). If we extend his ideas to cover all archaeological settlements they clarify the difference between Jackson's studies discussed above and more recent studies of faunal assemblages in Wessex. To Jackson a frog skeleton required no comment, he sensibly did not *assume* it was part of the diet but neither did he say it was not — all his comments related to animals used by people and were interwoven with current assumptions about the type of people who lived at that settlement type.

But the faunal remains, their state of preservation, fragmentation, and their final deposition are not necessarily related to human activity. Neither are they solely evidence of past ecosystems or kill populations of domestic animals.

An alternative theoretical framework can be based on what Binford calls the 'reality of the assemblage' (Binford 1978, 70). These ideas have been more fully discussed elsewhere for urban settlements (Coy 1982a, 108). The following sections should be seen in the light of these conceptual changes in archaeology and the consequent use of faunal remains as a tool for understanding the formation of archaeological assemblages.

The successive sources of bias and change which intervene between populations of animals exploited and the bone fragments available for study may be listed as 'cultural practices', 'disposal strategies', 'post-depositional taphonomic processes', 'methods of recovery and analysis', and 'research design' (Maltby, in preparation 1). These are dealt with in reverse order in the following sections as this order logically follows the investigative procedures involved.

Research design and archaeological excavation

Archaeological investigation in Wessex usually begins with a research design. Its significance to the study of bones will first be discussed under 'site choice' and then under 'retrieval strategies on site'. But it is necessary first to discuss 'sampling'.

Sampling

Sampling is an aspect of research design. It follows a deliberate decision to retrieve only a part of the available information and to use this to interpret the whole by invoking statistical sampling theory. The reliability with which the sample can be used to predict the whole is thus quantified. All archaeological research design involves sampling at some or all of the stages from site choice to sample treatment. Appreciation in Britain of the relevance of sampling theory to archaeology has been slow compared with its development in America. In 1977 a conference on sampling was held at Southampton and attended by many Wessex archaeologists (Cherry *et al.* 1978).

The bone analyst must be aware of the effects of these successive 'choices' on the sample finally received and aspects of sampling permeate any discussion of recent developments in archaeozoology. They form part of the middle range research already mentioned. Most middle range research uses virtually the same data needed for the final archaeological interpretations (animal species, utilisation, animal husbandry . . .) but uses it in different ways.

Sampling is often regarded as a way of studying only a part of the material and thus cutting costs but it is better to regard it as an aspect of research design. It should be possible to work out the sample size needed to answer each specific question and thus avoid unnecessary expense. For bones, however, with their very large variety in species, anatomical elements and fragment types, and types of evidence, there is no escape from the need to study thousands of fragments from each settlement, unless all that is required is a species list.

Although earlier bone workers appreciated that sampling occurred and often lamented the loss of certain material it is really only in the past decade that any systematic measurement of the relationship between samples and their original populations has played any part in animal bone studies in Wessex. The involvement of sampling theory is assumed throughout the following discussions.

Site Choice

Theoretical frameworks now control to some extent the policies behind site choice in Wessex. Rescue demands currently supply the other control. Site bias caused by rescue archaeology was discussed in 1976 (Coy, 1983b; the manuscript is AML Report 2649). Justification of site choice in Wessex has really only become an issue in the last few years and is related to the development of regional policies (Wessex Archaeological Committee n.d.) and the need to relate to DoE project funding.

Archaeozoological considerations do not usually form a major factor in site choice as the periods and places about which archaeologists know least tend to be gaps in archaeozoological knowledge too. As in archaeology in Wessex generally, however, there are some priorities and attempts are being made at FRP to stress the importance of some topics identified in the Research Aims of the FRP discussed earlier. They include a concentration on any new Bronze Age and Neolithic bones, that from specific period interfaces, and rural rather than urban material in the Roman and

Medieval (including Saxon) Periods. The need to answer even more specific archaeological and archaeozoological questions is also now more likely to influence site choice.

Retrieval Strategies on Site

Once sites are selected for excavation there is often now in Wessex a detailed discussion of excavation strategy; which parts of the area will be excavated and in what detail. Bone analysts are involved in this and advise on needs for sampling the different feature types for bones. The *sieving of bulk soil samples* may form a part of this.

Sieving strategies in Wessex over recent years have played an essential role in the evolution of a more scientific attitude towards research design on site. Retrieval strategies at Winchester in the 1970s were developed to include the sieving of bulk samples for botanical remains – a practice initiated by Green (1979). Parallel archaeobotanical work took place on rural Hampshire settlements and at Hamwic (Saxon Southampton) by Peter Murphy and Mick Monk, respectively. These affected bone retrieval as the samples were wet-sieved for bones as well. For bones, small scale sieving has advantages over the use of sieving machines and standard c5000cm^3 samples are now used for some excavations (Coy 1978a, 17).

Properly executed, such sieving can offer a baseline of total retrieval of all vertebrate species for a consistent but small sub-sample against which the rest of the bone from the same deposit can be seen in its 'manually' or 'normally' retrieved state.

Alterations in all aspects of sampling procedure, including sieving, prove necessary during excavation in order to cover particular feature types or because of the need to answer specific questions e.g. deposit volumes may be necessary in order to calculate the density of bone deposition. The relationship between any sieved samples and the original deposit in terms of volumes must be known.

One poorly investigated topic which bulk sampling is illuminating (by total retrieval of offcuts) is that of bone-working, as in analysis of the Roman bone-working activities at Crowder Terrace, Winchester, and mid-Saxon bone-working areas at Six Dials, Hamwic.

Doubts about the reliability of normal retrieval strategies for the interpretation of Saxon animal husbandry were expressed by Bourdillon and Coy (1980, 121) as a result of work in 1976 at Hamwic. Eventually this led to the excavation of a single pit at Hamwic by Sarah Colley in 1981 with complete sieving through 600mμ sieves (Colley AML Reports 3880 and 4071). The results of this study can now be used as a basis for the assessment of the quality of retrieval in the rest of Hamwic.

Comparison can be made between the type of material retrieved in the pit by the very careful trowelling with what was missed (and later retrieved by sieving). This is leading to a careful, quantitative assessment of the deposits in what the archaeologists suspect are different phases of pits and different pit types (Coy AML Report 3881). It also aids appreciation of the bias introduced at Hamwic by excavation. We had already suspected, for example, that 'normal' retrieval at Hamwic may bias against bones of immature animals but can now quantify this bias.

Bulk samples for sieving thus serve a number of functions. First, they monitor the relationship between identifiable and unidentifiable material in different contexts and thus check the efficiency of 'normal' retrieval. They can monitor horizontal and lateral distribution of bones, allowing a more accurate definition of specialised deposits. They provide evidence of fish, small birds, and small mammals. Finally, they immediately demonstrate that some layers or features are different in the quality and density of faunal remains and deserve careful attention.

The last function, especially, points to a need for continuous monitoring which provides fast feedback so that extra samples can be taken at the time if necessary. These *'quality assessment'* aspects of sieving also make it vital to ensure its continuity for inter-site comparability and such strategies are currently continuing at least in excavations in Wessex that involve Winchester City and District, Southampton Museums, Wessex Archaeological Committee, and Test Valley Archaeological Committee.

It is impossible to overstate the case for a *consistent* sieving methodology, not only through the different phases of occupation in one place but throughout any inter-settlement comparisons. If faunal remains are ever to demonstrate changes which do not mirror changes in the other finds the essential evidence may be missed if sieving has not played its part in the analysis.

In recent years Wessex archaeozoologists have gained new insight into the effect of both *quality of retrieval on site* and *intra-site variability* on results obtained from bone analysis. Techniques have been devised which allow testing of samples from different types of context and from different excavations in standard ways that will reveal differences due to excavation and preservation rather than to ancient human behaviour.

Important unpublished work on *contextual variability* has been carried out by Grant at Danebury, Bourdillon at Southampton (Bourdillon 1983), and Sheppard and Adams at Winchester. Griffith's work for FRP at Micheldever demonstrated considerable differences between pit and ditch contents and attempted to quantify them and assess the role of taphonomic factors (Griffith AML Report 2647; Coy AML Report 3288). Jon Driver working in medieval Southampton pointed to variations in context type and faunal remains at Westgate (Driver, personal communication).

Mark Maltby has confirmed in more detail the very different results obtained from fragment counts for Iron Age pits and ditches and the false results that intra-site variability within the sample can give in period comparisons (Maltby 1981a, 1 x 66). The variability both of context type and bone retrieval strategies makes comparisons between the archaeologists' phases and between different sites impossible unless the sampling methods are understood. This limits reliability of the picture which can be given of Iron Age to Anglo-Saxon animal husbandry (Maltby 1981a, 158) despite the large number of settlements excavated.

Even when retrieval methods are comparable, variability in results because of the constitution of the sample (its balance of context types) can be large (e.g. Maltby AML Report 3453; Coy AML Reports 3594 and 3876). But one recent advance is the use of certain bone indices to monitor the quality of bone retrieval in archaeozoological samples — making direct comparisons between contexts and sites more reliable (Maltby, in preparation 1). This has opened the possibility of bringing results from unsieved sites and backlog sites into the data corpus at least for limited comparisons.

From regarding the investigation of intra-site variability as a necessary nuisance to overcome, however, the variability revealed by faunal studies themselves is now becoming recognised by the archaeologist as an essential part of the evidence on a settlement. Bones, and even some marine molluscs, are useful indicators of retrieval efficiency, context similarity, and context history.

Recording procedures and data handling

Today's archaeologist has the advantage of data capture using readily-portable micro-electronic devices and access to an ever increasing range of microcomputers for handling and analysing these data. Ideally these can avoid much human error (especially if linked to devices for measuring bones), save recording time, and increase the scope of metrical and non-metrical analyses enormously.

Conversely, this equipment is often poorly engineered and inadequately backed-up and initially may prove frustrating.

For bones it is largely true that the data collected for answering the basic questions of animal husbandry and usage discussed later in this section are the same data that are used in 'middle range research' for analysing taphonomic factors, although the data may need to be handled in a different way. The frameworks set up by Jackson and Pitt-Rivers were thus to some extent the basis for middle range research. They include the identification of species and anatomical element, measurements, ageing and sexing data, fragmentation details, and the examination of bones for signs of butchery and gnawing.

Accurate *identification* of bone fragments can be improved by access to reliable modern comparative collections set up especially for archaeozoological work and the available anatomical monographs (Coy 1978b). Consistent accurate identification to species, genus, or a wider taxon has been slightly aided since Jackson's time by work on the comparative anatomy of some groups, some clarification of the morphometric effects of domestication, and wider availability of good comparative collections.

Bramwell and Eastham have ensured that bird bones have been collected and identified for the key Wessex sites in recent years (e.g. Bramwell 1975, and his contributions in all reports by Harcourt quoted; Eastham 1971; 1975; 1976; 1977). Work on fish in Wessex was pioneered by Wheeler (e.g. 1975) but it is only since the introduction of sieving techniques in the last five years or so that fish identification has become common practice in Wessex (Bourdillon and Coy 1980, 118; Bourdillon 1978, 209 and 1979, 182).

The level of identification of any bone fragment may vary from 'unidentifiable' to a specific identification where specific attributes are present. The level of identification will control to a large extent the comparability of data as it can affect many quantitative results from a bone assemblage (Coy 1980 and 1982a).

The comparability of *measurements* taken by different workers has been aided by the publication of the English version of von den Driesch's manual (v.d. Driesch 1976); the comparability of *ageing and sexing data* by a co-operative effort of British archaeozoologists (Wilson *et al.* 1982).

In Wessex, computer treatment of archaeozoological data began in the 1970s at Danebury by Grant, at Winchester Research Unit by Pauline Sheppard and Gina Adams, and at the Faunal Remains Project. In 1978 FRP began to use the Ancient Monuments Laboratory's computer coding system. This was devised by Roger Jones for Winklebury to tie in with the Central Excavations Unit's excavation recording techniques (Jefferies 1977; Jones R T 1977; Jones AML Report 2333).

The system was considerably expanded to include all likely mammal, bird, and fish species; to take into account the requirements for the very large sample from West Stow, Suffolk (Crabtree in press 1); to record the *fragmentation* and *state of preservation* of bones from Iron Age deposits at various Wessex settlements (Griffith AML Reports 2430 and 2647; Coy AML Report 3288; Coy 1978c; Maltby AML Report 2417); and to include coding for cattle, sheep, and pig *tooth wear* according to the method of Grant (1975, 437).

The current version of this system in use in Wessex thus records a wide range of data and is more applicable to the broad range of questions being asked today by Wessex archaeologists (Jones *et al.* AML Report 3342). In 1979 an account of the computerised system was given to Hampshire archaeologists (Coy 1981a, 101).

During 1981, programs written by Jones made the AML system capable of producing *contextually-based data* (as well as data ordered by species and anatomical element). Level III archive — organised data that will not necessarily be needed for the Level IV stage — can therefore be produced both in a zoological form (e.g. as metrical archive arranged by species which may be of primary value to specialists) and in a context-ordered form (e.g. by archaeological context in numerical order) which may be of more value to the archaeologist. Both are possible for the whole settlement, for any phase or feature type, or for any combination of layers required.

Level III archive can be made available to the archaeologist and to other bone specialists as print-out or in computer-readable form, in addition to the final report and its associated Level IV data. (For an explanation of these levels see DoE (1975). For their adaptation to bones see Coy (1978a, 31)).

The advantages of a computerised data base are: the possibility of easier reworking in the case of future rephasing by the archaeologist, the possibilities of detailed intra- and inter-site comparisons, easier rationalisation of what is produced at Levels III and IV, and the greater ease of sorting metrical and non-metrical data. In this way the data can lead to more reliable results for the topics discussed in the subsequent section on animal husbandry.

Post-depositional taphonomic processes

Recently there has been a growth in the systematic recording of features of bone collections which can result from, e.g., trampling, soil effects, weathering, and the behaviour of scavengers.

Current AML coding used in Wessex allows data for, for example, fragmentation, canid gnawing, and preservation to be compared both within and between settlements. This is valuable, provided that the influences from archaeological retrieval, including sampling strategies, are taken into account. The lack of comparability of archaeological retrieval in the past made it difficult to investigate post-depositional biases and this continues to be true to a large extent. Current FRP Iron Age work has reduced these and other methodological biases to a minimum by using a single worker to analyse a group of sites using a standard methodology but the problem of retrieval bias is large even when archaeologists are aware of its existence. It is important to stress this as some recent bone analyses elsewhere have used part of the taphonomic argument to suggest, for example, that certain assemblages are produced by particular 'cultural practices' or by particular 'post-depositional taphonomic processes' without detailing the retrieval methods, which might be a larger factor than either of the others in producing bias in a bone collection.

Subject to these most important methodological controls it is now becoming possible to identify evidence of post-depositional processes. To give some examples: it is possible to recognise when lack of dog *gnawing* could be due to swift and efficient burial of bones, not necessarily a lack of dogs. Bones subjected to *trampling* in their primary context may show a high degree of characteristic fragmentation. The absence of certain elements can be due entirely to *scavengers* or to differential *erosion* by acid groundwaters; species ratios can be affected by the same factors. The distribution of certain anatomical elements may be due entirely to the strategy of dog feeding within some settlements. Differential erosion, staining, and gnawing within a sample often indicate its *mixed origin.*

The investigation of such processes by Niall Griffith led to a series of studies where evidence for these factors was sought from a number of Wessex Iron Age settlements (Maltby 1981b; AML Reports 2918; 3289; 3453). These studies have shown that the assessment of post-depositional processes is complicated by retrieval bias (Maltby 1981a, 192; in preparation 1).

However, detailed recording and analysis of the evidence for differential preservation can enable us to quantify the effects of post-depositional factors on archaeological samples. For example, at Iron Age Winnall Down, Hampshire, there is strong correlation between the percentage of ovicaprid loose teeth and the number of weathered or chemically eroded fragments in the assemblages (Maltby in preparation 1, Table 2 and AML Report 3453). In general the better preservation of bones dumped in pits enables a more representative range of ovicaprid elements to be recovered although even the pits produce samples which are biassed in favour of the denser elements.

Similarly high fragmentation of limb bones and the loss of their articular ends are indicative of poor preservation so that ratios of shaft to end fragments can be calculated with interesting results. At Winnall shaft fragments of tibia, radius, and metapodia have survived better than other limb bones — these elements being better represented in poorly-preserved assemblages.

Several other factors of variation need isolation and this will only be achieved by extending similar techniques for monitoring archaeological retrieval, gnawing, erosion etc. to settlements of different types and periods. A detailed discussion of this is in Maltby (in preparation 1).

Bone analysis can also throw light on *post-depositional movement* of material. It is essential that bone analysis should take this into account as it may often affect interpretation and give a misleading picture of deposition. Analysis of the pit excavated in Hamwic is throwing further light on this process (Colley AML Reports 3880 and 4071).

Sorting out the various indices and counts which can give evidence of post-depositional effects, as opposed to retrieval effects, is tedious and time-consuming. Once they have been identified, however, computer-handling of the data collected on the AML system could be routine. The variability produced in archaeological assemblages by the combination of all these factors may seem to be an irritating complication but it is essential to understand the sources of such variability in order to understand the underlying cultural patterning.

Some of these cultural practices make it very difficult to clarify the role of post-depositional taphonomic processes. For example, we need to devise methods for analysing bone preservation which take into account the prior effects of butchery, bone-working, and refuse disposal. Maltby (in preparation 1) discusses, for example, the relevance of tibial indices to preservation analysis in the light of prior butchery. He concludes that it may be necessary to compare several such methods of analysis for the same site in order to isolate the effects of differential preservation from those caused by carcase utilisation.

This is only possible for sites where all the necessary details of fragmentation have been recorded and archaeological retrieval strategies are known, although some of the indices could be used to assess the degree to which results from any settlement might be worth inclusion in comparative studies.

Disposal strategies

Much ethnographic and experimental work on refuse disposal may be of greater relevance when deriving methods of analysis for prehistoric and historic Wessex than the projection of urban twentieth century behaviour which provides the unconscious model (Maltby 1980), as it does also for slaughter and carcase division discussed in the next section.

It is clear that on some prehistoric settlements a large amount of bone may have been left around the settlement and subjected to gnawing by dogs, trampling, and erosion (e.g. Coy AML Report 3591) whereas some was immediately buried in the most convenient place according to its nature. The density of bone deposition can give a clear picture of disposal patterns in each phase and this may illuminate use of the settlement, e.g., the use of the banjo settlement at Micheldever, Hampshire (Coy AML Report 3288) and the Iron Age settlement at Winnall Down, Hampshire (Maltby AML Report 3453).

Bone fragmentation and condition results from a combination of butchery, disposal, and post-depositional processes and their study is aided by the recognition of ancient breakages which show good fit. Finds of associated bone shafts and epiphyses suggest when bones were joined by ligaments or gristle at deposition (e.g. Colley AML Report 4071). Although the AML coding system was designed so that it could be used to record bones in random order it is essential for a full understanding of these processes that all the bone from a context (and possibly related contexts) is recorded and examined at the same time and in conjunction with the evidence from other specialists.

Accurate separation of different accumulations by the archaeologist is vital in disposal studies. For example, we now know that post-depositional sinkage is greater in Hamwic pits than had been suspected and that a number of non-contemporary pits have a very deep contemporary uppermost layer which was accumulated after the pits were in use.

Now that we aim to strip away the taphonomic overprint to gain a better understanding of cultural patterning it is *essential* that the complexities of site formation are thoroughly understood. In fact the nature of the bone assemblage in a layer may help to unravel these. This makes for closer and more efficient co-operation between archaeologist and bone analyst.

In the analysis of bones from the Sunken Feature Buildings at West Stow only layers contemporary with the building occupation were analysed to see whether bones could have fallen between floorboards (Crabtree in press 1). Conversely at Groundwell Farm, Wiltshire, bones in the wall trenches were not contemporary with the hut occupation and results for them must be treated for what they are — a residual collection, much of it probably a result of trampling on the later occupation surface. Pit and ditch contents, had they been available from the settlement, might have given a different picture of the relative importance of the species, anatomical elements, and age groups concerned (Coy AML Reports 3591 and 3594).

In order to investigate disposal strategies it is necessary to ensure adequate samples of bones from a variety of context types so that statistical techniques can be employed on comparable samples. Ideally this should be taken into consideration as part of the sampling design for an excavation.

Compared with prehistoric periods, Roman, medieval, and post-medieval bone deposits may provide evidence for more organised disposal strategies, such as specialised deposits which provide information on particular practices. The full range of variability in these periods has not been monitored. For example, very little attention has been paid to analysis of bone from cesspits in Wessex and it will be essential, not only to co-ordinate bone results with those from the archaeobotanists but to sample most carefully any new material of this type. Samples are available from Ludgershall Castle, Winchester, and Newbury but there has been insufficient archaeozoological input into sampling strategies for the investigation of this material apart from the systematic sampling that has taken place at Winchester since the 1970s — despite the fact that such analyses might reveal considerable variability which could be linked, for example, with social differences.

One result of this fuller consideration of disposal is that, whereas in the past we might have asked the question 'what does this bone assemblage represent in terms of past herds?' we would now ask 'what does this represent in terms of people's activities?' By asking the latter we can now reach a more accurate understanding of the pastoral economy (Coy AML Report 3881).

Other cultural practices

This section attempts to concentrate on species which we can assume were exploited by man either because they show evidence of usage or because there has been careful analysis of the anatomical elements present and their context. A 'period by period' approach is taken where possible. Much of this has already appeared in published form in Coy 1981a and 1982b and Maltby 1981a and Bourdillon and Coy 1980. These papers should be consulted for full bibliographic details which are omitted here when they do not refer to Wessex.

Wild Mammal Exploitation

Palaeolithic and Mesolithic Knowledge of faunal exploitation for the Palaeolithic of Wessex usually depends upon evidence other than bones or generalises from evidence from the rest of Europe. Shackley suggests for Hampshire that late Upper Palaeolithic game would have been horse (*Equus* sp.), reindeer (*Rangifer tarandus*), and giant deer (*Megaloceros giganteus*) and that open air sites of this period, such as Hengistbury Head, could have served as base camps to exploit migrating wild horses and reindeer in spring and autumn (Shackley 1981, 8).

Grigson, in surveying cave deposits, tentatively suggests *Megaloceros,* reindeer, horse, and *Bison* as the true Older Dryas fauna with *Megaloceros,* reindeer, and possibly red deer (*Cervus elaphus*) roe deer (*Capreolus capreolus*), and pig (*Sus scrofa*) in the succeeding Windermere. Younger Dryas evidence is more difficult but horse and reindeer seem the only likely ungulates (Grigson 1978, 48).

A consideration of this fauna for what were probably open, unwooded conditions is essential to any understanding of man's later exploitation of woodland in the same areas. The Pleistocene period involved an enormous complexity of climatic and vegetational change much of which is still very difficult to sort out: the woodland species which survived in Europe must, during this period, have been subjected to intensive selection by what was often extremely rapid change.

The ecology of some mammals may well have altered considerably during the Pleistocene as species adapted to a variety of biotopes (Stuart 1974, 259) and this includes the woodland species of the interglacials. Specific identification of Pleistocene mammalian remains is still too often inadequate. As Grigson suggests, more careful reworking of, for example, *Bos* and *Bison* remains, might clarify the picture and incidentally lead to more reliable evidence of size change within species during the Pleistocene. If size change were a common phenomenon during the Pleistocene some species may have been selected for high ability to achieve the most economic size either by the individual being more susceptible to external factors during its maturation than would otherwise be the case or by more rapid alteration of the whole ecotype during intensive natural selection. Climatic and vegetation changes, competition for food with other species, energy expenditure in migration, limitation of gene pools in isolation, and numerous other factors, could have caused alteration of size within species. Behavioural and territorial changes may have been linked with a lesser or greater degree of sexual dimorphism.

This Pleistocene adaptive ferment must to some extent have pre-adapted some species to the subsequent immense and rapid changes brought about by man.

Evidence for late Palaeolithic and Mesolithic diet shows red deer enjoying a unique place in Wessex as elsewhere. Their remains were found on 95% of the late Palaeolithic and Mesolithic sites in Europe available to Jarman in his analysis (Jarman 1972, 128). Wild boar comes a close second in number of occurrences, with aurochs (*Bos primigenius*) and roe deer frequent finds. Horse is more rarely found. Elk (*Alces alces*) distribution seems to have retreated from this area by the Pre-boreal although there are finds dating to the early Mesolithic from Wawcott and Thatcham, Berkshire. Reindeer had probably disappeared in the South by the Boreal or earlier (Grigson 1978, 50). Presence and absence statistics are often misleading and even when frequencies of each species are calculated, the weight of the individual species must be taken into consideration for any assessment of diet. For example, Jacobi points out that close analysis (e.g. for Thatcham) suggests that cattle provided most of the meat consumed (Jacobi 1981, 10).

A number of fur-bearing mammals, which are associated with woodland, such as beaver (*Castor fiber*), fox (*Vulpes vulpes*), badger (*Meles meles*), wildcat (*Felis silvestris*), marten (*Martes* sp.), and hare (*Lepus* sp.), occur on Mesolithic sites in the south. Some of these are also good to eat.

Any change from exploitation of grassland to exploitation of forest would involve man in considerable problems. Hunting mammals in dense forest, even with modern weapons and traps, is never easy. The animals are, first of all, difficult to detect because of the severe limitations of man's own sense of smell and hearing compared with those of the prey. The use of dogs to extend the reach of the human senses would indeed have been a very important adjunct at any period when woodland exploitation was essential; the early domestication of the dog in Northern Europe certainly fits this. Modern hunting in forest for deer and wild boar depends heavily on the carefully organised use of woodland clearings and dogs. Early clearance could therefore sometimes have had a significance for hunting but this sort of clearance would not necessarily have been any greater than settlement clearances, although cleared areas in use by hunters today in Europe are often several hundred metres across.

Mellars points out that the biomass of mammals in forested areas would be much less than that of open tundra and grassland and that forest species tend to be less gregarious in their habits than reindeer and horses (Mellars 1974, 80). People would have had to adapt to a substantially reduced food supply and to change their hunting techniques to suit the different habits of the forest species, if indeed they were the same people. Modern figures for the biomass of forest species, such as deer, low as they are, may give a falsely high figure as they are frequently influenced both by winter feeding (which is a tradition in central European hunting) and the proximity of agricultural land. The numbers of fur-bearers, where these are predators and therefore at the top of the biomass pyramid, would be extremely low, and their skins therefore highly prized, although the comparative ease with which some of the Mustelids can be trapped would partly cancel this out. Beavers and hares might be expected to be of greater significance throughout prehistoric Europe because as well as being edible and fur-bearing they are primary consumers. Any situation where not too swiftly flowing water was bordered by rich woodland could be expected to have supported beavers.

Forests represent a mosaic of zones of different stages of turnover of trees, wet areas, heath, and forest clearings. The latter are normally mediated by fires and sometimes brought into being by a single species. Obviously dense forest is not the only ecosystem available. Mellars points to the significance of swamps and watering places in Palaeolithic hunting strategies (Mellars 1974, 56). This could also apply in the Mesolithic, in areas where forests and wetlands were contiguous. The many different types of woodland available at different stages of the Post-glacial (in some areas successively dominated by birch, pine, hazel, and true deciduous forest) would again have led to a correspondingly complex faunal picture which we are nowhere near understanding.

The red deer is a highly adaptable species and would be capable of utilising all kinds of forest and open grassland, although one would expect changes in its life pattern to occur. Modern roe deer feed mainly on broadleaved trees and shrubs which form up to to 90% of the June/July diet. Hazel forms a very important part of the diet, where available, and any clearance, especially that associated with subsequent growth of hazel, would especially favour roe. In the early part of the year herbs are eaten to a larger extent. Roe is particularly partial to buds where soft vegetation is unavailable. It also drastically reduces its food intake in winter. These two factors are related to its being a relatively delicate feeder which cannot exist on low quality browse.

Interaction of wild mammals with Mesolithic woodland ecosystems would have been complex. These effects and natural oscillations in animal populations and ecosystems mean that it is often impossible, even today, to be certain that some effects are related to human interference. Some of the species already mentioned can quite 'naturally' have considerable effects on the ecosystems in which they live. The greater species diversity of some of these forests, compared with open conditions or single species stands, may in fact have made them extremely vulnerable except under constant favourable conditions. Past alterations in woodland ecosystems are often blamed on man though a modern ecologist might have difficulty proving his case.

Any breaks in woodland cover, especially those associated with wetlands, rivers, or providing a rich marginal interface with another ecosystem, could only have increased the possibilities for the exploitation of woodland species. There has been much discussion on the extent of clearance and its causes. Evans (1975, 96) provides a useful outline of the work of Simmons and others on late Boreal to Atlantic clearance and Jacobi discusses hazel in some detail (Jacobi 1978, 83). Increase in hazel would certainly benefit roe deer. Woodland species in central European forest today make good use of 'forest lawns' and of river banks and woodland edge where increased light allows colonisation by shrubs and herbs, and wild boar root after small mammals and frogs. Any control or extension of such areas by hunters could increase mammal populations, make the animals easier to catch, and increase man/mammal contact which could ultimately result in domestication. Such woodland management, even on a small scale, would enormously increase leisure as woodland hunting would have been extremely time-consuming. As improvement of comfort seems to be a basic human instinct, this, rather than population pressure, could have been the major pressure altering human behaviour at this time. Break up of continuous forest stand would obviously provide a higher proportion of forest edge.

While evidence of clearance might suggest management, the ages of the animals killed might give us more detailed evidence of the management of animals. Ryder has pointed out that Jarman's speculative development of the idea of incipient domestication first put forward for the reindeer by Zeuner could merely indicate the management that hunters would sensibly expend on a natural resource (Ryder 1981, 304).

The Neolithic and the Effects of Domestication and Agriculture Patterns of Neolithic woodland clearance and regeneration, or otherwise, are discussed in the volume referred to for Coy (1982b): Neolithic activity in Hampshire by Fasham and Schadla Hall (1981, 26). Exploitation of red deer in Wessex, especially for antler, continued in the Neolithic and subsequently, as shown by the bone, antler picks, and worked antlers found in settlements. The discrepancy between the large numbers of antler tools (frequently from shed antlers) and the relative scarcity of post-cranial bones of red deer has recently been discussed by Legge in connection with the antler tools from Grimes Graves. Legge concludes that, making allowance for the duration of the mining work, a standing population of only 120 deer would in fact be required (Legge 1981a, 100). Neolithic roe deer antlers and bones are found in small numbers in Wessex.

It is usually assumed that the numbers of deer would have rapidly decreased after the development of settled agriculture and associated forest clearance. But as shown above there could have been great advantages in clearance before settled agriculture.

Frequently overhunting is given as a reason for a decrease in deer numbers and a contributory cause of the spread of agriculture. This is a difficult area. Food plays a decisive role in establishing the density of animal populations. Deer populations can be kept artificially high by feeding and red and roe deer and, presumably, aurochs and boar too, would probably benefit not only from clearances made for agricultural purposes but from the increase in food diversity from agricultural produce itself. Farms and gardens are rich habitats compared with most natural ones, giving the highest figure, for example, for breeding bird density over all habitats studied.

Roe deer especially have responded positively to the development of agriculture in Europe and are in some areas far less dependent on woodland than before. They can adapt to a wide range of habitat by using their ability to vary their reproductive performance by natural selection (Rowe, personal communication).

Wild boar would no doubt travel out of the woodland before dusk as they do today in Central Europe, to feed on forest edge and marshy places, and would swiftly adapt to raiding crops. Aurochs we know less about because of their subsequent extinction but if modern cattle are any guide they could have caused havoc in early agricultural experiments.

Wild Mammals in Later Prehistory Once established, domestic cattle, pigs, and sheep would have a considerable effect on the extent of the woodland itself. Once sheep were present in any numbers they would have a considerable effect on deer, especially roe, which appear to avoid any sheep-grazed areas. Part of the explanation for domestic cattle size diminution (see below) could have been disappearance of woodlands with their possibilities for browse and winter feeding.

During the succeeding Bronze and Iron Ages in Wessex the bones of wild mammals turn up occasionally. Aurochs seem to disappear in the Bronze Age (Jewell 1962, 160). Large specimens of pig on Iron Age settlements are usually assumed to be domestic (e.g. Harcourt 1979a, 152) but, judging by size and sculpturing of the bones, there are pig bones from many sites of Bronze Age to Medieval date which could conceivably be from wild boar and, although this species may have been reintroduced to reinforce the Norman way of hunting, there is the possibility that small numbers survived from the original stocks even in southern England up to the final extinction in the seventeenth century AD.

There is still the occasional red and roe deer bone even from Iron Age settlements in Wessex and antler is a favoured material for working but most bones are those of domestic animals.

Pre-Iron Age horse material is rare and regarded as wild in bone reports (Harcourt 1971a, 350). Iron Age horses are discussed alongside the domestic species below.

Iron Age settlements produce remains of most of the fur-bearing mammals that were around in Britain until the last two centuries saw their extermination over large areas of the British Isles (Langley and Yalden 1977) such as the otter, *Lutra lutra,* marten, *Martes martes,* and polecat, *Mustela putorius.* There are also those that are still common today — fox, *Vulpes vulpes,* badger, *Meles meles,* stoat, *Mustela erminea,* and weasel, *Mustela nivalis.* The fate in the Iron Age of the brown bear, *Ursus arctos,* is unknown although it appears in the Neolithic at Ratfyn, Wiltshire (Stone 1935, 61). Beaver, *Castor fiber,* is still occasionally found e.g. at Durrington Walls, Wiltshire (Harcourt 1971a, 345) and at recent excavations at Coneybury Hill.

Evidence from bones of skinning is sometimes recognisable but not always sought, nor do we know how often such species were eaten, for example as badger hams. Some of them may have been killed because of their predatory activities rather than primarily for skins. Most of them are easy to catch and are usually hard hit if people have a reason for catching them.

The evidence for wolf, *Canis lupus*, wildcat, *Felis silvestris*, and polecat, *Mustela putorius* is complicated by the possibility of bones of related domestic species; respectively the dog, cat, and ferret. Wolf bones were found in early excavations at Balksbury (Harcourt 1969, 54).

A possible wildcat bone came from pre-barrow levels of R4 on the M3 excavations (Fasham 1979, 11). Kitten remains from the middle period of the Iron Age settlement at Gussage, Dorset (Harcourt 1979a) are, however, tentatively assessed as domestic.

Hares and rabbits, as well as having excellent fur, are important meat sources and significant factors in the lives of certain people at certain periods. Early bone reports do not distinguish between the different species of hare: the varying hare, *Lepus timidus,* and the brown hare, *Lepus capensis.* Prehistoric material probably represents the smaller *timidus,* for example, that at Windmill Hill, Wiltshire (Jope 1965, 143).

The Roman Period There are more extensive collections of red deer bone from Roman villa sites in Wessex than in the preceding Iron Age. This is especially true of the Isle of Wight villas (Gamble and Streeter, personal communications).

Otherwise the mammals exploited are the same as in the Iron Age. Cat carcasses at Roman Portchester are assumed to be domestic (Grant 1975, 384).

It is now becoming clear that many species which were in the past assumed to have been introduced by the Romans (including species that we know were exploited by them elsewhere, like the fallow deer, *Dama dama*) do not show up until medieval times. For zoologists there is no new evidence here as searching analysis such as that by Chapman and Chapman (1975) for fallow had already suggested this and Wessex results have no more than confirmed the current zoological picture (Corbet and Southern 1977; Yalden 1982). Despite this, such dateable remains of wild mammals from archaeological periods provide interesting records and are forwarded to the national data banks at the Biological Records Centre, Monks Wood, and the British Museum (Natural History).

The Saxon Period The only quantity of evidence from Wessex between the Roman Period and the Norman Conquest is from the Mid-Saxon Period which has produced little evidence for exploitation of wild mammals.

Mid-Saxon Melbourne Street's 80,000 bone fragments produced only 12 post cranial bones of red deer. Distinction of red deer and fallow deer is possible for some bones given supporting modern collections. Absence of fallow in the large Saxon collections from Southampton fits currently accepted theories that fallow was introduced, or reintroduced, to Britain after the Norman invasion (Bourdillon and Coy 1980, 113). The red/fallow distinctions are complicated by the remarkable similarity of antler coronets in the two species and the enormous variation in both species, which causes an overlap in size and large discrepancies between modern and archaeological material. This problem area highlights a major difficulty in archaeozoological work: for detailed anatomical studies it is necessary to have just the right modern comparative material not merely any specimen of the species involved (Coy 1978b).

Only seven roe deer fragments were found at Melbourne Street but contemporary Saxon material in Wiltshire at Ramsbury (Coy 1980), in a more rural setting, demonstrates some exploitation of young roe. More recent work by Colley on the Six Dials material from Hamwic has demonstrated that a high proportion of offcuts from bone working are of antler – probably all of red deer (Colley in press, and AML Report 4071).

The occasional large cattle and pig bone seen at Hamwic is probably from extra large domestic beasts (e.g. Bourdillon and Coy 1980, 40).

Of the fur-bearing mammals only results for beaver prove of interest. Remains from mid-Saxon Ramsbury show cranial knife cuts made in skinning (Coy 1980). Beaver had a long association with the Kennet valley and would have been difficult to exterminate from such a favourable stronghold. A charter of AD 944 refers to an island in the Kennet, near Brimpton, known as Beaver's Island (Peake 1935, 125). Beavers may have survived for longer in the Glastonbury region. The much-quoted record of a journey by the Archdeacon of Brecon in AD 1188 records the presence of this scarce beast in the river Teifi in Wales and suggests that at that time there were none left in England (Dimock 1868, 115).

The Ramsbury 'wolflike bones' are interpreted as possibly coming from hunting dogs (Coy 1980, 49) and the few remains of Saxon cats at Hamwic have some anatomical features in common with the wildcat but are surely domestic.

Post-Saxon Medieval and Post-Medieval Much of the evidence of wild species available from archaeological sites is from the Medieval Period and the presence of certain species can be used to some extent as an indicator of comparative wealth. Results for Okehampton include a discussion of this (Maltby 1982a) and the use of dietary variety as a social indicator in Southampton has been discussed by Platt (1972, 33).

Remains of red and roe deer continue to occur but they are usually outnumbered by bones of fallow, which appears to be a post-Norman introduction. This introduction seems to have coincided with an extension of forest for hunting but as fallow are also associated with the setting up of deer parks the presence of bones of fallow in Wessex deposits from the eleventh century AD is not necessarily indicative of extensive woodlands, although many deer parks were near forests. Fallow are well-suited to deer park life and may fatten better on poor land than red deer. One great advantage of the species is that they will graze alongside cattle.

The relationship between some of these wild mammals and people may have extended through various degrees of control up to and including full domestication. The investigation of these relationships makes some 'wild' species of particular cultural interest. There is now considerable confirmatory evidence from Wessex excavations that the rabbit, *Oryctolagus cuniculus,* now wild, was probably introduced (along with the system of warrening and the domestic ferret) after the Norman Conquest. Study of the bones of fallow deer, rabbit and ferret from early medieval castle, ecclesiastical, and manor sites should provide further evidence for the degree of control exercised over their populations by people. Documentary work on warrens, deer parks, and medieval hunting and management practices (which may have included castration of fallow deer) should go hand in hand with bone analysis. Contact with French medieval archaeologists who are studying bones of contemporary French settlements now makes it possible to compare native French hunting practices with those existing, for example, at Winchester, after the Conquest.

The control of landscape by hunters reached its climax in Britain in the management of the royal game forests of the Medieval period (Owen 1983). Any form of winter feeding, e.g. by cutting down browse for deer, would increase their numbers, preserve other trees from damage by bark stripping, and perhaps become the origin of pollarding. Man-influenced, highly developed, open forest as seen in the Medieval period would provide a more regular acorn and beechnut crop and this is crucial to the winter survival of roe deer and pigs (Remmert 1980, 146).

Finds of wild species, apart from deer and rabbit, are rare. Grant suspected wolf, *Canis lupus,* at medieval Portchester and there are occasional finds of large, well-sculptured pig bones which could be from wild boar (e.g. Coy and Winder AML Reports 1803 for Romsey, Hants).

Coastal sites in Wessex in all periods occasionally produce whalebone. There is some use of this in bone-working areas of Hamwic (Bourdillon and Coy 1980, 114; Colley AML Report 4071).

Non-Mammalian Wild Species

Unlike the account for mammals it is impossible to give a 'period by period' account of the exploitation of **birds** because of the difficulty of knowing whether material referred to in site reports had any evidence of exploitation. A number of bird reports have already been referred to earlier. The many different causes for the incorporation of bird bones in settlement debris have been discussed elsewhere (Coy 1983a). Since we do not understand the significance of most of these finds, and since many of the species of birds involved are those common in Britain today, no species lists are given here. Readers interested in particular species and their occurrence are referred to the extensive indices in our bound volumes of papers from the Faunal Remains Project (in the University of Southampton Library) and to the works in the bibliography of this paper by Bramwell and Eastham.

Any study of **falconry** is handicapped by the impossibility of distinguishing captive from wild birds and the anatomical similarity of some closely-related species of falcon (so that it will not be possible to prove importation of foreign species at, for example, Winchester).

Any remains of **fish**, however, are usually assumed to have been from food remains although there are other reasons for accumulations of fish bones on settlements (Colley, personal communication). Some papers with fish reports have been mentioned earlier. With a very few exceptions the fish represented are those found today off the Wessex coast and the comments made above about species lists applies. Additionally, in post-Saxon times there was considerable trade in marine fish (e.g. Coy 1982a). An additional complication is the lack of sieving on many sites so that only the larger fish species are represented. Only comparison of sites where comparable sampling and sieving strategies have been employed can yield reliable data on the role of fish in the diet. This is gradually becoming possible for Wessex, as a result of the retrieval strategies discussed in an earlier section.

The extent to which fish played a role in fulfilling nutritional and other needs is difficult to interpret although attempts have been made to discuss a number of biases which may influence their relative role (Coy 1982a, 112). Work in other countries has attempted to compare the role of different food sources, e.g., the role of shellfish in diet by Meehan (1975, 206). Most studies relate only to food weight, protein, and calories and the role of vitamins and minerals has not yet been looked at in any detail (Coy 1982a, 114).

Winder's work on the Hamwic oysters initiated her continuing studies of **marine shells** on Wessex settlements (Winder 1980) and her more recent work at Poole, Rockbourne Roman Villa, and Ludgershall Castle will shortly be published. A modern comparative collection of molluscan food species and their molluscan predators is essential for such work as well as access to modern quantitative data on some species. Local modern data may need to be collected if there is no useful published work.

In return, analysis of size, meat potential, and usage evidence can illuminate the role of these molluscs in the diet. A study of oyster shells can demonstrate whether they came from natural or cultivated populations, whether shells were cleaned for table (useful evidence of degree of affluence) and suggest place of origin by analysis of shell size, and predator and commensal frequency.

Analysis of oyster deposits (using randomised sampling in thick deposits) may make it possible to reconstruct activities on different parts of a settlement and provide an additional factor in the study of contextual variability. Recent work suggests how oysters might be used to distinguish food preparation areas (Winder, personal communication).

Shells on coastal sites in Dorset have provided information which, when combined with topographical knowledge, can lead to more information on ancient food gathering (Coy AML Report 3593).

Domestication

By the Neolithic in Wessex there are cattle, sheep, and pigs which show skeletal features associated with domestication. There is no doubt that we are not yet able to recognise the earliest stages of this process. The evidence for goat is more debatable because of the goatlike character of early sheep bones, which themselves are fairly scarce in Neolithic Wessex.

The investigation of the process of domestication itself is crucial to archaeozoology in Wessex. In Jackson's time assumptions were made about the introduction of domestic species from either nearby Europe or the mediterranean to fit diffusionist theories in archaeology (Jackson 1933). Such ideas die hard but, although it is probable that domestic sheep were brought to Britain (there being no evidence of an indigenous ancestor), there seems to be no need to rule out the possibility of indigenous domestication for pig and cattle. The habits of aurochs and wild boar mentioned in an earlier section and the extensive clearance in some areas would have brought people into the close contact with pigs and cattle at forest edge which might have favoured domestication. The same could apply to horses, which turn up in small numbers as bones in archaeological deposits throughout prehistory. Forest edge is seen by Harris as a favoured area for domestication and cultivation to have begun (Harris 1969, 7).

Cattle have been studied more than any other domestic species in Britain, mainly as a result of the work of Grigson who has pointed out that Jackson's smaller cattle from Neolithic Maiden Castle (Jackson 1943, 362) were probably female aurochs, *Bos primigenius* (Grigson 1969, 279). Grigson has made a detailed metrical study of modern domestic British cattle and fossil remains of *Bos primigenius*, concluding that these form a continuum. It is interesting that, although the problems of sex distinction within *Bos primigenius* and distinction between *Bos primigenius* and definite domestic cattle have now been solved, there is still resistance to the idea of indigenous domestication in Britain, especially of cattle. Quite recent papers still suggest introduction of the domestic Neolithic cattle by immigrant farmers along with the ideas of cultivation. Some resistance to indigenous cattle domestication may be a hangover from the traditional view of the European aurochs as a fierce giant incapable of being tamed (Clutton-Brock 1981, 65).

Size is the main criterion used to determine whether cattle and pigs were likely to have been wild or domestic. This, in isolation, is unsatisfactory and progress towards an understanding of early Wessex domestic animals is slow. We lack large samples from the earliest periods. Grigson found that the differences between the skulls of domestic cattle and aurochs were often allometric differences linked with sex and size. Domestication features, apart from smaller size, included an increase in variation (for example, greater skull breadth dimorphism between the sexes), and shorter horns in the bulls. Although the skulls she studied were modern domestic cattle, some of these features can be seen already in the early Neolithic material.

The work of the FRP has not contributed to studies on domestication for the major mammals as very little Neolithic and Bronze Age material has been studied and these and earlier periods are the key ones for such studies. The analysis of the bones from Hambledon Hill, Dorset, by Legge should shed more light on early domesticates and excavations by The Trust for Wessex Archaeology in the Stonehenge area and at Easton Lane, Hampshire, are contributing further.

The only domestic species likely to provide direct evidence of early changes consequent upon domestication in the later periods are goose and duck (Bourdillon and Coy 1980, 117; Coy 1981b, microfiche 207). The domestic fowl does not appear to have become established until the Late Iron Age (Coy 1983a, 2).

For studies of both the process of domestication itself and of *subsequent alterations and selective breeding* in the major domesticates Wessex is an important area. Initial introductions, early breeding, and subsequent shipments of domestic stock are all likely to have occurred there. Parallel studies with the south east of England are advisable.

In all such studies, once again, size is usually the major indicator used although sexual dimorphism and the amount of variation within the species are also used. Past discussions of these factors may well have overstressed the role of people and it might be useful in any future analysis to attempt application of some modern biological models relating to size and sexual dimorphism.

Other domestic species which appear in the archaeological record may, like sheep and domestic fowl, have been introduced as domesticates although with some like dog, goat, and goose, which have wild counterparts in the British

Isles, the situation is still obscure. With others, like the fallow, rabbit and ferret so popular with the Normans, introduction is likely even though the wild polecat provides a possible ancestor for the last.

Animal Husbandry

Once again a 'period by period' account will be attempted. The topics covered in this section are the species themselves and their size, specific ratios, ageing data, and aspects of exploitation. Only the Iron Age and Saxon periods have provided a good enough sample of data to make this worthwhile although evidence for the other periods is gradually accumulating.

Neolithic and Bronze Age Domestic cattle, sheep, and pigs have already been discussed above and the smaller size of cattle and pigs compared with that for possible wild individuals around at the same time has been mentioned. Legge has suggested that most of the observed subsequent size decrease in domestic cattle themselves between Neolithic and Iron Age occurs in the late Neolithic and early Bronze Age (Legge 1981a, 81). The relative abundance of the major species in the Neolithic forms a popular discussion point. Murray gives this a cultural significance (Murray 1970) but Jarman points to economic changes being geared to environmental conditions (Jarman 1972, 136). Recently, results from some Hampshire Iron Age sites have shown, as explained earlier, how apparent changes in economy can have a taphonomic explanation (Maltby 1981a, 165). An increase in pig exploitation in the late Neolithic is suggested by Grigson (1982, 306).

Ageing data have been little discussed for the Neolithic except both Grigson (1980) and Legge (1981b) have observed that there is a preponderance of old cows in both the Windmill Hill and Hambledon Hill assemblages. Legge (1981b, 179) has suggested that the cattle killed at these causewayed camps represented the surplus animals available from lowland-based cattle exploitation, in which milk production was of primary importance.

Sheep mandibles from Wessex excavations are being set aside for an investigation of *absolute age* from cementum lines as carried out earlier for cattle (Turner 1979; Coy *et al.* 1982). In that study interpretation of incremental growth lines in teeth of Saxon cattle from Hamwic was more difficult than expected. It is possible that considerable evidence on animal husbandry as well as age at death might eventually be forthcoming.

The more usual method is one of *relative ageing* dependent on assessing tooth eruption and wear. Most Wessex bone analysis makes use of Grant's methods for recording this (Grant 1975, 437). These techniques are all necessary if we are to elucidate the age structure of ancient herds. It is however essential to appreciate the part which is once again played by retrieval techniques as these and the balance of context types in any sample can cause considerable bias in ageing data (Maltby 1982b).

The frequency of different combinations of tooth wear stages within whole mandibles may ultimately provide a method for assessing feeding conditions in different areas and periods (Grant 1982, 106). Such data are now steadily accumulating for Wessex.

Once again it must be said that faunal results for the early prehistoric periods which have profited by recent methodological advances are few. Conclusions from Iron Age work can now, however, be turned to good account as soon as the opportunity of new Neolithic and Bronze Age material turns up so that we do not waste such opportunities. Results from Hambledon Hill, Easton Lane, and Coneybury Hill are awaited with interest.

Iron Age/Romano-British The apparently simple question of what domestic species were kept in the Iron Age and Romano-British periods is not as straightforward as it seems. There can be no doubt about the importance of cattle and sheep throughout and to a lesser extent pig, horse, and dog. The problem lies with the possible presence of other domestic species, in particular the goat, the donkey, the mule, and poultry.

Bone evidence suggests that **cattle** provided the major meat source in all periods in Wessex from the Iron Age although in later periods not necessarily for all classes of people.

Measurement of bones have been made in attempts to assess the relative sizes of the stock, to distinguish between the sexes, and to monitor the possible importation of new stock. Unfortunately, because of the haphazard nature of many of these studies and the variation of measurements taken by different analysts, such work has not produced the results that it has the potential to obtain. The advent of computer recording and attempts at standardisation of the measurements taken, described in a previous section, will improve the situation. For the time being, however, any analysis of past work is limited to comparisons of particular measurements. Single measurements are themselves unreliable because a combination of genetic, nutritional and sex factors can produce variations in size. Only by the study of several measurements from one bone and by comparisons of measurements from different bones will we be able to obtain a better understanding of the stature and variety of the domestic stock (e.g. O'Connor 1982, for sheep; and work on cattle and pig currently in progress at York).

Earlier studies of prehistoric and early historic cattle bones from Britain have been made. Jewell (1962) emphasised the diminutive form of Iron Age cattle and showed that similar small cattle were present during the Roman period. Iron Age cattle were mostly also small or short-horned but occasionally hornless (Armitage and Clutton-Brock 1976, 331). Jewell also noted that bones of larger cattle appeared in the Roman period and concluded that a larger breed of cattle was imported. Hodgson (1968) found that the same trends were apparent in the samples he compared. These surveys can now be supplemented by data obtained from more recent excavations in Wessex. Metrical analysis of the maximum length of the astragalus from Iron Age, Romano-British and Anglo-Saxon samples (Table 12) confirm the appearance of larger cattle in the Romano-British period. Apart from the small sample from Corstopitum and the two samples from Exeter, all the Romano-British assemblages produced a higher mean measurement than the Iron Age samples. Although the Romano-British and Anglo-Saxon samples contained some astragali as small as those from Iron Age sites, they also included others that were significantly larger than any found in the earlier assemblages. The same trend can be observed on other bones.

Table 12 Metrical Analysis of the Maximum Length of Cattle Astragali

Site	Date	N	Range	Mean	Source
Exeter	55–300	14	50.7–59.6	55.2	Maltby (1979)
Catcote	Iron Age	14	51–63	57.0	Hodgson (1968)
Gussage All Saints	Iron Age	54	54–62	57.0	Harcourt (1979a)
Winnall Down	MIA	7	53.1–61.0	57.3	Maltby (AML 3453)
Croft Ambrey	Iron Age	20	55–63	57.7	Whitehouse & Whitehouse (1974)
Balksbury 1973	MIA	12	55.0–63.1	57.9	Maltby (in prep 2)
Appleford	Iron Age	8	55–60	58.0	Wilson (1978)
Winnall Down	EIA	8	55.8–61.6	58.0	Maltby (AML 3453)
Corstopitum	Roman	9	53–63	58.0	Hodgson (1968)
Exeter	300–400	18	54.3–62.0	58.3	Maltby (1979)
Ashville	Iron Age	18	53–64	58.5	Wilson (1978)
Barley	Iron Age	13	54.1–62.1	58.5	Jarman et al. (1968)
Grimthorpe	EIA	8	56.3–61.5	59.5	Jarman et al. (1968)
Hamwic	Mid Saxon	167	49.2–71.5	60.9	Bourdillon & Coy (1980)
Baylham House	100–200	10	56.0–65.8	61.3	Maltby (in prep 3)
Alcester	Late Roman	30	53.9–67.6	61.4	Maltby (in prep 4)
Shakenoak Farm	Late Roman	44	53–72	61.6	Cram (1978)
Winnall Down	Early Roman	16	56.1–68.4	61.6	Maltby (AML 3453)
Ramsbury	Mid Saxon	6	51.5–66.5	61.9	Coy (1980)

All measurements in millimetres. EIA = Early Iron Age; MIA = Middle Iron Age. (From Maltby 1981a, 187).

Although most of the Romano-British samples listed in Table 12 are dated to the latter part of that period, there is some evidence that larger cattle were present in some areas during the early years of occupation. The astragali from Winnall Down, Hampshire included large specimens only in Phase 6 deposits dated to the first and second centuries AD (Maltby AML Report 3453). None of the astragali from the Iron Age features (Phases 3 and 4) attained the size of the largest Romano-British specimens (Figure 16).

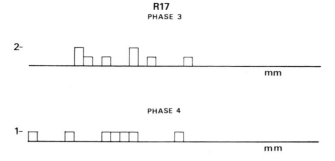

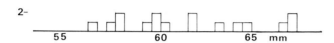

Figure 16   Maximum lengths of cattle astragali from early Iron Age, middle Iron Age and early Romano—British deposits at Winnall Down, Hampshire.
(From Maltby 1981a, 186).

More late Iron Age material is required for comparison but the present evidence suggests that the appearance of larger cattle did coincide with the Roman invasion. The possibility of the importation of cattle is therefore strong, although much more detailed analyses than these are needed to confirm this. Improvements in the size of the native stock may also have occurred during the Romano-British period but there may have been regional variations. Regional variation in the size of cattle in Roman Britain can be demonstrated elsewhere (Maltby 1981a, 188).

It is possible that there were environmental constraints on the size and type of cattle kept in some parts of Britain but the explanation may be more complex than this. It has been shown that large cattle appeared in Roman occupied territory in central and eastern Europe but were not found in contemporary settlements outside the area of Roman occupation. There were also variations in the number of large cattle found at different types of settlement within the Roman provinces. The degree of Roman influence on cattle farming in Britain may therefore account for the variability in cattle size observed in faunal samples. South West England may have been outside the area where larger cattle were introduced or bred.

It is believed that animal bone studies can establish the principal reasons why the various domestic species were kept and how intensively they were exploited. Cattle, for example, can be bred mainly as working animals, or as dairy producers or simply as providers of meat or a combination of all three. The kill-off patterns and the relative numbers of males, females and castrates kept will vary according to the particular regime of husbandry practised. By studying the ageing and sexing evidence of faunal samples, it is possible to investigate these topics. Once again there are problems in transforming the archaeozoological data into general statements about herd structures and exploitation patterns. Nevertheless some general patterns have begun to emerge from the ageing data of the major domestic species. The methods used are those discussed earlier for the Neolithic.

Analyses of the herd structures of cattle in Iron Age faunal samples have been limited by the fact that most of the largest and best studied assemblages have produced comparatively little ageing and sexing data. The picture of cattle exploitation is therefore very restricted. To take the evidence of tooth eruption and wear only, a few samples have produced a relatively large number of immature mandibles. In particular the sample from Phase 1 (Early Iron Age) at Gussage All Saints contained a very high percentage (36%) of jaws with at most only the deciduous premolars and first molar in wear (Harcourt 1979a, 151). Many of these must have belonged to calves under a year old and some were neonatal mortalities. Apart from these, most of the mandibles belonged to adult animals. Only 24 mandibles could be examined from the Ashville excavations (Hamilton 1978, 132), using the method of Grant (1975). Most of these had numerical values of less than 20 and accordingly did not have the second molar fully erupted. Sexing of the metapodia and distal radius suggested that most of the adult animals were cows (Wilson 1978, 135). Although mandibles of young calves were represented in both the early and middle Iron Age samples from Balksbury, Hampshire, the majority had numerical values of over 30 (Figure 17) and most of these had fully developed tooth rows, belonging to animals at least five years old and probably substantially older in many cases. A similar pattern was discerned from the Iron Age samples from Winnall Down (Maltby AML Report 3453) and Eldon's Seat, Dorset (Cunliffe and Phillipson 1968, 229). Another pattern of ageing appears in two late Iron Age samples. At Barton Court Farm, Oxfordshire, there was a concentration of mandibles with the first two molars in wear but the third molar unerupted (Hamilton 1978, 132), belonging to animals under three years of age on modern estimates. A small sample from first century AD deposits from the excavations at Baylham House, Suffolk (Maltby in preparation 3) also contained a number of mandibles at a similar stage of development, indicating the culling of young cattle for meat.

Other Iron Age faunal assemblages are difficult to compare because the methods of ageing are not fully explained. The variability of these samples could be the result of a combination of factors and it is premature to suggest significant changes in cattle husbandry during the Iron Age. Other factors such as regional variability, redistribution of stock, differences in disposal strategies and possible sampling, preservation and recovery biases could be involved. These factors cannot be examined on the existing data. A high kill-off of young calves and a predominance of adult cows in some assemblages may imply that dairying was an important element of cattle husbandry in some communities but much more sexing evidence is required before we can place any confidence in such statements.

BALKSBURY 1973

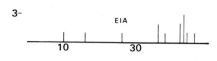

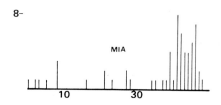

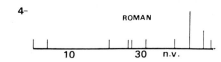

Figure 17   Ageing data from cattle mandibles in early Iron Age, middle Iron Age and Romano–British contexts from Balksbury 1973. n.v. = numerical value. Method of analysis follows Grant (1975). Estimated values are included. (From Maltby 1981a, 180).

Cattle ageing evidence from the Romano-British period is better documented, although the same limitations apply with regard to the possible explanations for the observed patterns. At least two recurring patterns can be observed from the studies of mandibular tooth eruption. The first contains mandibles of cattle of all ages, although mature individuals usually predominate. Examples can be found on villa and other rural sites. At Barton Court Farm a sample of 34 mandibles of Roman date included 16 which did not have the third molar erupted, including five of young calves (Hamilton 1978, 132). The mandibles from Sites C and K at the villa at Shakenoak Farm, Oxfordshire, dated mainly to the third and fourth centuries, contained 12 mandibles with at most the third molar in an early stage of wear and only six mandibles with fully erupted tooth rows (Cram 1978). The even smaller sample from Fishbourne also contained a relatively large number of immature cattle (Grant 1971, 385). The second century deposits at the roadside settlement at Baylham House, Suffolk included eight cattle mandibles that had not reached the stage when the third molar was fully erupted, 13 other jaws had fully erupted tooth rows. The late Roman deposits at Balksbury produced ten mandibles with fully erupted tooth rows but seven that had not reached dental maturity (Figure 17). Small samples of cattle mandibles from the roadside settlements of Margidunum, Nottinghamshire (Harman 1969, 101) and at Scole, Norfolk (Jones G, 1977, 210) also contained a relatively high proportion of immature specimens. Finally, the fourth century deposits from several sites in Exeter showed the presence of a significant number of immature cattle (Maltby 1979, 30, 155). Most of the young cattle represented in these samples were of a reasonable size for culling for meat, although not always fully grown. In most cases these were animals not required for breeding, working or dairying that were fattened for slaughter for their meat and hides.

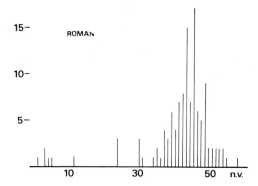

Figure 18 **Ageing data from cattle mandibles in Romano–British deposits at Portchester Castle.** Data adapted from Grant (1975, 1976). n.v. = numerical value. Method of analysis follows Grant (1975). Estimated values are included. (This figure is from Maltby 1981a, 181).

The second pattern of ageing is typified by the collection of mandibles from the Roman levels at Portchester Castle (Grant 1975). The great majority of mandibles recovered in the large sample belonged to adult animals and included very few jaws with numerical values of under 35 (Figure 18). Most of the cattle were therefore over five years of age and some had heavy toothwear which indicates that quite old animals were slaughtered. The predominance of mature cattle recurs in several other samples derived from military and urban sites. From the north of England, a large percentage (78.9%) of the 147 ageable mandibles from the excavations at Vindolanda possessed the third molar in wear (Hodgson 1977, 12). Of 132 ageable mandibles from deposits dated to the first to third centuries at Exeter only 10 definitely did not have the third molar in wear (Maltby 1979, 155–156). Analysis of the mandibles of fourth century date from the excavations at Angel Court, Walbrook in London produced similar results (Clutton-Brock and Armitage 1977, 92). Of the 155 mandibles of late Roman date examined from the excavations at 1, Bleachfield Street, Alcester, Warwickshire, under the direction of Paul Booth, only 10 did not have the third molar in wear (Maltby n.d. 4). Attempts to distinguish the sexes of the adult cattle by metrical analysis of the metapodia have been made on several of the samples and in each case it appears that cows were more commonly represented (Grant 1975, 401; Maltby 1979, 33–34; Clutton-Brock and Armitage 1977, 92), although the reliability of the various techniques of metrical analysis has yet to be established.

The evidence from all the Romano-British samples investigated to date would suggest that most cattle were allowed to reach maturity and it is unlikely that they were all raised simply for their meat, even allowing for slow rates of growth. Working and dairy cattle were probably important elements in the economy. Explanation of the variation in the number of immature cattle represented remains tentative. It is interesting, however, that the heaviest concentrations of adult cattle have so far appeared only on military and urban settlements. Organisation of cattle marketing and the need to provision these centres with meat may have resulted in the supply of particular types and age groups of cattle. Most of the other settlements may have been more self-sufficient and therefore their deposits included a higher percentage of immature cattle not required for breeding or working but also not in demand for redistribution to other centres. In Exeter, the increase in the number of immature cattle in the fourth century deposits coincided with evidence for a change in the settlement pattern and the presence of stock enclosures associated with houses within the walls, perhaps indicating an increase in the farming element of the population (Maltby 1979, 90). The evidence may also imply that there was a collapse of the former supply network of cattle brought to the town for slaughter. Most of the other settlements which contained higher proportions of immature animals were villas, rural settlements or settlements that did not need to be supplied with a large number of cattle brought in for slaughter from elsewhere. The possible dichotomy between the cattle represented on rural, urban and military sites remains a topic for further investigation.

It is clear that for an examination of effects, like Roman influence, results from a much wider area than Wessex need to be analysed. The above study provides a demonstration of the value of inter-regional studies and we are grateful to all our colleagues who have kept us supplied with their published work.

The presence of **horse** bones is attested from archaeological sites throughout the periods under consideration. Indeed, there is now abundant evidence that horsemeat made an important contribution to the diet in at least some parts of England during the Iron Age when ponies ranging from 10–14 hands were kept. Horse bones butchered for meat have been recorded, for example, at Ashville (Wilson 1978, 119, 122, 125), Tollard Royal, Dorset (Bird 1968, 147), Winnall Down (Maltby AML Report 3453) and Balksbury (Maltby in preparation 2). On some of these sites horse bones are very well represented and the importance of horses as working and riding animals has been pointed out by

223

several authors. Certainly most horse bones recovered on Iron Age sites belonged to mature animals and examinations of toothwear have shown that many of them were over 10 years of age. Meat production was not the primary purpose of their exploitation. The lack of immature specimens at Gussage All Saints led Harcourt (1979a, 158) to suggest that no breeding of horses was practised but that they were rounded up periodically when certain animals were selected for training. As horses are not suitable for working until three years of age, this type of round-up would have saved the expense of rearing and feeding the foals and allowed the processes of natural selection to take place. This hypothesis remains to be tested against a wider range of samples and several other explanations could account for the absence of very young horse bones from some Iron Age deposits. For example, Champion (1979, 384) has pointed out that the evidence for the production of horse gear at Gussage All Saints implies that a specialist was resident there. It is not beyond the bounds of possibility that there were also specialist horsebreeders on some settlements. If so, only adult horses may have been redistributed to other settlements. Nevertheless the importance of horses primarily as transport animals and secondarily as producers of meat appears consistent.

The poor representation of horse on Romano-British and Anglo-Saxon settlements may simply be the result of the decline in the horse's importance as a producer of meat. Certainly few horse bones have been found in Romano-British deposits in assemblages derived mainly from butchery waste and records of butchery on horse bones are rare. This does not necessarily imply that horses had become less important.

Most equid bones found on archaeological sites have been identified as horse. There is evidence, however, that both **mules** and **donkeys** were present from at least Roman times. A mandible of a mule has been identified from second century AD levels from the excavations at the Billingsgate Buildings in the City of London. Although this specimen may have belonged to an imported animal, its presence is interesting since there is good documentary evidence for the mule's employment as a draught animal and a beast of burden in the Roman Empire. Donkey has also been recorded occasionally on Romano-British sites, for example at Tripontium and possibly at the villa at Frocester Court, Gloucestershire. Because of the similarities of the skeletons of ponies, donkeys and mules, it is possible that mules and donkeys have been misidentified in some samples. Future studies of equid material should have regard for their possible occurrence.

Sheep can be distinguished from goats providing bones are sufficiently whole, although criteria vary from site to site and it is conceivable that the ease of separation itself may be linked to plane of nutrition and intensity of selection. It is assumed in the account below that all the ovicaprine bones discussed are from sheep. Goat will be discussed briefly later.

The most common measurement taken consistently on ovicaprine assemblages has been the maximum distal width of the tibia. The significance of this measurement as an indicator of size has yet to be adequately demonstrated and the size of the bone is to an extent determined by sexual dimorphism (Noddle 1980, 396). Nevertheless there has been some consistency in the results obtained to date. Results for sites from all over Southern Britain show that means from the Iron Age samples fall at the lowest end of the scale, with very few specimens measuring more than 25mm (Maltby 1981a, 190). Specimens of this size and larger have been found more commonly in Romano-British and Anglo-Saxon samples, although the smallest specimens were as small as the earlier ones. The means from the Romano-British samples fall between 22.8–25.5mm.

Other measurements of sheep bones support these observations, indicating an increase in the average size of sheep in the Romano-British and Anglo-Saxon periods. Possible introductions of stock could have taken place in both periods but improvements in the existing stock by better husbandry could also account for the variability. There is some evidence for an increase in the size of sheep within the Romano-British period on some sites (Maltby 1981a, 191).

There is certainly evidence for regional variation in sheep size in the Romano-British and Anglo-Saxon periods as described for cattle above. Sheep in the Southwest may have continued to be smaller after the Romano-British period, if the small Dark Age samples from Mawgan Porth, Cornwall (Clutton-Brock 1976) and Bantham Ham, Devon (Coy 1981c, 108) are typical.

The initial increase in size of some of the flocks in the Romano-British period may have parallels with the developments in cattle husbandry. The introduction or development of larger stock in some areas may be an indication of the rather nebulous concept of 'Romanisation'. If so, there may be a parallel with the situation in the Roman provinces of central and eastern Europe, where similar changes in sheep size took place.

Sheep produce meat, skins, manure, milk and wool. The relative importance of each plays some part in the manner in which they are husbanded. Both Cunliffe (1978, 183) and Bradley (1978, 36–37), using the published evidence available to them, concluded that sheep were exploited mainly for meat in some areas during the Iron Age and principally for wool in others. Rivet (1964, 123–124) and Applebaum (1972, 214–215) emphasised the importance of wool production on sheep rearing in the Romano-British period and Clutton-Brock (1976, 382) has suggested that large numbers of sheep were kept to provide enough wool for profitable trading in the Anglo-Saxon period.

Payne (1973) has shown that the kill-off patterns of sheep populations raised principally for wool, meat or milk should be quite different from each other. A substantial number of ewes and wethers would be allowed to reach maturity if wool production was predominant, to enable several annual growths of the fleece to be collected. On the other hand, only the animals selected for breeding would be required to reach maturity in a system that intensively exploited sheep for meat and the emphasis would be on the fattening and culling of young animals. Theoretically it should be possible to relate the ages of the bones found on archaeological sites to the regime of exploitation, although as Payne has pointed out, flocks are not usually kept for a single product, particularly in subsistence economies.

As for cattle, above, methods which employ epiphyseal fusion data will not be considered here, since differential preservation plays a dominant role in the survival of the fusion points and makes this method of analysing age structures most unreliable (Maltby, 1982b). Again the method of Grant (1975) has been used, with the limitations discussed in detail in Maltby (1981a, 171).

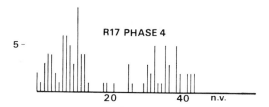

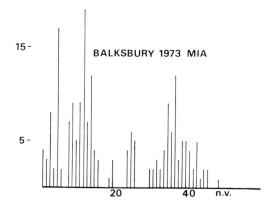

Figure 19   Ageing data from sheep/goat mandibles from middle Iron Age samples from Winnall Down and Balksbury 1973. n.v. = numerical value. Method of analysis follows Grant (1975). Estimated values are included. (Originally in Maltby 1981a, 173).

Several samples from Iron Age settlements in Wessex have now been examined. The analysis of two middle Iron Age samples from Hampshire, Winnall Down and Balksbury (material from the 1973 excavations directed by Geoffrey Wainwright) have produced very similar results (Figure 19). The diagram shows the number of mandibles scoring each of Grant's (1975) numerical values and includes estimated values from incomplete molar rows. It is important to emphasise that these values do not represent equal lengths of time. Changes in the toothwear stages of older mandibles are generally slower, although that is something of an over-simplification. As a guide, the first molar is in wear by c. n.v. 8, the second molar at c. n.v. 18 and the third molar at c. n.v. 30. In both samples, therefore, there was a concentration of very young mandibles, very few that were assigned values of 15–30 and then a broad concentration of older mandibles with fully erupted tooth rows. Several points need to be made about these samples. On both sites they were recovered almost exclusively from pits and contexts that preserved the mandibles extremely well. It is certain that had the samples derived from deposits that were less favourable to bone preservation, the survival rate of the youngest and most fragile jaws would have been seriously impaired. Secondly, it is uncertain whether these samples, although quite substantial, represent an accurate cross-section of the sheep kept by the inhabitants of the settlements. It is possible that there was redistribution of stock or carcasses between settlements. It is also conceivable that the mandibles in these pits were biased towards these age groups because of the particular disposal strategies employed by the inhabitants. A wider range of samples from contemporary neighbouring settlements is required to test these possibilities.

Assuming for the time being, however, that the samples are representative, what inferences can be drawn about sheep husbandry? The concentrations of young mandibles include those belonging to neonatal mortalities and those of lambs with their first molar not fully erupted or only in an early stage of wear. Absolute ageing is problematic but, even allowing for very slow eruption rates, it seems likely that the majority of these mandibles belonged to animals that died under a year old. Given the poor quality of the stock, a high rate of neonatal deaths is to be expected. Payne's models (1973, 282–284) allow for up to 30% of the lambs born each year to die of natural causes. High rates of young mortalities were prevalent in England in the Middle Ages (Miller and Hatcher 1978, 217). The older lambs represented at Winnall Down and Balksbury, although they were butchered for meat, were certainly not kept alive long enough to reach an optimum age and weight for culling for meat. In fact there were very few sheep of that age, as the low number of mandibles with numerical values of 15–30 indicates (Figure 19). Superficially, the observable age pattern fits more closely to Payne's model of milk exploitation, in which in addition to natural mortalities a high percentage of the flock are slaughtered in their first year leaving a few rams but mainly ewes for breeding purposes and their milk. Alternatively, it is possible to view the ageing pattern as evidence for a very low level of efficiency in sheep husbandry, in which only the stock selected for breeding were allowed to mature. This may indicate that there was a shortage of winter fodder for sheep or at least no incentive nor necessity to overwinter a significant proportion of the stock. In either case, although wool would have been provided by the older animals, the apparently high rates of immature mortalities suggest that wool production was not of primary importance in the exploitation of sheep at these settlements.

The smaller samples from the earlier Iron Age deposits from Winnall Down and Balksbury produced similar results to the one described above and these have parallels with other samples from southern England. The large samples from Phases 1–2 at Gussage All Saints contained a high proportion of sheep mandibles with, at most, only the first molar in wear, a low percentage of jaws with only the first and second molars in wear, and a larger group with fully erupted tooth rows (Harcourt 1979a, 152). The sample from Croft Ambrey contained a larger number of adult sheep but again a low number of mandibles at the stage when only the first and second molars are in wear (Whitehouse and Whitehouse 1974, 218–219). Similar results were obtained from the samples from Ashville and the late Iron Age deposits at Barton Court Farm, Oxfordshire (Hamilton 1978, 129).

Of the other large Iron Age samples, those from Eldon's Seat and Hawk's Hill cannot be compared directly with these since the data were grouped in a different way. The analysis of the mandibles from Barley, Hertfordshire, produced rather different results (Ewbank et al. 1964). Although mandibles of first year animals and adult stock still formed the largest groups, c. 20% of the sheep represented by complete mandibles were killed between the early wear stages of the second and third molars. Two late Iron Age samples from southern England also contained a higher percentage of mandibles at this age. At Gussage All Saints, 21% of the mandibles were at this stage of development (Harcourt 1979a, 152) and the excavations of the banjo enclosure in Micheldever Wood, Hampshire produced roughly equal numbers of these and those of the youngest age group (Coy AML Report 3288). Whether these samples provide evidence for a change in sheep husbandry that resulted in the culling of relatively more second and third year animals remains to be tested on other sites in the area.

Obviously the number of Iron Age samples is inadequate to provide information about the possibility of local, regional or temporal variation. The samples that have been examined so far do, however, have certain common traits. In all of them the number of first year mortalities represented is high compared to samples from later periods. Such jaws are small and fragile and are likely to be under-represented. Apart perhaps from the samples from Barley, Gussage All Saints and Micheldever Wood, all the Iron Age sites have produced few mandibles of sheep killed at an age when they would have provided a lot of meat for the amount of fodder they required. Efficient meat production was not, it seems, a characteristic of Iron Age sheep husbandry. How important wool production was depends on the interpretation of the relative number of young and old animals represented in the samples. Certainly all the adult animals could have provided wool and the occurrence of spindle whorls and loomweights at many sites testifies to textile manufacture. However, if first year mortalities were as high as suggested at sites such as Balksbury (Figure 19), the emphasis would have been more on the maintenance of a viable breeding stock rather than large scale wool production. Other sites have produced a greater proportion of adult animals. If it could be demonstrated that this was not merely a reflection of poorer preservation of the young mandibles, the case for the importance of wool would be strengthened. If not, an alternative hypothesis would regard sheep husbandry to be of a low standard, geared towards subsistence activities only, providing meat, milk, manure and wool but not at a commercial level.

It is interesting that the studies made at FRP, using a consistent methodology, have given a surprisingly consistent picture from the three Hampshire chalkland sites – Old Down Farm, Winnall Down, and Balksbury – for ageing results for sheep, despite the taphonomic and cultural factors which may bias the results (Maltby 1982b). It cannot, however, be assumed that the mortality profiles represented there are typical of the region. Redistribution of stock from producer to possible consumer settlements (none of which have been studied by the project) may have taken place. However, it is interesting to note that a simulation of the mortality profiles showed that they could have been produced by a self-contained viable herding strategy (Cribb, in preparation). The exploitation would appear to have been unspecialised, the main objective being to ensure the continuity of the stock, although meat and wool in particular would have been produced in some abundance.

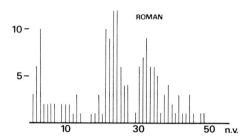

PORTCHESTER CASTLE

ROMAN

Figure 20   Ageing data from sheep/goat mandibles in Romano–British deposits at Portchester Castle (Groups 1–5). Data adapted from Grant (1975). n.v. = numerical value. Method of analysis follows Grant (1975). Estimated values are included. (Originally Maltby 1981a, 176).

Romano-British deposits have revealed fairly consistently a change in emphasis in sheep exploitation. The mandibles from Portchester Castle (Grant 1975) provide a good example (Figure 20). The number of mandibles with numerical values of 20–30 is high. A lot of the animals represented therefore were killed between the early wear stages of the second molar and the full eruption of the third molar. This corresponds roughly to Stages D and E in the method of Payne (1973, 293). If ageing estimates are correct, the sample shows an emphasis on the kill-off of second and third year animals for their meat. Many fewer first year animals are represented apart from some neonatal mortalities which were recovered mainly from wells (Grant 1975, 397–398). Samples from all types of Roman settlement have produced similar concentrations of mandibles of this age. These include urban centres such as Exeter (Maltby 1979, 42), military sites, for example Vindolanda (Hodgson 1977, 16), villas, for example Shakenoak Farm (Cram 1978, 128–135) and other rural sites, for example, Balksbury (Maltby in preparation 2). Generally fewer concentrations of mandibles belonging to first year mortalities have been found, although some early Roman sites have produced them in some numbers, for example, Winnall Down (Maltby AML Report 3453), Baylham House, Suffolk (Maltby in preparation 3) and the military deposits at Margidunum, Nottinghamshire (Harman 1969, 101). The change in emphasis to the culling of second and third year animals may therefore have been a gradual one, although there is a need to study a much wider range of samples before the pattern can be better understood.

Redistribution of stock and animal products undoubtedly took place in this period and it is conceivable that certain age classes will be found more commonly at some settlements than others. Nevertheless the present incomplete evidence suggests that meat production became more important in sheep management and there was a greater level of efficiency in sheep farming. A few samples have produced a relatively high number of mature animals, notably the villa at Barton Court Farm (Hamilton 1978, 129), the later levels at Fishbourne (Grant 1971, 384) and, to a lesser extent, Shakenoak Farm (Cram 1978, 128–135) and the Romano-British levels at Balksbury (Maltby in preparation 2). Once again it will be interesting to observe whether this pattern is typical of rural settlements and whether urban and military centres tended to attract a higher proportion of younger animals raised principally for their meat.

It is uncertain how important wool production became in the Romano-British period. Apart from the examples listed above, there is no evidence that adult animals were kept in numbers significantly above the level required to maintain the breeding stock, although investigations of other villa and rural assemblages may alter the picture. Change of emphasis in sheep farming may have occurred within the period but there is insufficient material to test this.

In the Iron Age **goat** was kept in small numbers. A detailed account of finds is given in Maltby (1981a, 159). In the Roman Period the pattern is similar although goats are generally better represented. The archaeological evidence suggests that goats were still of little importance in Roman Britain. They certainly provided little of the meat.

Pig had an important role in some Wessex settlements. By the Iron Age it is domestic pigs which make up the bone assemblages. The wild boar, *Sus scrofa*, occurs at many earlier Wessex sites and can be distinguished by its greater size especially in the third molar. Wessex Iron Age pigs show a withers height range of 50–60cm. Pigs tend to be killed young. Grant suggests that in all periods at Portchester Castle pigs were eaten in their second or third year (Grant 1977, 231).

The number of alternative exploitation strategies for domestic pigs is limited by the fact that almost all their value lies in their meat and lard. The high reproduction rates enable a substantial kill-off of young animals to take place and consequently relatively few animals are required to reach maturity. Thus the presence of large numbers of immature bones is to be expected and indeed is a feature of all the larger quantified assemblages under review. What is less certain is how intensive this exploitation was, how quickly the stock were fattened for slaughter, whether there were seasonal peaks in the culling of pigs and whether fattening processes relied solely on pannage or whether some sty husbandry was practised.

Evidence from the Iron Age is flimsy but there seems to have been no great intensity of pig exploitation on the settlement at Ashville, where 37% of 30 mandibles had the third molar in wear (Wilson 1978, 135) nor at Gussage All Saints, where between 33–47% of the mandibles had also reached that stage of development (Harcourt 1979a, 153). The Roman liking for suckling pig is well known and on some Romano-British sites it has been argued that there was a relatively high percentage of first year mortalities (Maltby 1979, 57; Grant 1971, 383). The better representation of pigs on most 'Romanised' sites (King 1978, 216) may also be significant here. Yet, even at Exeter and Fishbourne the proportion of mandibles with the third molar in wear was quite high and such jaws must have belonged to pigs at least two years old and possibly older.

Harcourt's (1974) review of the evidence for **dogs** on British archaeological sites included an extensive survey of metrical analysis. More recent studies have tended to support his observations. Measurements of Iron Age specimens revealed relatively little range in variation in the shape of the skulls and estimates of shoulder heights using conversion factors from the lengths of limb bones ranged between 35–58cm, mostly in the upper range, on material derived from 28 sites (Harcourt 1974, 163). The range has been increased slightly by the discovery of a partial skeleton of a dog in a late Iron Age deposit at Ashville that had an estimated shoulder height of 60cm (Wilson 1978, 125). Although articulated skeletons of dogs appear more frequently on Iron Age sites than those of other species, there is no doubt that dog meat was consumed at some settlements. Butchery marks on dog bones made during the disarticulation of the skeleton and the stripping of meat have been observed, for example, at Ashville (Wilson 1978, 122), Winnall Down (Maltby AML Report 3453) and Balksbury (Maltby in preparation 2). Some bones show skinning marks. The latter two sites also produced a relatively large number of bones of very young puppies, a phenomenon that also occurred at Gussage All Saints (Harcourt 1979, 154). It is possible that the number of dogs were controlled by killing some of the newborn puppies, although natural neonatal mortality could have accounted for some of these deaths.

The Roman period saw a significant increase in the variation of the types of dog kept. Estimates of shoulder heights ranged from 24–72cm and skull shapes showed much greater variation (Harcourt 1974, 164–166). The smallest dogs were regarded as lap dogs and the largest as hunting dogs.

The problem of differentiating the bones of the various species of **poultry** and their respective wild versions makes their discussion rather difficult. More research is needed on the metrical analysis and morphological distinctions of their skeletons before a clear picture can emerge. Bird bones are fragile and do not survive well but the rare occurrence of bird bones (including domestic fowl, large goose, and duck) on Iron Age sites is probably significant, since such sites contained some deposits that preserved bone well. Only Winklebury contained substantial numbers of domestic fowl bones but these include the bones of two skeletons (Jones R, 1977, 64). On all the other Iron Age sites on which bird bones have been quantified, those of domestic species were rare or absent and there is no certainty even that the duck and goose belonged to the domesticated varieties. Julius Caesar mentioned that the Britons kept chickens and geese but had a taboo on eating their flesh. Certainly there is as yet very little archaeological evidence that poultry was eaten by the Iron Age inhabitants of southern England. They may have provided eggs and feathers but contributed very little, if at all, to the meat diet.

In all the major Romano-British samples examined to date only domestic fowl were present consistently in any numbers. Once again it is not clear how many of the few bones of geese or duck that have been found belonged to domesticated birds.

The interpretation of the *relative number of animal bones of different species* has frequently been a principal component of faunal studies. Its main objectives have been the estimation of how much each species contributed to the meat diet and the assessment of the relative numbers of the different stock kept. There have been several attempts to generalise about the changes in the composition of the domestic herds in a region or within a period and these are worthy of consideration here.

Cunliffe (1978, 183–185) has stated that in broad terms there appears to have been a gradual increase in the numbers of sheep relative to cattle during the first millennium BC in southern England. In addition Cunliffe suggested that the large variation in the relative number of pig bones on Iron Age sites may be a reflection of ecological variation. The more suitable habitats for pigs would have been near woodlands rather than the open downland. Hence pig bones in assemblages on settlements on downlands were low.

Bradley (1978, 37–38) also pointed out the variability of pig remains on Iron Age sites citing Glastonbury and Croft Ambrey as extreme examples of low and high representation of the species in relation to sheep and thus questioned Clark's (1947) hypothesis that sheep gradually replaced pigs throughout prehistoric Britain as the woodlands were cleared. Like Cunliffe, Bradley suggests that regional and environmental factors were important considerations in the pig's importance. He also considered that there was a general increase in the proportion of sheep from the later Bronze Age to the later Iron Age.

The most comprehensive survey of Romano-British faunal material has been published by King (1978). He concludes from data from over a hundred sites that there was a distinct trend away from the keeping of sheep in the Roman period, probably due to the presence of more settlements in areas more suitable for cattle and pigs. Assemblages with more than 30% sheep bones were limited mainly to the lowland area of England and to dry, light soils. Secondly, the more 'Romanised' settlements such as villas, roadside settlements, towns and forts tended to have fewer sheep than the native sites which maintained the Iron Age pattern. Pig bones were more common on 'Romanised' settlements than on native sites, again partially indicating the presence of more settlements near woodland but also the probable influence of taxation and other cultural factors, such as the Roman's high regard for pork. Many military deposits contained high proportions of cattle bones.

The problems of quantification involved in such calculation of relative abundance are thoroughly discussed in Maltby (1981a, 164) and are seen as mainly those of methodology, intra-site variability, and inter-site variability. The rigorous methodology discussed in earlier sections has now been applied by FRP to Iron Age material from Old Down Farm, Balksbury, Winnall Down, Micheldever Wood banjo enclosure, and to smaller collections of material from Chilbolton Down, Cowdrey's Down, and Viables Farm, and more recently to a number of sites in Wiltshire and Dorset (Coy AML Reports 3591, 3592, 4070; Maltby AML Reports 2645, 3287, 3875).

On all these settlements cattle and sheep were the most abundant species followed by pig and horse. Wild species, goat, and poultry were poorly represented. Work on all these settlements demonstrated the fallacy of producing percentage figures for different species without taking the factors above into consideration. To give an example (discussed in detail in Maltby 1981a, 165) results for Winnall Down and Old Down Farm suggest that when these factors are taken into account there may in fact have been relatively little change in the relative numbers of the different species exploited between the early and middle Iron Age on these settlements.

To produce absolute percentages from such data, however, can be dangerously misleading as it is clear from the distribution of bones at Old Down Farm and Winnall Down, at least, that the carcases of the larger mammals (cattle and horse) may sometimes be stripped of meat in a primary butchery process that would result in fewer of their bones being incorporated into deposits used for the deposition of cooking waste. Such investigations have called into question Cunliffe's claim mentioned above of an increase in the importance of sheep for the Iron Age.

Another note of caution against such generalisations are the results from Groundwell Farm, Wiltshire (Coy AML Report 3591), a settlement not situated on chalk downlands, which produced a much greater proportion of pig bones than any of the above sites.

Little late Iron Age material has been collected and subjected to similar rigorous study as yet although the current study of Owslebury by Maltby should provide a large sample relevant to that period, augmenting the deposits from Winnall Down, Cleavel Point (Coy AML Report 3592), and Rope Lake Hole (Coy AML Report 4070).

The Romano-British period has, as can be seen above, provided a fruitful area of study and the changes in husbandry from what we can see in the middle Iron Age are of great interest. An additional problem in comparisons is the shallower burial and less good preservation on Romano-British sites favouring survival of large species over small. Possible changes within the Romano-British period itself provide a major new line of investigation. These areas are already under investigation by FRP and concentrate on the study of species representation, ageing data, butchery, and metrical analysis. Material from a variety of different site types is essential for analysis of the Romano-British material and we are fortunate in already having samples from major towns (Silchester, Winchester) and from several rural settlements in Hampshire and Dorset (Cleavel Point, Rope Lake Hole, Little Somborne (Maltby AML Report 2644), Balksbury, Winnall Down, Cowdery's Down, and Owslebury).

The Anglo-Saxon Period As for the Romano-British period there has been little time as yet for an integration of the knowledge we already have as material is still under study. Results will therefore be somewhat preliminary compared with those discussed above for the Iron Age. Most of the available material is mid-Saxon although small collections both of early Saxon material (from the recent M3 watching brief) and late Saxon material (from Winchester and Southampton) is now becoming available.

Large collections of mid-Saxon material from Melbourne Street, Southampton (Bourdillon and Coy 1980) and mid and late Saxon material from Portchester (Grant 1976) have set the scene but were not subjected to the same rigorous methodology as the Iron Age material already described.

The Melbourne Street, Hamwic, study established that mid-Saxon **cattle** at Southampton were comparable in size with those present in Southern Britain in the Roman Period (Bourdillon and Coy 1980, 106) and their close comparability with contemporary animals at Dorstat, Holland. Subsequent work in other parts of Britain shows a similar picture throughout the Saxon Period. Mid-Saxon samples from Hamwic and from rural Ramsbury, Wiltshire, are included in the cattle astragalus measurements in Figure 16.

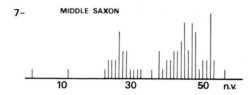

Figure 21   Ageing data from cattle mandibles in middle–late Saxon deposits at Portchester Castle. Data adapted from Grant (1975, 1976). n.v. = numerical value. Method of analysis follows Grant (1975). Estimated values are included. (Originally in Maltby 1981a, 181).

Of the few Anglo-Saxon samples examined, the age distribution of the mandibles from the middle–late Saxon levels at Portchester Castle (Grant 1976, 276) appears typical. Most cattle were mature, some having heavy wear on the teeth and including a high proportion of working, dairy and breeding stock. There was, however, a smaller but substantial group of mandibles in which the third molar was not erupted. These probably belonged to immature animals killed for their meat possibly between three and four years of age (Figure 21). A similar distribution occurred in the large sample of mandibles from Hamwic and the sexing evidence suggested that the majority of the immature specimens were males not required for breeding or working (Bourdillon and Coy 1980, 105). Another example of this age distribution has been discovered in the sample from the St. Peter's Street excavations in Northampton (Harman 1979, 331).

An attempt to obtain absolute ages for Saxon cattle and tie these in with tooth wear stages was made using material from Hamwic (Turner 1979; Coy, Jones and Turner 1982).

Although some attempt has been made already, in Hampshire at least, to investigate the relationship between the different types of Saxon settlement (in this case 'urban' Hamwic and a number of mid-Saxon rural settlements – Bourdillon 1983) larger samples and more intensive analysis of a consistent type is needed before any patterns both of cattle husbandry and the movement of cattle can emerge.

Metrical analyses of **horse** bones of Romano-British and Anglo-Saxon date have been limited by their rare occurrence on most sites. At present it seems that the smallest ponies represented in the Iron Age samples do not appear on later sites and some bones of larger horses have been recovered, although few appear to have been over 14 hands (e.g. Wilson 1978, 117–118; Bourdillon and Coy 1980, 104–105; Clutton-Brock 1976, 383).

The ages of the horses represented at Hamwic are usually those which correspond with maximum working ability. This and the great scarcity of bones suggests that horses were not bred there. Horse remains at rural Ramsbury are a greater proportion of the whole assemblage (Coy 1980). Occasional discoveries of butchered horse bones have been made on Anglo-Saxon sites, for example, at Sedgeford, Norfolk (Clutton-Brock 1976, 383) and Hamwic but again, where found, adult horses predominated the samples and their value as transport and pack animals continued to be the dominant feature of their exploitation.

Mid-Saxon **sheep** in Wessex give withers heights which can be as small as those in the Iron Age in Wessex but some Saxon sheep are larger than those found in the Iron Age. The sheep at Hamwic do not look particularly like those from Dorestad, Holland as is so for the cattle (Bourdillon, personal communication). Six of the seven samples of sheep tibia with the highest mean distal widths discussed by Maltby (1981a, 189) are from Anglo-Saxon sites in East Anglia and southern Britain.

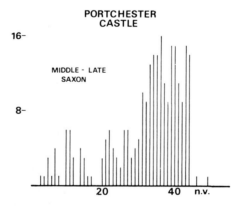

Figure 22   Ageing data from sheep/goat mandibles in middle–late Saxon deposits at Portchester Castle. Data adapted from Grant (1976). n.v. = numerical value. Method of analysis follows Grant (1975). Estimated values are included. (Originally in Maltby 1981a, 177).

Ageing evidence from Anglo-Saxon sites is more limited than that for Iron Age/Romano-British but it can be shown that wool production became more important in some areas during the latter part of the period. The sample from the middle–late Saxon deposits at Portchester Castle (Figure 22) included a concentration of mandibles with numerical values of over 30, indicating that the majority belonged to mature animals. The smaller sample from the late Saxon period at Portchester was similar (Grant 1976, 278). The contrast between this sample and the one from the Roman occupation of the fort (Figure 20) is marked. If these jaws accurately reflect the kill-off pattern, meat production was now only a secondary consideration to wool production. Of course it is again possible that the sheep represented at Portchester Castle do not contain a cross-section of the sheep kept in the area. It is interesting to note, however, that the urban deposits at Hamwic also produced a large proportion of mature animals (Bourdillon and Coy 1980, 87). Most of the mandibles from Ramsbury, Wiltshire also belonged to mature animals (Coy 1980). Several other samples, particularly from North Elmham, Norfolk (Noddle 1975, 257), the urban deposits from the St. Peter's Street excavations, Northampton (Harman 1979, 331), Walton, Aylesbury (Noddle 1976, 277) and Durham (Rackham 1979, 53) have produced high percentages of adult sheep. Only the sample from Sedgeford, Norfolk has not produced this pattern (Clutton-Brock 1976, 382). Although the number of samples is small, they have been derived from a wide range of settlement types in several parts of the country. It is tempting to equate this evidence with a large scale increase in the importance of wool production to enable extensive wool and cloth trading to take place. The origins of this development may lie in the early Saxon period but there is as yet little information about samples of that date, although results for the vast sample from West Stow, Suffolk are now available (Crabtree in press 1 and 2).

It is therefore possible to see long term changes in sheep exploitation. Once the possibility of regional, ecological, and cultural variability has been investigated the pattern will be better understood. At present there seems to have been an underlying trend from a low level of subsistence husbandry in the Iron Age, through improvements and emphasis on better meat production during the Romano-British period, to the development of wool production as the most important component of sheep husbandry by the late Saxon period.

The Anglo-Saxon period does at least provide some documentary evidence for the keeping of **goats**. Archaeological evidence would suggest that they continued to play only a small role as meat producers, although it is conceivable that they were kept mainly for their milk and skins and not butchered for meat. Goat bones were found consistently in small numbers at Hamwic (Bourdillon and Coy 1980, 111) but there is no evidence that large numbers of goats were exploited at any of the settlements excavated to date. Unmistakable at Hamwic are the large male goat horn cores which are common and may have been imported for hornworking.

Southampton Saxon **pigs** have an upper size limit somewhat higher than Wessex Iron Age pigs, with withers heights of 50–70cm compared with 50–60cm. At Melbourne Street, Hamwic, there was one large pig femur which could have been from a wild individual but otherwise pigs were obviously domestic, with ranges for third lower molar length of 25–34mm compared with figures of 45–50mm for continental *Sus scrofa* (Luhmann 1965, 21).

Such pigs were eaten young. At Hamwic 39% of pig jaws had not yet acquired third molars. This probably represented an age of less than three years (Silver 1969, 298–9).

The variation in skull shape of **dogs** appears to have decreased in the Anglo-Saxon period, if the specimens from the 11 sites examined by Harcourt (1974) are typical. The range in shoulder heights was similar to that for the Romano-British period but the majority of specimens belonged to large individuals. Domestic cats, first seen in the third to fourth century in Wessex, are occasional finds at Hamwic.

Geese as large as the wild greylag, *Anser anser,* and presumed domestic make their first real impact in Anglo-Saxon times. They are already of some importance at West Stow (Coy AML Report 3449) and are found consistently in all the Hamwic pits (Bourdillon and Coy 1980). By mid-Saxon times domestic fowl are of great variety and include bantams and capons (Bourdillon and Coy 1980, 44; Coy 1983) although the largest size ranges are from late Saxon Winchester. Analysis of sex ratios of fowl is beginning to show interesting results (Driver 1982; Coy 1983a).

King (1978) has suggested that Anglo-Saxon faunal material was not markedly different from Roman except for the high proportion of pig bones on a few sites. There was a trend which saw the increase in the proportion of sheep again towards the high levels attained in the Middle Ages. Obviously the same restraints apply to *the calculation of specific percentages* as they do for the periods discussed earlier. At Hamwic for example, cattle provided 52.5% of the domestic stock fragments, 72.1% of the weight of the identified bones and 31.4% of the minimum number of individuals estimated from the mandibles (Bourdillon and Coy 1980, 84–85). Corresponding fluctuations in the percentage of other species were found according to the method.

Detailed work at Hamwic now under way has investigated the effect of differential retrieval by the complete excavation of a pit and is now moving on to a study of the effect of contextual variability in Hamwic in the hope that removal of this constraint may allow (as it has already to some extent for the Iron Age results discussed above) a more accurate representation of specific percentages. It is fortunate that excavations there in the last year have produced specialised bone deposits, stratigraphic relationships, occupation layers in buildings, and the edge of the mid-Saxon town itself with its boundary ditch.

Post-Saxon Material The complexity of post-Saxon times and the lack of material from certain periods and for rural settlement means that again few conclusions can be presented.

The most intensive study in Wessex into post-Saxon material has been one by J Bourdillon for all post-Hamwic material from Southampton. This has demonstrated the post-Saxon diminution in size for **sheep** and **cattle** (Bourdillon 1980, 187) but at the same time has hinted at a complexity of fluctuations during the Medieval Period which only the analysis of further samples will sort out. Provisional results from some French excavations suggest that such a medieval size diminution did not occur there (Audoin, personal communication).

Recently the waterlogged riverside deposits of the Reading Abbey complex have produced **cattle** horn core material which has begun to give us a picture of cattle size and form from twelfth to eighteenth century AD. So far, however, only the early material has produced a large enough sample of material for an appreciation of the wide range of variation in animal type after the Saxon Period (Coy AML Report 4067). Increase in horn core size is correlated with a general increase in body size and the horn core types have been analysed for many London sites (Armitage 1982a). The establishment of such a framework for Wessex is essential if fluctuations in size are to be recognised and if animal size is to be used as an indicator of wealth as it conceivably might be (Armitage 1982b). Care must be taken, however, to build up an adequate framework as regional differences in size are already becoming evident (e.g. as in Dorset – Coy 1982c, AML Report 3877).

One exciting piece of sixteenth century evidence has been the opportunity this year to examine a very well-dated and specialised deposit from 19 July 1545 which provides superb evidence of what the best cattle and pig were really like at this time.

As discussed above under 'disposal strategies' we do not yet have material from the full range of contexts in this period. More organised refuse disposal in the Post-medieval Period means that such excavations have to be treated in a different way as far as the study of animal bones is concerned. Much of the material collected may throw little light upon the period in question so that there has to be a very careful search for meaningful contexts. This can mean that a lot of material needs to be collected initially but that much of it can later be discarded if it is not associated with reliable phasing evidence. Medieval and post-medieval archaeologists often need convincing that bones will produce any useful evidence and it is a great struggle to avoid unbiassed samples in these collections.

Apart from the usual remains of cattle, sheep, and pig from meals there is in post-Saxon times a wider range of wild species exploited (as already discussed in the section on the 'exploitation of wild species').

There are now opportunities to adapt what has been learnt from the intensive Iron Age and Saxon studies at FRP to material of these periods. Apart from the usual questions dealt with above of specific ratios, age structure of populations, and size there are particular problems of redistribution and specialisation which make it necessary to study material from a very wide range of context and site type and to do this in association with documentation of the period and in conjunction with the evidence from human skeletal material and botanical remains. There is a very large amount of scope here and it would be unwise to attempt conclusions at this stage.

Other Criteria Related to Animal Husbandry Apart from the analyses relating to specific ratios, usage, and size discussed in the whole of the 'animal husbandry' section there are some criteria which are computer coded by FRP and will ultimately lead to a greater understanding of animal husbandry in all periods. Some of these are metrical – such as the form of cattle metapodials and third phalanges which may eventually produce evidence of the use of cattle for traction. Others, like the horn core forms discussed above, are also non-metrical. The incidence of other genetic and epigenetic variation e.g. that relating to dental anomalies and atypical foramina, is probably the area with the most potential for study on the distribution of past animal stocks, the closed or open nature of flocks, and the origins of animals whose carcases are found in towns. Pathological changes are recorded but have been little studied to date. The distribution of calculus and periodontal disease in sheep was recently given a statistical treatment for three Wessex settlements: Atworth Roman Villa; Ower, Dorset; and Winnall Down (Backway 1981). This concluded that the frequency of these conditions varied greatly and that samples from a wider selection of periods and geographical areas were needed before explanations could be attempted.

Butchery and Bone-Working

Evidence for many cultural practices relating to all stages of food preparation can be found on both bones and shells. Using the word 'butchery' in the widest sense a number of marks may be distinguished which are due to the successive processes involved – slaughter, carcase division, meat removal both before and after cooking, and the use of knives or bone breakage for marrow extraction.

These data may be biased by successive taphonomic factors as already described. But just as an understanding of butchery must rest upon eliminating the effects of these subsequent events, so an understanding of those wider cultural issues for Wessex which relate to the food animals, such as redistribution of food within and between settlements, can never be recognised unless detailed studies have actually *defined* what we mean by Iron Age butchery, typical medieval skinning marks etc. We need as careful an analysis of these as Binford has achieved for the modern Nunamiut (Binford 1978).

Robert Foot produced a preliminary study of Iron Age butchery at Old Down Farm, Andover (Foot 1978). Apart from this the only systematic recording we know of has been the daily use of the AML coding system's butchery field for all bones recorded at FRP. Butchery is one of the pieces of evidence being used by Maltby in his attempts already mentioned above to discover changes within the *Iron Age and the Romano-British Periods.* The majority of Iron Age butchery was performed with a knife and usually left small, sharp incisions made during disarticulation, skinning or filleting. The Romano-British period saw a much wider range of butchery techniques. Similar knife incisions are found, particularly on sheep and pig bones but the use of a chopper and/or heavier use of the knife for disarticulation of certain joints on cattle become more common.

There is however a lot of variation between settlements. The most intensive butchery has been recovered from urban deposits at Silchester and Winchester and it appears to be these types of site where most chopping of bone occurs. It also seems that more use was made of marrow bones judging by the much greater fragmentation especially of cattle metapodia in Romano-British deposits generally and in urban deposits in particular, although analysis is complicated by taphonomic factors.

Maltby's work at Cowdery's Down makes some attempt to use butchery techniques as a cultural separator (Maltby AML Report 3875). More recent results will be published shortly (Maltby in press 2). Examination of specialised deposits of primary butchery waste at Silchester (Maltby AML Report 3595) and of bone-working waste which showed careful selection of bones for working at Western Suburbs, Winchester (Coy AML Report 4063) have made it clear that the Romano-British period provides a complicated but fruitful area of study for butchery and bone-working techniques.

The only other period where these matters have been studied in Wessex in any depth, apart from typological study of the bone objects associated with any period, is in analysis of *Saxon* material from Hamwic and Winchester. There is again, especially at Winchester, ample evidence of the use of very sharp and yet heavy knives to cut right through bones. In Late Saxon times in Winchester this technique seems to be a common way of dividing the smaller ungulates with cuts either side of the vertebral centrum. In much of the butchery of cattle at Hamwic, however, in the mid-Saxon period longbones appear to have been smashed midshaft and cut through the joints with a much heavier implement (Bourdillon and Coy 1980). Bone working debris at Six Dials, Southampton is found alongside food debris in the pits (Colley AML Report 4071) and consists of antler, cattle bone, and possibly whalebone. Sawing appears in connection with this and some of the debris may be connected with the manufacture of combs.

In the more detailed studies now taking place at Hamwic, Southampton Museums aim to both define the extent to which bone-working was a specialised activity and carry out a typological study of the bone objects produced. Only sieved deposits can yield reliable data for bone-working by allowing retrieval of all the small offcuts produced.

As in other regions one of the major developments in medieval butchery is the splitting of cattle carcasses down the midline. This had developed into an accurate art by post-medieval times. Only careful analysis of well-collected samples will reveal what happened to the rest of the carcase and primary butchery sites for the Medieval and Post-medieval periods for Wessex must be sought. Reading Abbey has recently provided some early medieval evidence for the bone assemblages that can be expected in sites where leather and horn were worked (Coy AML Report 4067).

The recognition of food preparation and cooking areas by the elements present and by burnt and 'ivoried' bone can be useful archaeologically, although the causes of 'ivorying' in bone need more detailed analysis – possibly using biochemical techniques (Coy 1975).

Art and Ritual

Worked bones, including all finished objects, need to be seen by the archaeozoologist so that species and anatomical element can be ascertained but there is also scope for stylistic analysis of worked bone in Wessex. This is not a part of the archaeozoologist's role and should ideally form part of a regional or wider study.

The interpretation of bone associations as being of ritual significance has been subjected to critical analysis in recent years. FRP deliberately encourages closer study of articulated bones, including whole skeletons, before they are raised. Many whole skeletons are from intrusive burials, some modern. Occasionally animals have died and the cause of death is known (Harcourt 1979a, 159, describes a cow which died in labour). Examination of some partial skeletons from the Iron Age has shown that meat had been removed prior to the disposal of the articulated bones (Maltby 1981b; AML Report 3287; Foot 1978). Dogs are sometimes carefully buried (Griffith AML Report 2430).

Animal remains are sometimes associated with human inhumations as at Viables Farm (Maltby AML Report 3287) and in the 'head and hooves' burials noted in Wessex Neolithic long barrows (Robertson-Mackay 1980, 147); and with cremations, as in the remains of flounders and a pig's trotter (Coy AML Report 2329), and birds' eggs found in Roman Winchester.

Evidence for sacrifice is difficult to pinpoint. Apart from a careful search for evidence of slaughter on the bones themselves, it can rest on archaeological context, the age and sex of the suspected victims, and the seasonality of the practice. Again this is something that depends upon the careful accumulation of detailed evidence (Grant in press).

With respect to the more general effects of ritual behaviour, bone analysis can only provide part of the evidence that can help to clarify economic and religious motives for food choice. The role of pigs in the Roman Period needs further investigation (Coy in press). The role of fish in the medieval diet, although often given religious significance, may also be functionally linked with changes in agriculture so that a careful analysis of the whole picture should include evidence from domestic stock, seeds, and documents. Once again such studies will profit from comparisons within and outside the region.

Wider Issues

Animal husbandry discussions above, especially those for the Romano-British and Saxon Periods have not been confined to individual settlements or even to Wessex and serve to show how bone evidence can be used to illuminate many wider issues. For example, analysis of large-scale accumulations of butchery waste, and variations in the age, sex, and type of animals represented in contemporary settlements can be used (with care) to investigate redistribution and trade of animals and their products (Maltby in preparation 1). This is seen at FRP as an integral part of the urban/rural investigations of our original aims. The impact of the Romans on animal husbandry in this country can be seen to some extent as part of the process of 'Romanisation', and may be monitored in the bones in the same way as the phenomenon has been monitored by many other types of archaeological data (Maltby in press 1). The evidence for these processes is being accumulated gradually. It depends upon using detailed inter-site comparisons and therefore requires some standardisation of methodology between sites.

Many of the detailed butchery and bone-working studies may throw important light on urbanisation by indicating the scale and distribution of these activities within a settlement.

The surrounding environment

Some elements of ecological information may be deduced from the *presence* of certain wild species in Wessex (whether they were exploited or not). Such clues may support or invalidate ecological and cultural models of change being considered for the domestic species. A mammalian example was the associated wild fauna including red deer, roe deer, and beaver, at mid-Saxon Ramsbury, Wiltshire, compared with the almost total absence of wild mammals at mid-Saxon Southampton (Coy 1980; 1982a, 210). But to what extent this gives us ecological or cultural information is difficult to clarify. A notable missing factor was the absence of a sieving programme so that the relative role of fish in the two assemblages could not be compared. Future study of mid-Saxon material from near the river Thames at Wraysbury, Berkshire, where an intensive sieving programme has been carried out, should prove more illuminating.

One piece of straightforward environmental evidence was provided by the roe antlers from Ramsbury, which Richard Prior of the Game Conservancy reckons are by modern British standards poor heads showing what are usually considered to be signs of poor nutrition in the spring.

The more precise identification of bird and fish remains which has taken place over the past few years has already been mentioned. Evidence for the presence of particular species of bird is often difficult to interpret as we do not know whether they were breeding or migratory individuals, unless bones contain medullary bone indicative of egg-laying (Coy 1983).

As has been pointed out earlier the presence of certain fish species in the medieval period gives valuable information about trade (as in the finds of large cod at Romsey (Coy AML Report 1803). The presence of other coastal material inland can be used as evidence for movement of resources even in prehistory as in the finds of kittiwake at Iron Age Gussage All Saints, Dorset (Harcourt 1979a, 155) and Danebury, Hampshire (Coy AML Report 3873).

Small mammal and amphibian remains require their own carefully designed sampling strategy which needs to be related to work on the surrounding modern ecosystems if it is to provide significant results. They also provide direct evidence of the history of archaeological features, e.g. pits may act as pitfall traps, and posts may be used by birds of prey as perches near which they produce pellets (Jewell 1958; Coy AML Report 3874). In some cases mice, as pests of stored products, could have lived in the features in which they are found. The small mammal and amphibian species present are normally extremely common species today and modern work demonstrates that ecological interpretations for the past could be dangerous without, for example, seasonal knowledge. If the remains are from pellets the results may indicate the species present in the total range of the bird of prey involved rather than just the immediate environment of the settlement. The volume and speed of recent rescue work in Wessex has not been conducive to intensive study of these species although they do represent an important if minor aspect which could lead to a greater understanding of the build-up of a deposit as much as they could provide environmental information.

Two species should, however, be mentioned. There is as yet insufficient evidence from modern data to prove that the ubiquity of the vole *Arvicola terrestris* on Wessex Iron Age sites on the chalk means that it has since changed its habits, as has frequently been suggested in the past. The current water vole survey being undertaken by the Mammal Society should clarify this issue. It is important that archaeologists should recognise its burrows during excavation as they may otherwise be misinterpreted. Remains of the house mouse, *Mus musculus* (a species probably imported inadvertently from Europe) have been found well-stratified on many Iron Age settlements in Wessex since it was identified at Gussage All Saints (Harcourt 1979a, 155), most recently in the early phases of Danebury (Coy AML Report 3874).

It has been pointed out recently that there is some scope for further study of sub-fossil small mammal remains which might help provide missing evidence for post-glacial distributions — perhaps by examining genetic and epigenetic disparities (Yalden 1982, 35). This might be considered, however, to be of more interest to zoology and geology than to archaeology and could equally well be applied to other wild mammal species. Archaeological evidence can thus fill a vital gap in knowledge of the origins of the present day vertebrate fauna. It does not follow, however that archaeological data can be used to reconstruct past ecosystems and we must not delude ourselves that vertebrate remains from archaeological settlements can be worked into simple ecological models.

To give an example, modern unpublished studies on plaice, *Platichthys platessa,* and flounder, *Platichthys flesus*, in the Solent, suggest that tidal migration strategies are used as a way of niche partitioning. It would be naive of us to imagine that we can say anything about the immediate state of the river tidal flats in the mid-Saxon period from the presence of these species at Hamwic. That is not to say that, when sufficient modern data are available, useful comparisons will not be possible.

Future developments

Assessment of achievements to date and their continuation

Not all the work going forward in Wessex is being carried out by the FRP but we hope that we have influenced some of it enough for a review of the status of our earlier aims to have relevance. It must be remembered that most of the key sites in Wessex are being worked by other faunal analysts and that we are therefore unable as yet to report on them. The Danebury work will shortly be published by Grant, and Legge has the Hambledon Hill analysis in hand. Winchester 1960–70 work is being published by Sheppard and Adams. Some of the earliest prehistoric material is being studied by Grigson and Noddle and all Southampton medieval material has been worked upon by Bourdillon and Driver. Sites with FRP input are shown in Figure 23.

As suggested earlier, although some progress has been made in analysis of *continuity and change* in the Iron Age, Romano-British and mid-Saxon Periods, the methodology evolved in these studies now needs to be put into action for samples from other periods as they become available and these must be priorities for the future. With resources as they are it will, however, be a question of choosing whether we do this or complete the analysis of the later prehistoric periods. We feel that Bronze Age and Neolithic material should have the highest priority and that time should be found for the analysis of the early material from Coneybury Hill, Stonehenge; Easton Lane, Hampshire; and Potterne, Wiltshire — the latter may possibly yield a large sample of Late Bronze Age material with superb preservation.

Further results from early Saxon West Stow will be of interest, (although it is not a Wessex site) and will be useful for any future analysis of the early Saxon material from Wessex. The small amount found on M3 has already been mentioned. Rural samples from all Saxon dates hold a high priority and the analysis of Wraysbury and Old Windsor due to take place in 1985 will be important. The vast amount of mid-Saxon material from Hamwic now provides great scope in the light of the breakthrough in understanding of this settlement made by the archaeologists in the last few months.

The additional needs for deeper understanding of the Iron Age and Romano-British Periods have been spelled out in the section on animal husbandry. Completion of the very large collection from Owslebury will answer some of them. After that they will have to compete for our attention with the early prehistoric work discussed above. It is very difficult to decide which should have priority, presumably the material from the early periods because of its relative scarcity.

Medieval and Post-medieval material is more difficult to control and the choice of samples and assessment of what has already been excavated needs more time than current staffing in Wessex can provide. So much urban excavation is occurring in Wessex that excavated samples from Poole, Dorchester, Alton, Newbury and Winchester lie unstudied and the next few years are likely to produce much more of this urban rescue material. But the quality of retrieval of the new material and recognition of what it represents are paramount and there is no point in anything but a reasoned retention of bones from dateable contexts and bone reports which set out to answer specific archaeological questions. It would be a waste of resources to process material of dubious origin. Archaeozoology must keep abreast of archaeological excavation if it is to solve the questions and the questions for post-Saxon periods will only be answered with the right samples. Rural medieval and post-medieval samples should again have priority, likewise early medieval, post-Conquest material.

The *urban/rural relationships* which have so far been investigated and their precursors in the Iron Age all suggest the need for more rural, or supplier, sites. Some of the questions discussed under 'wider issues' relate to this theme and we have made some progress in the analysis of the effect of 'Romanisation'. The relationships between other developments in settlement patterns and animal husbandry have not as yet been investigated in detail, for example the changes observed in the settlement pattern in some parts of England in the Late Iron Age may coincide with changes in species exploitation but again few samples of this date have been analysed. Similarly it should be possible to use faunal analyses to test the models for change in late Roman Britain. It may well be wise, as resources are limited, to concentrate on prehistoric and Roman models for this kind of work rather than to investigate the possibly complex patterns in the medieval data although ensuring that suitable material from medieval and post-medieval settlement is salvaged now.

The *wild/domestic* make-up of the faunal sample can only be assessed if methodology is rigorously defined (e.g. the 'level of identification' referred to earlier) and continuing attention is given to the skills of comparative anatomy which depend on a good comparative collection and literature as already stressed. These skills need constant vigilance and maintenance as do the collections themselves so that specialists are not being used for routine unskilled work. The collections built up at FRP are also used by many other specialists in Wessex and further afield, especially those who are not skilled in the identification of wild mammals, birds and fish.

Marine resources were of significance on many Wessex sites and our decision to include these has led to more insight into faunal assemblages. Fish are only now becoming of importance as the sites which produced sieved material are being analysed. Marine molluscs are lagging even further behind but as earlier comments demonstrate they can yield cultural and environmental evidence. Provision must be made for their study as soon as it is suspected that the site will produce them.

New techniques, such as tooth sectioning for the assessment of absolute age already discussed, may have a future but both this, and further morphometric work (which we made a start on in encouraging an undergraduate dissertation on the effect of domestication on cranial morphology — Burrell 1981) will need to wait on results from current studies taking place at Cambridge and York, respectively. New ways of using the data we collect on butchery, pathology, and genetic anomalies have been discussed a little and these could be developed and provide one of the main ways in which archaeozoology could say more about the movement of animals in the past. Even newer techniques such as those of MacGregor and Currey (1983) on bone tool technology and on $^{13}C/^{12}C$ ratios (see e.g. Schoeninger *et al.* 1983) could be exploited.

Pilot schemes, however, must be the province of other disciplines and may form suitable subjects for undergraduate and post graduate dissertations in, for example, Biology Departments of Universities. With their current resources archaeozoologists can only respond by organising collection of suitable samples of archaeological material and quickly recognising opportunities for such investigations. Part of the quick response may involve acquiring large modern samples of the same species. This too is the archaeozoologist's responsibility, even if it needs separate funding, as biologists and others cannot be expected to become too involved in answering archaeological questions.

But basic to any future progress must be the appreciation of the changes in concept which have occurred in archaeology and archaeozoology and which have resulted in a move from studying archaeological settlements as monuments, to studying assemblages, and finally the behaviour patterns which led to their accumulation. Concurrent with the continuation of present work discussed above must be the development of indices as discussed in the section on 'post-depositional taphonomic processes' which aid the separation of retrieval, post-depositional, and cultural effects. Continued computer-coding of metrical and non-metrical data (perhaps on a reduced scale), and the development of software for its swift appraisal, will allow both fine-grained intra-site analysis and work relating to wider geographical and temporal axes.

The quality of the data

It is essential to develop methods which will ensure that bones are studied in a scientific and comparable manner between different workers and different sites — ways which are independent of current theories and yet enable us to collect and analyse our data according to evolving archaeological concepts.

Control over the quality of the data recorded has already been discussed at some length. Computer recording, although it can provide a firmer basis for comparison of results collected by different workers and from different sites, does not begin to solve the problems of comparability. This can only be done by close co-operation between the workers themselves or by maintaining continuity of worker and method for a group of sites. As computerised recording spreads it will be essential to maintain close contact with users within and between regions. Ready access to modern collections and literature has also been stressed. Without all these, comparisons between the results of different workers would still be unwise.

The ability to handle these highly diverse data will increase as cheap microelectronic systems develop larger and larger storage facilities and good, relevant statistical packages. Analyses of the type discussed by Maltby (1981a, 165) have so far only been achieved by re-entering data onto the University of Southampton's ICL 2970 computer or by tedious manual working with a programmable calculator. Future data analysis could use more fully the data that *have* been computer recorded and make the study of the bones more cost-effective.

Even so, the balance of what is recorded against what is used is an important one; made more unwieldy by the fact that these data are both a museum record and a dynamic research tool. But this contrariety need not imply conflict and it should be possible to allow for sufficient safeguards to be maintained to allow future revision and pruning of these coding systems. Perhaps this time has now come.

In order to approach an understanding of continuity and change in animal husbandry it is essential to link animal bone variability with the variability shown by other factors in the archaeological record, especially those on which the archaeologist relies for providing a phasing framework for a site. The quality of the stratigraphic record and phasing ultimately controls the usefulness of faunal data (Harris 1979, 99). It is also difficult for bone coding systems to develop greater archaeological relevance without further progress and wider application of computer techniques in field archaeology itself as these systems have been devised to relate to the other evidence through the context number and for all but small sites manual correlations between faunal and other data would be too tedious.

A multidisciplinary approach

One important element in research design for the future is to achieve a multidisciplinary approach in Wessex, preferably starting before excavation. There has been virtually no policy in Wessex for retrieval and study of, for example, seeds and human bones, so that these have been retrieved and studied according to the sympathies of the individual excavator and individual specialists. Use of the same bulk samples for the retrieval of several kinds of biological evidence would often be more cost-effective than the collection of separate samples, and in addition such samples can yield archaeological information — e.g., on ceramics, coins, and bone- or metal-working.

Dietary and usage evidence is incomplete when only animal bones and shells are studied and a great deal more would be learnt if their information could be seen alongside the evidence from human bones and teeth and botanical remains. It is also impossible to separate, for example, considerations of manuring, development of orchards, gardens, changes in crops grown or their yields, species introductions . . . . . without a multidisciplinary approach involving all branches of 'environmental archaeology' and, for later periods, the existing documentation.

Equally, close co-operation during post-excavational study between bone analysts and those studying the pottery and other artefacts has already been discussed for its importance to 'phasing' but such co-operation may also lead to short cuts in the preparation of archive and publication.

Co-operation with the other sciences could result in use of a wide range of biological, veterinary, and statistical techniques in relation to specific identification, domestication, and nutritional status, for example. Some of these have been discussed as logical extensions of current work, and a few have been mentioned under 'new techniques'.

In the future it may be possible to fit detailed results from faunal analysis into the complex geographical variability outlined in the introductory geographical description of Wessex. This must always be our ultimate objective but it cannot be done prematurely and it would involve some selection of settlements for excavation because they lie in particular geographical contexts rather than for 'rescue' considerations.

To take just one aspect — *climate*, and its minor fluctuations within the region, through time, and according to distance from the coast must influence, for example, growing seasons, livestock growth, and the incidence and severity of livestock epidemics (University College of Wales 1958–66). If we can reconstruct topography, aspect, soil depth, and soil texture for archaeological settlements, and to some extent climate, it should be possible to make suggestions about comparative conditions for the growth of crops and raising of livestock. The mapping of such information and of natural resource availability and ecotones, is of value for both archaeological theory construction and interpretations, in both of which archaeozoology can play a role.

In some senses geographical sub-regions can be used as a background for theory testing, relating observed archaeological variability to differences in geology, topography, and climate or to ecological, social, administrative, and cognitive aspects of an area. In such studies some themes transcend sub-regional and regional boundaries. Others would use areas with a more secure historical basis than the geographical sub-regions defined earlier. Yet other themes may be related to variations within very small areas, perhaps aimed at investigating individual factors such as aspect, altitude, or specific cultural groupings. To date there has been even less of this small-scale analysis although logically it ought to come first.

Theories emanating from some of the cultural and behavioural evidence discussed under 'current themes' would be based initially on results from individual settlements and would develop outwards to relate to ecological and geographical constraints. Such constraints cannot in themselves therefore be regarded as a basis for theory testing but only as elements in the search for pattern in a very complex body of evidence.

Cost-effectiveness

Much of the previous section on 'current themes' discussed the ways in which archaeozoology in Wessex is attempting to come to grips with today's archaeological problems and various ways in which these studies could be made cost-effective have already been suggested.

The need to produce a complete archive for posterity may conflict here with bone studies and this matter is closely linked with whether bones should be studied 'blind' before final phasings are produced and thus perhaps have a greater input into the phasing process itself or whether bones should be analysed by groupings suggested by the final phasing of the site and only feed into the archaeologist's conclusions. There are two points here. First, in the present state of our understanding of faunal material it is only just now becoming possible to define what data we need to record from the bones so that the 'blind' type of study (which rests on using computers to make the final selection once phasing is completed) would have been unwise. Second, there is really no justification for recording bones which are from known modern contexts or from contexts that are so hopelessly mixed that there is no likelihood that they will ever be dated. Obviously though in the case of period interfaces with controversial artefacts the bones may play an important role and must be recorded and retained.

Thus a post-phasing study is in our opinion the only valid one at present and could be more cost-effective. We must not allow delays in producing bone reports, lamentable though they are, to force us to adopt wasteful and unscientific strategies.

Archaeozoology cannot be seen as providing only additional, background, environmental data for archaeologists, although it can do that. The main aim of the archaeozoological work being carried out in Wessex should be to relate very closely to archaeology and to help to solve the questions that archaeologists need answered. In the main material studied at FRP (Neolithic – Post-medieval) these are often questions relating to animal husbandry.

But these questions also range from fine-grained ones relating to people's activities and the build-up of particular deposits to wider questions relating to trade, redistribution, and economic change.

Archaeozoology can be no more precise than the excavation on which it depends. Both the high degree of bias introduced into the faunal data during excavation and the crucial relevance of archaeologists' phasing have been discussed. There is little value in studying the bones when these factors are not assessable. The archaeozoologist must know how the bones were excavated and the extent to which the final phasing is stratigraphically or typologically based. This is not to say that all 'backlog' material is worthless but the study of such material and the production of bone reports should not be a major aim in itself, whereas ensuring adequate retrieval from new excavations should.

Co-operation with other specialists and an awareness of archaeozoological progress in other regions and countries must be used to ensure that our thinly-spread archaeological resources are concentrated on projects which are both of prime archaeological and historical significance and are not repetitive. The emergence of national patterns in faunal data, as shown in our discussions of animal husbandry for the Iron Age, Romano-British, and Anglo-Saxon Periods above, reinforces this view.

Conclusion

Archaeology is in crisis. In 1970 Professor Cunliffe in his inaugural lecture in this university spoke of the rate of destruction of archaeological evidence in town and country. He drew the analogy of the systematic burning of a Public Record Office. This analogy is even more relevant today. What we had begun to regard as a run down of excavation two or three years ago has now become, once again, a desperate race against time as more capital projects get under way.

We cannot afford what Cunliffe in the same lecture called 'a scholarly pace' as we must quickly attempt to apply conclusions from unprocessed results in order to extract the maximum information from each new project (Cunliffe 1970).

Quite rightly there is now more rigorous selection of sites for excavation but most of these, for bones as for other fields, will be unique in some criteria and many of the opportunities will not come again. We have to adopt a scholarly approach at an unscholarly pace and prune our approach to meet the limits of our resources in time and people.

ACKNOWLEDGEMENTS

We are grateful to all those who commented on earlier drafts, especially colleagues in the Department of Archaeology, University of Southampton. We thank all Wessex archaeologists and all other specialists who have freely discussed with us their ideas, current aims, and unpublished results. Martin Oake drew Figure 23.

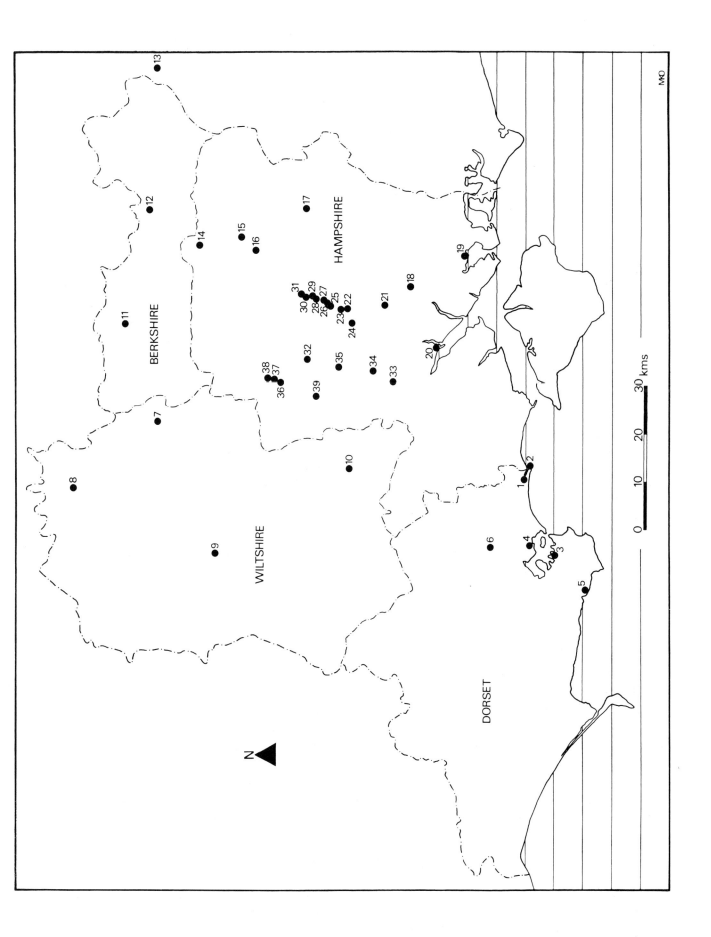

Figure 23   Animal bones studied by the Faunal Remains Project 1975–1983

List of Sites on Figure 23

Dorset

1   Christchurch
2   Hengistbury Head
3   Cleavel Point
4   Poole (birds and fish)
5   Rope Lake Hole
6   Wimborne

Wiltshire

7   Ramsbury
8   Groundwell Farm
9   Potterne
10   Clarendon Park

Berkshire

11   Beedon Manor Farm
12   Reading Abbey

Surrey

13   M25 sites

Sites Outside Wessex, not shown

Banwell, Somerset
Glastonbury, Somerset
Bantham Ham, Devon
West Stow, Suffolk (birds and fish)

Hampshire

14   Silchester
15   Cowdery's Down
16   Viables Farm
17   Alton
18   Bishop's Waltham
19   Portchester Castle (fish only)
20   Southampton (some)
21   Owslebury
22   Winnall Down (M3 site R17)
23   Easton Down (R7)
24   Winchester (birds and post–1970)
25   M3 R30
26   M3 R6
27   M3 R5
28   Micheldever Wood Barrow (R4)
29   Micheldever Wood Banjo (R27)
30   Stratton Park (R1)
31   London Lodge (R3)
32   Chilbolton Down
33   Romsey, Osbourne House
34   Braishfield Roman Villa
35   Little Somborne
36   Balksbury
37   Old Down Farm
38   Knight's Enham
39   Danebury (birds, small mammals)

BIBLIOGRAPHY

References in text

* FRP work
† FRP involvement

APPLEBAUM S, 1972   'Roman Britain', in Finberg H P R (ed) *The Agrarian History of England and Wales, Vol I.* Cambridge University Press, 1–277.

ARMITAGE P L, 1982a   'A system for ageing and sexing the horn cores of cattle from British post-medieval sites (with special reference to unimproved British longhorn cattle)', in Wilson *et al.* 1982, 37–54.

ARMITAGE P L, 1982b   'Studies on the remains of domestic livestock from Roman, medieval and early modern London: objectives and methods', in Hall A R and Kenward H K (eds) *Environmental archaeology in the urban context* Counc Brit Archaeol Res Rep 43, 94–106.

ARMITAGE P L, CLUTTON–BROCK J, 1976   'A system for the classification and description of the horn cores of cattle from archaeological sites', *J Archaeol Sci* 3, 329–48.

BACKWAY C J, 1981†   *Cause and effect of periodontal disease: a comparative study of four archaeological sites with respect to environmental causes of periodontal disease in sheep,* unpublished MSc dissertation, Department of Archaeology, University of Southampton.

BINFORD L R, 1978   *Nunamiut ethnoarchaeology,* Academic Press.

BINFORD L R, 1981   *Bones: ancient men and modern myths,* Academic Press.

BIRD P F, 1968   'Animal bones from Tollard Royal', in Wainwright G J, 'Excavation of a Durotrigian farmstead near Tollard Royal in Cranbourne Chase, Southern England', *Proc Prehist Soc* 34, 146–147.

BISHOP M J (ed), 1982   *The cave hunters: biographical sketches of the lives of Sir William Boyd Dawkins & Dr J Wilfrid Jackson,* Derbyshire Museum Service.

BOURDILLON J, 1978   In Walker J S F, 'Excavations in medieval tenements on the Quilter's Vault site in Southampton', *Proc Hampshire Fld Clb Archaeol Soc* 35, 207–12.

BOURDILLON J, 1979   'Town life and animal husbandry in the Southampton area as suggested by the excavated bones', *Proc Hampshire Fld Clb Archaeol Soc* 36, 181–91.

BOURDILLON J, 1983   *Animals in an urban environment,* unpublished MPhil thesis, Department of Archaeology, University of Southampton.

BOURDILLON J, COY J P, 1980†   'The animal bones', in Holdsworth P (ed) *Saxon Southampton: excavations at Melbourne Street 1971–6* Counc Brit Archaeol Res Rep 33, 79–121.

BRADLEY R, 1978   *The Prehistoric Settlement of Britain*, Routledge and Kegan Paul, London.

BRAMWELL D, 1975   In Platt C and Coleman-Smith R (eds) *Excavations in medieval Southampton: Vol I,* University of Leicester Press, 340–1.

BURRELL P J S, 1981†

The effects of domestication on skull morphology, unpublished undergraduate dissertation, Department of Biology, University of Southampton.

CHAMPION T C, 1979

'The Iron Age (c. 600 BC–AD 200). A. Southern Britain and Ireland', in Megaw J V S and Simpson D D A (eds) *Introduction to British Prehistory* University Press, Leicester 344–432.

CHAPMAN D, CHAPMAN N, 1975

Fallow deer, Terence Dalton, Suffolk.

CHERRY J E, GAMBLE C, SHENNAN S (eds), 1978

Sampling in contemporary British archaeology. Brit Archaeol Rep (Brit Ser) 50.

CLARK J G D, 1947

'Sheep and swine in the husbandry of prehistoric Europe', *Antiquity* 21, 122–136.

CLUTTON–BROCK J, 1976

'The animal resources', in Wilson D M (ed) *The Archaeology of Anglo-Saxon England,* London, Methuen, 373–392.

CLUTTON–BROCK J, 1981

Domesticated Animals from Early Times, Heinemann/British Museum, Natural History.

CLUTTON–BROCK J, ARMITAGE P L, 1977

'Mammal bones from Trench A', in Blurton T R, 'Excavations at Angel Court, Walbrook, 1974' *Trans London Middlesex Archaeol Soc* 28, 88–97.

CORBET G K, SOUTHERN H N (eds), 1977

The handbook of British mammals, second edition, Blackwell.

COY J P, 1975

'Iron Age cookery', in Clason A T (ed) *Archaeozoological studies,* Elsevier 426–30.

COY J P, 1978a*

First aid for animal bones, Rescue.

COY J P, 1978b*

'Comparative collections for archaeozoology', in Brothwell D R, Thomas K D and Clutton-Brock J (eds) *Research problems in zooarchaeology,* Institute of Archaeology, London, occasional publication 3, 143–5.

COY J P, 1978c*

'Animal bones studies and R27', in Fasham P (ed) *M3 Archaeology 1976–1977* 7–9.

COY J P, 1980*

'The animal bones', in Haslam J 'Excavation of a mid-Saxon iron smelting site at Ramsbury, Wiltshire', *Medieval Archaeol* 24, 41–51.

COY J P, 1981a*

'Animal husbandry and faunal exploitation in Hampshire', in Shennan S J and Schadla Hall R T (eds) *The Archaeology of Hampshire* Hampshire Fld Clb Archaeol Soc Monogr 1, 95–103.

COY J P, 1981b*

'The bird bones', in Williams J H and Shaw M 'Excavations in Chalk Lane, Northampton, 1975–1978', *Northamptonshire Archaeol* 16, microfiche pp 200–210.

COY J P, 1981c*

'The animal bones', in Silvester R J, 'An excavation on the Post-Roman site at Bantham, South Devon', *Devon Archaeol Soc Proc* 39, 106–110.

COY J P, 1982a*

'The role of wild fauna in urban economies in Wessex', in Hall A R and Kenward H K (eds) *Environmental archaeology in the urban context,* CBA Res Rep 43, 107–116.

COY J P, 1982b*

'Woodland mammals in Wessex: the archaeological evidence', in Limbrey S and Bell M (eds) *Archaeological aspects of woodland ecology,* Brit Archaeol Rep (International Ser 146, Association for Environmental Archaeology Symposium 2, 287–296.

COY J P, 1982c*

In Jervis K (ed) *Excavations in Christchurch 1969–1977* Dorset Natur Hist Archaeol Soc Monogr 5.

COY J P, 1983a*

'Birds as food in prehistoric and historic Wessex', in Clutton-Brock J and Grigson C (eds) *Animals and Archaeology: Volume 2 Shell middens, fishes and birds,* Brit Archaeol Rep, Proceedings of the International Committee for Archaeozoology.

COY J P, 1983b*

'The place of archaeozoology in rescue excavations in Britain', in Kubasiewicz M (ed), *Archaeozoology I.*

COY J P, in press*

'The role of pigs in Iron Age and Romano-British Wessex: recent faunal analyses', in Gilbertson D and Ralph N (eds) *AEA Conference Volume*, Brit Archaeol Rep.

COY J P, JONES R T, TURNER K A, 1982†

'Absolute ageing of cattle from tooth sections and its relevance to archaeology', in Wilson *et al.* listed below, 127–140.

CRABTREE P J, in press 1†

'Faunal remains', in West S, *West Stow: Part I the Anglo-Saxon settlement,* East Anglian Archaeol.

CRABTREE P J, in press 2

'The implications of intra-site variability in specific proportions at West Stow', in *Animals and Archaeology: Volume 4 Husbandry and the emergence of breeds* (see Coy 1983).

CRAM C L, 1978

'Animal bones', in Brodribb A C C, Hands A R and Walker D R *Excavations at Shakenoak Farm, near Wilcote, Oxfordshire. Part V: Sites K and E,* 117–178.

CRIBB R, in preparation

In Barker G and Gamble C (eds) *Beyond domestication.*

CUNLIFFE B W, 1970

The past tomorrow, University of Southampton.

CUNLIFFE B W, 1978

Iron Age Communities in Britain, Routledge and Kegan Paul; second edition, London.

CUNLIFFE B W, PHILLIPSON D W, 1968

'Excavations at Eldon's Seat, Encombe, Dorset', *Proc Prehist Soc* 34, 191–237.

DEPARTMENT OF THE ENVIRONMENT 1975

Principles of publication in rescue archaeology.

DIMOCK J F (ed), 1868

Giraldi Cambrensis Opera Vol VI Itinerarium Kambriae et Descriptio Kambriae Longmans, Green, Reader, and Dyer, London.

DRIESCH A VON DEN, 1976

A guide to the measurement of bones from archaeological sites, Peabody Museum Bulletin No. 1, Harvard University.

DRIVER J C, 1982

'Medullary bone as an indicator of sex in bird remains from archaeological sites', in Wilson *et al.* listed below, 251–4.

DYER K R, 1973

Estuaries: a physical introduction, John Wilson & Sons.

EASTHAM A, 1971

'The bird bones', in Cunliffe B W *Excavations at Fishbourne 1961–1969* Res Rep Soc Antiq London 27, Vol II, 388–393.

EASTHAM A, 1975

'The bird bones', in Cunliffe B W *Excavations at Portchester Castle, Volume I: Roman,* Res Rep Soc Antiq London 32, 409–415.

EASTHAM A, 1976

'The bird bones', in Cunliffe B W *Excavations at Portchester Castle, Volume II: Saxon,* Res Rep Soc Antiq London 33, 287–296.

EASTHAM A, 1977

'The bird bones', in Cunliffe B W, *Excavations at Portchester Castle, Volume III: medieval,* Res Rep Soc Antiq London 34, 233–238.

EVANS J G, 1975

The Environment of Early Man in the British Isles,
Elek, London.

EWBANK J M, PHILLIPSON D W,
WHITEHOUSE R D, HIGGS E S, 1964

'Sheep in the Iron Age: a method of study', *Proc Prehist Soc*
30, 423–426.

FASHAM P, 1979

'The excavation of a triple barrow in Micheldever Wood,
Hampshire', *Proc Hampshire Fld Clb Archaeol Soc* 35,
5–40.

FASHAM P J, SCHADLA HALL R T, 1981

'The Neolithic and Bronze Ages', in Shennan S J and
Schadla Hall R T (eds) *The Archaeology of Hampshire,*
Hampshire Fld Clb Archaeol Soc Monogr 1, 26–36.

FOOT R A, 1978†

*Traces of utilisation on the surface of animal bones: a case
study from the Iron Age,* unpublished undergraduate
dissertation, Department of Archaeology, University of
Southampton.

GRANT A, 1971

'The animal bones' (see Eastham 1971 above) 377–383.

GRANT A, 1975

'The animal bones' (see Eastham 1975 above) 378–408.

GRANT A, 1976

'The animal bones' (see Eastham 1976 above) 262–287.

GRANT A, 1977

'The animal bones' (see Eastham 1977 above) 213–239.

GRANT A, 1982

'The use of tooth wear as a guide to the age of domestic
ungulates', in Wilson *et al.* listed below, 91–108.

GRANT A, in press

'Survival or sacrifice: a critical appraisal of animal burials in
Britain in the Iron Age', in *Animals and Archaeology
Volume 4* (see Crabtree in press above).

GREEN F J, 1979

Medieval plant remains, unpublished MPhil dissertation,
Department of Archaeology, University of Southampton.

GRIGSON C, 1969

'The uses and limitations of differences in absolute size in
the distinction between bones of aurochs (*Bos primigenius*)
and domestic cattle (*Bos taurus*)', in Ucko P J and
Dimbleby G W (eds), *The domestication and exploitation
of plants and animals,* Duckworth 277–294.

GRIGSON C, 1978

'The Late Glacial and Early Flandrian ungulates of England
and Wales – an interim review', in Limbrey S and Evans J G
(eds), *The Effect of Man on the Landscape: the Lowland
Zone* CBA Res Rep 21 46–56.

GRIGSON C, 1980

'We need more than a laundry list', *Current Archaeol* 70,
334–5.

GRIGSON C, 1982

'Porridge and pannage: pig husbandry in Neolithic England',
in Bell M and Limbrey S (eds) *Archaeological Aspects of
Woodland Ecology* Brit Archaeol Rep (International Ser)
146, 297–314.

GRINSELL L, 1958

The archaeology of Wessex, Methuen.

HAMILTON J, 1978

'A comparison of the age structure at mortality of some
Iron Age and Romano-British sheep and cattle populations',
in Parrington M (ed), *The Excavation of an Iron Age Settlement, Bronze Age Ring-ditches and Roman Features at
Ashville Trading Estate, Abingdon, (Oxfordshire) 1974–76,*
Oxfordshire Archaeol Unit Rep 1, CBA Res Rep 28,
126–133.

HARCOURT R A, 1969

In Wainwright G J, 'The excavation of Balksbury Camp,
Andover, Hants', *Proc Hampshire Fld Clb Archaeol Soc*
26, 53–55.

HARCOURT R A, 1971a

In Wainwright G and Longworth I H, *Durrington Walls Excavations 1966–1968*, 338–350.

HARCOURT R A, 1971b

'The animal bones from Marden', in Wainwright G J, 'A late Neolithic enclosure at Marden', *Antiq J* 51, 234–5.

HARCOURT R A, 1974

'The dog in prehistoric and early historic Britain', *J Archaeol Sci* 1, 151–176.

HARCOURT R A, 1979a

'The animal bones', in Wainwright G J, *Gussage All Saints. An Iron Age settlement in Dorset,* DoE Archaeol Rep 10, HMSO, 150–160.

HARCOURT R A, 1979b

'The animal bones', in Wainwright G J, *Mount Pleasant, Dorset: Excavations 1970–1.* Res Rep Soc Antiq 37, 214–223.

HARMAN M, 1969

'The animal bones', in Todd M, 'The Roman settlement at Margidunum: excavations 1966–8, *Trans Thoroton Soc Nottinghamshire* 73, 96–103.

HARMAN M, 1979

'The mammalian bones' in J H Williams (ed) *St Peter's Street, Northampton, excavations 1973–1976,* Northampton Development Corp Archaeol Monogr 2, 328–332.

HARRIS D R, 1969

'Agricultural systems, ecosystems and the origins of agriculture', in Ucko P J and Dimbleby G W (eds), *The Domestication and Exploitation of Plants and Animals,* Duckworth London, 3–15.

HARRIS E C, 1979

Principles of archaeological stratigraphy, Academic Press.

HODGSON G W I, 1968

'A comparative account of the animal remains from Corstopitum and the Iron Age site at Catcote near Hartlepools, Co. Durham', *Archaeologia Aeliana* 46, 127–162.

HODGSON G W I, 1977

Vindolanda II. The Animal Remains 1970–1975, Vindolanda Trust, Hexham.

JACKSON J W, 1933

'Prehistoric domestic animals', *Man XXXIII,* 87.

JACKSON J W, 1943

'Animal bones', in Wheeler R E M, *Maiden Castle, Dorset* Soc of Antiq, 360–372.

JACOBI R M, 1978

'Population and landscape in Mesolithic lowland Britain', in Limbrey S and Evans J G (eds), *The Effect of Man on the Landscape: the Lowland Zone* Counc Brit Archaeol Res Rep 21, 75–85.

JACOBI R M, 1981

'The last hunters in Hampshire', in Shennan S J and Schadla Hall R T (eds) *The Archaeology of Hampshire* Hampshire Fld Clb Archaeol Soc Monogr No. 1, 10–25.

JARMAN M R, 1972

'European deer economies and the advent of the Neolithic', in Higgs E S (ed) *Papers in Economic Prehistory,* University Press Cambridge 125–147.

JARMAN M, FAGG A, with HIGGS E S, 1968

'Animal remains', in Stead I M, 'An Iron Age Hill-fort at Grimthorpe, Yorkshire, England', *Proc Prehist Soc* 34, 182–189.

JEFFERIES J S, 1977

Excavation records: techniques in use by the Central Excavations Unit, DAMHB Occasional Paper 1.

JEWELL P A, 1958

'Buzzards and barrows', *The Listener,* 13 February, 278–9, 282.

JEWELL P A, 1962   'Changes in size and type of cattle from prehistoric to medieval times in Britain', *Zeitschrift für Tierzüchtung und Züchtungsbiologie* 77, 159–167.

JONES G, 1977   'Zoological evidence', in Rogerson A, 'Excavations at Scole, 1973', *East Anglian Archaeol Rep* 5, 209–213.

JONES R T, 1977   'Animal bones', in Smith K, 'The excavation of Winklebury Camp, Basingstoke, Hampshire', *Proc Prehist Soc* 43, 58–69.

JOPE M, 1965   In Smith I F (ed), *Windmill Hill and Avebury Excavations by Alexander Keiller 1925–1939,* 142–145.

KING A, 1978   'A comparative survey of bone assemblages from Roman Sites in Britain', *Inst Archaeol Bull* 15, 207–232.

LANGLEY P J W, YALDEN D W, 1977   'The decline of the rarer carnivores in Great Britain during the nineteenth century', *Mammal Review* 7, 95–116.

LEGGE A J, 1981a   'The agricultural economy', in Mercer R J, *Grimes Graves, Norfolk. Excavations 1971–1972: Volume 1,* DoE Archaeol Rep No. 11, HMSO, 79–103.

LEGGE A J, 1981b   'Aspects of cattle husbandry', in Mercer R (ed), *Farming Practice in British Prehistory* Edinburgh University Press 169–181.

LUHMANN F, 1965   'Tierknochenfunde aus der Stadt auf dem Magdalensberg bei Klagenfurt in Kärnten: III die Schweineknochen', *Kärntner Museumsschriften,* XXXIX (4).

MACGREGOR A G, CURREY J D, 1983   'Mechanical properties as conditioning factors in the bone and antler industry of the 3rd to the 13th century AD', *J Archaeol Sci* 10, 71–77.

MALTBY J M, 1979   *Faunal studies on urban sites: the animal bones from Exeter 1971–1975,* Sheffield University.

MALTBY J M, 1980   'Modern refuse and ancient behaviour', *Nature* 284, 215–6.

MALTBY J M, 1981a*   'Iron Age, Romano-British and Anglo-Saxon animal husbandry: a review of the faunal evidence', in Jones M and Dimbleby G (eds), *The environment of man: the Iron Age to the Anglo-Saxon period,* Brit Archaeol Rep (Brit Ser) 87, 155–203.

MALTBY J M, 1981b*   'The animal bones', in Davies S M, 'Excavations at Old Down Farm, Andover, Part II; Prehistoric and Roman', *Proc Hampshire Fld Clb Archaeol Soc* 37, 81–165.

MALTBY J M, 1982a   'Mammal and bird bones', in Higham R A, Allan J P and Blaylock S R, 'Excavations at Okehampton Castle, Devon: Part 2: the bailey', *Proc Devon Archaeol Soc 40,* 114–135.

MALTBY J M, 1982b*   'The variability of faunal samples and their effects upon ageing data', in Wilson *et al.* listed below, 81–90.

MALTBY J M, in press 1*   'Animal bones and the Romano-British economy', in *Animals and Archaeology:* Volume 4 (see Crabtree in press above).

MALTBY J M, in press 2*   'Roman and Iron Age butchery', in Gilbertson and Ralph (see Coy J P in press above).

MALTBY J M, in preparation 1*   'Patterns in faunal assemblage variability', in Barker G and Gamble C (eds), *Beyond domestication.*

MALTBY J M, in preparation 2*   'The animal bones from the excavations at Balksbury, Hampshire, 1973'.

MALTBY J M, in preparation 3 — 'The animal bones from the excavations at Baylham House, Suffolk'.

MALTBY J M, in preparation 4 — 'The animal bones from the excavations of 1, Bleachfield Street, Alcester, Warwickshire'.

MEEHAN B, 1975 — *Shell bed to shell midden,* unpublished PhD thesis, Australian National University.

MELLARS P A, 1974 — 'The Palaeolithic and Mesolithic', in Renfrew C (ed), *British Prehistory – a New Outline* London: Duckworth 41–99.

MILLER E, HATCHER J, 1978 — *Medieval England: Rural Society and Economic Change 1086–1348,* Longman, London.

MURRAY J, 1970 — *A first European agriculture,* Edinburgh University Press.

NATIONAL ENVIRONMENTAL RESEARCH COUNCIL, 1980 — *The Solent estuarine system: an assessment of present knowledge,* NERC Series C, No. 22.

NODDLE B A, 1976 — 'Report on the animal bones from Walton, Aylesbury excavations 1973–4', *Rec Buckinghamshire* 20, 269–287.

NODDLE B A, 1980 — 'The animal bones', in Wade-Martins P, *North Elmham Park* East Anglian Archaeol Rep 9, volume 2, 375–412.

O'CONNOR T P, 1982 — *The archaeozoological interpretation of morphometric variation in British sheep limb bones,* unpublished PhD thesis, Institute of Archaeology, University of London.

OWEN C E, 1983 — 'The exploitation of the wild biomass for food in the medieval period', *Archaeozoology I,* Szczecin: Proceedings of the International Committee for Archaeozoology Kubasiewicz M (ed), 583–589.

PAYNE S, 1973 — 'Kill off patterns of sheep and goats: the mandibles from Asvan Kale', *Anatolian Stud* 23, 281–303.

PEAKE H J E, 1935 — 'The origin of the Kennet peat', *Trans Newbury Dist Fld Clb* 7, 116–126.

PIGGOTT S, 1938 — 'The early Bronze Age in Wessex', *Proc Prehist Soc* 4, 52–106.

PITT–RIVERS A H, 1887–1898 — *Excavations in Cranborne Chase,* Vols I, II, III and IV, privately printed.

PLATT C, 1972 (1974) — 'Colonisation by the wealthy: the case of medieval Southampton', *Proc Hampshire Fld Clb Archaeol Soc* 29, 29–35.

RACKHAM J, 1979 — 'Animal resources', in Carver M O H, 'Three Saxo-Norman tenements in Durham City' *Medieval Archaeol* 23, 47–54.

REMMERT H, 1980 — *Ecology,* Springer-Verlag, Berlin.

RIVET A L F, 1964 — *Town and Country in Roman Britain,* Hutchinson, 2nd edition, London.

ROBERTSON–MACKAY M E, 1980 — 'A 'head and hooves' burial beneath a round barrow with other Neolithic and Bronze Age sites, on Hemp Knoll, near Avebury, Wiltshire', *Proc Prehist Soc* 46, 123–176.

RYDER M L, 1981 — 'Livestock', in Piggott S (ed) *The Agrarian History of England and Wales. Volume I. i Prehistory* Cambridge University Press, 301–410.

SCHOENINGER M J, DENIRO M J, TAUBER H, 1983 — 'Stable nitrogen isotope ratios of bone collagen reflect marine and terrestrial components of prehistoric human diet', *Science* 220, 1381–3.

SHACKLEY M, 1981 — 'On the Palaeolithic archaeology of Hampshire', in Shennan S J and Schadla Hall R T (eds), *The Archaeology of Hampshire* Hampshire Fld Clb Archaeol Soc, Monogr 1 4–9.

SILVER I A, 1969 — 'The ageing of domestic animals', in Brothwell D and Higgs E S (eds), *Science in Archaeology,* Thames and Hudson, London, 283–302.

STONE J F S, 1935 — 'Some discoveries at Ratfyn, Amesbury, and their bearing on the date of Woodhenge', *Wiltshire Archaeol Natur Hist Mag* 47, 55–67.

STUART A J, 1974 — 'Pleistocene history of the British vertebrate fauna', *Biological Reviews* 49, 225–266.

TURNER K A, 1979† — *A comparison of certain age determination methods using teeth in two species: the stoat (Mustela erminea) and domestic cattle (Bos taurus),* unpublished undergraduate dissertation, Department of Biology, University of Southampton.

UNIVERSITY COLLEGE OF WALES, ABERYSTWYTH, DEPARTMENT OF GEOGRAPHY, 1958–1966 — *Symposia in Agricultural Meteorology,* Memorandum Series Nos 1–9.

WAINWRIGHT G J, 1982 — *An analysis of central government (DAMHB) support in 1982/3 for the recording of archaeological sites and landscapes in advance of their destruction,* Department of the Environment.

WESSEX ARCHAEOLOGICAL COMMITTEE, no date — *A policy for archaeological investigation in Wessex 1981 to 1985.*

WHEELER A, 1975 — In Platt C and Coleman-Smith R, *Excavations in medieval Southampton: Volume 1* University of Leicester Press, 342.

WHITEHOUSE R, WHITEHOUSE D, 1974 — 'The fauna', in Stanford S C, *Croft Ambrey* Hereford: privately printed, 215–221, 238–242.

WILSON R, 1978 — 'Methods and results of bone analysis/General conclusions and discussion of the bone sample', in Parrington M, *The Excavation of an Iron Age Settlement, Bronze Age Ring-ditches and Roman Features at Ashville Trading Estate, Abingdon (Oxfordshire) 1974–76,* Oxfordshire Archaeol Unit Rep 1, Counc Brit Archaeol Res Rep 28, 110–126, 133–139.

WILSON R, GRIGSON C, PAYNE S (eds), 1982 — *Ageing and sexing animal bones from archaeological sites,* Brit Archaeol Rep (Brit Ser) 109.

WINDER J, 1980* — 'The marine mollusca', in *Excavations in Melbourne Street* (see Bourdillon and Coy 1980 above), 121–127.

YALDEN D W, 1982 — 'When did the mammal fauna of the British Isles arrive?', *Mammal Review* 12 (1), 1–57.

ANCIENT MONUMENTS LABORATORY REPORTS

Animal bone and marine mollusc reports for Wessex

These reports are unpublished although some have since been rewritten for publication. They can be referred to by application to the AML and those produced by the Faunal Remains Project (marked *) are also available in bound volumes in the University of Southampton library. AML Reports often contain more detail than published reports.

*AML Report
Number*

1530	The animal bones from the Roman villa at Twyford, Hampshire. Raymond E Chaplin and John Atkinson 1958
1535	The animal bones from Winterslow. Miss J E King 1960
1550	Animal bones from Durrington Walls. R Harcourt
1555	Animal bones from Marden. R Harcourt
1569	Animal bones from Wilsford Down. R Harcourt 1971
1570	The dog bones from Portchester Castle. R Harcourt
1572	Animal bones from Southampton. J Clutton-Brock
1573	Animal bones from Bronze Age barrows, near Amesbury, Wiltshire. J Clutton-Brock
*1576	Report on animal bones from M25 sites. Jennie Coy and Jessica Winder. 1975, 10pp
1625	Animal remains, Balksbury Camp. R Harcourt 1969
1626	Animal remains. Longbridge Deverill. R Harcourt 1965
1627	Animal Bones, Mount Pleasant. R Harcourt 1971
1698	Animal bones: Brownsea Island, Poole Harbour, Dorset. R T Jones
*1801	Animal bones from the London Lodge Complex, Site R3, M3 Archaeological Rescue Committee. Jennie Coy and Jessica Winder 1975, 3pp
*1802	Animal bones from Hengistbury Head, Dorset. Jennie Coy and Jessica Winder 1975, 1 page.
*1803	Animal bones from the Osbourne House site, Romsey, Hampshire. Jennie Coy and Jessica Winder 1975, 7pp, 2 plates
1804	The animal bones from Gussage All Saints, Dorset. R Harcourt
1925	Animal bones: Long Bredy, Dorset. R T Jones
1984	Animal bones: Gussage 1972. R T Jones
2011	Animal bones: Ludgershall Castle. R T Jones
*2068	Animal bones from an Early Bronze Age Barrow; Site R4, M3 Archaeological Rescue Committee. Jennie Coy and Jessica Winder 1976, 1 page
*2069	Animal bones from Sites R5 and R6, M3 Archaeological Rescue Committee. Jennie Coy and Jessica Winder 1976, 1 page
*2070	Animal bones from a Bronze Age Barrow and Iron Age pits at Easton Down, Site R7, M3 Archaeological Rescue Committee. Jennie Coy and Jessica Winder 1976, 6pp.
2071	Animal bones; Avebury. R T Jones
2173	Animal bones; Winklebury. R T Jones
2246	Animal bones; Amesbury, Barrow 39. R T Jones
*2322	Animal bones from Site V; Bishop's Waltham, Hampshire. Jennie Coy 1977, 4pp
*2323	Bones of birds and non-domestic species from Melbourne Street sites I, IV, V, VI and XX of Saxon Southampton (Hamwic) and a Statistical Appendix (with J Bourdillon). Jennie Coy 1977, 50pp
*2324	Small mammal, bird, amphibian and fish bones from soil samples taken from Site VIII, Hamwic, Southampton. Jennie Coy 1977, 3pp
*2325	Bird bones from Upper Bugle Street, Southampton. Jennie Coy 1977, 2pp

*2326	Bird bones from Wirral Park Farm, 'The Mound', Glastonbury. Jennie Coy 1977, 2pp
*2327	Bird bones from the Town Cellars, Poole, Dorset. Jennie Coy 1977, 1 page
*2328	Small mammal and bird bones from Thames Street, Poole, Dorset. Jennie Coy 1977, 5pp
*2329	Fish bones from Hyde Street, Winchester. Jennie Coy 1977, 1 page
2333	Osteometric methodology. R T Jones
2364	Animal bone; Kings Somborne, near Winchester. Mrs A Locker
2365	Animal bone; Little Somborne, near Winchester. Mrs A Locker
*2417	Summary of additions and alterations to Roger Jones 'Computer codings for animal bones' (AML Report 2333). Mark Maltby 1977, 22pp
*2429	Animal bones from Ramsbury, Wiltshire. Jennie Coy 1977, 21pp, 3 figs
*2430	The animal bone remains from Knight's Enham, Andover, Hampshire. Niall Griffith 1977, 12pp
*2431	Report on the faunal remains from Wirral Park Farm (The Mound) Glastonbury. T C Darvill and J Coy 1977, 14pp, 1 fig
*2432	Fish bones from Upper Bugle Street Excavations, 1973, Southampton. Jennie Coy 1977, 2pp
*2433	Bird, fish and small mammal identifications from Upper Bugle Street, 1976 Excavations, Southampton. Jennie Coy 1977, 2pp
*2434	Fish bones and non-domestic birds from Quilter's Vault, Southampton. Jennie Coy 1977, 1 page
*2643	Animal bones from Christchurch, Dorset. Jennie Coy 1978, 37pp, 1 fig
*2644	Animal bones from the Roman site at Little Somborne, Hampshire. Mark Maltby 1978, 15pp
*2645	The animal bones from the Iron Age settlement at Chilbolton Down, Hampshire. Mark Maltby 1978, 12pp
*2646	A note on the animal bones from Beedon Manor Farm, Berkshire. Mark Maltby 1978, 1 page
*2647	Animal bones from R27, M3 Motorway Excavations. Niall Griffith 1978, 100pp, 5 figs
*2649	The place of archaeozoology in rescue archaeology. J Coy
*2651	A note on the animal bones from Stratton Park – M3 Archaeological Rescue Committee Excavations, R1. Mark Maltby 1978, 1 page
*2769	Animal bones from 58 French Street, Southampton. Jennie Coy 1977, 4pp
*2770	Report on 3 small collections of animal bones from ring ditches at R17, R30 and R363. M3 Motorway Rescue Excavations. Jennie Coy, Mark Maltby 1978, 2pp
*2771	Animal bones from Banwell, Somerset. Jennie Coy and Mark Maltby 1978, 4pp
2813	The animal bones from the Beaker Barrow of Hemp Knoll, Wiltshire. Dr Caroline Grigson
*2903	Animal husbandry and faunal exploitation in Hampshire. Jennie Coy 1979, 31pp
*2904	The role of wild fauna in urban economies in Wessex. Jennie Coy 1979, 32pp, 8 figs
*2916	The animal bones from Braishfield Roman Villa, Hampshire. J M Maltby and R Foot, 1979, 4pp
*2917	Summary of identifications of animal bone from Marc 3, R1, Stratton Park, Hampshire. J M Maltby 1979, 3pp
*2918	The animal bones from Balksbury, Old Down Farm and R17. J M Maltby 1979, 5pp
*3079	Additional notes on computer-coded bird bones from Chapel Road and Melbourne Street, Southampton. Jennie Coy 1979, 4pp
*3080	The variability of faunal samples and their effects upon ageing data. Mark Maltby 1980, 14pp, 5 figs
*3081	The bird bones from Westgate, Southampton. Jennie Coy 1980, 3pp
*3083	Fish bones from medieval and post-medieval layers of the Inner Bailey at Portchester Castle, Hampshire. Jennie Coy 1980, 19pp
*3287	The animal bones from Pit 5, Viables Farm, Hampshire. Mark Maltby 1980, 10pp
*3288	Animal bones from the Micheldever Wood Banjo, Hampshire, R27, M3 Motorway Rescue Excavations. Jennie Coy 1980, 24pp, 6 figs

*3289	Report on the animal bones from Old Down Farm, Hampshire. Mark Maltby 1980, 39pp, 10 figs
*3290	Iron Age, Romano-British and Anglo-Saxon husbandry — a review of the faunal evidence. Mark Maltby 1980, 63pp, 8 figs
*3291	Absolute ageing of cattle from tooth sections and its relevance to archaeology. J Coy, R Jones and K Turner 1980, 18pp, 3 figs
3342	Computer based osteometry; Data capture user manual. R T Jones *et al.* Supplement to AML Report 2333, 1980
*3449	Bird bones from West Stow, Suffolk. Jennie Coy 1981, 6pp, 4 figs
*3451	Animal bones and shells from Alton, Hampshire. Jennie Coy 1981, 6pp, 6 figs
*3452	The animal bones from Bantham Ham, Devon. Jennie Coy 1981, 14pp, 10 figs
*3453	The animal bones from Winnall Down (M3 Motorway Archaeological Rescue Committee, Site R17), Hampshire. Mark Maltby 1981, 34pp, 28 figs
*3591	Animal bones from Groundwell Farm, Blunsdon Street, Andrew, Wiltshire 1976. Level III Report. Jennie Coy 1981, 14pp, 22 figs
*3592	Animal bones from Cleavel Point, Ower, Dorset 1978. Level III Report. Jennie Coy 1982, 12pp, 13 figs
*3593	The marine shells from Cleavel Point, Ower, Dorset 1978. Jennie Coy 1981, 5pp, 2 figs
*3594	The animal bones: Groundwell Farm Level IV Report for *Wiltshire Archaeol Mag.* Jennie Coy 1982, 10pp, 2 figs
*3595	The animal bones from the 1974, 75 and 78 excavations at Silchester. Mark Maltby 1982, 12pp, 5 figs
*3596	Woodland mammals in Wessex — the archaeological evidence. Jennie Coy 1982, 13pp
3667	Animal bones, mollusc shells and carbonised plant remains from the Anglo-Saxon graves at Portway. Alison Locker *et al.* 1981
*3873	Bird bones from Danebury, Hampshire. Jennie Coy 1982, 6pp, 4 figs
*3874	Small mammals and amphibians from Danebury, Hampshire. Jennie Coy 1982, 3pp, 1 fig
*3875	The animal bones from Cowdery's Down, Basingstoke, Hampshire. Mark Maltby 1982, 12pp, 15 figs
*3876	Level IV Report for Ower Monograph, Dorset. The animal bones. Jennie Coy 15pp, 4 figs
*3877	Animal bones from excavations W5, W6, W7, W8, W9, W10 by the Wessex Archaeological Committee at Christchurch 1981. Jennie Coy 1982, 8pp, 6 figs
*3878	Birds as food in prehistoric and historic Wessex. Jennie Coy 1982, 17pp, 4 figs
*3879	Animal bones and the Romano-British economy. Mark Maltby 1982, 19pp
*3880	The Hamwic pit project — an interim report. Sarah Colley 1982, 11pp, 3 figs
*3881	Hamwic bones — old questions, new questions. Jennie Coy 1982, 11pp, 1 fig
*4063	The animal bones from the pre-Roman and Roman layers at Winchester, Western Suburbs, 1974–9. Jennie Coy 1983, 24pp, 15 page Appendix
*4064	Bird bones from Madison Street, 1979, excavations, Southampton Site 29. Jennie Coy 1983, 7pp
*4065	Animal bones from excavations at Wimborne, Dorset 1978–1981. Jennie Coy 1983, 5pp
*4066	Animal bones from trial excavations at Potterne, Wiltshire, by the Wessex Archaeological Committee, 1983, with recommendations for bone retrieval in proposed future excavations. Jennie Coy 1983, 5pp
*4067	A preliminary study of the animal bones from Sites A, B and C, Reading Abbey (WAC Site 12, 1981) with recommendations for future study, especially of the cattle horn cores. Jennie Coy 1983, 12pp, 7 tables, 1 fig
*4068	Fish bones from Madison Street. Sarah Colley 1983
*4069	Animal bone identifications from Clarendon Park, Vatcher Site 10. Jennie Coy 1983, 1 page
*4070	Animal bones and marine molluscs from Rope Lake Hole, Kimmeridge, Dorset. WAC Site. Jennie Coy 1983
*4071	Animal bones from the Hamwic Pit Project (Six Dials excavation, Site 31, F.2008). Sarah Colley 1983

Chapter 5 ENVIRONMENTAL ARCHAEOLOGY IN LONDON: A REVIEW

Philip L Armitage,* Alison Locker* and Vanessa Straker**
with a contribution by Barbara West

1 Introduction

1.1 Terms of reference

This review was produced at the request of the Science Panel of the DoE Ancient Monuments Board and is intended as a summary of the work on environmental archaeology already accomplished in London, as well as offering some proposals for the future in the light of this accumulated knowledge.

Following the recommendations laid down in *Principles of Publication in Rescue Archaeology* (DoE 1975) the presentation of the results of studies on the biological material from London's archaeological sites has been at two levels:

1. Full publication in scientific and archaeological periodicals, and

2. As Level III archival reports.

While other environmental archaeologists are kept fully informed of any new additions to the list of published papers produced by London's environmental archaeologists by means of synopses in such bibliographies as the CBA Abstracts and *Bibliographie Zur Archäo-Zoologie und Geschichte der Haustiere* (Berlin), there is no complete and readily available combined list of the unpublished reports held in the archives of DoE Ancient Monuments Laboratory and Museum of London. One of the purposes of this review is therefore to provide a reference list of this unpublished material for the use of other workers. This list appears as part of the gazetteer (pp 294–309). Brief synopses of all these archive reports are included in sections 3 and 4.

1.2 Structure of review document

The principal section of this review summarises the state of current knowledge of environmental archaeology in London. This is dealt with separately for the Greater London area and for the City. While the authors accept that such an artificial division should not persist in any future work programme (see p 288) they have decided to retain this scheme as previous studies have been carried out independently in the two areas, and it would be especially difficult now to attempt an integration. Within the two broad divisions of the Greater London area and the City, the different sorts of biological/environmental material (seeds, arthropods, animal bones etc) are treated systematically under chronological sequence (historical period). The numbers on Figures 25–27 and 29 refer to the sites mentioned in the text by name and number. The text was submitted in September 1983.

Historical introduction

2 Investigations into biological material from London sites from early times to the present day

London's citizens have from very early times shown occasional interest in the historical heritage that lies buried beneath the city and which has from time to time been accidentally revealed by workmen digging trenches for building foundations or sewers. Although this interest has in the main been centred on structural remains of ancient buildings and also on human skeletons, it has sometimes extended to faunal remains. One of the earliest recorded examples comes from the fourteenth century, when workmen digging in the grounds of St. Paul's Cathedral discovered a deposit of over 100 'ox-skulls' which scholars of that time interpreted as the remains of pagan sacrifices (Clark 1980, 6) – but probably was discarded debris from either horn or leather working.

In more recent times, chance finds of fossil animal bones excited the interest of seventeenth and eighteenth century antiquaries and natural philosophers, many of whom published accounts of such specimens. The earliest of these was by Bagford (1715) describing the 'body' of a Roman 'war elephant' found near Gray's Inn in 1690 – probably some fossil molars or tusks of a prehistoric mammoth or, more likely woodland elephant *Elephus antiquus* (Collins 1976a, 21). It was not until the nineteenth century that fanciful notions concerning fossil elephant and mammoth remains found in London were replaced by serious scientific interpretation (see, for example, Trimmer 1813, Lane Fox 1872, Brown 1888, and Hicks 1892), and a search through the early nineteenth century literature reveals that the Victorian naturalists, geologists and antiquaries were indeed very much interested in ancient (now extinct) faunal and floral material; very little attention being paid to organic remains from deposits of historic date. Their primary objective was the collection of relics for museum display and clearly the bones of Roman and medieval domestic livestock were poor substitutes for the tusks of mammoths or the antlers of extinct deer. Even when Roach-Smith, a London pharmacist and renowned amateur archaeological investigator, reported his discoveries of Roman deposits, the presence of biological

---

* DoE-funded contract workers, Institute of Archaeology, London.
** DoE-funded contract worker, University of Bristol.

material (he found) received only cursory mention: 'In one part of the Roman pit were loads of oyster shells; in another bones of cows, sheep and goats . . .' (Roach-Smith 1842). Slightly later, however, Lane Fox (1867) (later General Pitt-Rivers) showed a more enlightened approach during his investigations of Roman deposits near London Wall in 1866. As well as attempting to explain the significance of the 'peat' found in this part of the upper Walbrook valley, Lane Fox collected faunal material from the site and arranged for this to be examined by Professor Owen, who reported the presence of horse, red deer, roe deer, wild boar, dog and domestic cattle. Several of the cattle skulls rescued by Lane Fox from carts leaving the site for a nearby bone processing factory were subsequently used by Carter Blake (1868, 100) to prove the existence of *Bos longifrons, Bos trochocerus* and *Bos frontosus* as three very distinct races of Romano-British cattle — these specific names are now no longer considered valid by zoologists, however, as all non-humped cattle are of the same species *Bos taurus* (see Grigson 1982, 48). Twenty human skulls found at London Wall were also retained by Lane Fox. These skulls, which are now held in the collections of the Pitt-Rivers Museum in Oxford, as well as later finds of isolated groups of skulls from elsewhere in the Walbrook valley (in the collections of the Museum of London and Bank of England) have recently been published by Marsh and West (1981) (see p 286). Other human remains, of prehistoric date, and their associated fauna and flora, formed the basis of the book by Smith (1894) on *Man the Primaeval Savage* which deals with the theme of early man and his environment in the London region. Outside the City, the only faunal report of note appeared in Booth Latter (1858) who described the discovery at Camden Park, Chislehurst, in 1857 of a Romano-British shaft excavated in chalk. This was backfilled with domestic refuse including the bones of cattle, dogs, a small horse, pig and hedgehogs, as well as the shell remains of common snail *Helix nemoralis*.

The high standard set by Lane Fox in the recording and treatment of biological material found on archaeological sites in London continued into the early twentieth century with the work of Norman and Reader, two antiquaries who worked in partnership. Their detailed and well illustrated reports of Roman sites uncovered during building work in the City contain appended notes on faunal and floral material. These notes were contributed by such eminent specialists as Newton, FRS, Kennard, FGS, Woodward, FLS, Lyell, FSA and Clement Reid, FRS (see Reader 1903, Norman and Reader 1906, 1912). It was at this time that Kennard and Woodward demonstrated the value of non-marine mollusca on archaeological sites (Kennard and Woodward, 1902); using them to determine whether a Roman ditch was permanently filled with water or subject to periodic desiccation (Norman and Reader 1912, 331). Kennard and Woodward justified the inclusion of lists of non-marine molluscan faunas in archaeological reports: 'None of these records is of any great importance, yet certainly they have their value by throwing light on past physical conditions, we have therefore thought it advisable to record them'. Indeed, the study of molluscan fauna along the lines first suggested by Kennard and Woodward is continuing today as part of investigations into a fourth century defensive ditch at Crosswall (C49) (Davis 1983b).

Archaeological investigations were halted by the First World War, but Woodward in a lecture given to the South Eastern Union of Scientific Societies on 7 June 1917, and later published in *The Geological Magazine* (Woodward 1917), continued to stress the importance of biological material from London's archaeological record, making a special plea for the future collection of animal bones from historic deposits as well as those from the deeper fossil (Pleistocene) beds which had always attracted a great deal of scientific interest.

The immediate post-war period was marked by a resumption of building operations in the City which offered archaeologists the opportunity to investigate further Roman and medieval sites. Although archaeological research in London was during this period placed on a more secure footing, with the appointment by the Society of Antiquaries of a number of professional archaeologists to work in the City, no extensive environmental work was undertaken, apart, that is, from the continued interest shown by Kennard and other biologists in the molluscan and floral material associated with the marsh deposits near London Wall, in the upper Walbrook valley (Lambert 1921, 94–112). The limited study of biological remains from London's historic sites contrasts with the very detailed investigations into the Pleistocene fauna and flora of the Thames valley being carried out at this time (see King and Oakley 1936).

Again no real advances in environmental archaeology in London are evident during the post Second World War period, 1946 to 1957, and this despite the establishment by the Society of Antiquaries of a *Roman and Medieval Excavation Council* under the direction of Professor Grimes, then Director of the London Museum, (who was later to become director of the Institute of Archaeology, University of London). During his tenure as director of the Council, Professor Grimes made a very significant contribution to our knowledge of the early topographical development of the Roman and medieval City, but limited time and resources meant that he was unable to employ specialists to investigate floral and faunal remains from his sites. Grimes did, however, manage to collect some faunal material, including a large assemblage of cattle horn cores from beneath the Mithraeum, and these await analyses and publication (Geddes, pers. comm.).

One interesting piece of pioneering work carried out by Lowther in 1949 concerned the dendrochronological dating of timber structures from Roman and medieval deposits in London (Lowther 1949). Lowther's work possibly represents the earliest application of this technique in London.

Between 1949 and 1957, Noël Hume was appointed by the Guildhall as a museum clerk responsible for investigating archaeological material discovered on building sites in the City. Working under far from ideal conditions, and with only very limited resources, Noël Hume was unable to investigate properly organic deposits uncovered by workmen. In addition, pressure was apparently exerted by his employers, the library committee of the Corporation of London, for him to concentrate his efforts on the recovery of artefacts for the sole purpose of museum display (Noël Hume 1978, 16). Despite this, Noël Hume was nevertheless able to collect some human and animal bone from his sites for future study. One group, possibly a ritual deposit, comprising skulls of man, red deer, horse and cats, collected by Noël Hume from a first century well at Queen Street, has recently been examined by Armitage and West (forthcoming).

Noël Hume was succeeded in 1957 by Marsden whose many investigations in the City yielded groups of animal bone from Roman, medieval and post-medieval contexts. Again, this material had to wait some time before it was properly processed and identified. Although there is now a Level II archival report on this bone (West 1980a) none of the specimens has so far been published. One of Marsden's major sites was Baynard's Castle (C7), which in 1972–3 produced the largest faunal assemblage so far discovered from early Tudor London. This material was presented to the British Museum (Natural History) where a post-graduate student, Armitage, worked on it as a PhD research project, between 1974–77 (Armitage 1977a).

In Greater London, Canham was responsible for archaeology between 1966–75, under the auspices of the London Museum. In 1962, the Southwark Archaeological Excavation Committee (SAEC) was formed, under Sheldon (later Archaeology Officer for Greater London with the new Museum of London). SAEC later (1972) became the first full-time unit of professional archaeologists in London, and was shortly followed by a newly created unit for the City of London: the Department of Urban Archaeology (DUA) at the Guildhall Museum (later transferred to the new Museum of London when the Guildhall and London Museums amalgamated in 1975). Under the direction of its Chief Urban Archaeologist, Hobley, the DUA has grown to become the largest archaeological unit in Europe, currently employing over 50 full time field archaeologists and supporting specialist staff.

As a result of increased financial provision for rescue archaeology in Britain, further archaeological field groups ('units') were established in Greater London, either by museums or by societies such as the London and Middlesex Archaeological Society and the Surrey Archaeological Society (Sheldon 1976). These 'units' are as follows:

1. The Inner London Archaeological Unit for the seven Inner London Educational Authority Boroughs north of the Thames (1974).

2. West London Archaeological Field Group based in Brentford, employed by London Museum (1974).

3. The South West London team operating in Merton, Wandsworth and Richmond (under the auspices of the Surrey Archaeological Society) (1975).

In addition to these three, Passmore Edwards Museum provides staff to cover archaeological work in the London Boroughs east of the River Lea and the Kent Archaeological Rescue Unit also covers part of south east London.

With the establishment of these units and field teams, archaeological investigation intensified and excavations in the Greater London region and in the City area were carried out on a far more extensive scale than had hitherto been possible, resulting in the recovery of a wealth of biological material. It was clear that the study and interpretation of environmental and biological evidence from the many sites being excavated could no longer be adequately dealt with on an *ad hoc* basis by outside specialists from various museums and university departments. There was a distinct requirement for the provision of full-time specialists in geology, botany and zoology to be attached to London's archaeological teams. Accordingly in 1974 the DoE funded two environmental archaeology posts, one at the DUA, and the other to cover Greater London. A third post, to work for SLAEC, was funded by a private developer. These posts (which were filled by Willcox, Locker (nee Gebbels) and Spencer, respectively) were intended to cover work within personal expertise and to co-ordinate specialist work on other classes of material.

Over the past years there have been a number of staff changes and today (1983) the present London team consists of:

1. For Greater London: A Locker (faunal remains and co-ordinating other environmental work).

2. For Southwark: I Tyers (botanical remains, arthropods, wood and dendrochronology).

3. For the City: P Armitage[1] (Head of DUA Environmental Section, faunal remains)
   V Straker[2] (botanical remains – seeds, wood and carbonised grain)
   A Davis (botanical remains and arthropods)
   B West (human and animal bones).

---

[1] Now Principal Keeper of Natural Sciences, The Booth Museum of Natural History, Brighton, Sussex.
[2] Now at The Department of Geography, University of Bristol; replaced by G Jones (archaeobotanist).

254

Occasional assistance is provided by specialists employed on a short term basis (funded by developers), as well as polytechnic and university students, and there is still frequent liaison with external specialists especially regarding types of material not within the scope of the present team. Identifications of specimens are often checked using the reference collections of other institutions such as the British Museum (Natural History) and the Royal Botanic Garden, Kew.

Current knowledge

3   Greater London

3.1   Geology[1]

The solid and drift geological deposits which outcrop in Greater London are shown on Figure 24. The oldest rocks are of Upper Cretaceous age and are Upper Chalk. This is found on the north and south side of the Thames basin but is nearest to the City between Ewell and Croydon and Addington, with small exposures in Deptford (beneath drift) and Lewisham. The Thanet Beds rest on the chalk throughout London with the exception of the Hounslow area and consist of greyish green fine grained glauconitic quartz sand. The overlying Woolwich and Reading Beds are largely composed of sands, loams and pebbles with clays and sands above, and are succeeded in places by the Blackheath Beds which include pebbles, pebble sands and boulder beds rich in brackish, marine and freshwater shells. As well as outcropping at Blackheath, they also occur, for example, at Croydon and Beckenham. All these strata are of Palaeocene age and can be grouped together on the map. The thick London Clay rests on the Woolwich, Reading and Blackheath Beds and forms the main 'country rock' in Greater London, particularly the north western part. It consists of dark grey pyritous silty clays, sandy in parts and with courses of claystones, and weathers to brown or yellowish brown near the surface. The basal parts contain shallow water marine molluscan fauna. They are overlain by the Claygate Beds, which are a sandier deposit than the London Clay, and form hill-top outliers north and south of the river, as do the overlying Bagshot Beds. These yellow silty sands are of marine origin and cap high ground for example in Richmond Park, Highgate and Hampstead.

Many different drift deposits are exposed in the London area and are mostly of fluviatile origin and include older and newer tracts of the Thames flood plain forming generally flat terraces. Usually, the highest terraces are the oldest. The high level terrace deposits, consisting of sands, gravels and pebbles, may represent river deposits laid down before Thames drainage was established. They occur, for example, at Streatham and Norwood, Hendon and Southgate with the base of the deposits at 61 to 110m above OD. Mass wastage, generally in periods of intense cold, has formed Head deposits which occur, for example, in Clapham Park and in parts of Wimbledon and are derived from Claygate Beds or London Clay. Clay with flints is found on the Chalk, as at the exposure near Biggin Hill, and may be partly derived from the Chalk. Pebble Gravel, which outcrops near Barnet, for example, consists mostly of flint pebbles. Boulder Clay is of glacial origin, traditionally regarded as the ground moraine of an ice-sheet. It can be found in isolated patches in the northern and eastern part of Greater London such as near Finchley and on the outskirts of Romford. It consists of unsorted materials partly formed by erosion and the rock debris accumulated by weathering of the land surface.

The lower river terraces (numbered 1 to 4 on the map) are conventionally numbered from the lowest level upwards. Terms such as Boyn Hill and Taplow, used formerly, are now abandoned partly to aid correlation. Relatively few outcrops of Terrace 4 still survive (for example in Richmond Park and in patches from Wanstead to Romford in north east London) and comprise coarsely stratified gravel and sand. The third terrace in part formerly mapped as Boyn Hill is particularly extensive in the Hounslow area where stratified gravel and sand outcrops. Terraces one and two (often referred to in the past as the Flood plain Terrace) are the lowest terraces and youngest in age and occur in quite wide tracts both north and south of the river. The mammalian fauna contained in both terraces indicate both warm and cold conditions. Much of the terraces are capped with river brickearth which consists of a reddish brown loamy clay and may incorporate some material of wind blown origin. Patches of brickearth still exist throughout Greater London. The terraces represent periods of former high sea level in the interglacial of the last Ice Ages. The important Pleistocene deposits at Swanscombe, dated to the Hoxnian Interglacial, correspond in part to terrace three of the Thames in Greater London. The terraces are particularly difficult to date and correlate and therefore many tracts which have been mapped are left unclassified for the present and some which were formerly classified are now regarded as less certain. The age and stratigraphic relationships of the Thames terraces and the Pleistocene sequence of the London region have been described by numerous authors e.g. Collins (1976b, 1978) and King and Oakley (1936). The terraces are only described in general terms for the purpose of this review as their history is extremely complex and the subject of much research.

An extensive tract of soft fine grained alluvium overlies the younger gravel terraces and most of this represents an inundation deposit formed during the post-glacial rise in sea level. It comprises grey, blue or brown sandy clays with

---

[1] The information in this section is partly based on IGS sheet 270 1:50,000, (F G Berry and R C Rollin 1981).

stones, wood and peat lenses dated by Carbon 14 analysis from the prehistoric up to and including the Roman period. The drift geological deposits, particularly gravel and brickearth, are often rich in the remains of Pleistocene plants and animals which are essential to the dating of the deposits. A forthcoming paper by Delair (The Pleistocene Mammalia of Greater London: a bibliographic study) will provide a comprehensive review of this aspect of Pleistocene studies.

3.2 Palaeolithic to 8000 BC

Figure 25 shows the distribution of sites within the Greater London area. Many of the sites cannot be strictly termed as Palaeolithic since no stratified artefacts were found in association with environmental material — such sites are more accurately termed Pleistocene.

The distribution on the map may indicate a number of possibilities: — ideally it would suggest the direct association of Palaeolithic/Pleistocene sites with gravel and brickearth deposits, but the more likely explanation is that the distribution maps merely show the areas of extensive gravel extraction and brickearth workings (especially in the earlier part of this century). Because of the large-scale nature of these activities many archaeological sites have been found.

In the last century geologists showed much interest in these early sites, and recorded sections and finds in great detail. It is a result of this interest and detail which has permitted much of this early material (in both senses) to be later re-examined and reassessed.

For example, in 'Man the Primaeval Savage', Worthington Smith (1894) described the location of sites and their finds in the Stoke Newington area (117). Between Akham Road and Kyverdale Road in the gravel deposits he found bones, antler, teeth, chalk and driftwood in association with black sharp edged implements (Worthington Smith 1894). Hubbard (pers. comm.) suggests these two sites are Hoxnian or Swanscombe Interglacial in date, while Stoke Newington Common is Ipswichian and Late Devensian in date.

Plant remains were well preserved at many sites especially Trafalgar Square (61) (Franks *et al.* 1958), which produced the fruits and seeds of over 150 species. Pollen analysis was carried out, dating the deposits to the Ipswichian Zone IIb. Pollen was also examined from Ilford (158) (West *et al.* 1964) covering Ipswichian Zones I–II, and also from Yiewsley (6) by Hubbard (in Collins 1976a) from the Gouldsgreen gravel, Gouldsgreen loam, Stockley loam and the junction of Warrens Gravel and loam — these spectra were tentatively placed in the Ipswichian. At Ilford (158) (West *et al.* 1964) pollen analysis indicated typical conditions of the first half of the Ipswichian interglacial: the early treeless part and then a change to forested conditions with pine and oak. Macroscopic plant remains (and non-marine mollusca) suggested organic deposits within a large pond or small stream, i.e. a tributary of the Thames. There was a rise in base level (correlated to the sea level rise in zone I) when the Thames flood plain covered the deposits resulting in the occurrence of brickearth at 42 feet OD.

Another site where a multi-disciplinary approach has proved useful is at Aveley (164): — apart from the famous finds of fossil elephants (Blezard 1966), pollen analysis from sediments associated with the bones showed the elephants to be dated to the Ipswichian zones IIb and III (West 1969). A channel had been cut into London clay in quiet conditions as a meander or an ox bow, a suggestion also supported by the molluscan evidence (Cooper 1972); neither the ostracods or the beetles showed any marine influences (Hollim 1977). Most of the Ipswichian deposits are formed in the flood plains of rivers and represent many diverse plant communities and Godwin (1975) suggests that the herds of large mammals such as hippo and elephant may have contributed to this diversity.

At Willements Pit, Isleworth (14) the insect fauna indicated a temperate climate in a treeless landscape dating from the thermal maximum of the Upton Warren Interstadial, with a radiocarbon date of 43140 + 1520 — 1280 bp (Coope and Angus 1975). A treeless environment was also supported by the pollen evidence and reflects the slower recolonisation of trees compared with insects when temperatures began to rise. All the fossil groups represented (plant macrofossils, non-marine mollusca and ostracods) present a fairly consistent environmental picture (Kerney, Gibbard, Hall and Robinson 1982).

Insect remains were found at Trafalgar Square (61) (Franks *et al.* 1958) including dung beetles, chafers, ground and water beetles, and weevils; mollusca were also well preserved at this site — there were both land and freshwater shells, the latter including those which today have a more southerly distribution, generally suggesting that the Thames was a warm, swiftly flowing highly calcareous river. Snail evidence suggested the surrounding country was fairly open. Burchell (1935) studied a temperate molluscan fauna from Crayford (162), King and Oakley (1936) from interbedded sands and silty brickearth lying above the Lower Brickearth and correlated this with a flood loam section from Ebbsfleet. The Lower Brickearth at Crayford contained no molluscs but a cold mammal fauna and was compared with equivalent subaerial brickearths in the Ebbsfleet valley, where predominant molluscan species indicated bleak conditions.

Mammals are the most frequently occurring faunal type at Palaeolithic/Pleistocene sites, the structure and size of bones tending to favour preservation and recovery over other types. All the sites previously mentioned also produced animal bone. Trafalgar Square (61) (Franks *et al.* 1958 and 1960) included hippo, elephant and ox, i.e. a temperate

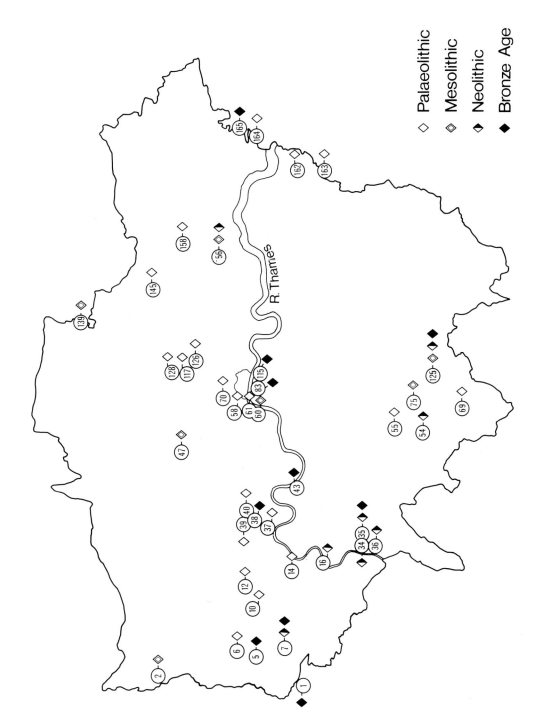

Figure 25   Greater London: distribution of Palaeolithic, Mesolithic, Neolithic and Bronze Age sites

Palaeolithic ◇

Mesolithic ◈

Neolithic ◆

Bronze Age ◆

R. Thames

fauna, whereas at Isleworth (14) a cold mammal fauna (bison, woolly rhino, reindeer and mammoth) was found in the same section as the temperate insect fauna previously mentioned, and reindeer was recovered from the same deposit as the insect fauna. The small form of bison (*Bison priscus* Boj.) is well known from the Last Glaciation (Coope and Angus 1975). These investigations emphasise the quick response of insects to rising temperature compared to mammals and also suggest the deposits were from the Upton Warren Interstadial within the last glacial period (Devensian) rather than an inter-glacial. A rich mammal fauna was found at Ilford (158) (Johnson 1900 and Rolfe 1958); mammal remains were also plentiful at Stoke Newington (117) from Worthington Smith's investigation, although there now seems some doubt as to whether the original identifications were correct, or whether several periods were amalgamated since the fauna shows an incompatible association of species (Collins 1976b).

At Brentford (37) a temperate fauna was identified (Zeuner 1945) including hippo, hyena, red deer, *Megalaceros, Bos primigenius, Bison priscus* and *Elephas antiquus,* while cold periods were indicated by the discovery of mammoth remains in association with implements at Norwood (12) and also at Southall (10) (Brown 1888). Implements were also found in association with *Elephas primigenius* in the gravels at Acton (Lane Fox 1872).

Small mammals react more quickly to climatic change than other mammals, and have been studied at a number of sites — much of the early work was covered by Hinton (1910 and 1926). At Crayford (162) a tundra environment was suggested by the small mammals found in association with a temperate fauna, but Zeuner explained this anomaly by suggesting that the rodents were part of a cold phase from the Upper Brickearth and had burrowed into the underlying sand (King and Oakley 1936).

All the Palaeolithic/Pleistocene sites within Greater London and the Lower Thames Valley have been used in conjunction with key sites just outside the area, i.e. Swanscombe, Ebbsfleet and Clacton-on-Sea to construct a chronology for this area. Recent work by Campbell (128) (1971 unpublished) and Gibbard and Harding (126) (in preparation), as well as trial trenching by the ILAU, have failed to rediscover the areas of good organic preservation in Stoke Newington which were found by Worthington Smith, especially the areas with quantities of mammal bones previously discovered; but it is hoped that pollen analysis from many borehole samples will yield evidence of the contemporary Pleistocene environment on sites where other biological materials have not been preserved or recovered.

3.3   Mesolithic, 8000–3500 BC, Figure 26

Well stratified Mesolithic artefacts in association with organic remains are not numerous in the Greater London area; although there are many references to antler and bone artefacts found in the Thames, these are not stratified (Lacaille 1961).

A stratified sequence was found at the Admiralty Buildings (60) in Westminster in 1890. The section contained derived Pleistocene mammal remains as well as microliths found in association with peat, plant remains, shells and bones. Two of the scrapers link this assemblage with those from the Colne and Lea Valleys. A fragment of carapace of a fresh water turtle, '*Emys*', was found in a marl and *Chara* bed overlying the deposit containing the flints, associated with large freshwater shells and is thought to date to the first half of the Atlantic, approximately 7–7500 bp. (Lacaille 1961).

The area around the Colne Valley is rich in Mesolithic finds: at the Sandstone Gravel Workings, which lie just outside the Greater London boundary, peat overlying gravel upon which flints had been found was dated to the late Boreal from the pollen by Dr G F Mitchell (Lacaille 1961). This period was typified by the expansion of forest cover and at the end of the Boreal began a phase of pronounced dryness that was to continue until the close of the Sub-Boreal. (Godwin 1975). On the other side of the river valley at Dewes Farm (2) pollen analysis was carried out on a peaty soil by Mrs Knox. The pollen was present in low frequencies, but indicated hazel, birch, willow, a little alder and much pine and fern, and this suggested to Lacaille a transitional period from Boreal to Atlantic, possibly of early Atlantic date (Lacaille 1961).

A more dubious find in the Lea valley at Seawardstone (139) was recorded in 1936:— molluscs from the bottom of a dugout canoe were examined including some derived shells incorporated in flood debris. A S Kennard, who examined the snails, felt that on their evidence the deposit could be Early Iron Age, but C W Phillips thought the marsh clay sealing the peat (which only produced a few pine pollen grains) compared well with that of Rikofs pit, Broxbourne, suggesting an Early Atlantic if not Boreal date, i.e. approximately 7–8000 bp. (Phillips 1936).

More recently an important Mesolithic site has been found on West Heath, Hampstead (47) and although the site itself lies on acid Bagshot sands, not conducive to organic preservation, a column of samples was taken from a permanently waterlogged boggy area 300m from the site. Complementary pollen analysis, seed and insect studies were carried out by Greig and Girling in 1977. The pollen diagram covered Zones VIIa–VIII and changes within the zones were matched by the seed and beetle assemblages. The forest appeared to be mainly composed of lime at the time of the earliest assemblage, and at the boundary between Zone VIIa and b, around 5000 bp (the beginning of the Neolithic) the pollen shows the elm decline and the introduction of cereals and weeds. Oak, lime and hazel also decrease; beech, holly and heather are introduced. Increased wetness was indicated by specific seeds and beetles, possible clearance episodes are indicated by charcoal; further heath formation and the appearance of dung beetles suggests herbivore grazing in Zone VIII (Iron Age). West Heath is the only Mesolithic site in this area where it has been possible to carry out this multidisciplinary approach and where a pollen diagram spans the Mesolithic to the Iron Age, showing the increasing effect of man's activities on the local environment.

Faunal remains were recovered from East Ham (156) in 1958 (Banks 1961):— peat deposits near Barking Creek contained part of the skull of *Bos primigenius* Bojanus, and from a tributary of Barking Creek, close to the first find, part of the skull, ribs, vertebrae and limb bones of a second individual were obtained. Pollen analysis by Franks dates the peat from the second find to Zones VIIa and VIIb; the bones were specifically linked to the upper part of Zone VIIa, around 5000 bp. Thus the lower part of these deposits in which the bones were found are Mesolithic in date, and the upper part belongs to the early Neolithic, including the elm decline.

The Atlantic was a period of increased warmth, which affected the distribution of many species, for example '*Emys*' (found at Admiralty Buildings (60)) had extended its range north of its present limits. The end of the Boreal and the Atlantic was the period of the highest temperatures in the Flandrian, and Godwin (1975) shows that forest trees and aquatic plants particularly responded to this rise in temperature by extending their ranges, including lime, previously only found in southern Britain, and holly and ash. A period of peat development ensued which preserved pollen and plant macrofossils.

Excavations of well stratified deposits yielding organic remains of Pleistocene and Mesolithic date have been infrequent in recent years. It is important that future work should focus on exposures that do not necessarily contain any artefactual material but are datable by some other means such as radiocarbon. Systematic bore-holing in areas that have produced Palaeolithic material in the past (such as Gibbard carried out at Stoke Newington) and on peat exposures for Mesolithic deposits should be carried out. Information on the environment could be gained initially from pollen work and then supplemented by larger scale sampling for other organic remains.

3.4 Neolithic, 3500–2000 BC, Figure 25

Neolithic features in the area are neither plentiful nor have favoured preservation of environmental remains. For example, the two Neolithic pits at the site of the Iron Age settlement and temple at Heathrow (Grimes 1960) have not produced any animal bones or plant material, although some charcoal flecks were noted in pit 1. In 1907 a possible Neolithic hearth was recorded from Wallington (54) and contained charred grains:— wheat, rye and good king henry (the latter is a common weed) were identified (Clinch 1907). However these identifications are of limited value as the dating is not secure. Current work on soil samples from a multi-period site at Stanwell, Heathrow (1), have shown few macroscopic remains from the Neolithic cursus ditch, whereas much plant and insect material was extracted from the Late Bronze Age features. However, with further excavation planned in Neolithic deposits at Stanwell it is hoped to carry out pollen sampling and further beetle and seed analysis.

In 1965 excavations at Eden Street, Kingston (34) revealed prehistoric occupation debris (Penn 1968), including Neolithic pottery. The sediments are thought to represent a section through a cut off river channel – a sub-channel of the Thames (Penn and Rolls 1981); this channel was also revealed during the 1974—77 excavations at Eden Walk (35). Molluscs at the base of these deposits suggested intermittent flow followed by a period of standing water. In the upper part plant material was well preserved in the dark clays. At the base of the black organic clay mid-Neolithic pottery was found with flint pot boilers and animal bone – the pottery is similar to that from Staines Causewayed camp, Putney and Twickenham. At the latter site (Church Street, Twickenham, 16) excavations revealed a Neolithic gully which contained some ox bones and an ovicaprid mandible (Sandford 1970).

A unique site, Staines Neolithic Causewayed Enclosure (just outside Greater London) was excavated in 1962; animal bone was found within the enclosure (Grigson in preparation) and outside a series of samples was taken from a section in a cable trench, which revealed a palaeochannel. These samples have yielded information on the environment prior to the camp's construction from terrestrial and freshwater Mollusca (Bell unpublished) and ostracods (Robinson unpublished). The shell marl in this section was particularly rich in molluscs:— in one column 39 species were identified; the dominant species *Valvata piscinalis* is common in running water, while other species favour thickly weeded stream courses; in this sample only 6% of the total were terrestrial molluscs. In the yellow/brown silty clay overlying the *Chara* marl there was a higher percentage of land molluscs including open country species and other species typical of swamp and marsh, which suggested to Bell (1983 unpublished) that this clay was laid down as a result of overbank flooding when the stream had adopted a different course and the landscape had been cleared by man.

An inhumation burial, probably prehistoric, was found at this site; radiocarbon results are awaited to confirm its date.

3.5   Bronze Age, 2000 to 600 BC, Figure 25

Bronze Age sites seem to be largely associated with cremations, such as Moor Hall Farm, Rainham (166) and Avenue Gardens, Acton (38), and other finds which are unstratified.

However in addition to well preserved Neolithic material, Eden Walk 111, Kingston (35) also produced some well preserved Bronze Age bone (Serjeantson, in preparation) and plant material which is currently being examined. To the east, pollen analysis of fen peats dated to the Late Bronze Age/Early Iron Age was carried out at Willsons Wharf, Southwark (115) (Scaife 1981) and indicated the dominance of herbaceous types throughout, with alder, oak and hazel present in low quantities. Scaife suggests the presence of a sedge fen with waste ground nearby which was later used for agriculture, and may indicate nearby settlement. At Stanwell, Heathrow (1), as previously mentioned, a number of Late Bronze Age features occurred, including a pit containing worked wood, the tip of a post, a post with notches cut, and a plank with a square cut hole (Watson 1981) — this wood was preserved in the fill of what may have been a pond. Many samples containing plant and insect material were taken from pits and a gully marking a trackway across the prehistoric field system. These samples are currently being examined and should provide much information about the landscape and available natural resources at the time of the occupation of the settlement.

It is important to consider where Neolithic and Bronze Age occupation is most likely to be found — to date the important concentrations are around Kingston and the Heathrow area. The numerous finds from the Thames suggest that the river banks were occupied but evidence for such occupation has only been found at Kingston. As well as evidence of the natural environment, man's manipulation of natural resources, such as woodland clearance, as suggested by Bell at Staines, and agricultural activities (arable and pastoral) should be investigated.

3.6   Iron Age, 600 BC to AD 43, Figure 26

Canham (1976) stated that current information is coming from 'a steadily growing list of settlement sites, located mainly on the gravel terraces that border the river'. However these sites have generally not been suitable for the preservation of plant and insect material, although animal bones have been recorded from a number of sites.

Topographically North Southwark was a riverside marsh during the prehistoric period and it has been suggested that these areas were at least visited if not permanently settled (Graham 1978). More recently pollen evidence from the upper levels of Willson's Wharf (Scaife 1981) showed an increase in cultigens and ruderals at the expense of wasteground species indicating more positive evidence of settlement than was available to Graham.

Pollen analyses were carried out at Caesar's Camp, Keston (149) by Professor G W Dimbleby, who found a rich pollen spectrum suggesting oak forest conditions when the rampart was constructed (hazel, birch, holly and oak) later giving way to more open vegetation (Piercy Fox 1969). The upper sample from the West Heath, Hampstead (47), pollen diagram corresponds to Zone VIII, encompassing the Iron Age, and is defined by a further steep fall in tree pollen and a rise in herbaceous pollen characteristic of pollen diagrams from the Iron Age onwards. The insect species from this Zone favour open land or waterside habitats (Girling and Greig 1977). Greig (1979) also analysed pollen from a section at Cromwell Green, Westminster (64) where three main vegetational types were present: (a) wetland vegetation, alder/oak carr; (b) dryland vegetation, meadows and arable land; (c) woodland, including the original lime, oak and elm woodland. Beech was also present, which since it is a relative latecomer to Britain, Greig suggests may have been encouraged by the clearance of lime forests. At New Palace Yard (63) the vegetation appears to have been similar to that of Cromwell Green, but owing to the small occurrence of beech and the higher percentage of lime, Greig suggests the New Palace Yard section belongs to an earlier period (Greig pers. comm. and in preparation).

The remaining sites in the gazetteer only produced animal bone:— St. Mary's Hospital, Carshalton (53), dated to the Early and Middle Iron Age (Lowther 1945) where Dr J W Jackson reported on horse, pig, sheep and ox being recovered from level 3 and a dog's skull from level 5 and at London Heathrow (3) excavated in 1969 (Sutton 1978) a small collection of bone was recovered, all from domestic species.

A multi-period site at Moor Hall Farm, Rainham (165) (recently excavated) contained two Iron Age wells — one, Middle Iron Age in date, contained plant material, a wooden stake and animal bone. The other was Late Iron Age in date and had well preserved plant material in the lower layers (Greenwood 1982). This material is being examined and has produced seeds (Vaughan unpublished); the animal bone awaits examination by the author.

Of all the different types of environmental evidence from the prehistoric period the most promising source for indicating the surrounding landscape and man's increasing effect on it comes from pollen. Cultural evidence from plant material and faunal remains has been scarce (excepting some of the Pleistocene sites such as Trafalgar Square (61) and Ilford (158)). Pollen analysis seems to be the most useful line to pursue, especially in conjunction with other disciplines such as insect studies, as at West Heath, Hampstead (47). The animal bones from Post-Pleistocene prehistoric sites would most usefully be examined as groups from sites of similar date and similar features in order to produce a statistically viable sample.

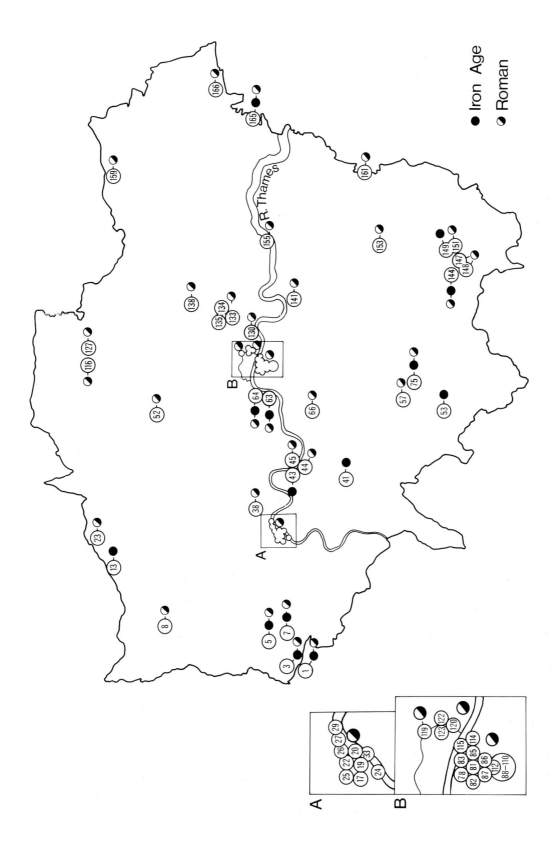

Figure 26   Greater London: distribution of Iron Age and Roman sites

Two Iron Age inhumations are known in Greater London, a late Iron Age flexed inhumation from 124–126 Borough High Street (Dean and Hammerson 1980) and the burial of a young male at the site of the Tower of London (Parnell 1977).

3.7 Romano-British, Figure 26, AD 43–500

In Sheldon and Schaaf (1978) the distribution of Roman sites in Greater London is attributed to a number of factors: – geologically and geographically sites are predominantly found on sand, gravel and mixed clays, with few sites occurring on the London Clay. Other important factors include proximity to water for transport, and the location of settlements close to roads, exemplified by the location of sites in Southwark.

A topographical and geological study of the North Southwark area was made by Graham (1978), who suggested that the river level in Late Iron Age/Early Roman times was + 1.30m OD. However this level then dropped in the Early Roman period resulting in down-cutting, (a level of – 0.5m OD was recorded in the District Heating Scheme Trench, 106, and + 0.70m OD at Chaucer House, 98), leaving a landscape of channels cut into clay and sandbanks. There is little evidence of developments taking place in the late Roman period; the dumping of dark earth deposits in the fourth century raised most of the land in Southwark to c + 2.0m OD.

Soil investigations have been carried out on the 'dark earth' which has been found on sites all over the country including York, Canterbury and London (both in the City and Southwark); these deposits have been dated from the late fourth to the ninth to eleventh centuries. Macphail (1980) has examined samples from three sites in the City (see p 275) and also from Arcadia Buildings, Southwark (90); Taylor (1978) looked at samples from Chaucer House, Southwark (98). The samples were subjected to a number of analyses including testing for alkali-soluble humus, micromorphology, pollen analysis and phytolith extraction. In summary, Macphail suggests that the London 'dark earth' may relate to a sparser population, and is an initially deliberately dumped artificial garden soil. In a more densely occupied urban environment, such as York, the 'dark earth' was less oxidised and was formed from continued urban refuse disposal; the relative organic nature of the dark earth reflects the intensity of the dumping.

The interpretation of the nature and purpose of these deposits is important in that they post-date a change in settlement that occurred at the end of the second century, and in some cases dark earth containing fourth century pottery overlies the remains of second century timber buildings, suggesting to Sheldon and Schaaf (1978) a change in land usage to agriculture; this reduction in population is also seen in the City (see p 272).

Regarding plant material recovered from Roman sites, some of the best preserved published material came from Southwark — many of the samples came from waterlain deposits, yielding information about the immediate local environment, and cultural evidence from food debris that had been thrown into stream channels. The preservation of plant and insect remains is due to semi-waterlogged and waterlogged conditions, and SLAEC have carried out extensive sampling on all their sites. For example at 93–95 Borough High Street, (99) dated to AD 200 (Dean 1978b) seeds from the waterlaid sediments included *Carex* sp. (sedges), *Apium graveolens* (wild celery), *Polygonum persicaria* (persicaria), *Polygonum aviculare* (Knotgrass) and *Polygonum convulvulus* (black bindweed) — plants one might expect to find on the margins of a fresh water channel. The plant remains from the main fill of the channel (pre-Flavian in date) at 201–211 Borough High Street (85) (Dean 1978a) suggested a variety of conditions including mud or wet soil and the proximity of wasteland.. Seeds from Ditch 2 (also pre-Flavian) on this site indicated a variety of habitats, including open water in the ditch itself, and dampness, wasteland and arable land from the surrounding area; the upper levels proved relatively barren. It is suggested from the combined evidence of seeds, insects and molluscs that the ditch contained water, then became stagnant and filled up with rotting vegetation, and the archaeological evidence also supports this.

Cultural evidence is provided by seeds and plant material from 1–7 St. Thomas Street (102) from a late second century timber-lined pit: – seeds recovered include *Morus nigra* (mulberry), *Ficus carica* (fig), *Camelina sativa* (gold of pleasure), *Prunus* sp. (plum type), *Pisum sativum* (pea), and *Olea europea* (olive) (Willcox 1978), suggesting both imported and locally cultivated species in the Roman period. The only features to indicate the local vegetation were three first century troughs, the seeds from which suggested fairly open wasteland.

A third century water storage tank from the site of the Roman signal station at Shadwell (130) contained many seeds in its fill, including *Chenopodium hybridum* (sowbane), *Chenopodium murale* (nettle leaved goosefoot), *Thlaspi arvense* (field pennycress), *Prunus domestica* (plum), and *Prunus cf. cerasus* (sour cherry). The first three species are weeds; the plums and sour cherries would have been imported at this period (Willcox 1977a). For further discussion on exotic plants imported into London in the Roman period see p 272. Samples taken from a section of silt at Tooley Street, Southwark contained pips of *Maloideae* sub. fam. (apple etc.), *Prunus domestica* (plum), *Linum usitatissimum* (flax), *Vitis vinifera* (grape), *Foeniculum vulgare* (fennel) and *Chrysanthemum segetum* (corn marigold). The plums and grapes were probably imported, although later in the medieval period they were grown in Britain; the other species are native (Willcox 1977a, Kennard and Warren 1903).

Carbonised grain has been identified (preliminary report) from Wall Garden Farm, Sipson Lane, Harlington (5):— the flue and stokehole of a late Roman corn drier containing *Hordeum* sp. (both the six-rowed hulled barley and the six-rowed naked barley), *Triticum dicoccum* (emmer) and *Triticum aestivum/compactum* (breadwheat) (Scaife 1980), provided evidence for the cultivated cereals of the period.

Wood and charcoal have also been identified from Southwark sites:— road timbers from 201—211 Borough High Street (85) were *Alnus* sp. (alder), the usual species found in road construction. *Ulmus* sp. (elm) was identified as the sleeper beam of a Romano-British hut at Churchfield Edmonton (Balfour Browne 1953). A variety of species were identified from charcoal found at the kiln site at Highgate Wood including *Quercus* sp. (oak), *Ilex aquifolium* (holly) *Salix* sp. (willow) (Locker unpublished); local wood was probably used as fuel. A quantity of *Corylus* sp. (hazel) charcoal was associated with the cremation of two lapdogs at Keston (47) (Piercy Fox 1967).

Fragments of charcoal can often be identified but it may be difficult to use the identifications in any constructive way unless they are associated with a definite feature such as a kiln or hearth where deliberate selection of certain species for fuel could be postulated.

Dendrochronological dating of wood samples has been carried out on wood from a number of Southwark sites; so far the most successful results have been from building piles from 15—23 Southwark Street (83) (Tyers in preparation) and it is hoped that in the future it will be possible to date some of the Roman road timbers.

Insect remains are usually found in deposits with similar preservation conditions as seeds and a number were found at 1—7 St. Thomas Street, Southwark (102); insect remains in the timber-lined pit, which was so rich in seeds, included *Blaps* sp. a beetle associated with cellars and graveyards, and *Trox* sp., often associated with dry bones and hide. Girling (1978) suggested that a suitable environment would be an enclosed pit with decaying animal and vegetable matter, such as a refuse pit also containing some dung. At 93—95 Borough High Street (99) insect remains from the waterway suggested both damp and wasteland conditions at the margins of freshwater (Dean 1978b). The possibility of herbivores grazing nearby was indicated by the presence of *Aphodius* sp., the dung beetle, and consistent with the presence of some food refuse in these sediments was *Trox* sp.

Southwark seems to have produced most of the molluscan evidence:— molluscs from the late pre-Roman/Early Roman waterlain clay at 106—114 Borough High Street (95) (Dean 1978d) yielded a number of aquatic species with different ecological requirements consistent with a slow moving or still body of water, occasionally drying out, with infusions of salt water. At Swan Street/Great Dover Street (88) the environmental evidence was entirely molluscan (Spencer 1978) from the fill of a Roman ditch (first to mid third century AD). The ditch was situated in open land, which was probably used for cultivation outside the main area of settlement and the results indicated aquatic conditions in the bottom of the ditch during the deposition of silt. Ostracods were also present in this sample, but were not identified.

At New Palace Yard, Westminster (63) building work revealed deposits which indicated the encroachment over a sandy river bank of estuarine clay, a bipartite peat bed and further estuarine clay (Limbrey pers. comm.). Evans (unpublished) examined shells from freshwater deposits overlying peat dated to the early third century BC to the fifth century AD — three zones were recognised:— a mixed zone of ecotypes suggesting freshwater with shaded woodland or scrub into which the land and marsh species were swept in times of flood, a zone of predominantly catholic and marsh species, suggesting a reed swamp environment, and zone C in which there is a return to open water conditions.

Oysters and other edible shellfish are often found with other food refuse; as they have seldom been collected consistently and their source cannot be identified, their presence or absence is usually all that has been recorded, although judging by the large numbers sometimes found they must have formed a substantial part of the diet.

Mammal bones have been recovered from a number of Roman sites throughout Greater London. After analysing bones from a number of sites, Rixson (1978) prepared a summary of the bones from all these sites suggesting that all the bones (except for those from one site) represented domestic meat consumption. The most common species were cattle, sheep, pig and domestic fowl; most bones showed evidence of butchery, rendering pieces small enough for domestic cooking, and all parts of the body were fairly evenly represented. The exception in Rixson's analysis was the bone from Ditch 2 (pre-Flavian) at 201—211 Borough High Street (85), where a relatively high proportion of lamb skull fragments were found. It has been suggested (Ferretti and Graham 1978) that this may indicate slaughtering nearby, and the removal of headless carcasses elsewhere, possibly as some commercial activity. Based on minimum numbers the contribution of pork to the diet in Southwark is only marginally less than mutton (with beef as the main meat). However, in the City pork was more popular, and was second only to beef (see p 273); in other areas of Greater London pork generally takes third place in frequency.

A similar synopsis was prepared by Sutton (1978) for a group of sites from Brentford High Street where the number of bones recovered from individual sites was too small for separate analysis. This is really the only feasible approach when publishing very small groups of bone from similarly dated sites in a given locality.

A group of sites from the Old Ford area, representing Late Roman settlement around the line of the Roman road to Colchester, including Parnell Road and Appian Road (134) (Rixson 1972) and Lefevre Road (133) (Rixson 1971) provided evidence that on both these sites cattle were dominant; the position of the sites allowed Rixson to speculate that the cattle were driven in from Essex to supply the City; this being an area which could be a convenient holding point on the journey. Bone was also found at Usher Road (135) (Locker 1979), where ox was dominant, although this was again a small group of bones (approximately 1100):— most bones showed signs of butchery, and the proportion of immature bones was small. A cremation burial from Lefevre Road (Cresswell and Sheldon 1979) also included some animal bone, sheep/goat, piglet and ? bird.

A small quantity of late Roman animal bone in dumped deposits at Goodmans Yard (122) (Locker 1980) showed a predominance of ox and the other usual domestic species; butchery marks were common. These deposits all seem to represent domestic food debris.

A Roman signal station at Shadwell (130) has been the subject of two excavations; the first by T Johnson in 1974 yielded a small quantity of animal bone (943 bones) (Locker 1983). The pre-dominance of ox is again apparent — in fact in all the Roman settlement sites examined in the area ox was the dominant species, both numerically and in terms of meat contribution. However it should be possible to comment on the bone from this site as a more statistically viable sample when the bones from the 1977 excavations by the ILAU have been examined.

In South London, animal bone has been recovered from excavations at Beddington Roman Villa (57) which is to be examined in the near future, and north of the Thames the site at Lincoln Road, Enfield (127) produced mainly cattle, pig, sheep and horse plus a few fragments of red and roe deer (Armitage 1977b). Many bones from Roman deposits at Fulham Palace Moat (45) (Clutton Brock 1978) were in a rolled condition except for the complete skulls of dog and horse, thought to be buried for a ritual purpose.

However when dealing with sites tentatively classified as 'ritual' the quantity of material is not of such importance. The area around Keston Warbank has long been excavated for Roman remains, and one of the more unusual features was the excavation of a 'ritual shaft' of third to fourth century date in 1960 (147). Within this shaft was a projection above which the cremation of 'a lapdog and a smaller dog' had taken place (Piercy Fox 1967); part of the report is devoted to investigating the ritual significance of the lapdog when it is depicted with goddess figures.

Later excavation in the same area by Philp in 1980 (147) of a similar shaft, dated to 70 AD, cut through chalk, revealed among the domestic debris a number of animal bones. At least twelve individuals of sheep were identified (both horned and naturally polled); these were not butchered. Also a few ox fragments, some domestic fowl bones, the skull of a house mouse and the femur of a vole. However the most interesting finds were the skeletons of two dogs:— one was a small stocky specimen which compared well with a modern beagle, and the other was a very small slender specimen of shoulder height 18.6 to 19.8cm (Locker unpublished), and compared fairly closely to a Pomeranian. It is well known that the Romans bred very small dogs, similar to our present day lapdogs, and it is interesting that these two closely related features produced some of the few examples of these small dogs in Britain. It cannot be ruled out that these animals were buried for some ritual purpose.

With regard to bird bones, the domestic species, i.e. domestic fowl, domestic duck and goose, are commonly found on sites where recovery is good and where sieving has also been carried out. In addition woodcock has been identified from Lincoln Road, Enfield (127) (Armitage 1977b) and the Bonded Warehouse, Montague Close (103) (Rixson 1978). *Haliaeetus albicilla* (white tailed sea eagle) was identified from a well fill at 8 Union Street (96) (Rixson 1978). *Milvus* sp. (kite) once a common scavenger in London was represented by a humerus and a tarsometatarsus identified by Bramwell from a ditch at Gay Street, Putney (44) (Locker unpublished).

As a result of the development of sieving as a standard procedure, fish bones are now frequently recovered from sites, although their more delicate structure makes them more susceptible to damage than mammal bones. A few bones representing ?sole and bream were recovered from Goodman's Yard (122) (Locker 1980). In Southwark at 201—211 Borough High Street (85) a cyprinid vertebral centrum and two eel vertebral centra, were recovered from two Roman ditches (Jones 1978), and one herring vertebral centrum was found in a late Roman pit at 106—114 Borough High Street (95) (Dean 1978d). Some of the most numerous fish remains from Southwark came from the timber-lined late second century pit at 1—7 St. Thomas Street (102) which also produced so much plant material. Herring, smelt, pike, cyprinid, dace, roach, gudgeon, chub, eel, cod, mackerel and haddock were identified (Jones 1978) as a result of extensive sampling through this feature. A Roman well at Hibernia Wharf (100) contained plaice or flounder and Spanish mackerel (*Scomber japonicus*); the latter's range extends north to the south-west coast of Britain, so presumably this fish must have been in some preserved state (dried or salted) by the time it reached Southwark (Locker unpublished). A Roman wreck of Claudian date, Port Vendres 11, discovered off the south-west coast of France, contained amphorae full of Spanish mackerel (Collis *et al.* 1977), indicating this species was of commercial importance in the Roman period. These species give some idea of the variety of fish available by a number of fishing methods to the inhabitants of Southwark and also introduces the possibility of fish being imported.

Roman burials have been frequently found in Greater London; the area around Old Ford contained inhumations as well as a cremation burial at Lefevre Road (133) (Sheldon 1979). A few cremation urns were found during the 1977 excavations at Shadwell Roman signal station (130). In Southwark both burials and cremations have been found; their provenance has been discussed by Dean and Hammerson 1980, as well as the distribution of pottery usually associated with burials (Dean 1981), and it is suggested that two areas of burial lay outside the settlement. Disturbed burials, believed to be from a Roman cemetery, have been found mixed with medieval material at Gardiners Corner, Aldgate (124) and Artillery Lane (119). A number of Roman stone coffins were discovered in East London at the end of the last century; in 1814 and 1837 stone coffins were found in the present grounds of Springfield Park, and in 1839 in Hackney Marsh. A white marble sarcophagus was discovered in Clapton in 1867 (Black).

Future work on Roman sites in Greater London should include a topographical study for the whole area on the same lines as that published for North Southwark by Graham (1978). Also further study of the changes that occurred between the second and fourth centuries AD, investigation of animal and plant material in conjunction with information from artefacts and structures should suggest whether this depopulation was exactly the same over the whole area shown by an increase in areas of agriculture.

3.8   Early Medieval, 500–900 AD, Figure 27

Evidence of Saxon occupation, especially with well preserved environmental material, is very scarce within the area.

The only plant material recovered came from a section at New Palace Yard (63) where a section through Early Medieval (tenth century) deposits was sampled for seeds. Paradine and Arthur (unpublished) suggested that the surrounding area was an aquatic environment, while on higher ground lay pasture or semi-wooded land.

Two pieces of oak plank were found in a stream bed at Cromwell Green, Westminster (64) and were dated to the seventh and eighth centuries by C14 (Mills 1980); pollen, snail and soil studies are being prepared to compare this section with those from the tenth century New Palace Yard deposits.

The site of the Early Medieval manor at Althorpe Grove, Battersea (50) produced a small quantity of animal bones (Locker 1983); approximately 300, the usual domestic species were found, and the vertebral centrum of a pilot whale was identified. Soil samples were also taken but did not contain any macroscopic remains of any interest.

A grubenhaus was excavated at Lower Warbank, Keston (146) dated to the fifth/sixth century AD; cattle, sheep, pig, roe and red deer were identified from a small group of 380 bone fragments (Harman 1973).

The most substantial quantity of Early Medieval bone in the area was found at Whitehall Palace (65); ninth century deposits contained cattle, sheep, pig, horse, fallow deer, dog and bird. Cattle were most important numerically (Chaplin 1971). Chaplin suggests selective killing of younger stock of cattle and pig, which were primarily raised for food, and the dispersal of selected joints from the site. He concludes that this Saxon farm appears economically competent, based on cattle rearing with the strong possibility of the provision of winter fodder.

Other finds of Early Medieval bone are limited to occasional association of bone in human burials, such as a dog skeleton found in a grave in a cemetery at Mitcham (51) (Bidder 1908), but in terms of interpreting the animal economy of this period our area is sparse in evidence compared with the preceding and following periods.

Other burials were found at Coulsdon (Moodie 1913) and Carshalton Road (Turner 1961). Three graves were found at Northolt Manor (11) and seven at Sewards Pit, Hanwell in 1886 (V.C.H.) — three of the latter were said to be men with spears.

3.9   Medieval, 900–1500 AD, Figure 27

A wide range of biological remains has been found from medieval sites, including plant material:— carbonised seeds and grains were found in eleventh and twelfth century deposits at Gatehouse Nurseries, West Drayton (4); in a preliminary report Scaife (1981) identified *Triticum aestivum* (breadwheat) predominantly, *Avena sativa* (oats), and *Pisum sativum* (pea); carbonised seeds included a large number of *Anthemis cotula* (stinking mayweed) and *Polygonum aviculare* (knotgrass), both associated with arable habitats. Carbonised seeds and grain were also identified from a number of medieval contexts from Eltham Palace (150) by Monk (1978):— *Triticum* sp. (wheat) grains were most numerous, followed by *Secale cereale* (rye), *Hordeum sativum* (barley) and *Avena sativa* (oats); however the interpretation was limited by the small number of samples. Monk states that bread wheat, barley, rye and peas were common medieval crops according to documentary evidence, but the presence of rye was interesting as it has rarely been found in carbonised deposits.

Charcoal was also identified from Eltham Palace (150) by Keepax (1978); the fill of a late twelfth century building contained *Crataegus* sp. (hawthorn type), *Quercus* sp. (oak), *Corylus avellana* (hazel), *Acer* sp. (maple) and *Prunus* sp.; the same species were found from a late twelfth century building. A demolition layer predating 1480 AD contained

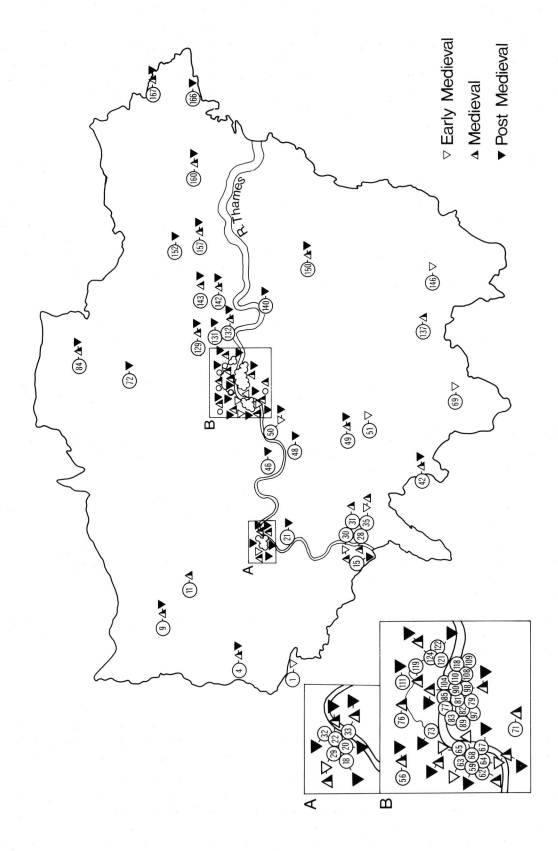

Figure 27 Greater London: distribution of early medieval, medieval and post—medieval sites

Quercus sp. (oak), *Taxus baccata* (yew), *Fraxinus excelsior* (ash), *Ilex aquifolium* (holly), *Betula* sp. (birch) and possibly *Lonicera* sp. (honeysuckle), showing a wide range of species in use from the twelfth to fifteenth centuries. Quantities of charcoal have also been identified from Merton Priory (49) (Keepax in preparation).

Samples have been submitted for dendrochronology from timbers from the Old Bridge Site, Kingston (28).

Bone makes up the remaining material recovered. Excavations in the sub-vault of the misericorde at Westminster Abbey (62) produced a small amount of mammal bone from the monastery; these included the usual domestic species plus red deer, rabbit and a porpoise tooth. Birds included domestic fowl, duck, jackdaw, pigeon, red grouse and goose, suggesting a varied diet and certainly not showing any change in diet resulting from the relaxation of monastic rule by the thirteenth century (Locker 1976). A number of fish bones were also recovered, mostly as a result of sieving (Jones 1976); a wide variety of species was present, including sturgeon, John Dory, bass, turbot and sole which were and are regarded as delicacies. In all, 21 species were identified representing fishing in the Thames to the Thames Estuary and the southern North Sea.

Further work on monastic sites to be undertaken include bones from Merton Priory (49), Clerkenwell Nunnery (76) and the Cistercian site at the Royal Mint which is to be excavated in the near future by the ILAU.

Manorial sites are represented by Northolt Manor (11) where, from the analysis of bone from deposits dated from 1050 to 1500 AD, King (1961) comments that no difference in size or distribution of the animals could be correlated to different layers (the sample size was small) and Jope (1961) identified domestic fowl, goose and partridge. The site of Tottenham Manor at Euston Road (56) produced a fifteenth century group of bones (Locker 1982); ox was dominant, sheep, pig, horse, cat, fallow deer, hare and rabbit were also present, starling was identified from a medieval wall, this also was a small group, as many of the features were yard surfaces which would be relatively clear of food debris.

Medieval deposits at Palace Gardens, Enfield (84), in a possible garden area (dated to the twelfth century) and associated with a gravel floor contained bones of horse, ox and fallow deer (Armitage 1978c). The hunting park of Enfield Chase was enclosed about AD 1136 which may be the source of the deer.

At Church Meadow, Addington (137) sheep are the dominant species; a sheep bell was also found (Thornhill 1978) and it is suggested that the keeping of sheep may have been the main local farming occupation here in the twelfth century.

Medieval cattle horn cores from the Eden Walk area of Kingston may represent industrial debris. These were found with the Neolithic deposits at Eden Street (34) and may be horn working waste as in many cases the horn tips had been sawn off (Penn, Field and Serjeantson 1983, forthcoming).

There were a few animal bones of medieval date from both Gardiners Corner, Aldgate (124) from the area of gravel workings (Locker in preparation) and also from Butcher Row, Ratcliffe (132) (Locker 1978), however post-Medieval activity had cut through these deposits.

The absence of quantities of well stratified medieval deposits is mainly due to their destruction by later activity. Material from monastic and palace sites has tended to be less disturbed, since the structural remains of some sites still exist as at Merton Priory (49) and Eltham Palace (150). Also the location of these sites is well documented so excavation can be directed towards very specific areas.

Burials have been found at Merton Priory (49) and form an interesting monastic group; other large groups include burials associated with a medieval hospital at Spital Square, excavated by the ILAU — these two sites in particular have provided valuable material for study.

3.10 Post Medieval, 1500 AD onwards, Figure 27

Organic preservation in the post-medieval period has been greatly assisted by the remains of industrial activities such as tanning and also the isolation of cess material within brick-lined pits such as garderobes; both these conditions which are usually accompanied by waterlogging and sometimes mineral replacement provide ideal preservation conditions. Another aspect of this later period is evidence of animal bones, more specifically horn cores used in structures.

Firstly regarding industrial activity, the site at Gardiners Corner currently being analysed (124) had many features, including four barrel-lined pits and a plank-lined pit with a ditch draining from it containing highly organic material from which many plant and insect remains have been recovered (Askew 1983). The barrels were made of oak with willow/poplar bindings, and the planks lining a pit were also made of oak (Watson 1982); animal hair was found, as well as leather and cloth. Horn core lined pits were seen in section, and were similar to those at Cutler Street nearby in the City (site No. c44) (Armitage 1979a); all these features could be associated with an industrial activity such as tanning.

Insect remains were found in a post-medieval pit from Chaucer House, Southwark (98) in deposits dated to the sixteenth and seventeenth centuries. Girling (1979) identified insects whose habitats indicate the presence of vegetable refuse and dung, old hides and dry carcasses and tree bark, which suggested to Girling that tanning was being carried out on the sites, the carcasses and hides being used as part of the raw material:— bark is used as a tanning agent and dung to produce supple leather.

Kenyon (1959b) in her excavations at King's Head Yard, Southwark (109) suggests that the Tudor ditches she found may have been associated with tanning. The locations of Gardiners Corner (124) and Chaucer House (98) would be consistent with the siting of such a strong smelling industrial activity away from densely inhabited areas, but the King's Head Yard Site is rather more doubtful.

The site at Broad Sanctuary, Westminster (59) must also have provided a rank atmosphere for the occupants of nearby houses shown on contemporary engravings. Pollen analysis (Scaife 1980) indicated a low presence of tree pollen and shrubs; the few instances of Ericaceous types (heathers) may be a result of animal bedding being brought into the area; the marginal aquatic and mire taxa could have grown along a stream channel which was the subject of excavation. Dominant were the ruderals typical of disturbed waste ground:— *Linum bienne* type pollen was present — the plant was used either for flax or linseed oil; *Cannabis sativa* may originate from the production of hemp, *Fagopyrum* (buckwheat), also present, has been rarely recorded in Britain. Graminacae and Cyperacae (grasses and rushes) are the dominant individual pollen types for which Scaife suggests a number of possible origins. In the upper samples were the eggs of nematodes *Trichuris* and *Ascaris* indicating cess associated with man and pigs. The animal bones from Broad Sanctuary (Locker 1982) were from three sixteenth century ditches; primary butchery waste, i.e. skulls and mandibles, were present, sheep being dominant over ox in terms of fragments (524 to 468 respectively), however in terms of meat weight this would be reversed. Twenty six sheep mandibles could be aged — these indicated fully mature animals; ox mandibles were more fragmented but also seemed to suggest mainly mature animals. Pig, fallow deer, dog, cat, rabbit and hare were also present. Domestic fowl, duck, goose, pigeon, swan and crow were the birds identified and the fish included conger eel, cod, gurnard and turbot. All these species were eaten; the most likely interpretation for the local environment around Broad Sanctuary is that of a wet area being used for the indiscriminate disposal of refuse.

Cess material was also evident from two pits at 201—211 Borough High Street, Southwark (85); one is dated to the second half of the seventeenth century and contained herring, smelt, eel and plaice as well as many dipterous puparia; the other cess pit (mid eighteenth century) contained the bones of eel, a cyprinid, dipterous puparia and the seeds of edible fruits including *Ficus carica* (fig) *Vitis vinifera* (grape), *Prunus spinosa* (sloe) and *Rubus idaeus* (raspberry).

A small sample (weight 270g) from a Tudor cess pit at the site of Tottenham Manor, Euston Road (56) contained over 300 fig seeds; *Prunus* sp., *Rubus* sp. and grape were also present. The abundance of wild plums, bullace and sloe and the profusion of walled vineyards in London during the medieval period is described by McLean (1981) and would have continued into the Tudor period — thus the sample from this site complements the documentary evidence.

Excavations at Abingdon Street, Westminster (67) (Green 1976) on the site of the south waterfront of the Palace, revealed a sixteenth century shoe in the mud which contained walnut shells, cherry stalks and stones. Samples were taken south and north of the piles of the waterfront and examined for diatoms (Ross 1976). The samples south of the pile contained species indicating still water with waterplants or reeds, with a discontinuity between the two samples. The samples taken north of the piles suggested an absence of water plants. The samples varied as to the likelihood of waterlogging depending on their position in relation to the piles, but nearly all the species identified were characteristic of fresh to slightly brackish water. The exception was the sample above the discontinuity which contained some brackish to marine forms; many of the latter were broken.

The animal bones from Nonsuch Palace (42) on the boundary of the area (Locker in preparation and Locker 1982) produced a very diverse fauna; many of the numerous species of small birds and fish were found in the garderobe pits and were meticulously recovered by hand picking. The bird species included heron, a variety of ducks, small birds such as finches, sparrows and thrushes, quail, crane, many waders, corvids as well as the domestic and game birds eaten today. The fish included sturgeon, turbot, salmon, carp and pike and many other fresh water and marine species. It is well known that in the sixteenth and seventeenth centuries virtually any type of bird was considered edible and contemporary recipe books describe elaborate ways of both cooking and presenting them at the table. The species identified from this site provide complementary evidence to the documentary sources of the varied diet enjoyed by the upper classes during this period. Work is also in progress on the animal bones from excavations at Greenwich Palace (140) (Harman in preparation) and it will be interesting to compare the two sites although they are not quite contemporary. A small collection of eighteenth to nineteenth century bone was found at Richmond Palace (21) (Harman 1975); cattle, sheep, horse, rabbit/hare, badger and domestic fowl were identified but the group was too small for any further comment to be made.

Later expansion of the medieval settlement at Butcher Row, Ratcliffe (132) (Locker 1977) revealed domestic food debris from 5 pits in Trench 1; cattle, sheep, pig, fallow deer, rabbit, duck, domestic fowl, swan, red grouse, oyster, mussel, cockle and whelk were identified but only in small quantities. The most interesting find from Butcher Row came from an eighteenth to nineteenth century well. Two articulated costal bones of a turtle (probably green turtle) were found. Armitage and McCarthy (1980) cite evidence for a thriving turtle trade between the West Indies and London by the second half of the eighteenth century.

Excavations at Palace Gardens, Enfield (84) produced animal bone from the seventeenth and nineteenth centuries. Armitage (1978c) was able to compare and contrast sheep humeri showing the differences in size between unimproved and improved sheep, the earlier animals being of small stature and build. However comparison of cattle from the same contexts showed little difference.

Five seventeenth century refuse deposits on the site of Fulham Pottery yielded 1013 mammalian, 36 bird and 40 fish bones, as well as the shell remains of 117 shellfish and land snails (Armitage forthcoming). In one rubbish pit of *c* 1660 date (predating the establishment of the pottery works in 1672) known to have been associated with a household of reasonable means, all the sheep bones from the fill were from small and medium sized animals, with a high proportion of elements from the legs and shoulders signifying best quality joints of meat. The presence of small sized sheep accords with the known preference shown by London's wealthier society for the succulent joints from short and middle woolled breeds such as Welsh sheep and the Dorset and Wiltshire horn: the meat from the longwool breeds was tougher and coarser grained and therefore generally only considered suitable for consumption by the urban working classes (see Armitage and Straker, 1983 forthcoming). Another deposit provided evidence of the variety of diet enjoyed by the reasonably well-off artisan in the late seventeenth century. In the cellar beneath the house once occupied by the owner of the pottery works, John Dwight, the food debris found included rabbit, hare, chicken, various sea and freshwater fish as well as shellfish. Terrestrial molluscs, such as common snail *Helix aspersa*, garden snail *Cepaea hortensis* and the grove snail *C. nemoralis*, were also recovered from the cellar. Although these land snails may originally have formed an integral part of the natural fauna on the site, their association with domestic (kitchen) rubbish could, however, mean that they were also food waste. Indeed it is known that the seventeenth century was marked in England by a revival in the consumption of many sorts of molluscs; the English cookery books of this period provide instructions on how to prepare snail pottages, fried and hashed snails and snail pie (Wilson 1976, 101).

The use of animal bone as building material has been much explored by Armitage using both documentary and bone evidence. Within Greater London cattle horncores have been found lining pits at Gardiners Corner, Aldgate (124), comparing well with similar features at Cutler Street (C44); the cores are from long horn cattle. Horncores were also used in land drains at 28–32 Upsdell Avenue, Enfield (72) where they were set in a continuous row east–west. Some were associated with black silt from water drainage: these cores were picked up at a number of points, and thought to channel excess water down a slope to a brook. The cores were from longhorn and medium horned cattle probably of late seventeenth to eighteenth century stock (Armitage, Coxshall and Ivens 1980) (see pp 281 and 285).

4   The City of London

4.1   Geology and Topography

The map showing solid and drift deposits (Figure 28) is intended to give a general idea of the distribution of the natural deposits which underlie the accumulation of almost 2000 years of deposits associated with the activities of man. The information is principally from a geological map (scale 1:25,000) based largely on borehole data, kindly supplied by Berry of the Institute of Geological Sciences. Additional information was obtained from Marsden (1972) and Bentley (pers. comm). A detailed survey of the natural deposits based on observations made during excavations is under way (see section 4.2). The nature of the deposits shown on Figure 28 is described in the section concerned with Greater London (3.1) and this should be referred to.

The oldest deposits to outcrop in the City are those of London Clay which can be seen in isolated areas, although in most places it is covered by drift deposits. The topographical features which dominate the City are two low gravel hills which are capped with brickearth. The western hill, known as Ludgate Hill, had a natural height estimated as + 12.95m above OD and is separated from the eastern, Cornhill (12.2m above OD), by the valley of the Walbrook. The brickearth has been extensively used in building, either as dumping to raise the ground surface, in wattle and daub walls, or in the manufacture of bricks (Merrifield 1965). The gravel terraces are exposed in much of the City where the brickearth capping has been removed through human and natural agencies. Much of the gravel that outcrops in the City is part of the second (formerly Higher Flood Plain) terrace of the Thames.

The natural topography was to some extent modified or taken advantage of as early as the Roman period; Merrifield (1965) states for example that the slope down towards the river was in places revetted artificially by the Romans. The Tower of London (just outside the eastern boundary of the administrative area, but at the eastern end of the Roman wall) is sited on an outcrop of second terrace gravel; an area presumably better drained than the surrounding alluvium and clay. That advantage was taken of stable ground may further be indicated by the fact that the alignment of the Roman bridge across the Thames makes use of patches of gravel and sand (first terrace) on both north and south banks of the river, and is particularly noticeable on the south side where the land is flat and low lying.

Alluvium, the most recent deposit, extends along the bank of the Thames and up the Fleet and Walbrook valleys. The term alluvium has a rather general meaning in parts of the City; in the Walbrook valley, for example, it is certainly used to describe several metres of peaty and organic layers which may contain cultural material. In other areas it is referable to the clays described in section 3.1.

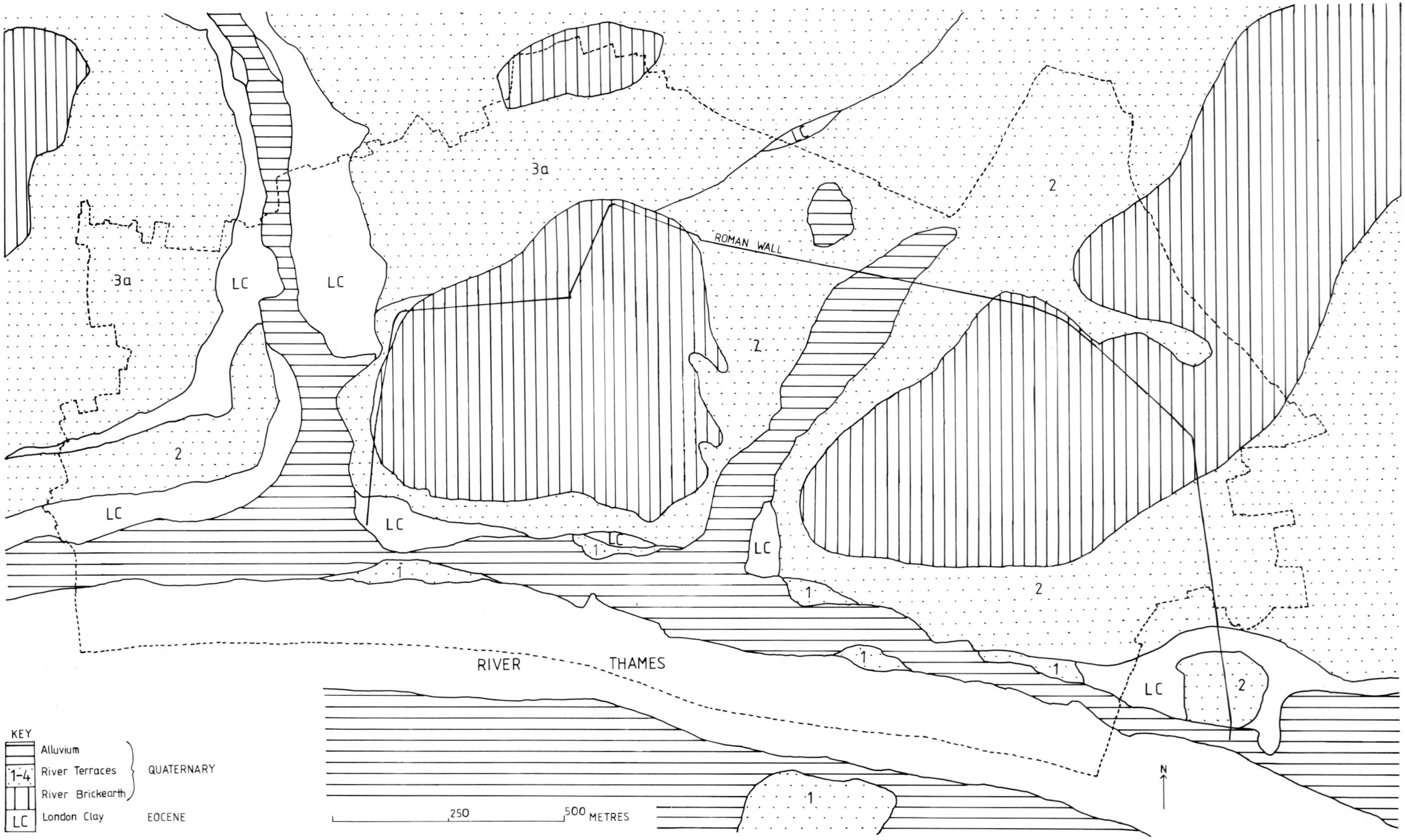
3a
3a
LC
LC
LC
LC
LC
LC
LC
LC
2
2
2
2
2
1
1
1
1
1
1
ROMAN WALL
RIVER THAMES
KEY
Alluvium
1-4 River Terraces
River Brickearth
LC London Clay
QUATERNARY
EOCENE
250
500 METRES
N

Figure 28 City of London: solid and drift geological deposits

In addition to the Fleet and Walbrook streams, which are relatively well known from archaeological and historical sources, observations of other channels have been made in the past; the positions of one of the larger ones are also shown on the map, located in the west of the City. Merrifield (1965) observed the beds of two streams, which, it is thought joined together, cutting brickearth into gravel to 31.5 feet below the present surface. The beds of these streams contained black mud and the remains of reeds and rushes. It is not known whether this stream flowed south to enter the Thames in the Puddledock area or west to join the Fleet. Streams in the City will be discussed in section 4.7.1.

4.2   Environment and vegetation before the development of the Roman settlement

One of the most important questions concerned with the archaeological study of the City of London is still largely unanswered. This concerns the nature of the environment (soils and vegetation) of the area which was later to become the Roman town. The natural soils of the area are formed on gravel or brickearth (Figure 28). Brickearth soils are usually regarded as fertile and capable of supporting woodland; however it is rare to encounter soils preserved in an urban archaeological context and none that can confidently be dated as pre-Roman have been preserved so far. A well developed brickearth soil at Lloyd's Bank (C39) was considered by Macphail (1980a) as being capable of supporting such woodland and although the soil was early Roman in date it may give an indication of immediately pre-Roman conditions.

Few deposits which would yield evidence of pre-Roman vegetation have been excavated. The most important to date is a deposit from stratigraphically below the earliest Roman levels at Peninsular House (C34) comprising peat and sediment divisible into three minerogenic and biogenic stratigraphical divisions (Scaife 1983 unpublished). A single 'spot' sample has been examined so far and the rest await analysis. The arboreal spectrum was dominated by *Pinus* (pine) (8% AP, 24% TP), *Betula* (birch) (10% AP), single grain occurrences of *Alnus* (alder) and *Quercus* (oak) and shrubs represented by *Corylus* (hazel) (18% AP) and *Salix* (willow). Gramineae represent 15% TP and Cyperaceae at 30% TP are the main herbaceous taxa. These are associated with a range of marginal aquatic herbs such as *Filipendula*, *Caltha*, *Lysimachia*, *Alisma* type, *Mentha* type as well as other groups less diagnostic for habitat reconstruction. There are also many *Dryopteris* spores. The high *Pinus* values would suggest that the deposit was early Flandrian (Boreal) in date, unless estuarine water conditions have been responsible for transporting the *Pinus* pollen, which is readily transported by water. Further work on the remaining samples and the result of C14 dating which is awaited should clarify the interpretation (Scaife 1983 unpublished).

An unusual molluscan fauna was recovered from an undated context at Pudding Lane (C32); the deposit in which it was found filled a small linear feature which was sealed by series of archaeological layers and cut on the west side by the foundation of a Roman bath-house, and it predated the earliest occupation of AD 160 on this part of the site. Some of the species are characteristic of calcareous soils, but the stratigraphical position of the deposit means that the molluscs could not have been imported with chalk or tufa as building material. The fauna contains species such as *Pomatias elegans,* not found in the clays and sands of the lower part of the Thames valley, and the fauna as a whole is one of moist calcareous woodland, undisturbed by man. This assemblage of species, and particularly the presence of *Vertigo pulsilla* and *Spermodea lamellata* suggests a date in the middle part of the post-glacial period, later than 5000 BC but before human clearance of the vegetation (Askew and Kerney 1983).

The suggestion that the vegetation of the City and environs was largely of woodland before the earliest settlement does have some support, although when the woodland was cleared is not known.

Other aspects of the natural environment, notably the river Thames and its tributaries, are also the subject of study and this topic is covered in section 4.7.1. Maps showing, where available, the natural contours of the land are presently being compiled in the Museum of London from the records of hundreds of natural deposits and their levels noted during excavations and in bore-hole investigations. Modern levels are sometimes very misleading, however, as in places up to seven metres of archaeological deposits have accumulated between the natural ground surface and the present ground level.

4.3   Romano-British (AD 43–500)

The natural soils which were present in London in the Roman period and before are virtually never encountered during the course of archaeological investigation and are assumed to have been removed completely during building activity throughout the City's history. Such soils would be an important source of information on the still inadequately understood details of the natural environment and vegetation in the City. One site which did produce remains of a soil in a Roman context, Lloyd's Bank (C39), has already been mentioned in section 4.2. The truncated argillic brown earth is described as evidence of a gently sloping area (2 to 3 degrees) which was under mature woodland during the major period of pedogenesis (Macphail 1980a). During a recent excavation at Rangoon Street (C47) another truncated soil of early or immediately pre-Roman date was found, also on brickearth which survives in patches in this part of the City. This deposit has not yet been fully analysed.

Another line of enquiry which it has not been possible to investigate on a large scale to date, is pollen analysis. Few of the deposits which survive in London are very suitable for pollen analysis. This is partly because of the problems of interpretation of pollen assemblages from pit fills and dump deposits, and also because preservation has been impaired, perhaps due to slightly alkaline conditions. The only work of this kind was carried out by Scaife (1981) on the samples collected by Professor Grimes from Walbrook deposits underlying the Temple of Mithras (C24),which was excavated in 1954. The flora was divided into several components: (1) the aquatic/marginal aquatic species which occurred in low frequencies indicating a fen type environment despite surprisingly low levels of *Alnus*,and possible derived pollen from upstream: (2) the arboreal/shrub element which also occurred in small quantity and included *Betula, Pinus, Quercus, Tilia* (lime), *Juglans* (walnut), *Corylus, Hedera* (ivy), *Ligustrum* (privet), *Sorbus* type (mountain ash type) and *Thelycrania* (dogwood). This suggests that if the area was forested before the Roman settlement was established, substantial deforestation had already taken place by the first to third centuries AD, the period represented by the study. Scaife (1981) comments that walnut is an interesting pollen record for this site as it is generally regarded as a Roman plant introduction to England (Godwin 1975). (3) ruderals/weeds made up the main vegetation adjacent to the site suggesting that the ground was waste or arable. The latter was also specifically indicated by cereal pollen which could reflect arable cropping outside the City's perimeter or crop processing, either near the site or in the stream catchment area.

Much of the botanical work for all periods in London has been concerned with macroscopic plant remains, in particular seeds. These have been preserved principally in wet or damp and anaerobic deposits and most provide details of economic rather than purely environmental character. Seeds have been extracted and identified from several sites in London from contexts dated from the first to third centuries as indicated in the gazetteer. It is not proposed to examine all this work in detail, but rather to select examples to make general points, or those of special interest. Willcox did much work to show the potential of London for the discovery of plants exotic to Britain and presumably imported as objects of trade. *Pinus pinea* (stone pine) bracts, nuts and cones have all been recovered from London sites (notably New Fresh Wharf and Billingsgate Buildings, C33 and C36). This species of pine is native to the Mediterranean countries and was imported as a delicacy. The New Fresh Wharf sites produced, among many other plants native to Britain, seeds and stones of peach, olive, fig, mulberry and grape. The mulberry was probably introduced here as the soft fruits would not travel well, and the others imported. Grapes were probably produced in this country as well as imported. Roman London has also produced the earliest evidence in Britain for the presence of cucumber (*Cucumis sativa*), a native plant of Africa (Willcox 1977a). Further work on Roman deposits in other parts of the City away from the waterfront has been carried out recently. Samples were collected from occupation layers, rubbish and cess pits excavated on the G.P.O. site (C11), Ironmonger Lane (C22), Milk Street (C16) and Watling Court (C17) (Davis 1983). Early Roman deposits at Watling Court contained seeds of coriander (*Coriandrum sativum*) as did New Fresh Wharf in its early and later Roman phases and another spice,dill (*Anethum graveolens*) was represented at Billingsgate Buildings (C36). Many species associated with waste places and disturbed ground are also present in these deposits, giving information on the background flora for comparison with that from later periods. The analysis of the plant macrofossils from Copthall Avenue (C27) has concentrated so far on the ditches and peat accumulations associated with the valley and drainage of the Walbrook which ran close to the site. About seven metres of stratigraphy were encountered, much of this of an organic nature derived from the 'marshy' deposits of the Walbrook valley. The deposits contain well preserved and abundant plant remains, some of economic importance but many, such as *Lemna* (duckweed), *Juncus* (rushes), *Ranunculus scleratus* (celery leaved crowfoot) and *Alima plantago-aquatica* (water plantain) giving a clear picture of the nature of the supposed Walbrook marsh itself (Askew and Moriarty 1982b). It is hoped that pollen analysis from this site as well as examination of Arthropods and further work on plant macrofossils will be carried out in the near future. As was mentioned above, all these sites also produce evidence of seeds from waste ground and disturbed places; typical 'urban' habitats and these compare well with examples from other urban excavations in Britain. Many of the plants in this category are useful in the sense that they yield raw materials for dyes, medicines, textiles etc, though in most cases this use can only be inferred.

Carbonised cereal grain is found in small quantities (often only isolated grains) from some of the Roman soil samples. Grain recovered in this way is of very limited value and where possible only permits the identification of the cereal type. However, two major deposits of carbonised grain have been recovered which allow much greater potential for the analysis of the crop components, methods and degree of processing of the crops, degree of infestation (if any) and even perhaps place of origin. The first such deposit was recovered during excavation of a site which included the south east corner of the Forum built in AD 60–90 (C37). The grain, which was over one metre thick in parts, was heaped against the eastern side of an internal mud brick wall of a building with a portico, along the main street of the Roman city. The building was at the corner of the main street and 'market square' and probably housed the workshop of a miller, baker or grain dealer (Marsden 1980). The destruction levels which contained the grain are attributed to the burning of London in AD 60 by the forces of Boudica. Most of the grain was wheat, principally *Triticum spelta* (spelt wheat) with smaller amounts of *T. dicoccum* (emmer), *T. aestivum* (bread wheat) and *T. monococcum* (einkorn). *Hordeum vulgare* (hulled barley), *Avena fatua* (wild oats), grasses, cereal crop weeds, *Lens culinaris* (lentils) and *Vicia ervilia* (bittervetch) were also recorded. (Boyd 1980, Straker in press). The presence of einkorn, lentil and bittervetch in small quantities suggests that the wheat may have been imported from the Mediterranean or Near East.

The other important deposit of carbonised grain was recovered from an excavation at Pudding Lane (C32) along the Roman waterfront. The sample is dated from the early to mid second century AD and was sealed within a dump of burnt building debris thought to represent the clearance of fire damaged structures along the waterfront. Most of the grain was spelt wheat with smaller amounts of hulled barley, oats, *Bromus* sp. and weed seeds. The composition of assemblage is consistent with local production and allows a comparison with that from the earlier Roman deposit described above (Straker in press). Both deposits give information on Roman farming techniques used in the processing of native and imported crops.

Many other types of plant remains are preserved in archaeological deposits in London. Leaves and stem fragments of box (*Buxus sempervirens*), for example, were found in deposits of Roman date at Copthall Avenue, and have been found on sites of similar date in other places including Roman York and Farmoor, Oxfordshire (Lambrick and Robinson 1979); they probably represent hedge clippings. Other contrasting examples of well preserved plant material are the ropes and cords that are often found in waterfront contexts and have been identified as being made of moss (*Polytrichum commune*, common hair moss).

Another aspect of palaeobotanical work is the identification of wood and charcoal from excavations. This is necessary partly because of the need to isolate timbers of oak for dendrochronological dating (this means that a lot of wood of a structural nature has been examined) and also because of the information on choice and availability of species that can be obtained. Most of the large structural timbers such as those used in Roman revetments are of oak, and it is important to ascertain the source. Some of it was presumably local, but pollen analysis of pre and early Roman deposits in and near the City would help to clarify this point. Apart from the waterfront, wooden structures preserved in Walbrook valley deposits at Copthall Avenue (C27) also revealed the limited use of ash (*Fraxinus excelsior*) for stakes and posts. One particularly interesting find from this site was a row of Roman stakes made of silver fir or cedar (*Abies/Cedrus* sp). These genera can be difficult to distinguish between when poorly preserved, but neither is native to Britain in the Roman period. These woods are usually found only as imported objects such as barrels or writing tablets and their presence at Copthall Avenue may suggest reuse of timber imported for some other purpose (Straker 1982a). A brushwood raft was laid as the foundation to a road surface on marshy land at this point in the upper Walbrook valley and young branches of oak and *Prunus* (cherry or sloe), about ten years old, were selected for this purpose. Another notable discovery from this site were tree stumps of willow/poplar (*Salix/Populus* sp.) preserved *in situ*. These trees can tolerate damp conditions and would have grown well beside a stream or drainage channel in this area (Straker 1982a). However, it is interesting to note that pollen of willow or poplar is absent from the assemblage previously described for the Mithraeum, lower in the Walbrook valley. On sites which do not benefit from waterlogged conditions, wood is more often preserved in the form of charcoal. As part of a project investigating the evidence for early Roman buildings and topography in the western part of the City, much charcoal from first and second century contexts was identified, principally from the G.P.O. site (C11). As was expected, structural wood was largely of oak, with smaller amounts of hazel, ash and willow/poplar and this was also reflected in the destruction debris. Charcoal associated with hearths was oak, *Pomoidae* (hawthorn type) and holly and in pit fills *Acer* sp. (field maple type), hazel, *Prunus* sp. and *Pomoidae*. All the taxa mentioned above were represented in the charcoal from accumulations on floors. This work suggests that the wood which was being used in the first phases of urban development in London could very well have been of local origin; all the varieties are easy to obtain in southern England (many are hedgerow species).

Although many studies of molluscs from Roman sites were carried out by Kennard and Woodward between 1902–21 (see p 253), little recent work has been done and the most useful has been that by Willcox (1980a) who looked at seeds and molluscs from deposits associated with the Roman Riverside Wall. The evidence from the molluscs (identified by Spencer) showed that in the Roman period the wall was only marginally affected by the river, species such as *Theodoxus fluviatilis* and *Bithynia* sp. were present as well as terrestrial varieties including *Discus rotundatus* and *Cepea nemoralis*. However, in front of the medieval revetment and to the south of the Roman wall, a rich assemblage of freshwater mollusca such as *Bithynia* sp., *Lymnaea peregra* and *L. truncatulata*, *Planorbis* and *Valvata piscinalis*, clearly river deposited, provide good evidence for the rise in river level since the Roman period.

The study of microflora and microfauna from the Thames and its tributaries will be discussed in section 4.7.1.

Information on the diet of Londoners in the Roman period is coming from the study of animal bones found, the bulk of which are the discarded waste from slaughteryards and households. The following general observations may be drawn from the material studied so far (see Gazetteer for list of sites): beef formed the largest part of the meat eaten, followed by pork; very little mutton appears to have been consumed before the late Saxon period. Davies (1971) stressed the important part played by bacon and lard in the Roman military diet and, on the evidence collected, it is clearly demonstrated that the inhabitants of London also had a predilection for pig-meat (Armitage 1982b, 96). Of the variety of birds served at table, domestic chickens, goose and duck were the most common (Clutton-Brock and Bramwell 1975, Gask 1977, Carey and Armitage 1979, Cowles 1981, West 1983a). Among the fish species eaten were ling (*Molva molva*), cod (*Gadus morhua*), dory (*Zeus faber*) and bass (*Dicentrarchus labrax*) (Jones 1977, Wheeler 1977 and 1981, Locker 1981). Evidence for a home-produced substitute for *garum* (a strong fish sauce frequently used in

Roman cooking) based on the fermentation of locally caught white bait (herring *Clupea harengus* and sprat *Sprattus sprattus*) was found at Peninsular House (C34) where a fish processing factory is thought ot have operated on the waterfront from the second to early fourth century (Bateman and Locker 1982). As for the exploitation of wild game animals such as red deer (*Cervus elaphus*), roe deer (*Capreolus capreolus*) and hare (*Lepus* sp.) the archaeological record reveals that in the Roman (and later) times this was only carried out on a small scale; their meat was never an important feature of the Londoner's diet but only supplemented it. The discovery in a Hadrianic fire debris deposit at Watling Court (C17) of a sacrum of a female fallow deer (*Dama dama*) is likely to arouse the interest of zoologists since this is the first securely dated specimen of this species from a Romano-British site. Zoologists have always believed that after the species became extinct in Britain during the last Glaciation (Würm, which lasted from about 80,000 to 10,000 BP) it was not re-introduced until the eleventh century (West 1983a).

Documentary sources reveal that, contrary to popular belief, London from the thirteenth century had a reasonably well organised refuse disposal system that included the regular collection of household and other (non-domestic) rubbish which was carted away for burial in municipal dumps (Sabine 1937). It would be interesting to determine whether a similar system was in existence in Roman London from the study of the spatial distribution of buried organic refuse and the analysis of the contents of the rubbish to ascertain whether domestic (kitchen) waste was mixed in with, for example, stable sweepings, butcher's debris or bone-working waste, or whether these non-domestic waste materials were disposed of (treated) in a special way. Although the majority of the dumps investigated so far suggest that domestic and non-household refuse was generally thrown into the same rubbish deposits, a pit of early second century date discovered at Sir John Cass Primary School (C48) contained only the waste from a butcher's shop. This was attested by the presence of pieces of skull and the extremity bones of the feet of cattle (i.e. the first parts removed by the butcher during preparation of a carcase for disjointing) (King 1973, Armitage 1979b). On the other hand, at St. Swithins House and the Bank of England, two sites in the Walbrook valley, Roman refuse deposits of first to second century date were found to contain very little in the way of slaughteryard and household rubbish and the material was mostly derived from industrial sources; comprising sawn red deer metatarsal bones and deer antlers, probably waste from the manufacture of knife-handles, together with sawn sections of ox metatarsal bones from the manufacture of lathe-turned cylinders or hinges (Armitage in press).

Excavations of Roman sites have from time to time produced, in addition to domestic and industrial rubbish, the occasional enigmatic faunal assemblage or single unusual specimen; as for example, during investigations carried out by Marsden inside a Roman turret at the Central Criminal Court site (C3) in 1966–9, where, in levels dated to the third century, the skeletons of at least nine adult dogs were found together with moulds used by a coin forger (Armitage 1979c). The presence of so many dogs in one place is not easily explained, and remains a mystery. Another example comes from the Tower of London, where Parnell found an ox tibia with an iron ballista-bolt shot through it; possibly evidence of target practice by troops manning the artillery pieces mounted in the bastions that formed part of the defences in this part of the Roman city (Armitage 1982a).

With two notable exceptions discussed below (Fenchurch Street and Crosswall), the level of recovery of skeletal remains of small wild animals such as mice, shrews and frogs, from Roman (and later) sites in the City has been extremely poor; in marked contrast to the very large quantities of bones of domestic livestock collected from them. The paucity of small animal bones may be attributed in part to the absence of any systematic programme for the on-site bulk sieving of deposits, which although widely recognised as being essential for the successful recovery of such material, is not usually practicable given the very limited time and resources available to investigate urban rescue sites. Only very rarely have small bones been acquired through careful hand sorting during excavation, as for example at the General Post Office site (C11) where six bones of frog and the almost complete skeleton of a grass snake (*Natrix natrix*) (identified by Stimson, BM (NH)) were recovered from a late Roman timber-lined well (West 1983a). On two other occasions only have small animal bones been recovered by hand during excavation of Roman sites in the City of London. At Sir John Cass Primary School (C48) an ulna of a field or bank vole (*Microtus agrestis/Clethrionomys glareolus*) was found in a first century occupation level (Armitage 1979b) and, near St. Bartholomew's Hospital (C5) the sacrum and cervical vertebra of a field mouse *Apodemus sylvaticus* (identified by Armitage) were found mixed in with cremated human remains in a Roman cinerary urn (see Bentley and Pritchard 1982).

The deficiency in records of small animal bones from London's archaeological sites cannot entirely be the result of inadequate recovery techniques but probably also genuinely reflects the very low incidence of such remains in the majority of deposits that have been excavated so far. This was demonstrated by the negative results obtained when an on-site bulk sieving experiment was conducted by Armitage on the General Post Office site (C11) during excavation of occupation levels inside Roman buildings of early second century date. No small animal bones were found during this exercise and the only specimen of this category eventually recovered from the buildings, the jawbone of a house mouse (*Mus musculus domesticus*) (identified by Armitage) was extracted from the residue of a soil sample taken from around a hearth area as part of the general sampling strategy for the collection of seeds and charcoal (see Davis 1983a).

In addition to the sites referred to above which have produced one or two small animal bones only, there are two more sites which proved more rewarding, and which deserve special mention for their important contribution to our knowledge of the small mammal fauna of the City in Roman times. The first site, 5–12 Fenchurch Street (FS), has provided the earliest evidence so far of black rat (*Rattus rattus*) in Britain. The skeletal remains of three rats (an adult, sub-adult and juvenile) were found with the bones of several house mice in a third century well. The recovery of all these specimens was entirely due to bulk sampling and wet sieving (1mm mesh) of the well fills. The location of the Fenchurch Street site immediately south of the forum and basilica may explain why rats and mice would have been attracted to this part of the City. As the focal centres for the administration and commercial life of the Roman city, these two major public buildings were surrounded by the highest concentration of settlement, including granaries and warehouses containing stored food products; all of which would have formed an ideal environment for infestation by rodents (Armitage *et al.* 1984). The second site, Crosswall (C49) also yielded evidence of black rats, this time in a fourth century defensive ditch outside the City wall. Here the remains of at least two rats were found together with bones of both field and house mouse. In addition to these three commensals, the ditch also contained the limb bones and teeth of mammalian species more commonly associated with rural habitats; including Water vole (*Arvicola terrestris*), field vole and common shrew (*Sorex araneus*). The rural component of the assemblage was further emphasised by the presence of frog and grass snake (identified by Clarke and McCarthy, both of the BM (NH)). Although the final interpretation of the environment of the Roman ditch at Crosswall must await the results of analyses currently being carried out on the other biological remains found (e.g. plants and molluscs) the fauna does suggest that the ditch contained running water, at least for a time, and that dense ground cover covered the banks or grew nearby (Armitage 1983a). Perhaps even more importantly, the presence of a mixed urban and rural faunal assemblage clearly demonstrates the existence of an abrupt transition just beyond the eastern defensive wall between the city and the open countryside (fields and woods) outside. All of this faunal material from Crosswall came from sieved residues of soil samples that had been taken from the ditch fills as part of the general sampling strategy for the collection of seeds and other organic remains (see Davis 1983b).

In general, there has been only a limited amount of work on biological material (botanical and zoological) from late Roman London compared with the earlier period. This is partly because of the genuine deficiency of such material in the archaeological record, due to the reduced urban community (as discussed below, in section 4.4).

4.4   Early Medieval, AD 500–800

There is very little evidence to indicate the nature of the Dark Age and early Saxon settlement in the City of London. Archaeological work hints at a reduced community starting as early as the third quarter of the second century (Sheldon 1975, Merrifield 1983, 147) and there is only scanty evidence of continuity of occupation within the Roman city walls for the fifth and sixth centuries. Signs of occupation by 'squatters', for example, were found in the ruins of the former Roman palace in Bush Lane and in the Roman bathhouse at Billingsgate (Marsden 1980). Recent excavations carried out at St. Peter's Hill (C9), Miles Lane (C30), Pudding Lane (C32) and Peninsular House (C34) have also revealed human activity in the City during the fifth and sixth centuries. However, it is presumed that much of the City was abandoned and lay derelict until the seventh century, when documentary evidence indicates that by about AD 601–4 the City was already of some importance, as it was chosen as a centre by the Christian mission sent to Britain by Augustine. Seventh century port and wharf facilities have not yet been located but may possibly lie in the area south of St. Paul's Cathedral. The dearth of information for this period was first highlighted in *Rescue's* survey of London (Biddle *et al.* 1973) and the study of early medieval London still remains an important priority.

On many excavations this period is represented by a thick accumulation of a dark coloured anthropogenic deposit often referred to as 'dark earth'. On some sites this type of accumulation has replaced earlier buildings by the end of the second century which, as Dyson and Schofield (1981) point out, only emphasises the uncertain nature of late Roman occupation in the City and Greater London. Soil analyses have been carried out on dark earth in London and other cities such as Gloucester, Norwich, York and Carlisle (Macphail 1981 and this volume). The sites he has considered in the City so far include the G.P.O. sites (C11 and C12) and St. Bartholomew's Hospital (C6) (Macphail 1980b, c, d and 1981). The result of this work (which has included study of soil colour (wet and dry), pH, loss on ignition, and grain size and pollen analyses as well as tests for alkali soluble humus estimation of the extractable phosphorus content and the manufacture of thin sections for micromorphological analysis), is to conclude that dark earth can be divided into two main types: (1) waterlogged and often dumped deposits, and (2) dry, agricultural deposits which often include dumped material, but may possibly have been used for agriculture within urban areas (Macphail 1981; 1982, Roskams and Schofield 1978 and Roskams 1981). This division is based principally on micromorphological studies as pollen preservation, especially in dry 'dark earth' deposits such as those found in London, is poor (Scaife in Macphail 1981, Scaife 1980). The best potential source of environmental information from a London 'dark earth' is felt to be a waterlogged deposit where organic remains including pollen will be better preserved and possibly helpful in identifying evidence of agriculture within the City area.

At Rangoon Street (C47) in the east of the City a large part of the site was covered with dark earth of a roughly similar type to that seen in other parts of the City. This material, when excavated, revealed two crouched burials which were sealed within the 'dark earth'. Preliminary examination of these skeletons suggests one is probably female aged

35–45, and the other is possibly a male aged 17–25 (identified by West). Radiocarbon dating is in progress to determine the date of the skeletons which do not seem to be in a definable cut within the dark earth (see p 287).

In consequence of the lack of surviving archaeological evidence for late Roman to Middle Saxon London, virtually no other environmental work has been done. At Pudding Lane (C32) work on seeds and molluscs is currently in progress to establish the nature of a deposit which was sealed by the latest Roman deposits in that part of the site, but was itself sealed by layers dated to the ninth century. This deposit is probably waterlain in origin and may indicate a change in urban land use in the area for some centuries (Milne and Bateman pers. comm.).

4.5   Medieval, AD 800–1500

The majority of the environmental work in London for this period concerns the analysis of plant macrofossils from deposits dated to the earlier phases. Most of the contexts sampled were pit fills some of which are dated by the pottery to the tenth to early twelfth centuries, the mid to late twelfth century and a few are stratigraphically within 'dark earth' but dated to AD 750–1000. The site sampled was Milk Street (C16) and during the excavation over 100 pits were recorded carefully with a view to studying their form and function. For all the pits' characteristics such as lining (clay, wattle plank, unlined), shape, depth, alignment and fill were examined by de Hoog (DUA). The range and quantity of inclusions was also noted and it was hoped that analysis of the results would produce groups that could be related to the functions or uses of pits, the aim being that a decision about the level of future site recording of these features which occur so commonly on urban excavations could be made. (A detailed statistical analysis using plant remains and other aspects of the pits is under way to try to examine those questions). As part of the study 58 contexts from 24 of the pits were sampled for environmental analysis and so far it has only been possible to study the plant macrofossils, although it is hoped that a limited amount of pollen and arthropod analysis will be undertaken. All the pits at Milk Street contained some residual pottery and it is hoped that the present statistical analysis being carried out by Orton will emphasise particular problems in this respect, as although it is usually thought that bone, pottery and charcoal and some carbonised plant remains could be considered residual it is not clear whether some of the less durable plant remains might also fall into this category. As a whole, the Milk Street assemblage provides much useful information on the use and availability of a wide range of plants to Londoners at this time and the assemblage can be briefly described on the basis of the habitat preferences and possible uses of the plants (Straker and Davis 1982):

1.   Weeds of cultivated land include seeds of the poisonous corn cockle (*Agrostemma githago*), a former pest of cereal fields and *Camelina cf. sativa* (gold of pleasure) often found in association with flax, also found at Milk Street.

2.   The plants of waste places and disturbed ground comprise a large group including many common species often recorded on urban excavations.

3.   Only a few plants representative of woods, hedgerows and scrub are included and some of these are edible fruits such as some of the members of the Roseaceae family.

4.   The grassland plants include some sedges which may have been used as flooring material and perhaps were brought in from damp meadows and some of the plants from wetter habitats, such as rushes, may also have been brought in for this purpose.

5.   The edible wild plants comprise a diverse group including blackberries, sloes, hazelnuts, elderberries and many others, including many herbaceous plants such as members of the Chenopodiaceae (goosefoot, fat hen) and nettles.

6.   The pitfalls in assuming that specific plants were used medicinally are well known and reference to a herbal will show that in the past almost every plant was regarded as having magical or medicinal properties of some sort.

Papaver somniferum (opium poppy) which contains powerful alkaloids was found at Milk Street in large quantities in some pits and *Hyoscyamus niger* (henbane), known as a hypnotic and brain sedative (Grigson 1975), was found in very large amounts in one pit and smaller quantities in others. Many dye plants and those with other properties of industrial use were identified but most also occur commonly as weeds. Flax and hemp are well known fibre producing plants and nettles too were a useful source of fibres in the past (Grigson 1975). It is likely that dyes were brought to the town in a partly processed state only detectable by chemical analysis and that the seeds of these plants only indicate their presence as weeds (however cf evidence from Trig Lane, below). The cultivated plants available to medieval Londoners include oats, wheat, barley, rye, figs, mulberries and grapes; the figs were probably imported as they do not grow well in this country (Willcox 1977a) and some grapes may have been imported though they were grown in Britain as Domesday charts the presence of 38 vineyards in southern Britain (Harvey 1981) and one of these was in Westminster. Other vegetables (apart from the many edible wild plants) are represented by seeds of (wild) carrots and (wild) celery (*Apium graveolens*) as well as members of the *Brassiceae* (cabbages etc); however these plants are often utilised before they set seed and they may be under represented in the archaeological record. Legumes are poorly represented and only the presence of the bean weevil (*Bruchus* sp.) identified by Kenward suggests that beans or peas were a component of the diet. Herbs are present in the assemblage, notably dill (*Anethum graveolens*) and alexanders (*Smyrnium olusatrum*), the latter identified by Mark Robinson. This was a potherb favoured by the Romans, but (it is thought) not previously recorded in a medieval context (Straker and Davis 1982). The background flora that a study of this sort indicates gives some details of the urban environment and the composition of this can provide a useful comparison with that from other stages in the development of the City.

Little work has been done on plant macrofossils from cultural deposits later in the medieval period with the exception of the waterfront site of Trig Lane (C13) where Willcox (unpublished) looked at the composition of the closely dated backfill deposits associated with the structures, and foreshore deposits which contained freshwater mollusca as well as food and other plants from fifteenth century deposits, many of which are also recorded from the earlier Milk Street assemblage. Dyer's rocket (*Reseda luteola*) is singled out as of particular importance as it occurred in vast quantities in some samples; this plant yields the yellow dye weld and historical sources show that this part of the site belonged to dyers (Willcox unpublished). Organic layers from deposits dated to the late fourteenth/early fifteenth century at Baynard's Castle (C8), later the palace of Henry VII, built on the north bank of the Thames near Blackfriars, were thought to consist of stable sweepings (Davis 1982); many seeds including rushes, sedges, grasses and buttercups were contained as well as a quantity of horsehair (Armitage 1981a) and a curry comb.

The fill contained in drainage ditches excavated at Copthall Avenue (C27) throws light on a different aspect of medieval London. This site in the upper Walbrook valley (see also sections 4.3 and 4.7.1) produced a complex series of ditches which represent repeated attempts to drain the area, which was marshy. The ditches contain seeds including *Ranunculus sceleratus* (celery leaved crowfoot), *Rorippa islandica* (marsh yellow cress), *Rorippa nasturtium-aquaticum* (watercress), *Alisma plantago-aquatica* (water plantain), *Oenanthe* sp. (water dropwort), *Lemna* sp (duckweed), *Carex* sp. etc. (sedges) and *Juncus* sp. (rushes) in the assemblages; these are aquatic and bankside species (Askew and Moriarty 1982). The presence of freshwater ostracods and their juveniles in one ditch in addition to the plant macro-fossils, indicates fairly open water, still or stagnant with a muddy bottom (Whittaker 1982 unpublished) and the presence of *Chara* Oospheres, (algae) in another ditch also evidences clear, though still, water. The 'peaty' organic layers which represent the marsh itself include more of the waste and disturbed ground species, with occasional economic plants represented as well as many species representative of wet ground such as rushes and sedges. The preliminary picture suggested by the plant remains seems to be one of a naturally marshy area with domestic rubbish also thrown into it (many artefacts, notably leatherwork, are also present). There is still much work to do on this site and one aspect, the analysis of the Arthropod remains, has not yet been investigated at all.

Wood has been identified from several medieval sites. Baynard's Castle, mentioned above, was built on numerous piles of elm (*Ulmus* sp.), a wood which, along with oak and others, is durable in wet conditions. In the medieval city ditch at Ludgate Hill two wooden hurdles were preserved and studied in some detail. These objects are of interest as they occur in other parts of the City as well and from their analysis suggestions about woodland management may be made; information on choice of wood used and method of construction can also be obtained. Although such objects were probably brought to the City ready made, there were probably suitable woodlands near the City and coppicing was, according to Rackham (1978) well established in southern Britain by the time of the Domesday survey of AD 1086. The techniques of construction of the two hurdles from Ludgate varied and this was also reflected in the choice of wood. The rods, for example, in one hurdle were of hazel with smaller quantities of oak and birch, whereas in the next they were almost entirely of oak. The age range of the rods is wide for both hurdles — they may have been selected by the process of drawing in which rods are chosen on the basis of the size required for the particular purpose in hand (Straker 1982d). Hurdles of approximately the same date preserved at Billingsgate should make an interesting comparison.

Environmental work on molluscs and arthropods is noticeably lacking for the medieval period and while work on plant macrofossils has received some attention, further work on deposits in parts of the City not previously studied would be useful for the tenth to twelfth centuries, but the thirteenth to fifteenth centuries have been studied in less detail in all parts of the City than the earlier period.

Some attempt has been made to use the documentary sources which are available for London and these are very scarce for the ninth to twelfth centuries, but progressively much better thereafter. The information they contain is of use when the interpretation of an assemblage is being made, particularly, for example, where industries such as dyeing or other processes which leave uncertain traces in the archaeological record are being considered. The historical sources also document, to some extent, movement by ship of goods in and out of the City and occasionally importation and exportation of, for example, foodstuffs.

All deposits pertaining to an understanding of the changes in the natural environment of the City, especially those whose analysis may help to answer specific archaeological questions, will continue to be a high priority. Work on micro-floral and microfaunal assemblages is also fairly limited for the later medieval period.

Work on Saxon Thames foreshore deposits at Swan Lane and fourteenth century Fleet deposits at Tudor Street are not mentioned in this section but are described in section 4.7.1.

Apart from small groups of animal bone from St. Mildreds Church (C15) (Clutton-Brock 1975, Bramwell 1975b), New Fresh Wharf (C33) (Armitage 1979d) and Billingsgate Buildings (C36) (Armitage 1980e) and the one horse skeleton described below, very little has been done on late Saxon and Saxo-Norman faunal remains. It is hoped that the forthcoming study of the animal bones collected from pits at Milk Street (C16), dated AD 750–early twelfth century, will fill in the gap in our knowledge of the livestock types, diet of Londoners etc, of this period. One interesting find of a late tenth century horse skeleton at Ironmonger Lane (C22), one of only four complete articulated horse skeletons recorded so far for late Saxon Britain, has provided valuable information on the size and conformation of Saxon horses. The animal, a male aged between 7 and 8 years, with an estimated withers height of 139cm, was discovered lying on its side at the bottom of a cesspit cut into the underlying natural gravel (Armitage 1981b). Among the more interesting bird bones found on late Saxon and Saxo-Norman sites have been the following wild species: sparrow hawk (*Accipiter nisus*), pigeon (*Columba* sp.) and raven (*Corvus corax*) from St. Mildred's Church, Bread Street (C15) (Bramwell 1975b, 208); woodcock (*Scolopax rustica*) and curlew (*Nemenius arquata*) from New Fresh Wharf (C33), (Carey and Armitage 1979); and white-tailed sea eagle (*Haliaetus albicilla*) from Billingsgate Buildings (C36) (Cowles 1980, 163).

For the later medieval period (late thirteenth to fifteenth century) the faunal evidence is slightly better, and small to medium sized assemblages (100+ to 3,000 bones) from a number of sites have been examined; for example from Tudor Street (C1), Baynard's Castle (C7), Angel Court (C29), New Fresh Wharf (C33) and Custom House (C40) (see Gazetteer for details of levels III and IV reports on these sites). In addition to these assemblages, West has examined the large quantities of faunal material (20,000 + bones) from the medieval waterfront dumps at Trig Lane (C13).

Of the wild mammalian species that have been able to adapt and thrive in the urban environment in the City of London, the most successful has undoubtedly been the black rat; this is demonstrated by the frequency of the discovery of their skeletal remains at medieval sites in London. Black rat is infamous for spreading bubonic plague in London during the Black Death of 1348–51, and later outbreaks of plague (including the Great Plague of 1665). In view of its importance in human history, the osteological and documentary history of the black rat in London is the subject of a special study being carried out by Armitage, some of the preliminary results of which are discussed below (see also pp 275).

The discovery of a single immature tibia of rat in a late tenth century context at New Fresh Wharf (C33) (Armitage 1979d) may not at first seem of any significance, but when considered with the recent finds of rat bones in the eighth to tenth century levels in Lincoln and York (O'Connor 1982, 40; 1983 pers. comm.) the London specimen provides important evidence for a second wave of invasion by black rats into Britain — following their initial arrival in this country during the Roman period (see p 275). This second invasion was probably one of the unforeseen consequences of the expansion of international trade during the Anglo-Saxon and Anglo-Scandinavian periods, when merchant ships unwittingly carried this unwelcome visitor across the Channel from continental Europe. The presence of this animal in other European ports as early as the eighth to eleventh century is well attested; rat bones have been found at Stettin, Poland (Brodniewicz 1969), Haitabu on the Baltic (Rechstein 1974) and Lund, Sweden (Bergquist 1957).

Evidence that the storage warehouses along the City of London waterfront district were, in the later medieval period, infested by colonies of black rats is provided by the large numbers of their bones found in the stone-lined dock basin that once lay to the west of Baynard's Castle (C7) (Armitage 1977a, 125–130); these animals had presumably been killed and thrown into the dock along with other domestic refuse. Preservation of organic material in the dock basin was very good, due to anaerobic conditions created by waterlogging, and one skeleton of a rat excavated still retained some of its fur, in which there was found a flea identified by Hutson (BM (NH)) as human flea *Pulex irritans* which is known to act as a vector for *Yersinia pestis* (the bacterium responsible for bubonic plague) although less effectively than the rat flea *Xenopsylla cheopis*. A short note describing the human flea from Baynard's Castle site (a rare archaeological find) has been published in *New Scientist* (see Marsh 1982). The fur of the rat also contained the following mites (identified by Macfarlane, Commonwealth Institute of Entomology): *Eulaelaps stabularis; Alliphis halleri* and *Trichoribates trimaculatus*. The first mite (*Eulaelaps stabularis*) infests stored products and is also a predator of nest debris (Girling pers. comm.) and, it may be supposed, had been accidentally picked up when the rat visited its nest. The other two mites were probably also accidentally picked up, from the soil and vegetation (*Alliphis halleri* is a soil mite which lives in a wide range of soil types, while *Trichoribates trimaculatus* is a plant mite found especially in grassland — Girling pers. comm.).

4.6   Post-Medieval: AD 1500 onwards

In marked contrast to the widescale investigations carried out into biological remains from London's Roman and medieval sites, there has been comparatively little work done on plant macrofossils, arthropods, molluscs and microflora for the post-medieval period. A number of studies on faunal remains of this period have, however, been carried out (see below) but even here there is a need for more detailed and systematic research.

The paucity of information on biological remains from the post-medieval period reflects the limited opportunities in the City for the excavation of early modern levels. Apart from the waterfront sites such as Baynard's Castle (C7) and the occasional deep well shaft or cesspit such as those found at the General Post Office site (middle area) (C12), almost all post-medieval features and occupation surfaces within the walls no longer survive intact. This is because of previous building activity, and in particular the digging of deep basements in the nineteenth century, which has truncated much of London's later archaeological record, either disturbing or completely removing all but the deepest and earliest (Roman and medieval) levels of occupation. Only outside the walls in the suburban areas does the evidence of the recent past survive sufficiently extensively to justify investigation, as for example at Aldgate (C50) and Cutler Street (C44).

Where plant and faunal remains have been recovered from post-medieval deposits, evidence has been found which demonstrates how the range of imported foods and raw materials diversified greatly during the early modern period as British merchants came into contact with those parts of the world not previously exploited.

Oryza sativa (rice) husks were identified in a cesspit at Billingsgate (C35) of late seventeenth century date (Askew and Moriarty 1982a); this has not been previously recorded from London, but was found prior to this date in other parts of Britain (it is native to the tropics but can be grown in the Mediterranean region). *Ribes nigrum* (blackcurrant) was found with other more common seeds in the same deposit; this also has not been found in London before. A preliminary examination of a drain fill from a seventeenth century context at Baynard's Castle (C8) contained, as well as the seeds of British plants, evidence of importation from both the Old and New World. *Piper* sp. (pepper) and *Cucurbita* sp. (pumpkin or marrow) were brought from these areas though attempts at cultivation of such plants in this country, using artificially improved growing conditions, were also attempted on a small scale. The enormous numbers of plant introductions that were made into Britain by and during this recent period are of biological interest; however this can make the palaeobotanist's task increasingly difficult as the range of plants that can be expected in the archaeo-logical record becomes so large.

Further evidence of trade between London and the New World is provided by animal bones. For example, the skull, mandibles and costal bones of three Green turtles *Chelonia mydas* from the Caribbean which were found in an eighteenth century well during redevelopment of Leadenhall Buildings in 1923. They represent the discarded waste from the manufacture of turtle soup, a traditional dish frequently served at ceremonial banquets organised by the Lord Mayor of London and others. Although the sale of turtle soup in early modern London is well documented, very little precise information is known about the organisation of the trade in live turtles to the City from the West Indies in the late eighteenth century. For instance, records of age, weight and sex of turtles sold in London at this time are very scanty and the Leadenhall group has therefore provided useful information on these aspects: the skull from Leadenhall is identified as a sub-adult with an estimated weight of 60lb (27kg) (Armitage and McCarthy 1980).

Another exotic faunal specimen recently found, a jawbone of a monkey, not only provides evidence of trade links with the New World but is also of intrinsic zoological interest. This jawbone, which was found in a mid to late seven-teenth century deposit at Brooks Wharf, has been identified as a South American Weeper capuchin *Cebus nigrivitatus* (Wagner 1848). This is the earliest record in Britain of a New World (Platyrrhine) monkey as well as the first record in Europe of a Weeper capuchin: the species was not officially recognised and described by the scientific community until AD 1767 when de Buffon published an illustrated account of this animal which he called *Le Sai*. X-radiographs taken of the London jawbone reveal that the internal bony structure is poorly developed and 'spongy', indicating that the animal had been kept in captivity for a number of years. Probably the monkey was brought to London live in a merchant ship returning from Guiana where the English were attempting to establish trading posts and plantations in the seventeenth century (Armitage 1983e).

It was apparently not only plants and mammals which were transported to Britain; other, unwelcome, visitors were also brought in unwittingly as a result of worldwide shipment of goods; and these included arthropods. The first evidence for the presence in Britain of *Pythris pubis* (crab louse), an unpleasant human ectoparasite, was discovered at Cutler Street (C44) in a late seventeenth—early eighteenth century cess fill in a pit (Girling 1982). This species of louse is known from Old World sources, but is not native to Britain (Girling pers. comm.). Other examples of newly introduced parasitic species no doubt await discovery and it is important therefore that the sampling strategy adopted for post-medieval (and earlier) sites should allow for the recovery of this sort of evidence (see Jones 1982).

Analyses of the few faunal assemblages recovered so far from post-medieval sites in London has started to make significant contributions to a number of priority areas identified by the Department of Urban Archaeology, Museum of London, in a recent review of archaeological research in the City. Among the topics of post-medieval archaeology considered the most interesting and worthwhile were the following three: (1) The palaces of Henry VII and VIII: (2) The Dissolution of the monasteries and other religious estates in AD 1532–40: and (3) Growth of the East End with special reference to domestic and industrial development in the area. In all of these areas of study, the evidence provided by animal bones can play an important part, as demonstrated below:—

1   The palaces of Henry VII and VIII

Excavations carried out at Baynard's Castle (C7) in 1972–3 produced a very large assemblage of animal bones (over 20,000 mammalian and 4,000 bird bones). This particular castle was once owned by Richard III's mother, and later by Henry VII who converted it into a palace. Work on the animal bone has provided evidence for a difference in the quality of the diet enjoyed by the nobles (and other occupants) of the castle and the common people outside. This was demonstrated by measurement of the cattle metacarpal bones found in the refuse pits located within the castle grounds (c AD 1520), which were much larger and more robust than those recovered from the municipal rubbish dump of contemporaneous date (c AD 1450) situated just outside the west wall of the building. Clearly, the cattle eaten by the castle inhabitants were much larger and probably carried more flesh than those consumed by the other, less wealthy, citizens of London (Armitage 1977a, 54). Analyses of the wild bird bones by Bramwell (1975d) and domestic fowl by Carey (1982) provided additional evidence for a difference in the quality of the diet of the two social classes. The variety of wild bird species was far greater in the castle refuse deposits and included such 'exotic' birds as peafowl (*Pavo cristatus*), crane (*Grus grus*) and great bustard (*Otis tarda*); species frequently served at banquets. The identification by Bramwell of Great Bustard, represented by a femur from a male bird, is the only well-dated record for a sub-fossil bone of this species found so far in Britain: the great bustard became extinct in Britain about AD 1838. Carey (1982) found little difference in the proportions of juvenile and adult chickens eaten by the two social groups, with both the castle inhabitants and the common people consuming mostly adult birds; the former group, however, apparently did prefer goslings to adult geese. Whether the fish bone will also show evidence of a difference in the diet of the two social classes remains to be determined as their investigation continues (Wheeler, BM (NH) in progress). An interim report on the fish bone reveals, however, that cod (*Gadus morhua*), conger eel (*Conger conger*), ling (*Molva molva*) and turbot (*Scophalalmus maximus*) were the most abundant species eaten by the castle inhabitants, with sturgeon (*Acipenser sturio*), roach (*Rutilus rutilus*) and salmon (*Salmo salar*) consumed in smaller numbers.

2   Dissolution of the religious estates

Evidence of past land use associated with the period in London of the dissolution of the religious houses has come from a deep chalk-lined well at the General Post Office site (middle area) (C12), in a part of the City which was once the garden of the Greyfriars. According to the dates of the pottery from this well, it had apparently fallen out of use and been infilled about AD 1500, while the dumping of refuse had at first been gradual leaving the well open but unused for some time before the shaft was completely filled in. Whilst still open, the well had acted as a giant pitfall trap into which unwary small creatures from the surrounding garden area had fallen and were unable to climb out. Over 3,000 bones of these creatures, mostly small mammals but with some frogs, were recovered from the well by on-site bulk sieving (1.5mm mesh), and these are now the subject of a special study (Armitage in progress). Research into this material has revealed the presence in the garden of an exceptionally diverse small mammal fauna that included weasel (*Mustela nivalis*), black rat (*Rattus rattus*), house mouse (*Mus musculus domesticus*), field mouse (*Apodemus sylvaticus*), yellow necked field mouse (*A. flavicollis*), water shrew (*Neomys fodiens*), common shrew (*Sorex araneus*), pygmy shrew (*Sorex minutus*), water vole (*Arvicola terrestris*), field vole (*Microtis agrestis*), bank vole (*Clethrionomys glareolus*) and hedgehog (*Erinaceus europaeus*). Comparisons are currently being made between the fauna from the General Post Office site and data on small mammals from modern urban, suburban and rural habitats obtained by live trapping experiments. Preliminary findings suggest that the G.P.O. assemblage includes species associated with thick ground cover (dense scrub), suggesting that the friars were neglecting the cultivation of their garden in the period just prior to the dissolution of their estate in c AD 1538. The presence of species associated with aquatic habitats (water shrew and water vole) may indicate that the friars were also failing to maintain the drainage of the area; allowing the gutter running through the garden (known from documentary sources) to become blocked and excess water to spill over into the garden to form a pond.

In addition to the small mammal and frog bones, the well also yielded large quantities of bones of domestic livestock and a wide variety of wild birds. It is believed that these represent food debris from the Greyfriars kitchens and so will provide important evidence of the friars' diet (West in progress).

3   Growth of the East End with special reference to domestic and industrial development in the area

Post-medieval deposits of domestic refuse excavated in the East End of the City sometimes provide important clues as to the social status of the household (or households) from which the material derived. Although such information generally comes from the study of the pottery and other artefactual evidence recovered, recent work has demonstrated how the associated faunal remains can sometimes provide important supporting evidence. Two examples illustrate this sort of contribution:

(i)   *Crosswall (C49)* Among the contents of a post-medieval brick-lined cess pit (infilled c AD 1770) at Crosswall (C49) was found a skeleton of a very large domestic rabbit which was subsequently identified as an Angora (Armitage 1981d and e). Ownership of such an uncommon breed suggests that the household from which the animal derived must have been reasonably well-off; an observation that is fully in accordance with the status of the other artefactual evidence from the same pit (the contents of which are believed to represent the wholesale clearance of possibly a single household) which included fine quality imported Chinese porcelain (Vince 1981, Pearce 1981, 165–168). Further evidence of the prosperity of the Crosswall inhabitants was provided by the high proportion of immature cattle, sheep, pig and chicken bones; a poorer family would presumably have eaten the cheaper meat from older animals.

(ii)   *Aldgate (C50)* The evidence for the consumption of good quality meat at Crosswall in the late eighteenth century may be compared with the site at Aldgate (C50) located in a poorer quarter of the East End, where the faunal material recovered from cesspits and a cellar associated with a row of late seventeenth/early eighteenth century tenements was found on analysis to comprise very high proportions of bones from the head and feet of sheep, including an unusually large number of sheep jawbones (Armitage 1983h, in press). All these bones have very little flesh on them and so represent cuts of meat of the lowest quality and therefore the ones traditionally purchased only by the poorer households (see Jones 1976, 90). Equally significant were the remains of Leicester and Lincolnshire longwool sheep found. These animals were supplied to London in large numbers throughout the late seventeenth and early eighteenth century and were the principal source of mutton for the urban working classes, because although tough and coarse grained, joints from them were cheap and comparatively large (Perkins 1977, 7 and 45, Armitage 1983c). The assessment, based on the faunal remains, of low status households at Aldgate is consistent with the evidence of the other finds from the tenements. As discussed by Grew (in Thompson *et al.* in press) nowhere is there any evidence to indicate a lifestyle of luxury or refinement; the knives, for example, have plain wood handles, and fine glassware is almost totally lacking; more prosperous Londoners of this time would have worn clogs and not the pattens found at Aldgate. The only evidence apparently contradicting this general picture of low status households comes from the bird bones found, which include swan (*Cygnus olor*) and peacock (*Pavo cristatus*), both very costly and usually only served at feasts of the wealthier classes (West 1983c).

Studies of faunal remains excavated from post-medieval sites in the East End have also provided information on industrial activity in the area, for example at Cutler Street (C44). Excavations carried out on this site between 1978 and 1980 revealed the floors of seventeenth century workshops (including a smithy) and other post-medieval debris of a wide variety of industries (bell founding, glass and clay tobacco pipe making, bone-working and ivory turning) sealed beneath East India Company warehouses (built at the end of the eighteenth century) whose shallow cellars ensured the survival of this evidence. In the northern part of the site, buried beneath the warehouses, was a series of at least thirteen pits whose function remains unknown. All of these pits, which are dated to the late seventeenth/early eighteenth century, had their sides lined with cattle horn cores in distinct courses, with their tips all aligned one way (pointing outwards) and bonded with clay. Five of the pits had traces of wooden planks (possibly pine) and oak joists projecting from the lining of horn cores, suggesting the possibility that either the structures were lined with wood, in the form of an enclosed wooden tank, or that they had originally been fitted with lids (Armitage and O'Connor Thompson, in progress). All the pits were filled with the same dark silty material that on analysis was found to contain very little artefactual or biological material. Samples of the seeds examined by Straker and Davis (1982) were identified as common components of urban plant macrofossil assemblages. In addition to the seeds, the fills contained arthropods including wood-boring weevils and various beetles which live on dung and carrion, with a small number of phytophagus beetles hinting at the presence of vegetation used for bedding or stalling animals (Girling 1982). Chemical analysis carried out by Evans (North East London Polytechnic) revealed that the pit fills were certainly not cess and that some of them contained traces of residue from bronze casting. Human, cattle and rabbit hair fibres, identified by Armitage, were also extracted from the fills. Despite the detailed investigation into the nature of the material filling these pits, their function remains unknown but presumably they were used for some industrial purpose, for example as casting (founding pits) or as soak-aways. Further examples of horn core lined pits in the eastern suburbs of London have been found at Crosswall (C49), Mansell Street (C51) and Gardeners Corner (Greater London site 124). The cattle horn cores used in the construction of all these pits probably came from the horners' workshops situated along Petticoat Lane (now Middlesex Street) and the butchers' shops in Aldgate High Street. The only known parallel for the London pits was discovered at Greyfriars in Oxford, where a cesspit dated between *c*1750 and 1800 had been lined with horn cores obtained from a nearby tanyard (Armitage 1983g, in press).

In addition to their use as a substitute for bricks in the construction of industrial pits, cattle horn cores were also employed in farming in the late seventeenth century. Evidence for this comes from excavations carried out by the Enfield Archaeological Society in the back gardens of 28 to 32 Upsdell Avenue, Greater London site 72 (see p 269) in 1978 and 1980, which uncovered traces of two parallel agricultural land drains of late seventeenth century date, lined with cattle horn cores (Armitage, Coxshall and Ivens 1980). Similar land drains were found by workmen in the grounds of Forest House Estate, near Leyton, in 1896 (McKenny Hughes 1896). As the large quantities of horn cores used in the drainage systems at Upsdell Avenue and Forest House Estate could not have been supplied by the local butchers it may be suggested that arable farmers from Middlesex and Essex who visited London to sell their produce sometimes returned home with carts loaded with horn cores obtained from City slaughteryards and horners' workshops, and that these were used by them to line their land drains in place of the more traditional materials such as brushwood and straw 'ropes' used at this time (the production of relatively cheap mass-produced unglazed tile-pipes was not possible until about 1840). Research into the archaeological and documentary evidence for the use in post-medieval Britain of animal bone as building material continues (Armitage in progress).

4.7   Special projects

4.7.1   *The natural environment – studies on the Thames and its tributaries*

The Thames London's function as a port was already established by the second half of the first century AD and clearly the nature of the river as well as the topographical advantages of the situation selected on the north bank (see section 4.1) must have influenced the decision to establish the Roman settlement there.

The course, level and position of the tidal limit of the Thames are subject to change and the reasons for this and a statement of the current knowledge of the nature of the Thames in the first century AD in the area of the City are the subject of a paper (Milne *et al*. forthcoming), intended to update the useful starting point made by Willcox (1975). Papers by West (1972), Dunham (1972), D'Olier (1972) and Devoy (1977, 79 and 80) and others are noted. The recent work of Devoy (ibid) in the lower Thames estuary has helped to clarify some of the changes in the level and tidal nature of the river. Devoy made a stratigraphic study of post-glacial biogenic and inorganic deposits (between Crossness and the Isle of Grain) and the heights of relative sea-level movement were calculated from this work. By plotting these values against time the rate of relative sea-level change and subsidence trends for the Thames and southern England were shown. According to Devoy (1977, 79, 80) five marine transgressions and five phases of regression can be recognised in the pattern of sea-level rise over the last 10,000 years.

Although the changes in sea-level and the problem of subsidence in the Thames estuary have been the subject of much research, changes in the course of the river are less well known. In a recent study of the development of the river Thames in central London during the post-glacial period, Nunn (1983) has been able to propose five chronological stages in the predominantly northwards movement of the river. According to Nunn (1983) the five chronological stages he proposes may possibly be compatible with the Tilbury I–V regressions identified by Devoy. Nunn suggests that the regressions caused a halt in the lateral migration of the Thames in central London and initiated downcutting. If this is to be accepted, there are clear implications for the selection of archaeological sites throughout Greater London as it is possible that prehistoric 'waterfront' sites would lie at some distance from the present course of the river, along the channels proposed by Nunn, for the stages in the migration of the river. It is also possible that such areas may be promising from the point of view of environmental work as conditions for preservation of organic material may be favourable.

Recent work in London: river level and tidal influence Excavations along the waterfront in the City of London have attempted to determine the level of the Thames in the Roman period and later by establishing the height of structures and associated working surfaces (Milne and Milne 1979, 1982, and Willcox 1975 and 1981). In the past 2,000 years the mean high water level has risen by about 3m relative to the land; in the first century AD the mean high water level reached to between 1 and 1.5m above O.D. (Milne *et al*. forthcoming) and from excavation of a series of medieval waterfront structures at Trig Lane (C13), it could be shown that the level had risen further, that for the highest astronomical tide in the fourteenth century being estimated at *c* + 2m below the present day level (Milne and Milne 1982). It was mentioned above that a regression has been noted for the lower Thames estuary downstream of the City in about AD 200 and it is possible that this may be detectable in the City area although at present no estimation has yet been given from excavated waterfront structures of this period. Willcox (1980) stated that at this period the river level could have been so low that the river was not tidal; this hypothesis has yet to be tested as it is not known whether the effects of Tilbury V would have been felt so far upstream. Sheldon (1978) writing about the evidence for former river level from excavations on the south bank at Southwark stated that it was not possible to locate the Roman river bank on the south shore of the Thames at Southwark owing to erosion and the fact that it could have lain well out into the present river. The evidence for Roman river level in Southwark is forthcoming from the surface of silts as high as + 1.20m above O.D. which lay on the margins of sandy islands at the time of the Roman conquest (Sheldon 1978, Yule in Milne *et al*. forthcoming). The question of whether or not the Thames was tidal in the first century AD when the Roman port was established has been the subject of controversy for some time; this is an important point as there are obvious disadvantages to a port which does not benefit from tidal rise and fall such as increased silting up, the need to travel upstream without an incoming tide for assistance etc. Wheeler (1928) considered that it was likely that the Roman town was sited at or near the tidal head of the river, whereas Akeroyd (1972) stressed that in her opinion the river was <u>not</u> tidal and that freshwater conditions existed as far downstream as Dagenham and Crossness; this view has also been expressed by more recent writers. At the present day the Thames is tidal as far as Teddington, some 25 miles upstream of the City.

In order to examine this question, Thames foreshore deposits associated with waterfront structures of different periods were sampled for diatom analysis to assess the salinity level of the river at different times and thus build up a picture of changes in the tidal nature of the river over the last 2,000 years. Several first century foreshores were sampled at Pudding Lane (C32) and a Saxon deposit from Swan Lane (C26). The analysis was carried out by Battarbee (Battarbee 1981 unpublished, 1983 and in Milne *et al*. forthcoming). The dominant taxon at all levels in the Pudding

Lane assemblage was *Cyclotella striata*; this brackish species is a common planktonic diatom in European river estuaries including the contemporary Thames. Other brackish taxa include *Nitzschia sigma*, *Synedra tabulata* var. *affinis* and *Bacillaria paradoxa*. There is a small number of marine taxa such as *Cymatosira belgica*, *Raphoneis surirella*, *R. amphiceros* and *Cocconeis scutellum* which were probably carried up river on high or flood tides. The majority of the taxa are freshwater forms; some of the most common such as *Fragilaria pinnata*, *Surirella ovata*, *Cocconeis placentula* are also encountered in weakly brackish conditions.

Battarbee (1983 and in Milne *et al.* forthcoming) concludes that the river adjacent to the first century site was estuarine during the period the deposits were accumulating, contrary to earlier opinion. *Cyclotella striata* was also abundant in the Saxon deposit from Swan Lane (Battarbee 1981 unpublished) though rather more of the assemblage (11%) was euhalobous at this site than the 2% of marine forms at Pudding Lane. Battarbee suggests that this may indicate that the tidal head of the river was closer to the City in the Roman than medieval period. The recent Billingsgate excavation will provide a further opportunity to examine the diatoms from Thames foreshore deposits of a later date than those from Pudding Lane. The sequence from Billingsgate (C35) (late Roman to Medieval) will allow expansion of the emerging picture of the movement of the tidal head of the river although comparative studies of the modern river and consideration of effects of bridges etc will have to be taken into account.

Having established that the first century river was tidal and had a tidal amplitude of at least 1.5m (Milne *et al.* forthcoming) the approximate width of the river during high and low tides can be suggested (Milne ibid). It is considered that the river could have been up to 1,000m wide to the south of the Roman city at high tide, decreasing to about 275m wide at its narrowest point at low tide (the present day channel is about 200m wide). The effect of this is that much of the south bank in the area of the City must have been inter-tidal marsh as the land is flat and the topography very different from that on the north bank.

It is hoped that dated deposits from other parts of the Thames and its tributaries will form the subject of similar enquiries so that the movement of the tidal head of the river and its effect upon settlement can be assessed.

The course of the Thames It has been suggested by Nunn (1983) as cited above that the course of the Thames has migrated northwards naturally. It is also true, however, that the effects of artificial reclamation over the last 2,000 years have resulted in the advancing of the north bank of the Thames in the area of the City southwards. In an article by Milne and Milne (1979) the advancement of the river is summarised. Since the publication of that paper, first century waterfronts have been excavated at Miles Lane, Peninsular House and Pudding Lane (C30, 32 and 34) demonstrating that the present river front is now about 100m to the south of its position 2,000 years ago. This movement of the north bank southwards is considered to be an artificial encroachment; the reasons for this are discussed in a paper by Milne (1981).

The Fleet In his book 'The lost rivers of London' Barton (1962) describes the Fleet as the longest tributary of the Thames in central London, running from its source at two heads on Hampstead Heath to the Thames at Blackfriars, where it flows through a sewer. There was a wide strip of marsh on the west side of the mouth of the stream in the medieval period known from documentary evidence as London Fen which was later reclaimed. Although this stream is well attested historically, it has not been studied thoroughly by archaeologists, with the exception of some fourteenth century waterlaid deposits excavated at Tudor Street (C1) in the area of the mouth of the Fleet. These sediments formed the subject of detailed study by Boyd (1981b) who identified a wide range of freshwater, brackish and marine flora and fauna from them including diatoms, seeds, charophytes, foraminifera, sponges, molluscs, bryozoans and ostracods. Boyd (1981b) describes the early evidence from these and other organisms for anthropogenic eutrophication and pollution in the river which he also found evident from contemporary documentary sources. He draws attention to the importance of examining more than one taxonomic or size group of organisms from such environments to give fully representative data. It is hoped that further analysis of deposits associated with the Fleet will be examined and such areas should, perhaps, form a priority when site selection is being exercised.

The Walbrook This short tributary has played an important part in the development of the City and has been mentioned in sections 4.1, 4.3 and 4.5 above. The stream does not flow above ground today, but what remains of it flows into the Thames through a sewer at Dowgate. Barton (1962) suggests that Holywell, Shoreditch may have been the source of the stream, though the exact course in the upper part of the valley is not completely understood. Merrifield (1965) has mapped the position of what are considered to be tributaries of the Walbrook; these are indicated on Figure 30. Dyson (1977) suggests that the name Walbrook is a generic term for a network of convergent south bound streams. Many references to the Walbrook are made in documentary sources from the thirteenth century onwards. There have been two main excavations near the course of the stream, at Angel Court (Blurton 1977) and Copthall Avenue (C27) excavated by Cathy Maloney. At the former site, revetted banks were excavated and it was suggested that the stream bed may have silted up as a result of dumping or a rise in the level of the Thames (Blurton 1977). At Copthall Avenue several metres of deposits including peaty and silty layers were excavated and the abundant plant macrofossils contained in them are the subject of current work. These deposits presumably form part of the 'marshy' area in the upper part of the Walbrook valley, cut by numerous drainage ditches and channels, several of which were excavated at Copthall Avenue. In a paper written in 1903, Reader discusses the Walbrook stream and valley including the marshy area to the north of the City wall known as Moorfields. He considered that the building of the City wall impeded the natural drainage of the area, the wall acting as a dam and causing a swamp to form. On present evidence, the wall was not constructed until the early third century AD. It is still not clear whether the Walbrook marsh area (including Moorfields) started to develop before the Roman period or only during and after this time, but it is certain, on the basis of recent and past excavation and observation, that much dumping of refuse into the marsh took place, and owing to the good preservation conditions, many organic remains such as wood and leather have survived along with the fruits and seeds of natural wild and cultivated plants described in sections 4.3 and 4.5.

Grimes (1968), Merrifield (1965) and Marsden (1980) discuss the nature of the Walbrook valley and its development in terms of building. The Moorfields area built up more slowly than that inside the City wall; its final drainage did not take place until the sixteenth century (Reader 1903). Kennard (in Reader 1903) examined deposits from Moorfields in the Finsbury House/Blomfield Street area and identified domestic refuse containing bones, edible molluscs and other freshwater and land snails. In the eastern part of the area he examined he described a possible bed of a stream, noting gravel, fine sand and peaty loam. He considered that dumping caused the stream to overflow its banks forming a large mire which was gradually drained to form a marsh and eventually dry land; more recent observation has modified this idea.

The current analysis of samples from the excavation at Copthall Avenue in the Walbrook valley will go some way to clarify some of the hypotheses that have been advanced for the development of the valley, but other parts of the area need to be examined to supplement this work and are a priority for future environmental work in the City.

The tributaries of the Thames as well as the main river itself would repay detailed examination and when site selection has to be exercised, such areas would form an important priority for environmental work throughout the City and Greater London.

4.7.2   *Identification of artefacts made from wood and bone*

The rising river level discussed in section 4.7.1 has provided ideal conditions for the preservation of wood along the Thames waterfront and apart from the identification of wood of a structural nature to determine the choice and availability of this essential raw material, many artefacts are also examined. A wide range of such objects as bowls, spatulas, spoons, pattens, knife and weapon handles, combs, boxes, barrels and even chesspieces are identified to genus or species level so that the most applicable conservation method can be selected. The use of wood as a building material and the importance of oak in particular has been discussed in sections 4.3, 4.5 and 4.7.5 which deal with the Roman and Medieval periods and dendrochronology.

Objects made of animal tissues recovered from sites, for example combs, buttons and knife handles, are also routinely examined to ascertain the source material used (horn, bone or ivory); as for wooden objects, this information is often required by the Museum of London's conservationists to enable them to carry out the most appropriate treatment. In addition, the study of such objects, together with pieces of sawn horn, bone and ivory identified as the discarded waste from their manufacture, is providing important information on the past techniques of working with animal tissues. One study of 190 sawn cattle metapodial bones from a late fifteenth century deposit at Baynard's Castle (C7) for example, has revealed the precision achieved by the later medieval bone-worker in removing the shaft from the unwanted proximal and distal ends; on each bone the position and direction of sawing was nearly always the same (Armitage 1977a, 143–147; 1982b, 104). The shaft of the ox metapodial bone is long and straight, with thick walls, and therefore formed an ideal raw material for the manufacture of knife handles, pins and bodkins; while the flat posterior side sawn from the shaft formed a good template from which circular discs could be cut out for use either as beads or buttons. Bull metacarpal bones, with their extra wide and uniformly flat posterior face, were apparently exploited in later medieval times in the manufacture of spectacle frames as demonstrated by the pair of bone spectacles from Trig Lane (C13), the earliest known in Britain (cAD 1440) (Armitage 1982e).

MacGregor, in Addyman *et al.* (1976), discussed the possibility of using certain types of artefact found on archaeological sites as indicators of past climate. He quoted as an example of this the work of Radley (1971), who had interpreted the large numbers of bone skates from the Anglo-Saxon deposits in York as evidence of long hard winters. In view of the York evidence, it is notable that the seven bone skates from well stratified contexts in London recently examined by West (1982d) (from Pudding Lane (C32), Swan Lane (C26), Lloyds (C39), Watling Court (C17) and General Post Office (C11) are all firmly dated between eleventh to thirteenth century, the period of climatic deterioration which led in the mid thirteenth century to the onset of a 'little ice age'. The frequency with which low-lying bodies of shallow water in London froze in winter at this time is attested by William Fitzstephen's famous eyewitness description (cAD 1170–83) of skaters on the frozen marshy area of Moorfields printed by Stowe in his *Survey of London* (Wheatley 1970, 85). A similar period of climatic deterioration, resulting in very cold winters in south eastern England in late Roman times, is apparently suggested by the recent discovery of two bone skates, one fashioned from an ox radius, the other from a sheep metapodial bone (presumably a child's skate) at the General Post Office site (C11) (West

1982d). The presence of ice skates in Roman London is extremely interesting as it is always presumed that temperatures at this time were warmer, not colder, than today. However, caution must be exercised in directly attributing the presence of these two skates to the occurrence of a little ice age in Roman Britain. As pointed out by MacGregor, shallow bodies of water will readily freeze over under conditions of increased continentality of the climate with frequent anticyclones of light winter winds. Perhaps it was this sort of climatic change rather than the arrival of more severe (much colder) conditions which accounts for the presence of bone skates at the General Post Office site; the study of botanical and arthropod remains may provide more direct information on past changes in climate and so help clarify this point.

As well as providing data on the exploitation of woodland and animal resources, the routine identification of wood and bone objects is accumulating information on trade. For example, study of the barrels and writing tablets from Roman sites has revealed that many of them are made of woods not native to Britain, indeed often not introduced until hundreds of years later. Barrels of *Abies* sp. and *Cedrus* sp. (cedar and silver fir) have been found on several waterfront sites. These same woods, as well as larch or spruce (*Larix/Picea* sp.) were apparently also used in the manufacture of writing tablets, examples of which have come from New Fresh Wharf (C33), Pudding Lane (C32) and other waterfront sites. Presumably these writing tablets were imported ready-made into Britain (Straker in preparation). The information which this sort of study can provide compares well with that of other objects brought to Britain in the Roman period, such as combs made from elephant ivory (identified by Armitage, unpublished), together with the exotic foodstuffs already mentioned (pp 272 and 273), and even the importation of commodities such as olive oil, wine and fish sauce in amphorae.

Evidence for the importation of exotic deer antler, presumably from Scandinavia, in the late medieval period is provided by a sawn piece of elk (*Alces alces*) antler (a species extinct in Britain since Mesolithic times) found at Baynard's Castle (Armitage 1977a). Objects recovered from even later (post-medieval) sites show how the range of imported goods diversified when tropical areas of the world were exploited. Two wooden objects, a box and knife handle, from seventeenth century levels at Cutler Street (C44) illustrate this; both were identified at the Royal Botanic Garden, Kew, as being of *Entandophragma* sp., a kind of false mahogany probably from Africa. Seventeenth and eighteenth century levels at Cutler Street also yielded other examples of imported organic materials from tropical latitudes; including sawn pieces of elephant ivory (waste from ivory-turning) and strips of tortoiseshell from the hawksbill turtle (*Eretmochelys imbricata*) (identified by Armitage, unpublished).

4.7.3 *Reconstruction of British livestock husbandry from London's faunal remains*

The bulk of faunal material found in London comprises the remains of domestic livestock, largely cattle, sheep and pigs. Such material can provide valuable information on developments in livestock husbandry in different historic periods. It is now widely accepted that major urban sites, like London, can contribute considerably more information on this subject than rural sites. As stressed by Addyman (1982, 4) faunal assemblages from rural sites are unlikely to reflect more than the local livestock types and it is only in the larger cities that the archaeological record will contain a truly representative selection of types from a whole region. It is also important to appreciate that due to the late seventeenth and eighteenth century practice of driving cattle over long distances to the meat markets of London, the bones of a wide variety of unimproved breeds of cattle will be found on early modern sites in the City; including Scottish and Welsh runts, Dutch shorthorns (from Lincolnshire), Lancashire longhorns and red Devon and Sussex cattle (Armitage 1978a, 1982b, 98). Sheep were also sent 'on the hoof' into London; the principal areas of mutton supply being in the north, in Lincolnshire and part of Leicestershire, as recorded by Defoe (1724, reprinted 1974; Vol. 1, 125 and Vo. 2, 89). The skeletal remains of these unimproved Lincolnshire and Leicestershire longwool sheep have recently been identified from the late seventeenth century deposits at Aldgate (C50) (Armitage 1983h, in press) (see below).

In London, deposits of cattle horn cores representing the discarded waste from horners' workshops and tanyards have proved especially valuable in tracing developments in British livestock husbandry from Roman times to the present day. The potential of such material was first recognised by Chaplin (1971: 141) who believed that once an adequate series of located and dated horn core types was established it would then be possible to reconstruct the way in which regional livestock types (and later, breeds as we would know them) developed. To this end, Armitage and Clutton-Brock (1976) devised a system for the classification and description of horn cores from archaeological contexts of Roman to early Tudor date. This system was based largely on London material, from Baynard's Castle (C7) and Angel Court (C29). Already the application of the system to London material has revealed that in south eastern England, by the Tudor period, methods of keeping and breeding cattle were much improved, culminating in the emergence on the larger more progressive farms of large sized longer horned cattle (Armitage 1980d) — whose presence, although suspected by historians (Dyer 1982, pers. comm.), is nowhere mentioned in the contemporary books on livestock husbandry. In order that the later history of British cattle may be traced from the archaeological evidence, Armitage (1982c) revised and extended the original classification system of Armitage and Clutton-Brock (1976) to cover specimens from London's seventeenth and early eighteenth century sites. Application of this system has allowed reconstruction of the appearance of the unimproved British longhorn cattle, information on which is lacking in the contemporary documentary sources. Further studies of cattle horn cores from London and other British archaeological sites have confirmed the view of Jewell (1963) that the larger strains of cattle found on many Romano-British sites 'were encouraged into ascendancy by the Roman organisation for agriculture'; that is, the larger sized cattle were the result of an upgrading of the existing stocks of British cattle and not the progeny of improved breeding stock specially imported from Italy as other writers have suggested (Armitage 1982d).

Sheep bones from Baynard's Castle (C7) have been used in conjunction with iconographic sources to reconstruct the appearance of late medieval 'primitive longwool sheep' (Armitage and Goodall 1977). Other sheep bones, from late seventeenth century contexts at Aldgate (C50) have provided information on the conformation of the unimproved Lincoln and Leicester longwool sheep. These Aldgate sheep predate the improvements made by Robert Bakewell to the English longwool breed (between AD 1760–1790) and their discovery therefore provided a unique opportunity to compare directly the skeleton of the unimproved longwool with their modern improved counterparts/descendants. Measurements of the metatarsal bones from Aldgate reveal that the unimproved longwool was far taller and more slender-legged than the modern animal; selection for a meat-producing animal rather than a wool-producer, in modern longwool breeds, has resulted in a smaller, shorter-legged beast with a barrel-shaped body (Armitage 1983c).

Study of the wool fibres from textiles derived from grubenhaus and cesspits at Milk Street (C15), Ironmonger Lane (C22) and New Fresh Wharf (C33) has provided important information on fleece types in late Saxon and Saxo-Norman (ninth to eleventh century) sheep. This research by Frances Pritchard of the Finds Section, DUA, was assisted by Armitage, who provided advice on the recording and description of the wool fibres, and their identification and interpretation (Pritchard in preparation). Earlier work by Ryder on a sample of raw wool (a comparatively rare archaeological find) from the thirteenth century deposits, Roman Riverside Wall (C6) has provided the first direct evidence for the fineness of medieval wool; it is not known whether this sample was from a local sheep or was imported, however (Ryder 1977, 1980, 114).

Evidence of maltreatment (rough handling, poor care and feeding etc) in livestock is occasionally found in faunal material from London and can tell us something about the standard of husbandry in different historic periods. For example, the presence of dwarf short horned cattle in Saxo-Norman and High medieval contexts in London suggests that the high standard of cattle husbandry initiated by the Roman farmers and continued in the Saxon period (at least in south eastern England) had deteriorated by this time (Armitage 1980d, 1982d). An example of rough handling in Roman mules is provided by a jawbone from Billingsgate Buildings (C36) which exhibits an area of eroded bone on the outer surface. This was the result of pressure atrophy probably caused by a rope halter or muzzle being tied too tightly round the nose, chafing the underside of the jaw where there is little flesh to cushion and protect the underlying bone (Armitage and Chapman 1979). A further example of harsh treatment in a Roman equid comes from Miles Lane (C30) where the fused lumber vertebrae of an adult male horse, aged 7 to 8 years, suggests that the animal was frequently ridden or used to haul heavy loads (Armitage 1981c). Ankylosis of vertebrae is only found in domestic horses and mules that have been constantly worked by man and is nowhere found in free-living wild equids such as wild asses and zebras (Stecher and Goss 1961).

4.7.4   *London's past inhabitants: studies of human skeletal remains by Barbara West*

There have been many finds of small groups of human bone in the City over the years, usually discovered accidentally during construction work on building sites, but as none of these was properly recorded or dated, they yield little or no useful information. Following the formation of the DUA and its development of scientific methods for recording human skeletal material (see Morgan 1978 and Thompson 1980), it has been possible for specialists (DUA and external) to carry out detailed studies of the groups recovered from rescue sites in the City. The aim of these continuing studies (which yield information on diet and nutrition, longevity, stature, disease and injury etc) is to build up a picture of the populations which occupied London during different historical periods, and to compare them with populations of similar date from other British and European urban and rural sites.

Prehistoric (to AD 43) The Museum of London's collection of unpublished skulls from the Thames was examined for comparison with the skulls from the Walbrook valley (see below). Many of these skulls are believed to be Mesolithic, by association with various flint implements (Macdonald pers. comm.), but they have never been securely dated; however, arrangements are now being made to obtain radiocarbon dates for them.

Roman (AD 43–500) The groups of human inhumations recovered from the Roman cemetery sites at St. Bartholomew's Hospital (C5) (Bentley and Pritchard in press) and Cutler Street (C44) (West 1981b) are too small for any general conclusions to be drawn about the population of Roman London; but the information provided by these groups will be valuable when combined with that from future sites of Roman date. A study of the 48 skulls found in or near the Walbrook stream proved to be more immediately fruitful, as it was concluded that these were possibly associated with Celtic head rituals linked with a water religion (Marsh and West 1981) and not, as previously believed, victims of the Boudiccan massacre in AD 60.

Early Medieval (AD 500–800) The only properly recorded (presumed) Saxon human material from the City is represented by two skeletons from the dark earth deposit at Rangoon Street (C47), for which a radiocarbon date is being obtained from the Research Laboratory of the British Museum[1]. A large collection of well-dated but poorly recorded material from a Saxon site in Mitcham has been stored in the Museum of London since the 1920s, but these still await further study.

Medieval (AD 800–1500) The medieval period is numerically better represented. In addition to a small group of skeletons from Holy Trinity Priory (C45) (Downs 1979b), a large group comprising 233 articulated skeletons from St. Nicholas Shambles (General Post Office site C11) is currently under investigation by White (part time MPhil student at the University of London) (White 1983). Another, but smaller, medieval group from Billingsgate (C35) has recently been examined by West (1983b).

Post Medieval (AD 1500 onwards) Examination of over 72 inhumations from a post-medieval burial ground at Mansell Street (C51) (West 1982a) yielded no surprises as to the conditions of the individuals represented, with evidence of poor dental health and vitamin deficiency (rickets, for example) to be expected in an eighteenth century urban population. Of greater interest, however, was the fact that the entire group (with all ages represented) were apparently deposited together at one time, neatly stacked directly beside and above one another. Historical records are being searched in an attempt to solve this mystery. One of the Mansell Street skulls has the top half removed by sawing, possibly a post-mortem. Other evidence of sawn human bones comes from St. Bartholomew's Hospital (C5) where three femora and one mandible were found buried together in an eighteenth century pit. These sawn bones were probably from practice amputations and dissections carried out (illegally in the eighteenth century) by students in the nearby anatomy school (West 1980b, West and Armitage 1980).

4.7.5 *Dendrochronology*

Structural timbers which have been identified as oak are catalogued and checked for their suitability as dendrochronological samples. The annual rings are counted to ensure that there are sufficient to provide a good chance of obtaining a date and other advantageous factors such as the presence of sapwood are also noted.

Excavations, particularly along the Thames waterfront, have provided hundreds of samples for tree-ring analysis; Brett, Fletcher and Morgan have carried out some of this work in the past but the work is now done in the DoE funded laboratory at Sheffield University by Hillam. Dendrochronological reports are available for the following sites:

C1	Tudor Street (Hillam 1980d) and Bridewell (Hillam 1980f) and Kingscote Street (Hillam 1980g).
C4	Mermaid Theatre (Hillam 1979a, Hillam and Herbert 1980).
C6	Riverside Wall (Hillam and Morgan 1979, Morgan 1980b).
C13	Trig Lane (Brett 1982).
C16	Milk Street (Hillam 1980b).
BW	Bull Wharf (Hillam 1981b).
C17	Watling Court (Hillam 1980e).
C19	Thames Street Tunnel (Hillam 1980c).
C23	Masons Avenue (Hillam 1980a).
C28	Seal House (Morgan 1977 and Morgan and Schofield 1978).
C30	Miles Lane (Hillam 1982a).
C33	New Fresh Wharf (Morgan 1977, Hillam and Morgan 1979, 1981a).
C34	Peninsular House (Hillam 1982b).
C36	Billingsgate Buildings (Morgan 1980a).
C40	Custom House (Fletcher 1974 and 1975, and Hillam 1979b).

Dendrochronology aims to provide an absolute date for a structure but relative dating is also a great benefit to the archaeologist and tree-ring analysis is regarded in London as of paramount importance in the evaluation of often very complex structures. It also provides dating for groups of artefacts that otherwise may be poorly tied into a chronology. Tree-ring analysis does not only allow accurate dates to be produced, but also gives information on the age, size and origin of the wood (Hillam and Morgan 1981b) and how it was used by man. Similar ring patterns might suggest the exploitation of the same woodland resource. The age and size of timber adds to knowledge of the woodland itself and in some cases the width of rings may suggest whether the woodland was dense or open, and details such as season of felling may be forthcoming (Hillam and Morgan 1981b). Study of tree rings may also provide data of use in palaeoclimatic studies (Morgan and Schofield 1978).

---

[1] Results obtained (December 1983): BM-2214 ref. 1090, 1050 ± 45bp; BM-2215 ref. 1157, 980 ± 50bp. Calibrated (Klein *et al.* 1982) AD900–1145 (combined date at 95% confidence level) (Amber pers. comm.)

In addition to the obvious vital contribution to some aspects of the interpretation of archaeological sites, the hundreds of timbers from London have themselves provided valuable data which is used in the construction of general chronologies which can in turn be used to date further samples from Britain. Hillam (1981a) has recently published an English Tree Ring Chronology from AD 404–1216 in which Saxon timbers from London and Essex were used to date the Old Windsor–Portchester sequence to produce a curve which can now date Saxon as well as medieval timbers. A radially split plank from Tudor Street containing 237 rings was dated from AD 682–918, and at present provides the only link which extends the tree-ring curve for England back beyond cAD 770; a major step towards a continuous English chronology extending over the last 2,000 years (Hillam 1981a). The need to date the Roman waterfront structures has produced floating tree-ring sequences for the London area, but absolute dates also are now available for Roman London and other places on the basis of a chronology constructed by averaging ring widths from several London sites and comparing the resultant chronology with German curves using a computer program (Hillam and Morgan 1981c). It is hoped that the samples from the sites which remain to be studied (Pudding Lane, St. Peter's Hill, Copthall Avenue, Swan Lane and Billingsgate, C32, 9, 27, 26, 35) will be able to provide further useful material in the construction of a 2,000 year chronology, particularly the gap still existing between the Roman and Saxon chronologies.

5   Future prospects in environmental archaeology in London

5.1   Introduction

All aspects of environmental enquiry in London have, until recently, been pursued in a piecemeal fashion (see sections 3 and 4); the results in some areas may therefore appear fragmented and to lack a defined apparent framework. However, existing results should be seen as part of a continuing cumulative process of information gathering, and there is no doubt that previous studies, although often on a small scale and largely unco-ordinated, have indeed provided a most valuable data base for subsequent investigations.

The best way of now using the evidence already collected would be to amalgamate and compare selected information relating to botanical and faunal remains from discrete features on different sites where these are allied by date, function and context, focusing attention on a number of clearly defined themes (e.g. diet, farming, palaeodemography). In addition, work must continue on selected samples from the store of backlog material. Again this should follow the same thematic approach (with clearly defined objectives in mind) based on several sites rather than simply following a series of routine site by site analyses which do not attempt to integrate the collected information in any meaningful way.

This does not mean, however, that all work aimed at answering specific problems of archaeological interpretation raised by individual sites should cease. We fully recognise that this 'service aspect' is one of the essential roles of the environmental archaeologist in London (and indeed elsewhere in Britain) and should certainly continue. There will always be a requirement for environmental archaeologists in London to provide a closely integrated scientific 'back-up', interpretative and advisory service to field archaeologists, finds researchers and others. But the point which must be stressed is that, as well as undertaking this sort of general work, the environmentalist should carry out a systematic/ thematic programme of investigation aimed at obtaining a broader picture of past human activity and living conditions.

Although investigations carried out so far have provided a wealth of information, there are certain important problems concerning London's past (see section 5.2 below) which will only be resolved by the collection of new material from sites chosen specifically for their potential for environmental archaeology. It is vital therefore that environmental/biological criteria are considered in any future programme for site selection. After selection, the site should then be carefully and systematically investigated and adequate environmental/biological samples taken, perhaps ensured by use of on-site bulk sieving. However, it is appreciated that under urban rescue conditions it is not always practicable to expect full recovery of the biological evidence nor possible in every case to implement a recovery operation entirely as planned in advance of the excavation. Any recovery programme must be flexible and provision be made for 'opportunist' sampling of unexpected deposits that may prove exceptionally rich in well preserved organic remains, even — perhaps especially — where such material may not necessarily fit into any current research strategy.

In order to maximise the potential of the environmental/biological material from sites in London, some ancillary investigations of a more fundamental nature will be required. Two fields may be suggested:

1.   The development of new techniques and methods for the sampling and collection of material, and

2.   Modern comparative ecological study of flora and fauna in urban, suburban and rural contexts (to serve as a basic analytical tool and as a useful reference framework for aiding interpretation of archaeological deposits and assemblages).

The present study of the City and Greater London areas as two separate entities is highly unsatisfactory in practice — from a scientific viewpoint the division is wholly artificial and irrelevant.

For example, the study of pollen on Greater London sites could reveal important changes in vegetation over time, indicating how the growth of the City affected its hinterland (e.g. provide a measure of the extent of deforestation to provide fuel and raw material). Conversely, studies of the remains of domestic (kitchen) refuse on City sites may reveal changes in the pattern of meat consumption by the urban population and so help explain shifts in livestock production observed in the rural settlements and farmsteads in the Greater London area.

Considerations such as these render the present arrangements inappropriate and undesirable, and there is, we believe, a distinct need for the integration of studies on environmental/biological material from both areas to give a balanced overview of the City — the historic 'core' of London — and the surrounding countryside and settlements.

5.2   Areas of specific academic priority

Many of the more general questions requiring biological investigation in London have already been covered in sections 3 and 4 above. The reader's attention is also directed to the list of thematic priorities drawn up by the York Environmental Unit (see Kenward *et al.* in press) many of which are applicable to London. On the basis of work carried out so far, certain specific areas of high priority may be suggested for London. These are presented here under chronological sequence:

Prehistoric period (Palaeolithic to Iron Age)

(i)   The natural and man-made landscape of the London region.

Very little is known about the natural landscape (vegetation and topography) and land-use in the London region in early times. Borehole investigations should provide further data required to refine existing geological and topographical maps. At the same time, studies of sediments and ostracods and diatoms contained in them will clarify past changes in the course, level and tidal limit of the Thames.

Other important questions for this period include: where Palaeolithic and Mesolithic communities chose to live and why and the possibility of constructing a predictive model, based on existing knowledge of site locations, to assist archaeologists in their search for prehistoric sites as yet undiscovered, that are presumed to be in the region.

As there is generally a paucity of mammalian and molluscan material on Palaeolithic and Mesolithic sites, the main evidence for the local and regional environment will therefore probably come from studies of pollen and insect remains.

(ii)   Early farming economies.

Very little is known of livestock and arable farming systems of the London region in the Neolithic, Bronze and Iron Ages, and efforts should therefore be made to recover further faunal and botanical remains from sites of these periods.

(iii)   Human inhabitants of the London region in prehistoric times.

The few human skeletal remains from this period require systematic study and, in some cases, confirmation of date by radiocarbon.

The Romano-British period

(i)   Studies on the Thames and its tributaries.

Changes in the level and tidal limit of the Thames and their effect on waterfront development in the City remain an important priority. Studies also need to be carried out on the local effects of flooding and silting on other settlements located near river courses. Dr Morris (pers. comm.) for instance, believed that flooding of the Lea at Enfield may have been a contributory factor in the relocation of the settlement from the floodplain in the post-Roman period and may also have severely disrupted traffic using the local Roman road (Ermine Street).

(ii)   Supply of food and raw materials to Londinium.

Despite the persistent belief that an important prehistoric settlement once stood on the present site of the City of London, there is no archaeological evidence of this; the area before the arrival of the Romans was uninhabited. Unlike most other Roman towns in Britain whose origins lay in existing major Iron Age settlements, Londinium was therefore a completely new city founded by the Roman government for the specific purpose of administering newly-conquered Britain. As there was no predecessor to the Roman city there would have been no established system for the procurement of food (grain and livestock) and other essential supplies (e.g. timber for fuel or building purposes). It is important to know how these requirements were met, and what effect the sudden appearance of a large urban centre had on the farming economies in the surrounding area. As a flourishing international port, early Roman London may have imported much of its food and raw materials from overseas rather than from local sources. With the storage of food products on a large scale, ideal environmental conditions were created for infestation by pests (rodents and insects). The biological material from sites may tell us about the arrival in London of these pests and provide indirect evidence for the presence of certain stored foodstuffs even where these may not themselves have survived in the archaeological record.

(iii)   Refuse disposal.

It would be useful to know if this was organised, or that the inhabitants of Roman London and other settlements simply dumped rubbish in the nearest convenient place (disused well, cesspit or ditch), and if the waste from industrial processes (e.g. leatherworking) was treated differently.

(iv)   Studies on the human population.

Systematic studies of human skeletal material need to be carried out and the investigation of Roman cemeteries is considered to be of a high priority; the value of such work in elucidating the health and longevity etc of Romano-British populations has been amply demonstrated by the recent survey carried out at Cirencester (McWhirr *et al.* 1982). There is very little human bone currently available in London for such detailed study and every effort must be made to obtain further material.

Late Roman, Dark Age and Early Saxon period

(i)   ? the end of Roman London.

The question of the fate of the City and of the survival of urban life into the sub-Roman and early Saxon period remains a high priority, including investigation of how much of the City lay derelict as wasteland and the significance of the presence of 'dark earth' which may, as some people have suggested, be the result of cultivation within the walls. If the City itself was largely abandoned, where its previous inhabitants went to is of interest and there may be for example, evidence from the size of cemeteries in rural settlements of an increased population outside. With the disappearance of such an important centre of trade and commerce, the effect on the farming economies of the rural settlements and farmsteads should be ascertained – there may have been, for instance, a return to subsistence farming. The high standards of livestock husbandry initiated by the Romans may have persisted, or, alternatively, stock degenerated.

(ii)   The arrival of Germanic peoples in the London area.

Genetic 'distance' calculated from non-metrical variant frequencies in human skulls can be used to distinguish ethnic affinities and thus reveal human population movements. Studies of human skulls from fifth and sixth century cemeteries using such techniques may provide evidence of the presence of Germanic peoples in the London region thus substantiating the artefactual evidence. Similarly, multivariate techniques may be able to show the degree of inter-marriage between the British and invading Anglo-Saxons.

Medieval period

(i)   Effects on the natural environment of urban growth.

With the 'rebirth' of the City of London by the late seventh century there followed a period of urban growth, especially rapid from the tenth century. By the fifteenth century, London was the most densely populated city in Europe and the biological/environmental effects of this growth are of importance, e.g. which species of wild animals and plants, if any, managed to adapt to the urban environment and which failed to survive and whether microevolutionary trends and adaptations can be detected in, for example, urban small mammals, that are not present in their rural relatives. As discussed by Brothwell and Jones (1978, 54), modern studies on regional samples of black rat in Delhi suggest that variation may occur even within the same urban complex and there may be evidence in the numerous black rat remains from medieval London of a similar genetic divergence.

(ii)   Early medieval livestock husbandry.

Very little is known about early medieval livestock husbandry and the study of faunal remains from Greater London sites of this period is therefore considered of high priority.

(iii)   Patterns of food consumption and social status.

As discussed by Brothwell (1982, 128), social heterogeneity in towns is reflected in contrasting food habits, which differ not only between castle and monastic house, but extend to neighbourhoods, ethnic groups and so forth. It may be that these differences in diet can be detected in the archaeological record for the City of London. It would also be informative to compare evidence of differences in quality and quantity of diet enjoyed by Londoners and their rural counterparts e.g. evidence from food debris for differences in economic status of the various rural settlements and towns throughout the Greater London region in medieval times.

(iv)   Palaeodemographic studies of medieval cemeteries.

Studies of human skeletons recovered from medieval cemeteries can reveal important information relating to infant and adult mortality, life expectancy and age group composition of the different social classes and ethnic origins. One line of research that could prove especially informative, would be to compare human remains from the City with those from the surrounding towns and villages, in order to see if people living in crowded urban conditions were subjected to greater health hazards and consequently a reduced life expectancy and a higher rate of infant mortality, how far social position or wealth of the city dweller influenced their health, well-being and life expectancy and if the same determinants could be detected in the rural population.

(v)   Evidence of international trade.

As London merchants came into contact with those parts of the world not previously exploited, the range of imported foods and raw materials diversified greatly; the botanical and faunal evidence from London may have much to reveal about the expansion of this trade from the medieval period onwards. Possibly the identification of certain ethnic groups in cemeteries may also throw some light on this subject.

Post-medieval period

All too often this period is regarded as of low priority and dismissed as being 'too modern' and therefore fully comprehensive from research into documentary sources. There are a number of areas, however, where archaeological investigation can make an important contribution, and indeed in some instances represent the only source of information available. Two examples may be suggested:

(i)   Livestock husbandry and the evolution of our modern breeds of cattle and sheep.

It is well known that the growth of London from the seventeenth century down to the present day has provided an important stimulus to the development of British livestock husbandry. As Fisher (1935) said, the livestock breeders and graziers throughout Britain at this time 'all looked to the London market as the hub of their economic universe'. It is very appropriate therefore that the remains of cattle and sheep from post-medieval sites in London are used in the reconstruction of livestock husbandry; indeed, as has already been discussed in section 4.7.3, groups of bone from large urban centres like the City of London offer the greatest potential for such studies.

It is often assumed that the later developments in British livestock husbandry (of the eighteenth and early nineteenth century) are very well documented and that there is therefore no need for further study of animal remains. This assumption is false. As shown by Clutton-Brock (1982), documentary evidence is indeed remarkably detailed, even to the extent of providing individual weights and body measurements of animals. But these data, valuable though they are to the agricultural historian, are highly biased and relate only to a small proportion of carefully nurtured pedigree beasts. Only examination of the skeletal remains from the archaeological record will fill in the gaps by providing the missing information on the other, common (non-pedigree), stock excluded from contemporary documentary sources.

(ii)   Spatial analysis of the suburban environment of the City of London (sixteenth to eighteenth century).

The suburban environment in the most conspicuous areas of urban growth in London – the East and West Ends – between late sixteenth and end of the seventeenth century has been the subject of special study by several scholars in recent years (Schofield in Thompson *et al.* in press). Although information on the character of London's suburbs has mainly come from documentary sources, the recent study of the structural, artefactual and biological evidence from Aldgate (C50) has demonstrated the value of archaeological investigation in this field (see p 281). From studies of the domestic refuse (including food debris and waste from industries such as tanning, horn and bone working) from cesspits, wells and rubbish pits, it should prove possible (when combined with the artefactual evidence) to draw up distribution maps for the suburban areas to show the areas occupied by the wealthier classes, middle class tradesmen and skilled craftsmen, and the poorer unskilled artisans. These maps may then be compared with contemporary maps, surveys, property deeds and other written sources (e.g. Hearth Tax returns) to build up a detailed picture of the suburban environment.

5.3   Organisation and funding of future environmental archaeology in London

It seems quite clear that the interests of both the DUA and the new Greater London unit, as well as those of the Passmore Edwards Museum would be best served by a single environmental team, possibly organised along the lines first suggested by Keeley and Sheldon as long ago as 1976 (Keeley and Sheldon 1976) with some modification in the light of the changed level of archaeological excavation. It is important that such a team maintains close ties with the field archaeologists and finds researchers; only by an interdisciplinary approach will the potential of London archaeology be adequately achieved. The beneficial result of co-operation between environmental archaeologists and others is succinctly summarised by Willcox (1976): 'The importance in gaining an understanding of London's natural past as an integral part of historical reconstruction cannot be overstressed. The archaeological, historical and environmental data are inseparable. Together they can help form a more complete picture of the past'.

ACKNOWLEDGEMENTS

We would like to thank the many people who have provided information and also for their helpful comments, in particular; J Musty, Dr Helen Keeley (DoE Ancient Monuments Laboratory), Professor J Evans, Professor D Harris (Institute of Archaeology, London), Dr Juliet Clutton-Brock (British Museum (Natural History)), Jennifer Hillam (University of Sheffield), B Hobley, J Schofield, A Dyson, Dr H Chapman, Anne Davis, Barbara West and D Bentley (Department of Urban Archaeology, Museum of London), T Wilkinson (Department of Natural Sciences, Hatfield Polytechnic), H Sheldon, D Whipp, S McCracken, M Hammerson, Laura Schaaf and J Cotton (Greater London Archaeological Unit), Pat Wilkinson (Passmore Edwards Museum), and B Philp (Kent Archaeological Rescue Unit).

Special thanks are due to Dr F Berry (Institute of Geological Sciences) for providing unpublished information on the geology of the area and also for his comments. Thanks must also go to Gwen Profit who typed the original manuscript.

CITY OF LONDON

Key to map showing location of sites (sites C1–52, BW & FS) on Figure 29

C	1	Tudor Street	C	27	Copthall Avenue
	2	Ludgate Hill		28	Seal House
	3	Central Criminal Court		29	Angel Court
	4	Mermaid Theatre		30	Miles Lane
	5	St. Bartholomew's Hospital		31	Clements Lane
	6	Upper Thames Street (Riverside Wall)		32	Pudding Lane
	7	Baynard's Castle 1972		33	New Fresh Wharf (3 sites)
	8	Baynard's Castle 1981		34	Peninsular House
	9	St. Peter's Hill		35	Billingsgate
	10	Horn Tavern		36	Billingsgate Buildings
	11	G.P.O. 1975		37	Forum South East
	12	G.P.O. middle area 1979		38	28–38 Bishopsgate
	13	Trig Lane		39	Lloyds, Leadenhall
	14	Foster Lane		40	Custom House
	15	St. Mildreds Church		41	Harp Lane
	16	Milk Street		42	Aldermans House
	17	Watling Court		43	Bevis Marks
	18	Well Court		44	Cutler Street
	19	Thames Street Tunnel		45	Holy Trinity Priory
	20	Cannon Street		46	Dukes Place
	21	College Hill		47	Rangoon Street
	22	Ironmonger Lane		48	Sir John Cass School
	23	Mason's Avenue		49	Crosswall
	24	Temple of Mithras		50	Aldgate
	25	Cannon Street 1981		51	Mansell Street
	26	Swan Lane		52	Finsbury Circus

BW   Bull Wharf
FS   Fenchurch Street

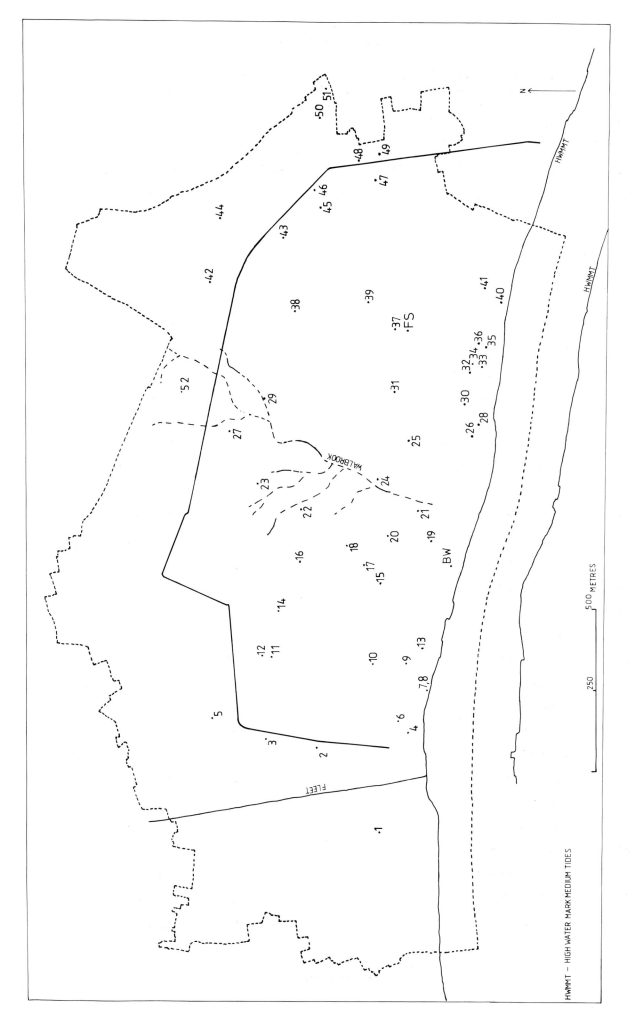

Figure 29 City of London: map to show the location of archaeological sites from which environmental samples have been taken

293

GAZETTEER

SITES 1–168 (GREATER LONDON) (A Locker)

ABBREVIATIONS

LR	Ancient Monuments Laboratory Report
SURREY ARCH. UNIT	Surrey Archaeological Unit
WLAFG	West London Archaeological Field Group
ILAU	Inner London Archaeological Unit
CEU	Central Excavation Unit
SWLU	South West London Unit
KING. MUS.	Kingston Museum
WANDS. HIST. SOC.	Wandsworth Historical Society
HENDON ARCH. SOC.	Hendon Archaeological Society
ENFIELD ARCH. SOC.	Enfield Archaeological Society
SLAEC	Southwark and Lambeth Archaeological Excavation Committee
WKAFG	West Kent Archaeological Field Group
PEM	Passmore Edwards Museum

	Site	*Grid*	*Excavator*	*Evidence and date*
1.	Stanwell, Heathrow, 1980, 1981	TQ 053745	Surrey Arch. Unit	LBA, EIA, RB, EARLY MED. Seeds, insects, pollen in prep. worked wood, Watson 1981 LR
2.	Dewes Farm	TQ 054884	Lacaille	MES Pollen Knox in Lacaille 1961
3.	London, Heathrow	TQ 055765	WLAFG	IA, RB Animal bone Sutton 1978
4.	Gatehouse Nurseries, West Drayton (Church Road)	TQ 062795	WLAFG	MED. AND TUDOR Carbonised grain and seeds Scaife 1979 LR Animal bone Sutton in prep. human bone
5.	Wall Gdn. Farm, Sipson Lane, Harlington	TQ 077782	WLAFG	LBA, EIA, ROMAN Carbonised Grain Scaife 1980 LR Animal bone
6.	Barnfield Pit, Warren Lake, Yiewsley	TQ 082808 081805	Collins	PALAEOLITHIC Pollen Hubbard 1976
7.	Bedfont, Heathrow	TQ 087766	Alexander and Farrent	NEO. BA, EIA, ROMAN Charcoal Keepax 1973
8.	Manor Farm, Ruislip	TQ 091879	Bowlt	ROMAN Animal bone (Teeth pers. comm.)
9.	Ruislip Vicarage	TQ 092875	Bowlt	14th century onwards Animal bone (pers. comm.)
10.	Southall	TQ 119797	Brown	PALAEOLITHIC Animal bone Brown 1888
11.	Northolt Manor	TQ 130845	Hurst	MED. Animal bone King 1961 Birds Jope 1961
12.	Norwood Green	TQ 139793	Brown	PLEISTOCENE Animal bone Brown 1888
13.	Grims Dyke	TQ 141928	ILAU	IA Soil sample, residual

Site	Grid	Excavator	Evidence and date
14. Willement's Pit, Isleworth	TQ 157764		PLEISTOCENE Plant remains Shotton and Williams 1973
	TQ 158746 TQ 157747		Insects Coope and Angus 1975 Fauna and dating Callow *et al.* 196
15. Hampton Court Palace	TQ 158685	CEU	POST MED. Animal bone Langley LR
16. Church Street, Twickenham	TQ 165733	Sandford	NEO. Animal bone Sandford 1970
17. Northumberland Wharf, Brentford	TQ 172772	WLAFG	ROMAN Animal bones Sutton 1976
18. Ham Recreation Ground, Brentford	TQ 173771	WLAFG	POST MED. Animal bone Sutton 1978
19. 141–147 Brentford High Street	TQ 173772	WLAFG	ROMAN Animal bones Sutton 1978
20. 184–187 Brentford High Street	TQ 174773	WLAFG	ROMAN, TUDOR Animal bone Sutton 1978
21. Richmond Palace	TQ 174748	Dixon	POST MED. Animal bones Harman 1975
22. 136 Brentford High Street	TQ 174773	WLAFG	ROMAN, MED. POST MED. Animal bones Sutton 1978
23. Brockley Hill	TQ 172937 172934 17494 175939	Castle	ROMAN Charcoal Cutler 1970 Animal bone Gentry 1971 Charcoal Cutler 1971 Charcoal Stant 1975
24. Syon Reach Foreshore	TQ 178769 approx.	WLAFG	ROMAN Animal bone Sutton 1978
25. 219–113 High Street, Brentford	TQ 176774	WLAFG	ROMAN Animal bone Sutton 1978
26. 209–215 High Street, Brentford	TQ 176774	WLAFG	ROMAN Animal bone Sutton 1978
27. Catherine Wheelhouse, High Street, Brentford	TQ 176773	WLAFG	ROMAN Animal bone Sutton 1978
28. Old Bridge Street Kingston	TQ 177694	SWLU King. Mus.	MED. Wood dendro in prep.
29. 233–246 High Street, Brentford	TQ 178775	WLAFG	ROMAN, EARLY MED. MED Animal bone Sutton 1978
30. 29 Thames Street, Kingston	TQ 178693	King. Mus.	SAXON, MED. Soil samples Locker unpub. Animal bones Serjeantson in prep.
31. Horsefair site, Kingston 1981	TQ 178694	SWLU King. Mus.	MED.
32. 181–189 High Street, Brentford	TQ 178776	WLAFG	POST MED. Animal bone Sutton 1978
33. Old England, Brentford	TQ 179770	Wheeler	ROMAN, MED. POST MED. Animal bone Wheeler 1929

	Site	Grid	Excavator	Evidence and date
34.	Kingston Beneath Eden St. 1966	TQ 181692		NEO. Animal bone in Macdonald 1976
35.	Eden Walk, Kingston	TQ 181692	King. Mus.	NEO. BA, SAXON, MED. Animal bone Serjeantson in prep.
36.	Kingston Electricity Works	TQ 188691 approx.		NEO. Animal bone 1930
37.	Brentford	TQ 194784		PLEISTOCENE Animal bone Zeuner 1945
38.	Avenue Gardens	TQ 199796	WLAFG	BA, ROMAN
39.	Creffield Rd., Acton 1974–5	TQ 202802	Burleigh	PALAEOLITHIC
40.	130–4 Shakespeare Road, Acton, Chaucer Road and Myrtle Road	TQ 202804	Pitt Rivers	PALAEOLITHIC Fauna in Lane Fox 1872
41.	Caesar's Camp, Wimbledon	TQ 225710	Lowther	IA Charcoal Lowther 1945
42.	Nonsuch Palace, 1959	TQ 230630	Biddle	MED. POST MED. Animal bone Locker in prep. Fish bone Locker 1980 LR
43.	Beverley Brook	TQ 235763	Wands. Hist. Society	LBA, IA Soil samples Locker in prep.
44.	Felsham Road, Gay Street, Bemish Street	TQ 241755	Wands. Hist. Society	ROMAN Animal bone Locker unpub. 1977
45.	Fulham Palace Moat, 1972–3	TQ 241759	Arthur & Whitehouse	ROMAN Animal bone Clutton-Brock 1978 Charcoal Richardson 1978 Mollusca Cooper 1978
46.	Fulham Potteries	TQ 245772	Green	POST MED. Biological remains Armitage and Straker 1983, forthcoming
47.	West Heath, Hampstead	TQ 256867	Hendon Arch. Soc. & Collins	MES. Pollen and insects Girling and Greig 1977
48.	Wandsworth High Street 1963 and 1973	TQ 257746	Wands. Hist. Soc.	POST MED. Animal bone
49.	Merton Priory	TQ 265699	SWLU	MED. POST MED. Soil samples Locker in prep. Animal bones Locker future work Human bones Henderson future work Charcoal Keepax in prep.
50.	Althorpe Grove, Battersea	TQ 268770	SWLU	EARLY MED. POST MED. Animal bones Locker 1983
51.	Mitchum	TQ 275680	Bidder	EARLY MED. Animal bone in Bidder 1908
52.	Highgate Woods	TQ 283885	Brown & Sheldon	ROMAN Charcoal Locker unpub.
53.	Queen Mary's Hospital, Carshalton	TQ 280625	Lowther	IA Animal bones Jackson 1944–5

	Site	Grid	Excavator	Evidence and date
54.	Wallington	TQ 288640	Clinch	NEO ? Grain Clinch 1907
55.	Mitchum Terrace	TQ 290665		PLEISTOCENE Insects in Mitchell *et al.* 1973
56.	Tottenham Manor Euston Road	TQ 293824	ILAU	MED. POST MED. Seeds Locker 1982 LR Animal bones Locker 1982 LR
57.	Beddington Roman Villa	TQ 298658	Addy	ROMAN Animal bones Addy 1874
	1981–1982		Adkins	Animal bones Locker future work
58.	Endsleigh Street, Euston	TQ 298824		PLEISTOCENE Mammoth Hicks 1982
59.	Broad Sanctuary, Westminster	TQ 299796	ILAU	POST MED. Pollen Scaife 1980 LR Animal bones Locker 1983 LR
60.	Admiralty Building Spring Gardens	TQ 300804	Abbott	MES. Fauna, flora, mollusca in Lacaille 1961
61.	Trafalgar Square	TQ 300804	Franks	PLEISTOCENE Fauna etc. Franks *et al.* 1958, 1960
62.	Westminster Abbey	TQ 300794	ILAU	MED. Animal bone Locker 1975 Fish bone Jones 1975
63.	New Palace Yard	TQ 301795	Davison	IA, RB, EARLY MED. Seeds Paradine unpub. LR Mollusca Evans unpub. LR Pollen Greig unpub. Soil Limbrey in prep.
64.	Cromwell Green, Westminster	TQ 301795	ILAU	IA, ROMAN, EARLY MED. MED. POST MED. Animal bones Locker 1979 LR Pollen Greig 1979 LR Wood Watson 1978 LR
65.	Whitehall Treasury	TQ 302798	Green	EARLY MED. MED. TUDOR Animal bones Chaplin 1971 Molluscs Evans unpub.
66.	Clapham	TQ 303762 294747 290740	Imber	ROMAN Animal bone Rixson unpub.
67.	Abingdon Street Westminster, 1963	TQ 303795	Green	POST MED. Diatoms Ross 1976
68.	Westminster Hall	TQ 305795	ILAU	MED. Animal bone Locker unpub.
69.	Coulsdon	TQ 310600 ?	Moodie	PLEISTOCENE, EARLY MED. Preglacial hippo Moodie 1913
70.	Kings X Road	TQ 310830		PALAEOLITHIC
71.	Black Princes Palace, Kennington	TQ 310775	Dawson	MED. Animal bones in Dawson 1976

	Site	Grid	Excavator	Evidence and date
72.	28–32 Upsdell Avenue, Palmers Green	TQ 312917	Enfield Arch. Soc.	POST MED. Cattle horncores Armitage *et al.* 1980
73.	Fetter Lane	TQ 312812	ILAU	POST MED. Animal bone Locker 1976
74.	Roupell Street Hatfield Street Lambeth	TQ 314804	SLAEC	POSS. PREHISTORIC, POST MED. Seeds, insects in Densem 1979
75.	Waddon, Croydon	TQ 315648	Reid	MES. IA, ROMAN Animal bone Reid 1954 Plant remains Reid 1954
76.	Clerkenwell Nunnery	TQ 315823	ILAU	MED. Animal bone Locker future work Soil samples Locker future work
77.	Bankside Power Station 1960	TQ 320805	Marsden	TUDOR Molluscs Castell 1971 Wood Taylor 1971
78.	38–42 Southwark Bridge Road	TQ 322802	SLAEC	ROMAN Wood White unpub. Soil samples future work
79.	244–245 Borough High Street	TQ 323796	Celoria & Thorn	MED. Animal bone in Celoria and Thorn 1974
80.	5–15 Bankside	TQ 323804	SLAEC	PREHISTORIC, POST MED. Wood Tyers unpub. Pollen Scaife in prep.
81.	170–194 Borough High Street	TQ 324798	SLAEC	ROMAN, POST MED. Wood Slack unpub. White unpub.
82.	223–237 Borough High Street	TQ 324797	SLAEC	ROMAN, MED. Pollen samples future work Soil samples future work
83.	15–23 Southwark Street 1981–3	TQ 325801	SLAEC	BA, IA, ROMAN, MED. Animal bone future work Soil samples future work
84.	Palace Gardens, Enfield	TQ 325965	Enfield Arch. Soc.	MED. TUDOR Animal bones Armitage 1978c
85.	201–211 Borough High Street	TQ 325798	SLAEC	ROMAN, MED. Insects Girling 1978 Fish Jones 1978 Animal bone Rixson 1978 Seeds Dean 1978a
86.	64–70 Borough High Street	TQ 325800	SLAEC	ROMAN Grain Arthur unpub. Wood Slack and Tyers unpub. Insects Girling unpub.
87.	88 Borough High Street	TQ 325800	SLAEC	ROMAN Grain Arthur
88.	1–5 Swan Street/ 7–14 Great Dover Street	TQ 325795	SLAEC	ROMAN Molluscs Spencer 1978 Animal bone Rixson 1978

Site	Grid	Excavator	Evidence and date
89. 107–115 Borough High Street	TQ 325800	SLAEC	ROMAN, MED. Wood Tyers unpub. Dendro Tyers unpub. Soil samples future work
90. Arcadia Buildings (Sylvester Street/ Tabard Street) 1979	TQ 325796	SLAEC	ROMAN, MED. TUDOR Soil analysis Fisher 1980 Dark earth sample MacPhail 1980
91. 84–86 Borough High Street	TQ 325800	SLAEC	ROMAN Seeds Paradine unpub. Fish Locker unpub.
92. 175–177 Borough High High	TQ 325799	SLAEC	ROMAN Wood Slack unpub. Sediment analysis Gardiner 1977 Soil samples future work
93. 199 Borough High Street	TQ 325798	SLAEC	ROMAN Insects Girling and Tyers in prep. Seeds Tyers in prep. Fish Jones 1981 Animal bone Rixson, Locker in prep.
94. Silvester Buildings	TQ 325797	SLAEC	ROMAN Soil samples future work
95. 106–114 Borough High Street	TQ 325799	SLAEC	ROMAN Organic data Dean 1978d
96. 8 Union Street	TQ 325800	SLAEC	ROMAN Seeds, wood, insects, mollusca in Dean 1978c Animal bone Rixson 1978
97. 199 Borough High Street 1962	TQ 325798	Orton & Turner	ROMAN, POST MED. Animal bone Chaplin and Harman 1979
98. Chaucer House Tabard St/Pilgrimage St.	TQ 326796	SLAEC	ROMAN, MED. POST MED. Soil samples future work Insects Girling 1979 LR Wood Slack unpub.
99. 93–95 Borough High St.	TQ 326800	SLAEC	ROMAN Fish Jones 1978 Seeds Dean 1978b Insects Girling 1978 Animal bones Rixson 1978
100. Hibernia Wharf	TQ 326803 327803	SLAEC	ROMAN Wood Slack, Tyers, White unpub.
101. Southwark Cathedral	TQ 327802	SLAEC	ROMAN Animal bone in Hammerson 1976
102. 1–7 St. Thomas Street	TQ 327801	SLAEC	ROMAN Seeds Willcox 1978 Insects Girling 1978 Fish Jones 1978 Animal bone Rixson 1978

Site	Grid	Excavator	Evidence and date
103. Bonded warehouse Montague Close	TQ 327803	SLAEC	ROMAN, MED. Seeds, wood, insects in Dean 1978e Animal bone Rixson 1978
104. New Hibernia Wharf	TQ 327803	SLAEC	ROMAN, MED. Molluscs
105. Hibernia Chambers	TQ 327803	SLAEC	ROMAN Seeds
106. District Heating Scheme Tooley Street	TQ 327803 330802	SLAEC	ROMAN Seeds Paradine unpub. Grain Arthur unpub.
107. New Guy's House 1951	TQ 328799	Marsden	Roman boat Shell Castell 1965 Plant remains in Marsden 1965
108. 20 Southwark Street	TQ 328804 ?	Kenyon	LATE ROMAN, TUDOR Fish Barfield in Kenyon 1959 Birds Lawford in Kenyon 1959
109. Kings Head Yard	TQ 328803	Kenyon	ROMAN, MED. Animal bone in Kenyon 1959
110. Toppings & Sun Wharves 1970–2	TQ 328803	SLAEC	LATE PREHISTORIC, ROMAN, MED. Animal bone Rixson 1974 Shellfish Thomas 1974
111. Bonhill Street Finsbury Square	TQ 329821	ILAU	POST MED. Soil samples Locker unpub.
112. Rephidim Street	TQ 329792	SLAEC	ROMAN Soil samples unpub.
114. Grounds of Guy's Hospital	TQ 330798 approx.	Spurrell	ROMAN Plant remains Spurrell 1885
115. Willsons Wharf	TQ 331802	SLAEC	LBA, EIA Pollen Scaife 1981 LR Seeds Slack in prep.
116. Churchfield, Edmonton	TQ 326949	Gillam	RB Wood Balfour Brown 1953
117. Stoke Newington	TQ 334868 342869	Worthington Smith	PALAEOLITHIC Animal bone Worthington Smith 1894 Wood Worthington Smith 1894
118. Mark Browns Wharf, 1973	TQ 334801	SLAEC	POST MED. Wood Slack in prep. Soil samples in prep.
119. 27–33 Artillery Lane	TQ 335817	ILAU	ROMAN, MED. DISTURBED Animal bones Locker unpub.
120. Tower Hill 1978	TQ 336807	ILAU	ROMAN Animal bone Locker 1980 Shellfish Locker 1980
121. The Postern, Tower Hill, 1978	TQ 336807	ILAU	POST MED. Animal bones Locker future work

	Site	Grid	Excavator	Evidence and date
122.	Goodmans Yard 1978	TQ 337809	ILAU	ROMAN, TUDOR Animal bone Locker 1980 Human bone Locker 1980 Shellfish Locker 1980 Fish Locker 1980
123.	Tower of London Jewel House	TQ 338805	Pearce	ROMAN Animal bones Harcourt unpub.
124.	Gardiners Corner, Aldgate 1980	TQ 338812	ILAU	MED. POST MED. Animal bone Locker in prep. Soil samples Locker in prep. Cattle horn cores Armitage in prep. Wood Watson 1982 LR
125.	Croyham Hurst, Croydon 1968/9	TQ 338631	Drewett	MES. NEO. BA Pollen not preserved in Drewett 1970
126.	55 Northwold Road, 1980	TQ 340862	ILAU	PALAEOLITHIC Pollen Gibbard & Harding in prep.
127.	Lincoln Road, Enfield	TQ 341949	Enfield Arch. Soc.	ROMAN Animal bone Armitage 1977b
128.	Stoke Newington 1971	TQ 342360	Campbell	PALAEOLITHIC Campbell and Cook in prep.
129.	Shore Road, E9	TQ 351841	ILAU	MED. POST MED. Animal bone Locker unpub.
130.	Shadwell 1974	TQ 353808	Johnson	ROMAN Animal bones Locker 1983 LR Seeds Willcox 1977 Animal bones Locker future work
131.	High Street, Stepney	TQ 358815	ILAU	POST MED. Animal bones Locker 1983
132.	Butcher Row, Ratcliffe	TQ 359809	ILAU	MED. POST MED. Animal bone Locker 1977 Turtle Armitage and McCarthy 1980
133.	Le Fevre Road, Old Ford, 1969–70	TQ 368835	Sheldon	ROMAN Animal bone Rixson 1971
134.	Parnell Road/Appian Road, 1971	TQ 369836	Sheldon	ROMAN Animal bones Rixson 1972
135.	Usher Road, 1972–5	TQ 369835	SLAEC	ROMAN Animal bones Locker 1979
136.	Chestnuts Megalithic Tomb, Addington	TQ 371642	Alexander	PREHISTORIC Animal bone Barfield 1961
137.	Church Meadow Addington	TQ 372638	Thornhill	MED. Animal bone in Thornhill 1972
138.	Church Road, Leyton	TQ 375868	PEM	ROMAN Animal bone, insects, wood in Locker 1978
139.	Sewardstone	TQ 375970	Phillips	MES ? CANOE Snails Kennard 1936

	Site	Grid	Excavator	Evidence and date
140.	Greenwich Palace	TQ 385780	Dixon	POST MED. Animal bones Harman in prep.
141.	Greenwich Park 1978–9	TQ 390775	SLAEC	ROMAN Buried soil Fisher in Sheldon and Yule 1979
142.	Bakers Row West Ham, 1974	TQ 391831	PEM	MED. POST MED. Animal bone Locker future work Soil samples Locker future work
143.	West Ham Church Street 1973	TQ 391836	PEM	MED. POST MED. Animal bone Locker future work Soil samples Locker future work
144.	North Pole Lane, West Wickham	TQ 401640	WKAFG	IA, RB Animal bone Harman 1973
145.	South Woodford	TQ 405900 approx.	Wymer	PALAEOLITHIC Bone in text Wymer 1980
146.	Lower Warbank, Keston	TQ 414632	WKAFG	EARLY MED. Animal bone Harman 1973
147.	Keston Ritual Shaft, 1960 1980	TQ 415632	Piercy Fox Philp	ROMAN Animal bone in Piercy Fox 1967 Charcoal in Piercy Fox 1967 Animal bone Locker unpub.
148.	Keston 1854	TQ 415632	Corner	ROMAN Animal bones in Corner 1854
149.	Caesar's Camp Keston	TQ 423638	Piercy Fox	IA Soil in Piercy Fox 1967 Pollen in Piercy Fox 1967
150.	Eltham Palace	TQ 424740	Woods	MED. TUDOR Charcoal Keepax 1978 Seeds Monk 1978 Seeds Paradine 1980
151.	Warbank Keston	TQ 424636	Piercy Fox	RB Animal bones Caweek & Davis 1955
152.	Ilford Hospital 1959	TQ 435863	PEM	POST MED. Animal bone future work Human bone
153.	Camden Park Chiselhurst	TQ 435705	Latter	ROMAN Animal bone in Latter 1858
154.	Ilford Maison Riche 1959	TQ 435865	PEM	POST MED. Animal bone future work
155.	Albert Dockyard	TQ 440800		ROMAN CANOE Wood 1890
156.	East Ham 1958	TQ 440835	Banks	LATE MES/EARLY NEO. Animal bone Banks 1961 Pollen Franks 1961
157.	Barking Abbey 1971	TQ 440840	PEM	MED. POST MED. Animal bone future work

	Site	Grid	Excavator	Evidence and date
158.	Ilford	TQ 453871	West *et al.*	PLEISTOCENE Pollen West *et al.* 1964 Flora West *et al.* 1964 Fauna Rolfe 1958, Woodward and Davies 1874, Hinton 1900, Johnson 1900
159.	Havering Park, 1975	TQ 499929	PEM	ROMAN Animal bone future work
160.	Dagenham Church St. 1976	TQ 500846	PEM	MED. POST MED. Animal bone future work Charcoal future work
161.	Joydens Wood, Bexley	TQ 500715	Eunston	ROMAN Charcoal Erwood 1928
162.	Crayford	TQ 517761		PLEISTOCENE Kennard 1944 Chandler 1914 Burchell 1935
163.	Bowmans Lodge	TQ 518738	Tester	PALAEOLITHIC Oysters in Tester 1951
164.	Aveley	TQ 552807	Blezard	PLEISTOCENE Pollen West 1969 Mollusca Cooper 1972 Fauna Blezard 1966
165.	Rainham Moor Hall Farm 1977, 1979	TQ 555815	PEM	BA, IA, ROMAN Soil samples future work Locker Animal bone future work Locker
166.	Stubbers Youth Camp, Havering 1972	TQ 575847	PEM	ROMAN, POST MED. Animal bone future work
167.	Beredens (M25) 1976	TQ 577897	PEM	MED. POST MED. Animal bone future work
168.	Tilbury Fort	TQ 651755	PEM	POST MED. Soil samples future work

ABBREVIATIONS

E. Med	Early Medieval
Med.	Medieval
Post—Med.	Post—Medieval
DUA	Department of Urban Archaeology
GM	Guildhall Museum
GRIMES	Professor Grimes
LII	Level two (catalogue sheets, species lists, photographs etc.)
LIII	Level three (unpublished archival report)
LIV	Level four (published report)

No.	Site & date	Grid Ref.	Unit	Evidence
1	Tudor Street 1978	TQ 3152 8095	DUA	Med. Post Med. Soil samples, bone, dendro LII: animal bone (Armitage & West 1978–80) LIII: fish bone (Locker 1980a) Dendro (Hillam 1980d) LIV: microfossils (Boyd 1981b) also: Ripscote St. LIII dendro (Hillam 1980g) Bridewell LIII dendro (Hillam 1980f)
2	Ludgate Hill 1974, 1982	TQ 3178 8118	DUA	Roman, Med. Soil samples, bone, wood LIII: wooden hurdles (Straker 1982d) Med. Equid bones (Wilkinson 1983)
3	Central Criminal Court 1966–69	TQ 3180 8135	GM	Roman, Med. Bone LIII: animal bone (Armitage 1979c)
4	Mermaid Theatre 1979	TQ 3182 8090	DUA	Roman Soil samples, dendro LIII: dendro (Hillam 1979a) fish bones (Jones unpublished) LIV: dendro (Hillam & Herbert 1980)
5	St. Bartholomew's Hospital 1979	TQ 3186 8152	DUA	Roman, Post—Med. Soil samples, bone LII: Roman human bone (Downs 1979a; West 1980b) Roman animal bone (Armitage 1980c) LIII: soil analysis (MacPhail 1980c) LIV: Post—Med. sawn human bone (West and Armitage 1980) Roman human skeletons (Downs 1980; West and Downs in Bentley and Pritchard in press)
6	Upper Thames Street 1975 (Roman riverside wall)	TQ 3190 8088	DUA	Roman, Med. Post—Med. Soil samples, bone, dendro LIV: seeds and molluscs (Willcox 1980a) mammal bones (King 1980) fish bones (Jones 1980) wool (Ryder 1977, 1980) dendro (Hillam and Morgan 1979, Morgan 1980b)

No.	Site & date	Grid Ref.	Unit	Evidence
7	Baynard's Castle 1972–3	TQ 3195 8084	GM	Med., Post–Med. Bone LIII: mammalian bone (Armitage 1977a) LIV: computer recording system for animal bones (Armitage 1978b) bird bone (wild) (Bramwell 1975a) bird bone (domestic) (Carey 1982) Med. rat flea (Marsh 1982)
8	Baynard's Castle 1981	TQ 3195 8084	DUA	Med., Post–Med. Soil samples, bone, wood LII: wood (Straker 1981a) animal hair (Med.) (Armitage 1981a) LIII: seeds, straw/grass and rushes (Med.) (Davies 1982) seed (Med.) (Pritchard 1982)
9	St. Peter's Hill 1981	TQ 3198 8092	DUA	Roman, E. Med., Med. Soil samples, bone, dendro, wood LII: wood (Straker), rest unprocessed
10	Horn Tavern 1982	TQ 3203 8101	DUA	E. Med. Soil samples, bone, all unprocessed
11	General Post Office, 1975	TQ 3204 8135	DUA	Roman, E. Med., Med. soil samples, bone, charcoal LII: wood and charcoal (Squirrell) LIII: seeds and charcoal (Roman) (Davis 1983a, Straker 1982c) animal bone (Roman) (West 1983a) human skeletons (Med.) (White 1983) soil analysis (Macphail 1980d) LIV: human bone (Med.) (Morgan 1978) soil analysis (Macphail 1981)
12	G.P.O. middle area, 1979	TQ 3206 8136	DUA	Med., Post–Med. Soil samples, bone LII: fish bone (Post–Med.) (Locker 1982b) large mammal and bird bones (Post–Med.) (West 1982b) small mammal bone (Post–Med.) (Armitage 1983 in progress) LIII: soil analysis (Macphail 1980d) LIV: soil analysis (Macphail 1981)
13	Trig Lane 1974	TQ 3208 8086	DUA	Med. Post–Med. Soil samples, bone, wood LII: wood (Squirrell) LIII: seeds (Willcox) fish bone (Jones) LIV: Med. bone spectacles (Armitage 1982e) Dendro (Brett 1982 in press)
14	Foster Lane 1982	TQ 3219 8131	DUA	Roman, E. Med., Med., Post–Med. Soil samples, bone, all unprocessed
15	St. Mildred's Church 1973	TQ 3228 8099	GM	Roman, E. Med. Bone LIV: mammal bone (Clutton-Brock 1975) bird bone (Bramwell 1975)

No.	Site & date	Grid Ref.	Unit	Evidence
16	Milk Street 1976	TQ 3235 8124	DUA	Roman, E. Med., Med. Soil samples, bone, dendro, charcoal LII: hairs from Med. textiles (Armitage 1983d) LIII: Roman seeds (Davis 1983a) charcoal (Straker 1982c) Roman animal bone (West 1983a) E. Med. seeds (Straker and Davis 1982) dendro (Hillam 1980b)
17	Watling Court 1978	TQ 3235 8105	DUA	Roman, E. Med., Med. Soil samples, bone, dendro LII: charcoal (Squirrell) LIII: Roman seeds (Davis 1983a) dendro (Hillam 1980e) Roman animal bones (West 1983a)
18	Well Court 1979	TQ 3245 8108	DUA	E. Med., Med. Soil samples, bone, all unprocessed
19	Thames Street Tunnel 1978	TQ 3241 8083	DUA	Roman Soil samples, dendro LIII: dendro (Hillam 1980c)
20	Cannon Street 1975	TQ 3244 8097	DUA	Roman Animal bone LIII: animal bone (Bird and Armitage 1979a) LIV. animal bone, summary only (Bird and Armitage 1979b) human bone (Morgan 1979)
21	College Hill 1981	TQ 3250 8087	DUA	Med. bone LII: human bone (West 1981a)
22	Ironmonger Lane 1980	TQ 3250 8124	DUA	Roman, E. Med. Soil samples, bone LIII: Saxon horse skeleton (Armitage 1981b) Roman seeds (in progress)
23	Mason's Avenue 1978	TQ 3258 8137	DUA	Roman Soil samples, bone LIII: dendro (Hillam 1980a)
24	Temple of Mithras 1954	TQ 3260 8090	Grimes	Roman Soil sample LIII: pollen (Scaife 1981c)
25	Cannon Street 1981	TQ 3272 8090	DUA	Roman Soil samples, bone, all unprocessed
26	Swan Lane 1981	TQ 3273 8070	DUA	E. Med., Med. Soil samples, bone, wood, dendro LIII: wood (Straker 1982f) diatoms (Battarbee 1981)

No.	Site & date	Grid Ref.	Unit	Evidence
27	Copthall Avenue 1981	TQ 3275 8148	DUA	Roman, E. Med., Med., Post–Med. Soil samples, bone, wood, dendro LII: seeds from selected contexts (Roman and Med.) (Askew and Moriarty 1982b) LIII: ostracods (Med.) (Whittaker, 1982) wood (Straker 1982a)
28	Seal House 1974	TQ 3277 8067	DUA	Med. Bone, dendro LIV: dendro (Morgan 1976, 1977, Morgan and Schofield 1978)
29	Angel Court 1974	TQ 3283 8136	DUA	Roman, Med. LIV: animal bone (Clutton-Brock and Armitage 1977) fish bone (Wheeler 1977) bird bone (Gask 1977)
30	Miles Lane 1979	TQ 3284 8075	DUA	Roman, E. Med. Soil samples, bone, dendro, wood LIII: Roman horse skeleton (Armitage 1981c) dendro (Hillam 1982a) Wood (Straker 1981b)
31	Clements Lane 1981	TQ 3287 8095	DUA	Roman, Med. Soil samples, bone, charcoal LII: Roman charcoal (Straker 1982b)
32	Pudding Lane 1981	TQ 3294 8072	DUA	Roman, E. Med., Med. Soil samples, bone, wood, dendro LII: sub-Roman seeds and molluscs (Moriarty, Askew, Straker) LIII: diatoms (Battarbee 1983)
33	New Fresh Wharf 1974, 5 and 8	TQ 3295 8066	DUA	Roman, E. Med., Med. Post–Med. Soil samples, bone, dendro, wood LII: wood (Squirrell) Roman leather (Armitage 1983b) LIII: mammal bones (Armitage 1979d) bird bone (Carey and Armitage 1979) fish bone (Locker 1979c) LIV: Roman seeds (Willcox 1977)
34	Peninsular House 1979	TQ 3295 8070	DUA	Roman, E. Med. Soil samples, bone, wood, dendro LIII: wood (Straker 1980) dendro (Hillam 1982b) pollen (Scaife 1983) LIV: fish bones (Roman) (Bateman & Locker 1982)
35	Billingsgate 1982	TQ 3304 8065	DUA	Roman, E. Med., Med., Post–Med. Soil samples, bone, dendro LII: human skeletons (West 1983b)
36	Billingsgate Buildings, 1974 (formerly known as the 'Triangle')	TQ 3301 8069	DUA	Roman, Med. Bone, seeds, dendro LIV: mammal bones (Armitage 1980e) Roman mule (Armitage and Chapman 1979)

No.	Site & date	Grid Ref.	Unit	Evidence
36 (contd)	Billingsgate Buildings, 1974 (formerly known as the 'Triangle')	TQ 3301 8069	DUA	LIV: fish bone (Wheeler 1980) bird bone (Cowles 1980) oyster shells (Llewellyn–Jones and Pain 1980) human bone (Morgan 1980) seeds (Roman) (Willcox 1977) environment (Willcox 1980b) dendro (Morgan 1980a)
37	Forum South East 1976	TQ 3306 8095	DUA	Roman carbonised grain LIII: grain (Boyd 1980) LIV: grain (Straker in press)
38	Bishopsgate 1982	TQ 3310 8126	DUA	Roman, Med. Soil samples, bone, all unprocessed
39	Lloyds, Leadenhall, 1978	TQ 3314 8104	DUA	Roman, Med. Soil samples, bone LIII: soil analysis (Macphail 1980a) LIV: Med. bone skate (West in press)
40	Custom House 1973	TQ 3315 8061	GM	Roman, Med. Organic, molluscs, bone, dendro, wood LII: wood (Squirrell) LIV: molluscs (Rigby 1974) organic remains (Dimbleby 1974) animal bone (Fleck–Abbey and King 1975) dendro (Fletcher 1974, 1975, Hillam 1979b)
41	Harp Lane 1974	TQ 3316 8067	DUA	Roman Bone, unprocessed
42	Alderman's House 1982	TQ 3321 8153	DUA	Roman, Post–Med. Bone, unprocessed
43	Bevis Marks 1980	TQ 3335 8130	DUA	Roman, Med. Post–Med. Soil samples, bone, all unprocessed
44	Cutler Street 1978	TQ 3340 8150	DUA	Roman, Med., Post–Med. Soil samples, bone, cattle horn cores LII: human skeletons (Roman) (West 1981b) LIII: seeds (Post–Med.) (Straker and Davis 1981) cattle horn cores (Post–Med.) (Armitage 1979a) arthropods (Post–Med.) (Girling 1982) LIV: horn core lined pits (Armitage and O'Connor Thompson in prep.)
45	Holy Trinity Priory, 1979	TQ 3345 8118	DUA	Med. Bone LII: human skeletons (Downs 1979b)
46	Dukes Place 1977	TQ 3349 8120	DUA	Roman, Med., Post–Med. Soil samples, bone, all unprocessed

No.	Site & date	Grid Ref.	Unit	Evidence
47	Rangoon Street 1982	TQ 3352 8101	DUA	Roman, E. Med., Med., Post–Med. Soil samples, bone LII: human skeletons
48	Sir John Cass School 1972	TQ 3353 8105	GM	Roman, Med., Post–Med. Bone LIII: animal bone (Armitage 1979b)
49	Crosswall 1979	TQ 3360 8100	DUA	Roman, Post–Med. Soil samples, bone, cattle horn cores LII: cattle horn cores (Armitage 1979e) small mammal bones (Roman) (Armitage 1983a) seeds (Roman) (Davis 1983b) LIV: fish bone (Post–Med.) (Locker 1981a) bird bone (Post–Med.) (West 1981c) mammal bones (Post–Med.) (Armitage 1981e) Angora rabbit (Post–Med.) (Armitage 1981d)
50	Aldgate 1974	TQ 3371 8118	DUA	Med., Post–Med. Bone LIII: mammal bones (Armitage 1983f) bird bone (West 1983c) fish bone (Locker 1982c) LIV: faunal remains (Armitage 1983h in press)
51	Mansell Street 1982	TQ 3388 8116	DUA	Post–Med. bone, cattle horn cores LIII: human skeletons (West 1982a)
52	Finsbury Circus	TQ 3285 8152	–	Roman Seeds LIV: seeds (Willcox 1977)
BW	Bull Wharf	TQ 3233 8077	DUA	LIII: dendro (Hillam 1981b)
FS	Fenchurch Street 1983	TQ 3303 8092	DUA	Roman, Med., Post–Med. Soil samples, bone LIV: Roman rat bones (Armitage, West and Steedman 1984) rest unprocessed

REFERENCES

ADDY J, 1874

'Account of a Roman Villa lately discovered at Beddington, Surrey', *Surrey Archaeol Collect* 6, 118–121.

ADDYMAN P V, 1982

'The archaeologist's desiderata', in Hall A R and Kenward H K (eds), *Environmental Archaeology in the Urban Context*, Counc Brit Archaeol Res Rep No. 43, 1–5.

ADDYMAN P V, HOOD J S R, KENWARD H K, MACGREGOR A, WILLIAMS D, 1976

'Palaeoclimate in urban environmental archaeology at York, England: problems and potential', *World Archaeol* 8, 220–33.

AKEROYD A V, 1972

'Archaeological and historical evidence for subsidence in Southern Britain', *Phil Trans Roy Soc London A* 222, 151–169.

ARMITAGE P L, 1975

'The extraction and identification of opal phytoliths from the teeth of ungulates', *J Archaeol Sci* 2, 187–97.

ARMITAGE P L, 1977a

The Mammalian Remains from the Tudor Site of Baynard's Castle, London: A Biometrical and Historical Analysis, unpublished PhD Thesis, University of London.

ARMITAGE P L, 1977b

'The animal bones from areas 149 and 5', in Gentry A *et al.* 'Excavations at Lincoln Road, London Borough of Enfield, November 1974–March 1976', *Trans London Middlesex Archaeol Soc* 28, 181–187.

ARMITAGE P L, 1977c

'The Faunal Remains', in Ivens J and Deal G, 'Excavations in Roman Enfield', *London Archaeol* 3 (No. 3), 59–65.

ARMITAGE P L, 1978a

'Hertfordshire cattle and London meat markets in the seventeenth and eighteenth centuries', *London Archaeol* 3 (No. 8), 217–223.

ARMITAGE P L, 1978b

'A system for the recording and processing of data relating to animal remains from archaeological sites', in Brothwell D, Thomas K, Clutton-Brock J (eds), *Research Problems in Zooarchaeology* Institute of Archaeology London Occasional Publication No. 3, 39–45.

ARMITAGE P L, 1978c

'The Faunal Remains', in Armitage P and Ivens J, 'Excavations at Palace Gardens, Enfield 1977', *London Archaeol* 3 (No. 6), 143–148.

ARMITAGE P L, 1979a

Preliminary report on the cattle horn cores from the trial hole, number two, Cutler Street Warehouses, London (CUT 78), Level III report, AML Report 2803.

ARMITAGE P L, 1979b

The mammalian remains from the Roman, medieval and post medieval refuse pits; Sir John Cass Primary School, London, (CASS 72, ER 1358). Level III report, AML Report 2804.

ARMITAGE P L, 1979c

The mammalian remains from the Roman and medieval levels; Central Criminal Court Extension (1966–69), Level III report, AML Report 2805.

ARMITAGE P L, 1979d

The mammalian remains from the Roman, Medieval and Early Modern levels; St Magnus, City of London, Level III Report, AML Report 2806.

ARMITAGE P L, 1979e

Cattle horn cores from post–medieval pits, Crosswall 1979, unpublished level II archival report, Museum of London.

ARMITAGE P L, 1979f

'A preliminary description of British cattle from the late 12th to the early 16th century AD', in Kubasiewicz M (ed) *Archaeozoology Vol. 1,* (Proceedings of the IIIrd Archaeo-zoological Conference, Szczecin, Poland 1978), Szczecin, Poland: Agricultural Academy, 402–414.

ARMITAGE P L, 1980a

Report of the study carried out on the spectacles from Trig Lane, City of London. (TL 74). AML Report 3127.

ARMITAGE P L, 1980b

Report on the study of the Diptych showing the Crucifixion of Christ, from Baynard's Castle, City of London, AML Report 3128.

ARMITAGE P L, 1980c

Identifications of mammalian bone from Roman levels, St Bartholomew's Hospital site, (BAR 79), City of London, AML Report 3129.

ARMITAGE P L, 1980d

'A preliminary description of British cattle from the late twelfth to the early sixteenth century', *The Ark,* (Journal of the Rare Breeds Survival Trust), 7 (No. 12), 405–12.

ARMITAGE P L, 1980e

'Mammalian remains', in Jones D M and Rhodes M (eds) *Excavations at Billingsgate Buildings, (Triangle), Lower Thames St. London 1974,* London Middlesex Archaeol Soc Special Paper No. 4, 149–161.

ARMITAGE P L, 1980f

Report on the animal hairs found attached to metal 'leaves' from the medieval levels, Trig Lane. (TL 74), AML Report 3126.

ARMITAGE P L, 1981a

Report on the Animal Hairs from Baynard's Castle (BYD81), unpublished level II archival report, Museum of London.

ARMITAGE P L, 1981b

Late Anglo-Saxon Horse Skeleton from Ironmonger Lane 1980, unpublished level III archival report, Museum of London.

ARMITAGE P L, 1981c

Roman Horse Skeleton from Miles Lane 1979, unpublished level III archival report, Museum of London.

ARMITAGE P L, 1981d

'Remains of an Angora rabbit from a late 18th century pit at Crosswall', *London Archaeol* 4 (No. 4), 87–95.

ARMITAGE P L, 1981e

'Faunal Remains' in Maloney J (ed) 'The contents of a late 18th century pit at Crosswall, City of London', *London Middlesex Archaeol Soc* No. 32, 159–181.

ARMITAGE P L, 1982a

Report on the animal bone with ballista bolt from the Tower of London, unpublished level II archival report, Museum of London.

ARMITAGE P L, 1982b

'Studies on the remains of domestic livestock from Roman, Medieval and Early Modern London; objectives and methods', in Hall A R and Kenward H K (eds), *Environmental Archaeology in the Urban Context. Counc Brit Archaeol Res Rep* No. 43, 94–106.

ARMITAGE P L, 1982c

'A system for ageing and sexing the horn cores of cattle from British post—medieval sites with special reference to unimproved British longhorn cattle', in Wilson B, Grigson C and Payne S (eds), *Ageing and Sexing Animal Bones from Archaeological Sites, Brit Archaeol Rep (Brit Ser)* 109, 37–54.

ARMITAGE P L, 1982d

'Developments in British cattle husbandry from the Romano—British period to early modern times', *The Ark* 9 (No. 12), 50–54.

ARMITAGE P L, 1982e

'Note on the source of the material used in the manufacture of the spectacles', in Rhodes M 'A pair of fifteenth-century spectacle frames from the City of London', *Antiq J* 62, 67–73.

ARMITAGE P L, 1983a

Report on the Faunal Remains from the Sieved Soil Samples from the Roman Ditch, Crosswall 1979, unpublished level II archival report, Museum of London.

ARMITAGE P L, 1983b

Identification of the Leather from the Roman Contexts New Fresh Wharf (NFW74) and St. Magnus (SM75), unpublished level II archival report, Museum of London.

ARMITAGE P L, 1983c

'The early history of English longwool sheep', *The Ark* 10 (No. 3), 90–97.

ARMITAGE P L, 1983d

Report on the Animal Hair Fibres from Medieval Textiles, Milk Street 1976, unpublished level II archival report, Museum of London.

ADMITAGE P L, 1983e

'Jaw of a South American monkey from Brooks Wharf, City of London', *London Archaeol* 4 (No. 10), 262–270.

ARMITAGE P L, 1983f

The Mammalian Bones from the Post—Medieval Contexts, Aldgate 1974, unpublished level III archival report, Museum of London.

ARMITAGE P L, 1983g in press

'Preliminary report on the cattle horn cores from Greyfriars (Site B) Oxford', in Hassall T, 'Post—medieval material from the St. Ebbes survey area of Oxford', *Oxoniensia.*

ARMITAGE P L, 1983h in press

'The mammalian bones', in Thompson A, Schofield J and Grew F, 'Excavations at Aldgate 1974', *Post Medieval Archaeol.*

ARMITAGE P L, CHAPMAN H, 1979

'Roman Mules', *London Archaeol* 3 (No. 13), 339–346 and 349.

ARMITAGE P L, CLUTTON-BROCK J, 1976

'A system for classification and description of the horn-cores of cattle from archaeological sites', *J Archaeol Sci* 3, 329–48.

ARMITAGE P L, O'CONNOR THOMPSON S, in preparation

Late 17th and early 18th Century horn-core lined pits from Cutlers Gardens, City of London.

ARMITAGE P L, DAVIS A, STRAKER V, WEST B, 1983

'Bugs, bones and botany', *Popular Archaeol* 4 (No. 9), 24–34 and 4 (No. 10), 24–27.

ARMITAGE P L, GOODALL J, 1977

'Medieval horned and polled sheep: The archaeological and iconographic evidence', *Antiq J* 57, 73–89.

ARMITAGE P L, IVENS J, 1980

'28–32 Upsdell Avenue, N13', in Armitage P, Coxshall R and Ivens J 'Early agricultural land drains in the former parishes of Edmonton and Enfield', *London Archaeol* 3 (No. 15), 408–415.

ARMITAGE P L, McCARTHY C, 1980 — 'Turtle remains from a late 18th century well at Leadenhall Buildings', *London Archaeol* 4 (No. 1), 8–15.

ARMITAGE P L, STRAKER V, 1982 — *Report on the Biological Remains,* in Green C 'Excavations at Fulham Pottery, London SW6 1971–9', forthcoming.

ARMITAGE P L, WEST B A, 1980 — *The Faunal Remains from the Medieval and Tudor Levels, Tudor Street 1978,* unpublished level II archival report, Museum of London.

ARMITAGE P L, WEST B A, 1982 — 'Report on the mammalian remains from the two Roman wells, Queen Street 1954 (ER81 and ER254)', in Wilmott T, 'Excavations on Queen Street 1953–60 and Roman timber lined wells in London', *Trans London Middlesex Archaeol Soc* 33, 74–76.

ARMITAGE P L, WEST B A, STEEDMAN K, 1984 — 'New evidence of Black rat in Roman London', *London Archaeol* 4 (No. 14), 375–383.

ARTHUR J B, PARADINE P A, 1976 — *New Palace Yard, the seeds.* AML Report 1783.

ASKEW P, 1983 — *A Molluscan Fauna with Pomatias elegans from Pudding Lane, London,* Level II archival report, Museum of London.

ASKEW P, MORIARTY D, 1982a — *Billingsgate: Level II report on plant remains from post–medieval contexts,* Museum of London.

ASKEW P, MORIARTY D, 1982b — *Copthall Avenue: Roman and Medieval seeds (selected contexts from pits, ditches and peat layers,* Level II Archive, Museum of London.

ASKEW P, KERNEY M, 1983 — 'A molluscan fauna with *Pomatias elegans* from an archaeological site in the City of London', *Conchologist's Newsletter* No. 84, 65–6.

BAGFORD J, 1715 — *De Rebus Britannicus Collectanae,* London.

BANKS C, 1961 — 'Report on the Recently discovered Remains of the wild ox (*Bos primigenius* Bojanus) from East Ham', *London Naturalist* 41, 54–59.

BARFIELD L, 1961 — 'The Animal Bone' in J Alexander 'The Excavation of the Chestnuts Megalithic Tomb at Addington', *Archaeol Cantiana* 76, 1–57.

BARTON N J, 1962 — *The Lost Rivers of London,* London: Phoenix House.

BATEMAN N, LOCKER A, 1982 — 'The Sauce of the Thames', *London Archaeol* 4 (No. 8), 204–207.

BATTARBEE R, 1982 — *Swan Lane,* unpublished report, Museum of London.

BATTARBEE R, 1983 — *Pudding Lane: diatoms from Roman Thames foreshore deposits,* unpublished report, Museum of London.

BELL M, 1983 — *Mollusca from a Palaeochannel beside the Staines Causewayed Camp Surrey,* AML Report 3907.

BENTLEY D, PRITCHARD F, 1982 — 'The Roman Cemetery at St Bartholomew's Hospital', *Trans London Middlesex Archaeol Soc* 33, 134–172.

BERGQUIST H, 1957 — 'Skeletal finds of Black rat from the early middle ages', in Bergquist H and Lepiksaar J, *Animal Skeletal Remains from Medieval Lund,* Archaeology of Lund vol. I, 98–103, Sweden.

BIDDER F, 1908 — 'Excavations in an Anglo Saxon Burial Ground at Mitcham, Surrey', *Surrey Archaeol Collect* 21, 1–25.

BIDDLE M, HUDSON D, HEIGHWAY C, 1973 — 'The Future of London's Past: a survey of the archaeological implications of planning and development in the nation's capital', *Rescue Publication No. 4.*

BIEK L, 1961 'Scientific Evidence', in Hurst J, 'The Kitchen area of Northolt Manor, Middlesex', *Medieval Archaeol* 5, 254–299.

BIRD C, ARMITAGE P L, 1979a *The Mammalian Remains from the Roman and Medieval contexts, Cannon Street, London,* unpublished level III archival report, Museum of London.

BIRD C, ARMITAGE P L, 1979b 'Notes on the mammalian remains from the Roman, Saxon and medieval levels', in Boddington A, 'Excavations at 48–50 Cannon Street, City of London, 1975', *Trans London Middlesex Archaeol Soc* Vol. 30, 34.

BLACK G *The Archaeology of Tower Hamlets.*

BLEZARD R C, 1966 'Field meeting at Aveley and W Thurrock', *Proc Geol Ass* 77, 273–6.

BLURTON T R, 1977 'Excavations at Angel Court, Walbrook, 1974', *Trans London Middlesex Archaeol Soc* 28, 14–100.

BOYD P D A, 1980 *Carbonised cereals and associated weed seeds from Roman London AD 60,* AML Report 3135.

BOYD P D A, 1981a 'The Palaeoecology of Estuarine deposits associated with archaeological sites with particular reference to the City of London', in Brothwell D and Dimbleby G (eds), *Environmental Aspects of Coasts and Islands Symposium for the Association of Environmental Archaeology, Brit Archaeol Rep* International Ser No. 94, 84–88.

BOYD P D A, 1981b 'The micropalaeontology of medieval estuarine sediments from the Fleet and Thames in London', in Neale J W (ed), 'Micropalaeontology of shelf seas — fossil and recent', *Occasional publication of the British Micropalaeontological Association,* 274–292.

BRAMWELL D, 1975a 'Bird remains from medieval London', *London Naturalist* 54, 15–20.

BRAMWELL D, 1975b 'Bird remains', in Marsden P, Dyson T and Rhodes M, 'Excavations on the site of St. Mildred's Church, Bread Street, London, 1973–74', *Trans London Middlesex Archaeol Soc* 26, 207–208.

BRETT D W, 1982 'Dendrochronology', in Milne G and C, *Medieval Waterfront Development at Trig Lane, London,* London Middlesex Archaeol Soc Special Paper, in press.

BRODNIEWICZ A, 1969 'Das problem der Rattenbekämpfung in Polen während der letzen zwie Jahrzehnte (1945–1966)', *Schriftenreihe des Vereins für Wasser –, Boden – und Lufthygiene. Berlin* 32, 71–92.

BROTHWELL D, 1982 'Linking urban man with his urban environment', in Hall A R and Kenward H K (eds), *Environmental Archaeology in the Urban Context,* Counc Brit Archaeol Res Rep No. 43, 126–129.

BROTHWELL D, JONES R, 1978 'The relevance of small mammal studies to archaeology', in Brothwell D R, Thomas K D and Clutton-Brock J (eds), *Research Problems in Zooarchaeology,* Institute of Archaeology London Occasional Publication No. 3, 47–57.

BURCHELL J P, 1935 'Some Pleistocene deposits at Kirmington and Crayford', *Geol Mag* 72, 327–331.

BROWN J A, 1888   'On the discovery of Elephas primigenius, associated with flint implements, at Southall', *Proc Geol Ass London* 10, 361–372.

CALLOW W J *et al.*, 1964   'National Physical Laboratory Radiocarbon measurements II', *Radiocarbon* 6, 25–30.

CALLOW W J *et al.*, 1966   'National Physical Laboratory measurements IV', *Radiocarbon* 8, 340–7.

CAMPBELL J   *Excavations in 1971 north of Stoke Newington Common,* in prep with Mrs G M Cook.

CANHAM R, 1976   'The Iron Age', in Collins *et al., The Archaeology of the London Area; Current knowledge and Problems,* London Middlesex Archaeol Soc Special Paper No. 1, 42–49.

CANHAM R, 1978   'Some priorities and problems in the Prehistoric Archaeology of the Thames Basin', *Collectanea Londinensia. Studies presented to Ralph Merrifield,* London Middlesex Archaeol Soc Special Paper No. 2, 32–38.

CAREY G, 1982   'Ageing and sexing domestic bird bones from some late medieval deposits at Baynard's Castle, City of London', in Wilson B, Grigson C and Payne S (eds), *Ageing and Sexing Animal Bones from Archaeological Sites,* Brit Archaeol Rep (Brit Ser) 109, 263 268.

CAREY G, ARMITAGE P L, 1979   *The Bird Bones from the Roman, Medieval and Early Modern Levels, St. Magnus 1975,* unpublished level III archival report, Museum of London.

CARTER BLAKE C, 1868   'Bos longifrons', *Geol Mag* 5, 100–102.

CARWEEK I N, DAVIS A G, 1955   In Piercy Fox N 'Warbank, Keston: a Romano British site', *Archaeol Cantiana* 69, 96–116.

CASTELL C P, 1965   'The Molluscs', in Marsden Peter R V, 'A boat of the Roman period discovered on the site of New Guys House, Bermondsey 1951'. *Trans London Middlesex Archaeol Soc* 21, Pt II, 118–131.

CASTELL C P, 1971   'The Molluscs', in Marsden Peter R V 'Report on recent excavations in Southwark Part II', *Trans London Middlesex Archaeol Soc* 23, 19–41.

CELORIA F S C, THORN J C, 1974   'Excavations at 244–246 Borough High Street', *Trans London Middlesex Archaeol Soc* 25.

CHANDLER R H, 1914   'The Pleistocene deposits of Crayford', *Proc Geol Ass* 25, 61–71.

CHAPLIN R E   'Report on Animal Bone from a Saxon Occupation site, Whitehall, London', *Archaeozoological Research Report No. 2.*

CHAPLIN R E, 1971   *The Study of Animal Bones from Archaeological Sites,* London.

CLARK J, 1980   'Saint Erkenwald: Bishop and London archaeologist', *London Archaeol* 4 (No. 1), 3–7.

CLINCH G, 1907   'Recent discoveries at Wallington', *Surrey Archaeol Collect* 20, 233–5.

CLUTTON–BROCK J, 1975   'Mammalian remains', in Marsden P, Dyson T and Rhodes M, 'Excavations on the site of St. Mildred's Church, Bread Street, London 1973–74', *Trans London Middlesex Archaeol Soc* 26, 207–208.

CLUTTON–BROCK J, 1978   'The Animal Bones', in Arthur P and Whitehouse K, 'Report on Excavations at Fulham Palace Moat 1972–3', *Trans London Middlesex Archaeol Soc* 29, 45–72, 69–70.

CLUTTON–BROCK J, 1982   'British cattle in the 18th century', *The Ark* 9 (No. 2), 55–59.

CLUTTON–BROCK J, ARMITAGE P L, 1977   'Mammalian Remains from Trench A', in Blurton T R and Rhodes M (eds), 'Excavations at Angel Court, Walbrook, 1974', *Trans London Middlesex Archaeol Soc* 28, 88–97.

CLUTTON–BROCK J, GASK J, 1976   'Identification of the bones', in Marsden P 'Two Roman Public Baths in London', *Trans London Middlesex Archaeol Soc* 27, 68–9.

COLLINS D, 1976a   *The Human Revolution: From Ape to Artist,* London.

COLLINS D, 1976b   'Palaeolithic and Mesolithic', in Collins *et al. The Archaeology of the London Area: Current knowledge and problems,* London Middlesex Archaeol Soc Special Paper No. 1, 1–18.

COLLINS D, 1978   *Early Man in West Middlesex.* HMSO.

COLLS D, ETIENNE R, LEQUEMENT R, LIOU B, MAYET F, 1977   'L'Épave Port-Vendres II et le Commerce de la Bétique a l'epoque de Claude', *Archaeonautica* I, 40–43.

COOPE G R, ANGUS R B, 1975   'An ecological study of a temperate interlude in the middle of the last glaciation, based on fossil coleoptera from Isleworth', *J Animal Ecology* 44 (No. 2), 365–391.

COOPER J, 1972   'Last Interglacial (Ipswichian) non marine mollusca from Aveley, Essex', *Essex Naturalist* No. 33, 9–14.

COOPER J, 1978   *The Conchologist Newsletter*, No. 57, 490–492.

CORNER G R, 1854   'Excavations on the site of Roman Buildings at Keston, near Bromley, Kent', *Archaeologia* 36, pt 1.

COTTON J, 1981   'Excavations in Church Road, West Drayton 1979–80', *London Archaeol* 4 (No. 5), 121–129.

COWLES G, 1980   'The Bird Bones', in Jones D M (ed), *Excavations at Billingsgate Buildings (Triangle), Lower Thames Street, London 1974,* London Middlesex Archaeol Soc Special Paper No. 4, 163.

CUTLER D F, 1971   'The Charcoal', in Castle S A, 'Excavations at Brockley Hill, Middlesex 1970', *Trans London Middlesex Archaeol Soc* 23, 148–159.

CUTLER D F, 1974   In Castle S A 'Excavations at Brockley Hill, Middlesex, March–May 1970', *Trans London Middlesex Archaeol Soc* 25, 251–263.

DAVIS R W, 1971   'The Roman military diet', *Britannia* 2, 122–42.

DAVIS A, 1982   *Seeds, Straw/Grass and Rushes from Context 36 (? Stable Sweepings), Baynard's Castle (BYD81),* unpublished level II archival report, Museum of London.

DAVIS A, 1983a   *Plant Remains from Early Roman Buildings, West of the Walbrook,* unpublished level III archival report, Museum of London.

DAVIS A, 1983b   *Environmental Evidence from the Roman Defences, City of London,* unpublished level III archival report, Museum of London.

DAWSON G J, 1976   *The Black Prince's Palace at Kennington, Surrey,* Brit Archaeol Rep 26.

DEAN M, 1978a   'Organic data', in Feretti E and Graham A H, '201–211 Borough High Street', *Southwark Excavations 1972–4, Pt II, London Middlesex Archaeol Soc, Surrey Archaeol Soc*, Joint Publication No. 1, 168–170.

DEAN M, 1978b   'Organic data', in Sheldon H, '93–5 Borough High Street', *Southwark Excavations 1972–4, Pt II, London Middlesex Archaeol Soc, Surrey Archaeol Soc,* Joint Publication No. 1 465–467.

DEAN M, 1978c   'The Organic data', in Marsh G '8 Union Street', *Southwark Excavations 1972–4, Pt II. London Middlesex Archaeol Soc, Surrey Archaeol Soc,* Joint Publication No. 1, 231.

DEAN M, 1978d   'Organic data', in Schwab. I, '106–114 Borough High Street', Southwark Excavations 1972–4, Pt I, London Middlesex Archaeol Soc, Surrey Archaeol Soc, Joint Publication No. 1, 219–220.

DEAN M, 1978e   'Seeds, wood, insects, and molluscs' in Graham A, 'The bonded warehouse, Montague Close', Southwark Excavations 1972–4, Pt I, London Middlesex Archaeol Soc, Surrey Archaeol Soc, Joint Publication No. 1, 287.

DEAN M, 1981   'Evidence for more Roman burials in Southwark', *London Archaeol* 4 (No. 2), 52–3.

DEAN M, HAMMERSON M, 1980   'Three inhumation burials from Southwark', *London Archaeol* 4 (No. 1), 17–22.

DEFOE D, 1724 reprinted 1974   Cole G D H and Browning D C (eds), *A Tour Through the Whole Island of Great Britain,* London.

DELAIR J B, forthcoming   *The Pleistocene Mammalia of Greater London; a bibliogeographic study.*

DENSEM R, 1979   'Recent work in Lambeth', *London Archaeol* 3 (No. 9), 236.

DEVOY R J N, 1977   'Flandrian sea-level changes in the Thames Estuary and the implications for land subsidence in England and Wales', *Nature* 270, 712–715.

DEVOY R J N, 1979   'Flandrian sea-level changes and vegetational history of the Lower Thames Estuary', *Phil Trans Roy Soc London B* 285, 355–407.

DEVOY R J N, 1980   'Post-glacial Environmental Change and Man in the Thames Estuary: a synopsis', in Thompson F H (ed), *Archaeology and Coastal change, Soc Antiq Occasional Paper 1* (New Series). 134–148.

DIMBLEBY G W, 1974   'Analysis of organic remains', in Tatton–Brown T (ed), 'Excavations at the Custom House site, City of London 1973', *Trans London Middlesex Archaeol Soc* 25, 117–220.

D'OLIER B, 1972   'Subsidence and sea-level rise in the Thames Estuary', *Phil Trans Roy Soc London A* 272, 121–130.

DOWNS D L, 1979a   *Human Skeletal Remains, St. Bartholomew's Hospital 1979,* unpublished level II archival report, Museum of London.

DOWNS D L, 1979b   *Human Skeletal Remains, Holy Trinity Priory 1979,* unpublished level II archival report, Museum of London.

DOWNS D L, 1980   'Archaeology at Barts: Human skeletal remains', *The Bart's Journal,* Spring 1980, 20–23.

DUNHAM K C, 1972   'The Evidence for Subsidence', *Phil Trans Roy Soc London A* 272, 81–86.

DYSON T, SCHOFIELD J, 1981 — 'Excavations in the City of London, second interim report, 1974–1978', *Trans London Middlesex Archaeol Soc* 32, 24–81.

ERSTON ERWOOD F C, 1928 — 'Excavations at Joydens Wood, Bexley', *J Brit Archaeol Soc* 34, New Series. 165–197.

EVANS J — *New Palace Yard Molluscs,* AML Report 1785.

FERRETTI E, GRAHAM A, 1978 — '201–211 Borough High Street', *Southwark Excavations 1972–4, pt II, London Middlesex Archaeol Soc, Surrey Archaeol Soc,* Joint Publication No. 1, 63.

FISHER F J, 1935 — 'The development of the London food market, 1540–1640', *Economic History Review* V, 46–64.

FISHER P, 1979 — In Sheldon H and Yule B 'Excavations in Greenwich Park 1978–79', *London Archaeol* 3 (No. 12), 311–317.

FISHER P, 1980 — In Dean M, 'Excavations at Arcadia Buildings, Southwark', *London Archaeol* 3 (No. 14), 367–373.

FLECK–ABBEY A, KING A, 1975 — 'The Animal Bones', in Tatton Brown T, 'Excavations at the Custom House site, City of London', 1973, part II', *Trans London Middlesex Archaeol Soc* 26, 167–169.

FLETCHER J, 1974 — 'The dendrochronology', in Tatton Brown T, 'Excavations at the Custom House site, parts I and II', *Trans London Middlesex Archaeol Soc* 25, 211–215, Vol 26, 169–170.

FRANKS J, 1961 — 'Pollen analysis of peat from the Oaken Trough (section B) at East Ham Sewage Works', in Banks C, 'Report on the Recently Discovered Remains of the Wild Ox (*Bos primigenius* Bojanus) from East Ham', *London Naturalist* 41, 58.

FRANKS J W, SUTCLIFFE A J, KERNEY M P, COOPE G R, 1958 — 'Haunt of elephant and rhinoceros, the Trafalgar Square of 100,000 years ago – new discoveries', *Illustrated London News* 232, 1011–1013.

FRANKS J W, SUTCLIFFE A J, KERNEY M P, COOPE G R, 1960 — 'Interglacial deposits at Trafalgar Square', *New Phytol* 59, 149–152.

GASK J S, 1977 — 'The Bird Bones from Trench A', in Blurton T R and Rhodes M (eds), 'Excavations at Angel Court, Walbrook 1974', *Trans London Middlesex Archaeol Soc* 28, 88–97.

GENTRY A W, 1971 — 'The Animal Bone', in Castle S A, 'Excavations at Brockley Hill, Middlesex 1970', *Trans London Middlesex Archaeol Soc* 23, 148–159.

GIBBARD P L, COOPE G R, HALL A R, PREECE R C, ROBINSON J E, 1981 — 'Middle Devensian deposits beneath the upper floodplain terrace of the River Thames at Kempton Park, Sunbury, England', *Proc Geol Soc* 93(3), 275–289.

GILLAM G R, 1953 — *A Romano–British site at Edmonton, Middlesex,* No. 1, Sponsored by the Edmonton Hundred Historical Society.

GIRLING M, 1978a — 'The Insects', in Feretti E and Graham A H, '201–211 Borough High Street', *Southwark Excavations 1972–4, pt II, London Middlesex Archaeol Soc Surrey Archaeol Soc,* Joint Publication No. 1, 170.

GIRLING M, 1978b — In Dean M, 'The Organic data', in Sheldon H '93–5 Borough High Street, Southwark', *Southwark Excavations 1972–4, pt II. London Middlesex Archaeol Soc, Surrey Archaeol Soc,* Joint Publication No. 1, 465–467.

GIRLING M, 1978c   'The Insects from pits F28 and F29', in Dennis M G, '1–7 St Thomas' Street', *Southwark Excavations 1972–4 pt II, London Middlesex Archaeol Soc, Surrey Archaeol Soc,* Joint Publication No. 1, 414–415.

GIRLING M, 1979   *The Entomological Evidence for tanning from a post–medieval pit at Southwark,* AML Report 2735.

GIRLING M A, 1982   *The Arthropod Assemblage from Cutler's Gardens, London,* AML Report 3670.

GIRLING M, GREIG J, 1977   'Palaeoecological investigations of a site at Hampstead Heath, London', *Nature* Vol 268, No. 5615, 45–47.

GODWIN H, 1975   *A History of the British Flora,* Cambridge.

GOULD T H, 1948–51   'Finds on two sites by the Walbrook 1940 and 1946', *Trans London Middlesex Archaeol Soc* 10, 151–154.

GRAHAM A, 1978   'The Geology of North Southwark and its topographical development in the post–pleistocene period', *Southwark Excavations 1972–74, London Middlesex Archaeol Soc, Surrey Archaeol Soc,* Joint Publication No. 1, 501–517.

GREENSMITH J A, TUCKER E V, 1973   'Holocene transgressions and regressions on the Essex coast outer Thames Estuary', *Geol en Mijnb* 52, 193–202.

GREENWOOD P, 1982   'Excavations at Moor Hall Farm, Rainham', *London Archaeol* 7, 185–193.

GREIG J R A, 1979   *Report on Pollen Spectra from Cromwell Green, London,* AML Report 2745.

GRIGSON C, 1975   *The Englishman's Flora,* Everyman.

GRIGSON C, 1982   'Cattle in prehistoric Britain', *The Ark* 9 (No. 2), 47–49.

GRIMES W F, 1960   *Excavations on Defence sites 1939–45,* 1, 186–197.

GRIMES W F, 1968   *The Excavation of Roman and Medieval London,* London.

HARCOURT R   *Tower of London; Jewel House; the Animal Bones,* AML Report 1568.

HARMAN M, 1973   'The Animal Bones', in Philp B, 'A Romano–British site in North Pole Lane, West Wickham, Kent', *Excavations in West Kent 1960–1970,* 68–76.

HARMAN M, 1973   'The Animal Bones', in Philp B 'An Anglo-Saxon hut at Lower Warbank, Keston, Kent', *Excavations in West Kent 1960–1970,* 156–163.

HARMAN M, 1975   'The Animal Bones', in Dixon P 'Excavations at Richmond Palace, Surrey', *Post Medieval Archaeol* 9.

HARVEY J, 1981   *Medieval Gardens,* Batsford.

HICKS H, 1892   'On the discovery of mammoth and other remains in Endsleigh Street and on sections exposed in Endsleigh Gardens, Gordon Street, Gordon Square, and Tavistock Square, London', *Quarterly J Geol Soc London,* 48, 453–468.

HILL C, MILLET M, BLAGG T, 1980   *The Roman Riverside Wall and Monumental Arch in London,* London Middlesex Archaeol Soc Special Paper No. 3.

HILLAM J, 1979a   *Tree-ring dating in London: The Mermaid Theatre site (THE 79).* Interim Report. AML Report 3008.

HILLAM J, 1979b   *Tree-ring Analysis of further samples from the Medieval Custom House,* AML Report 3009.

HILLAM J, 1980a

Mason's Avenue: Interim dendrochronology report, AML Report 3255.

HILLAM J, 1980b

Milk Street: Interim dendrochronology report, AML Report 3256.

HILLAM J, 1980c

Thames Street Tunnel: Interim dendrochronology Report, AML Report 3257.

HILLAM J, 1980d

Tudor Street: Interim dendrochronology Report, AML Report 3258.

HILLAM J, 1980e

Watling Court: Interim Dendrochronology Report, AML Report 3259.

HILLAM J, 1980f

Dendrochronology; Bridewell, unpublished.

HILLAM J, 1980g

Kingscote Street (KSC 77) — Final Tree-ring Report.

HILLAM J, 1981a

'An English Tree-ring Chronology AD 404–1216', *Medieval Archaeol* 25, 31–44.

HILLAM J, 1981b

Bull Wharf — Interim Dendrochronology Report, AML Report 3560.

HILLAM J, 1982

Peninsular House; Dendrochronology Report, unpublished Level 3.

HILLAM J, HERBERT P, 1980

'Tree-ring dating: The Mermaid Theatre, City of London', *London Archaeol* 3 (No. 16), 439–444.

HILLAM J, MORGAN R A, 1979

'The dating of the Roman riverside Wall at three sites in London', *London Archaeol* 3 (No. 11), 283–288.

HILLAM J, MORGAN R, 1981a

Tree-ring analysis of timbers from New Fresh Wharf, London, AML Report 3562.

HILLAM J, MORGAN R A, 1981b

'What value is dendrochronology to waterfront archaeology?', in *Waterfront Archaeology in Britain and Northern Europe, Counc Brit Archaeol Res Rep No. 41,* 39–46.

HILLAM J, MORGAN R, 1981c

'Dendrochronology dates from Sheffield', in '*Absolute Chronology* 252 BC–209 AD', *Current Archaeol* 3 (No. 9), 286–287.

HILLAM J, 1982a

Miles Lane: dendrochronology, Level III Archive.

HINTON M A C, 1900

'The Pleistocene deposits of the Ilford and Wanstead district', *Proc Geol Ass* 16, 271–281.

HINTON M A C, 1926

'Monograph of the Voles and Lemmings (Microtinae)', *British Museum Catalogue* 1.

HOBLEY B, SCHOFIELD J, 1977

'Excavations in the City of London 1974–5', *Antiq J* 57, 31–66.

HOLLIM J T, 1977

'Thames Interglacial sites, Ipswichian sea levels and Antarctic ice surges', *Boreas* 6 (No. 1), 33–52.

HUBBARD R N L B, 1982

'The Environmental evidence from Swanscombe and its implications for Palaeolithic archaeology', in Leach P (ed), *Archaeology in Kent to AD 1500,* Counc Brit Archaeol Res Rep No. 48, 3–7.

HUBBARD R, 1976

'Pollen analysis; Interim results', in Collins D, *Early Man in West Middlesex,* HMSO, 15–19.

NOËL HUME I, 1978

'Into the jaws of death ..... walked one', in Bird J, Chapman H and Clark J (eds), *Collectanea Londiniensia. Studies in London archaeology and history presented to Ralph Merrifield,* London Middlesex Archaeol Soc Special Paper No. 2, 7–22.

INSTITUTE OF GEOLOGICAL SCIENCE, 1981 — *Solid and Drift Geology Map Sheet,* No. 270, F G Berry and K C Rollin. Scale 1:50,000.

JEWELL P, 1963 — 'Cattle from British archaeological sites', in Mourant A E and Zeuner F E (eds), *Man and Cattle,* London, 80–91.

JOHNSON J P, 1900 — 'Additions to the Palaeolithic fauna of the Uphill Brickyard, Ilford, Essex', *Essex Naturalist* II, 209–212.

JONES P E, 1976 — *The Butchers of London,* London.

JONES A K G, 1976 — 'The Fish Bones', in Black G, 'Excavations in the sub-vault of the misericorde of Westminster Abbey February–May 1975', *Trans London Middlesex Archaeol Soc* 27, 135–178.

JONES A K G, 1978a — 'The Fish', in Ferretti E and Graham A H, '201–211 Borough High Street', in *Southwark Excavations 1972–4 Pt II, London Middlesex Archaeol Soc, Surrey Archaeol Soc,* Joint Publication No. 1, 171.

JONES A K G, 1978b — In Dean M, 'Organic data', in Sheldon H '93–95 Borough High Street', *Southwark Excavations 1972–4, Pt II,* London Middlesex Archaeol Soc. Surrey Archaeol Soc, Joint Publication No. 1, 465–466.

JONES A K G, 1978c — 'The Fish remains', in Dennis M G, '1–7 St Thomas Street', *Southwark Excavations 1972–4, Pt II,* London Middlesex Archaeol Soc. Surrey Archaeol Soc, Joint Publication No. 1 414–416.

JONES A K G, 1980 — 'Fish bones from the Upper Thames Street section', in Hill C, Millett M and Blagg T, *The Roman Riverside Wall and Monumental Area in London,* London Middlesex Archaeol Soc Special Paper No. 3, 87–88.

JONES A K G, 1982 — 'Human parasite remains: prospects for a quantitative approach', in Hall A R and Kenward H K (eds), *Environmental Archaeology in the Urban Context,* Counc Brit Archaeol Res Rep No. 43, 66–70.

JONES A K G — *Mermaid Theatre: The Fish Bones,* Level III, unpublished, Museum of London.

JONES A K G — *Trig Lane: Fish Bones,* Level III, unpublished, Museum of London.

JOPE M, 1961 — 'The Bird Bones', in Hurst J, 'The Kitchen Area of Northolt Manor Middlesex', *Medieval Archaeol* 5, 254–299. Also AML Report 1529.

KEELEY H, SHELDON H, 1976 — 'Environmental Archaeology: a policy for London', *London Archaeol* 2 (No. 16), 415–416.

KEEPAX C, 1973 — 'Report on Environmental Investigations', in Alexander J and Farrant N, *Excavations at Bedfont 1971–2,* privately circulated.

KEEPAX C, 1978 — *Charcoal Identifications from Eltham Palace.* AML Report 2558.

KEEPAX C, 1980 — *Identification of a charcoal sample; Eltham Palace,* AML Report 3242.

KENNARD A S, 1936 — In Phillips C W, 'A dugout canoe from the Lea Valley', *Proc Prehist Soc* 2, 144.

KENNARD A S, 1944 — 'The Crayford Brickearths', *Proc Geol Ass* 55, 121–169.

KENNARD A S, WOODWARD B B, 1902 — 'On the non-marine mollusca from the Holocene deposits at London Wall and Westminster', *Proc Malacological Soc London 1902–3,* vol. 5, 180–182.

KENYON K, 1959a — '20 Southwark Street', in *Excavations in Southwark,* Res Papers Surrey Archaeol Soc No. 5, 27.

KENYON K, 1959b — 'Kings Head Yard', in *Excavations in Southwark,* Res Papers Surrey Archaeol Soc No. 5, 24.

KERNEY M P, GIBBARD P L, HALL A R, ROBINSON J E, 1982 — 'Middle Devensian river deposits beneath the 'Upper Floodplain' terrace of the River Thames at Isleworth, West London', *Proc Geol Ass* 93(4).

KING W B R, OAKLEY K P, 1936 — 'The Pleistocene Succession in the Lower part of the Thames valley', *Proc Prehist Soc* 2, 52–76.

KING J, 1961 — 'The Animal Bone', in Hurst J, 'The kitchen area of Northolt Manor Middlesex', *Medieval Archaeol* 5, 254–299. Also AML Report 1544.

KING A C, 1980 — 'Mammal Bones from the Upper Thames Street Section', in Hill C, Millet M and Blagg T (eds), *The Roman Riverside Wall and Monumental Arch in London,* London Middlesex Archaeol Soc Special Paper No. 3, 83–87.

KINGSTON ELECTRICITY WORKS, 1930 — *Surrey Archaeol Collect* 38, Pt II, 227.

KINGSTON BENEATH EDEN STREET, 1966 — *Surrey Comet.* October 22nd.

KINGSTON BENEATH EDEN STREET, 1968 — *Kingston Geol Soc Review* No. 1, 1–6.

KINGSTON BENEATH EDEN STREET, 1976 — In MacDonald J, 'The Neolithic', *London Middlesex Archaeol Soc Special Paper No. 1,* 20.

KINGS CROSS ROAD — *Proc Geol Ass* 63, 271–2, Figure 1.

LACAILLE A D, 1961 — 'Mesolithic facies in Middlesex and London', *Trans London Middlesex Archaeol Soc* 20, Pt 3.

LAMBERT F, 1920 — In *London Middlesex Archaeol Soc* 3, Pt III, 246.

LAMBERT F, 1921 — 'Some recent excavations in London', *Archaeologia* 71, 94–112.

LANE FOX A, 1867 — 'A description of certain piles found near London Wall and Southwark, possibly the remains of pile buildings', *J Anthrop Soc London* 5, 71–80.

LANE FOX A, 1872 — 'On the discovery of Palaeolithic implements in association with *Elaphus primigenius* in the gravels of the Thames Valley at Acton', *Quart J Geol Soc London* 28, 449–465.

LATTER R, 1858 — 'Discovery of fragments of Ancient British, Romano–British and Roman pottery found in a chalk cavern in Camden Park, Chislehurst near Bromley, Kent', *Archaeologia Cantiana* 1.

LEESON J R, LAFFAN G B, 1894 — 'On the geology of the Pleistocene deposits in the valley of the Thames at Twickenham', *Quart J Geol Soc London* 50, 453–62.

LEWIS ABBOTT W J, 1890 — In Lacaille A D 1961, 'Mesolithic facies in London and Middlesex', *Trans London Middlesex Archaeol Soc* 20, Pt 3, 126.

LLEWELLYN–JONES J, PAIN C, 1980 — 'Oyster shells', in Jones D M, *Excavations at Billingsgate Buildings 'Triangle', Lower Thames Street, 1974,* London Middlesex Archaeol Soc Special Paper No. 4, 147–148.

LOCKER A, 1976 — 'The Animal Bones', in Black G, 'Excavations in the sub-vault of the misericorde of Westminster Abbey February to May 1975', *Trans London Middlesex Archaeol Soc* 27, 135–178.

LOCKER A, 1977 — 'The Animal Bones', in Schwab I and Nurse B, 'Butcher Row, Ratcliffe E14', *Trans London Middlesex Archaeol Soc* 28, 249–250.

LOCKER A, 1978a — 'The Animal Bones', in Siegal J 'Excavations at Fetter Lane 1976', *Trans London Middlesex Archaeol Soc* 29, 73–90.

LOCKER A, 1978b — 'The Environmental Evidence', in Greenwood P, 'Excavations at Church Road, Leyton', *Essex J* 14, No. 3.

LOCKER A, 1979a — 'The Animal Bones', in McIsaac W, Schwab I and Sheldon H, 'Excavations at Old Ford 1972–5', *Trans London Middlesex Archaeol Soc* 30, 39–96.

LOCKER A, 1979b — *Cromwell Green, Westminster; The Animal Bones*, AML Report 3121.

LOCKER A, 1979c — *New Fresh Wharf: The Fish bones.*

LOCKER A, 1980a — *Tudor Street; the Fish Bone*, AML Report 3168.

LOCKER A, 1980b — *Nonsuch Palace; The Fish Bones*, AML Report 3124.

LOCKER A, 1980c — 'The Animal Bones', in Whytehead R, 'Excavations at Goodmans Yard 1978', *Trans London Middlesex Archaeol Soc* 31, 29–46.

LOCKER A, 1980d — 'The Animal Bones', in Whipp D, 'Excavations at Tower Hill 1979', *Trans London Middlesex Archaeol Soc* 31, 47–67.

LOCKER A, 1981a — 'Fish Bone', in Maloney J (ed), 'The Contents of a Late 18th Century Pit at Crosswall, City of London', *Trans London Middlesex Archaeol Soc* 32, 175 and 176.

LOCKER A, 1981b — *High Street Stepney; the Animal Bones*, AML Report 3852.

LOCKER A, 1982a — *Euston Road; The Animal Bones*, AML Report 3665. (The seeds are attached to this report).

LOCKER A, 1962b — *GPO Middle: the fish bone*, unpublished Level III Archival Report, Museum of London.

LOCKER A, 1982c — *Fish bone from Aldgate 1974*, unpublished Level III Archival Report, Museum of London.

LOCKER A, 1983a — *Broad Sanctuary; The Animal Bone*, AML Report 3850.

LOCKER A, 1983b — *Shadwell; the Animal Bones*, AML Report 3848.

LOCKER A, 1983c — *Althorpe Grove, Battersea; The Animal Bones*, AML Report 3849.

LOWTHER A W G, 1949 — 'Dendrochronology', *Archaeol News Letter* 11, 1–3.

MACDONALD J, 1976 — 'Neolithic', in Collins D *et al., The Archaeology of the London Area: Current Knowledge and Problems*, London Middlesex Archaeol Soc Special Paper No. 1, 19–29.

MACPHAIL R I, 1980a — *Report on a soil in a Romano–British context at Lloyds Merchant Bank, London (LLO 78)*, unpublished report, Museum of London.

MACPHAIL R I, 1980b — *Soil Report on a 'dark earth' at GPO Middle (POM 79) London*, AML Report 3055.

MACPHAIL R I, 1980c — *Soil Report on the 'dark earth' at St Bartholomew's Hospital, London*, AML Report 3059.

MACPHAIL R I, 1980d — *Soil Report on the 'dark earth' at GPO 75, London*, AML Report 3060.

MACPHAIL R I, 1980e — *Soil Report on the 'dark earth' at the Arcadia Buildings, Southwark, London*, AML Report 3057.

MACPHAIL R I, 1980f — *Soil and Botanical Studies of the 'dark earth'*, AML Report 3106.

MACPHAIL R I, 1981   'Soil and Botanical Studies of the 'dark earth', in Jones M and Dimbleby G (eds), *The Environment of Man; the Iron Age to the Anglo–Saxon Period*, Brit Archaeol Rep 87, 309–332.

MARSDEN D, 1972   'Mapping the Birth of Londinium', *Geographical Magazine* 44, 840–845.

MARSDEN P, 1980   *Roman London*, London.

MARSH P, 1982   'Flea-bitten rat gives new clues to Black Death', *New Scientist* 94, 492.

MARSH G, WEST B, 1981   'Skullduggery in Roman London?', *Trans London Middlesex Archaeol Soc* 32, 86–102.

McCLEAN T, 1981   *English Medieval Gardens*, London.

McKENNY HUGHES T, 1896   'On the more important breeds of cattle which have been recognised in the British Isles in successive periods', *Archaeologia* 55, 125–158.

McWHIRR A, VINER L, WELLS C, 1982   *Cirencester Excavation II: Romano–British Cemeteries at Cirencester*, Cirencester.

MERRIFIELD R, 1965   *The Roman City of London,* London.

MERRIFIELD R, 1983   *London: City of the Romans*, London.

MILNE G, MILNE C, 1978   'Excavations on the Thames Waterfront at Trig Lane, London 1974–76', *Medieval Archaeol* 22. 84–104.

MILNE G, MILNE C, 1982   *Medieval Waterfront Development at Trig Lane, London*, London Middlesex Archaeol Soc Special Paper No. 5.

MILNE G, BATTARBEE R, STRAKER V, YULE B, 1983   'The River Thames in the mid 1st Century AD', *Trans London Middlesex Archaeol Soc*, in press.

MITCHELL G F, PENNY L F, SHOTTON F W, WEST R G, 1973   *A correlation of Quaternary deposits in the British Isles*, Geol Soc London Special Rep 4.

MONK M, 1978   *Eltham Palace; Plant Remains*, AML Report 2654.

MOODIE J M, 1913   'Animal remains and Saxon burials found near Coulsdon, Surrey', *Surrey Archaeol Collect* 26, 139–140.

MORGAN M, 1978   'Excavation and recording techniques used at the cemetery of St. Nicholas Shambles (1975–78)', *London Archaeol* 3 (No. 8), 213–216.

MORGAN M, 1979   'Human bones', in Boddington A, 'Excavations at 48–50 Cannon Street, City of London, 1975', *Trans London Middlesex Archaeol Soc* 30, 34–36.

MORGAN M, 1980   'Human bones', in Jones D M, *Excavations at Billingsgate Buildings 'Triangle', Lower Thames Street, 1974* London Middlesex Archaeol Soc Special Paper No. 4, 164.

MORGAN R, 1976   'Tree-ring dating of the London Waterfronts', *London Archaeol* (1977) 3 (No. 2), 40–45. Also AML Report 2118.

MORGAN R A, 1980a   'Tree-ring analysis of timbers', in Jones D M, Rhodes M (eds) *Excavations at Billingsgate Buildings (Triangle), Lower Thames Street, London 1974*, London Middlesex Archaeol Soc Special Paper No. 4, 28–33.

MORGAN R, 1980b   'The carbon 14 and Dendrochronology', in Hill *et al.*, *The Roman Riverside Wall and Monumental Arch in London*, London Middlesex Archaeol Soc Special Paper No. 3, 88–94.

MORGAN R, SCHOFIELD J, 1978   'Tree-rings and the Archaeology of the Thames Waterfront in the City of London', in Fletcher J (ed), *Dendrochronology in Europe*, Brit Archaeol Rep No. 51, 223–238.

NORMAN P, READER F W, 1906   'Recent discoveries in connection with Roman London', *Archaeologia* 60, 169–250.

NORMAN P, READER F W, 1912   'Further discoveries relating to Roman London 1906–12', *Archaeologia* 63, 257–333.

NUNN P, 1983   'The development of the River Thames in Central London during the Flandrian', *Trans Inst British Geogr* N.S.8, 187–213.

O'CONNOR T P, 1982   'Animal bones from Flaxengate, Lincoln *c* 870–1500', *The Archaeology of Lincoln*, 18 – Part 1, 1–52.

ORTON C, 1983   *Statistical Analysis of Seed Samples from the Milk Street Pit Project*, unpublished Level III Archival Report, Museum of London.

PARADINE P J, 1980   *Eltham Palace Site; Seeds*, AML Report 3239.

PARNELL G, 1977   'Excavations at the Tower of London', *London Archaeol* 3 (No. 4), 97–99.

PEARCE J E, 1981   'Chinese porcelain', in Maloney J (ed), 'The contents of a late 18th century pit at Crosswall, City of London', *Trans London Middlesex Archaeol Soc* 32, 165–68.

PENN J, 1968   'Evidence of Neolithic Man in Kingston', *Kingston Geological Review* I.

PENN J S, ROLLS J D, 1981   'Problems in the Quaternary development of the Thames Valley around Kingston; a framework for Archaeology', *Trans London Middlesex Archaeol Soc* 32, 1–12.

PENN J, FIELD D, SERJEANTSON D, 1983   'Evidence of Neolithic Occupation in Kingston. Excavations at Eden Walk 1965', *Surrey Archaeol Collect* forthcoming.

PERKINS J A, 1977   'Sheep farming in eighteenth and nineteenth century Lincolnshire', *Occasional Papers Lincolnshire Hist Archaeol* 4, 6–58.

PHILLIPS C W, 1936   'A dugout canoe from the Lea Valley', *Proc Prehist Soc* 2, 144.

PIERCY FOX N, 1967   'The Ritual Shaft at Warbank, Keston', *Archaeol Cantiana* 82 184–191.

PIERCY FOX N, 1969   'Caesar's Camp, Keston', *Archaeol Cantiana* 84, 185.

PRICE J E, 1866–70   'Notes on Roman Remains discovered in London and Middlesex', *Trans London Middlesex Archaeol Soc* 3, 492–531.

PRITCHARD C, 1982   *Seeds from Context 122 (14th century drain-fill), Baynard's Castle (BYD81)*, unpublished Level II Archival Report, Museum of London.

RACKHAM O, 1978   *Trees and Woodland in the British landscape*, J W Dent and Sons.

RADLEY J, 1971   'Economic aspects of Anglo–Danish York', *Medieval Archaeol* 15, 37–57.

READER F W, 1903   'Pile structures in the Walbrook near London Wall', *Archaeol J* 60, 137–203, 213–235.

RECHSTEIN H, 1974 — 'Bemerkungen zur Verbreitungs–geschichte der Hausratte (*Rattus rattus* Linee, 1758) an hand jüngerer Knochenfunde aus Haitabu (Ausgraben 1966–9)', *Die Heimat*, 81 113–114.

REID A B L, 1954 — 'The Excavation of a fourth cave at Waddon', *Proc Croydon Natur Hist Sci Soc* , 144–151.

RICHARDSON G, 1978 — 'The Charcoal', in Arthur P and Whitehouse K, 'Excavations at Fulham Palace Moat 1972–3', *Trans London Middlesex Archaeol Soc* 29, 45–72.

RIGBY J E, 1974 — 'The Mollusca', in Tatton–Brown T, 'Excavations at the Custom House Site, City of London, 1973', *Trans London Middlesex Archaeol Soc* 25, 215–218.

RIXSON D, 1970 — 'The Animal Bones', in Sheldon H, 'Excavations at Lefevre Road, Old Ford, E3, Sept 1969–June 1970', *Trans London Middlesex Archaeol Soc* 23, 42–77.

RIXSON D, 1974 — 'The Animal Bones', in Sheldon H, 'Excavations at Toppings and Sun Wharves 1970–2', *Trans London Middlesex Archaeol Soc* 25, 1–116.

RIXSON D, 1978a — 'The Animal Bones', in Sheldon H, 'Excavations at Parnell and Appian Road, Old Ford, E3, Feb–April 1971', *Trans London Middlesex Archaeol Soc* 23, 101–147.

RIXSON D, 1978b — 'The Animal Bones', in Sheldon H, '93–95 Borough High Street', *Southwark Excavations 1972–4, Pt II, London Middlesex Archaeol Soc, Surrey Archaeol Soc*, Joint Publication No. 1, 467–468.

RIXSON D, 1978c — 'The Animal Bone', in Marsh G, '8 Union Street', *Southwark Excavations 1972–4. Pt II, London Middlesex Archaeol Soc, Surrey Archaeol Soc*, Joint Publication No. 1, 231–232.

RIXSON D, 1978d — 'The Animal Bones', in Graham A, 'Swan St/Gt Dover St', *Southwark Excavations 1972–4. Pt II, London Middlesex Archaeol Soc, Surrey Archaeol Soc*, Joint Publication No. 1, 494–495.

RIXSON D, 1978e — 'The Animal Bones', in Ferretti E and Graham A H, '201–211 Borough High Street', *Southwark Excavations 1972–4. Pt II, London Middlesex Archaeol Soc, Surrey Archaeol Soc*, Joint Publication No. 1, 173–176.

RIXSON D, 1978f — 'The Animal Bones', in Dennis M G, '1–7 St Thomas Street', *Southwark Excavations 1972–4. Pt II, London Middlesex Archaeol Soc, Surrey Archaeol Soc,* Joint Publication No. 1, 418–422.

ROACH–SMITH C, 1842 — 'Observations on further Roman remains discovered in London', *Archaeologia 29* (Part 2), 267–274.

ROLFE W D I, 1958 — 'A recent temporary section through Pleistocene deposits at Ilford', *Essex Naturalist* 30, 93–103.

ROSKAMS S, 1980 — 'GPO Newgate Street, 1975–9; the Roman Levels', *London Archaeol* 3 (No. 13), 405–7.

ROSKAMS S, SCHOFIELD J, 1978 — 'The Milk Street Excavation, Part 2', *London Archaeol* 3 (No. 9), 227–234.

ROSS R, 1976 — 'Diatom Report', in Green H J M, 'Excavations of the Palace Defences and Abbey Precinct Wall at Abingdon Street, Westminster 1963', *J Brit Archaeol Soc* 129, 59–76.

RYDER M L, 1977   'Some miscellaneous ancient fleece remains', *J Archaeol Sci* 4, 177–181.

RYDER M L, 1980   'The wool', in Hill C, Millett M and Blagg T, *The Roman Riverside Wall and Monumental Arch in London,* London Middlesex Archaeol Soc Special Paper No. 3, 114–116.

SABINE E L, 1937   'City cleaning in medieval London', *Speculum* 12, 19–43.

SANDFORD R, 1970   'Excavations in Church Street, Twickenham, 1966', *London Archaeol* 1 (No. 9), 199–201.

SCAIFE R, 1980a   *Preliminary analysis of carbonised grain from Harlington, Wall Garden Farm,* AML Report 3000.

SCAIFE R, 1980b   *Pollen analytical investigation of Broad Sanctuary, Westminster,* AML Report 3070.

SCAIFE R, 1980c   *Pollen analysis of some dark earth samples,* AML Report 3001.

SCAIFE R, 1981a   *Willson's Wharf, Southwark. Pollen analysis; the vegetation of Southwark in the later Bronze Age,* AML Report 3499.

SCAIFE R, 1981b   In Cotton J, 'Excavations in Church Road, West Drayton 1979–80', *London Archaeol* 4 (No. 5), 121–129. Also *Identification of 11th and 12th Century carbonised crop remains from Gatehouse Nurseries, West Drayton Manor House, Middlesex,* AML Report 3517.

SCAIFE R, 1981c   *Pollen analysis of the Walbrook Stream Channel underlying the Temple of Mithras,* AML Report 3502.

SCAIFE R, 1983   *Peninsular House: pollen analysis,* unpublished Level III Report, Museum of London.

SCHOFIELD J, 1983 in press   See Thompson A, Schofield J and Grew F, 1983.

SHELDON H, 1975   'A decline in the London settlement A.D. 150–250?', *London Archaeol* 2 (No. 11), 278–284.

SHELDON H, 1976   'Recent developments in the archaeology of Greater London', *Roy Soc Arts* 124, 411–423.

SHELDON H, 1978   'The 1972–74 Excavations: Their contribution to Southwark's history', in *Southwark Excavations 1972–74, London Middlesex Archaeol Soc, Surrey Archaeol Soc,* Joint Publication No. 1, 11–49.

SHELDON H, SCHAAF L, 1978   'A Survey of Roman sites in Greater London', *Collectanea Londinensia. Studies presented to Ralph Merrifield,* London Middlesex Archaeol Soc Special Paper No. 2, 59–87.

SHOTTON F W, WILLIAMS R E G, 1973   'Birmingham University Radiocarbon dates V1', *Radiocarbon* 15, 451–468.

SPENCER P J, 1975   'St Thomas' Street, Southwark; Environmental work; Interim Report', *London Archaeol* 2 (No. 11), 273–11.

SPENCER P, 1978   'The Molluscs', in Graham A '1–5 Swan St/7–14 Gt Dover St', *Southwark Excavations 1972–4, Pt II, London Middlesex Archaeol Soc, Surrey Archaeol Soc,* Joint Publication No. 1, 493–494.

SPURRELL F J, 1885   'Early sites and embankments on the margins of the Thames Estuary', *Archaeol J* 42, 269.

SQUIRRELL J, unpublished   *Wood identifications from the General Post Office 1975, Watling Court, Custom House, Trig Lane and New Fresh Wharf sites.*

STANT M Y, 1975

'The Charcoal', in Castle S A, 'Excavations in Pear Wood, Brockley Hill, Middlesex, 1948–73', *Trans London Middlesex Archaeol Soc* 26, 267–77.

STECHER R M, GOSS L J, 1961

'Ankylosing lesions of the spine', *J American Veterinary Medical Ass* 138 (No. 5), 248–255.

STRAKER V, 1980

Peninsular House: Wood identification (Roman to Medieval), unpublished Archive Report, Museum of London.

STRAKER V, 1981a

Baynard's Castle: wood identification, unpublished Level III Report, Museum of London.

STRAKER V, 1981b

Miles Lane: wood identification, unpublished Level III Report, Museum of London.

STRAKER V, 1982a

Copthall Avenue: Identification of wood, Roman and Medieval, unpublished Level III Report, Museum of London.

STRAKER V, 1982b

Clements lane: Roman and Medieval Charcoal identification (selected contexts), unpublished Level III Report, Museum of London.

STRAKER V, 1982c

Identification of charcoal from 1st and 2nd century contexts at the GPO and Milk Street sites, unpublished Level III Report, Museum of London.

STRAKER V, 1982d

Report on the wooden hurdles from the Medieval City ditch at Ludgate Hill, unpublished Level III Report, Museum of London.

STRAKER V, 1982e

St Peter's Wood identification (Roman), unpublished Level III Report, Museum of London.

STRAKER V, 1982f

Swan Lane; wood identification, unpublished Level III Report, Museum of London.

STRAKER V, in press

'First and second century carbonised cereal grain from Roman London', in Van Zeist W, and Casparie W A (eds), *Plants and Ancient Man: Studies in Palaeoethnobotany*.

STRAKER V, DAVIS A, 1981

'Environmental Report', in Armitage P and O'Connor Thompson S, *Late 17th and Early 18th Century horn-core lined pits at Cutlers Gardens, City of London*, in preparation.

STRAKER V, DAVIS A, 1982

Milk Street; Plant Remains from early Medieval Pits, unpublished Level III Report, Museum of London.

SUTTON M, 1976

'The Animal Bones', in Lawes A, 'Excavations at Northumberland Wharf; Brentford', *Trans London Middlesex Archaeol Soc* 27, 179–205.

SUTTON M, 1978

'Animal Bone', in Canham R, *2000 years of Brentford*, HMSO, 139–146.

TATTON–BROWN T, 1974

'Excavations at the Custom House Site, City of London', *Trans London Middlesex Archaeol Soc* 25, 117–220.

TATTON–BROWN T, 1975

'Excavations at the Custom House Site, City of London, part 2', *Trans London Middlesex Archaeol Soc* 26, 285–292.

TAYLOR Sir C, 1971

'Plant Remains', in Marsden Peter R V, 'Report on Recent Excavations in Southwark Part II', *Trans London Middlesex Archaeol Soc* 23, 19–41.

TESTER P J, 1951 — 'Palaeolithic implements from Bowman's Lodge Gravel Pit, Dartford Heath', *Archaeol Cantiana* 63, 122—134.

THOMAS K D, 1974 — 'The Molluscs', in Sheldon H, 'Excavations at Toppings and Sun Wharves 1970—2', *Trans London Middlesex Archaeol Soc* 25, 1—116.

THOMPSON A, 1980 — 'Recording human skeletons', in Schofield J (ed), *Site Manual Part 1: The Written Record*, Mus London DUA Handbook, 36—45.

THOMPSON A, SCHOFIELD J, GREW F, 1983 in press — 'Excavations at Aldgate 1974', *Trans London Middlesex Archaeol Soc.*

THORNHILL L, 1972 — 'A Medieval site at Addington', *London Archaeol* 2, 8—11.

TRIMMER W K, 1813 — 'An account of some organic remains found near Brentford, Middlesex', *Phil Trans Roy Soc London 1813*, 131.

TURNER J D, 1963 — 'Excavations at Merton Priory, Merton, Surrey', *London Naturalist* 42, 79—92.

VINCE A, 1981 — 'Recent research on post—medieval pottery from the City of London', *London Archaeol* 4 (No. 3), 74—80.

WATSON J, 1979 — *Cromwell Green, Westminster; the Wood*, AML Report 3172.

WATSON J, 1981 — *Identification of waterlogged wood from Stanwell, Heathrow Airport*, AML Report 3552.

WATSON J, 1982 — *Identification of waterlogged wood from Gardiners Corner, Aldgate*, AML Report.

WEST B A, 1980a — *Catalogue of animal bones from London Excavations (ER series) 1957—72*, unpublished Level II Archival Report, Museum of London.

WEST B A, 1980b — *Sawn Human Bone from St. Bartholomew's*, Level II Archival Report, Museum of London.

WEST B A, 1981a — *Medieval and Post—Medieval Human skeletons, College Hill 1981*, unpublished Level II Archival Report, Museum of London.

WEST B A, 1981b — *Roman Human Skeletal Remains, Cutler Street 1978*, unpublished Level II Archival Report, Museum of London.

WEST B A, 1981c — 'Bird bone', in Maloney J (ed) 'The contents of a late 18th century pit at Crosswall, City of London', *Trans London Middlesex Archaeol Soc* 32, 175—176.

WEST B A, 1982a — *Human Skeletal Remains, Mansell Street 1982*, unpublished Level III Archival Report, Museum of London.

WEST B A, 1982b — *Faunal evidence from a medieval garden well of the Greyfriars, London: large mammal and bird bones*, unpublished Level III Archival Report, Museum of London.

WEST B A, 1982c — 'Spur development: recognising caponised fowl in archaeological material', in Wilson B, Grigson C and Payne S (eds), *Ageing and Sexing Animal Bones from Archaeological Sites*, Brit Archaeol Rep Brit Ser 109, 255—261.

WEST B A, 1982d — 'A note on bone skates from London', *Trans London Middlesex Archaeol Soc* 33, 303.

WEST B A, 1983a — *The Roman Buildings West of the Walbrook Project: Human, and Animal Bones*, unpublished Level III Archival Report, Museum of London.

WEST B A, 1983b — *Medieval and Post–Medieval Human Skeletons, Billingsgate 1982*, unpublished Level II Archival Report, Museum of London.

WEST B A, 1983c — *Bird Bones from Aldgate 1974*, unpublished Level III Archival Report, Museum of London.

WEST B A, 1984a — *Trig Lane 1974: the animal and bird bones*, unpublished Level II Archival Report, Museum of London.

WEST B A, 1984b — 'Ivory Towers: tooth wear in three dimensions', *Circaea* 2, No. 3, 135–8.

WEST B A, ARMITAGE P L, 1980 — 'Sawn Human Bones from St Bartholomew's Hospital', *The Barts J*, Spring 1980, 24–8.

WEST B A, DOWNS D — *Human Bones: St Bartholomew's*, Level II. (Also published in Bentley D and Pritchard F, forthcoming).

WEST R G, 1969 — 'Pollen analysis from interglacial deposits at Aveley and Grays, Essex', *Proc Geol Ass London* 90, 271–82.

WEST R G, 1972 — 'Relative land-sea level changes in South eastern England during the Pleistocene', *Phil Trans Roy Soc London A* 272, 87–98.

WEST R G, LAMBERT C A, SPARKS B W, 1964 — 'Interglacial deposits at Ilford, Essex', *Phil Trans Roy Soc B* 247, 185–212.

WHEATLEY H B (ed), 1970 — *John Stow. The Survey of London*, London.

WHEELER R E M, 1929 — 'Old England, Brentford', *Antiquity* 3, 20–32.

WHEELER A C, 1977 — 'The Fish Remains', in Blurton T R and Rhodes M (eds), 'Excavations at Angel Court, Walbrook, 1974', *Trans London Middlesex Archaeol Soc* 28, 88–97.

WHEELER A C, 1980 — 'The Fish Remains', in Jones D M (ed), 'Excavations at Billingsgate Buildings (Triangle), Lower Thames Street, London 1974', *London Middlesex Archaeol Soc, Special Paper* No. 4, 161–162.

WHITE W J, 1983 — *The Cemetery of St. Nicholas-in-the-Shambles, City of London (GPO site, Newgate Street, 1975–8): Report on the Human Skeletons*, unpublished Level III Archival Report, Museum of London.

WHITE W J, in preparation — *The Cemetery of St. Nicholas-in-the-Shambles, City of London (GPO site, Newgate Street, 1975–8): Report on the Human Skeletons*, London Middlesex Archaeol Soc Special Paper.

WHITTAKER J, 1982 — *Copthall Avenue: analysis of ostracods from a medieval ditch fill*, unpublished report, Museum of London.

WILFRED JACKSON J, 1944–5 — 'The Animal Bone', in Lowther A W G, 'Report on the excavations at Carshalton Surrey', *Surrey Archaeol Collect* 49, 56–74.

WILKINSON T S, 1983 — *The Equid Bones from the Medieval Ditch at Ludgate (LUD 82)*, unpublished Level III Archival Report, Museum of London.

WILLCOX G H, 1975 — 'Problems and possible conclusions relating to the history and archaeology of the Thames in the London region', *Trans London Middlesex Archaeol Soc* 26, 285–92.

WILLCOX G H, 1976 — 'Environmental Aspects of London's Past', *London Archaeol* 2 (No. 15), 388–389.

WILLCOX G H, 1977a — 'Exotic plants from Roman waterlogged sites in London', *J Archaeol Sci* 4, 269–282.

WILLCOX G H, 1977b — 'Environmental Research', in Hobley B and Schofield J, 'Excavations in the City of London 1974–5', *Antiq J* 57, 60–61.

WILLCOX G H, 1978 — 'The Seeds from the late 2nd Century Pit F28', in Dennis G, '1–7 St Thomas' Street', *Southwark Excavations 1972–4, Pt II, London Middlesex Archaeol Soc, Surrey Archaeol Soc,* Joint Publication No. 1, 411–413.

WILLCOX G H, 1980a — 'The Environmental Evidence', in Hill C, Millet M and Blagg T (eds), *The Roman Riverside Wall and Monumental Arch in London*, London Middlesex Archaeol Soc Special Paper No. 3, 78–83.

WILLCOX G H, 1980b — 'Environmental Evidence', in Jones D M and Rhodes M, 'Excavations at Billingsgate Buildings (Triangle), Lower Thames Street, London, 1974', *London Middlesex Archaeol Soc Special Paper* No. 4, 24–27.

WILLCOX G H, unpublished — *Trig Lane; the seeds*, Level III Report.

WOODWARD A S, 1917 — 'On mammalian bones from excavations in the London district', *Geol Mag* 4 (No. 9), 422–424.

WOODWARD H, DAVIES W, 1874 — 'Notes on the Pleistocene deposits yielding mammalian remains in the vicinity of Ilford', *Essex Geol Mag* II, 390–398.

WORTHINGTON SMITH , 1894 — *Man the Primaeval Savage.*

WYMER J J, 1980 — 'The Palaeolithic of Essex', in Buckley D (ed), *Archaeology in Essex to AD 1500*, Counc British Archaeol Res Rep No. 34, 8–11.

ZEUNER F, 1945 — *The Pleistocene Period*, The Ray Society, 126 and 266.

Chapter 6   A REVIEW OF SOIL SCIENCE IN ARCHAEOLOGY IN ENGLAND

R I Macphail

1   Introduction

1.1   Foreword

A Review cannot help but reflect the experience and preferences of the author, and so although many aspects of soil science in archaeology will, it is hoped, be covered, some approaches will undoubtedly be given more weight. The contents also reflect the kind of information which has been sought, in the experience of the author, by archaeologists.

The number of sites and subjects referred to has also been limited by constraints of time, lack of access to unpublished material, and a deliberate decision to avoid repetition with other Reviews. Where possible English sites are used to illustrate soil changes in each of the soil environments, with details presented in a tabular form. However, when English sites are lacking, for example in the Neolithic on Moorland areas, other sites in the British Isles have been referred to so that no artificial gaps appear in our understanding of soil development. Similarly, important interpretative advances from Scottish (Romans and Robertson) and European workers have also been included especially in the field of micromorphology, so that English sites can be better interpreted. As an illustration, Limbrey (1975) commented on the large number of thin sections from important archaeological sites, which had been made by Dr Cornwall at the Institute of Archaeology, before our present day improved techniques of micropedological analysis. Some of these, which have not been referred to in publication have themselves been reviewed, with Dr Cornwall's blessing.

At present the author, as a contract soil scientist working for the Ancient Monuments Laboratory (Department of the Environment), may be called out to any rescue archaeological excavation funded by the Department. This entails both fieldwork during excavation and laboratory analysis as part of the post excavation process. Findings are submitted to the excavators who produce the final archaeological reports. Soil reports are also added to the Ancient Monuments Laboratory Report series as a source of reference.

The Review commences with a brief outline of the information on the present soil cover of England available to archaeologists. An introduction to basic soil processes is given so that the pedological changes through time, which are the core of the Review, can be appreciated by non-soil scientists. A background to periglacial effects and early soil formation is also outlined to warn the archaeologist of this source of confusion. Major soil environments are dealt with separately and this is followed by a section on topics related to soils and archaeology, and field and laboratory techniques. Areas for future work which are outlined for each environment are summarised at the end.

1.2   Introductory Information

The 1:1,000,000 (Avery *et al.* 1975) and 1:250,000 (Soil Survey England and Wales, 1983) Soil Maps of England, are a complement to geological and Ordnance Survey maps of the country. Some areas and counties are covered by more detailed soil maps at the scales of 1:25,000 and 1:63,650[1].

Maltby (in Bell in press I) has already summarised the benefits of such a cover, therefore suffice it to say their usefulness lies in their ability to reflect geology, physiography and climate in soil formation under the impact of man (Bridges 1978).

English soils are classified according to Avery (1980) and Clayden and Hollis (in press), the Soil Survey Field Handbook (Hodgson 1976) and the Soil Survey Laboratory Methods (Avery and Bascomb 1974). The Soil Survey of England and Wales also provides other information applicable to archaeology such as land use classification (Bibby and Mackney 1972) and average maximum potential cumulative soil moisture deficit, the latter being considered crucial to the timing of aerial photography (Jones 1979 – See 10.1). As another example, land use capability classification was used to look at the relationship between soil distribution and Bronze Age settlement on Shaugh Moor, Dartmoor (Keeley and Macphail 1981a), and to characterise, using a 'workability' classification (after Fordham and Green 1980), soil types in East Sussex for the Cuckmere Valley Project (Macphail 1982, AML Report 3763). Moreover, many Soil Survey staff have provided information for archaeological sites (Jones 1979, Robson in Beresford 1975, Robson 1980, Allen and Sturdy 1980) or acted as advisors.

---

[1] Full details and list of publications from: Soil Survey of England and Wales, Rothamsted Experimental Station, Harpenden, Herts.

Archaeologists however, may increase their own understanding of soils by reference to the Soil Handbook for Archaeologists (Keeley and Macphail 1981b) or to the more detailed World Soils (Bridges 1970) and Soil Science and Archaeology (Limbrey 1975).

2 General Soil History

2.1 Pleistocene heritage

Devensian glacial deposits are easily recognised, with the separation of Devensian and Anglian deposits depending on palaeopedological evidence of a warm (interglacial) stage:— whilst earlier glacial deposits are less easily discerned as, for example, the use of Palaeolithic artefacts for dating tills is not always satisfactory (Catt 1979). Relic soil features (Bullock and Murphy 1979) from an interglacial stage and periglacial effects and deposits (Evans 1968, Catt 1979) need to be differentiated from Flandrian and anthropogenic soil fabrics and deposits (Weir et al. 1971, Mücher and De Ploey 1977, Kwadd and Mücher 1979, Bolt et al. 1980).

Periglacial effects can be summarised as follows (after Catt 1979) (i) mass movement on slopes to produce head deposits; (ii) the development of non-diastrophic structures such as valley bulges, and patterned ground; (iii) aeolian deposition of locally derived coversand and silt (loess) from more distant areas; and (iv) considerably enhanced fluvial activity, with extensive aggravation of gravel terraces along most major lowland rivers.

(i)   Soils are commonly formed on Head deposits on valley sides and this parent material should not be confused with colluvium, as in the latter very coarse material from the underlying geological strata, and features of patterned ground (frost wedges, involutions etc) will be absent.

(ii)   Possible confusion between archaeological features and periglacial structures and patterned ground are discussed by Evans (1968) and Williams (1973). Periglacial activity in the form of cryoturbation is also recorded in the soil by the way microfabrics produced during warm interglacials have become disrupted, for instance in Boulder Clay, Essex (Sturdy et al. 1979), and in Plateau Drift in Oxfordshire (Bullock and Murphy 1979). Such horizons, where clay translocation occurred in pre Post Glacial times, are designated paleo-argillic horizons (Avery 1980) and can be recognised on landscapes unaffected by Devensian ice, eg those carrying Clay-with-Flints (Hodgson et al. 1971, Catt 1979). In Essex, lessivage and rubification dating to the Cromerian interglacial have also been identified (Rose et al. 1977). It is useful to differentiate between pre Flandrian micromorphological features (9.3v) and those attributable to the Flandrian (Weir et al. 1971, Bullock and Murphy 1971, Sturdy et al. 1979, Macphail 1981a), if the soil history on archaeological sites is to be understood.

(iii)   There has been correlation of brown earth formation in the Older Loess (Pre-Devensian) with Lower Paleolithic culture, for example at Ebbsfleet, Kent (Zeuner 1955). Other early studies of paleosols in loess are listed by Dalrymple (1957, 1958). At present, three phases of brown earth soil formation buried by Weichselian loess are being studied at a Palaeolithic site at Belvedere quarry (Maastricht, Belguim) by Mücher (Wil Roebroeks pers comm). Such work has been aided by a scheme of experimental micromorphological investigation (See 10.3i).

One effect of coversands is to produce an unstable environment after clearance (Catt 1977), such as at West Heslerton, North Yorkshire where Neolithic to modern soils have been both eroded, and buried by blown sand (Radley and Simms 1967, Macphail 1982, AML Report 3706). Prehistoric sites on the Brecklands of Norfolk have similarly suffered, e.g. West Stow where a humoferric podzol in an Iron Age/Saxon context has been buried by blown sand (Macphail 1979, AML Report 2747), or at Thetford where a 1st century Icenian fort has been eroded down to the ditch fills (Macphail 1981, AML Report 3566).

Similarly, the distribution of loess (Perrin et al. 1974), much of which was deposited in the Late Devensian (see earlier) and reworked by solifluction and stream flow of this last glacial period, was also attractive to Neolithic and later farmers (Evans 1975; Catt 1978). On clays, loess had the effect of lightening the soil, while on acid sandstone substrates loess produced more fertile soils (Catt et al. 1971, Limbrey 1975). Similar 'loam terrains' in the South East have been correlated with intense prehistoric occupation (Wooldridge and Linton 1933).

(iv)   Many Pleistocene gravel deposits contain Palaeolithic artefacts e.g. Wymer (1961).

Cave sediments, which also contain Palaeolithic finds, as old as the Cromerian interglacial (Bishop 1978) also reflect changing climatic conditions during the Pleistocene and later periods (Laville 1976, Goldberg 1979a, 1979b, Courty 1982). However, there are a number of complications in this kind of study, as for example a natural roof-fall will produce a 'clastic' deposit, while human occupation by altering the cave's interior temperature and humidity may indicate climatic conditions unrelated to the outside environment (Simon Collcott pers comm).

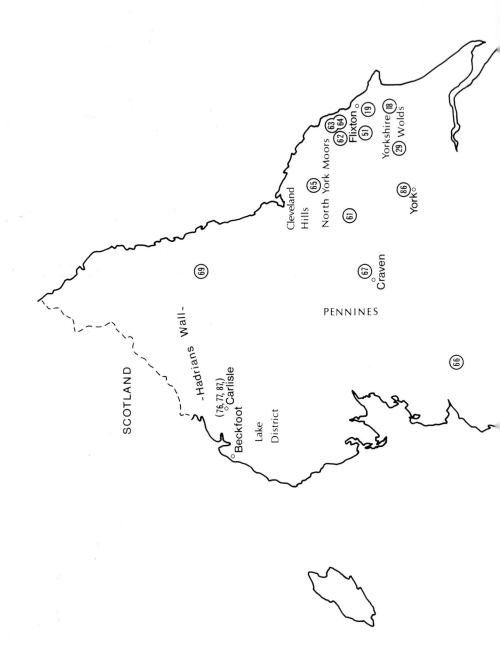

SCOTLAND

-Hadrians Wall-

(76, 77, 87,)
°Carlisle
°Beckfoot

Lake
District

PENNINES

⑥⑨

⑥⑦ °Craven

⑥⑥

Cleveland
Hills

North York Moors

⑥⑤

⑥①

⑧⑥
York°

⑥③
⑥②⑥④
Flixton°
⑤① ⑲

⑱
Yorkshire ⑲
⑳ Wolds

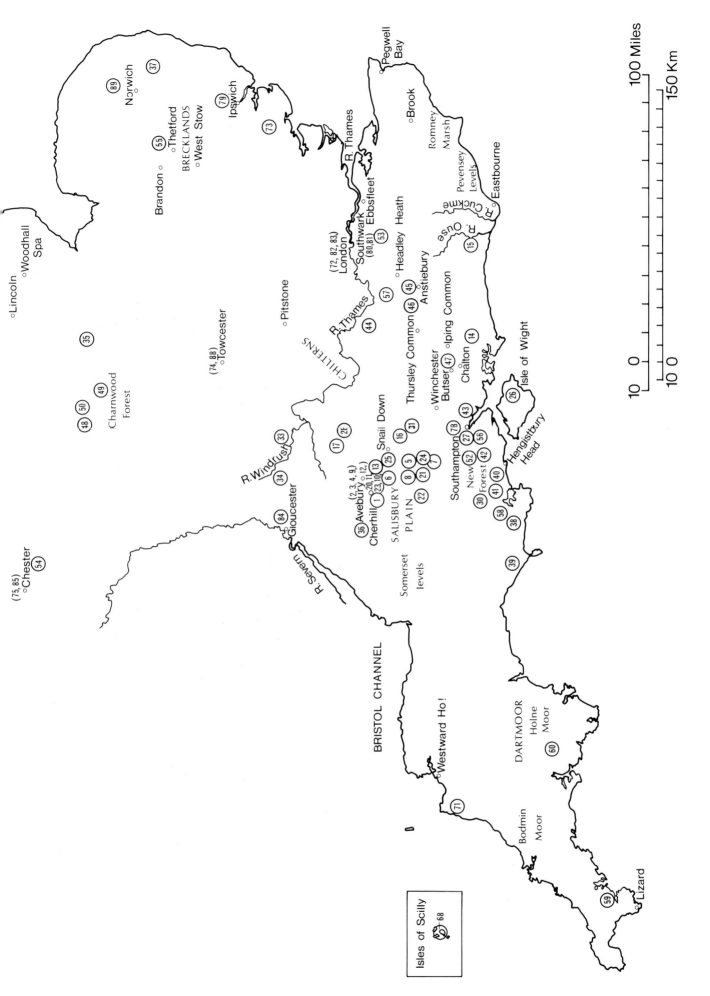

Figure 30   Map showing sites referred to in Tables 13–16

2.2 Post Glacial Soil Development

Soil development was affected by the nature of the soil parent material, the activities of man and whether the soils lay in the lowland or highland zone. Thus details of soil development in different environments are dealt with under the headings of 'Chalk and Lowland Limestone', 'Heathlands', 'Moorlands and Upland Limestone', 'Claylands' and 'Alluvial Soils and Coastlines' — the latter encompassing the effects of sea-level changes. Soils in the urban context and man-made soils are discussed separately. Firstly, however a general understanding of soil formation during this period is presented by first identifying basic soil processes.

2.3 Soil processes

Soil development can be divided into (i) homogenisation, (ii) (a) A horizon formation and (b) soil ripening, (iii) decalcification, (iv) B horizon formation (erdefication after Conacher and Dalrymple, 1977), (v) clay translocation, (vi) podzolisation, (vii) gleying, (viii) peat formation, and (ix) soil erosion (Weir *et al.* 1971, Buol *et al.* 1973, Conacher and Dalrymple 1977, van der Meer 1982, Keeley 1982).

(i) *Homogenisation* Layered or discrete material of *in situ* geological material or of glacial origin is mixed by periglacial slope movements and plant and faunal activity, for example (van der Meer 1982) during soil formation.

(ii)(a) *A horizon formation* This is the primary weathering and humus accumulation under a vegetation cover, and at present this type of soil formation is limited to rankers for example, occurring on fresh surfaces and at high altitude (Ball 1975). An archaeological example can be cited from Towcester where micromorphological analysis identified a mull humus developed in a ditch-fill prior to burial by a Roman wall (Dalrymple 1958).

(b) *Soil ripening* Soil ripening as the first pedogenesis in exposed alluvial soils, e.g. Romney Marsh (Catt 1979) occurs as aeration and oxidation of surface horizons, together with weathering and biological activity. At present a narrow organic horizon developed on alluvial deposits at Brayfords Warf, Lincoln is under scrutiny, because here soil ripening spans the late Roman to Saxon periods (Macphail in preparation).

(iii) *Decalcification* Van der Meer (1982) suggests this occurs at a rate of 0.03–0.04% loss of calcium carbonate a year on calcareous glacial beach sands, with increasing depth with time, and this is in approximate agreement with earlier work on English coastal sand dunes (Salisbury 1925). As an example, late Middle Weichselian loess at Pegwell Bay was decalcified by early Post Glacial times (Weir *et al.* 1971). Low temperature (as in the early Post Glacial) and high percolation favour calcium carbonate dissolution, while in the later warmer Holocene the rate of dissolution decreased (Catt 1979, van der Meer 1982).

(iv) *B horizon formation* This encompasses fundamental processes which produce Bw (Avery 1980) and A horizons (excluding podzol Ah horizons) of Brown Earths (Conacher and Dalrymple 1977). Briefly, in the Bw horizon the soil undergoes alteration by weathering, leaching and/or structural re-organisation *in situ*; by wetting and drying and faunal mixing of mineral and organic materials (Conacher and Dalrymple 1977, Avery 1980). This soil process, prior to clay translocation was identified in loess in South-East England (Dalrymple 1962).

(v) *Clay translocation* This occurs through the dispersion of clay, its translocation and deposition. Briefly, organic acids disperse clay, which is often associated with iron and organic matter, and move it down-profile where it is redeposited along ped and pore surfaces. Recently, both Fisher (1982) and van der Meer (1982) have looked at this subject and their reviews show that lessivage may take place in a soil that is not decalcified. Certainly, Duchaufour (1958) has shown that soils on limestone, clay and sand, develop a uniform slightly acid A horizon under an oak cover — only the B horizons differ. In such circumstances lessivage may be initiated. It is useful here to differentiate between limpid (Bullock *et al.* in press) argillans produced for example under stable woodland, and dusty argillans (Courty and Federoff 1982) and agricutans (Jongerius 1970) which develop through clearance and tillage (see 3iv, 3ii).

(vi) *Podzolisation* During this process aluminium, iron and/or organic matter chemically migrate from the upper soil to the B horizon under acid soil conditions, which may be severe enough to destroy clay. This may occur both under forest or heath (Dimbleby 1962, Valentine and Dalrymple 1975) although it has been argued that biological activity still remains greater under a woodland cover (Simmons and Tooley 1981).

(vii) *Gleying or hydromorphism* Here iron is reduced under anaerobic 'waterlogged' conditions producing bleached zones (e.g. Eag horizons), and mottled horizons which contain ferric and manganiferous concretions. Under such conditions organic materials are preserved as metabolic rates decrease (Pearsall 1952 – Figure 31). Besides natural soil progression, for instance in upland areas (Ball 1975), 'earthworks' may cause post-burial deposition of iron and manganese (Limbrey 1975, Keeley 1982) while land use changes may raise water tables — waterlogging soils which were once freely-drained, as at York (Addyman *et al.* 1976).

336

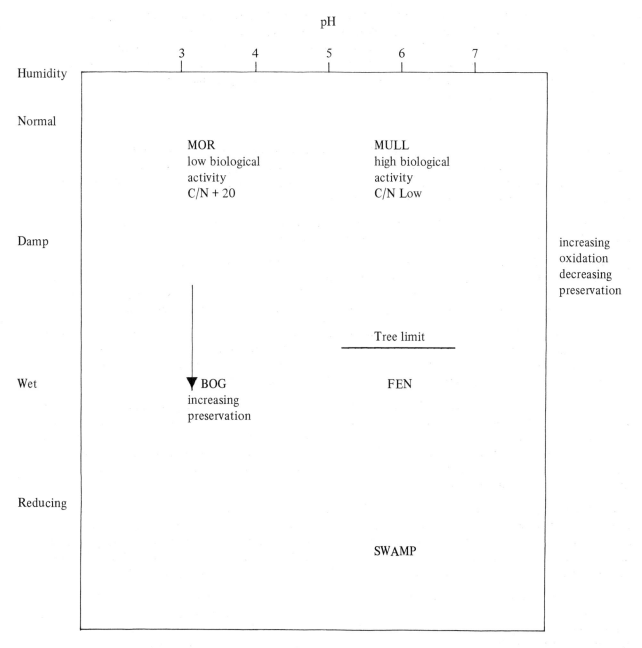

Figure 31 Generalised relations between soil pH, humidity, and humus types (after Pearsall 1952)

(viii) *Peat formation* As in the above, waterlogging both in base rich (Fen) and acid (Bog) environments, low metabolic rates allow organic matter to accumulate.

(a)   Prehistoric man, sometimes in conjunction with climatic deterioration, may have been responsible for decreasing evapotranspiration rates in upland areas on acid substrates or even on limestone, sufficiently for peat to form, or

(b)   the natural drainage of a basin may have been interfered with, or

(c)   natural sea-level changes may have induced the formation of coastal swamps (Simmons and Tooley 1981, Smith in press).

(ix)   *Soil erosion* Major erosion has been inferred from Iron Age colluvium and alluvium, with also examples from the Neolithic being cited, as evidence of man's activities (Simmons and Tooley 1981). Some small amounts of Mesolithic disturbance have also been identified (Simmons 1975), while very large accumulations of inorganic sediments of Boreal age are also tentatively related to anthropogenic activity (Scaife 1982). However, it should be noted that significant amounts of soil can be lost downslope under purely natural woodland conditions (Imeson *et al.* 1980) (See 3.3iii; 4.2iii; 9.3i).

2.4   General soil development

The above processes can be viewed in several ways. Mechanisms such as lessivage and increasingly poor drainage, and the sequence of acidification, podzolisation and peat formation may be seen as degradational. Soil erosion may be a last stage in the degradation sequence but more fertile horizons can be exposed (Smith 1975, Macphail 1979), while fertile colluvium can bury unproductive soils.

The general trends of soil formation from prehistoric to historic times have been reviewed (Keeley 1982, Bridges 1978, Evans 1975, Limbrey 1975, Dimbleby 1976, Simmons and Tooley 1981), but some of the basic aspects of pedogenesis, listed above (2.3), have been missed, while little consideration has been given to early soil formation.

Ball (1975) suggests there could have been little soil formation in the late Glacial sub-arctic conditions until the Pre-Boreal. However, soil formation had taken place during the temperate Allerød Interstadial.

Soil development, for example, over a maximum of 16,000 years in tills and glacial beach sands at Fribourg, Switzerland (van der Meers 1982) and in loess of up to 14,000 years old at Pegwell Bay, Kent (Weir *et al.* 1971) have been investigated. In the early stages the raw soils were at their most heterogeneous, with later soil processes tending to homogenise soil profiles (Catt 1979). However, Smith (in press) argues that in the Craven district of Yorkshire a uniform cover of drift over acid substrates and limestone, first produced a similar soil cover, and that later pedogenesis and human activity with erosion led to either a cover of wet peaty soils or dry limestone pavement.

There is little mention of Boreal soils in the literature (Evans 1972), but as parent materials such as loess and calcareous beach sands are considered to have been decalcified (see 3iii) by early post-Glacial times and B horizon formation including lessivage had commenced prior to the Atlantic (van der Meer 1982, Weir *et al.* 1971), then many brown soils would have been in existence during the Boreal (Ball 1975). As previously noted, inorganic alluvial sediments of this age have been identified, and a Mesolithic influence inferred (Scaife 1982). In the same way, later Mesolithic activity has been linked to soil erosion and blanket peat initiation in upland areas in the Atlantic (Simmons and Tooley 1981), as well as to early podzolisation caused by localised clearance of present day heaths (Dimbleby 1962).

Major clay translocation has been identified in the Atlantic and Sub-Boreal (Catt 1979, Kwaad and Mücher 1977, Langohr and Van Vliet 1979, Valentine and Dalrymple 1975), although it is generally accepted that clay has continued to move subsequently (Fisher 1983). In the later Flandrian podzolisation, gleying and peat formation became more important (Catt 1979, Simmons and Tooley 1981), and can be related to man's activities on heaths (Dimbleby 1962, 1976) and moorlands (Simmons 1969, Keeley and Macphail, in Balaam *et al.* 1982, Smith in press). In addition, on claylands, deteriorating drainage due to agriculture has been inferred by Evans (1975), while the stripping of upland limestone of its soil cover is also blamed on agricultural practices (Smith in press, Drew 1982).

Soil Environments

3   Chalk and lowland Limestone

This review of mainly base-rich soils in lowland areas covers the Chalk (e.g. Yorkshire Wolds, Chilterns, Salisbury Plain), and the Jurassic Limestone (e.g. Cotswolds, Leicestershire, Northamptonshire), but also has to include areas of less freely draining acid superficial deposits, such as Plateau Drift and Clay-With-Flints, that occur on the Chalk. Non-pedological evidence of environmental change has been provided mainly by molluscan, and to a much lesser extent by pollen analyses (Evans 1972, Evans and Dimbleby 1976, Thomas 1982, Waton 1982).

3.1   Soil development on the Chalk

In the South and East many of the areas under study had Late Devensian loessic covers and although these were mainly eroded off in Late Devensian and Early Flandrian times (Catt 1977, 1979) some loess remained in areas of Plateau Drift and also became mixed with Clay-With-Flints material (Hodgson *et al.* 1967). Thus, some parts of the Chalk were covered by varying thicknesses of easily decalcified and acidified superficial materials over a base-rich geological stratum. The effects of pedogenesis on these and the Chalk is considered below.

Chalk and other limestone may contain very little mineral material and thus form very shallow soils (Rendzinas). More mineral rich limestone (e.g. Lower Chalk) and colluvial deposits may produce thicker soils (Calcareous brown earths). Profiles developed on heavier textured superficial deposits on the Chalk develop argillic horizons (Argillic brown earths) which are slowly permeable – and may contain paleo-argillic horizons (Avery 1980) at depth, dating from Interglacial soil formation on pre-Devensian surfaces.

Allerød Interstadial soil development is reported from Pitstone, Buckinghamshire (Evans 1972) and from Brook, Kent – where a marshy soil formed (Kerney *et al.* 1963). Some Mesolithic occupation soils of Boreal age (e.g. Cherhill, Wiltshire) were noted by Evans (1972). Additionally, the Rivers Medina (Isle of Wight), Sussex Ouse and Cuckmere (Sussex) which drain the chalk contain significant inorganic sediments of Boreal age (Scaife 1982) which appear to be originally aeolian in origin (Burrin and Scaife in press). It is problematical whether these are a result of erosion caused by Mesolithic activity (Scaife 1982) or mainly, or in part relate to natural erosion – such as demonstrated both experimentally and in the field in areas of loess in Luxembourg and the Netherlands (Mücher and Vreeken 1981, Imeson *et al.* 1980).

The decalcification and soil development in loess at Pegwell Bay, Kent (Weir *et al.* 1971) has already been considered (See 2.3iii; 2.4), and suffice it to say that by the Sub-Boreal (Neolithic) a mature argillic brown earth had formed. Not surprisingly, a number of Neolithic monuments (Table 13) when burying soils developed on superficial deposits have been found to bury argillic brown earths e.g. Marden, Wiltshire (Evans 1972), Nutbane, Hampshire (De Mallet Morgan 1959). Other Neolithic monuments may bury rendzinas e.g. Horslip, Wiltshire (Ashbee *et al.* 1979), or nearly totally decalcified calcareous brown earths e.g. Willerby Wold, North Yorkshire (Cornwall in Manby 1963) where superficial deposits are absent; or rendzinas together with argillic brown earths where there is a partial cover of superficial deposits e.g. Beckhampton, Wiltshire (Ashbee *et al.* 1979). Environmental evidence reveals that the monuments were constructed usually sometime after woodland clearance on grassland (Evans 1972, Evans and Dimbleby 1976), occasionally after a phase of arable agriculture, which at South Street, Wiltshire, was also revealed by the presence of cross-cut plough marks (Ashbee *et al.* 1979). A micromorphological review of buried soils beneath long barrows and evidence of soil disturbance and agriculture, from Willerby Wold, North Yorkshire, Fussells Lodge, Wiltshire and Nutbane, Hampshire (thin sections by Cornwall) will be presented later (10.3iv). The original wooded nature of the chalk has been identified by rare pollen profiles and by snail evidence from tree hollows (Evans 1972, Waton 1982, Scaife this volume). The suggestion that Neolithic agriculture actually gave rise to argillic brown earths on superficial deposits on the chalk e.g. at Marden, and Kilham, North Yorkshire (Evans 1972, Limbrey 1975) and its critical review by Fisher (1982) are discussed in a later section (iv).

Further snail evidence from Sussex has shown that the environs to Neolithic monuments were often wooded e.g. Offham Hill (Thomas 1977, 1982) but as mollusca from buried soils and ditch fills are very localised, a wider environmental appraisal can be given by molluscan distributions in valley colluvium. Evidence of major Neolithic clearance and erosion on the chalk is present at Brook, Kent (Burleigh and Kerney 1982) and later at Pitstone, Buckinghamshire (Evans and Valentine 1974, Valentine and Dalrymple 1976). The hillwash at Pegwell Bay is also believed to be of Neolithic age (Weir *et al.* 1971). Pollen analyses by Waton (1982) reveal a variation in landuse of the chalk, with arable declining in favour of grassland in mid-Neolithic to late Neolithic times at Winchester, while at Snelsmore on the Clay-With-Flints and Plateau Gravels there was only limited disturbance of the woodland cover until the early Iron Age. Bell (1981a) notes that areas of Clay-With-Flints were less cultivated and less settled in prehistory, perhaps as suggested by Waton (1982) because they are base deficient (stoniness and poor drainage may also be a contributory factor) unlike areas of loess which make the attractive 'loam terrains' identified by Wooldridge and Linton (1933).

Thus, by the Bronze Age much of the chalk may well have been deforested and in use for arable or grassland e.g. Gallibury Down, Isle of Wight (Scaife in Tomalin 1979), while areas such as those with a Clay-With-Flints cover were still wooded. Where woodland regeneration took place it was possible for soil changes to occur, such as at South Lodge Camp, Wiltshire, where argillic brown earths developed in the positive lynchets (Fisher 1983).

Anthropogenic activity on the chalk probably helped to produce a mainly shallow soil cover, as shown by the large number of monuments that bury rendzinas, associated with grassland conditions (see Table 13). Detailed analyses of colluvium from Kiln Coombe, Eastbourne, and Itford Bottom in Sussex and Chalton, Hampshire by Bell (1981b) give the impression that hillwash earlier than the Bronze Age had been lost down-valley in these sites; and only Bronze Age, Iron Age and later colluvium, as dated by artefacts, remained. In the valley bottom at Chalton a truncated paleo-argillic brown earth contains micropedological evidence of clearance and probable agriculture prior to burial (Macphail 1981a). Continued erosion on the chalk through later prehistory was also identified at Brook (Kerney *et al.* 1964), while the development of strip lynchets is believed to relate to renewed intensive arable agriculture in the Iron Age and Romano-British period (Wood 1961, Macnab 1965, Fowler and Evans 1967, Waton 1982) – related alluvial evidence is presented later (7.1). Such losses of soil material are made apparent by Bronze Age barrows burying soils of greater thickness (*c*25cm) than those present locally (*c*8cm) e.g. Arreton Down, Isle of Wight (Alexander *et al.* 1960), or where barrows bury brown soils in areas with only a rendzina cover (Evans 1975). Besides erosion, losses due to weathering of the chalk have been calculated at 50cm over 3,200 years from the Bronze Age barrow at Snail Down (Jewell 1958) and 53cm over 5,000 years at Fussells Lodge long barrow, Wiltshire (Cornwall in Ashbee 1966). Iron Age forts generally bury rendzinas e.g. Badbury earthwork, Dorset (Evans 1972), but where they occur on chalk slopes the embankments may bury calcareous brown earths (Plate 1), and colluvium may be accumulated against the ramparts downslope e.g. Balksbury Camp, Hampshire (Macphail in preparation). Bell (1981b) suggests a general movement off the chalk in Roman and Saxon times, although Abrahams (1977, AML Report 2360) found quantities of Saxon and Medieval pottery in hillwash at Wharram Percy, North Yorkshire, and Cornwall (1958) measured 1.5m of hillwash deposited between the fourth and fourteenth centuries at Lullingstone, on the edge of the North Downs.

Table 13 Chalk and lowland limestone

No.	Site and Location	Feature	Age	Buried Soil	Environment	Author
	CHALK					
1	Cherhill, Wilts SU 025703	Occupation	Mes	(buried by hillwash)		Evans 1972
2	Horslip, Wilts SU 08607052	L. barrow	N.	rendzina	open grass (Sn)	Ashbee *et al.* 1979
3	Beckhampton, Wilts SU 06666773	L. barrow	N.	rendzina, argillic brown earth	open (local arable and woods) (Sn)	Ashbee *et al.* 1979
4	South Street, Wilts SU 09026928	L. barrow	N.	rendzina	open (arable previously) (Sn)	Ashbee *et al.* 1979
5	Durrington Walls, Wilts SU 153435	Henge	N.	rendzina	open (arable previously) (Sn)	Evans 1971a
6	Marden, Wilts SU 090583	Enclosure	N.	argillic brown earth	arable-pasture (Sn)	Evans 1971b, Evans 1972
7	Fussells Lodge, Wilts SU 19203246	L. barrow	N.	rendzina		Cornwall in Ashbee 1966
8	Robin Hoods Ball, Wilts SU 102460	Causewayed camp	N.	rendzina		Cornwall in Thomas 1964
9	Windmill Hill, Wilts SU 087715	Enclosure	N.	rendzina	open (Sn)	Evans 1972
10	West Kennet, Wilts SU 105677	L. barrow	N.	rendzina	open (Sn)	Evans 1972
11	Silbury Hill, Wilts SU 100685	R. barrow	N.	brown earth (rendzina turves)	arable prior to grassland (Sn)	Evans 1972
12	Avebury Henge, Wilts SU 101698	Henge	N.	calcareous brown earth	grass (after clearance (Sn)	Evans 1972
13	Knap Hill, Wilts SU 121636	Enclosure	N.	rendzina	wooded (Sn.P.)	Dimbleby and Evans 1974

No.	Site and Location	Feature	Age	Buried Soil	Environment	Author
	CHALK (continued)					
14	The Trundle, W Sussex SU 877110	Enclosure	N.	rendzina	local woods (Sn)	Thomas 1982
15	Offham Hill, Sussex TQ 399118	Enclosure	N.		open (local woods) (Sn)	Thomas in Drewett 1977
16	Nutbane, Hants SU 330495	L. barrow	N.	argillic brown earth		De Mallet Morgan 1959
17	Wayland's Smithy, Berks SU 281854	L. barrow	N.	rendzina	open grass (Sn) (Kerney)	Evans 1972
18	Kilham, Yorks TA 056673	L. barrow	N.	argillic brown earth, rendzina	open (arable previously (Sn.P.)	Evans and Dimbleby in Manby 1976
19	Willerby Wold,Yorks TA 029761	L. barrow	N.	brown earth		Cornwall in Manby 1963
20	Hemp Knoll, Wilts SU 06856733	R. barrow	B.A.	rendzina	open grass (Sn)	Evans in Robertson-Mackay 1980
21	Amesbury, Wilts SU 184419	R. barrow	B.A.	rendzina	open grass (Sn)	Kerney in Christie 1967
22	Lamb Down, Wilts ST 989395	R. barrow	B.A.	rendzina		Dorrell and Cornwall in De Mallet Vatcher 1961
23	Roughridge Hill, Wilts SU 060660	R. barrow	B.A.	rendzina	open grass (Sn)	Evans 1972
24	Earls Farm Down, Wilts SU 170415	R. barrow	B.A.			
25	Down Farm, Wilts SU 187566	R. barrow	B.A.	rendzina		Dorrell and Cornwall in De Mallet Vatcher 1960
26	Arreton Down, IOW SZ 530860	R. barrow	B.A.	50 cm clayey loam	open grass (Sn) (Sparks)	Alexander *et al.* 1960
27	Edmondsham, Dorset SU 04611155	Bell barrow	B.A.	rendzina		Proudfoot 1963
28	Lambourn, Berks SU 330826	R. barrow	B.A.	truncated gleyic brown earth		Macphail 1979, AML Report 2927

No.	Site and Location	Feature	Age	Buried Soil	Environment	Author
	CHALK (continued)					
29	Callis Wold, Humberside SE 832559	R. barrow	B.A.	truncated rendzina		Keeley 1979, AML Report 2924
30	Badbury Earthwork, Dorset ST 956030	Fort	I.A.	rendzina	open grass (Sn)	Evans 1972
14	The Trundle, W Sussex SU 877110	Fort	I.A.	rendzina	local woods (Sn)	Thomas 1982
31	Balksbury Camp, Hants SU 362451	Fort	I.A.	calcareous brown earth, argillic brown earth		Macphail in preparation
32	Overton Down, Wilts	Experimental Earthwork	Modern	rendzina		Jewell and Dimbleby 1966
	JURASSIC LIMESTONE					
33	Ascot-under-Wychwood, Oxon SP 299175	L. barrow	N.	brown earth	open woodland (Sn.P)	Dimbleby and Evans 1974
34	Hazleton, Glos SP 073134	L. barrow	N.	argillic brown earth	locally shady (Sn), possible arable (S)	Bell in preparation Macphail, in preparation
35	Sproxton, Leics SK 857278	R. barrow	B.A.	truncated calcareous brown earth, turves	open grass (Sn.S)	Wainwright; Macphail 1981b
36	Burywood Camp, Wilts ST 817740	Fort	I.A.	calcareous ploughsoil (Cornwall*)		Grant King 1963

Abbreviations in Tables 13-16

Age Mes. Mesolithic; N. Neolithic; B.A. Bronze Age; I.A. Iron Age; R. Roman; S. Saxon; Med. Medieval.

Environmental Evidence Sn. Snails; P. Pollen; S. Soils.

*unpublished

3.2 Examples from the Jurassic Limestone

At the Neolithic long barrow at Ascott-Under-Wychwood, Evans (1972) found a buried brown calcareous earth with a history of grassland after recent woodland clearance — and this small amount of soil disturbance was reflected in the soil microfabric (author's review of Cornwall's thin section (Plate 2). Preliminary results from the long barrow at Hazleton, Gloucestershire, suggest the local area was shady (Bell in press, I), although buried argillic brown earths give evidence of clearance, domestic fires and possible agriculture (Macphail in preparation, Plates 3, 4 and 5). Bell (in press) has already dealt with the later land use of the Cotswolds. In Leicestershire, a Bronze Age barrow at Sproxton, buried truncated brown calcareous soils developed in loessic material over limestone. Micromorphological analyses of turves preserved in the barrow, and snail evidence indicate a pastural environment (Macphail, Wainwright in Clay 1981, Macphail 1979, AML Report 2926). An example of a buried Iron Age cultivated soil (thin section by Cornwall) can also be cited from Bury Wood Camp, Wiltshire (Grant King 1963).

3.3 Topics

(i) *Earthworks* A large variety of earthworks have been constructed on lowland limestone (see Table 14). Jewell (1958) estimated the size of the area needed to be stripped to construct a turf-stack barrow, and calculated the barrow may compact by 40%. Such practices as stripping turf for barrows give rise to truncated soils (Cornwall 1958), which when buried may give rise to a new drainage regime e.g. Lamborn, Berkshire, where the junction is marked by an iron-enriched streak (Macphail 1979, AML Report 2927). Proudfoot (1963) found turves were placed grass to grass at Edmondsham, Dorset; while turves at Sproxton were right way up (Macphail 1981b). Turves have also been identified in long barrows (Ashbee *et al.* 1979). To study the deterioration of earthworks on chalk Experimental Earthworks have been constructed at Overton Down, using inverted turves (Proudfoot 1965, Jewell and Dimbleby 1966), and at the Butser Ancient Farm (Reynolds 1981).

(ii) *Earthworms* The effect of earthworms on monuments and buried materials has been identified by Jewell and Dimbleby (1966), and Dimbleby and Evans (1974). A review by Atkinson (1957), found most earthworms occur in the upper 20cm of the soil, but discovered they may penetrate to a depth of 2m. By the action of surface casting species and their undermining of objects, these same objects may be moved downprofile at a rate of 30cm in 30 years, although this rate decreases rapidly with depth. This phenomenon has led archaeologists to infer buried stone-free zones may relate to periods of pasture, after cultivation (See iii).

(iii) *Colluvium* This material defined by Avery (1980) was studied by Bell (1981a, 1981b) in dry valleys where it formed deep calcareous brown earths over periglacially deposited head. Stone-free zones were regarded as representing pastural phases between periods of agricultural disturbance — the latter producing stony horizons. Some layers containing more organic matter than the soil material which buries it were considered as standstill phases (Bell 1981a) (see earlier for environmental histories based on molluscan sequences in colluvium). At present colluvial material separated into stone-free and stony layers in the quarries that flank the long barrow at Hazleton are under study (Bell in preparation). However, fine colluvium may well be deposited in stone-free horizons by rain-splash erosion on bare ground or even under woodland, by pluvial and runoff deposition (Mücher and Breeker 1981, Imeson *et al.* 1980) (See 5.2iii). Lastly, a preliminary study may indicate palaeomagnetic secular variation dates may coincide with artefact dating of colluvium at Eastbourne, and possibly, that source of colluvium affects magnetic susceptibility (Allen 1983).

(iv) *Lessivage* The review (See 3.3v) has already shown how clay translocation cannot only occur in calcareous soils but was well developed prior to burial by Neolithic monuments on superficial deposits; and lessivage *sensu stricto* was not initiated by acidification relating to clearance and agriculture (Evans 1972), but occurred earlier through natural pedogenesis (Fisher 1982) under the Post Glacial forest cover. Interestingly, a review (by the author) of a thin section of the buried Bt horizon at the long barrow at Kilham (made by Cornwall in Evans and Dimbleby 1976) revealed no limpid argillans such as form under woodland, but a plasma dominated by dusty argillans and agricutans — the probable result of clearance and agriculture prior to the construction of the barrow. In this case the fabric of the soil does seem to relate to anthropogenic activity (See 4.1; 9.3).

3.4 Future Work

(i) The early (Boreal) movement of aeolian material into rivers in the South (Scaife 1982) questions the impact of Mesolithic man, in relation to natural processes of erosion (See 3.3iii), and the stability of early soils. More work, both experimental and on-site or in alluvium, needs to be carried out before the fate of windblown material — areas of which were attractive to prehistoric man and affected other areas such as heaths (See 4.2iii; 7.2) can be properly ascertained.

(ii) It is still necessary to estimate the impact of Neolithic man on the lowland limestone landscape, so that the questions of initiation of lessivage (Evans 1972) or 'agric horizons' (see above), and Neolithic erosion of the Eb horizon as suggested by Limbrey (1975) can be fully evaluated. By detailed pedological, molluscan and possible pollen studies of a large expanse of buried soil beneath the long barrow at Hazleton, together with the local area, it is hoped to clarify these problems in the Cotswolds.

(iii)   Related to (ii) is the estimation of the importance of Neolithic erosion as for example identified by Burleigh and Kerney (1982); and because much of the resulting colluvium of this date has disappeared down-valley, the colluvial/alluvial interface should be closely examined for evidence of it (Bell 1981a, 1981b) (See 8.2)

(iv)   Later prehistoric soil changes, such as those found at South Lodge Camp (Fisher 1983) should not be ignored. One present study from Balksbury Camp is underway, where Iron Age buried soils and residuals soils developed in tree hollows are being investigated.

(v)   The above study will also allow the investigation of the ageing of buried turf material in a base-rich environment (see Sproxton, Macphail 1979, AML Report 2926). Material from the Experimental Earthwork at Overton Down will be of future use (See 5.2ix, 5.3) and will allow comparisons, for example, with barrow stack turves from Earls Farm Down, Wiltshire, and the perfectly preserved buried soil turf from Silbury Hill, Wiltshire (thin sections by Cornwall) — the latter reflecting the affects of anaerobic conditions (See 10.3iv).

(vi)   As discussed in this chapter, the mosaic of woodland and cleared areas on the chalk may relate to the persistence of forests on such parent materials as the Clay-With-Flints. An assessment of human impact on such 'difficult' soils would be of use (See 6.2).

4   Heathlands

These are lowland areas where soils have developed on acid substrates such as coarse drift material (e.g. Charnwood Forest, Midlands), sandy and gravelly superficial deposits (e.g. Headley Heath on the Chalk, Surrey; Blackheath in Kent), blown sand (e.g. West Heslerton, North Yorkshire; the Brecklands, East Anglia), and coarse geological formations such as the Lower Greensand and Eocene sands (e.g. Surrey, Sussex, Hampshire and Dorset heaths). Acid soils developed in upland, high rainfall regions will be considered later (See 5).

4.1   Soil development on heathlands

Classical soil degradation sequences have been described by Mackney (1961), Dimbleby (1962) and Duchaufour (1965, 1977), who suggest the following order of soil deterioration: argillic brown earth — brown podzolic soil — podzol (ferric podzol — humo-ferric podzol) (See 2.3, Anderson et al. 1982). Thus on freely-draining parent materials clay is moved or destroyed in an acidifying environment, prior to the eluviation of sesquioxides and organic matter. Dimbleby (1954, 1962) suggested the character of the primeval forest, under which, according to Duchaufour (1965, 1977) the 'climax soil' (argillic brown earth) developed, prior to its degradation under the impact of early clearance and agriculture and the invasion of heath plants. The resulting depletion of soil nutrients and progressive soil acidification generated by the loss of woodland cover, burning and accelerated leaching have been detailed by Dimbleby (1962), and are regarded as the major trigger of podzolisation under heathland vegetation in the later Flandrian (Catt 1979).

However, there are instances of podzolisation under an uninterrupted woodland cover by the Atlantic period at Woodhall Spa, Lincolnshire (Valentine and Dalrymple 1975), by the Bronze Age near the Hardy Monument, Black Down, Dorset (Dimbleby in Thompson and Ashbee 1957) (Table 15); by the Iron Age, at Keston Camp (Dimbleby 1962); and by the present (Dimbleby and Gill 1955, Mackney 1961, Guillet 1975). Alternatively, Mesolithic activity at High Rocks, Sussex (Dimbleby 1962) and at Flixton, Yorkshire (Cornwall 1958) may have led to early podzolisation locally, while at Iping Common, Sussex, Mesolithic clearances allowed heath plants to invade (Keef et al. 1965). Other evidence of the early popularity of the heathlands comes from Mesolithic artefacts (Dimbleby 1965), which because of worm working before the soil acidified, occur within heathland soil profiles, such as at Oakhanger, Hampshire (Dimbleby 1960a), or at West Heath, West Sussex (Drewett 1976).

Although in Holland Neolithic monuments bury podzols (Limbrey 1975), many soils on British heathlands were probably not podzolised by the Neolithic. This is illustrated from Rackham, Sussex where artefacts were worm-worked to a depth of 15—20cm prior to podzolisation (Dimbleby and Bradley 1975); and from Broome Heath, Norfolk, where a Neolithic settlement buried brown earths, protecting them from the cultivation and soil impoverishment which led to the podzolisation of the surrounding soils (Dimbleby and Evans in Wainwright 1972).

However, by the Bronze Age the majority of heathland soils were podzolised or podzolising (see Table 14) giving credence to the idea of how early usage of the heaths had degraded the soils from brown earths to podzols (Dimbleby 1962). Yet evidence of actual Neolithic occupation is very sparse (exceptions are e.g. Broome Heath, above, and West Heslerton, North Yorkshire (Macphail 1982, AML Report 3706)), even though some heathland soils buried by Bronze Age barrows were only incipiently podzolised e.g. Burley, Hampshire (Dimbleby 1962), Wallis Down, Dorset (Cornwall in Case 1952, Cornwall 1958), Canford Heath, Dorset (Cornwall 1956a) and Lockington, Leicestershire (Cornwall in Pomansky 1955). At West Heslerton (above) it is considered that the Bronze Age barrows buried brown earths.

Table 14 Heath

No.	Site and Location	Feature	Age	Buried Soil	Environment	Author
37	Broome Heath, Norfolk TM 344912	Occupation	N.	brown soil	open heath (recent wood-land) (P)	Dimbleby and Evans in Wainwright 1972
38	Chicks Hill, Dorset SY 869859	R. barrow	B.A.	humo-ferric podzol		Dimbleby 1962
39	Black Down, Dorset SY 600850	R. barrow	B.A.	podzol	primary wood-land (P)	Dimbleby in Thompson and Ashbee 1957
40a	Wallis Down, Dorset SZ 980950	R. barrow	B.A.	podzol		Cornwall in Case 1952
40b	Wallis Down, Dorset SZ 980950	R. barrow	B.A.	incipient podzol		Cornwall 1953
41	Canford Heath, Dorset SZ 980950	R. barrow	B.A.	podzol		Cornwall 1953
42	Burley, Hants SU 212052	R. barrow	B.A.	immature podzol	open heath (P)	Dimbleby 1962
43	Moorgreen, Hants SU 4766 1465	R. barrow	B.A.	immature podzol	not fully cleared (P)	Dimbleby 1965
44	Ascot, Berks SU 914687	R. barrow	B.A.	humo-ferric podzol	arable-heath (P)	Bradley and Keith-Lucas 1975
45	Wotton, Surrey TQ 1185 4805	R. barrow	B.A.	podzol		Corcoran 1963
46	St Martha's Hill, Surrey TQ 029 483	Earth circle	B.A.?	podzol		Wood 1956
47	West Heath, W Sussex SU 786226	Nine R. barrows	B.A.	humo-ferric podzols	heath-local woodland (P)	Drewett 1976 Macphail 1981 AML Report 3586 Scaife 1982
48	Swarkeston, Derby SK 368 285	R. barrow	B.A.	podzol		Cornwall 1956b
49	Parwich, Derby SK 5717	site	B.A.–I.A.	podzolic brown earth		Cornwall in Lomas 1962

No.	Site and Location	Feature	Age	Buried Soil	Environment	Author
50	Lockington, Leics SK 465287	R. barrow	B.A.	incipiently podzolised brown earth		Cornwall in Posnansky 1955
51	West Heslerton, N Yorks SE 910760	Two R. barrows	B.A.	probable brown earth, later, humo-ferric podzol	possible arable followed by woodland, clearance and heath (S)	Macphail 1982, AML Report 3706
52	Dark Hat, Hants SU 232160	Bank	I.A.?	paleo-argillic brown earth/podzol	woodland (P)	Eide 1982
53	Keston Camp, Kent TQ 421637	Fort	I.A.	humo-ferric podzol	primary woodland (P)	Dimbleby 1962 Cornwall 1958
54	Beeston Castle, Cheshire SJ 550610	Fort	I.A.	humo-ferric podzol		Macphail 1980 AML Report 3235 Macphail 1981, AML Report 3565
55	Gallows Hill, Norfolk TL 870830	Turf stack	R	gleyic sand ranker		Macphail 1979, AML Report 2799
56	The Ridge, Hants SU 312079	Bank	Med.	humo-ferric podzol	open heath (P)	Dimbleby 1962
57	Ockham Common, Surrey TQ 0090590	Ridge and Furrow	Med.?	humo-ferric podzol		Macphail 1982 AML Report 3738
58	Wareham, Dorset SY 911623	Experimental earthwork	Modern	humo-ferric podzol	heath	Evans and Limbrey 1984

Recent pedological and pollen analyses of buried soils from the Bronze Age barrow cemetery at West Heath, Sussex show a mosaic of clear areas surrounded by woodland (Scaife 1982) had developed a variety of fully eluviated humo-ferric podzols (Macphail 1981 AML Report 3586). Equally, an immature podzol at Moorgreen, Hampshire had formed in an area which was not fully cleared by the Bronze Age (Dimbleby 1965).

Dimbleby (1962) also noted that unfortunately the early history of heathlands was not recorded by soil pollen because the pollen at that stage was destroyed by earthworms and the base-rich character of the original brown soil. Some direct evidence of Bronze Age clearances, however, has been found at Ockley Bog, Thursley Common, Surrey, together with indications of agriculture and soil erosion (Wilmott 1968, Moore and Wilmott 1976). Other indications of pre-barrow Bronze Age agriculture on the heath occur at Ascot, Berkshire (Bradley and Keith-Lucas 1975).

There was a general movement off the heaths in the Iron Age, during which time mainly only forts were built (Macphail 1979). These Iron Age features tend to exclusively bury degraded soils e.g. Beeston Castle, Cheshire (Macphail 1980, AML Report 3235, 1982, AML Report 3565), and Keston Camp, Kent (Cornwall 1958) — the latter developed under woodland (Dimbleby 1962). It is worth noting that late Bronze Age to early Iron Age field boundaries bury podzolised paleo-argillic brown earths at Dark Hat in the New Forest (Eide 1982); and that Iron Age levels at West Stow in the Brecklands occur beneath layers of unstable bleached blown sand (Macphail 1979, AML Report 2747) — a phenomenon which continued into Saxon times. Nearby at Fisons Way, Thetford, the Romano-British ditches which were cut in podzols, subsequently eroded (Macphail 1981, AML Report 3566). Continued podzolisation between phases of cultivation has also been recorded in soils and blown sand deposits from Bronze Age, Iron Age and Roman levels at West Heslerton, North Yorkshire (Macphail 1982, Macphail in preparation). In addition, Eide (1982) found that continued post Iron Age cultivation of New Forest soils led to structural deterioration and the formation of a fragipan at Dark Hat, while other soils were probably converted from podzols to brown podzolic soils by the ameliorating effects of agriculture.

Investigations of the age of Bh horizons by C14 dating (See 9.5) suggested mainly Iron Age podzolisation in the Brecklands of East Anglia, while pollen studies suggested heathlands had commenced at least as early as the Neolithic (Perrin et al. 1964). More recently, in France, Righi and Guillet (1977) have shown that the apparent ages of Bh horizons vary according to the particular part of the horizon sampled. The upper, biologically active part (de Coninck 1980) shows a younger age (e.g. 770 ± 80 apparent age) than the lower more cemented zones (e.g. $2810 \pm 70 - 3390 \pm 80$ apparent ages). A Bh horizon of mainly inert character (Macphail 1981, AML Report 3586) from beneath a Bronze Age barrow at West Heath, Sussex was dated at 3770 ± 150 bp, as a comparison to the known age of barrow construction (Macphail in preparation).

The land uses of heathlands based on burning, grazing and the cutting of turf for fuel (Brayley 1850) were established as Commoners Rights in Surrey in the reign of Edward III, after Henry III had tried to re-afforest areas (Manning and Bray 1804). However, some field boundaries had been established in some areas of the New Forest in Medieval times and earlier, on poor soils (Dimbleby 1962, Eide 1982), while at Ockham Common in Surrey a ridge and furrow system constructed on humo-ferric podzols may also relate to agricultural expansion during the Middle Ages (Macphail 1982, AML Report 3738). Eighteenth century enclosures also affected the heathlands (Commonlands) (Manning and Bray 1804), but most probably because of the poor quality of the soil these were not always taken up, e.g. Chately Heath, Surrey (Macphail 1979).

Summary of heathland soil development   It may be considered that:

1.   some areas of heathland were podzolising under woodland by the Atlantic,

2.   a mosaic of podzolisation had been initiated by Mesolithic clearances,

3.   primary or secondary clearance and utilisation of heathlands in Neolithic times continued to encourage podzolisation, and

4.   by the Bronze Age final and major woodland clearance and use of most heaths — perhaps originally for agriculture but progressively mainly as a source of grazing and fuel to the nineteenth century — allowed the character of heathland podzols to develop to their present character (Dimbleby 1962, Macphail 1979).

4.2   Topics

(i)   *Earthworks*   Unlike in lowland limestone areas few Neolithic monuments occur on heaths. Most environmental work has been carried out on Bronze Age barrows (See Table 14), and little attention has been paid to later earthworks such as Iron Age hill-forts — three of which were excavated without environmental analyses recently in Surrey (Thompson 1979). This is regrettable as pollen and micropedological investigations of Keston (Caesar's) Camp, Kent showed the buried humo-ferric podzol to have developed under primary woodland (Cornwall 1958, Dimbleby 1962).

The soil, pollen character and barrow structure have been investigated from a number of heath sites, and although buried soils may be superficially similar, a variety of Bronze Age environments has been revealed (Dimbleby 1962, Bradley and Keith-Lucas 1975, Scaife and Macphail in preparation). Large (40cm) and 15–18cm thick inverted turves were identified at the Bronze Age barrow at Ascot, Berkshire, which from an estimated barrow height of 1.3m required the stripping of 370sq m of the local area (Bradley and Keith-Lucas 1975). Individual inverted turves (the Ah and underlying Ea horizons) were studied in thin section and by absolute pollen counts from West Heath barrow cemetery, Sussex (Scaife and Macphail in preparation). This allowed, for example, the differentiation of the buried Ah horizon and the Ah horizon of the first inverted turf. Maximum compression occurred in this first turf, perhaps by 600%, if effects of wetness are ignored (Macphail 1981, AML Report 3586). In comparison, organic matter in the buried Ah horizon from the Experimental Earthwork at Marden Bog, Wareham, Dorset (now Hampshire) (Evans and Limbrey 1974) is much less aged and compacted (Macphail 1981, AML Report 3587), while probable 'turf material' in Bronze Age barrows from West Heslerton, North Yorkshire, appear to have been converted to Bh horizon material by later podzolisation (Macphail 1982, AML Report 3706).

(ii)   *Earthworms* As detailed earlier worm-working of Mesolithic and Neolithic artefacts below the present day soil surface of now worm-free, acid soils, has been cited as evidence of (1) brown earths occurring on heaths prior to podzolisation — and (2) soils being originally insufficiently acid to preserve pollen.

(iii)   *Loess and Colluvium* Limbrey (1975) suggested the probable occurrence of loess on heathlands, but considered that although it could have acted as a buffering agent it was rapidly destroyed by podzolisation on coarse siliceous substrates. The presence of fine sand and silt in upper soils on coarse parent materials has been used as possible evidence of a loess input on Blackheath, Kent (Burnham and McRae 1974). A relic loessic cover and silty colluvium in receiving sites were recognised on some Surrey heaths, and it was argued that erosion of this fine material in prehistory may have initiated podzolisation (Macphail 1979). Boreal alluvial sediments of probable loessic origin have already been discussed (3iii), but these also may relate to the erosion of loess from heaths.

Periodic wind erosion on blown sand areas can be identified from the Bronze Age to the present at West Heslerton, North Yorkshire (Radley and Simms 1967, Macphail 1982, AML Report 3706), and in the Brecklands (Murphy in press I). The common occurrence of wind-sorted ditch fills of Bronze Age sites led Cornwall (1953) to suggest a dry phase in the Sub-Boreal, but the evidence from North Yorkshire and East Anglia indicate sand becomes wind blown as soon as surface horizons are breached.

Colluvium from acid soils is often less easy to date than from chalk soils, for example, because pottery fragments may dissolve. At Beeston Castle, Cheshire, seemingly homogeneous colluvium (Macphail 1981, AML Report 3565) was found to bury and contain prehistoric features. Mücher (1974) developed a micromorphological classification of colluvial deposits and was able to date acid colluvium, using pollen and mineralogical techniques, to late Medieval deforestation of the Belgium Ardennes (Kwaad and Mücher 1977, 1979). This study has been allied to experiments in the effects of anthropogenic activity on the stability of soils (Imeson and Jongerius 1974, 1976, Imeson *et al.* 1980, Bolt *et al.* 1980) (see 9.3i). Using the above techniques deeply buried (by colluvium) anthropogenically disturbed truncated argillic brown earths were identified at Wotton Common, Surrey; and as podzols of perhaps Bronze Age ancestry have developed in the overlying colluvium, early cultivation is suspected of encouraging soil degradation and erosion (Macphail and Scaife in preparation). The erosion of eluvial horizons and the accumulation of bleached sand colluvium at West Heath barrow cemetery, Sussex, has already been mentioned (Scaife and Macphail in preparation).

4.3   Future work

(i)   See 3.4(i) and Colluvium above.

(ii)   Podzolisation produced under primary woodland has been demonstrated, but more work needs to be carried out on the initiation of podzolisation by Mesolithic and later activity, especially as regards a. the possible erosion of loess (see i) and b. the prehistoric utilisation of heaths — especially in the light of the paucity of Neolithic activity on heathlands and the general degraded nature of the soils by the Bronze Age.

(iii)   It is believed there is still plenty of information to be gleaned from buried soils, even under Iron Age and later earthworks.

(iv)   There has been little inquiry into the effects of agriculture which may have expanded on to the heathlands in the Medieval period.

(v)   The investigation into the ageing of organic matter (see 4.4v) in an acid regime, as at West Heath, West Sussex, and the Experimental Earthwork at Wareham (Macphail 1981, AML Report 3587) is important, because the character of the original organic matter has to be understood, if buried surface horizons are to be interpreted properly.

5   Moorlands and Upland Limestone

In this section, areas of the South West (e.g. Dartmoor, Cornwall, the Isles of Scilly) will be covered (see Maltby in Bell in press I), in addition the North (see Donaldson and Rackham in press I) will include the Lake District, Pennines and the North York Moors. These parts of the country are affected by cool, wet climates related to both exposure and high altitudes, and have either acid (e.g. granite, Millstone Grit, siliceous drift) or base-rich parent materials (e.g. Carboniferous Limestone).

5.1   Soil development on moorlands and upland limestone

On acid substrates the soil degradation sequence is similar to that on heaths, but the cooler, wetter climatic conditions commonly lead to waterlogging in the upper soil of the podzol, leading to the development of a thin iron-pan (iron-pan stagnopodzol), if the subsoil remains oxidised (Anderson *et al.* 1982). Increased hydromorphism will produce stagno-humic gley soils and peats, especially in receiving sites (Crompton 1952). With clearance, the loss of woodland cover decreases evapotranspiration and increases both surface wetness, infiltration, and thus leaching and gleying are encouraged, e.g. Shaugh Moor (Keeley and Macphail in Balaam *et al.* 1982). At the highest altitudes soil formation is limited to the development of rankers (Ball 1975) (see 3.3). The pedogenic sequence on limestone is often related to the nature of any superficial deposits. Deep deposits give an eventual cover of podzols and peats, while very shallow deposits give rise to calcareous brown earths or rendzinas — the erosion of which quickly produces dry limestone pavements (Drew 1982, Smith in press).

5.2   Moorlands

Since the beginning of the Flandrian soil formation on upland areas has been influenced by westerly exposure, altitude and latitude, producing a pattern of earlier development of podzols and blanket peat in western and northern areas (Durno and Romans 1969, Romans and Robertson 1975a, Ball 1975).

Ball (1975) has also emphasised the natural inclination of upland soils towards podzolisation and hydromorphism, and climatic deteriorations in later prehistory (Sub-Atlantic) more plainly affected these soils (Keeley 1982) than those of the lowland zone. Nevertheless, there is evidence of soil degradation and blanket peat formation on Dartmoor (Simmons 1969, 1975, Simmons and Tooley 1981), and early soil gleying and erosion in the Cleveland Hills and the Pennines (Dimbleby 1961, Dimbleby 1976) being initiated by Mesolithic man.

Neolithic effects were more dramatic. In the South West Neolithic clearances on Bodmin Moor (Maltby in Bell in press I), Dartmoor (Simmons and Tooley 1981) and Isles of Scilly (Dimbleby *et al.* 1981) produced increasingly acidified soils (Clayden and Manley 1964, Simmons 1969, Staines 1979). Their general pre-Bronze Age character has been discussed by Clayden (1964) and Maltby (in Bell in press I) and Caseldine and Maguire (1982), but one example may be cited from the Isles of Scilly. On St Mary's it is considered that Neolithic clearances led to the erosion of brown earths developed on granitic head (Dimbleby 1976/77, Scaife 1980, AML Report 3047) and that later podzolisation developed in the truncated subsoils, for example at Bar Point (Macphail 1981, AML Report 3299).

In the North West woodland clearances increased both runoff and soil erosion (Pennington 1975), while in Scotland, acid brown forest soils were converted to podzols after a phase of 'slash and burn' as at Daladies, or just leached by cultivation and grazing, as at Strathallan, as identified from buried soil microfabrics (Romans and Robertson 1975a, in press a). However, the best example of the result of clearance and tillage comes from Goodland and Torr Townlands, Northern Ireland, where soil deterioration, ironpan formation and peat initiation all occurred within the Neolithic (Proudfoot 1958). Contrastingly, not all early agriculture led to soil degradation, as illustrated from Shetland where the first phase of agriculture little affected the local brown forest soils (Romans and Robertson in press b). At Trefignath, Anglesey soils had already deteriorated by the Neolithic, while at Gwernvale, Powys on more base rich parent materials local and buried soils remain as brown earths (Keeley 1982).

By the Bronze Age, areas such as Dartmoor had suffered both Neolithic and secondary Bronze Age clearances (Smith *et al.* 1981). Typically, the Bronze Age barrow at Crig-a-mennis, Cornwall (Table 15) had been constructed in a clearing in scrub (Dimbleby 1960b). Soils buried beneath Bronze Age huts and enclosure walls, and two reaves were examined from Shaugh Moor and showed that ironpan stagnopodzols (Plate 6) had formed and peat had begun to accumulate; and it was suggested that the present soil cover on this part of Dartmoor was most probably developed by the Iron Age (Keeley and Macphail in Balaam *et al.* 1982). Local soil mapping indicated the poorest soils coincided with low density of prehistoric settlement, and that the moor had not been used for cultivation in the Bronze Age (Keeley and Macphail 1981a). A comparable study, using detailed soil mapping, micropedological and pollen analytical methods has been carried out on nearby Holne Moor (Fleming and Ralph 1982) on prehistoric reaves and Medieval field systems, but as yet full results are unavailable (Ralph pers comm).

The importance of noting the variation in development of two contemporaneous buried Bronze Age soils from Colliford, Bodmin Moor has been presented by Maltby (in Bell in press I) (see Cornwall 1956a for similar situation in Dorset). The close juxtaposition of a large number (approximately 8) of Early Bronze Age burial mounds at Brenig Valley, Clwyd allowed many contemporaneous buried soil profiles to be examined from contrasting physiographic positions, and these revealed that a mainly uniform cover of ironpan stagnopodzols had formed under primarily open conditions (Keeley 1982).

In Lancashire and Yorkshire, Dimbleby (1962) examined a suite of six profiles beneath Bronze Age barrows and these varied from a leached brown earth developed under scrub at Bickley Moor (see Table 16) to an ironpan stagnopodzol formed under open woodland at Winter Hill. These with the presence of another buried brown soil at Springwood led Dimbleby (1962) to suggest the original brown earth character of upland soils prior to Bronze Age clearances. Soil degradation appears to have been generally earlier on Shaugh Moor, Dartmoor than in these northern moorlands, but it is interesting to note that in both cases heath was quite a late invader (Iron Age) (Dimbleby 1962, Smith *et al.* 1981).

However, Atherden (1976) has argued that the major impact of clearance on the North York Moors came later in the Iron Age and Romano-British times – perhaps accounting for the lack of full degradation in some buried Bronze Age soils (Dimbleby 1962) – when settlements became permanent. This clear felling, with more advanced technology, is believed to have caused the real onset of leaching and podzolisation, especially as it coincided with a climatic deterioration (Atherden 1976). It may also be linked to intensified agriculture and the spread of heath from 350 BC onwards at Craven, Yorkshire (Smith in press). However, farther north in Scotland podzolisation was felt to be well advanced already by the Sub-Atlantic, even at low altitudes (Romans and Robertson 1975a).

Romano-British usage of the uplands varied with pastoralism in an area of podzols at Fortress Dike Camp (Tinsley and Smith 1974) and cultivation of a gleyed brown soil at Carlisle (Keeley 1979, AML Report 2887) and of a stagnogley at Throckley, Tyne and Wear – as evidenced in the latter by ardmarks beneath Hadrian's Wall (Keeley 1981, AML Report 3401). Also prior to the construction of Hadrian's Wall at Lannerton Farm, Cumbria, considerable human activity had disturbed the gley soil locally (Keeley 1980, AML Report 3101).

Agricultural utilisation of moorlands continued in Anglo-Saxon and Viking times (Smith in press), but the next major environmental impact occurred through the massive deforestation and spread of grasses as encouraged by the expansion of sheep grazing by the Medieval Cistercian monasteries; and this led to accelerated hydromorphism and peat formation (Romans and Robertson 1975b, Bridges 1978, Smith in press).

5.3   Upland Limestone

At Craven, Yorkshire, Smith (in press) noted direction of soil formation related to thickness of drift (see earlier). Actual cultivation of soils at Malham on Carboniferous Limestone, when this led to erosion, made the soils less acidic and more fertile (Smith 1975). The development of Karstic scenery is undated in the Pennines, but it is believed to have formed in Iron Age to Dark Age times on the Burren, Ireland, through the erosion of the original shallow calcareous brown earths, into hollows and swallow holes that had been promoted by soil acidity (Drew 1982).

5.4   Topics

(i)   *Earthworks* Under the high rainfall conditions of the uplands, buried soils may become affected by leaching of the overburden e.g. Cowesby Moor, North Yorkshire (Abramson 1980). Often buried surfaces become the focus of ironpan formation e.g. Embury Beacon, Devon (Limbrey in Jefferies 1974) (Limbrey 1975, Keeley and Macphail 1981b), and buried soils become affected by a rise in water table (Romans and Robertson in press a), and the deposition of manganese (Keeley and Macphail 1979, Keeley 1982). Some attempts have been made to distinguish the pedogenic character and ageing of buried ditch clearance phases, which had developed organic surface horizons, by micromorphological techniques in reaves on Shaugh Moor, Dartmoor (Keeley and Macphail in Balaam *et al*, 1982) (see 10.3).

5.5   Future Work (See 3.4, 4.3)

(i)   Onset of soil degradation appears to vary in date from the Bronze Age on Shaugh Moor, Dartmoor to the Iron Age and Romano-British periods in parts of North Yorkshire; with some areas not being affected until the Middle Ages. The latter suppositions need to be tested by the analysis of buried soils. Present work on Holne Moor, Dartmoor where soils beneath Medieval field boundaries are being examined is thus relevant to this question.

(ii)   Little micromorphological analysis has been carried out on buried soils to calculate degree of 'soil degradation' apart from 'bleached stone rim' measurements (Romans and Robertson 1975b, in press a) (see 10.5iv). Relic brown earth fabrics have also been identified by the above authors in Scotland, but as yet little similar work has been carried out in the upland zone in England (see Maltby in Bell in press I), although a thin section programme is underway at Holne Moor.

Table 15 Moorland and Upland Limestone

No.	Site and Location	Feature	Age	Buried Soil	Environment	Author
59	Crig-a-mennis, Cornwall 7575282	R. barrow	B.A.		clearing in scrub (P)	Dimbleby 1960b
60	Shaugh Moor, Devon SX 560630	Settlement,Reaves	B.A.	stagnopodzols, stagnohumic gleys, shallow peats	secondary clearance, pasture (P)	Beckett; Balaam; Keeley and Macphail 1981a, Balaam et al. 1982
61	Cowesby Moor, N Yorks SE 480890	R. barrow	B.A.	contaminated		Abramson 1980
62	Bickley Moor, N Yorks SE 904906	R. barrow	B.A.	'possible leached argillic brown earth'	scrub (P)	Dimbleby 1962
63	Springwood, N Yorks SE 953939	R. barrow	B.A.	'leached brown earth'		Dimbleby 1962
64	Reasty Top, N Yorks SE 965943	R. barrow	B.A.	'weak ferric podzol'	scrub and heath (P)	Dimbleby 1962
65a	Burton Howes, N Yorks NZ 608033	R. barrow	B.A.	ironpan stagnopodzol	forest clearing (P)	Dimbleby 1962
65b	Burton Howes, N Yorks NZ 608032	R. barrow	B.A.	stagnogley podzol		Dimbleby 1962
66	Winter Hill, Lancs SD 658149	R. barrow	B.A.	ironpan stagnopodzol	open woodland (P)	Dimbleby 1962
67	Fortress Dike Camp, Yorks SE 179732	Fort	R/B	podzol	pasture (P)	Tinsley and Smith 1974
68	Bar point, St Marys, Isles of Scilly SV 921 127	Walls	R/B	podzols/ploughsoils	arable (S)	Macphail 1981, AML Report 3299
69	Throckley, Tyne and Wear NZ 125680	Hadrian's Wall	R	cambic stagnogley	arable (S)	Keeley 1981, AML Report 3401
70	Lannerton Farm, Cumbria	Hadrian's Wall	R	truncated gley		Keeley 1980, AML Report 3101
71	Embury Beacon, Devon SS 218197	Fort	D.A.?	gleyic podzol		Limbrey in Jefferies 1974

(iii)   Results from the Shaugh Moor Project highlighted the probable differences between the prehistoric land use of the uplands in comparison to the surrounding lowlands – which most probably supported a higher population. Thus, the environmental archaeology, including buried soils, of the lowland zone needs to be examined if highland/lowland interaction in prehistory (e.g. transhumance) is to be understood.

6   Claylands

These include areas such as the London Clay and Weald Clay in the South East, the Lias Clay in the South West, the Gault in the Midlands, and Boulder Clay in East Anglia and the North (see Clay-With-Flints, 4.1).

6.1   Soil development on the claylands

This varies according to the base status and clay mineralogy present in the soil. Thus some soils may develop as acid stagnogley soils, or more base-rich varieties may have 'vertic' qualities, as pelo-stagnogley soils.

There is little site information on the prehistoric character of clay soils. Most literature is based on the inference that these soils were unattractive to prehistoric man (Wooldridge and Linton 1933) – thus the paucity of sites. Evans (1975) has conjectured that natural claylands were well drained but Neolithic cultivation – in the absence of liming and manuring – rapidly led to loss of nutrients and structure, and eventually resulted in waterlogging. Duchaufour (1958) suggested that a loss of woodland cover with the disappearance of humus allowed the packing of the surface soil, producing a temporary perched water table and a saturated organic surface horizon. However, in stagnogleyic (paleo) argillic brown earths natural clay translocation may have already decreased soil porosity.

The review of Bridges (1978) indicated that finer textured soils were not properly taken up until Anglo-Saxon times when better technology allowed them to use these more difficult soils. (Difficulty Classification – see Fordham and Green 1980). Some attempts have been made to link claylands with Medieval ridge and furrow, but rather than relating to soil type, this field pattern can now be seen as old pasture associated with imperfectly or poorly drained soils (Bridges 1978). Modern Soil Survey of England and Wales estimates of arable farming conditions at the deserted Medieval villages of Goltho and Barton Blount, Lincolnshire, suggest that the three and two field system – with frequent fallow and little or no drainage – would create severe soil problems in the form of soil compaction (Beresford 1975). The clay soil would need to be worked when dry as wet conditions may deflocculate the soil infilling its pores – worsening the drainage problem. Soils present on sites of large number of deserted villages were classified, but as Barton Blount occurred on the easier worked Keuper Marl, in comparison to Goltho on the more difficult Boulder Clay, no conclusion over agricultural cause of abandonment was obvious (Robson, Thomasson in Beresford 1975).

6.2   Future Work

(i)   There is an obvious need to find suitable clayland sites for studies of soil development in prehistory. Currently, in clay areas of the Weald very low density of prehistoric occupation has been recorded, but by field-walking it is hoped to ascertain if this is a real phenomenon (Peter Drewett, Cuckmere Valley Project Sussex, pers comm).

(ii)   Present day problems of heavy soil management are being studied by the Soil Survey and other bodies, and good estimates of workability should be obtainable for most areas (Macphail 1982, AML Report 3763).

(iii)   The technology of ridge and furrow appears to be geared for improved drainage, e.g. at Raunds, Northamptonshire (Macphail unpublished note), but as yet this has not been fully investigated (see Ockham Common).

7   Alluvial Soils and Coastlines

This section includes islands, coastlines, estuaries and river valleys. Details of environmental change in these zones in the South West (Bell in press, volume I), East Anglia (Murphy in press, volume I), the South (Scaife, volume II) and the North (Donaldson and Rackham in press, volume I) are presented elsewhere.

7.1   Soil Development

Both coastlines and alluvial deposits have been affected by sea-level changes, and these have been identified in the lower Severn Valley (Beckinsale and Richardson 1964) the Bristol Channel (Kidson and Heyworth 1978), the South (Akeroyd 1972) and the North West (Simmons and Tooley 1981), for example. These changes have given rise to submerged forests and coastal peats, e.g. Westward Ho!, where they overlie a Mesolithic Midden, (Churchill 1965). Alluvium and long shore drift, in contrast, have allowed some coastlines to accrete, e.g. Romney Marsh, Sussex; and after drainage to be reclaimed e.g. Pevensey Levels, Sussex, or Somerset Levels, (Coles and Orme 1980). Anthropogenic influences, however, are more readily noticeable in the character of river sediments, as erosion has produced increased deposition of inorganic alluvium.

Newly exposed sediments are first affected by soil ripening (see 3.3ii), and some typical micromorphological features have been identified in Holland (Miedema et al. 1974). In general, freely drained alluvium in river valleys develop as ground water (alluvial) gley soils (Avery 1980). The study of organic debris in alluvium have allowed some river sediments to be associated with deforestation and agriculture in the later Bronze Age on the Lower River Severn (Shotton 1978) and to the Iron Age on the River Windrush (Hazelden and Jarvis 1979). Details of Boreal alluvium have already been presented (see 4; 5). Brown (1982), working on River Severn peats and sediments, also found that there was a lag between deforestation and the deposition of alluvium. His suggestion that *sol lessives* (argillic brown earths) which were more prone to erosion, developed after deforestation, needs to be more critically examined (see 4.3iv). Later, at York, post Roman reclamation, and increasingly restricted river channel in Medieval times, combined with probable deforestation and erosion in the catchment led the Ouse to continually flood (Addyman et al. 1976). At Farmoor, Oxfordshire, Iron Age to 4th century AD (Thames) alluvial deposition led Robinson (1981) to suggest middle to late Iron Age agricultural expansion in the Cotswolds.

Some recent site examples may be given. A base rich alluvial gley soil had developed in mixed inorganic and organic sediments deposited on Iron Age timbers sunk in fen peat at Fiskerton, Lincolnshire (Macphail 1982, AML Report 3658). At Lincoln, itself, post Roman–pre Saxon organic soil ripening of alluvium was noted in the River Witham (Macphail in preparation). In Suffolk, a Saxon village in a river valley site at Brandon, had been inundated by blown sand, but it was difficult to identify the buried soil because of subsequent ground water fluctuations (Macphail 1981, AML Report 3568). In Norwich, urban sediments of Saxon age ('dark earth', see 9.2) at Whitefriars waterfront (River Wensum) were scrutinised in thin section. Although the presence of well-preserved organic matter suggested waterlogging (Murphy, volume I), some soil-ripening in the form of oxidation had occurred, producing spherical pyrite and vivianite (Macphail 1981, AML Report 3256, Macphail 1982), and possibly jarosite (Miedema et al. 1974).

The changing sea levels around the Isles of Scilly (Fowler and Thomas 1979) may have influenced the blowing of sand on the north coast of St Marys. At Bar point, blown sand was incorporated in the plough soil, but eventually the site became buried in post-Romano-British times (Macphail 1981, AML Report 3299) (Plate 7). These plough soils occur down to sea level, and presumably plough soils over larger areas have become submerged and eroded (Macphail 1981, AML Report 3299).

In Cumbria, on the Solway lowland coast, sand blowing began as early as 8500 BP (Mathews 1982), and blown sand later buried Roman soils (1690 and 1540 Bp) at Beckfoot. Buried brown podzolic soils coincided with Roman occupation, otherwise only decalcified skeletal soils had developed by Roman times (Bellhouse 1982). However, there was no evidence of soil improvement (see 9.3) either by marling, or seaweed, especially as the latter does not occur locally (Bellhouse 1982, Bellhouse, pers comm).

Large mounds of silty beach deposits, which were identified as salterns in Lincolnshire were produced after beach deposits had been desalted, mainly in the eleventh to fourteenth centuries (Robson 1980). Other samples of salt working can be cited from the Lizard, Cornwall (McAvoy et al. 1979).

7.2 Future Works

(i) It would be useful to more closely correlate human activity, colluvium and alluvial deposits (see 5.3; 5.5). Some results may be forthcoming from the current Cuckmere Valley Project, Sussex.

(ii) There appears to be plenty of scope in studying the effects of exploitation of the coastal area. At present, the Mesolithic midden at Westward Ho! now under scrutiny, is a very early example of coastal exploitation after the exposure of estuarine silts, before peat formation, forest growth and marine submergence in the late Boreal/Atlantic periods.

(iii) The soil-ripening effect on waterlogged urban sediments is as yet, poorly understood. The origins of such minerals as vivianite need to be identified, as it can occur both naturally in ripening marine alluvium, or represent a cess input (see 9.2).

8 Urban and Man-Made Soils

This section includes natural soils present in urban contexts, urban soils or sediments such as those defined as 'dark earth', and man-made soils such as plaggens.

8.1 Natural soils

Examples (Table 16) can be given of Roman soils at Carlisle (Keeley 1979, AML Report 2887) and Lloyds Merchant Bank, London (Macphail 1980, AML Report 3045) where there is evidence of cultivation, and pre-Roman soils which were truncated, as at Princess Street, Chester (Macphail 1982) and Gryme's Dyke, Colchester (Taylor 1978, AML Report 2470), prior to burial by a Roman feature. Keeley (1977, AML Report 2228) also noticed that Roman buried soils at Tarraby, Carlisle did not differ from the present local soils, while Dalrymple (1958) reported that enough time had elapsed from the infilling of a ditch, to its burial by a wall, for an A horizon to develop at Roman Towcester. Saxon occupation levels, also bury a brown podzolic soil at Ipswich (Keeley and Macphail 1978, AML Report 2691) and Saxon plough soil at Madison Street, Southampton (Keeley 1980, AML Report 3211).

8.2   Urban soils

Post-Roman, Saxon and Viking deposits called 'dark earth' have been characterised (Macphail 1981c, 1982, AML Report 3633, 1982), unlike the later Medieval and post Medieval deposits which may well continue up into Victorian garden soils in some cities, and have received little attention. 'Dark earth', once seen as a flood deposit (Kenyon 1959), can be divided into two types of artificial deposits:

1   Probably relating to continuous, as based on pottery evidence (Orton 1978, Wilson *et al.* 1979), refuse disposal in a densely occupied urban environment, resulting in organic rich deposits, sometimes waterlogged and containing cess material, for example Keays Lane, Carlisle; The Bedern, York; Whitefriars, Norwich (Macphail 1983, 1982).

2   A generally well-drained 'dark earth' thought to be soil deliberately dumped, for within wall urban cultivation, possibly in the late Roman period (Roskams and Schofield 1978, Roskams 1981), for example, GPO London; St Barts, London; Tanners Hall, Gloucester (Macphail 1983, 1982); Southwark (Sheldon 1978).

The differentiation of these two sediments is important to an understanding of human activity in Britain at this time. Reece (1980) argued that Roman cities had begun to decline from 300 AD onwards – the deposition of 'dark earth' possibly before the end of the second century at GPO Newgate Street, London has been seen as relating to the changing function of settlement in the late Roman period (Roskams 1981). Direct evidence of within-wall urban cultivation is rare however (Macphail 1981c, 1983), but micromorphological data from Tanners Hall, Gloucester and Towcester (Plate 8) indicated cultivation and possible mixing-in of organic matter (Macphail 1982, 1983, AML Report 3922) (see 10.3iii). Taylor (1978, AML Report 2493), in contrast, had suggested 'dark earth' from Chaucer Street, Southwark contained too little organic matter for agriculture. Yet it has been argued that post depositional oxidation of organic matter by earthworm activity implies present quantities of organic carbon do not relate to original amounts (Macphail 1981c, 1982).

In the case of wet sediments, as at York, the accumulation of archaeological deposits by the agencies of digging pits and wells and rubbish disposal for example, and the breakdown of the Roman drainage system raised the water table, allowing Viking and later deposits to be well preserved by waterlogging (Addyman *et al.* 1976). In contrast, a fall in the water table at London has allowed many deposits to oxidise, except for those in riverside sites, for instance Billingsgate. The environmental character of Viking York (Kenward *et al.*, volume I), Saxon Ipswich and Norwich (Murphy, volume I) and other early cities (Bell in press, volume I; Armitage *et al.*, this volume) is presented elsewhere. Suffice it to say that these analyses will help understand the environmental contexts in which the 'dark earth' was deposited. Later urban sediments, which often merge with the 'dark earth' and lumped as Medieval and Post Medieval, also give an indication of land use; for example Princess Street, Chester. Here areas of 'dark earth' were possibly used for grazing since the thirteenth century (Macphail 1982, AML Report 3741). Again, botanical analysis of local waterlogged sediments allow some understanding of the urban environments at this time, for instance Broad Sanctuary London (Scaife 1980, AML Report 3001).

8.3   Man-Made Soils

Examples of soil amelioration, using seaweed and calcareous sand for plaggens, have been quoted from the South West and the North (Bell in press, volume I; Romans and Robertson, in press c). The probable prehistoric use of seaweed for example in Sussex has also been discussed by Bell (1981c). Detailed analyses of a number of Irish plaggens showed additions of calcareous sand and dung gave increments of P, K, Mg and Na to Ap horizons nearly one metre thick developed on podzol subsoils and these probably enabled a wider range of crops to be grown (Conry 1971). Additions of wood and peat ash to acidic soils on superficial deposits and moorland areas in prehistoric times, can be cited (Bell 1981a, Romans and Robertson, in press b), while heathland soils were probably converted to brown earths at Wotton Common, Surrey, by marling in the Medieval period (Bunting and Green 1964).

8.4   Future Work

(i)   The scarcity of preserved buried soils in urban areas give them great importance for an understanding of pre-urban and early urban conditions, which is of both archaeological and pedological interest.

(ii)   The above is relevant to a proper interpretation of 'dark earth' as this deposit includes material from original local soils, which according to their alteration gives clues to usage of this urban sediment. However, corroboratory environmental information is best sought in local contemporaneous waterlogged deposits.

(iii)   Soil amelioration and management in prehistory has often been suggested from sites, but no overall review has yet been carried out.

Table 16   Urban and Man-Made Soils

No.	Site and Location	Feature	Age	Buried Soil	Environment	Author
	Natural Soils					
72	Lloyds Bank, London	Occupation	'R'	argillic brown earth	probable arable (S)	Macphail 1980, AML Report 3045
73	Gryme's Dyke, Colchester, Essex	Wall	R	truncated brown soil		Taylor 1978, AML Report 2470
74	Towcester, Northants	Wall	R	'immature mull humus'		Dalrymple 1958
75	Princess Street, Chester, Cheshire	Road—Wall	R	truncated typical brown sand		Macphail 1982, AML Report 3741
76	Tarraby, Carlisle, Cumbria	Vallum	R	gleyed brown soil		Keeley 1977, AML Report 2228
77	Carlisle, Cumbria	Wall	R	abandoned plough soil	arable (S)	Keeley 1979, AML Report 2887
78	Madison Street, Southampton, Hants	Occupation	S	ploughsoil over earlier gleyed cultivated brown earth	arable (S)	Keeley 1980, AML Report 3211
79	Ipswich, Suffolk	Occupation	S	brown podzolic soil		Keeley and Macphail 1978, AML Report 2691
	Urban Soils					
80	Chaucer Street, Southwark, London	Occupation	Late R—Med	'Dark Earth'		Taylor 1978, AML Report 2493
81	Arcadia Buildings, Southwark, London	Occupation	Late R—Med	'Dark Earth'	possible garden soil (S)	Macphail 1981c
82	St Bartholomew's, London	Occupation	Late R—11th C	'Dark Earth'	possible garden soil (S)	Macphail 1981c, 1982
83	GPO, London	Occupation	Late R—Med	'Dark Earth'	possible garden soil (SP)	Macphail 1981c, 1982

No.	Site and Location	Feature	Age	Buried Soil	Environment	Author
84	Tanners Hall, Gloucester	Occupation	Late R–Med	'Dark Earth'	probable cultivated soil (S)	Macphail 1982
85	Princess Street, Chester	Occupation	Late R–Med	'Dark Earth'	possible garden soil – later pasture (S)	Macphail 1982, AML Report 3741
86	The Bedern, York	Occupation	Late R–Med	'Dark Earth'	probable dump (SP)	Macphail 1983
87	Keays Lane, Carlisle	Occupation	Late R–Med	'Dark Earth'	possible dump (S)	Macphail 1981c
88	Towcester, Northants	Occupation	Late R–Med	'Dark Earth'	probable cultivated soil (S)	Macphail 1983, AML Report
89	Whitefriars, Norwich	Occupation	S–Med	'Dark Earth'	probable dump (SP)	Macphail 1982, Scaife 1981

9 Topics

9.1 Crop Marks

Crop marks and soil marks seen in aerial photographs (Wilson in press) pick out crop responses to soil variations relating to archaeological features and are best developed in:

(i) arable areas of eastern and southern England, and eastern Scotland;

(ii) where bare soil-marks relate to the occurrence of light coloured subsoils (e.g. chalk); and

(iii) where shallow loamy soils have rooting depths between 30–60cm and crop marks are caused by soil moisture deficit interacting with nutrient supply and soil depth (Jones and Evans 1975).

Marks are better recorded in cereals than grasses, appearing first in shallow soils when the potential soil moisture deficit, which occurs when water transpired by a crop exceeds rainfall, is greater than the amount of water in the soil is available to the plant (Evans and Jones 1977). More faint crop marks also occur in wet years, probably because of waterlogging (Evans and Jones 1977), which may lead to nitrogen shortage, or archaeological features may cut through drainage impedance levels, also producing a crop mark (Bellhouse 1982). Soil conditions, crop marks and potential soil moisture deficit have been linked from an Iron Age site survey at Fisherwick, Staffordshire, where for instance there was better plant growth over a ditch, because the deeper soil allowed plants to reach greater available water (Jones and Smith 1979, Jones 1979). Taylor (1979) reported ploughsoils above ditches at Winchester maintained their character after repeated ploughing of level areas, although deep ploughing removed shallow features. Difference in crop marks between soil series, for example Clifton series and Salop series were noted by Bellhouse (pers comm), who also suggests crop marks occur through the poaching of grass.

9.2 Earthworks and other building (see 3.3i, 4.2i, 5.4i relevant 'environments')

Buried soils at Barnard's Castle, County Durham (Keeley 1979, AML Report 2911) and at Beeston Castle, Cheshire (Macphail 1980, AML Report 3235) suffered dramatic increases in pH as calcium carbonate was washed in from mortar above, reducing the likelihood of pollen preservation.

9.3 Buried Soils

This section highlights the importance of buried soils both in understanding (a) the environment under which the soils developed prior to burial, and (b) pedogenesis in the different types of environments through time, as discussed earlier. The interest in buried soils lies in their unique ability to preserve the soil as it was (if well sealed), and to provide a soil profile which can be dated. Normally, dating is archaeological (e.g. monument and/or artefact typologies, radiocarbon dates of included organic materials), but occasionally sites may be dated through radiocarbon dating of organic matter in the buried land surface (see 9.6). Thus, for instance, the character of an Atlantic age argillic brown earth from beneath colluvium was investigated at Pegwell Bay, Kent (Weir *et al.* 1971), soil formation up to Neolithic times was studied on Chalk from three long barrows at Avebury, Wiltshire (Ashbee *et al.* 1979), and the development of podzols by the Bronze Age was established from soils buried beneath round barrows by Dimbleby (1962). Later monuments, such as Hadrian's Wall (Keeley 1981, AML Report 3401), and Medieval banks in the New Forest (Eide 1982), also covered soil profiles containing evidence of local agriculture; while the soils beneath the Iron Age ramparts at Keston Camp, Kent (Cornwall 1953, Dimbleby 1962) revealed a podzol formed under primary woodland. Another advantage of studying soils from a buried landscape may be cited from Dartmoor, where podzolisation and incipient peat formation were dated to the Bronze Age at Shaugh Moor (Keeley and Macphail in Balaam *et al.* 1982), whereas previously soil scientists had suggested major soil degradation in the post–Bronze Age period (Clayden and Manley 1964). Finally, it is worth noting that buried soils may also provide corroborative evidence through pollen or molluscan analysis; and it may also be possible to discriminate post burial soil effects, such as gleying (see 2.3.vii) from features relating to pre-burial land use, especially by micromorphology (see 9.4.iv).

9.4 Micromorphology

i.   *Soil erosion and soil aggregate stability*
Forest soil aggregates were found to be more stable than farmland soil aggregates under rainsplash – the latter slaking, while forest soil micro-aggregates, which are more porous and contain more organic matter, may be transported by splash (Imeson and Jungerius 1976). On both acid and calcareous soils Grieve (1980) found that grassland developed a more stable A horizon than that under woodland, because of the greater root density and intimate mixture of organic matter under grass, but that woodland provided a better protective cover. Protection of the soil by forest canopy was also noted in the Luxembourg Ardennes, where a lack of erosion even on the steepest slopes was associated with woodland cover – the removal of which led to soil disturbance, erosion and colluviation (Imeson and Jungerius 1974). Further experimental work has identified that erosion of a loess soil may actually take place even under an oak/beech woodland, principally when soil becomes exposed, through a number of agencies, in the early autumn – perhaps

357

producing 6cm of colluvium every hundred years (Imeson *et al.* 1980). The mode of origin of this colluvium, whether rainsplash, overland flow and rainsplash, or afterflow, have been characterised by micromorphology (Imeson *et al.* 1980, Mücher *et al.* 1981). The character of transported materials in thin section have been listed by Mücher (1974) and include, papules, sharply bounded glaebules and rounded soil aggregates from other horizons. Such criteria were used to identify colluvium resulting from erosion after Medieval deforestation and cultivation in the Luxembourg Ardennes (Kwaad and Mücher 1977, 1979).

ii.   *Agricutans*
Soil disturbance (see above) also produces micro-features known as agricutans (Jongerius 1970) – and phases of woodland clearance followed by cultivation have been identified from these in both sandy (Kwaad and Mücher 1979) and loessic (Bolt *et al.* 1980) soils in Europe. Briefly, in some circumstances, land use can be associated with micromorphological features, as follows: woodland – limpid argillans (Plate 9); clearance – dusty argillans (Plate 10), charcoal; cultivation – agricutans (Plate 11), silt and charcoal (Slager and van der Wetering 1977, Jongerius 1970, Courty 1982, Bullock *et al.* in press). It should also be remembered that podzolisation as shown in the field and in thin sections may also occur under woodland (see Keston Camp – 5.i), and that some 'dusty' argillans may relate to clay decomposition (Brinkman *et al.* 1973).

Agricutans are thought to only occur relatively near the soil surface (just beneath the Ap) through the slaking of soil aggregates, but in heavy, deeply cracking soils they may reach 70cm (Jongerius 1970). The presence of agricutans at a depth of 160cm led Kwaad and Mücher (1979), who reviewed the origin and character of agricutans, to conclude that in their sandy soils agricutans were formed during the deposition of the overlying colluvium – under the agency of human cultivation. On Lower Greensand, at Wotton Common, Surrey, similar reasoning indicates that agricutans buried by over a metre of colluvium may relate to prehistoric agriculture (see 4.2iii, Macphail and Scaife in preparation).

Little experimental study has been made of prehistoric cultivation and these microfeatures, but variation in depth of maximum clay deposition in pores led Romans and Robertson (in press b, in press c) to suggest at Strathallan, Perthshire, that different cultivation methods were used. In cultivation ridges maximum deposition occurred at 4–5cm while below a henge bank maximum deposition was at 12cm, indicating shallow hoeing of the former and deeper ard ploughing of the latter. Micromorphology also showed the close similarity between the modern plough soil and the buried Neolithic soil at Barnack-Bainton Northamptonshire, again suggesting probable early agriculture (French 1983).

In dug soils (alluvial plaggens) in Holland matri-argillans (agricutans) were also present (Miedema *et al.* 1978). At Tanners Hall, Gloucester, and Towcester 'dark earth' contained evidence of the addition of several different soil types, the mixing-in of organic matter, and cultivation in the form of agricutans and organans (Macphail 1982, 1983). Some coatings may also be related to the disturbance of the soil caused by dumping, as Romans and Robertson (in press b) were able to detect two sequences of construction in a prehistoric mound at Strathallan, by two phases of clay deposition, and these should not be confused with agricutans.

iii.   *Archaeological deposits*
The development of limpid argillans in pit-fills not only indicated a wooded phase at sites in Germany and France, but also suggested increased deposition of fine clay because the high K content of the fill relating to the presence of ashes (Slager and van der Wetering 1977, Courty and Federoff 1982b). Clearance and fires tend to produce heterogeneous micro-coatings of badly sorted charcoal and silt, while occupation fires (hearth) give rise to fine well sorted charcoal (Courty, pers comm). Courty (in press) carried out an experimental examination of oak and pine burned for various lengths of time and the layers produced by a large wood fire; and has related these to archaeological layers on sites. In a complete burn the upper layer is comprised of white ashes of poorly formed calcite crystals, over a 'reddened' soil layer. Beneath, the soil is 'blackish' containing not fully oxidised charcoal. These layers become compressed after about six months, but the fragile white ash layer may be well preserved, even after millenia, if burial conditions are dry and calcareous. On acid and wetter soils, the calcite ashes are replaced, probably by a phosphate residue (Courty, in press). 'Blackish' layer material has been found in thin sections from the Neolithic long barrow at Hazleton and most probably relate to pre-barrow occupation (Macphail in preparation). Similarly, thin sections (made by Cornwall) of a hearth from a Bronze Age barrow at Earls Farm Down, Wiltshire, on chalk, include the fabrics described by Courty (above), but in addition have been partially reworked by earthworms (Plate 12).

Charcoal in the soil, from clearance or stubble burning, for example, is commonly coarse near the surface, but becomes increasingly fragmented by biological activity, and may be included in dusty argillans (Courty and Federoff 1982b). The blackish colour of 'dark earth' has been related to the intimate mixing of fine charcoal with soil, and numerous inclusions of anthropogenic origin, such as pottery, oyster shell, bone and mortar (Macphail 1981c, 1982). A scanning electron microscope x-ray analysis of 'dark earth' from GPO London revealed, besides large amounts of the soil forming elements, Si, Al, Fe and Mg, much Ca and K, with less Ma and P, suggesting a very fertile environment (Macphail 1982, AML Report 3633).

Equally, the micromorphology of cave sediments (see 2.1) indicates that they can be biogenic and anthropogenic, rather than sedimentary in origin (Goldberg 1979a, 1979b).

iv.   *Buried soils*

Beneath Bronze Age barrows at West Heslerton, Yorkshire, limpid argillans preceded dusty coatings and sequioxidic (from podzolisation) coatings which contained fine charcoal, indicating a phase of stable, probably wooded conditions (after original clearance on the site) predated clearance, burning and podzolisation (Macphail 1982, AML Report 3706).

A review of thin sections (made by Cornwall) from beneath long barrows (Table 2) showed only minor pre-barrow soil disturbance at Ascott-under-Wychwood, Wiltshire, Nutbane, Hampshire and Fussells Lodge, Wiltshire – although the latter contained burned soil and possibly ashes, compared with Willerby Wold, Yorkshire. In the mound of the latter, soil fabrics probably relating to pre-barrow woodland, clearance, cultivation and burning were present. The agricutans present in the Bt horizon of the buried soil at the long barrow at Kilham, Yorkshire, have already been mentioned (see 3.3iv).

Cornwall also made thin sections from Bronze Age barrow turves, for example Earls Farm Down, Wiltshire and from buried Iron Age cultivation soils, for example, Burywood Camp, Wiltshire. Turves from the Bronze Age barrow at Sproxton, Leicestershire had a relic lamina fabric picked out by manganese relating to a densely rooted mull horizon (Macphail 1981b) – although very little organic matter remained probably because of base rich conditions (Macphail 1979, AML Report 2926). The unique nature of buried turf (thin section by Cornwall) at Silbury Hill, Wiltshire, occurred through exceptional preservation of the grass turf in a brown earth, because of the anaerobic conditions produced by burial.

In comparison, buried turf from acid soils have been examined from beneath a Bronze Age barrow at West Heath, Sussex and the Experimental Earthwork at Wareham, Dorset. Besides the much greater organic matter preservation overall on acid soils, thin sections from West Heath show organic matter to be much more dense, black (melanic – Dinc *et al.* 1976) and amorphous than the recently buried turf at Wareham (Macphail 1981, AML Reports 3586, 3587).

Buried organic horizons from a moorland Bronze Age site (Saddlesborough Reave, Dartmoor) generally show similarly aged acid organic matter, but one part was affected by earthworm activity – probably produced by the regeneration of the moorland soil by the dumping of unweathered spoil (Keeley and Macphail in Balaam *et al.* 1982). Ways of calculating degree of 'soil degradation' or upland podzolisation in moorland areas has been carried out by measuring bleached stone rims, and the depth to which they occur in correlation with soil profile macromorphology (Romans and Robertson 1975b, in press c). The original presence of earthworms in a brown forest soil – prior to podzolisation on moorland, has been corroborated by the movement of stones down profile and the occurrence of rewelded porous fabrics (Romans and Robertson 1975b).

v.   *Relic features*

Micromorphological features relating to the last interglacial and earlier soil formation were disrupted by cryoturbation during the Devensian and can be differentiated, for example from post-Glacial pedogenesis – by often forming discreet bodies such as papules, rounded fossil aggregates, and perhaps clay concentrations produced by compression (Bullock and Murphy 1979).

9.5   Phosphorus and Body Stains

Anomalously high quantities of phosphorus (P) are commonly associated with (a) occupation areas, because of the accumulation of organic wastes, domestic refuse and ashes, and (b) with burials, because of the presence of bone (Proudfoot 1976, Faul and Smith 1980, Keeley 1980, AML Report 3095, Keeley and Macphail 1981b). Topsoil usually contains higher quantities of P than the subsoil except generally when extraneous material has been added (Faull and Smith 1980). Keeley (1980, AML Report 3095) in her review found enhanced P, measured semi-quantitatively, could be related to flint miners' debris at Grimes Graves, Norfolk; occupation deposits at St Martins, Nornour and Samson, Isles of Scilly; probable inhumations at Watch Hill, St Austell, Cornwall and Saxon, Norman and Medieval occupation levels at St Peters Street, Northampton, for example. Semi-quantitative analysis also tended to show greater P in 'wet' 'dark earth' than 'dry' 'dark earth' (Macphail 1981c). Phosphate spot tests were also used in conjunction with field and soil survey and crop mark interpretation at Fisherwick, Staffordshire (Jones and Smith 1979).

The location of possible ecclesiastical sites, based on place-name information in Yorkshire were checked by quantitative phosphate analysis (Faul and Smith 1980). They felt, after a discussion of the various types of P in soil, that their phosphate data could be best interpreted if the variation in natural soils, physiography and drainage were all taken into consideration. Both Proudfoot (1976) and Keeley (1980, AML Report 3095) also considered methods of phosphorus analysis but stated as yet there was no way of differentiating between natural P and human P.

Baker (1976) discussed the effects of pedogenesis on P, suggesting considerable amounts are complexed by organic matter and could be moved to a depth of 1m in 10,000 years. However, Romans and Robertson (in press b), quoting other workers and their own site evidence, suggested P may move significantly within archaeological time, i.e. 1cm per 20–40 years.

Phosphate surveys have (a) discriminated between arable and village (occupation) areas in the deserted Medieval village at Low Buston Northumberland (Alexander and Roberts 1978), (b) been used to interpret usage of Romano—British hut-circles in Clwyd using trend surface analysis (Conway in press) and (c) been used to identify possible stock areas in a Bronze Age enclosure on Dartmoor (Balaam and Porter in Balaam *et al.* 1982), for example. Phosphate analysis is also being used to trace prehistoric drove-ways elsewhere on Dartmoor (Ralph pers comm).

Trace element analysis of body stains at Spong Hill, Norfolk were associated with higher P than the surrounding soil, but amounts of copper (Cu) were obscured by the presence of grave goods (Keeley 1979, AML Report 2902). However, at Mucking, Essex, Anglo-Saxon body stains were related to concentrations of P, Mn and Cu — manganese (Mn) which was absorbed from the soil, acted as the best indicator of skeletal areas (Keeley *et al.* 1977).

9.6   Organic matter and C14 dating

Problems of dating soils (Tamm and Ostlund 1960) using radiocarbon techniques have been described (Scharpenseel 1971, Valentine and Dalrymple 1976, Goh and Molloy 1978). They suggest that different organic matter fractions and soil environments influence the dates measured. Two major sources of organic matter radiocarbon dates can be highlighted. These are buried surface organic matter horizons and Bh horizons.

The radiocarbon age of a buried A horizon does not represent the date of burial, because organic matter which it contains is already old. The half-life of organic matter fractions vary, and further differ, with more rapid decomposition in neutral soils than in acid soils (Jenkinson 1977, Jenkinson and Rayner 1977, Cerri and Jenkinson 1981). In a steady state of organic matter turnover at Rothamsted (Harpenden, Hertfordshire) an A horizon will record a predicted radiocarbon age of 1240 years (Jenkinson and Rayner 1977). Weir *et al.* (1971) used figures of around 1200 and 1300 years to give their buried soil, which had an apparent age of 6120 ± 250 years, an approximate age of burial at 5000 Bp. Eide (1982) quotes a figure of 1450 ± 95 years to be subtracted from her buried soil dates.

Sources of contamination in buried soils has been examined (Valentine and Dalrymple 1976) and Limmer and Wilson (1980) suggest they can differentiate fossil amino acids from any later contamination.

Dates of organic matter in Bh horizons represent mean residence time of the organic matter (Valentine and Dalrymple 1976). Scharpenseel (1971) suggested dates vary little within the upper, middle and lower Bh horizons, but significant age differences by Righi and Guillet (1977) refute this (see 4.i). Bh horizons in East Anglia were dated by Perrin *et al.* (1964) to have apparent ages varying from 1580 ± 200 to 2860 ± 200 years, indicating podzolisation took place well after the onset of heath in about 5500 BP. However, if mean residence time is taken into consideration, a relatively (biologically) inert Bh horizon dated at 3770 ± 150 BP years at West Heath, Sussex, indicated podzolisation commenced in the late Mesolithic (Scaife and Macphail in preparation). Here the apparent Bronze Age date was aided by the humo-ferric podzol being buried beneath a Bronze Age barrow — causing very diminished or eventual cessation of organic matter illuviation.

Other soil dating methods include paleomagnetic and thermoluminiscence analysis which have been utilised in Hungarian loess (Pecsi *et al.* 1979), for instance. Currently, attempts at using thermoluminiscence to date wind blown sand at the Palaeolithic site at Hengistbury Head, Hampshire are being made (Barton, pers comm).

9.7   Environmental materials in soils See 2.3vii for preservation of organic matter, seeds, wood etc, and Dimbleby and Evans (1974) and Scaife and Thomas (Volume II) for pollen and snails.

Phytoliths, because they can provide botanical evidence where soil pollen is poorly preserved have attracted much attention in England (Smithson 1958) and abroad (Twiss *et al.* 1969, Rovner 1971, Geiss 1973, Bartoli and Guillet 1977). Some general information has been obtained on 'Dark Earth' (Macphail 1981c) and an East Anglian heathland area (Murphy, volume I in press), but detailed botanical identifications have also been carried out using S.E.M. (Palmer 1976) in preference to light microscopy.

9.8   Preservation of artefacts

The variation in preservation of pottery in various soil environments have been discussed earlier. Effects of soil conditions on corrosion of buried tin-bronzes and copper may be mentioned. Tylecote (1979) found that acid soils were aggressive, alkaline soils were benign, and strangely that peats were also benign, in spite of their acidity — probably due to the protective action of polyphenols.

10   Techniques

These can be divided into:

10.1   Field
(a)   Remote sensing, such as aerial photographic interpretation of crop and soil marks (see 9.1).

(b)   Survey in the form of (i) grid survey, for example for soil phosphorus content (see 9.5), (ii) auger survey, for example for depth and extent of such deposits as colluvium and (iii) soil mapping, to relate soil type at the excavation site to the soil landscape and the effects of slope, in relationship to landuse capability and workability classification (see 1.2).

(c)   Profile (section) description of buried soil horizons and archaeological layers (see 1.2).

(d)   Sampling, for (i) bulk samples (3–500gm) for particle size and general chemical analysis, (ii) specific spot sampling (10–100gm) for instance for phosphate analysis, and (iii) undisturbed samples (in Kubiena boxes –6.5 x 7.5cm or monolith boxes –10 x 50cm) for thin section (micromorphological) analysis.

10.2   Laboratory

Here the number of techniques employed per site varies according to the specific problems posed by the archaeologist and the time and resources available to the soil scientist. Different sites require different methods and as resources are very limited a pragmatic approach is necessary. Some useful techniques include the following:

(i)   *Chemical*

(a)   *pH* measured (see 1.2) on site or in the laboratory, will provide information on the likelihood of pollen and molluscan preservation, general soil conditions and any contamination from overlying levels (see 9.2).

(b)   *Organic Matter* (i) Alkali Soluble Humus (Cornwall 1958) does not measure all (ii) Organic Carbon (Avery and Bascomb, 1974) and some relatively organic rich horizons e.g. in podzol Bs horizons, are very poor in humus (Anderson *et al.* 1982), while (iii) Loss on Ignition includes the charcoal content of a soil – the latter being important in the understanding of anthropogenic deposits. Thus, a generally useful approach is a combination of (i) or (ii), with (iii). As examples, organic matter analysis allows buried A horizons or plough soils to be differentiated from B horizons; dumped materials to be characterised e.g. in pits, ditches, waterlogged sites and urban sites and in addition, permit thin sections to be more accurately interpreted – as organic matter is not always obvious.

(c)   *Iron* (and aluminium) Full analysis (Avery and Bascomb 1974) is desirable (Maltby in Ball, volume I) but not always available, and large overall variations, such as in buried podzols may be identified by adhesive tape soil ignition profiles (Dimbleby 1962), in which obscuring organic matter is removed and amounts of iron show up clearly after being oxidised – a technique easily combined with loss on ignition.

(d)   *Phosphate* (see 9.5).

(e)   *Other chemical analyses* include Cation Exchange Capacity and measurement of Exchangeable Cations (Avery and Bascomb 1974) such as Ca, K, Mg and Na, which with nitrogen (N) and phosphate (P) analysis provide data on potential fertility of archaeological soils, identify contamination from marine influences, or explain fine clay illuviation in pits by the presence of ashes (Slager and van der Wetering 1977, Courty and Federoff 1982b).

(ii)   *Physical*

(a)   *Grain size analysis* This allows overall characterisation of the physical nature of the soil, and in addition may give information such as burial by blown sand, for example at Bar Point, Isles of Scilly (Macphail 1981, AML Report 3299); on alluvial deposits, for example, of the Sussex Ouse (Burrin and Scaife, in press); or identify the possible addition of loess to sandy soils at Selmeston, Sussex (Macphail 1983, AML Report 3982). Ditch (Evans and Limbrey 1974) and pit fills, and colluvium may also be interpreted by grain size analysis.

(b)   *Heavy mineral analysis* Few sites have been investigated by this technique (Macphail 1979, AML Report 2926, Conway 1980, French 1983) – although mineralogical analysis is commonplace in fabric analysis of pottery. Heavy mineral analysis gives specific information on soil weathering and presence of such influential materials as loess (Catt 1979).

(iii)   *Micromorphological*

The analysis of thin sections (Bullock *et al.* in press) gives data on both the physical and chemical composition of the soil. However, it gives a better overall understanding of the soil and may be more specific (Fisher and Macphail in press). For instance, a soil, bulk sampled and analysed by grain size as a loam in fact may comprise separate fabric areas of clay, and areas of sand and silt – for example where different soils were dumped together at Tanners Hall, Gloucester (Bell and Macphail in Heighway, in press). The occurrence and character of the iron content, the organic matter fraction, the mesofauna (by their excrements) and the state of weathering in the soil, for example, may all be recognised in thin section. In addition, the smallest areas of fabric may be chemically analysed by microprobe.

Other analytical techniques (10.2.i, ii) and quantitative analysis of the microfabric, together give a clear understanding of the soil, but micromorphology as shown earlier (see Soil Environments; 9.4) can also provide much information about past environments and anthropogenic activity. Micromorphology, which was first related to archaeology by Cornwall (1958) is now beginning to be an exact science (Bullock *et al.* in press) in pedology. Moreover, such past occurrences as erosion, clearance, burning, cultivation and dumping may also be identified in the microfabric of buried soils and archaeological deposits. Much careful work has yet to be carried out in the field of micromorphology in archaeology and this should be carried out in close correlation with other sources of environmental data to produce substantiated interpretations.

10.3   Future Work

(i)   *Field* It would be useful for sites not to be studied in isolation but related to the landscape as a whole, with a basic understanding of the local and on-site soils gained by the excavator — who should also be competent to take the full range of soil samples (see 10.1).

(ii)   *Laboratory* There is a great deal of potential for improving the understanding of particular archaeological soils by judicious use of physical and chemical analyses, but as ever this must be with regard to the requirements and worth of individual sites.

(iii)   *Micromorphology* Future studies may do well to establish the types of micromorphological fabrics per soil environment — in (a) contemporary soils e.g. as available reference collections at Rothamsted Experimental Station, Hertfordshire and the International Soil Museum, Wageningen, Holland — as compared to (b) dated buried soils. In this instance besides current work being carried out by the author and others (Romans and Robertson, Courty, Goldberg, Fisher etc) the reference collection of thin sections by Cornwall, at the Institute of Archaeology, should be examined in detail. In addition, attempts should be made to classify specific micro-features (see 9.4) and their relationship to environments and land use (a research programme to examine soil coatings developed under various land uses, such as old woodland, pasture and arable, is about to commence at the Soil Survey under Thompson); and how soil materials may alter through time.

11   Summary of Future Work

1.   In the coastal zone there is scope to investigate, with other environmentalists, Boreal/Atlantic shorelines submerged in Mesolithic times, as well as later marine inundations which affected river valleys. Use of coastal resources, such as shell sand and seaweed for soil amelioration, as identified in the South West (Bell, in press volume I) may also warrant further attention.

2.   Former covers of loess have been identified on areas of Chalk and heath, for example, and from studies of alluvium it is likely that in some areas quantities were not eroded off into rivers until the Boreal. The possibility of areas of loess attracting man have been stated, but as yet there is little data on the effects of loess on heathlands and Chalk areas in prehistory, or its identification in similarly dated colluvium.

3.   The impact of early agriculture on soil, which is associated with the above loess question, has not been fully established — as for example the consequences to soil formation — such as the suggestion that lessivage was initiated by cultivation of superficial deposits on Chalklands. Secondly, although soil erosion has been recognised and dated on these Chalklands, areas of colluvium from cultivation of heathlands, prior to podzolisation, have yet to be recognised.

In addition, major alluvial sedimentation is dated to the Iron Age, with as yet few observations of what was happening to the Neolithic and Bronze Age colluvium in dry valleys (Bell 1981a).

In this context, some heed could be paid to studies of prehistoric land management and conservation (Bell 1981a, 1981c).

4.   The difference in date of the onset of podzolisation and peat formation (in the Bronze Age, Iron Age or as late as Medieval) vary on moorland areas across the country, and this pattern is worthy of further investigation.

5.   In both the lowland and upland zones, the history of soil formation and land use in intervening valleys and claylands is sparsely understood in comparison to hill and upland areas.

6.   Very little is known about the effects of prehistoric man on clayland soils, although Soil Survey data indicates the difficulty of working such land in the much later Saxon and Medieval periods.

7.   Much useful information could be gained from the examination of buried soils from the later periods, such as was the case at Keston Camp, Kent. Some examples may include the relationship between Romano–British soils, lynchets and colluvium; medieval agricultural expansions onto marginal land, or the variety and use of ridge and furrow.

8.   A gradual understanding of the formation and utilisation of man-made soils in urban areas and elsewhere is arising, but as yet there is still a need for data on the role of the original or local natural soils, and the correlation of those man-made deposits with urban history.

9.   The constituents of urban sediments of a purely refuse or dumped origin are of more interest to other environmentalists, but post depositional pedogenesis relating to water-logging or oxidation may produce characteristics of pertinence to archaeology — such as the mineral vivianite, which can be associated with cess or 'marine soil' ripening.

10.   When examining buried soils, barrow mounds or other archaeological deposits it is important to appreciate how soils may alter through time, according to base status, fauna, or degree of anaerobism, as these govern the quality of soil preservation. It is increasingly necessary as interpretations become more precise for field and laboratory techniques to be able to identify post-depositional changes. Both micromorphological and chemical techniques may be used to do this.

11.   In the future soil science methods, whether in the field or laboratory should be problem-orientated rather than just providing 'data'; so that chemical techniques such as phosphate analysis can be applied to surveys of possible cemeteries or animal stocking areas, micromorphology may be used as a guide to a soil's history as preserved in a buried microfabric, or soil mapping may allow comparison of prehistoric and present day landscapes.

12   Conclusions

1.   Soil science provides an extremely valuable background to environmental studies in archaeology. Firstly, in identifying basic site characteristics (i.e. relationship of soil type to site), and secondly, by reflecting the site environment (i.e. chemical and physical properties of the buried soil may indicate pedological history and pre-burial land use) and later soil changes (i.e. variations between buried and local soils). Other branches of soil science furnish useful information on land use classification, and problems with tillage and drainage, for example on modern soils, which may be directly comparable to prehistoric landscape economies.

2.   Soil science also enables early soil formation to be appreciated, especially if type sites such as Pegwell Bay are utilised, through the comprehension of fundamental soil processes. This basic understanding is crucial if the Mesolithic and Neolithic effects on soils, for example, are to be interpreted properly.

3.   Areas least altered by modern cultivation (i.e. chalk and lowland limestone; heathlands; and moorlands), and containing the most sites, provide the greatest quantity of information on prehistoric soils. Intervening areas, such as valleys and lowlands have fewer sites by reason of being possibly unattractive to prehistoric man, e.g. claylands — or by being obscured by later agriculture and alluvium, and thus their early soil history is mainly speculative. An important environmental problem is therefore the linking of these two zones, so that landscapes can be understood as a whole. For instance, the early (Bronze Age/Iron Age) soil degradation on Shaugh Moor, Devon cannot be extrapolated to the South Hams.

4.   One possible way of linking the two zones identified in 3, is by identifying land use changes through studies of colluvium and alluvium — as these reflect the intensity of soil disturbance in a river catchment.

5.   In the urban environment two main topics can be isolated. These are (a) the corroboration of possible within-wall cultivation in the late Roman period — and this is also related to the pre-urban soils and studies of man-made soils in general; and (b) the further understanding of the preservation and pedogenic alteration of dumped material in an urban context.

6.   Various techniques related to soil science, which are useful to archaeology, have been briefly commented on. The kinds of scientific disciplines mentioned are very wide ranging, but have been successfully applied to archaeology. In this context, a certain amount of experimental work and close comparison of site results, needs to be carried out if these techniques are to be accurately employed to their full potential.

ACKNOWLEDGEMENTS

The author wishes to thank the following for their help with the Review;

P Abrahamson, M A Alexander, R H Allen, N Balaam, G Barclay, M Bell, R Bellhouse, P Bullock, C P Burnham, J A Catt, J S Conway, W Corbett, I Cornwall, M A Courty, R Evans, N Federoff, P F Fisher, C A I French, H George, J Hazelden, J Hollis, M G Jarvis, R J A Jones, H C M Keeley, S Limbrey, E Maltby, J J M van der Meer, A Moffat, H J Mücher, C P Murphy, N Ralph, D N Riley, D Robson, W Roebroeks, J C C Romans, R G Scaife, J Sevink, R T Smith, R G Sturdy, D R Wilson, C A Whiteman and A Whittle.

REFERENCES

ABRAMSON P, 1980
A study of the pedological and vegetational development within and beneath the mounds of two round barrows on the North Yorkshire Moors, unpublished MA Thesis, University of Bradford.

ADDYMAN P V, HOOD J S R, KENWARD H K, MacGREGOR A, WILLIAMS D, 1976
'Palaeoclimate in urban environmental archaeology at York, England', *World Archaeology* 8, 2, 220–233.

AKEROYD A V, 1972
'Archaeological and historical evidence for subsidence in southern Britain', *Phil Trans Roy Soc London A* 272, 151–169.

ALEXANDER J, OZANNE P C, OZANNE A, 1960
'Report on the investigation of a round barrow on Arreton Down, Isle of Wight', *Proc Prehist Soc* 26, 263–302.

ALEXANDER M J, ROBERTS B K, 1978
'The deserted village of Low Buston, Northumberland'. A study in soil phosphate analysis', *Archaeol Aeliana,* Series 5, VI, 107–116.

ALLEN R H, STURDY R G, 1980
'The environmental background', in Buckley D G (ed), *Archaeology in Essex to AD 1500,* Counc British Archaeol Res Rep No. 34, 1–7.

ALLEN M J, 1983
Sediment analyses and archaeological data as evidence of the palaeoenvironments of early Eastbourne. The Bourne Valley Excavation, unpublished BSc dissertation, Institute of Archaeology, University of London.

ANDERSON H A, *et al.,* 1982
'A reassessment of podzol formation process', *J Soil Sci* 33, 1, 125–136.

ARMITAGE P, LOCKER A, STRAKER V, forthcoming
'Environmental Archaeology in London: A Review', Chapter 5, this volume.

ASHBEE P, SMITH I F, EVANS J G, 1979
'Excavation of three Long Barrows near Avebury, Wiltshire', *Proc Prehist Soc* 45, 207–300.

ATHERDEN M A, 1976
'Vegetation of the North York Moors', *Trans Inst British Geographers* 1, 3, 284–300.

ATKINSON R J C, 1957
'Worms and weathering', *Antiquity* 31, 219–233.

AVERY B W, BASCOMB C L (eds), 1974
Soil Survey Laboratory Methods, Soil Survey Technical Monograph 6, Harpenden.

AVERY B W, FINDLAY D C, MACKNEY D, 1975
Soil Map of England and Wales 1:1,000,000, Ordnance Survey, Southampton.

AVERY B W, 1980
Soil Classification for England and Wales, Soil Survey Technical Monograph 14, Harpenden.

BAKER R T, 1976
'Changes in the chemical nature of soil organic phosphate during pedogenesis', *J Soil Sci* 27, 504–512.

BALAAM N D, PORTER H M, 1982
In Balaam N D, Smith K and Wainwright G J, 'The Shaugh Moor Project: Fourth Report – Environment, context and conclusion', *Proc Prehist Soc* 48, 203–278.

BALL D F, 1975
'Processes of soil degradation: a pedological point of view', in Evans J G, Limbrey S and Cleere H (eds), *The effect of man on the landscape: the Highland Zone,* Counc Brit Archaeol Res Rep No. 11, 20–27.

364

BARTOLI F, GUILLET B, 1977

'A comparative study of phytoliths and pollen diagrams of a sandy podzol in the Vosges', *Comptes Rendus Hebdomadaires des Seances de l'Academie des Sciences* D, 284, 5, 353–356.

BECKINSALE R P, RICHARDSON L, 1964

'Recent findings on the physical development of the Lower Severn Valley', *Geo J* 130, 1, 87–105.

BELL M, 1981a

Valley sediments as evidence of prehistoric land use: a study based on dry valleys in south east England, unpublished PhD thesis, Institute of Archaeology, University of London.

BELL M, 1981b

'Valley sediments and environmental change', in Jones M and Dimbleby G (eds), *The environment of man: the Iron Age to the Anglo-Saxon Period,* Brit Archaeol Rep (Brit Ser) 87, 75–91.

BELL M, 1981c

'Seaweed as a prehistoric resource', in Brothwell D and Dimbleby G (eds), *Environmental aspects of coasts and islands,* Brit Archaeol Rep (Intern Ser) 94, 117–126.

BELL M, in press

'Environmental archaeology in south west England', in Keeley H C M (ed), *Environmental Archaeology: A Regional Review,* Vol I, DAMHB Occasional Paper No. 6.

BELLHOUSE R L, 1982

'Soils and archaeology', in Alexander M J (ed), 'Soils, archaeology and land use history of the Solway Lowlands of Cumbria', *North of England Soils Discussion Group, Proceedings* 17, 41–47.

BIBBY J S, MACKNEY D, 1969

Land Use Capability Classification, Soil Survey Technical Monogr No. 1, Harpenden.

BISHOP M J, 1978

'Earliest record of man's presence in Britain', *Nature* 253, 5487, 95–97.

BOLT A J J, MÜCHER H J, SEVINK J, VERSTRATEN J M, 1980

'A study on loess-derived colluvia in southern Limburg (the Netherlands)', *Netherlands J Agric Sci* 28, 110–126.

BRADLEY R, KEITH–LUCAS M, 1975

'Excavation and pollen analysis on a bell barrow at Ascot, Berkshire', *J Archaeol Sci* 2, 95–108.

BRIDGES E M, 1970

World Soils, Cambridge University Press.

BRIDGES E M, 1978

'Interaction of soil and mankind in Britain', *J Soil Sci* 29, 125–139.

BRINKMAN R, JONGMANS A G, MIEDEMA R, MAASKANT P, 1973

'Clay decomposition in seasonally wet, acid soils: micro-morphological, chemical and mineralogical evidence from individual argillans', *Geoderma* 10, 259–270.

BROWN A G, 1982

'Human impact on the former floodplain woodlands of the Severn', in Bell M and Limbrey S (eds), *Archaeological aspects of woodland ecology,* Brit Archaeol Rep (Intern Ser) 146, 93–104.

BULLOCK P, MURPHY C P, 1979

'Evolution of a paleo-argillic brown earth (Paleudalf) from Oxfordshire, England', *Geoderma* 22, 225–252.

BULLOCK P, *et al.,* in press

Handbook for soil thin section description, Waine Research Publications.

BUNTING B T, GREEN R D, 1964

The soils and geomorphology of an area around Dorking. Guide to London excursions, in Clayton K M (ed), 20th International Geographers Congress London, 71–78.

BUOL S W, HOLE F D, McCRACKEN R J, 1973

Soil Genesis and Classification, Iowa State University Press, Ames.

BURLEIGH R, KERNEY M P, 1982   'Some chronological implications of a fossil molluscan assemblage from a Neolithic site at Brook, Kent, England', *J Archaeol Sci* 9, 29–38.

BURNHAM C P, McRAE S G, 1974   'The relationship of soil formation to geology in an area south-east of London', *Proc Geol Ass* 85, 1, 79–89.

BURRIN P, SCAIFE R G, in press (1983)   'Floodplain development in and the vegetational history of the Sussex High Weald and some archaeological implications', *Sussex Archaeol Collect* 121.

CATT J A *et al.*, 1971   'Loess in the soils of north Norfolk', *J Soil Sci* 22, 4, 444–452.

CATT J A, 1977   'Loess and coversands', in Shotton F W (ed), *British Quaternary; Recent Advances,* Clarendon Press.

CATT J A, 1978   'The contribution of loess to soils in lowland Britain', in Limbrey S and Evans J G (eds), *The effect of man on the landscape: The lowland zone, Counc Brit Archaeol Res Rep* 21, 12–20.

CATT J A, 1979   'Soils and Quaternary geology in Britain', *J Soil Sci* 30, 607–642.

CERRI C C, JENKINSON D S, 1981   'Formation of microbial biomass during the decomposition of ^{14}C labelled ryegrass in soil', *J Soil Sci* 32, 619–626.

CHURCHILL D M, 1965   'The kitchen midden site at Westward Ho!, Devon, England: ecology, age and relationship to changes in land and sea level', *Proc Prehist Soc* 5, 74–84.

CLAYDEN B, 1964   'Soils of Cornwall', in *Present views on some aspects of the geology of Cornwall and Devon,* Roy Geog Soc Cornwall, 311–330.

CLAYDEN B, MANLEY D J R, 1964   'The soils of the Dartmoor Granite', *Dartmoor Essays,* 117–140.

CLAYDEN B, HOLLIS J, in press   *Criteria for Differentiating Soil Series,* Soil Survey Technical Monogr No. 17, Harpenden.

CORCORAN J, 1963   'Excavation of the bell barrow in Deerleap Wood, Wotton', *Surrey Archaeol Collect* 60, 1–18.

COLES J M, ORME B J, 1980   *Prehistory of the Somerset Levels. Somerset Levels Project,* Austin and Sons Ltd, Hertford.

CONACHER A J, DALRYMPLE J B, 1977   'The nine unit land surface model: an approach to pedogeomorphic research', *Geoderma* 18, 1–2, 1–154.

DE CONINCK F, 1980   'Major mechanisms in formation of spodic horizons', *Geoderma* 24, 101–128.

CONRY M J, 1971   'Irish plaggen soils, their distribution, origin and properties', *J Soil Sci* 22, 401–416.

CONWAY J S, 1980   'Heavy mineralogy of soils from Cremlyn standing stone, Anglesey', *Trans Anglesey Antiq Soc,* 124.

CONWAY J S, in press   'An investigation of soil phosphorus distribution within occupation deposits from a Romano–British hut group', *J Archaeol Sci.*

CORNWALL I W, 1952   In Case H, 'The excavation of two round barrows at Poole, Dorset', *Proc Prehist Soc* 2, 9, 148–159.

CORNWALL I W, 1953   'Soil science and archaeology with illustrations from some British Bronze Age monuments', *Proc Prehist Soc* 2, 129.

CORNWALL I W, 1955   In Posnansky M, 'The excavation of a Bronze Age round barrow at Lockington', *Trans Leicestershire Archaeol Hist Soc* 31, 17–29, Appendix II.

CORNWALL I W, 1956a   In Ashbee P, 'Excavation of a barrow on Canford Heath', *Proc Dorset Natur Hist Archaeol Soc* 76, 39–50.

CORNWALL I W, 1956b   In Posnansky M, 'The Bronze Age round barrow at Swarkeston, Derbyshire', *J Derbyshire Archaeol Natur Hist Soc*, Vol , 10–26.

CORNWALL I W, 1958   *Soils for the archaeologist*, Phoenix House Ltd, London.

CORNWALL I W, 1959   In De Mallet Morgan F, 'The excavation of a long barrow at Nutbane, Hampshire', *Proc Prehist Soc* 25, 2, 15–51.

CORNWALL I W, 1962   In Lomas J, 'A Bronze Age site at Parwich, Derbyshire', *Derbyshire Archaeol J* 82, 91–99.

CORNWALL I W, 1963   In Manby T G, 'The excavation of the Willerby Wold long barrow, East Riding, Yorkshire', *Proc Prehist Soc* 29, 173–203.

CORNWALL I W, 1964   In Thomas N, 'The Neolithic causewayed camp at Robin Hood's Ball, Shrewton', *Wiltshire Archaeol Natur Hist Mag* 59, 1–27.

CORNWALL I W, 1966   In Ashbee P, 'The Fussells Lodge long barrow excavations 1957', Appendix IV, *Archaeologia*, 100, 74.

COURTY M A, 1982   *Etudes geologiques de sites archeologiques Holocenes: definition des processus sedimentaires et post-sedimentaires, caracterisation de l'impact anthropique. Essai de Methodologie*, unpublished PhD Thesis, L'Universite de Bordeaux I.

COURTY M A, FEDEROFF N, 1982   'Micromorphology of a Holocene dwelling', in *Proceedings of the 2nd Nordic Conference of Scientific Methods in Archaeology, Denmark, 1981*, 2, 7, II, 257–277.

COURTY M A, in press   'Formations et evolution des accumulations cendreuses – Approche micromorphologique', in *Colloque Interegional sur le Neolitique de l'Est de la France*, Le Puy, 3–4 Oct 1981.

CROMPTON E, 1952   'Some morphological features associated with poor soil drainage', *J Soil Sci* 3, 277–289.

DALRYMPLE J B, 1957   'The Pleistocene deposits of Penfold's Pit, Slindon, Sussex, and their chronology', *Proc Geol Ass* 68, 4, 294–303.

DALRYMPLE J B, 1958   'The application of soil micromorphology to fossil soils and other deposits from archaeological sites', *J Soil Sci* 9, 2, 199–205.

DALRYMPLE J B, 1962   'Some micromorphological implications of time as a soil-forming factor, illustrated from sites in south east England. Zeitschrift für pflanzenernahring', *Dungung und Bodenkunde* 98 (143) 3, 232–239.

DIMBLEBY G W, 1954   'The origin of heathland podzols and their conversion by afforestation', *Report of the 8th Botanical Congress* 13, 74–80.

DIMBLEBY G W, GILL J M, 1955   'The occurrence of podzols under deciduous woodland in the New Forest', *Forestry* 28, 95–106.

DIMBLEBY G W, 1957   In Thompson M W and Ashbee P, 'Excavation of a barrow near the Hardy Monument, Black Down, Portesham, Dorset', *Proc Prehist Soc* 23, 6, 124–136.

DIMBLEBY G W, 1960a	In Rankine W F and Rankine W M, 'Further excavations at a Mesolithic site at Oakhanger, Selborne, Hants', *Proc Prehist Soc* 26, 246–262.
DIMBLEBY G W, 1960b	In Christie P M, 'Crig-a-mennis: a Bronze Age barrow at Liskey, Perranzabuloe, Cornwall', *Proc Prehist Soc* 26, 76–97.
DIMBLEBY G W, 1961	'The ancient forest of Blackamore', *Antiquity* 35, 123–128.
DIMBLEBY G W, 1962	*The development of British heathlands and their soils,* Oxford, Clarendon Press.
DIMBLEBY G W, 1965	'Post glacial changes in soil profiles', *Proc Roy Soc Ser B* 161, 355–362.
DIMBLEBY G W, EVANS J G, 1972	In Wainwright G J, 'The excavation of a Neolithic settlement on Broome Heath, Ditchingham, Norfolk, England', *Proc Prehist Soc* 38, 1–97.
DIMBLEBY G W, EVANS J G, 1974	'Pollen and land snail analysis of calcareous soils', *J Archaeol Sci* 1, 117–133.
DIMBLEBY G W, BRADLEY R J, 1975	'Evidence of pedogenesis from a Neolithic site at Rackham, Sussex', *J Archaeol Sci* 2, 179–186.
DIMBLEBY G W, 1976	'Climate, soil and man', *Phil Trans Roy Soc London Ser B* 275, 197–208.
DIMBLEBY G W, 1976/77	'A buried soil at Innisdigen, St Mary's, Isles of Scilly', *Cornish Stud* 4/5, 5–10.
DIMBLEBY G W, GREIG J R A, SCAIFE R G, 1981	'Vegetational history of the Isles of Scilly', in Brothwell D and Dimbleby G W (eds), *Environmental aspects of coasts and islands,* Brit Archaeol Rep (Intern Ser) 94, 127–144.
DINC U, MIEDEMA R, BAL L, PONS L T, 1976	'Morphological and physico-chemical aspects of three soils developed in peat in the Netherlands and their classification', *Netherlands J Agric Sci* 24, 247–265.
DONALDSON A M, RACKHAM D J, in press	'Environmental work in Northern England (Cumbria, Durham, Northumberland, Tyne and Wear, Cleveland)', in Keeley H C M (ed), *Environmental Archaeology: A Regional Review,* Vol I, DAMHB Occasional Paper No. 6.
DORELL P, CORNWALL I W, 1960	In De Mallet Vatcher F, 'The excavation of a group of barrows at Down Farm, Pewsey, Wiltshire', *Wiltshire Archaeol Natur Hist Mag* 57, 339–352.
DORELL P, CORNWALL I W, 1961	In De Mallet Vatcher F, 'The Excavations of the barrows on Lamb Down, Codford St Mary', *Wiltshire Archaeol Natur Hist Mag* 58, 211, 417–441.
DREW D P, 1982	'Environmental archaeology and Karstic terrains: the example of The Burren, Co Clare, Ireland', in Bell M and Limbrey S (ed), *Archaeological aspects of woodland ecology,* Brit Archaeol Rep (Intern Ser) 146, 115–127.
DREWETT P, 1976	'The excavation of four round barrows of the second millenium BC at West Heath, Harting, 1973–75', *Sussex Archaeol Collect* 14, 126–150.
DUCHAUFOUR Ph, 1958	*Dynamics of forest soils under the Atlantic climate. Lectures in Surveying and Forest Engineering,* Quebec – L'institut Scientifique Franco-Canadien, 80pp.
DUCHAUFOUR Ph, 1965	*Precis de Pedologie,* Masson and Cie, Paris.
DUCHAUFOUR Ph, 1977	*Pedology: Pedogenesis and Classification,* George Allen and Unwin, London.

DURNO S E, ROMANS J C C, 1969   'Evidence for variations in the altitudinal zonation of climate in Scotland and northern England since the Boreal Period', *Scottish Geog Mag* 85, 1, 31–33.

EIDE K S, 1982   *Some aspects of pedogenesis and vegetation history in relation to archaeological sites in the New Forest,* unpublished PhD Thesis, Institute of Archaeology, University of London.

EVANS J G, 1968   'Periglacial deposits on the Chalk of Wiltshire', *Wiltshire Archaeol Natur Hist Mag* 63, 12–26.

EVANS J G, 1971a   'The pre-henge environment', in Wainwright G J and Longworth I H, *Durrington Walls excavation,* Res Rep Soc Antiq London 29, 329–337.

EVANS J G, 1971b   In Wainwright G J, Evans J G and Longworth I H, 'The excavation of a late Neolithic enclosure at Marden, Wiltshire', *Proc Prehist Soc* 51, 177–239.

EVANS J G, 1972   *Land snails in archaeology,* Seminar Press, London.

EVANS J G, VALENTINE K W G, 1974   'Ecological changes induced by prehistoric man at Pitstone, Buckinghamshire', *J Soil Sci* 1, 343–351.

EVANS J G, 1975   *The environment of early man in the British Isles,* Paul Elek, London.

EVANS J G, DIMBLEBY G W, 1976   In Manby T G, 'Excavation of the Kilham long barrow, East Riding of Yorkshire', *Proc Prehist Soc* 42, 111–159.

EVANS J G, 1980   In Robertson-Mackay M E, 'A "head and hooves" burial beneath a round barrow, with other Neolithic and Bronze Age sites, on Hemp Knoll, near Avebury, Wiltshire', *Proc Prehist Soc* 46, 123–176.

EVANS R, JONES R J A, 1977   'Crop marks and soils at two archaeological sites in Britain', *J Archaeol Sci* 4, 63–76.

FAULL M L, SMITH R T, 1980   'Phosphate analysis and three possible Dark Age ecclesiastical sites in Yorkshire', *Landscape History* 2, 21–38.

FISHER P F, 1982   'A review of lessivage and Neolithic cultivation in southern England', *J Archaeol Sci* 9, 3, 299–304.

FISHER P F, 1983   'Pedogenesis within the archaeological landscape at South Lodge Camp, Wiltshire, England', *Geoderma,* 93–106.

FISHER R F, MACPHAIL R I, in press   'Studies of archaeological soils and deposits by micromorphological techniques', in Fieller W R J, Silbertson D and Ralph N, *Proc Ass Environmental Archaeology, Brit Archaeol Rep.*

FLEMING A, RALPH N, 1982   'Medieval settlement and land use on Holne Moor, Dartmoor', *Medieval Archaeol* 26, 101–137.

FORDHAM S J, GREEN R D, 1980   *Soils of Kent,* Soil Survey Bulletin No. 9, Harpenden.

FOWLER P J, EVANS J G, 1967   'Plough-marks, lynchets and early fields', *Antiquity* 41, 289–301.

FOWLER P J, THOMAS C, 1979   'Lyonese revisited: the early walls of Scilly', *Antiquity* 53, 175–189.

FRENCH C A I, 1983   *An environmental study of the soil, sediments and molluscan evidence associated with prehistoric monuments on river terrace gravels in north west Cambridgeshire,* unpublished PhD Thesis, Institute of Archaeology, University of London.

GEISS J W, 1973 — 'Biogenic silica in selected species of deciduous angiosperms', *Soil Sci* 116, 113–119.

GOH K M, MOLLOY B P J, 1978 — 'Radiocarbon dating of palaeosols using soil organic matter components', *J Soil Sci* 29, 567–573.

GOLDBERG P, 1979a — 'Micromorphology of Pech-de-l'Aze II sediments', *J Archaeol Sci* 6, 17–47.

GOLDBERG P, 1979b — 'Micromorphology of sediments from Hayonim Cave, Israel', *Catena* 6, 167–181.

GRANT KING D, 1963 — 'Bury Wood Camp, Report on excavations, 1960', *Wiltshire Archaeol Natur Hist Mag* 210, 185–208.

GREIG J, COLLEDGE S, this volume — 'A review paper on environmental archaeology in the Midlands and the surrounding area of England'.

GRIEVE I C, 1980 — 'Some contrasts in soil development between grassland and deciduous woodland sites', *J Soil Sci* 31, 137–145.

GUILLET B, 1975 — 'Forested podzols and degraded podzols: relationship between vegetation history and podzol development on the Vosges Triassic Sandstone', *Revue d'Ecologie et du Biologie du Sol* 12, 1, 405–414.

HAZELDEN J, JARVIS M G, 1979 — 'Age and significance of alluvium in the Windrush valley, Oxfordshire', *Nature* 282, 5736, 291–292.

HODGSON J M, CATT J A, WEIR A H, 1967 — 'The origin and development of Clay-with-Flints and associated soil horizons on the South Downs', *J Soil Sci* 18, 1, 85–102.

HODGSON J M, 1974 — *Soil Survey Field Handbook,* Soil Survey Technical Monogr No. 5, Harpenden.

IMESON A C, JUNGERIUS P D, 1974 — 'Landscape stability in the Luxembourg Ardennes as exemplified by hydrological and (micro) pedological investigations of a catena in an experimental watershed', *Catena* 1, 273–295.

IMESON A C, JUNGERIUS P D, 1976 — 'Aggregate stability and colluviation in the Luxembourg Ardennes: An experimental and micromorphological study', *Earth Surface Processes* 1, 259–271.

IMESON A C, KWAAD F J P M, MÜCHER H J, 1980 — 'Hillslope processes and deposits in forested areas of Luxembourg', in Cullingford R A, Davison D A and Lewin J, (eds), *Timescales in Geomorphology,* John Wiley and Sons, 31–42.

JENKINSON D S, 1977 — 'Studies on the decomposition of plant material in soil V. The effects of plant cover and soil type on the loss of carbon from ^{14}C labelled Ryegrass decomposing under field conditions', *J Soil Sci* 28, 424–434.

JENKINSON D S, RAYNER J H, 1977 — 'The turnover of soil organic matter in some of the Rothamsted classical experiments', *Soil Sci* 123, 5, 298–305.

JEWELL P A, 1958 — 'Natural history and experiment in archaeology', *Brit Ass Advancement Sci* 59, 165–172.

JEWELL P A (ed), 1963 — *The experimental earthwork on Overton Down, Wiltshire, 1960,* Brit Ass Advancement Sci, London.

JEWELL P A, DIMBLEBY G W (ed), 1966 — 'The experimental earthwork on Overton Down, Wiltshire, England: the first four years', *Proc Prehist Soc* 32, 313–342.

JONES R J A, 1979	'Crop marks induced by soil moisture stress at an Iron Age site in Midland England UK', *Proceedings of the 18th International Symposium for Archaeometry and Archaeological Prospection, Bonn, March 1978*, 656–668.
JONES R J A, EVANS R, 1975	'Soil and crop marks in the recognition of archaeological sites by air photography', in Wilson D R (ed), *Aerial Reconnaissance for Archaeology,* Counc Brit Archaeol Res Rep 12, 1–12.
JONES R J A, 1979	'Soil and crop marks', in Smith C (ed), *Fisherwick: The reconstruction of an Iron Age landscape,* Brit Archaeol Rep (British) Ser 61, 10–17, 195–207.
JONGERIUS A, 1970	'Some morphological aspects of regrouping phenomena in Dutch soils', *Geoderma* 4, 311–331.
KEEF P A M, WYMER J J, DIMBLEBY G W, 1965	'A Mesolithic site on Iping Common, Sussex, England', *Proc Prehist Soc* 31, 85–92.
KEELEY H C M, HUDSON G E, EVANS J, 1977	'Trace element contents of human bones in various states of preservation 1. The soil silhouette', *J Archaeol Sci* 4, 19–24.
KEELEY H C M, MACPHAIL R I, 1981a	'A soil survey of part of Shaugh Moor, Devon', in Smith K, Coppen J, Wainwright G J and Beckett S, 'The Shaugh Moor Project: Third Report – Settlement and environmental investigations', *Proc Prehist Soc* 47, 205–273 (240–245).
KEELEY H C M, MACPHAIL R I, 1981b	*A soil handbook for archaeologists,* Inst Archaeol Bull No. 18, 225–244.
KEELEY H C M, MACPHAIL R I, 1982	'Soils of the Saddlesborough Reave area, Shaugh Moor', in Balaam N D, Smith K and Wainwright G J, 'The Shaugh Moor Project: Fourth Report – Environment, context and conclusion', *Proc Prehist Soc* 48, 203–278 (219–220), Microfiche, 4–20.
KEELEY H C M, 1982	'Pedogenesis during the later prehistoric period in Britain', in Harding A F (ed), *Climatic change in later prehistory,* Edinburgh University Press.
KENWARD H K, HALL A R, JONES A K G, O'CONNOR T P, in press	'Environmental archaeology at York in retrospect and prospect', in Keeley H C M (ed), *Environmental Archaeology: A Regional Review* Vol I, DAMHB Occasional Paper No. 6.
KENYON K M, 1959	*Excavations at Southwark (1945–47),* Research Papers Surrey Archaeol Soc 5, Guildford.
KERNEY M P, BROWN E H, CHANDLER T J, 1963	'The Late Glacial and Post Glacial History of the Chalk escarpment near Brook, Kent', *Phil Trans Roy Soc London B,* 745, 248, 135–204.
KERNEY M P, 1967	In Christie P M, 'A barrow-cemetery of the second millenium BC in Wiltshire, England', *Proc Prehist Soc* 33, 336–366.
KIDSON C, HEYWORTH A, 1978	'Holocene eustatic sea level changes', *Nature* 273, 748–750.
KWAAD F J P M, MÜCHER H J, 1977	'The evolution of soils and slope deposits in the Luxembourg Ardennes near Wilts', *Geoderma* 17, 1–37.
KWAAD F J P M, MÜCHER H J, 1979	'The formation and evolution of colluvium on arable land in northern Luxembourg', *Geoderma* 22(2), 173–192.
LANGOHR R, VANKLIET B, 1979	'Clay migration in well to moderately well drained acid brown soils of the Belgium Ardennes: morphology and clay content determination', *Pedologie* 29, 367–385.

LAVILLE H, 1976	'Deposits in calcareous rock shelters: analytical methods and climatic interpretation', in Davidson D A and Shackley M L (eds), *Geoarchaeology,* Duckworth.
LIMBREY S, 1974	In Jefferies J S, 'An excavation at the coastal port of Embury Beacon, Devon', *Proc Prehist Soc* 40, 136—156.
LIMBREY S, 1975	*Soil Science and Archaeology,* Academic Press.
LIMBREY S, 1978	'Changes in quality and distribution of the soils in lowland Britain', in Limbrey S and Evans J G (eds), *The effect of man on the landscape: the lowland zone,* Counc Brit Archaeol Res Rep 21, 21—26.
LIMMER A W, WILSON A T, 1980	'Amino acids in buried paleosols', *J Soil Sci* 31, 147—153.
DE MALLET MORGAN F, 1959	'The excavation of a long barrow at Nutbane, Hampshire', *Proc Prehist Soc* 25, 2, 15—51.
MANNING O, BRAY W, 1804	*The History and Antiquities of the County of Surrey,* John White, London.
McAVOY F, MORRIS E L, SMITH G H, 1979	'The excavation of a multi-period site at Carngoon Brank, Lizard, Cornwall', *Cornish Archaeol* 19, 31—62.
MACKNEY D, 1961	'A podzol development sequence in oakwoods and heath in central England', J Soil Sci 12, 1, 23—40.
MACNAB J W, 1965	'British strip lynchets', *Antiquity* 39, 279—290.
MACPHAIL R I, 1981a	In Bell M, *Valley sediments as evidence of prehistoric land use: a study based on dry valleys in south east England,* unpublished PhD Thesis, Institute of Archaeology, University of London.
MACPHAIL R I, 1981b	In Clay P, *Two multi-phase barrow sites at Sproxton and Eaton, Leicestershire,* Archaeol Rep No. 2, Leicester Museum.
MACPHAIL R I, 1981c	'Soil and botanical studies of the 'Dark Earth' ', in Jones M and Dimbleby G, *The Environment of Man: the Iron Age to the Anglo-Saxon Period,* Brit Archaeol Rep (Brit Ser) 87, 309—331.
MACPHAIL R I, 1983	'The micromorphology of 'Dark Earth' from Gloucester, London and Norwich: an analysis of urban anthropogenic deposits from the Late Roman to Early Medieval Periods in England', in Bullock P and Murphy C P (eds), *Soil Microscopy. 6th International Working-Meeting Soil Microscopy, London 1981,* AB Academic Publishers, Berkhamsted, 245—252.
MACPHAIL R I, SCAIFE R G, in preparation	'Geographical and environmental background', in Bird J and Bird D, 'The archaeology of Surrey (from the Palaeolithic to 1500)', *Surrey Archaeol Collect.*
VAN DER MEER J J M, 1982	*The Fribourg area, Switzerland. A study in Quaternary geology and soil development,* Fys Georgr Bodemk Lab Univ Amsterdam, Nr 32.
MIEDEMA R, JONGMANS A G, SLAGER S, 1974	'Micromorphological observations on pyrite and its oxidation products in four Holocene soils in the Netherlands', in Rutherford S K, *Soil Microscopy, Proceedings of the 4th International Working-Meeting Soil Micromorphology, Kingston, Ontario,* Limestone Press, 772—794.

MIEDEMA R, VAN ENGELDEN E, PAPE Th, 1978 — 'Micromorphology of a toposequence of Late Pleistocene fluviatile soils in the eastern part of the Netherlands', *Proceedings of the 5th International Working-Meeting Soil Micromorphology, Granada*, I, 469–500.

MOORE P, WILMOTT A, 1976 — 'Prehistoric forest clearances and the development of peatlands in the uplands and lowlands of Britain', *Proceedings of the 5th International Peat Conference, Poznan, Poland*.

MÜCHER H J, 1974 — 'Micromorphology of slope deposits: the necessity of a classification', in Rutherford G K (ed), *Soil Microscopy. 4th International Working-Meeting Soil Micromorphology Kingston, Ontario*, Limestone Press, 553–556.

MÜCHER H J, DE PLOEY J, 1977 — 'Experimental and micromorphological investigation of erosion and redeposition of loess by water', *Earth Surface Processes* 2, 117–124.

MÜCHER H J, VREEKEN W J, 1981 — '(Re)deposition of loess in Southern Limbourg, The Netherlands 2). Micromorphology of the Lower Silt Loam Complex and comparison with deposits produced under laboratory conditions', *Earth Surface Processes and Landforms* 6, 337–363.

MÜCHER H J, DE PLOEY J, SAVAT J, 1981 — 'Response of loess materials to simulated translocation by water: micromorphological observations', *Earth Surface Processes and Landforms* 6, 331–336.

MURPHY P, in press — 'Environmental archaeology in East Anglia 1977–1980; a review', in Keeley H C M (ed), *Environmental Archaeology: A Regional Review* Vol I, DAMHB Occasional Paper No. 6.

ORTON C, 1978 — 'Sequence of Medieval and Post-Medieval pottery', in Sheldon H L (ed), *Southwark Excavations 1972–74*, Joint Publication No. 1, Southwark and Lambeth Archaeological Excavation Committee, London and Middlesex Archaeological Society, Surrey Archaeological Society, 140–146.

PALMER P G, 1976 — 'Grass cuticles: a new palaeoecological tool for East African lake sediments', *Canadian J Botany* 54, 15, 1725–1734.

PEARSALL W H, 1952 — 'The pH of natural soils and its ecological significance', *J Soil Sci* 3, 1, 41–51.

PENNINGTON W, 1975 — 'The effect of Neolithic man on the environment in north west England: the use of absolute pollen diagrams', in Evans J G, Limbrey S and Cleere H (eds), *The effect of man on the landscape: the highland zone*, 74–85.

PERRIN R M S, WILLIS E H, HODGE C A H, 1964 — 'Dating of humus podzols by residual radiocarbon activity', *Nature*, London 202, 165–166.

PERRIN R M S, DAVIES H, FYSH M D, 1974 — 'Distribution of Late Pleistocene aeolian deposits in eastern and southern England', *Nature*, London, 248, 320–323.

PESCI M, SZEBENYI E, PEVZNER M A, 1979 — 'Upper Pleistocene litho- and chronostratigraphical type profile from the exposure at Mende', *Acta Geologica Academiae Scientiarum Hungaricae, Tomus* Vol 22 (1–4), 371–389.

PROUDFOOT E V W, 1963 — 'Report on the excavation of a bell barrow in the Parish of Edmondsham, Dorset, England, 1959', *Proc Prehist Soc* 29, 13, 395–425.

PROUDFOOT V B, 1958 — 'Problems of soil history. Podzol development at Godland and Toor Townlands, Co Antrim, Northern Ireland', *J Soil Sci* 9, 2, 186–198.

PROUDFOOT V B, 1965 — 'The study of soil development from the construction and excavation of experimental earthworks', in Hallsworth E G and Crawford D V (eds), *Experimental Pedology Proceedings 11th Easter School in Agricultural Science, Nottingham, 1964,* Butterworths, London, 282–294.

PROUDFOOT V B, 1976 — 'The analysis and interpretation of soil phosphorus in archaeological contexts', in Davidson D A and Shackley M L (eds), *Geo-archaeology: earth science and the past,* Duckworth, London 93–113.

RADLEY J, SIMMS C, 1967 — 'Wind erosion in East Yorkshire', *Nature* 216, 20–22.

REECE R, 1980 — 'Town and Country: the end of Roman Britain', *World Archaeology* 12, 1, 77–92.

REYNOLDS P J, 1981 — 'New approaches to familiar problems', in Jones M and Dimbleby G W (eds), *The Environment of Man: the Iron Age to the Anglo-Saxon Period,* Brit Archaeol Rep (Brit Ser) 87, 19–49.

RIGHI D, GUILLET B, 1977 — 'Datations par le Carbonne — 14 natural de la matiere organique d'horizons spodiques de podzols des Landes du Medoc (France)', in *Soil Organic Matter Studies,* II, International Atomic Energy Agency, Vienna 187–192.

ROBINSON M, 1981 — 'The Iron Age to Early Saxon environment of the Upper Thames Terraces', in Jones M and Dimbleby G (eds), *The Environment of Man: the Iron Age to the Anglo-Saxon Period,* Brit Archaeol Rep (Brit Ser) 87, 251–286.

ROBSON D, 1975 — In Beresford G, *The Medieval Clay-Land Village: excavations at Goltho and Barton Blount,* Soc Medieval Archaeol Monogr Ser No. 6, London, 101–102.

ROBSON D, 1980 — 'Salterns: collaborative work with archaeologists in Lincolnshire', *Rothamsted Experimental Station Report,* Part I, Harpenden, 224–225.

ROMANS J C C, ROBERTSON L, 1975a — 'Soils and archaeology in Scotland', in Evans J G, Limbrey S and Cleere H (eds), *The effect of man on the landscape: the Highland zone,* Counc Brit Archaeol Res Rep No. 11, 37–39.

ROMANS J C C, ROBERTSON L, 1975b — 'Some genetic characteristics of the freely drained soils of the Ettrick Association in East Scotland', *Geoderma* 14, 297–317.

ROMANS J C C, ROBERTSON L, in press a — 'Some notes on the soils at Scord of Brouster Shetland', in Whittle A, *Excavation at Scord of Brouster.*

ROMANS J C C, ROBERTSON L, in press b — 'Soils appendix', in Barclay G, 'An excavation report on the mount and henge at North Mains, Strathallen', Proc Soc Antiq of Scotland.

ROMANS J C C, ROBERTSON L, in press c — 'The Environment of North Britain: Soils', in *Proceedings of The George Jobey Conference: Settlement in North Britain 1000 BC–AD 1000.*

ROVNER I, 1971 — 'Potential of opal phytoliths for use in palaeoecological reconstruction', *Quaternary Research* 1, 343–359.

ROSE J, STURDY R G, ALLEN P, WHITESIDE C A, 1977 — 'Middle Pleistocene sediments and palaeosols near Chelmsford, Essex', *Geol Ass Fld* Meeting Rep (7 Nov 1976), 91–96.

ROSKAMS S, SCHOFIELD J, 1978 — 'The Milk Street excavation, Part 2', *London Archaeol* 3, 9, 227–234.

ROSKAMS S, 1981 — 'GPO Newgate Street, 1975–9; the Roman levels', *London Archaeol*, 403–407.

SALISBURY E J, 1925 — 'Note on the edaphic succession in some dune soils with special reference to the time factor., *J Ecology* 13, 322–328.

SCAIFE R G, 1982 — 'Late-Devensian and early Flandrian vegetation changes in southern England', in Bell M and Limbrey S (eds), *Archaeological aspects of woodland ecology, Brit Archaeol Rep* (Intern Ser) 146, 57–74.

SCAIFE R G, MACPHAIL R I — 'The post-Devensian development of heathland soils and vegetation', *Seesoil*.

SCHARPENSEEL H W, 1971 — 'Radiocarbon dating of soils — problems, troubles, hopes', in Yaalon D H (ed), *Paleopedology; origin, nature and dating of paleosols. International Society Soil Science*, Israel 77–88.

SHELDON H L, 1978 — *Southwark Excavations, 1972–74*, Southwark and Lambeth Archaeological Excavation Committee, Joint Publication No. 1, London and Middlesex Archaeological Society, Surrey Archaeological Society.

SHOTTON F W, 1978 — 'Archaeological inferences from the study of alluvium in the lower Severn-Avon valleys', in Limbrey S and Evans J G (eds), *The effect of man on the landscape: The lowland zone*, Counc Brit Archaeol Res Rep 21, 27–32.

SIMMONS I G, 1969 — 'Environment and early man on Dartmoor, Devon, England', Proc Prehist Soc 35, 203–219.

SIMMONS I G, 1975 — 'The ecological setting of Mesolithic man in the highland zone', in Evans J G, Limbrey S and Cleere H (eds), *The effect of man on the landscape: the Highland Zone*, Counc Brit Archaeol No. 11, 57–63.

SIMMONS I G, TOOLEY M, 1981 — *The environment in prehistory*, London, Duckworth.

SLAGER S, VAN DE WETERING H T J, 1977 — 'Soil formation in archaeological pits and adjacent loess soils in southern Germany', *J Archaeol Sci* 4, 259–267.

SMITH K, COPPEN J, WAINWRIGHT G J, BECKETT S, 1981 — 'The Shaugh Moor Project: Third Report — Settlement and environmental investigations', *Proc Prehist Soc* 47, 205–273.

SMITH R T, 1975 — 'Early agriculture and soil degradation', in Evans J G, Limbrey S and Cleere H (eds), *The effect of man on the landscape: the Highland Zone*, Counc Brit Archaeol Res Rep No. 11, 27–37.

SMITH R T, in press — 'Aspects of the soil and vegetation history of the Craven district of Yorkshire', in Raistrick A, *Archaeology in the Pennines*, Brit Archaeol Rep.

SMITHSON F, 1958 — 'Grass opal in British soils', *J Soil Sci* 9, 1, 148–154.

SOIL SURVEY ENGLAND AND WALES, 1983 — *1:250,000 Soil Map of England and Wales*, Soil Survey England and Wales, Harpenden. (Ordnance Survey).

STAINES S, 1979 — 'Environmental change on Dartmoor', *Proc Devon Archaeol Soc* 37, 21–47.

STURDY R G et al., 1979 — 'Palaeosols developed on Chalky Boulder Clay in Essex', *J Soil Sci* 30, 117–137.

TAMM C O, OSTLUND H G, 1960 — 'Radiocarbon dating of soil humus', *Nature* 4714, 706–7.

TAYLOR T P, 1979 — 'Soil mark studies near Winchester, Hampshire', *J Archaeol Sci* 6, 93–100.

THOMAS K D, 1977 — In Drewett P, 'The excavation of a Neolithic causewayed enclosure on Offham Hill, East Sussex 1976', *Proc Prehist Soc* 43, 201–241.

THOMAS K D, 1982 — 'Neolithic enclosures and woodland habitats on the South Downs in Sussex, England', in Bell M and Limbrey S (eds), *Archaeological aspects of woodland ecology*, Brit Archaeol Rep (Intern Ser) 146, 147–170.

THOMASSON A J, 1975 — In Beresford G, *The Medieval clay-land village: excavations at Goltho and Barton Blount*, Soc Medieval Archaeol Monogr Ser No. 6, London, 100.

THOMPSON F H, 1979 — 'Three Surrey hillforts: excavations at Anstiebury, Holmbury and Hascombe, 1972–1977', *Antiq J* 59, 245–318.

TINSLEY H M, SMITH R T, 1974 — 'Ecological investigations at a Romano-British earthwork in the Yorkshire Pennines', *Yorkshire Archaeol J* 46, 23–33.

TYLECOTE R F, 1979 — 'The effect of soil conditions on the long-term corrosion of buried tin-bronzes and copper', *J Archaeol Sci* 6, 345–368.

TWISS P C, SUESS E, SMITH R M, 1969 — 'Morphological classification of grassphytoliths', *Soil Sci Soc America Proc* 33, 109–114.

VALENTINE K W G, DALRYMPLE J B, 1975 — 'The identification, lateral variation, and chronology of two buried palaeocatenas at Woodhall Spa and West Runton, England', *Quarternary Research* 5, 551–590.

VALENTINE K W G, DALRYMPLE J B, 1976a — 'The identification of a buried palaeosol developed in place at Pitstone, Buckinghamshire', *J Soil Sci* 27, 541–553.

VALENTINE K W G, DALRYMPLE J B, 1976b — 'Quaternary buried paleosols: A critical review', *Quaternary Research* 6, 209–222.

WAINWRIGHT A, 1981 — In Clay P, *Two multi-phase barrow sites at Sproxton and Eaton, Leicestershire*, Archaeol Rep No. 2, Leicester Museum.

WATON P V, 1982 — 'Man's impact on the Chalklands: some new pollen evidence', in Bell M and Limbrey S, *Archaeological aspects of woodland ecology*, Brit Archaeol Rep (Intern Ser) 146, 75–91.

WEIR A H, CATT J A, MADGETT P A, 1971 — 'Post-glacial soil formation in the loess of Pegwell Bay, Kent (England)', *Geoderma* 5, 131–149.

WILLIAMS R B G, 1973 — 'Frost and the works of man', *Antiquity* 47, 19–31.

WILLMOT A, 1968 — *The palynological and stratigraphical record of Ockley Bog, Thursley Common*, unpublished BSc dissertation, Kings College, University of London.

WILSON B, THOMAS R, WHEELER A, 1979 — 'Sampling profile of town soil accumulation 57, East Street, Helen's Street, Abingdon', *Oxoniensia* 44.

WILSON D R, in press — *Air Photo Interpretation for Archaeologists*, Batsfords.

WOOD E S, 1956 — 'The earth circles on St Martha's Hill, near Guildford', *Surrey Archaeol Collect* 54, 10–46.

WOOD P D, 1961 — 'Strip lynchets reconsidered', *Geog J* 127, 4, 449–459.

WOOLDRIDGE S W, LINTON D L, 1933 — 'The loam terrains of south east England and their relation to its early history', *Antiquity* 7, 297–310.

WYMER J, 1961 — 'The Lower Palaeolithic succession in the Thames valley and the date of the ancient channel between Caversham and Henley, Oxfordshire', *Proc Prehist Soc* 27, 1, 1–27.

ZEUNER F E, 1955 — 'Loess and Palaeolithic chronology', *Proc Prehist Soc* 21, 51–64.

ANCIENT MONUMENTS LABORATORY REPORTS

ABRAHAMS P, 1977 — 'Soil report for Wharram Percy, North Yorkshire', AML Report 2360.

KEELEY H C M, 1977 — 'Interim soil report, Tarraby, Carlisle', AML Report 2228.

KEELEY H C M, MACPHAIL R I, 1978 — 'Report on a soil at Ipswich, Suffolk', AML Report 2691.

KEELEY H C M, 1979 — 'Report on a soil column from Carlisle', AML Report 2887.

KEELEY H C M, 1979 — 'Spong Hill, Norfolk — A report on trace element analysis of soil samples from two graves', AML Report 2902.

KEELEY H C M, 1979 — 'A report on 2 sections examined at Barnard Castle, County Durham', AML Report 2911.

KEELEY H C M, 1979 — 'Report on a series of soil samples from Callis Wold, Humberside', AML Report 2924.

KEELEY H C M, 1980 — 'Recent work using soil phosphorus analysis in archaeological prospection', AML Report 3095.

KEELEY H C M, 1980 — 'A section through Hadrian's Wall, Lannerton Farm, Appletree, Cumbria', AML Report 3101.

KEELEY H C M, 1980 — 'Report on soils at Madison Street, Southampton', AML Report 3211.

KEELEY H C M, 1981 — 'Soil columns from Throckley, Tyne and Wear', AML Report 3401.

MACPHAIL R I, 1979 — 'Soil report on the barrow and buried soil at Sproxton, Leicestershire (IL400, 1978)', AML Report 2926.

MACPHAIL R I, 1979 — 'Soil report on the barrow and buried soil at Lambourn, Berkshire (LB 78)', AML Report 2927.

MACPHAIL R I, 1979 — 'Soil report on turf stack and buried soil at Gallows Hill, Thetford, Norfolk', AML Report 2799.

MACPHAIL R I, 1980 — 'Report on a soil in a Romano-British context at Lloyds Merchant Bank, London (LL078)', AML Report 3045.

MACPHAIL R I, 1981 — 'Soil report on Bar Point, St Marys, Isles of Scilly', AML Report 3299.

MACPHAIL R I, 1981 — 'Soil report on Beeston Castle, Cheshire', AML Report 3565.

MACPHAIL R I, 1981 — 'Soil report on Fisons Way, Thetford, Norfolk', AML Report 3566.

MACPHAIL R I, 1981 — 'Soil report on Brandon, Suffolk, near Thetford', AML Report 3568.

MACPHAIL R I, 1981 — 'Soil report on West Heath Cemetery (1980), West Sussex. Part I and Part II', AML Report 3586.

MACPHAIL R I, 1981 — 'Soil report on the micromorphology, and first turf of the turf stack at the Experimental Earthwork on Marden Bog, Wareham, Dorset', AML Report 3587.

MACPHAIL R I, 1982 — 'Special soil report on the micromorphology of 'Dark Earth' from Gloucester, London and Norwich. An analysis of urban anthropogenic deposits from the Late Roman to Early Medieval Periods', AML Report 3633.

MACPHAIL R I, 1982 — 'Soil report on Fiskerton, near Lincoln, Lincolnshire', AML Report 3658.

MACPHAIL R I, 1982   'Soil report on West Heslerton, near Malton, North Yorkshire', AML Report 3706.

MACPHAIL R I, 1982   'Soil report on Ockham Common (M25), Surrey', AML Report 3738.

MACPHAIL R I, 1982   'Soil report on Princess Street, Chester', AML Report 3741.

MACPHAIL R I, 1982   'Preliminary soil report on the Cuckmere Valley Project', AML Report 3763.

MACPHAIL R I, 1982   'Preliminary soil report on Hengistbury Head, Bournemouth, Hants', AML Report 3811.

MACPHAIL R I, 1983   'Soil report on Towcester, Northamptonshire (Sewer Trench across North Defences)'.

MACPHAIL R I, 1983   'Soil report on Selmeston, East Sussex (Cuckmere Valley Project)', AML Report 3982.

MACPHAIL R I, in preparation   'Soil report on Balksbury Iron Age Camp, Andover, Hampshire'.

MACPHAIL R I, in preparation   'Soil report on Hazleton Long Barrow, Gloucestershire'.

SCAIFE R G, 1980   'Pollen analytical investigation of Broad Sanctuary, Westminster', AML Report 3070.

TAYLOR T P, 1978   'Gryme's Dyke, Colchester. 10 BC to 43 AD. The base of the rampart', AML Report 2470.

TAYLOR T P, 1978   'Preliminary report on the black earth deposit at Chaucer Street, Southwark', AML Report 2493.

Plate 1   Balksbury Camp, Hampshire
South Rampart (1st and 2nd stages); buried calcareous brown earth on chalk; Iron Age.

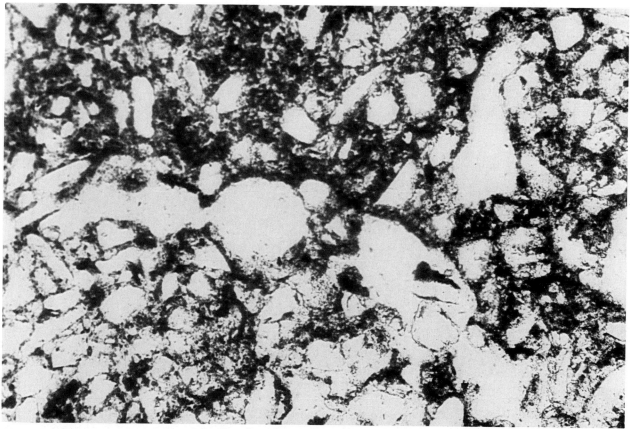

Plate 2   Photomicrograph; Ascott-Under-Wychwood, Long Barrow, Oxfordshire
Buried soil; thin dusty void argillans; Neolithic; Plane Polarised Light (PPL); length of figure 1.348mm.
(Thin section by Cornwall).

Plate 3   Hazleton Long Barrow, Gloucestershire
Barrow buries tree hollow (basal part contains Atlantic molluscan woodland fauna; Bell, pers. comm.);
Neolithic.

Plate 4   Hazleton Long Barrow, Gloucestershire
Barrow buries decalcified brown soil on Jurassic Oolitic Limestone; Neolithic.

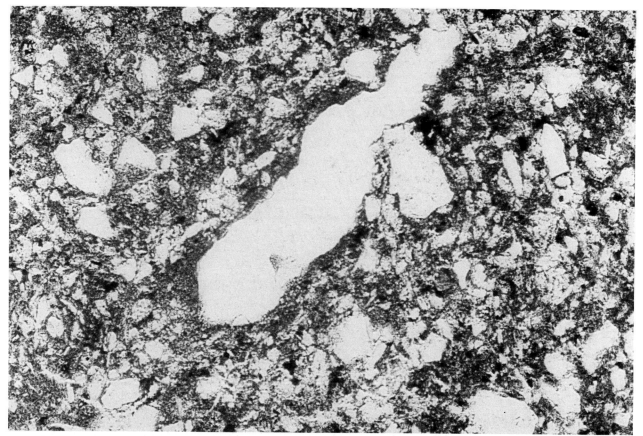

Plate 5   Photomicrograph; Hazleton Long Barrow, Gloucestershire
Buried soil — A(g) horizon; significant dusty void argillans. Neolithic. PPL; length of figure 1.348mm.

Plate 6   Saddlesborough Reave, Shaugh Moor, Dartmoor, Devon
Reave buries organic horizons formed on ditch upcast and the original stagnogley. Bronze Age.

Plate 7   Bar Point, St Mary's, Isles of Scilly
East/West wall with contemporary plough soil, over earlier plough soil and truncated ferric podzol; all buried by blown sand. Romano–British.

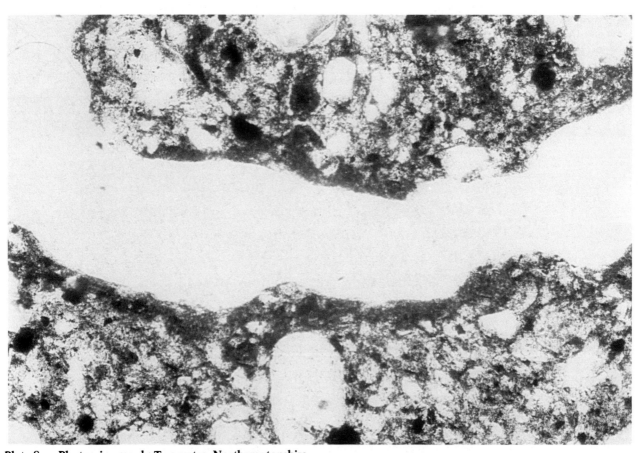

Plate 8   Photomicrograph; Towcester, Northamptonshire
'Dark Earth'; 'agricutan type' void coatings; 2nd Century AD. PPL; length of figure 1.348mm.

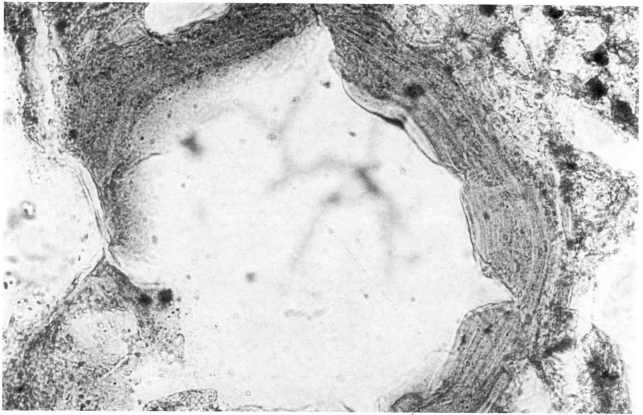

Plate 9   Photomicrograph; Selmeston, Sussex
Lower Greensand; brown earth, Bt(g)2 horizon; a clay argillan; PPL; length of figure 0.340mm. Mesolithic to Saxon soil.

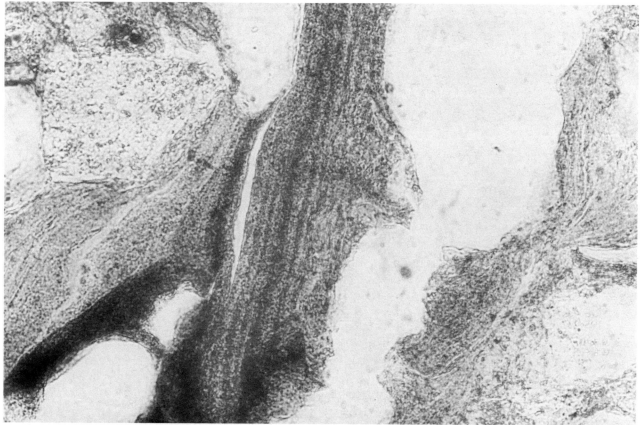

Plate 10   Photomicrograph; Selmeston, Sussex
Lower Greensand; brown earth, Bt(g)2 horizon; a banded dusty argillan; PPL; length of figure 0.340mm. Mesolithic to Saxon soil.

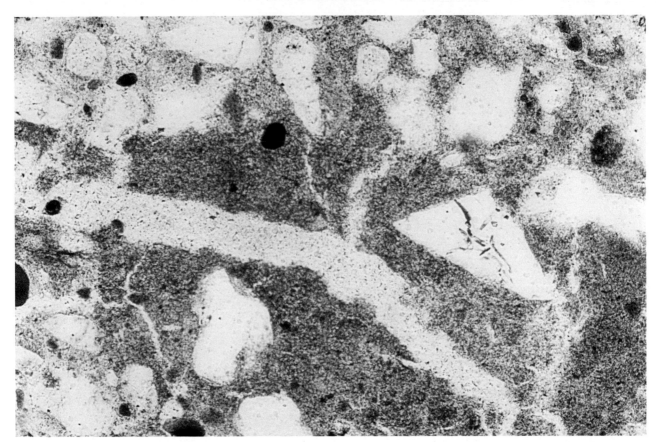

Plate 11 Photomicrograph; Wotton Common, Surrey
Lower Greensand, undated soil beneath colluvium; 6 Bt gsm 3 horizon; an 'agricutan' type void infill; PPL; length of figure 0.340mm.

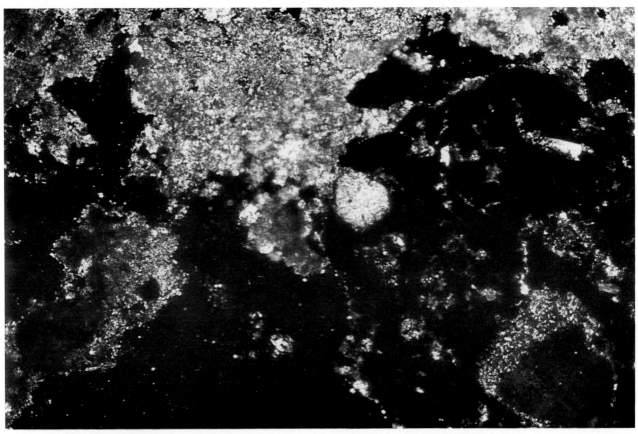

Plate 12 Photomicrograph; Earls Farm Down, Round Barrow, Wiltshire
Ashes from central hearth. Crossed polarised light; length of figure 5.225mm. (Thin section by Cornwall).

HISTORIC BUILDINGS AND MONUMENTS
COMMISSION FOR ENGLAND

Occasional Paper no. 1

90 0749079 8

ENVIRONMENTAL ARCHAEOLOGY

A REGIONAL REVIEW

VOLUME II

Edited by

H C M KEELEY

ISSN 0141-6596
ISBN 1 85074 040 2